EXPLORING CAREERS

A Young Person's Guide to 1,000 Jobs

THIRD EDITION

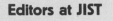

Editors at JIST

Exploring Careers, Third Edition
A Young Person's Guide to 1,000 Jobs

Published by JIST Works, an imprint of JIST Publishing, Inc.
8902 Otis Avenue
Indianapolis, IN 46216-1033

Phone: 800-648-JIST Fax: 800-JIST-FAX
E-mail: info@jist.com Web site: www.jist.com

Instructional Support Materials Available

Substantial resource materials are available to help instructors use *Exploring Careers* in a group setting or with individuals. Call 1-800-648-JIST or visit www.jist.com for more information.

1. **An instructor's guide** (ISBN 1-56370-626-1) features helpful guidance on using *Exploring Careers* with your students for career exploration, for connecting school to work, and more. It includes presentation ideas, discussion questions, suggested projects, and transparency masters.
2. **An activities workbook** (ISBN 1-56370-964-3, package of 10) helps students use *Exploring Careers* to interactively learn about career and education options, the job search process, employability skills, character education, and more.
3. **A companion video** (1-56370-999-6) is available to introduce and reinforce the information in the book.
4. **A self-directed assessment** called *The World of Work and You* (1-56370-865-5, package of 10) covers the same interest areas as *Exploring Careers* and leads students through career and learning options.
5. **A CD-ROM and Web site** with information on over 14,000 jobs, including those in *Exploring Careers,* is available through CareerOINK.com. The Web site offers information at free and subscription program levels.

Quantity discounts are available for JIST products. Please call 1-800-648-JIST or visit www.jist.com for a free catalog and more information.

Visit www.jist.com. Find out about our products, order a catalog, and link to other career-related sites.

Content Advisor: Michael Farr
Acquisitions and Development Editor: Susan Pines
Editors: Lori Cates Hand, Veda Dickerson, Rodine L. Dobeck, Stephanie Koutek, Lisa S. Williams
Database Work: Laurence Shatkin
Cover and Interior Designer: Aleata Howard
Photo Coordinator: Trudy Coler
Proofreaders: David Faust, Jeanne Clark

Printed in Canada

07 06 05 04 03 9 8 7 6 5 4 3 2 1

ISBN 1-56370-488-9

Exploring Careers Takes You to Work

Every day you see adults all around you on their way to work. What do they do all day? How did they know which career path to follow? What training and education do they have? Do they like their jobs?

These questions are important because you will one day enter the world of work. *Exploring Careers* helps you answer the questions above, learn more about the jobs that interest you, and perhaps even decide on a career.

Deciding on a career is like climbing a ladder: Take it one rung at a time, and you will steadily and surely get to your goal. Skip a rung or two, and you may feel shaky and unsure about reaching the top. *Exploring Careers* is a rung on the ladder of your career decision-making and planning.

WHAT MAKES THIS BOOK UNIQUE?

Unlike dry reference books, *Exploring Careers* was written especially for you. It helps you explore career options through a unique combination of real information in an interesting style.

- It helps you consider connections between your interests, favorite subjects, and possible jobs.
- It features 49 detailed profiles of people at work, so you'll feel like you're right next to them on the job.
- It offers 19 skill samplers that discuss the skills important in certain jobs, so you'll learn if a career may be right for you.
- It includes over 1,000 job descriptions with information on education, job growth, annual openings, annual earnings, and skill levels required in math, English, and science. These facts help you pinpoint jobs to consider more seriously.

GETTING STARTED IS EASY

Exploring Careers is organized into 14 interest areas. Review the Table of Contents and each interest area's opening pages to decide if you want to know more about the related jobs. It's an easy and interesting way to start your journey through *Exploring Careers*.

After using *Exploring Careers,* you'll be ready for other rungs on your ladder to a career choice. They include talking to people who work in jobs that interest you; planning your high school classes to match your path; working in a field of interest part-time, as a volunteer, or as an intern; and pursuing further education and training. Good luck.

Quick Summary of Contents

Exploring Careers provides information on over 1,000 jobs organized into 14 interest areas. Each interest area includes interesting profiles of real workers, skill samplers that describe the skills required in certain jobs, and a section with facts and descriptions of all related jobs.

Here are the main sections of this book. Just turn to the pages listed to begin *Exploring Careers*.

Table of Contents

Introduction

THIS IS A BIG BOOK, BUT IT IS EASY TO USE

Exploring Careers is designed to help you explore and focus in on career options. It is a big reference book with lots of solid facts, but here's what's most important:

It's easy to use and fun to read. It contains real-life information about jobs and what they're like. Use the Table of Contents to find the sections and the profiles that interest you most. Then read how various workers spend a typical day. You can go on to the skill samplers and facts about all related jobs in each section for even more information.

If you want to know more about this book, including specific details on how it is organized, what the data in the job descriptions means, and what else you can learn from these pages, please read the rest of this introduction.

HOW *EXPLORING CAREERS* IS ORGANIZED

This book is organized into fourteen main sections, each representing an "interest area." The interest areas are from the *Guide for Occupational Exploration* (JIST Publishing), a separate book that arranges jobs by interests for easier study. The GOE system of interests was originally developed by the U.S. Department of Labor to provide young people with an intuitive way to explore career options. The fourteen interest areas are as follows:

1. Arts, Entertainment, and Media
2. Science, Math, and Engineering
3. Plants and Animals

4. Law, Law Enforcement, and Public Safety
5. Mechanics, Installers, and Repairers
6. Construction, Mining, and Drilling
7. Transportation
8. Industrial Production
9. Business Detail
10. Sales and Marketing
11. Recreation, Travel, and Other Personal Services
12. Education and Social Service
13. General Management and Support
14. Medical and Health Services

Each interest section is easy to use. Here is a summary of what you will find in each section.

SECTION OPENER

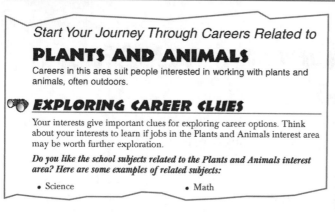

Start Your Journey Through Careers Related to

PLANTS AND ANIMALS

Careers in this area suit people interested in working with plants and animals, often outdoors.

EXPLORING CAREER CLUES

Your interests give important clues for exploring career options. Think about your interests to learn if jobs in the Plants and Animals interest area may be worth further exploration.

Do you like the school subjects related to the Plants and Animals interest area? Here are some examples of related subjects:

- Science
- Math

Opening pages help you "Start Your Journey Through Careers" related to the particular interest area. First, you read a brief description of the interest area. Next, "Exploring Career Clues" covers school subjects and free-time activities related to the interest area. This material helps you consider whether jobs in the interest area may be a good fit for you.

Then, "Exploring Job Groups" gives a list of more specific job groupings. These groups put related jobs together so that you can study them all at once.

For example, Visual Arts is a job group in the Arts, Entertainment, and Media interest area. In the job descriptions, all jobs related to Visual Arts are grouped together and described in alphabetical order. The Visual Arts job group includes such careers as cartoonist, fashion designer, interior designer, multi-media artist and animator, sculptor, set designer, and sketch artist.

At the end of each opener, "Exploring Career Possibilities" offers examples that connect specific interests to specific jobs to get you thinking about your future.

JOB PROFILES

PROFILE

Chris Choi—Graphic Designer

Chris Choi put down the phone and took a moment to think. His boss had called with a big change to a brochure that Chris was designing.

"In an artistic job, you have to keep your ego under control," Chris said. "It takes confidence and commitment to remain cooperative at all times. This is true especially when a client says your creation isn't

A graphic artist must listen carefully to create a brochure that pleases the client.

Three to five job profiles follow each opener. They are the heart of this book. The profiles—forty-nine in all—describe real people as they go about their daily work. These individuals discuss the jobs they do, the challenges they face, their training and education, their work environment, and what they like and sometimes don't like about the work. Sometimes the workers give advice to students interested in the career about what to study and how to get started.

The profiles were written by different people, so you may notice a variety of writing styles that adds richness to the stories. The content is based on actual interviews with workers and is enhanced with information from government resources. All names have been changed.

SKILL SAMPLERS

One to three skill samplers follow the job profiles. Each skill sampler–nineteen total–features a person who discusses the skills needed for his or her job. Questions appear after each skill to help you learn if the career may suit you.

SKILL SAMPLER

Catherine Rodriguez–Registered Nurse

Catherine Rodriguez works as a registered nurse in a hospital intensive care unit. She takes care of patients who are in serious condition following surgery. "I observe every little thing about my patient's condition, and I have to understand what I see."

Catherine discussed the skills and knowledge needed by registered nurses. She offers several tips to help you decide if you are suited for a career in nursing.

Registered nurses must be con- ... **lth.**

Catherine Rodriguez responds calmly to the tense, highly charged atmosphere of

JOB DESCRIPTIONS

MECHANICAL WORK

These workers install, service, and repair various kinds of machinery. Some machinery is large, such as the bodies and engines of cars, trucks, buses, airplanes, and ships; furnaces and air conditioners; office machines; and home appliances. Others are small, such as locks, watches, medical instruments, power tools, and musical instruments. These workers are hired by manufacturers, service companies, and businesses that use machines.

Aircraft Body and Bonded Structure Repairers. Repair body or structure of aircraft according to specifications. **Education and Training:** Postsecondary career and technical education. **Skills:** Math—Medium. English—Medium. Science—Medium. **Yearly Earnings:** $$$$ **Job Growth:** ★★★ **Yearly Openings:** 🚶🚶🚶

"Facts About All Major Jobs" marks the start of the job description section for each interest area. Jobs are organized into groups of related jobs. The job groups, as mentioned earlier, are from another book called the *Guide for Occupational Exploration.* A brief definition of each job group is provided to give you an overall sense of the work it covers.

A total of 1,093 jobs are described. These job descriptions come from the U.S. Department of Labor's Occupational Information Network (O*NET) database, a vast electronic resource packed with up-to-date job information.

Each job description includes the following information in an easy-to-use format.

- Job title.
- Description of the job's main duties.
- Education and training. This section tells you the education and training levels that most employers expect for someone starting out in the job. Almost all jobs require a high school diploma, so we do not include "high school graduate" as an option. Instead, we list the additional training and education the average high school graduate needs to get the job. Here are the education and training levels used and what they mean:
  - *Short-term on-the-job training.* Lasts one month or less.
  - *Moderate-term on-the-job training.* Lasts one to twelve months.
  - *Long-term on-the-job training.* Lasts more than twelve months. Includes apprenticeships.
  - *Work experience in a related occupation.*
  - *Postsecondary career and technical education.* Formal vocational or technical training after high school. Leads to certificate or other award.
  - *Associate's degree.* A two-year college degree.
  - *Bachelor's degree.* A four-year college degree.
  - *College degree, plus work experience.* Usually for management-related jobs that require a college degree and experience in a related nonmanagerial position.
  - *Master's degree.* A bachelor's degree plus one or two years of additional education.
  - *Doctoral degree.* A bachelor's degree plus three or more years of additional education.
  - *Professional degree.* A bachelor's degree plus at least three years of specialized education (for example, attorney or veterinarian).
- Skills. To show the relationship of basic school subjects to a job, we list skill levels required in math, English, and science. We set the levels at high, medium, and low, based on how experts rated the occupations in the O*NET database.

- Yearly earnings. Dollar signs represent the approximate range of average earnings for a job.

  $ = $20,000 or less per year
  $$ = $20,001 to $30,000 per year
  $$$ = $30,001 to $40,000 per year
  $$$$ = $40,001 to $50,000 per year
  $$$$$ = $50,001 or more per year

- Job growth. Stars represent the percentage of job growth through 2010. The percentage is the overall increase in the number of people employed in an occupation.

  ★ = 2% or less growth, or a decline
  ★★ = 3% to 9% growth
  ★★★ = 10% to 20% growth
  ★★★★ = 21% to 35% growth
  ★★★★★ = 36% or more growth

- Yearly openings. "People" represent the annual number of job openings. You may notice that some occupations, such as "computer and information scientists, research," have a high growth rate but a low number of openings. Other jobs, like "cooks, fast food," have many openings every year but a low growth rate overall.

  🯅 = 5,000 or fewer openings per year
  🯅🯅 = 5,001 to 10,000 openings per year
  🯅🯅🯅 = 10,001 to 50,000 openings per year
  🯅🯅🯅🯅 = 50,001 to 100,000 openings per year
  🯅🯅🯅🯅🯅 = 100,001 or more openings per year

We used the most reliable data available for the job descriptions. The data is helpful and gives you a general idea about earnings, job growth, and other measures. But because it is from a huge database of compiled and cross-referenced information, it can also be misleading at times. Take, for example, the yearly earnings information. This is highly reliable data from a very large U.S. working population sample. But many people in these jobs may earn much more or much less, depending on factors such as their experience, location, and employer size. So please keep this point in mind as you review the job descriptions. In addition, when you see the statement "no data available," it means that data has not yet been collected or processed for that particular measure.

OTHER MATERIAL

After the fourteen interest sections, appendixes describe sources of additional information for more research, give career tips for students, and discuss the importance of core school subjects and your career. Finally, an index of job titles helps you find specific jobs by page number.

OTHER INFORMATION YOU'LL LEARN FROM THIS BOOK

In addition to the details on what people do at work, this book offers other information in the profiles, skill samplers, and job descriptions. By reading the content, you will learn the following:

- **The connection between school subjects and work.** In the profiles, workers discuss how the things they learned in school became the foundation for their success.
- **The importance of matching your skills, interests, and values to a career.** People who like and are successful in their jobs are usually using their interests and best talents at work.
- **The importance of the right education and training for a job.** Deciding on a career path and then pursuing the right training or education have led the workers in the profiles and skill samplers to success.
- **The need to develop employability skills.** By developing and improving the skills that all jobs require, workers in the profiles and skill samplers have become valued employees. The skills that all employers want include basic ones, such as writing or listening; personal qualities, such as honesty; thinking skills, such as problem solving; interpersonal skills, such as teamwork; and technology skills.
- **The need for lifelong learning.** Many people in the profiles discuss how they continue to study and learn about their fields long after their formal education or training ends. Lifelong learning is important to stay current with changes on the job, with technology, and with your career field.
- **How character education carries over into the workplace.** Workers in the profiles discuss the importance of character at work.

Fairness, respect, initiative, teamwork, finishing projects, caring about people, trustworthiness, and honesty are keys to success with bosses, coworkers, and customers.

FINAL THOUGHTS

Exploring Careers helps you develop many of the basic "competencies" in the National Career Development Guidelines for high school students, including those on self-knowledge, educational and occupational exploration, and career planning.

What this means is that as you read this book, you are using your time wisely and learning about yourself, the working world, and how you will someday be an important part of it.

Acknowledgments

This reference is a complete revision of an earlier work by the same title. While this third edition features a new organizational structure, new or substantially revised job profiles, and new job descriptions, it would not have been possible without the effort of the many people involved in the original *Exploring Careers* by the U.S. Department of Labor. Other information sources used to develop this edition of *Exploring Careers* include JIST Publishing's *Guide for Occupational Exploration* and the U.S. Department of Labor's Occupational Information Network (O*NET) 4.0 database, the *Occupational Outlook Handbook,* and the *Occupational Outlook Quarterly.*

Special thanks to the reviewers of this edition: Ronda Ballinger, Sue Doell, and Linda Woodstrom.

Exploring Careers:

Arts, Entertainment, and Media

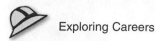

Start Your Journey Through Careers Related to

ARTS, ENTERTAINMENT, AND MEDIA

Careers in this area suit people interested in creatively expressing feelings or ideas, in communicating news or information, or in performing.

EXPLORING CAREER CLUES

Your interests give important clues for exploring career options. Think about your interests to learn if jobs in the Arts, Entertainment, and Media interest area may be worth further exploration.

Do you like the school subjects related to the Arts, Entertainment, and Media interest area? Here are some examples of related subjects:

- English
- Composition and writing
- Literature
- Speech
- Foreign language
- Art
- Photography
- Music
- Chorus
- Band
- Physical education

Do you like the free-time activities related to the Arts, Entertainment, and Media interest area? Here are some examples of related activities:

- Reading and writing articles, stories, poems, or plays
- Writing letters and e-mails to friends and family
- Keeping a journal or diary
- Working on your school newspaper or yearbook
- Taking photographs
- Painting
- Drawing
- Making short films or videos
- Designing sets for school or community plays
- Making costumes or clothes
- Playing a musical instrument
- Performing in a play
- Singing
- Dancing
- Being on the debate team
- Doing crafts
- Desktop publishing
- Creating Web pages

- Working on radios and TVs
- Doing makeup and hair for school plays, for friends, and for family
- Cheerleading
- Participating in baseball, basketball, football, hockey, soccer, running, gymnastics, and other sports
- Coaching sports activities

EXPLORING JOB GROUPS

Jobs related to the Arts, Entertainment, and Media interest area fit into ten groups. Read through the list to see which groups sound interesting to you.

- Managerial Work in Arts, Entertainment, and Media
- Writing and Editing
- News, Broadcasting, and Public Relations
- Visual Arts
- Performing Arts
- Craft Arts
- Graphic Arts
- Media Technology
- Modeling and Personal Appearance
- Sports: Coaching, Instructing, Officiating, and Performing

EXPLORING CAREER POSSIBILITIES

You can satisfy your interest in the Arts, Entertainment, and Media area through jobs that include creative, verbal, or performing activities. Here are a few examples of career possibilities:

If you enjoy literature, perhaps a writing or editing career would appeal to you. Do you prefer the performing arts? If so, you could direct or perform in drama, music, or dance.

If you especially enjoy the visual arts, you could become a graphic designer. You may want to use your hands to create products. You may prefer to model clothes or develop sets for entertainment.

You may want to participate in sports professionally as a coach or combine writing and sports as a sports reporter.

Turn the page to meet people working in the Arts, Entertainment, and Media interest area→

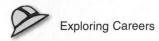

PROFILE

Kevin Kruse—Coach

"I love sports and coaching, but I am a teacher first."

The morning air was still and damp. The Seaview High School football field was slippery and rather muddy. On the sidelines, Coach Kevin Kruse was keeping students from cutting across it on their way to classes. A breeze ruffled his hair, and a patch of blue suddenly appeared in the sky. Coach Kruse smiled.

"It'll be fine by afternoon."

He headed back to his office in the gym and phoned the maintenance department.

"Mornin', Zack. Kruse here. The field should be dry in a couple of hours. Can you guys please restripe it before our practice? Great! Thanks, Zack."

Coach Kruse knew how important this game would be and how important it was to maintain good relations with the town's only newspaper.

He picked up a clipboard and checked the roster for the afternoon's practice. He then called Grace Wells in the school's main office to be sure no team members were absent. She told him they were all there and also that Sammy Wong had arrived.

Wong, a reporter for the *Seaview Sandpiper,* was there to get a background story before the upcoming game against Rio Seco. The friendly rivalry between the two schools was a community tradition.

Coach Kruse tried to avoid talking to reporters during school hours, but he knew how important this game would be and how important it was to maintain good relations with the town's only newspaper.

"People interested in high school coaching must realize that they will be teachers first and coaches second."

Paths to the Playing Field

"Coach Kruse, our readers know all about how you came here and turned a losing team around," Wong began. "You've won four conference and three state titles. You've been an inspiration. What would you tell someone who wants to follow in your footsteps?"

"There are many ways to become a high school football coach," Coach Kruse replied. "Some people go from playing in college to assistant coaching and teaching at a college or high school. A person can start at the high school level as an assistant, but often he or she first must be hired as a teacher."

"I know of several professional ball players who have gone into coaching when their playing career ended," Wong commented.

"So do I," the coach said. "But people interested in high school coaching must realize that they will be teachers first and coaches second. Education is more important than any sport because it can open far more opportunities for more people."

"What was your path, Coach?"

"My route carried me from being an assistant at the high school level to being an assistant coach at two colleges before I took a head coaching position at a state college for three years."

About that time, Coach Kruse said, he also realized that he would like to stay with one team, settling down in one place, to have more stability for himself and his family. He believed he would find that by returning to high school coaching. "I did a lot of looking, found Seaview, and here I am.

"You know, Sammy," the coach said, "many college students think a physical education major is the most direct path to coaching. Not so. I majored in life sciences rather than PE because I could always pick up the phys ed knowledge I needed for coaching by selecting specific courses.

"Graduates who are interested in coaching and have majors in the sciences or math would have a better chance at getting hired at most schools because there are more openings for these skills than there are for phys ed."

"Graduates who are interested in coaching and have majors in the sciences or math would have a better chance at getting hired at most schools because there are more openings for these skills than there are for phys ed.

"Many colleges also select assistant coaches for their teaching skills and experience rather than their coaching or playing records."

What the Fans Don't See

The reporter asked Coach Kruse to give his readers a glimpse into the daily life of a football coach.

"Most coaches and their assistants work ten- to twelve-hour days in season. They're out there six days a week–rain or shine. Off season, I log almost as many hours as I do during the season," Coach Kruse continued. "Inventorying equipment, being sure it's all in good repair, reviewing schedules, meeting with other conference coaches, and setting goals with each football player take up most of my time."

Coach Kruse and his players set goals for their physical and athletic development *and* for academics, identifying obstacles and ways to overcome those. Together, they review the goals throughout the year.

"Aren't all those responsibilities stressful?"

Coach Kruse laughed. "Would you believe it's winning that actually causes me the most stress?

Coach Kruse and his players set goals for athletic development and for academics.

"I have to believe my team can do it, even though I know in my heart that most people don't expect a win every week. After a few wins, I get to the point of constantly expecting to do well."

Why Coaching?

"Has football always been your first love?" Wong asked.

"As a kid, I drew plays, followed my favorite teams, and played every chance I could get. It's been like a lifetime hobby, so I reasoned that it would be great to get paid for it.

"An athlete who cares about his team, the game, and himself is not as likely to get into the dangerous stupidity of drugs and gangs."

"I thoroughly enjoy working with my staff, the other teachers, the kids, and their parents. It's exciting to see hard work pay off and to bring about changes in kids, especially those who might have gone in the wrong direction."

"Can you talk about that some more?" asked Wong.

"Our main purpose as educators and coaches is to teach our students outside the classroom. I think sports have positive, long-lasting effects on kids. An athlete who cares about his team, the game, and himself is not as likely to get into the dangerous stupidity of drugs and gangs.

"Through the things provided in football–like discipline, teamwork, and sacrifice–they learn some important life skills."

Sammy Wong tapped his pencil against his notepad thoughtfully. "Coach, let's say your star quarterback gets caught stealing right before a championship game. Would you play him?"

"No, I would not. I have standards and values that cannot be compromised. It's great to wear a championship ring. It's good for the ego, which all coaches seem to have. It feels good to be invited to seminars, banquets, and clinics. But I get more satisfaction when I can influence a young man who might be heading for some serious problems."

Coach Kruse then related the story of Bill, a sophomore with a troubled home life and some brushes with the law. A year ago, Coach Kruse and his staff decided to intervene.

"Since then, Bill has become part of our 'team family.' He's productive in school and is on the right path for a varsity position."

Preparing for the Big Game

Wong turned to the game against Rio Seco: How would the coach prepare his team now?

"All the physical conditioning is behind us," said Coach Kruse, "but we have to make sure we take care of the mental preparation. We want each player to feel good in knowing that he and his teammates are ready when they meet the preparation goals they set for themselves.

"We try to make it the players' team, their program, their victories, their championship. I let them know that it doesn't matter how much I want it. They are the people who will make the difference."

"We try to make it *the players'* team, *their* program, *their* victories, *their* championship. I let them know that it doesn't matter how much *I* want it. *They* are the people who will make the difference."

"Coach, I don't think Rio Seco has a chance this year!" exclaimed Wong.

The coach grinned. "Neither do I, Sammy. But don't quote me!"

PROFILE

Chris Choi—Graphic Designer

Chris Choi put down the phone and took a moment to think. His boss had called with a big change to a brochure that Chris was designing.

"In an artistic job, you have to keep your ego under control," Chris said. "It takes confidence and commitment to remain cooperative at all times. This is true especially when a client says your creation isn't what he or she had in mind."

A graphic artist must listen carefully to create a brochure that pleases the client.

Chris should know. He has dealt with many clients in his ten years as a graphic designer at a small public relations firm. "You have to realize that your work on a project sparks ideas for the other people working on the project. It's not a rejection of your work. It's a move in the right direction.

It's the designer's job to deliver a project that pleases the client, communicates clearly, and is attractive to the public.

"Looking at it that way keeps the job in perspective," Chris said. "You make contributions as the project goes from concept to rough sketches and then to a final look and layout."

It's the designer's job to deliver work that pleases the client. The project must also communicate clearly and be attractive to the public.

Chris said that new designers must keep in mind that often the client is correct. "Maybe that headline *should* be larger. Maybe the photo isn't right or the color needs to be brighter. The client best understands the message he or she wants the public to see."

Drawing on Natural Talent

"As a kid, I loved to doodle. In time, my doodles became decent-looking art that I put on birthday cards for my family.

"While signing up for my sophomore classes in high school," Chris said, "I was told all the electives I wanted were full. So I took an art class and met an inspiring teacher.

"Several months later, a neighbor who worked for a design company saw sketches of a house that I did as a class project. She encouraged me to keep drawing.

"Not long after that, my neighbor had several rush projects at work and needed freelance artists fast. She hired me at minimum wage. I didn't care because I was happy to be a professional. I worked after school and on Saturdays," Chris said.

"As I explored art as a possible career, I learned of the many options for designers."

After that, Chris took every art course that his high school offered. He also worked on the design and layout of his high school yearbook.

"As I explored art as a possible career, I learned of the many options for designers. You can work in print media, illustration, animation, or multimedia or on the Web."

Creativity with Computers

The occupation is influenced strongly by the computer, so anyone considering it should take courses in computer graphics. "The digital arts are very important. Drawing-board designers are rare." Chris pointed around the office. Each designer had a computer.

The occupation is influenced strongly by the computer, so anyone considering it should take courses in computer graphics.

"It's essential to select a college that is keeping pace with technology," Chris continued. "Though drawing classes are crucial, graphic design departments stress the use of computer graphics.

"With the computer, I can deliver three design options in a few hours. Doing them on a drawing board would take me all day."

College and Beyond

When it came time for college, Chris was careful about choosing one with a good graphic arts and design program.

"Then I started doubting my talent. I shared my doubts with my favorite instructor. My instructor said, 'Chris, do you think when an author sits down to write a novel, he writes until he's done? Or how about the artist who crosses out a dozen sketches before the work begins to take form?'

"My teacher continued. 'Do you *like* all aspects of what you're studying–the planning, the initial sketching, the constant changing, and the final developing?' As my head nodded in agreement, I realized that I was doing what I wanted to be doing.

"After college, I went looking for a job. I was armed with a perfect resume and a portfolio of what I considered my best work," Chris explained. "The interviewer placed my resume to one side. But she looked over my portfolio upside, downside, sideways, every way. That's what she wanted

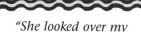

"She looked over my portfolio upside, downside, sideways, every way. That's what she wanted to see."

to see. That was the proof of my ability. I carry that lesson with me–pack a good portfolio."

Many Options for Graphic Designers

At that moment, Rosie, a department intern, called Chris to take another phone call. "I'm interning here while I'm taking graphic design and art classes. I'm getting terrific hands-on experience. I have to keep up with the other staff and learn to deal with deadlines," Rosie said.

"A young designer should look at fields that are closely related. Fields such as set design, medical illustration, merchandise display, photography, multimedia work, Web page design–even things like camera operation and lighting–could be of interest."

"Being an intern is a good reality check," Rosie continued. "I heard that last summer, another intern was given small jobs that he handled well. After that, he moved up to a project creating designs for a newsletter.

"But instead of showing off his talents, it turned out to be his moment of truth. He couldn't produce what was expected of him," Rosie noted. "He discovered early on, without more expense or frustration, that this wasn't his field. When he returned to school in the fall, he changed his major to interior design. I hear he's doing great.

"There's a good lesson there," Rosie said. "A young designer should look at fields that are closely related. Fields such as set design, medical illustration, merchandise display, photography, multimedia work, Web page design–even things like camera operation and lighting–could be of interest."

Bill Thomas, another experienced designer, stopped at Rosie's desk to look at her latest work. "Rosie, you can't learn from a better designer than Chris. Designers each develop a style, yet Chris's projects have a fresh look. Each assignment he takes on is like the most important one of his career."

Chris had explained to Rosie that a designer can choose to work for an agency, a design studio, or in a business with a design department. Chris also said that graphic designers can work their way up to assistant art director, art director, design director, or creative director of an art or design department. They can be freelancers. Or they can specialize in one area, such as science, technical, or medical work.

Always Learning and Improving

Chris said that designers must stay alert for developments. He suggests memberships in design groups that sponsor workshops. "Participation in these groups is fun and helps me improve my skills."

Outside, the city lights were coming on. The rush hour was beginning, but there was no sign of leaving. Several coworkers were sharing ideas to be used in the revisions that had to be done before anyone could go home.

"O.K.," Chris said to no one in particular as he turned back to his work. "Let's get this finished."

PROFILE

Linda Anderson-Miller—Reporter

Linda Anderson-Miller picked up the phone on the second ring. "The *Messenger,* good morning. May I help you?" she said quickly.

Her deadline was near. She was in a hurry. But any call might be *the* call—the one leading to the story of the century. Well, the story of the week, anyway.

A small voice said that this was Joey, that he was nine years old, and that he had news. A tree in his yard had fallen during the weekend rainstorm, and two squirrels had been left homeless. Linda was caught off guard and muffled a laugh.

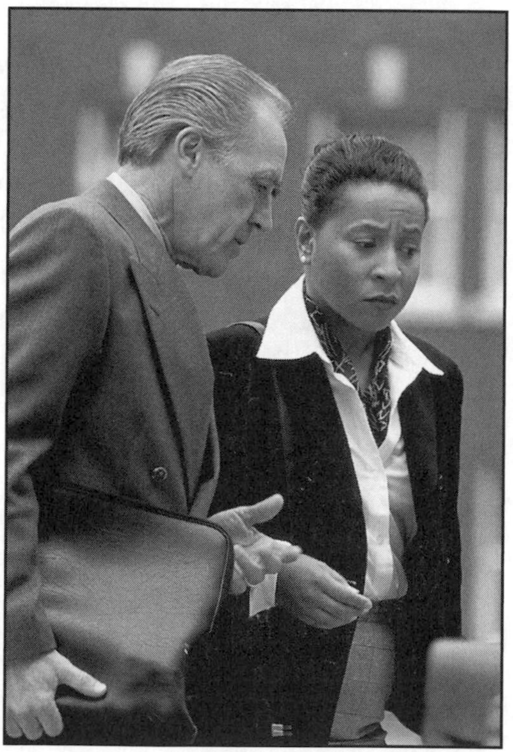

Linda investigates leads for new stories and confirms facts.

Today she was busy with last-minute details on stories for the next issue. The paper was coming out in just two days, on Thursday, as it always did. It wasn't too late to look into a new story. But it would have to be about something bigger.

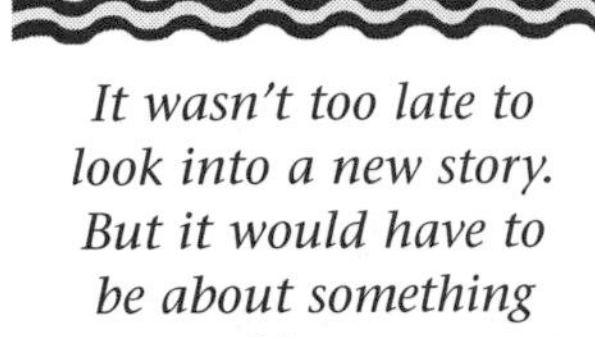

It wasn't too late to look into a new story. But it would have to be about something bigger.

"Thank you, Joey," she said. "But the *Messenger* has enough stories now. Perhaps you should tell your school newspaper."

A Weekly's Workers

The *Messenger* is a weekly newspaper. It serves a community of 35,000 readers. Like other weeklies, it has a small staff. Fortunately, the two staff reporters aren't responsible for all the articles that go into each edition. The newspaper buys some articles and columns. These come from a *syndicate,* an organization that sells stories to different newspapers for publication at the same time.

The newspaper also uses *stringers,* self-employed writers who cover specific topics, such as club and church activities and community meetings. Press releases sent in by local government agencies, political officials, local firms, and community groups also provide material.

A Busy Business

Linda called hello to her fellow reporter, Bill Leahy, who had just come in.

"Hi, Linda!" he called back, sitting down at his computer. "Just organizing these notes from my interview with Chester Deems. He's running for school board, you know."

Looking at Bill's paper-filled desk, Linda was suddenly aware of other keyboards clicking and several phones ringing. Linda finds that working in this busy environment motivates her. Working closely with the other staff also keeps her involved in all aspects of producing the newspaper.

"My work week begins Thursday morning and doesn't end until Wednesday night when the newspaper staff 'puts the paper to bed' by finishing it," she said.

Linda, Bill, and the managing editor, Craig Mead, meet each Thursday to create the weekly list of stories. Stories are assigned for each *beat,* which is a news source that a reporter covers regularly.

"I like to uncover the inside story, to find out what is really going on in the community."

Linda's beat is large. "I cover the state legislature, the city council, transportation, the fire and police departments, and parks and recreation.

"Covering so many different areas is one of the things that I like best about working at the *Messenger.* The job requires broad knowledge of the community," Linda said.

"If I were working on a city paper, I'd probably cover just one area of news–business, perhaps, or education." Linda enjoys the variety that the *Messenger* provides.

Digging Deep

"I like to uncover the inside story, to find out what is really going on in the community," Linda explained.

Linda advises people interested in a career as a reporter to work on their school newspaper and to read newspapers.

This side of reporting is the most interesting and challenging part of her work. It is also the most difficult, even with her bachelor's degree in journalism, which the job required. Through experience, has she learned how much research is involved in reporting, especially for a small weekly paper.

"We may not have the advantage of publishing a big story as soon as it breaks," she stated. "But Bill and I make up for it by doing extra investigation or by giving a new slant on a story. And we get to take more of a human-interest approach."

To keep up-to-date on what is happening on her beat, Linda often has to work nights as well as days, attending meetings of the city council, the parks and recreation department, and citizens' groups.

"Covering meetings is not easy," Linda said. But she has learned some helpful techniques over time. "I do research before a meeting to find out what is scheduled and to explore the different sides of each issue."

Attending meetings is just one way of gathering details for stories. Linda also uses leads from people who are in a position to know something useful. Developing these sources or contacts in the right places is another part of Linda's job. Leads also come from strangers who call in with questions, complaints, or information. *Like Joey,* she chuckled.

Linda spends a large part of her time checking out these leads. But only a few result in articles. Sometimes she does research at the library or on the Internet. Other times she examines police records or public records at the courthouse. Most of the time, though, she uses the phone or e-mail to check out leads.

The Write Moves

Linda has a curious nature and has always enjoyed writing. In high school, she explored public relations as a career option but decided on newspaper reporting instead.

Linda advises people who are interested in a career as a reporter to work on their school newspaper and to read newspapers. It is also helpful to get part-time or summer work on a newspaper while still in high school or during college.

Pulling It All Together

Linda looked at her notes from a lead received last Friday. "Hello? Are you a reporter at the *Messenger*?" the caller had asked.

When Linda replied that she was, the caller said, "I want to know what's going on with the construction that's begun in Crane Park. That land is owned by the county."

Linda had wanted to know, too. She'd quickly found the right people to talk to: the director and the public information officer of the county parks department.

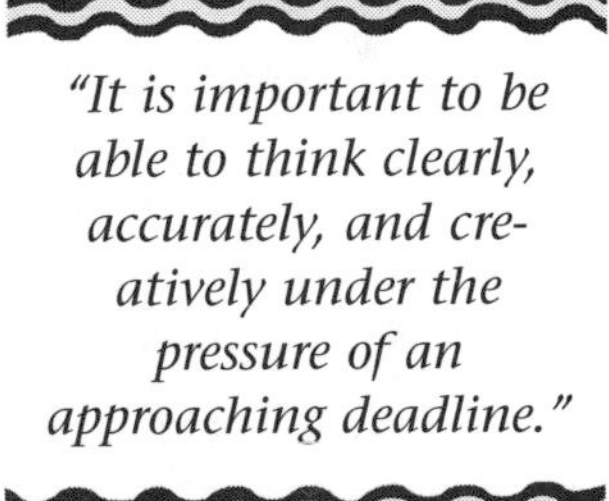

"It is important to be able to think clearly, accurately, and creatively under the pressure of an approaching deadline."

After that, she talked with the county's lawyers and then with the land developer. Finally, she went back to the park authorities. Just yesterday Linda learned that the county had decided to take the developer to court.

Linda gathered her notes from the stories she had followed during the past week. Many notes were scribbled down from phone conversations and interviews.

Knowing that people depend on her for news gives Linda a sense of responsibility.

"I end up doing most of my writing at the computer," Linda said. "It is important to be able to think clearly, accurately, and creatively under the pressure of an approaching deadline.

"I create a first draft and return to it later, rewriting and polishing it. Thank goodness I don't have to redo my drafts as much as when I was first starting out."

The articles had to be ready by the next morning so that they could be edited. They would then be given to the newspaper's compositor, who would lay them out on his computer.

Linda began rewriting the lead paragraph of the article about the land developer, thinking that she was proud of this story.

Bill looked over her shoulder. "That looks like an interesting piece."

"Thanks, Bill. I think that the community will find it worthwhile," she added.

Knowing that people depend on her for news gives Linda a sense of responsibility. Though she was looking forward to putting the week's paper to bed so that she could get some rest, Linda felt a big sense of satisfaction.

SKILL SAMPLER

Edna Tower—Broadcast Technician

Edna Tower attended a technical school after high school and is now working on a degree in electronics from a nearby college. She is a broadcast technician at radio station WPLA. "I'm behind the scenes, so the better I do my job the less I'm noticed."

Edna talked about the skills that broadcast technicians need. She offers these tips to help you decide if a career as a broadcast technician might be right for you.

Broadcast technicians must train their ears to pick out imperfections in the recordings they make and in the broadcasts they engineer.

- Do you like to listen closely to music and pick out its different parts?
- Can you tell a good-quality recording from a poor one?
- When listening to the radio, do you adjust the tuning to get the best sound from the station?

Broadcast technicians often have odd work schedules.

- Would you mind working nights, early mornings, or weekends?
- Could you adjust to having different working hours each day of the week?

Broadcast technicians often must operate controls continually through long broadcasts.

- Can you sit still and keyboard your school papers?
- Are you patient during classes that don't really interest you?
- Do you play long games such as Monopoly?
- Do you watch TV programs that last longer than an hour?

Broadcast technicians usually spend most of their workday in a few small studio rooms.

- Would you be satisfied working inside all day long?
- Would it bother you to spend the day in a small room with no outside windows?

Broadcast technicians often are given new tasks before they finish their current ones.

- Are you able to successfully handle projects and homework assignments from several different classes?
- Do you enjoy being involved in various activities outside of school each week?
- Is it easy for you to exit a computer program or game when one of your parents asks you to help with something?

Broadcast technicians must think and act quickly if something unexpected happens during a broadcast.

- Can you stay calm and act sensibly if the electricity goes off or some other emergency occurs at home?
- Do you know whom to call if something goes wrong when your parents are away?
- Can you adjust quickly if your friend has to cancel your plans at the last minute?

Broadcast technicians must keep an eye on several things at once.

- Can you cook a whole meal yourself and have everything ready at the same time?
- Do you enjoy watching sports, such as football, basketball, soccer, or hockey, in which you have to keep track of many players at once?
- Do you play complex computer games?

Broadcast technicians work with their hands.

- Do you have hobbies or crafts that require fine handiwork?
- Are you good with tools?
- Do you play a musical instrument?

SKILL SAMPLER

Bob Owens—Musician

Bob Owens has been a professional guitarist for five years. "I formed my own small band and hire for as many gigs as I can get. I've been successful because our band can play a variety of music, from rock to blues to jazz to mellow."

Bob talked about the skills that musicians need and offers some tips on how to know if music may be a good career for you to consider.

Musicians have to be devoted to their music.

- Do you love listening to music?
- Do you often get caught up with the music you hear?
- Would you rather go to a concert than to a movie?
- Would you rather play your musical instrument or sing than participate in sports or read a book?
- Do you ever think of songs that express your feelings?
- Do you ever write songs?
- Do you relate to characters in stories or movies who are musicians?
- Do you ever daydream about playing in front of an audience?

The music Bob Owens plays is easy to listen to and appeals to a large audience.

Musicians must be good at recognizing and reproducing sound differences. They need a good ear for music and rhythm.

- Can you tell when someone is singing off-key? Can you tell when someone plays a flat note on a musical instrument?
- Can you pick up a beat after hearing just a few bars of music? Can you remember the beat to a song the next day? Do you like to tap out rhythms on desktops and armchairs?
- Can you pick out a tune you know on a piano or guitar without reading the music?

Musicians spend many hours practicing. Musical ability is partly a matter of talent; practice is responsible for the rest.

- Can you stick with a task to perfect it? Do you rewrite your English compositions or rework your math homework?
- How willing are you to practice the skills you have now? Do you practice with your musical instrument or your singing?

Musicians, like all performing artists, have to be comfortable in front of an audience.

- Do you like being the center of attention?
- Can you speak in front of the class without getting embarrassed?
- Are you good at telling jokes?

Musicians need to be good at memorizing the words or music they perform.

- Is it easy for you to memorize words and tunes to popular songs?
- Do you have a good memory for names, phone numbers, and addresses?
- Can you remember the right keys to hit when you're at a computer keyboard?
- Are you good at memorizing?

Musicians sometimes have to perform when they don't want to or perform pieces they've grown tired of.

- Can you put your own wishes aside to please other people?
- Can you find the energy to meet your commitments, even if you don't feel like following through?

Now learn about all major jobs in the Arts, Entertainment, and Media interest area→

Facts About All Major Jobs Related to

ARTS, ENTERTAINMENT, AND MEDIA

In addition to the jobs covered in the profiles and skill samplers, other careers in the Arts, Entertainment, and Media interest area may appeal to you. This section describes and gives facts about all major jobs in the Arts, Entertainment, and Media interest area. For an explanation of the $, ★, and 🚶 symbols, see page 6.

MANAGERIAL WORK IN ARTS, ENTERTAINMENT, AND MEDIA

These workers manage people who work in arts, entertainment, and media. They oversee performers and performances in the arts and sports. They work for radio, television, and motion picture production companies and for artists and athletes.

Agents and Business Managers of Artists, Performers, and Athletes. Represent and promote artists, performers, and athletes to potential employers. May handle contract negotiation and other business matters for clients. **Education and Training:** College degree, plus work experience. **Skills:** Math—Medium. English—Medium. Science—Medium. **Yearly Earnings:** $$$$$ **Job Growth:** ★★★★ **Yearly Openings:** 🚶

Art Directors. Create design concepts and presentation approaches. Direct workers engaged in artwork, layout design, and copywriting for magazines, books, newspapers, packaging, and other visual media. **Education and Training:** College degree, plus work experience. **Skills:** Math—Medium. English—Medium. Science—Medium. **Yearly Earnings:** $$$$$ **Job Growth:** ★★★★ **Yearly Openings:** 🚶🚶

Producers. Plan and coordinate various aspects of radio, television, stage, video, or motion picture production, such as selecting scripts, coordinating writing, directing, editing, and arranging financing. **Education and Training:** College degree, plus work experience. **Skills:** Math—Medium. English—High. Science—Medium. **Yearly Earnings:** $$$$ **Job Growth:** ★★★★ **Yearly Openings:** 🚶🚶🚶

Producers and Directors. Produce or direct stage, television, radio, video, or motion picture productions for entertainment, information, or instruction. Responsible for creative decisions, such as interpretation of script, choice of guests, set design, sound, special effects, and choreography. **Education and Training:** College degree, plus work experience. **Skills:** Math—Medium. English—Medium. Science—Medium. **Yearly Earnings:** $$$$ **Job Growth:** ★★★★ **Yearly Openings:** 🚶🚶🚶

Program Directors. Direct and coordinate activities of personnel engaged in preparation of radio or television station program schedules and programs, such as sports or news. **Education and Training:** College degree, plus work experience. **Skills:** Math—Medium. English—High. Science—Medium. **Yearly Earnings:** $$$$ **Job Growth:** ★★★★ **Yearly Openings:** 🚹🚹🚹

Technical Directors/Managers. Coordinate activities of technical departments, such as taping, editing, engineering, and maintenance, to produce radio or television programs. **Education and Training:** Long-term on-the-job training. **Skills:** Math—Medium. English—Medium. Science—Medium. **Yearly Earnings:** $$$$ **Job Growth:** ★★★★ **Yearly Openings:** 🚹🚹🚹

WRITING AND EDITING

These workers write or edit prose or poetry. Some use knowledge of a technical field to write manuals. Most work for publishers, in radio and television studios, and in the theater and motion picture industries. Some are self-employed and sell their stories and plays to publishers.

Copy Writers. Write advertising copy for use by publication or broadcast media to promote sale of goods and services. **Education and Training:** Bachelor's degree. **Skills:** Math—Medium. English—High. Science—Medium. **Yearly Earnings:** $$$$ **Job Growth:** ★★★★ **Yearly Openings:** 🚹🚹🚹

Creative Writers. Create original written works, such as plays or prose, for publication or performance. **Education and Training:** Bachelor's degree. **Skills:** Math—Low. English—High. Science—Medium. **Yearly Earnings:** $$$$ **Job Growth:** ★★★★ **Yearly Openings:** 🚹🚹🚹

Editors. Perform variety of editorial duties, such as revising, laying out, and indexing content of written materials in preparation for final publication. **Education and Training:** Bachelor's degree. **Skills:** Math—Medium. English—High. Science—Medium. **Yearly Earnings:** $$$ **Job Growth:** ★★★★ **Yearly Openings:** 🚹🚹🚹

Poets and Lyricists. Write poetry or song lyrics for publication or performance. **Education and Training:** Bachelor's degree. **Skills:** Math—Low. English—High. Science—Medium. **Yearly Earnings:** $$$$ **Job Growth:** ★★★★ **Yearly Openings:** 🚹🚹🚹

Technical Writers. Write technical materials, such as equipment manuals, appendices, or operating and maintenance instructions. May assist in layout work. **Education and Training:** Bachelor's degree. **Skills:** Math—Medium. English—High. Science—Medium. **Yearly Earnings:** $$$$ **Job Growth:** ★★★★ **Yearly Openings:** 🚹

Writers and Authors. Originate and prepare written material, such as scripts, stories, advertisements, and other material. **Education and Training:** Bachelor's degree. **Skills:** Math—Medium. English—Medium. Science—Medium. **Yearly Earnings:** $$$$ **Job Growth:** ★★★★ **Yearly Openings:** 🧍🧍🧍

NEWS, BROADCASTING, AND PUBLIC RELATIONS

These workers write, edit, translate, and report factual or persuasive information. They use their language skills and knowledge of special writing techniques to communicate facts or convince people of a point of view. They work for radio and television stations, newspapers, publishing firms, and advertising agencies. Some translators travel with visiting foreign business people or diplomats; others work in courtrooms and law firms.

Broadcast News Analysts. Analyze, interpret, and broadcast news received from various sources. **Education and Training:** Bachelor's degree. **Skills:** Math—Low. English—High. Science—Medium. **Yearly Earnings:** $$ **Job Growth:** ★ **Yearly Openings:** 🧍🧍

Caption Writers. Write caption phrases of dialogue for hearing-impaired and foreign language-speaking viewers of movie or television productions. **Education and Training:** Moderate-term on-the-job training. **Skills:** Math—Low. English—Medium. Science—Medium. **Yearly Earnings:** $$$$ **Job Growth:** ★★★★ **Yearly Openings:** 🧍🧍🧍

Interpreters and Translators. Translate or interpret written, oral, or sign language text into another language for others. **Education and Training:** Long-term on-the-job training. **Skills:** Math—Low. English—High. Science—Medium. **Yearly Earnings:** $$$ **Job Growth:** ★★★★ **Yearly Openings:** 🧍

Public Relations Specialists. Engage in promoting or creating good will for individuals, groups, or organizations by writing or selecting favorable publicity material and releasing it through various communications media. May prepare and arrange displays and make speeches. **Education and Training:** Bachelor's degree. **Skills:** Math—Medium. English—High. Science—Medium. **Yearly Earnings:** $$$ **Job Growth:** ★★★★★ **Yearly Openings:** 🧍🧍🧍

Reporters and Correspondents. Collect and analyze facts about newsworthy events by interview, investigation, or observation. Report and write stories for newspapers, news magazines, radio, or television. **Education and Training:** Bachelor's degree. **Skills:** Math—Low. English—High. Science—Medium. **Yearly Earnings:** $$ **Job Growth:** ★ **Yearly Openings:** No data available.

VISUAL ARTS

These workers draw, paint, or sculpt works of art or design consumer goods in which visual appeal is important. They work for advertising agencies, printing and publishing firms, television and motion picture studios, museums, and restoration laboratories. They also work for manufacturers and in retail and wholesale trade. Many operate their own commercial art studios or do freelance work.

Cartoonists. Create original artwork using any of a wide variety of mediums and techniques, such as painting and sculpture. **Education and Training:** Long-term on-the-job training. **Skills:** Math—Low. English—Medium. Science—Medium. **Yearly Earnings:** $$$ **Job Growth:** ★★★ **Yearly Openings:** 🯅

Commercial and Industrial Designers. Develop and design manufactured products, such as cars, home appliances, and children's toys. Combine artistic talent with research on product use, marketing, and materials to create the most functional and appealing product design. **Education and Training:** Bachelor's degree. **Skills:** Math—Medium. English—High. Science—Medium. **Yearly Earnings:** $$$$ **Job Growth:** ★★★★ **Yearly Openings:** 🯅 🯅

Exhibit Designers. Plan, design, and oversee construction and installation of permanent and temporary exhibits and displays. **Education and Training:** Bachelor's degree. **Skills:** Math—Medium. English—Medium. Science—Medium. **Yearly Earnings:** $$$ **Job Growth:** ★★★★ **Yearly Openings:** 🯅

Fashion Designers. Design clothing and accessories. Create original garments or design garments that follow fashion trends. **Education and Training:** Bachelor's degree. **Skills:** Math—Medium. English—Medium. Science—Medium. **Yearly Earnings:** $$$$ **Job Growth:** ★★★ **Yearly Openings:** 🯅

Fine Artists, Including Painters, Sculptors, and Illustrators. Create original artwork using any of a wide variety of mediums and techniques, such as painting and sculpture. **Education and Training:** Long-term on-the-job training. **Skills:** Math—Medium. English—Medium. Science—Medium. **Yearly Earnings:** $$$ **Job Growth:** ★★★ **Yearly Openings:** 🯅

Floral Designers. Design, cut, and arrange live, dried, or artificial flowers and foliage. **Education and Training:** Moderate-term on-the-job training. **Skills:** Math—Medium. English—Medium. Science—Medium. **Yearly Earnings:** $ **Job Growth:** ★★★ **Yearly Openings:** 🯅 🯅 🯅

Graphic Designers. Design or create graphics to meet specific commercial or promotional needs, such as packaging, displays, or logos. May use a variety of mediums to achieve artistic or decorative effects. **Education and Training:** Bachelor's degree. **Skills:** Math—Medium. English—Medium. Science—Medium. **Yearly Earnings:** $$$ **Job Growth:** ★★★★ **Yearly Openings:** 🯅 🯅 🯅

Interior Designers. Plan, design, and furnish interiors of residential, commercial, or industrial buildings. Formulate design that is practical, attractive, and fitting for intended purposes, such as raising productivity, selling merchandise, or improving lifestyle. **Education and Training:** Bachelor's degree. **Skills:** Math—Medium. English—Medium. Science—Medium. **Yearly Earnings:** $$$ **Job Growth:** ★★★ **Yearly Openings:** 🧍🧍

Merchandise Displayers and Window Trimmers. Plan and erect commercial displays, such as those in windows and interiors of retail stores and at trade exhibitions. **Education and Training:** Moderate-term on-the-job training. **Skills:** Math—Low. English—Low. Science—Low. **Yearly Earnings:** $$ **Job Growth:** ★★★ **Yearly Openings:** 🧍🧍🧍

Multi-Media Artists and Animators. Create special effects, animation, or other visual images using film, video, computers, or other electronic tools and media. The art is used in products or creations, such as computer games, movies, music videos, and commercials. **Education and Training:** Bachelor's degree. **Skills:** Math—Medium. English—Medium. Science—Medium. **Yearly Earnings:** $$$$ **Job Growth:** ★★★★ **Yearly Openings:** 🧍🧍

Painters and Illustrators. Paint or draw to produce original artwork or illustrations, using watercolors, oils, acrylics, tempera, or other paint mediums. **Education and Training:** Long-term on-the-job training. **Skills:** Math—Low. English—Medium. Science—Medium. **Yearly Earnings:** $$$ **Job Growth:** ★★★ **Yearly Openings:** 🧍

Sculptors. Design and construct three-dimensional artworks, using materials such as stone, wood, plaster, and metal and employing various manual and tool techniques. **Education and Training:** Long-term on-the-job training. **Skills:** Math—Low. English—Low. Science—Medium. **Yearly Earnings:** $$$ **Job Growth:** ★★★ **Yearly Openings:** 🧍

Set and Exhibit Designers. Design special exhibits and movie, television, and theater sets. May study scripts, confer with directors, and conduct research to determine appropriate architectural styles. **Education and Training:** Bachelor's degree. **Skills:** Math—Medium. English—Medium. Science—Medium. **Yearly Earnings:** $$$ **Job Growth:** ★★★★ **Yearly Openings:** 🧍

Set Designers. Design sets for theatrical, motion picture, and television productions. **Education and Training:** Bachelor's degree. **Skills:** Math—Medium. English—Medium. Science—Medium. **Yearly Earnings:** $$$ **Job Growth:** ★★★★ **Yearly Openings:** 🧍

Sketch Artists. Sketch likenesses of subjects according to observation or descriptions to assist law enforcement agencies in identifying suspects, to depict courtroom scenes, or for entertainment purposes of patrons. Sketch artists use mediums such as pencil, charcoal, and pastels. **Education and Training:** Long-term on-the-job training. **Skills:** Math—Low. English—Medium. Science—Medium. **Yearly Earnings:** $$$ **Job Growth:** ★★★ **Yearly Openings:** 🧍

PERFORMING ARTS

These workers direct or perform for the public in works of drama, music, dance, or other entertainment. They are employed by motion picture, television, and radio studios, stock companies, nightclubs, theaters, orchestras, bands, choral groups, music publishing and recording companies, carnivals or circuses, and amusement parks. They may compose, arrange, or orchestrate musical compositions, choreograph dance routines, or plan the presentation of performances. In addition to the time spent on stage, performers must spend a large portion of their time auditioning for parts and rehearsing their performances.

Actors. Play parts in stage, television, radio, video, or motion picture productions for entertainment, information, or instruction. Interpret serious or comic role by speech, gesture, and body movement to entertain or inform audience. **Education and Training:** Long-term on-the-job training. **Skills:** Math—Low. English—Medium. Science—Medium. **Yearly Earnings:** $$ **Job Growth:** ★★★★ **Yearly Openings:** 🚹🚹🚹

Choreographers. Create and teach dance. May direct and stage presentations. **Education and Training:** Work experience in a related occupation. **Skills:** Math—Low. English—Medium. Science—Medium. **Yearly Earnings:** $$ **Job Growth:** ★★★ **Yearly Openings:** 🚹

Composers. Compose music for orchestra, choral group, or band. **Education and Training:** Master's degree. **Skills:** Math—Low. English—Medium. Science—Medium. **Yearly Earnings:** $$$ **Job Growth:** ★★★ **Yearly Openings:** 🚹🚹

Dancers. Perform dances. May also sing or act. **Education and Training:** Long-term on-the-job training. **Skills:** Math—Low. English—Low. Science—Medium. **Yearly Earnings:** $$ **Job Growth:** ★★★ **Yearly Openings:** 🚹

Directors—Stage, Motion Pictures, Television, and Radio. Interpret scripts, conduct rehearsals, and direct activities of cast and technical crew for stage, motion pictures, television, or radio programs. **Education and Training:** College degree, plus work experience. **Skills:** Math—Medium. English—Medium. Science—Medium. **Yearly Earnings:** $$$$ **Job Growth:** ★★★★ **Yearly Openings:** 🚹🚹🚹

Music Arrangers and Orchestrators. Write and transcribe musical scores. **Education and Training:** Bachelor's degree. **Skills:** Math—Low. English—Medium. Science—Medium. **Yearly Earnings:** $$$ **Job Growth:** ★★★ **Yearly Openings:** 🚹🚹

Music Directors. Direct and conduct instrumental or vocal performances by musical groups, such as orchestras or choirs. **Education and Training:** Master's degree. **Skills:** Math—Medium. English—Medium. Science—Medium. **Yearly Earnings:** $$$ **Job Growth:** ★★★ **Yearly Openings:** 🚹🚹

Music Directors and Composers. Conduct, direct, plan, and lead instrumental or vocal performances by musical groups, such as orchestras, choirs, and glee clubs. Includes arrangers, composers, choral directors, and orchestrators. **Education and Training:** Master's degree. **Skills:** Math—Medium. English—Medium. Science—Medium. **Yearly Earnings:** $$$ **Job Growth:** ★★★ **Yearly Openings:** 🚹🚹

Musicians and Singers. Play one or more musical instruments or entertain by singing songs in recital, in accompaniment, or as a member of an orchestra, band, or other musical group. Musical performers may entertain on stage, radio, TV, film, or video or record in studios. **Education and Training:** Long-term on-the-job training. **Skills:** Math—Medium. English—Medium. Science—Medium. **Yearly Earnings:** $$$ **Job Growth:** ★★★ **Yearly Openings:** 🚹🚹🚹

Musicians, Instrumental. Play one or more musical instruments in recital, in accompaniment, or as members of an orchestra, band, or other musical group. **Education and Training:** Long-term on-the-job training. **Skills:** Math—Low. English—Medium. Science—Low. **Yearly Earnings:** $$$ **Job Growth:** ★★★ **Yearly Openings:** 🚹🚹🚹

Public Address System and Other Announcers. Make announcements over loudspeaker at sporting or other public events. May act as master of ceremonies or disc jockey at weddings, parties, clubs, or other gathering places. **Education and Training:** Associate's degree. **Skills:** Math—Medium. English—Medium. Science—Medium. **Yearly Earnings:** $ **Job Growth:** ★ **Yearly Openings:** 🚹🚹🚹

Radio and Television Announcers. Talk on radio or television. May interview guests, act as master of ceremonies, read news flashes, identify station by giving call letters, or announce song title and artist. **Education and Training:** Moderate-term on-the-job training. **Skills:** Math—Low. English—Medium. Science—Medium. **Yearly Earnings:** $ **Job Growth:** ★ **Yearly Openings:** 🚹

Singers. Sing songs on stage, radio, television, or motion pictures. **Education and Training:** Long-term on-the-job training. **Skills:** Math—Low. English—Medium. Science—Low. **Yearly Earnings:** $$$ **Job Growth:** ★★★ **Yearly Openings:** 🚹🚹🚹

Talent Directors. Audition and interview performers to select most appropriate talent for parts in stage, television, radio, or motion picture productions. **Education and Training:** Long-term on-the-job training. **Skills:** Math—Medium. English—Medium. Science—Medium. **Yearly Earnings:** $$$$ **Job Growth:** ★★★★ **Yearly Openings:** 🚹🚹🚹

CRAFT ARTS

These workers create visually appealing objects from clay, glass, fabric, and other materials. Their jobs demand considerable skill. Some are employed by manufacturing firms, but many are self-employed, selling items they have made through galleries, gift shops, and Web sites.

Craft Artists. Create or reproduce handmade objects for sale and exhibition. Craft artists use a variety of techniques, such as welding, weaving, pottery, and needlecraft. **Education and Training:** Associate's degree. **Skills:** Math—Medium. English—Medium. Science—Medium. **Yearly Earnings:** $$ **Job Growth:** ★★ **Yearly Openings:** 🚹🚹

Glass Blowers, Molders, Benders, and Finishers. Shape molten glass according to patterns. **Education and Training:** Long-term on-the-job training. **Skills:** Math—Medium. English—Low. Science—Medium. **Yearly Earnings:** $$ **Job Growth:** ★★ **Yearly Openings:** 🚹🚹

Potters. Mold clay into ware as clay revolves on potter's wheel. **Education and Training:** Long-term on-the-job training. **Skills:** Math—Low. English—Low. Science—Medium. **Yearly Earnings:** $$ **Job Growth:** ★★ **Yearly Openings:** 🚹🚹

GRAPHIC ARTS

These workers produce printed materials, specializing in text, in pictures, or in combining both. Some of them use precision engraving and etching equipment and use considerable manual dexterity. Others use computerized or photographic equipment and rely more on technical skills. All of them have a good sense of what is visually appealing. They are employed by manufacturing firms, printing and publishing companies, and the publications departments in businesses of all kinds.

Camera Operators. Operate process camera and related darkroom equipment to photograph and develop negatives of material to be printed. **Education and Training:** Long-term on-the-job training. **Skills:** Math—Medium. English—Low. Science—Medium. **Yearly Earnings:** $$$ **Job Growth:** ★ **Yearly Openings:** 🚹🚹🚹

Desktop Publishers. Format text and graphic elements using computer software to produce publication-ready material. **Education and Training:** Postsecondary career and technical education. **Skills:** Math—Low. English—Medium. Science—Low. **Yearly Earnings:** $$$ **Job Growth:** ★★★★★ **Yearly Openings:** 🚹

Dot Etchers. Increase or reduce size of photographic dots by chemical or photomechanical methods to make color corrections on halftone negatives or positives to be used in preparation of printing plates. **Education and Training:** Long-term on-the-job training. **Skills:** Math—Low. English—Low. Science—Medium. **Yearly Earnings:** $$$ **Job Growth:** ★ **Yearly Openings:** 🚹🚹🚹

Electronic Masking System Operators. Operate computerized masking system to produce stripping masks used in production of printing plates. **Education and Training:** Long-term on-the-job training. **Skills:** Math—Low. English—Low. Science—Medium. **Yearly Earnings:** $$$ **Job Growth:** ★ **Yearly Openings:** 🯅🯅🯅

Engravers, Hand. Engrave designs and identifying information onto rollers or plates used in printing. **Education and Training:** Long-term on-the-job training. **Skills:** Math—Medium. English—Low. Science—Medium. **Yearly Earnings:** $$ **Job Growth:** ★★★ **Yearly Openings:** 🯅

Engravers/Carvers. Engrave or carve designs or lettering onto objects, using hand-held power tools. **Education and Training:** Long-term on-the-job training. **Skills:** Math—Medium. English—Low. Science—Medium. **Yearly Earnings:** $$ **Job Growth:** ★★★ **Yearly Openings:** 🯅

Etchers and Engravers. Engrave or etch metal, wood, rubber, or other materials for identification or decorative purposes. Includes such workers as etcher-circuit processors, pantograph engravers, and silk screen etchers. **Education and Training:** Postsecondary career and technical education. **Skills:** Math—Medium. English—Medium. Science—Medium. **Yearly Earnings:** $$ **Job Growth:** ★★★ **Yearly Openings:** 🯅

Etchers, Hand. Etch patterns, designs, lettering, or figures onto a variety of materials and products. **Education and Training:** Moderate-term on-the-job training. **Skills:** Math—Medium. English—Low. Science—Medium. **Yearly Earnings:** $$ **Job Growth:** ★★★ **Yearly Openings:** 🯅

Etchers. Etch or cut artistic designs in glass articles, using acid solutions, sandblasting equipment, and design patterns. **Education and Training:** Long-term on-the-job training. **Skills:** Math—Medium. English—Low. Science—Medium. **Yearly Earnings:** $$ **Job Growth:** ★★★ **Yearly Openings:** 🯅

Pantograph Engravers. Affix identifying information onto a variety of materials and products, using engraving machines or equipment. **Education and Training:** Moderate-term on-the-job training. **Skills:** Math—Medium. English—Medium. Science—Medium. **Yearly Earnings:** $$ **Job Growth:** ★★★ **Yearly Openings:** 🯅

Paste-Up Workers. Arrange and mount typeset material and illustrations into pasteup for printing reproduction, based on artist's or editor's layout. **Education and Training:** Long-term on-the-job training. **Skills:** Math—Medium. English—Medium. Science—Low. **Yearly Earnings:** $$$ **Job Growth:** ★ **Yearly Openings:** 🯅🯅🯅

Photoengravers. Photograph copy, develop negatives, and prepare photosensitized metal plates for use in letterpress and gravure printing. **Education and Training:** Long-term on-the-job training. **Skills:** Math—Medium. English—Low. Science—Medium. **Yearly Earnings:** $$$ **Job Growth:** ★ **Yearly Openings:** 🯅🯅🯅

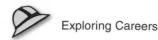

Precision Etchers and Engravers, Hand or Machine. Engrave or etch flat or curved metal, wood, rubber, or other materials by hand or machine for printing, identification, or decorative purposes. Includes etchers and engravers of both hard and soft metals or materials and jewelry and seal engravers. **Education and Training:** Long-term on-the-job training. **Skills:** Math—Medium. English—Low. Science—Medium. **Yearly Earnings:** $$ **Job Growth:** ★★★ **Yearly Openings:** 🚶

MEDIA TECHNOLOGY

These workers perform the technical tasks that create the photographs, movies, and videos; radio and television broadcasts; and sound recordings that provide entertainment and information for all of us. They are employed by local and network broadcasters, film studios, and independent film or video production companies, recording studios, and photography studios.

Audio and Video Equipment Technicians. Set up or set up and operate audio and video equipment, including microphones, sound speakers, video screens, projectors, video monitors, recording equipment, connecting wires and cables, sound and mixing boards, and related electronic equipment for concerts, sports events, meetings and conventions, presentations, and news conferences. May also set up and operate lighting. **Education and Training:** Long-term on-the-job training. **Skills:** Math—Medium. English—High. Science—Medium. **Yearly Earnings:** $$$ **Job Growth:** ★★★ **Yearly Openings:** 🚶

Broadcast Technicians. Set up, operate, and maintain the electronic equipment used to transmit radio and television programs. Control audio equipment to regulate volume level and quality of sound during radio and television broadcasts. Operate radio transmitter to broadcast radio and television programs. **Education and Training:** Postsecondary career and technical education. **Skills:** Math—Low. English—Medium. Science—Medium. **Yearly Earnings:** $$ **Job Growth:** ★★★ **Yearly Openings:** 🚶

Camera Operators, Television, Video, and Motion Picture. Operate television, video, or motion picture camera to photograph images or scenes for various purposes, such as TV broadcasts, advertising, video production, or motion pictures. **Education and Training:** Moderate-term on-the-job training. **Skills:** Math—Medium. English—Medium. Science—Medium. **Yearly Earnings:** $$ **Job Growth:** ★★★★ **Yearly Openings:** 🚶

Film and Video Editors. Edit motion picture soundtracks, film, and video. **Education and Training:** Bachelor's degree. **Skills:** Math—Low. English—Medium. Science—Low. **Yearly Earnings:** $$$ **Job Growth:** ★★★★ **Yearly Openings:** 🚶

Photographers. Photograph persons, subjects, merchandise, or other commercial products. May develop negatives and produce finished prints. **Education and Training:** Long-term on-the-job training. **Skills:** Math—Medium. English—Medium. Science—Medium. **Yearly Earnings:** $$ **Job Growth:** ★★★ **Yearly Openings:** 🚶 🚶 🚶

Professional Photographers. Photograph subjects or newsworthy events, using still cameras, color or black-and-white film, and variety of photographic accessories. **Education and Training:** Long-term on-the-job training. **Skills:** Math—Medium. English—Medium. Science—Medium. **Yearly Earnings:** $$ **Job Growth:** ★★★ **Yearly Openings:** 🧍🧍🧍

Radio Operators. Receive and transmit communications using radiotelegraph or radiotelephone equipment in accordance with government regulations. May repair equipment. **Education and Training:** Long-term on-the-job training. **Skills:** Math—Medium. English—Medium. Science—Medium. **Yearly Earnings:** $$ **Job Growth:** ★★ **Yearly Openings:** 🧍

Sound Engineering Technicians. Operate machines and equipment to record, synchronize, mix, or reproduce music, voices, or sound effects in sporting arenas, theater productions, recording studios, or movie and video productions. **Education and Training:** Postsecondary career and technical education. **Skills:** Math—Medium. English—Medium. Science—Medium. **Yearly Earnings:** $$$ **Job Growth:** ★★★ **Yearly Openings:** 🧍

MODELING AND PERSONAL APPEARANCE

These workers pose before a camera or a live audience, or they prepare the makeup or costumes for models or performers. Models display clothing, hairstyles, and commercial products; appear in fashion shows and other public or private product exhibitions; and pose for artists and photographers. They and their makeup artists work for manufacturers, wholesalers, and retailers. Some are employed by motion picture and television studios. Many models are self-employed or get jobs through model agencies or unions. Makeup artists and costume attendants who assist performers work for theaters and motion picture and television studios.

Costume Attendants. Select, fit, and take care of costumes for cast members and aid entertainers. **Education and Training:** Moderate-term on-the-job training. **Skills:** Math—Medium. English—Medium. Science—Low. **Yearly Earnings:** $ **Job Growth:** ★★★ **Yearly Openings:** 🧍🧍

Makeup Artists, Theatrical and Performance. Apply makeup to performers to reflect period, setting, and situation of their role. **Education and Training:** Postsecondary career and technical education. **Skills:** Math—Medium. English—Medium. Science—Medium. **Yearly Earnings:** $ **Job Growth:** ★★★ **Yearly Openings:** 🧍🧍🧍🧍

Models. Model garments and other apparel to display clothing before potential buyers at fashion shows, private showings, and retail establishments or for photographers. May pose for photos to be used for advertising purposes. May pose as subject for paintings and other types of artistic expression. **Education and Training:** Moderate-term on-the-job training. **Skills:** Math—Low. English—Low. Science—Low. **Yearly Earnings:** $ **Job Growth:** ★★★★ **Yearly Openings:** 🚶

SPORTS: COACHING, INSTRUCTING, OFFICIATING, AND PERFORMING

These workers participate in professional sporting events, such as football, baseball, and horse racing. Included are contestants, trainers, coaches, referees, and umpires. Some work at private recreational facilities, such as ski resorts, tennis courts, and gymnasiums.

Athletes and Sports Competitors. Compete in athletic events. **Education and Training:** Long-term on-the-job training. **Skills:** Math—Low. English—Low. Science—Low. **Yearly Earnings:** $$$ **Job Growth:** ★★★★ **Yearly Openings:** 🚶

Coaches and Scouts. Instruct or coach groups or individuals in the fundamentals of sports. Demonstrate techniques and methods of participation. May evaluate athletes' strengths and weaknesses as possible recruits or to improve the athletes' technique to prepare them for competition. **Education and Training:** Long-term on-the-job training. **Skills:** Math—Medium. English—Medium. Science—Medium. **Yearly Earnings:** $$ **Job Growth:** ★★★ **Yearly Openings:** 🚶🚶🚶

Fitness Trainers and Aerobics Instructors. Instruct or coach groups or individuals in exercise activities and the fundamentals of sports. Demonstrate techniques and methods of participation. Observe participants and inform them of corrective measures necessary to improve their skills. **Education and Training:** Postsecondary career and technical education. **Skills:** Math—Low. English—Medium. Science—Medium. **Yearly Earnings:** $$ **Job Growth:** ★★★★★ **Yearly Openings:** 🚶🚶🚶

Umpires, Referees, and Other Sports Officials. Officiate at competitive athletic or sporting events. Detect violations of rules and decide penalties according to regulations. **Education and Training:** Long-term on-the-job training. **Skills:** Math—Medium. English—Medium. Science—Medium. **Yearly Earnings:** $ **Job Growth:** ★★★★ **Yearly Openings:** 🚶

Exploring Careers:

Science, Math, and Engineering

Start Your Journey Through Careers Related to

SCIENCE, MATH, AND ENGINEERING

Careers in this area suit people interested in researching, analyzing, and applying scientific, mathematical, engineering, and technological knowledge to real-world problems. Some of these workers are interested in discovering, and analyzing information about the world, the environment, or societies. Others enjoy applying scientific research to problems in medicine, the life sciences, and the natural sciences. Some like to work with and manipulate data. Others enjoy employing technology and computers in a wide range of activities.

EXPLORING CAREER CLUES

Your interests give important clues for exploring career options. Think about your interests to learn if jobs in the Science, Math, and Engineering interest area may be worth further exploration.

Do you like the school subjects related to the Science, Math, and Engineering interest area? Here are some examples of related subjects:

- Science
- Chemistry
- Biology
- Geology
- Physics
- Geography
- Math
- Algebra
- Geometry
- Calculus
- Computers
- History
- Social studies
- Sociology
- Psychology
- English

Do you like the free-time activities related to the Science, Math, and Engineering interest area? Here are some examples of related free-time activities:

- Playing chess or solving complex puzzles
- Researching things that sound interesting to you
- Belonging to a computer or science club
- Installing, wiring, and upgrading personal computers and other electronic equipment

- Writing computer programs
- Helping friends with math
- Creating Web pages
- Calculating sports statistics
- Participating in science fairs
- Studying and collecting rocks, minerals, fossils, or plants
- Observing and studying the stars, the weather, insects, birds, or wildlife
- Doing experiments with chemistry sets and science kits
- Building robots, electronic devices, or working models
- Taking apart or fixing mechanical and electronic devices
- Visiting museums and historic sites
- Reading about topics related to technology, computers, science, or medicine

EXPLORING JOB GROUPS

Jobs related to the Science, Math, and Engineering interest area fit into eight groups. Read through the list to see which groups sound interesting to you.

- Managerial Work in Science, Math, and Engineering
- Physical Sciences
- Life Sciences
- Social Sciences
- Laboratory Technology
- Mathematics and Computers
- Engineering
- Engineering Technology

EXPLORING CAREER POSSIBILITIES

You can satisfy your interest in the Science, Math, and Engineering area through jobs that focus on the knowledge and processes of the sciences, mathematics, computers, and engineering. Here are a few examples of career possibilities:

You may enjoy researching and developing new knowledge in mathematics. Or perhaps solving problems in the physical or life sciences would appeal to you. You may wish to study engineering and help create new machines, processes, and structures. If you want to work with scientific equipment and procedures, you could seek a job in a research or testing laboratory. If you are good with computers, you could work as a computer programmer.

Turn the page to meet people working in the Science, Math, and Engineering interest area→

PROFILE

Anita Braxton—Archeologist

Anita Braxton pushed open the double doors and grabbed her lab coat. Her energetic style disguised the scholar within: She holds a master's degree in archeology and a doctoral degree in anthropology.

In Anita's lab, shelves of labeled boxes line the walls. There are sinks for washing "finds," or artifacts. Next to them are counters where artifacts are placed on grates to dry. Artifacts are also weighed, measured, and compared to other items found at the sites, or "digs."

The other side of the room houses a laboratory for determining the age of the artifacts and how they were made. They are eventually analyzed, labeled, rebagged, and shipped to a museum.

There is a feeling of excitement in this large room. The joy of discovery that began on sites in far corners of the world continues here.

The Puzzle of the Past

Anita poured herself a steaming mug of coffee and leaned comfortably against a sink.

"My job is searching for what was left by human beings from the past. That could be fossil remains, such as bones. It could be artifacts like carvings, jewelry, pottery, or coins. We look at the remains of structures, which could be their homes, buildings, monuments.

"These remains help us to learn as much as we can about a past society's behavior and culture. It's like putting together a wonderful, complex puzzle.

"This is an exciting part of my job. 'Life' begins to emerge from those objects. We begin to picture the society that used them. For me, it's like being transported back in time."

Raiders of the Lost Ark?

"You know," she said, "people think archeologists are like Indiana Jones. We do put up with bugs, snakes, and scorpions. But it isn't always an adventure. Sometimes it's boring.

"Going out in the field has some hardships. In some countries, electricity is available only in larger towns. The same can be true for running water.

"It's especially important to be patient and very respectful of the people and their customs and traditions."

"You can really miss home cooking. At a site in Ghana, we missed it so much that we made a cake on top of a kerosene burner. Still, it's especially important to be patient and very respectful of the people and their customs and traditions. Living in a small African village, for example, in no way compares to *any* town in the United States."

Roads to Travel

Anita is the lab director for an archeological consulting firm. Her duties include keeping the projects on schedule, editing and writing reports, and checking supplies and equipment.

In the field of archeology, various types of work are available. On the academic side, teaching positions allow for fieldwork in the summer. The other career area, consulting, offers a wider variety of positions. A person can be involved solely in lab work or fieldwork or can combine the two.

"I know people who want to work only in the field. They travel from one project to the next. Others find they'd rather work in the lab than live out of suitcases."

Anita's work experience has been a mix. She's worked on many digs. She has also spent time as a research assistant in a radiocarbon lab where they study the age of materials. Anita's worked as an analyst of stone tools and of animal remains and has been a computer consultant.

Digging into This Career

"The days of hands-on experience being enough are over," said Anita. "You'll need a bachelor's degree for this career. If you want to direct an excavation, you'll need a master's or doctoral degree.

"Of course, you also need field experience. Most degree programs require fieldwork. That can be gained by attending a field school for a summer or semester. The work involves excavating, surveying, and mapping sites. Usually these programs include lab work and artifact analysis.

"There are some amateur societies that offer annual digs," added Anita. "They're lots of fun. It's a good chance to meet interesting, experienced people.

"When I went out on my first field assignment, I worked on the Alaska Highway excavating an old trading post. One of my jobs was looking through nearby farm fields for artifacts exposed by plowing. When I was finished with that project, I was hooked into this career."

Anita strongly advises learning a second language in school. "That can be a big asset if you want to get work at sites outside of the United States. I have learned Swahili."

Location is not the only career choice that archeologists make. Anita pointed out that students usually develop an interest in a specific time period and in working with certain materials, such as pottery, tools, or animal bones.

"However, it's better to develop into a jack-of-all-trades. Getting people to overseas sites has become so expensive that many companies would rather send one person to do two or three specialized tasks."

Life in the Field

"When I go on trips in the field, I try to gather as much information as I can about the area and what is available. I like to reduce surprises.

"I'd say fieldwork is the hardest and yet the most rewarding part of the job. We get up at the crack of dawn, and everyone on the crew is assigned a specific task. Then the work really begins. Eight to ten hours of manual labor!

"Working with shovels, trowels, brushes, and screens can be backbreaking. We often deal with heat, humidity, sunburns, sore muscles, bugs, and frustration. People in this field have spent entire days on their hands and knees without finding a single thing.

"When a dig becomes frustrating, it's especially important to be able to get along with people. There's a good deal of companionship on-site–sharing of past experiences and wonderful stories by the old-timers.

"As we excavate, we must document. We record everything we find, how we found it, and what it's made of. We take many photos along the way,

which help us later when we try to link artifacts with one another. Keep in mind that once a site has been excavated, it's destroyed. Notes and photos become crucial."

Computers have become a major asset to archeology, Anita said. "All reports are done on computers, as well as cataloguing and some analysis. Laptops now follow the archeologist into the field."

Discovery!

"This business is educational. Since starting out twenty years ago, I've had so many wonderful experiences in different sites, regions, and countries. I love it."

Suddenly someone in the lab gave a loud whoop. Lab technicians and scientists hurried over. A technician had just made a perfect match between an arrowhead and a puzzling mark he'd been studying on a rib bone.

The expression on Anita's face showed that at this moment the years of study, sore muscles, and mosquito bites were well worth it.

PROFILE

Maxwell Mullen—Computer Programmer

The beeping of the pager finally got through to Max. He rolled over sleepily, clicked on the lamp, and glanced at the clock. Midnight!

Who would be calling me at this hour? Max wondered.

As his mental fog cleared, he remembered. Of course. It was his turn to be on call if anything went wrong with the computers down at Fischer Financial.

"As a computer programmer, I'm the one who figures out how to tell a brainless piece of machinery how to work."

Maxwell Mullen is a computer programmer working for a small computer systems and software company located in a medium-sized city.

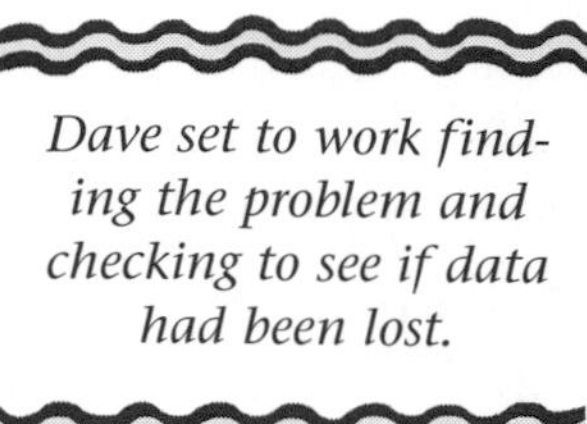

Dave set to work finding the problem and checking to see if data had been lost.

It was his own fault that he'd barely had fifteen minutes of sleep so far. He'd been so absorbed by working on a software concept that he'd forgotten he was on call.

Grabbing the phone, he dialed the number at "Fish Fin" (as he called the company) that would connect him with the computer area in the basement of the downtown high-rise.

A Midnight Run

"Dave? That you? This is Max. What's up?"

"Oh, hi, Max. Hey, I'm sorry to wake you up, but the tape storage machine failed again. I think it's a software problem, and I'm not sure if we've lost data. Can you help me?"

"Sure, Dave. Give me about a half hour and I'll come get you running again. That's what they pay me for."

At "Fish Fin," Max found Dave nursing a cup of lukewarm coffee and looking unhappy.

"Hi, Max–thanks for coming down. This is the third time this thing has failed on my watch. I'd give it a kick, but I'm afraid it'll bite me."

"I know how you feel, Dave. Sometimes this stuff seems to have a mind of its own."

Max set to work finding the problem and checking to see if data had been lost. "Okay, Dave, you're up and running again," said Max before long. "I've run the backup program, and everything's there. I'm going back to bed where I belong."

It had taken Max an hour and a half, including his driving time, to do the fix. Knowing how to do that fix is what made him so valuable.

The Brains Behind the Computer

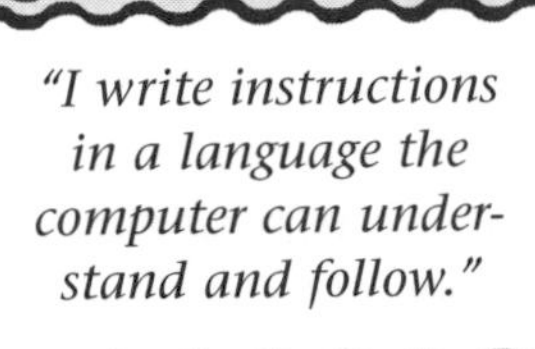

"I write instructions in a language the computer can understand and follow."

A few hours of sleep later, he entered his office–feeling a bit more awake after a hot shower, a shave, a change of clothes, and some breakfast. Brilliant sun flooded the office suite he shared with two other computer software development specialists, a national sales manager, and one receptionist.

"As a computer programmer, I'm the one who figures out how to tell a brainless piece of machinery how to work," Max said.

"When a computer needs to be told how to do a task, whether it's something new or a change in some existing program, I break the project down into a series of simple, logical steps. Then I write those steps, or instructions, in a language the computer can understand and follow.

"Once I've written it, then I've got to test it to see if the computer will do what I told it to do. If it doesn't, then I've got to go back through the program I wrote, find out where the 'bug' is, and fix it. Then I test it again.

"I may have to retest it several times, especially if it's a complicated program, before I'm sure that a computer will properly read the instructions I've given it.

"You know, a computer isn't smart. It doesn't think, at least not in human terms. It's just super-fast. And it doesn't always work as we want it–as proven by last night.

"So one of the things I've been working on is to program–'teach'–Fish Fin's computer to run a full backup in a situation like that."

How to Get with the Program

Max, who holds a bachelor of science degree in computer sciences, says that a college degree is not an absolute requirement to become a computer programmer. Without one, however, the road is a lot more difficult.

"Believe me, programmers without college degrees are the exception," he said. "It's one of those circles you get trapped in. If you lack the degree, you must have the equivalent in solid, hands-on experience. But it's almost impossible to get the experience without the degree.

"If you want to be a computer programmer, go for the technical curriculum in college," he advised. "Be sure to learn as much as you can about a variety of current programming languages. It doesn't hurt to learn the analytical side of this business, either. But your main focus should be on the technical.

"Be sure to learn as much as you can about a variety of current programming languages."

"Get some good on-the-job experience along with your courses. You need exposure to less-than-perfect computer environments so you'll be able to recognize problems when you run into them again.

"Once you're in a job, you've got to keep up with the advances in technology. There are seminars that your company will usually pay all expenses to have you attend.

"And read! I subscribe to several monthly trade magazines and schedule daily reading time just to keep up."

Max points to some framed documents on his wall. "There are no licensing requirements for programmers. However, a number of companies offer certifications, like these. Companies are aware of this and will look very carefully at your background. So it pays to give yourself every competitive edge you can."

Programming Paths

"Many programmers work for companies, but more and more they're being employed on a contract basis," Max noted. "For example, some company may need a programmer to come in and debug or rewrite a program of theirs, and that's the end of their need.

"So they turn to a consulting firm or temporary help agency instead. Some temporary jobs can last for months or even years, and I know some programmers who prefer to work on that basis.

"Like anything else, it has its pros and cons, but it's something to know about and consider when you're looking for work as a programmer.

"A lot of time commitment and stress can go along with some programming jobs. Computers run twenty-four hours a day, and I know some programmers who have turned down high-paying jobs because of the stress

and family disruption that would be involved in being responsible for keeping those machines running."

Max believes that this is a good time to go into computer programming because the field is growing and changing dramatically.

"One government report I read recently said that the employment of programmers will slow somewhat as more software that users can run by themselves becomes available. On the other hand, many programmers make their living from designing that software–from computer games to personal finance and educational software.

"The enormous growth of the World Wide Web has meant more jobs for programmers, too, as organizations depend more and more on good Web sites to attract and inform people.

"As I see it, computer technology is changing and growing so fast that there will be a demand for programmers who are educated and skilled enough to make that technology work."

PROFILE

Jon Cisnero— Environmental Specialist

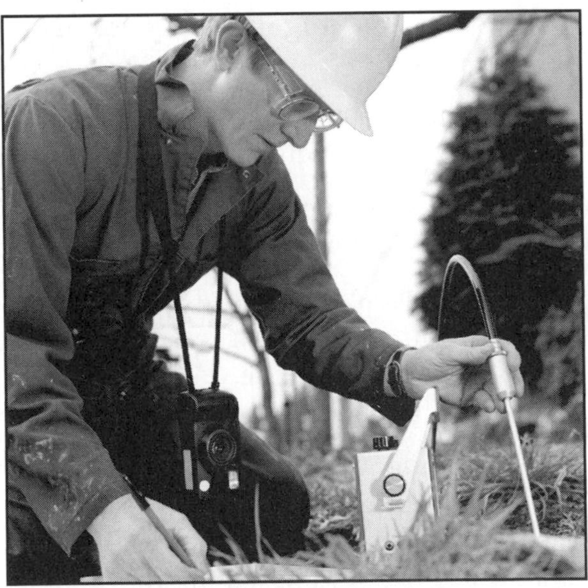

Jon's work makes the world cleaner and safer for everyone.

The morning frost shines on autumn leaves around the manhole cover where Jon Cisnero is kneeling.

Jon is an environmental specialist on assignment to inspect the city's combination sewers. These sewers are designed to carry both rainwater and sanitary waste. He's looking for illegal connections that dump hazardous chemicals into the sewer.

"My career takes me into interesting places, some of which I enjoy. Sewers are not one of them," Jon said.

Checking sewers for illegal connections is of major concern to managers at the local wastewater treatment plant. Hazardous chemicals could destroy the delicate biological process inside the treatment plant. The plant makes wastewater safe for release into rivers and streams.

If Jon finds illegal sewer connections, the guilty party must be located and stopped. That party could face big fines–even jail.

Going "Down Under"

Jon opens the manhole cover with a pry bar. He instantly senses warm, foul air from the sewer below. Jon then shouts, "Watch your toes," as he flips the heavy manhole cover on its side.

Protective clothing, flashlight, hard hat, and breathing mask (in case of fumes) complete Jon's safety gear.

Covering his shirt pocket with one hand, Jon leans over the manhole. "I can't tell you how many times I've forgotten to cover my pocket and watched my pens fall in," he said.

Using a flashlight, he peers inside. Jon then straightens up and takes a few notes. He asks Connie Stenson, his assistant, for vials to take samples.

"I've been in dozens of sewers this week looking for illegal connections," Jon said. "Not the most pleasant assignment."

Storm sewer inspection can be dangerous, too. One time, Jon was suspended from a safety harness and lowered into a sewer with deep water rushing through it. "The water was rushing by at three feet a second. If my safety line had snapped, I would have been in trouble."

This morning, Connie helps Jon into his harness. The harness is attached to a nylon rope that will lead Jon back to the manhole should he become disoriented from gases, darkness, or an accident. Protective clothing, flashlight, hard hat, and breathing mask (in case of fumes) complete Jon's safety gear.

This manhole shaft drops twelve feet to where the brick sewer tunnel branches off in each direction. Jon shines his flashlight into the hole. He then descends the steps into the darkness.

Above Ground, But Not Always Aboveboard

Out in the daylight again and on the way back to his office, Jon explained that sewers can seem serene compared to some locations–for example, a metal-finishing factory.

"The floor is one big puddle of oil, water, and chemicals. Machines are swinging big mechanical arms, and forklifts are buzzing by. You have to watch out.

"You have to watch out for some companies, too. One tried to dodge the laws by shutting off the flow of wastewater whenever it was inspected. A massive tank that stood about fifteen feet off the shop floor held this wastewater. They shut off its drain for inspections.

"Once when I was there, they shut off the drain but forgot to turn off the pump that was filling it. Suddenly there was a loud noise. I looked up to see water gushing out of the tank."

What It Takes

For students with an interest in chemistry, math, or the natural sciences, environmental science is a good career to consider. A four-year college degree, often in some type of engineering, is needed.

Some large industries employ environmental specialists on staff. Other specialists work for large environmental consulting firms or, like Jon, as independent consultants.

"Smaller companies don't usually have environmental specialists on staff," Jon explained. "They need independents like me to help them understand what changes they have to make in their treatment of wastes to comply with the laws.

"That means I need a solid knowledge of the hundreds of federal, state, and local pollution regulations. To do that, I read industry publications and reports.

"Some clients are resentful and reluctant to speak with me," Jon said. "I tell them I'm trying to help them. I'm not there to turn them in.

"I need to communicate problems and solutions to clients clearly, both verbally and in writing."

"I need to communicate problems and solutions to clients clearly, both verbally and in writing. It helps that I've taken courses in communications and public speaking."

Fines for businesses that do not obey environmental laws can be in the millions of dollars. The Environmental Protection Agency has jailed some executives found guilty. When customers are cited for violations, Jon must often take part in hearings.

"I'm there to lessen the risk to my customers," he said. "Hearing officers are usually tolerant if you're cooperative. But you'll be monitored more often to make certain you're following the law."

Jon Shares His Findings

Back at his office, Jon showers and dresses in a clean shirt. He then shares his thoughts with colleagues. They include a chemical engineer, a chemist, a geologist, and several general and environmental engineers.

Jon takes out the clipboard he carried into the sewer and flips through his notes. "I found an illegal tap about a hundred feet into the line," he said. He holds up a vial with yellowish fluid inside. "This is the stuff coming from the tap line. Looks like some sort of acid, but we'll take it to our lab for analysis."

Once the sample is identified, finding the tap begins. The sample helps Jon identify the manufacturing processes that create such wastes. Then, using a study of the manufacturers in the area, he identifies the potential violators. Along with Jon, officials from the wastewater treatment facility will investigate those companies.

Violators could face fines. They could be required to correct the tap and then construct proper connections to handle the hazardous waste.

"Sometimes a business owner will blame me for hurting the business by citing these abuses. But more often people are amazed to learn that what they've been doing is illegal."

"I get a lot of satisfaction from helping to make our world a cleaner and safer place."

Jon believes that most industries want a clean environment. He said most companies go to great lengths to make their operations as pollution-free as possible.

A Great Environment

As pollution laws continue to change, the demand for environmental specialists should grow. "Regulations are often phased in slowly. This gives industry time to address the solutions and creates opportunities for people like me," said Jon.

"If you're willing to learn and work hard, the environmental field offers variety, challenge, and financial rewards. And I get a lot of satisfaction from helping to make our world a cleaner and safer place."

PROFILE

Gregory Bloom—Home Inspector

As a home inspector, Gregory Bloom searches to uncover defects in dwellings before someone buys them. He helps buyers beware so their dreams of home ownership don't collapse into nightmares.

Most buyers, Gregory explained, lack the expertise needed to assess the condition of a house, condominium, or other dwelling. They seek aid from a home inspector.

"Some buyers got the idea of asking an architect or builder friend to look over a house and give an opinion about its soundness," he said. "The profession evolved from there."

A home inspector checks wiring, plumbing, and other structural components of a house.

In the beginning, home inspectors checked only for major structural problems, such as sinking foundations. Then they began to inspect things like wiring, plumbing, major kitchen appliances, roofing, and attic ventilation.

"The trend," said Gregory, "has been increasing coverage of inspections and expectations of customers."

Checking, Climbing, and Crawling

Gregory receives calls from home buyers requesting his services. To inspect thoroughly, Gregory considers every aspect of a house. He climbs on roofs, descends into basements, and ventures into attics and crawl-spaces, besides exploring the main living areas.

"You need to be fairly physically fit for the job," said Gregory. "Physical strength isn't required as much as agility."

The work requires use of special tools. "We're famous for a couple of tools," said Gregory. "The biggest one is our folding ladder." This triple-jointed ladder has four sections. Gregory can configure it in a variety of ways for interior and exterior use. When completely folded, the ladder fits nicely into Gregory's car. Inspectors use moisture meters to check for water seepage. They also use electrical outlet testers and other more common tools.

Inspection work presents some risks. Climbing on roofs, working with electricity, and doing other home inspecting tasks pose obvious hazards.

"Most inspectors have gotten an electrical shock at least once," said Gregory. "They've likely been singed by flames coming from a furnace, too." When delving into attics and crawlspaces, inspectors may find broken glass, rodents, or other disagreeable things. On Gregory's least lucky day, a basement sump pump blew up near him, making his ears ring and splattering him with scummy water.

Gregory enjoys the technical challenges of inspections. They vary by size, complexity, and age of the building and whether it's currently occupied. Poor maintenance or do-it-yourself improvements add difficulty as well.

Gregory likes mixing the technical and the interpersonal in his work. He educates prospective buyers. They usually watch as he inspects the house. "It gives me great satisfaction," he said, "to teach buyers about technical matters addressed by the inspection. They are things most people are unfamiliar with. I strive to do so with excellence."

Inspectors must support the interests of their customers, the buyers. On completing an inspection, Gregory gives the customer a written report. He does not discuss these findings with sellers or their agents unless the buyers give permission. The information he provides may give buyers their last chance to back out of a bad deal.

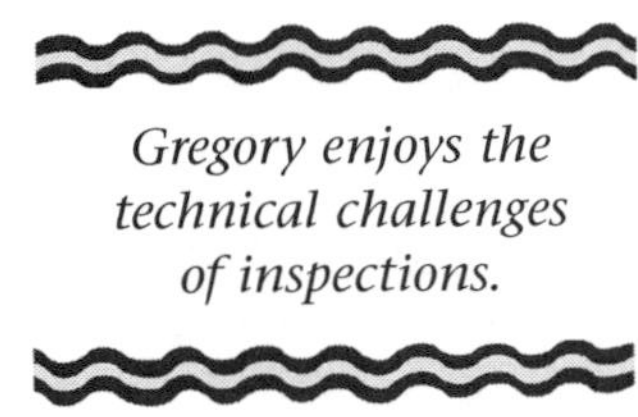

Gregory enjoys the technical challenges of inspections.

The most troubling aspect of the job arises for Gregory when an inspection fails to reveal a major defect that becomes apparent after the sale. Some defects are hard to spot. For example, detecting leaks sometimes proves impossible unless it's raining during the inspection and the wind is blowing a certain way. "There are legitimate oversights," said Gregory. "But whenever that happens, I feel awful about it."

The Home Inspection Business

According to the American Society of Home Inspectors, most home inspectors work as independent contractors either full or part time.

Successful inspectors wanting to expand their business use subcontractors instead of hiring workers. An inspecting contractor refers work to subcontractors. The contractor schedules the inspections on their behalf and claims an agreed-on share of fees earned. This way, the contractor and subcontractor share liability.

Losing a lawsuit can drown inspectors in debt. Some opt for liability insurance. But Gregory said it does not guarantee protection. This is because current laws do not address unique issues inspectors face.

The fortunes of home inspectors shift with the seasons and with interest rates. Both affect the amount of home buying and, thus, the number of customers. When sales are booming, Gregory might work a six-day week. He may conduct as many as four inspections between 8 a.m. and 7 p.m. each day. He then returns home to do paperwork for the next day.

When the housing market slumps, Gregory's seventy hours per week may drop to thirty. But most home inspectors do not earn by the hour. They charge by the job. They set a fee according to the selling price of the house or its square footage. "During busy periods, we home inspectors are all fed, so to speak," Gregory said. "During slow times, we're in competition."

Building a Home Inspection Career

According to Gregory, many architects, engineers, builders, and contractors begin inspecting homes as a result of their related experience. Some of them continue in their first careers at the same time.

Students interested in researching the field should look up job titles such as construction and building inspector, home inspector, architectural inspector, and electrical inspector.

Gregory thinks he benefited by learning about principles of electricity and heat conduction while earning his bachelor's degree. Being a home inspector does not require a college degree. His work experience mattered more.

After graduating from college, Gregory manufactured solar collector panels. He then conducted energy audits for several years. "I had half the skills home inspectors need," he said. "I still had to learn lots of things."

Like the occupation itself, the preparation of inspectors is largely unregulated. Inspectors add to their work experience through brief instruction. They also observe more experienced inspectors.

Many home inspectors take instruction that the American Society of Home Inspectors sponsors to prepare for its two exams. They are required for membership. Some unaccredited private schools also offer training.

Gregory improvised. He spent about 250 hours reading books and studying on his own to gain the required knowledge. He then arranged an unpaid one-month apprenticeship with a home inspection company. Gregory observed about a hundred inspections. The company then began to use him as a subcontractor.

Over time, he became more independent. A few years ago, he founded his own company. He hopes to work with subcontractors of his own in the future.

Gregory had intended to do home inspection for three years and then move on. But after twelve years in the field, he finds that homes are still where his heart is.

Many architects, engineers, builders, and contractors begin inspecting homes as a result of their related experience.

PROFILE

Carolyn Coleman—Urban Planner

Carolyn Coleman gazed out her office window at the town below. "You know," she said, "a community is a living thing. It wakes and sleeps, uses energy and produces waste, just as you do.

"Like other living things, communities grow and change. Farmland gives way to towns. Towns expand outward to become cities. Old brick buildings make way for glass and steel skyscrapers."

As an urban planner, Carolyn wears many hats. "In one day I may talk with a transportation engineer, a lawyer, and an architect."

Communities grow up and grow old, just as people do. Just like people, they need care. Many people take care of a community in different ways. Who keeps track of how the community is changing? Who watches to see that in ten years it will be the kind of home its residents want?

That job belongs to the urban and regional planners. They provide the information that citizens and governments need to make good choices.

Seeing Both Sides

"Planning is a balancing act," said Carolyn. "As individuals, citizens want to use their land as they please, but the public also wants the land used in a way that will benefit the whole community. The planner has to balance these two sides."

Carolyn's current balancing act is the new master plan for the area around her town. It shows how each piece of land should be used: for heavy industry, commercial business, single-family homes, farms, recreation, or some other purpose.

"A master plan is a blueprint for the future, guiding a community's growth," she said.

Carolyn knows it's vital to be in touch with local citizens from the start. At a public meeting, she talks to citizens and sets up an advisory committee. It's a two-way street: The committee will see that the people understand how the master plan will affect their lives and in turn will advise Carolyn of what the citizens want.

Carolyn must have the answers to a long list of questions before she can begin writing the plan. "I need to know about the area's natural features, the nature of the population, transportation routes and traffic, and how the land is presently being used," she said.

"John Casey–the urban planner who works with me–and I get answers to our questions from many places," explained Carolyn.

"To find out how the land is being used, we study aerial photos. For a closer look, we visit the neighborhoods. We read studies done by other divisions of the planning staff, other county agencies, and the federal government. Not to mention gathering tips from citizens!

"Speaking of citizens, we're holding a series of public meetings throughout the plan-writing process. I ask them how they'd like to see the community grow, what kinds of changes are important, and what changes *shouldn't* be made."

Carolyn knows there are almost as many answers to these questions as there are people in the town. That's why the planners also hold several meetings to talk with specific groups.

Bringing Ideas into Focus

Once she has a good idea of what the people want, Carolyn starts writing. "As a planner, you must know how to write well. The citizens will read your plan, so you have to keep it clear and simple."

And with the writing begins the balancing act of how to use the land in a way that is best for everyone. If that seems easy, think again.

"Planning is an art, not a science," Carolyn pointed out. "There's no formula you can use to answer a question or solve a problem. There are only basic principles of good planning. The rest is creativity, hard work, and common sense. But that's what makes the job challenging and fun."

Carolyn draws on the knowledge of other people on the county planning staff. The experts in other divisions help Carolyn solve many problems.

"A planner wears many hats," she said. "In one day I may talk with a transportation engineer, a lawyer, and an architect, so I must know a little about each of those career areas."

Planning to Be a Planner

"There are only basic principles of good planning. The rest is creativity, hard work, and common sense. But that's what makes the job challenging and fun."

Carolyn's interest in planning cities started in childhood. The daughter of an Air Force officer, she traveled widely in the United States and Europe. "I saw many cities," she recalled, "and I noticed that some were nicer than others. I began to wonder why."

In college, as a political science major, she studied urban politics. After college, she got a job as a research assistant in a planning office. "I thought I could work my way up. But I just couldn't pick up what I needed to know." So Carolyn went back to college for two more years to earn a master's degree in urban planning.

The town's master plan promises to be a major step for Carolyn in developing a specialty as a planner. The area has grown very quickly in the last few years, eating up the surrounding farmland. With the new plan, Carolyn hopes to slow the town's growth and save the rural area.

One strategy is to require that every new home have at least five acres of land–quite a bit more than in most towns. But this rule, like every rule, makes someone unhappy.

In this case it is a couple who bought twenty acres of land years ago. They expected the town to grow and planned to sell the land to a developer who would build many new homes on it–not just the four that the plan would allow. The plan will make their land less valuable.

Carolyn knows it will be hard to face this couple: "They feel this part of the plan will harm them. And I have to explain why it's necessary."

Communication Is Key

Many people come in to ask about the new plan. Others call or send letters or e-mail for information. Carolyn spends much time communicating with each of them. Do these contacts stop when she has finished writing the plan?

"Not at all! They *increase*, because the plan is not a final version. The people will have a chance to read it and react to it. This means more phone calls, letters, visits, and public meetings.

"Public speaking ability is so important. After all, I'm telling people how to use their land. I have to expect some opposition. I have to convince people that the plan makes good sense. It won't sell itself."

The staff members make changes in the sketch plan, based on the public's reactions. Then they give the new version to the planning board. After the planning board approves the plan, it goes to the county council for adoption as official policy.

Carolyn's work is still not finished! To put the new plan into effect, much of the area must be rezoned for different kinds of land uses. That means many county council sessions and more public meetings.

As the plan's author, Carolyn must be there to explain it. The meetings continue until rezoning is finished and the new plan takes effect.

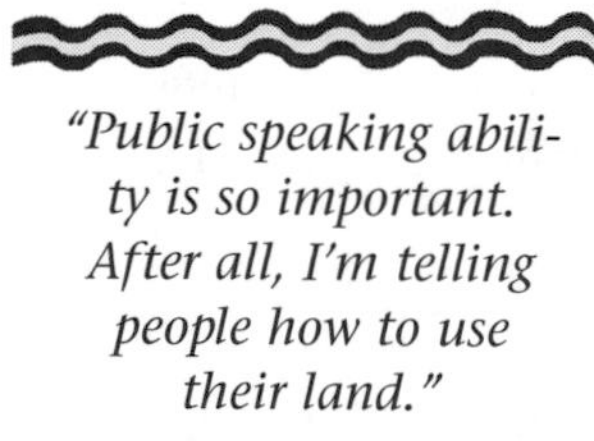

"Public speaking ability is so important. After all, I'm telling people how to use their land."

Where does that leave Carolyn? With other projects to do, more letters and e-mails to answer, more people to speak with. And with the satisfaction of knowing she's helped improve her environment.

"And that," she said, "is the best part."

SKILL SAMPLER

Georgia Catravas—Biochemist

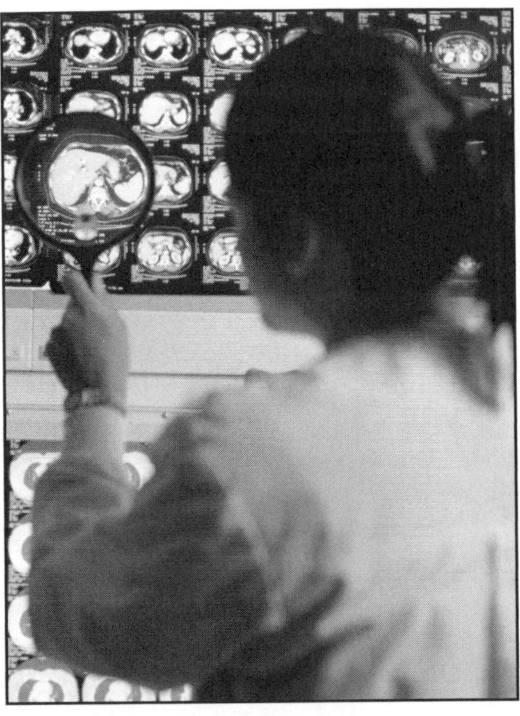

Dr. Catravas's plans took several twists and turns before she decided on biochemistry. "I didn't even like chemistry in high school," she said.

Georgia Catravas is a biochemist at a government-run research institute. Her world is one that most of us will never see. Dr. Catravas's days are filled with planning and coordinating research experiments and supervising her team of laboratory technicians. "Molecules don't cheat. They remain the same, waiting for you to figure them out."

Dr. Catravas described the skills needed by a biochemist. She offers the following tips to help you determine if you are suited for a satisfying career in biochemistry.

Biochemists are curious about the wonders and mysteries of life.

- Do you enjoy using a magnifying glass or microscope to look at leaves, insects, flowers, and other ordinary things?
- Do you read books or search the Internet for information about nature?
- Are you interested in what your body, the earth, or the stars are made of?

Biochemists continue learning all their lives.

- Do you like to read?
- Do you use your dictionary to look up words you don't know?
- Do you like to browse in the new book section of your library?
- Do you belong to a science club?

Biochemists must think like detectives to solve the mysteries of science.

- Do you like to solve puzzles, riddles, and brain teasers?
- When you don't understand something, do you try to figure it out before asking for help?

Biochemists work with numbers and advanced mathematics.

- Do you do well in math?
- Do you enjoy working with numbers?
- Do you like to calculate sports statistics or automobile mileage?

Biochemists do experiments that may take weeks, months, even years to finish. They must be very patient.

- Do you enjoy crafts, painting, or needlepoint?
- Do you like putting together large jigsaw puzzles?
- Do you like long projects such as growing vegetables or putting on a play?

Biochemists pay attention to detail when they do research.

- Can you follow the instructions correctly to assemble toys for your younger siblings?
- Can you follow the steps for making a casserole or sewing clothes from a pattern?
- Did you assemble your own computer table or other furniture or equipment?
- Can you give someone else detailed instructions?
- Can you read a road map?

SKILL SAMPLER

Gene Blue—Electrical Engineer

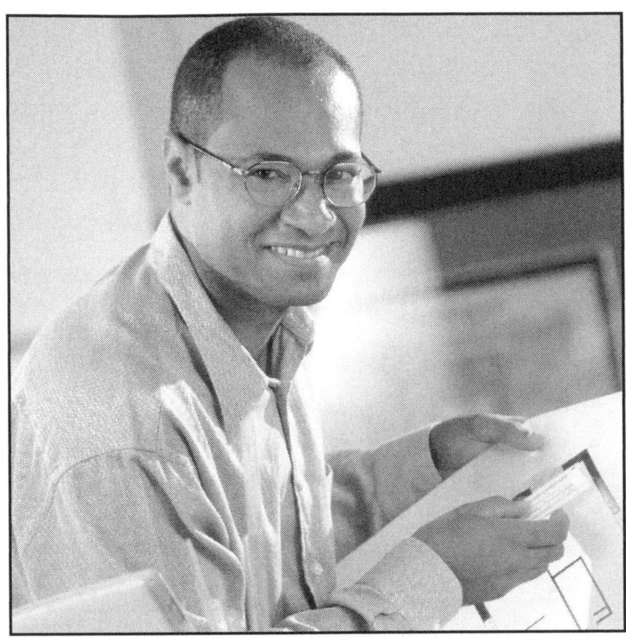

Gene uses his knowledge and skills to develop new sound-equipment products.

Gene Blue is vice-president of engineering for one of the country's largest manufacturers of sound equipment for cars and other vehicles. He has a bachelor's degree in engineering and a master's in business administration. "A career in engineering has given me the opportunity to express myself creatively."

Gene talked about electrical engineering and the skills and knowledge his career requires. He listed some tips to help you decide if electrical engineering is the career for you.

Electrical engineers must deal with complex devices and understand how they work.

- Do you enjoy taking things apart to see how they work?
- Do you sometimes fix your younger brothers' and sisters' toys?
- Are you good at repairing things around the house?
- Do you like to read about new inventions?

Electrical engineers apply what they know to solve problems in a practical way.

- Do you like word problems in math?
- Are you good at things like putting up a shelf or arranging your computer equipment in a small space?

- Is it important to you to know how your school subjects relate to the real world?
- Are you more likely to study if you think a subject has practical value?

Electrical engineers deal with many ideas and objects that cannot be seen or felt. They must be able to think abstractly.

- When you keyboard a term paper, can you picture what the printed version will look like?
- Can you see something in a store and imagine how it would look in your room?
- Can you look at machines such as automobiles or medical equipment and visualize their inner workings?

Electrical engineers look for creative answers to problems.

- Do you play games of strategy such as checkers or chess?
- Do you play electronic games of strategy?
- Do you enjoy solving puzzles?
- Do you like to think of new ways to do things around the house?

Electrical engineers must pay attention to detail.

- Do you enjoy checking computer files for spelling, grammar, and punctuation errors?
- Are you able to memorize complicated plays in the sports you participate in?
- Do you enjoy doing craft projects or building things from kits?
- Do you go over your homework carefully before you hand it in?

Electrical engineers must continually read and learn, because new discoveries and inventions are made all the time.

- Do you like to read for pleasure?
- When you are curious about something, do you go to the library or check the Internet for more information?
- Do you like to read popular scientific or technical magazines?
- Do you use a dictionary to look up words you don't know?

Electrical engineers must be able to write clearly.

- Can you write street directions or recipes?
- Do you write your math or science homework clearly enough for your teachers to read it?

Electrical engineers must be able to discuss technical subjects.

- Can you express yourself verbally?
- If a teacher doesn't answer your question exactly, do you ask it again in a different way?
- Do you ever help your brothers, sisters, or friends with their homework?

SKILL SAMPLER

Paula Ivy—Forester

As a forester for a forest products company, Paula Ivy manages more than 60,000 acres of company timberland scattered over a ten-county area. "I've always liked being outdoors, and I started thinking about a forestry career after visiting several of our national parks while I was in college."

Paula talked about the skills and abilities needed by a forester. She offers the following tips to guide you in considering whether you are suited for a career in forestry.

Foresters must be well organized and able to set priorities.

- Are you able to plan your time efficiently?
- Do you keep lists of things to do?
- Do you find yourself able both to finish your homework and have time left for recreation?
- Do you keep a diary?
- Is it easy for you to decide between different things to do?
- Do you take part in extracurricular activities at your school?

Foresters must be patient. They have to wait for a long time to see the end results of their work.

- Do you enjoy long-term projects such as gardening?
- Do you ever think about or plan what you will be doing five years from now?
- Do you enjoy playing electronic games that require several sessions to complete?
- Do you save your money for things you want?

Foresters often must work with other people. There's a lot more to the job than just being out in the woods.

- Do you like to speak in front of your class?
- Do you enjoy working with other people on class projects?
- Do you join organizations and take an active part in them?
- Do you like to help organize activities such as trips, parties, sports events, picnics, and dances?

Foresters must have a genuine love of the outdoors and a respect for the environment.

- Do you enjoy outdoor activities such as camping, fishing, gardening, and hiking?
- Does it bother you when you see a polluted river?
- Do you ever try to think of ways to clean up the environment?
- Do you throw your trash in trash cans?

Now learn about all major jobs in the Science, Math, and Engineering interest area→

Facts About All Major Jobs Related to

SCIENCE, MATH, AND ENGINEERING

In addition to the jobs covered in the profiles and skill samplers, other careers in the Science, Math, and Engineering interest area may appeal to you. This section describes and gives facts about all major jobs in the Science, Math, and Engineering interest area. For an explanation of the $, ★, and 🚶 symbols, see page 6.

MANAGERIAL WORK IN SCIENCE, MATH, AND ENGINEERING

These workers manage scientists who are doing research and engineers who are applying scientific principles to solve real-world problems. They set goals, oversee financial and technical resources, and evaluate outcomes. They work for industries, government agencies, universities, and hospitals.

Computer and Information Systems Managers. Plan, direct, or coordinate activities in such fields as electronic data processing, information systems, systems analysis, and computer programming. **Education and Training:** College degree plus work experience. **Skills:** Math—High. English—High. Science—Medium. **Yearly Earnings:** $$$$$ **Job Growth:** ★★★★★ **Yearly Openings:** 🚶🚶🚶

Engineering Managers. Plan, direct, or coordinate activities in such fields as architecture and engineering. Manage research and development in these fields. **Education and Training:** College degree plus work experience. **Skills:** Math—High. English—High. Science—High. **Yearly Earnings:** $$$$$ **Job Growth:** ★★ **Yearly Openings:** 🚶🚶🚶

Natural Sciences Managers. Plan, direct, or coordinate activities in such fields as life sciences, physical sciences, mathematics, and statistics. Manage research and development in these fields. **Education and Training:** College degree plus work experience. **Skills:** Math—High. English—High. Science—High. **Yearly Earnings:** $$$$$ **Job Growth:** ★★ **Yearly Openings:** 🚶

PHYSICAL SCIENCES

These workers are concerned mostly with non-living things, such as chemicals, rocks, metals, and movements of the earth and stars. They conduct scientific studies and perform other activities requiring knowledge of math, physics, or chemistry. Some workers investigate, discover, and test new theories. Some develop new or improved materials or processes for use in production and construction. Some do research in such fields as geology, astronomy, oceanography, and meteorology. Workers base their conclusions on information that can be measured or proven. Industries, government agencies, and large universities employ most of these workers in research facilities.

Astronomers. Observe, research, and interpret celestial and astronomical phenomena to increase basic knowledge and apply information to practical problems. **Education and Training:** Doctoral degree. **Skills:** Math—High. English—High. Science—High. **Yearly Earnings:** $$$$$ **Job Growth:** ★★★ **Yearly Openings:** 🚶

Atmospheric and Space Scientists. Investigate atmospheric phenomena and interpret meteorological data gathered by surface and air stations, satellites, and radar. Prepare reports and forecasts for public and other uses. **Education and Training:** Bachelor's degree. **Skills:** Math—High. English—High. Science—High. **Yearly Earnings:** $$$$$ **Job Growth:** ★★★ **Yearly Openings:** 🚶

Chemists. Conduct chemical analyses or chemical experiments in laboratories for quality control or process control or to develop new products or knowledge. **Education and Training:** Bachelor's degree. **Skills:** Math—High. English—High. Science—High. **Yearly Earnings:** $$$$$ **Job Growth:** ★★★ **Yearly Openings:** 🚶 🚶

Geographers. Study nature and use of areas of earth's surface, relating and interpreting interactions of physical and cultural phenomena. Conduct research on physical aspects of a region, including land forms, climates, soils, plants, and animals. Conduct research on the spatial implications of human activities within a given area. Research interdependence between regions. **Education and Training:** Bachelor's degree. **Skills:** Math—Medium. English—High. Science—Medium. **Yearly Earnings:** $$$$ **Job Growth:** ★★★ **Yearly Openings:** 🚶

Geologists. Study composition, structure, and history of the earth's crust. Examine rocks, minerals, and fossil remains to identify and determine the sequence of processes affecting the development of the earth. Apply knowledge of chemistry, physics, biology, and mathematics to explain these phenomena and to help locate mineral and petroleum deposits and underground water resources. Prepare geologic reports and maps. Interpret research data to recommend further action for study. **Education and Training:** Bachelor's degree. **Skills:** Math—High. English—High. Science—High. **Yearly Earnings:** $$$$$ **Job Growth:** ★★★ **Yearly Openings:** 🚶

Geoscientists, Except Hydrologists and Geographers. Study the composition, structure, and other physical aspects of the earth. May use geological, physics, and mathematics knowledge in exploration for oil, gas, minerals, or underground water or in waste disposal, land reclamation, or other environmental problems. May study the earth's internal composition, atmospheres, and oceans. May study the earth's magnetic, electrical, and gravitational forces. Includes mineralogists, crystallographers,

paleontologists, stratigraphers, geodesists, and seismologists. **Education and Training:** Bachelor's degree. **Skills:** Math—Medium. English—Medium. Science—Medium. **Yearly Earnings:** $$$$$ **Job Growth:** ★★★ **Yearly Openings:** 🚶

Hydrologists. Research the distribution, circulation, and physical properties of underground and surface waters. Study the form and intensity of precipitation and its rate of infiltration into the soil, movement through the earth, and return to the ocean and atmosphere. **Education and Training:** Bachelor's degree. **Skills:** Math—High. English—High. Science—High. **Yearly Earnings:** $$$$$ **Job Growth:** ★★★★ **Yearly Openings:** 🚶

Materials Scientists. Research and study the structures and chemical properties of various natural and manmade materials, including metals, alloys, rubber, ceramics, semiconductors, polymers, and glass. Determine ways to strengthen or combine materials or develop new materials with specific properties for use in a variety of products and applications. **Education and Training:** Bachelor's degree. **Skills:** Math—High. English—High. Science—High. **Yearly Earnings:** $$$$$ **Job Growth:** ★★★ **Yearly Openings:** 🚶

Physicists. Conduct research into the phases of physical phenomena. Develop theories and laws on the basis of observation and experiments. Devise methods to apply laws and theories to industry and other fields. **Education and Training:** Doctoral degree. **Skills:** Math—High. English—High. Science—High. **Yearly Earnings:** $$$$$ **Job Growth:** ★★★ **Yearly Openings:** 🚶

LIFE SCIENCES

These workers do research and conduct experiments to find out more about plants, animals, and other living things. Some study methods of producing better species of plants or animals. Some work to find ways of preserving the natural balance in the environment. Others conduct research to improve medicine, health, and living conditions for human beings. These jobs are found in manufacturing plants, government agencies, universities, and hospitals.

Agricultural and Food Science Technicians. Work with agricultural scientists in food, fiber, and animal research, production, and processing. Assist with animal breeding and nutrition work. Under supervision, conduct tests and experiments to improve yield and quality of crops or to increase the resistance of plants and animals to disease or insects. Includes technicians who assist food scientists or food technologists in the research, development, production technology, quality control, packaging, processing, and use of foods. **Education and Training:** Moderate-term on-the-job training. **Skills:** Math—Medium. English—Medium. Science—Medium. **Yearly Earnings:** $$ **Job Growth:** ★★★ **Yearly Openings:** 🚶

Agricultural Technicians. Set up and maintain laboratory and collect and record data to assist scientist in biology or related agricultural science experiments. **Education**

and Training: Associate's degree. **Skills:** Math—Medium. English—Medium. Science—Medium. **Yearly Earnings:** $$ **Job Growth:** ★★★ **Yearly Openings:** 🧍

Animal Scientists. Conduct research in the genetics, nutrition, reproduction, growth, and development of domestic farm animals. **Education and Training:** Bachelor's degree. **Skills:** Math—High. English—High. Science—High. **Yearly Earnings:** $$$$ **Job Growth:** ★★★ **Yearly Openings:** 🧍

Biochemists. Research or study chemical composition and processes of living organisms that affect vital processes such as growth and aging. Determine the chemical action of foods, drugs, or other substances on body functions and tissues. **Education and Training:** Doctoral degree. **Skills:** Math—High. English—High. Science—High. **Yearly Earnings:** $$$$ **Job Growth:** ★★★★ **Yearly Openings:** 🧍

Biochemists and Biophysicists. Study the chemical composition and physical principles of living cells and organisms, their electrical and mechanical energy, and related phenomena. May conduct research to further understanding of the complex chemical combinations and reactions involved in metabolism, reproduction, growth, and heredity. May determine the effects of foods, drugs, serums, hormones, and other substances on tissues and vital processes of living organisms. **Education and Training:** Doctoral degree. **Skills:** Math—Medium. English—Medium. Science—Medium. **Yearly Earnings:** $$$$ **Job Growth:** ★★★★ **Yearly Openings:** 🧍

Biologists. Research or study basic principles of plant and animal life, such as origin, relationship, development, anatomy, and functions. **Education and Training:** Doctoral degree. **Skills:** Math—High. English—High. Science—High. **Yearly Earnings:** $$$$ **Job Growth:** ★★★★ **Yearly Openings:** 🧍

Biophysicists. Research or study physical principles of living cells and organisms, their electrical and mechanical energy, and related phenomena. **Education and Training:** Doctoral degree. **Skills:** Math—High. English—High. Science—High. **Yearly Earnings:** $$$$ **Job Growth:** ★★★★ **Yearly Openings:** 🧍

Conservation Scientists. Manage, improve, and protect natural resources to maximize their use without damaging the environment. May conduct soil surveys and develop plans to eliminate soil erosion or to protect rangelands from fire and rodent damage. May instruct farmers, agricultural production managers, or ranchers in best ways to conserve soil and water; in the number and kind of livestock and forage plants best suited to particular ranges; and in range and farm improvements, such as fencing and reservoirs for stock watering. **Education and Training:** Bachelor's degree. **Skills:** Math—Medium. English—Medium. Science—Medium. **Yearly Earnings:** $$$$ **Job Growth:** ★★ **Yearly Openings:** 🧍

Environmental Scientists and Specialists, Including Health. Conduct research or perform investigation for the purpose of identifying, abating, or eliminating sources of

pollutants or hazards that affect either the environment or the health of the population. Using knowledge of various scientific disciplines, may collect, study, report, and take action based on data derived from measurements or observations of air, food, soil, water, and other sources. **Education and Training:** Bachelor's degree. **Skills:** Math—High. English—High. Science—High. **Yearly Earnings:** $$$$ **Job Growth:** ★★★★ **Yearly Openings:**

Epidemiologists. Investigate and describe the causes and distribution of disease, disability, and other health outcomes. Develop the means for prevention and control. **Education and Training:** Doctoral degree. **Skills:** Math—High. English—High. Science—High. **Yearly Earnings:** $$$$$ **Job Growth:** ★★★★ **Yearly Openings:**

Food Science Technicians. Perform tests to determine physical or chemical properties of food or beverage products. **Education and Training:** Associate's degree. **Skills:** Math—High. English—High. Science—High. **Yearly Earnings:** $$ **Job Growth:** ★★★ **Yearly Openings:**

Food Scientists and Technologists. Use chemistry, microbiology, engineering, and other sciences to study the principles underlying the processing and deterioration of foods. Analyze food content to determine levels of vitamins, fat, sugar, and protein. Discover new food sources. Research ways to make processed foods safe, palatable, and healthful. Apply food science knowledge to determine best ways to process, package, preserve, store, and distribute food. **Education and Training:** Bachelor's degree. **Skills:** Math—High. English—Medium. Science—High. **Yearly Earnings:** $$$$ **Job Growth:** ★★★ **Yearly Openings:**

Foresters. Manage forested lands for economic, recreational, and conservation purposes. May inventory the type, amount, and location of standing timber, appraise the timber's worth, negotiate the purchase, and draw up contracts for procurement. May determine how to conserve wildlife habitats, creek beds, water quality, and soil stability and how best to comply with environmental regulations. May devise plans for planting and growing new trees, monitor trees for healthy growth, and determine the best time for harvesting. Develop forest management plans for public and privately owned forested lands. **Education and Training:** Bachelor's degree. **Skills:** Math—High. English—High. Science—High. **Yearly Earnings:** $$$$ **Job Growth:** ★★ **Yearly Openings:**

Medical Scientists, Except Epidemiologists. Conduct research dealing with the understanding of human diseases and the improvement of human health. Engage in clinical investigation or other research, production, or technical writing. **Education and Training:** Doctoral degree. **Skills:** Math—High. English—High. Science—High. **Yearly Earnings:** $$$$$ **Job Growth:** ★★★★ **Yearly Openings:**

Microbiologists. Investigate the growth, structure, development, and other characteristics of microscopic organisms, such as bacteria, algae, or fungi. Includes medical microbiologists who study the relationship between organisms and disease or the effects of antibiotics on microorganisms. **Education and Training:** Doctoral degree. **Skills:** Math—Medium. English—High. Science—High. **Yearly Earnings:** $$$$ **Job Growth:** ★★★★ **Yearly Openings:** 🚶

Plant Scientists. Conduct research in breeding, production, and yield of plants or crops and control of pests. **Education and Training:** Bachelor's degree. **Skills:** Math—High. English—High. Science—High. **Yearly Earnings:** $$$$ **Job Growth:** ★★★ **Yearly Openings:** 🚶

Range Managers. Research or study range land management practices to provide sustained production of forage, livestock, and wildlife. **Education and Training:** Bachelor's degree. **Skills:** Math—Medium. English—Medium. Science—High. **Yearly Earnings:** $$$$ **Job Growth:** ★★ **Yearly Openings:** 🚶

Soil and Plant Scientists. Conduct research in breeding, physiology, production, yield, and management of crops and agricultural plants, their growth in soils, and control of pests. Study the chemical, physical, biological, and mineral composition of soils as they relate to plant or crop growth. May classify and map soils and investigate effects of alternative practices on soil and crop productivity. **Education and Training:** Bachelor's degree. **Skills:** Math—Medium. English—Medium. Science—Medium. **Yearly Earnings:** $$$$ **Job Growth:** ★★★ **Yearly Openings:** 🚶

Soil Conservationists. Plan and develop coordinated practices for soil erosion control, soil and water conservation, and sound land use. **Education and Training:** Bachelor's degree. **Skills:** Math—High. English—High. Science—High. **Yearly Earnings:** $$$$ **Job Growth:** ★★ **Yearly Openings:** 🚶

Soil Scientists. Research or study soil characteristics. Map soil types. Investigate responses of soils to known management practices to determine use capabilities of soils and effects of alternative practices on soil productivity. **Education and Training:** Bachelor's degree. **Skills:** Math—High. English—High. Science—High. **Yearly Earnings:** $$$$ **Job Growth:** ★★★ **Yearly Openings:** 🚶

Zoologists and Wildlife Biologists. Study the origins, behavior, diseases, genetics, and life processes of animals and wildlife. May specialize in wildlife research and management, including the collection and analysis of biological data to determine the environmental effects of present and potential use of land and water areas. **Education and Training:** Doctoral degree. **Skills:** Math—Medium. English—High. Science—High. **Yearly Earnings:** $$$$ **Job Growth:** ★★★★ **Yearly Openings:** 🚶

SOCIAL SCIENCES

These workers gather, study, and analyze information about individuals, groups, or entire societies. They conduct research into all aspects of human behavior, including abnormal behavior, language, work, politics, lifestyle, and cultural expression. They are employed by schools and colleges, government agencies, businesses, museums, and private research foundations.

Anthropologists. Research or study human origins and physical, social, and cultural development. Study the behavior of humans and the cultures and organizations they have created. **Education and Training:** Bachelor's degree. **Skills:** Math—High. English—High. Science—High. **Yearly Earnings:** $$$$ **Job Growth:** ★★★ **Yearly Openings:** 🚶

Anthropologists and Archeologists. Study the origin, development, and behavior of humans. May study the way of life, language, or physical characteristics of existing people in various parts of the world. May engage in recovery and examination of material evidence, such as tools or pottery remaining from past human cultures, in order to determine the history, customs, and living habits of earlier civilizations. **Education and Training:** Bachelor's degree. **Skills:** Math—Medium. English—Medium. Science—Medium. **Yearly Earnings:** $$$$ **Job Growth:** ★★★ **Yearly Openings:** 🚶

Archeologists. Conduct research to reconstruct record of past human life and culture from human remains, artifacts, architectural features, and structures recovered through excavation, underwater recovery, or other means of discovery. **Education and Training:** Bachelor's degree. **Skills:** Math—Medium. English—High. Science—High. **Yearly Earnings:** $$$$ **Job Growth:** ★★★ **Yearly Openings:** 🚶

City Planning Aides. Compile data from various sources, such as maps, reports, and field and file investigations. Data is used by city planner in making planning studies. **Education and Training:** Associate's degree. **Skills:** Math—High. English—Medium. Science—Medium. **Yearly Earnings:** $$$ **Job Growth:** No data available. **Yearly Openings:** No data available.

Economists. Conduct research, prepare reports, or formulate plans to aid in solution of economic problems arising from production and distribution of goods and services. May collect and process economic and statistical data. **Education and Training:** Bachelor's degree. **Skills:** Math—High. English—High. Science—High. **Yearly Earnings:** $$$$$ **Job Growth:** ★★★ **Yearly Openings:** 🚶

Historians. Research, analyze, and interpret the past as recorded in sources such as government and institutional records, newspapers, photographs, interviews, films, and unpublished manuscripts, including personal diaries and letters. **Education and Training:** Bachelor's degree. **Skills:** Math—Medium. English—High. Science—Medium. **Yearly Earnings:** $$$$ **Job Growth:** ★★★ **Yearly Openings:** 🚶

Industrial-Organizational Psychologists. Apply principles of psychology to personnel, administration, management, sales, and marketing problems. Activities may include policy planning; employee screening, training, and development; and organizational development and analysis. May work with management to reorganize the work setting to improve worker productivity. **Education and Training:** Master's degree. **Skills:** Math—High. English—High. Science—High. **Yearly Earnings:** $$$$ **Job Growth:** ★★★ **Yearly Openings:** 🧍🧍🧍

Political Scientists. Study the origin, development, and operation of political systems. Research a wide range of subjects, such as relations between the United States and foreign countries, the beliefs and institutions of foreign nations, or the politics of small towns or a major city. May study topics such as public opinion, political decision making, and ideology. May analyze the structure and operation of governments as well as various political entities. May conduct public opinion surveys, analyze election results, or analyze public documents. **Education and Training:** Master's degree. **Skills:** Math—High. English—High. Science—Medium. **Yearly Earnings:** $$$$ **Job Growth:** ★★★ **Yearly Openings:** 🧍

Social Science Research Assistants. Assist social scientists in laboratory, survey, and other social research. May perform publication activities, laboratory analysis, quality control, or data management. Normally, these individuals work under the direct supervision of a social scientist and assist in routine activities. **Education and Training:** Associate's degree. **Skills:** Math—Medium. English—Medium. Science—Medium. **Yearly Earnings:** $$$ **Job Growth:** No data available. **Yearly Openings:** No data available.

Sociologists. Study human society and social behavior by examining the groups and social institutions that people form, as well as various social, religious, political, and business organizations. May study the behavior and interaction of groups, trace their origin and growth, and analyze the influence of group activities on individual members. **Education and Training:** Master's degree. **Skills:** Math—High. English—High. Science—Medium. **Yearly Earnings:** $$$$ **Job Growth:** ★★★ **Yearly Openings:** 🧍

Survey Researchers. Design or conduct surveys. May supervise interviewers who conduct surveys in person or over the telephone. May present survey results to client. **Education and Training:** Bachelor's degree. **Skills:** Math—Medium. English—Medium. Science—Medium. **Yearly Earnings:** $$ **Job Growth:** ★★★★ **Yearly Openings:** 🧍

Urban and Regional Planners. Develop comprehensive plans and programs for use of land and physical facilities of towns, cities, counties, and metropolitan areas. **Education and Training:** Master's degree. **Skills:** Math—High. English—High. Science—Medium. **Yearly Earnings:** $$$$ **Job Growth:** ★★★ **Yearly Openings:** 🧍

LABORATORY TECHNOLOGY

These workers use special laboratory techniques and equipment to perform tests in such fields as chemistry, biology, and physics; then they record information resulting from their experiments and tests. These reports are used by scientists, medical doctors, researchers, and engineers. Hospitals, government agencies, universities, and private industries employ these workers in their laboratories and research activities.

Biological Technicians. Assist biological and medical scientists in laboratories. Set up, operate, and maintain laboratory instruments and equipment, monitor experiments, make observations, and calculate and record results. May analyze organic substances, such as blood, food, and drugs. **Education and Training:** Associate's degree. **Skills:** Math—Medium. English—Medium. Science—Medium. **Yearly Earnings:** $$$ **Job Growth:** ★★★★ **Yearly Openings:** 🚶🚶

Chemical Technicians. Conduct chemical and physical laboratory tests. These tests assist scientists in analyzing solids, liquids, and gaseous materials for purposes such as research and development of new products or processes, quality control, maintenance of environmental standards, and other work involving experimental, theoretical, or practical application of chemistry and related sciences. **Education and Training:** Associate's degree. **Skills:** Math—High. English—Medium. Science—High. **Yearly Earnings:** $$$ **Job Growth:** ★★★ **Yearly Openings:** 🚶🚶🚶

Environmental Science and Protection Technicians, Including Health. Perform laboratory and field tests to monitor the environment and investigate sources of pollution, including those that affect health. Under direction of an environmental scientist or specialist, may collect samples of gases, soil, water, and other materials for testing. Take corrective actions as assigned. **Education and Training:** Associate's degree. **Skills:** Math—High. English—Medium. Science—High. **Yearly Earnings:** $$$ **Job Growth:** ★★★★ **Yearly Openings:** 🚶

Geological and Petroleum Technicians. Assist scientists in the use of electrical, sonic, or nuclear measuring instruments in both laboratory and production activities to obtain data indicating potential sources of metallic ore, gas, or petroleum. Analyze mud and drill cuttings. Chart pressure, temperature, and other characteristics of wells or bore holes. Investigate and collect information leading to the possible discovery of new oil fields. **Education and Training:** Associate's degree. **Skills:** Math—Medium. English—Medium. Science—Medium. **Yearly Earnings:** $$$ **Job Growth:** ★★ **Yearly Openings:** 🚶

Geological Data Technicians. Measure, record, and evaluate geological data, using sonic, electronic, electrical, seismic, or gravity-measuring instruments to prospect for oil or gas. May collect and evaluate core samples and cuttings. **Education and Training:** Associate's degree. **Skills:** Math—Medium. English—Medium. Science—High. **Yearly Earnings:** $$$ **Job Growth:** ★★ **Yearly Openings:** 🚶

Geological Sample Test Technicians. Test and analyze geological samples, crude oil, or petroleum products. One purpose is to detect petroleum, gas, or mineral deposits indicating potential for exploration and production. Another purpose is to determine physical and chemical properties to ensure that products meet quality standards. **Education and Training:** Associate's degree. **Skills:** Math—Medium. English—Medium. Science—High. **Yearly Earnings:** $$$ **Job Growth:** ★★ **Yearly Openings:** 🚹

Nuclear Equipment Operation Technicians. Operate equipment used for the release, control, and utilization of nuclear energy to assist scientists in laboratory and production activities. **Education and Training:** Associate's degree. **Skills:** Math—High. English—Medium. Science—High. **Yearly Earnings:** $$$$$ **Job Growth:** ★★★ **Yearly Openings:** 🚹

Nuclear Technicians. Assist scientists in both laboratory and production activities by performing technical tasks involving nuclear physics, primarily in operation, maintenance, production, and quality control support activities. **Education and Training:** Associate's degree. **Skills:** Math—Medium. English—Medium. Science—Medium. **Yearly Earnings:** $$$$$ **Job Growth:** ★★★ **Yearly Openings:** 🚹

Photographers, Scientific. Photograph variety of subject material to illustrate or record scientific/medical data or phenomena. Use knowledge of scientific procedures and photographic technology and techniques. **Education and Training:** Long-term on-the-job training. **Skills:** Math—Medium. English—Medium. Science—High. **Yearly Earnings:** $$ **Job Growth:** ★★★ **Yearly Openings:** 🚹 🚹 🚹

MATHEMATICS AND COMPUTERS

These workers use advanced math, statistics, and computer programs to solve problems and conduct research. They analyze and interpret numerical data for planning and decision making. Some of these workers determine how computers may best be used to solve problems or process information. Businesses and industries, colleges, research organizations, and government agencies hire these workers. Some programmers work as consultants on changing assignments.

Actuaries. Analyze statistical data, such as mortality, accident, sickness, disability, and retirement rates, and construct probability tables to forecast risk and liability for payment of future benefits. May determine premium rates required and cash reserves necessary to ensure payment of future benefits. **Education and Training:** College degree plus work experience. **Skills:** Math—High. English—High. Science—Medium. **Yearly Earnings:** $$$$$ **Job Growth:** ★★ **Yearly Openings:** 🚹

Computer and Information Scientists, Research. Conduct research into fundamental computer and information science as theorists, designers, or inventors. Solve or develop solutions to problems in the field of computer hardware and software.

Education and Training: Doctoral degree. **Skills:** Math—Medium. English—Medium. Science—Medium. **Yearly Earnings:** $$$$$ **Job Growth:** ★★★★★ **Yearly Openings:** 🧍

Computer Programmers. Convert project specifications and statements of problems and procedures to detailed logical flow charts for coding into computer language. Develop and write computer programs to store, locate, and retrieve specific documents, data, and information. May program Web sites. **Education and Training:** Bachelor's degree. **Skills:** Math—Medium. English—High. Science—Medium. **Yearly Earnings:** $$$$$ **Job Growth:** ★★★ **Yearly Openings:** 🧍🧍🧍

Computer Security Specialists. Plan, coordinate, and implement security measures for information systems. Purpose is to regulate access to computer data files and prevent unauthorized modification, destruction, or disclosure of information. **Education and Training:** Bachelor's degree. **Skills:** Math—Medium. English—Medium. Science—Medium. **Yearly Earnings:** $$$$$ **Job Growth:** ★★★★★ **Yearly Openings:** 🧍🧍🧍

Computer Support Specialists. Provide technical assistance to computer system users. Answer questions or resolve computer problems for clients in person, via telephone, or from remote location. May provide assistance concerning the use of computer hardware and software, including printing, installation, word processing, electronic mail, and operating systems. **Education and Training:** Associate's degree. **Skills:** Math—Medium. English—High. Science—High. **Yearly Earnings:** $$$ **Job Growth:** ★★★★★ **Yearly Openings:** 🧍🧍🧍

Computer Systems Analysts. Analyze science, engineering, business, and other data processing problems for application to electronic data processing systems. Analyze user requirements, procedures, and problems to automate or improve existing systems and review computer system capabilities. May analyze or recommend software. May supervise computer programmers. **Education and Training:** Bachelor's degree. **Skills:** Math—Medium. English—High. Science—High. **Yearly Earnings:** $$$$$ **Job Growth:** ★★★★★ **Yearly Openings:** 🧍🧍🧍

Database Administrators. Coordinate changes to computer databases. Test and implement the database, applying knowledge of database management systems. May plan, coordinate, and implement security measures to safeguard computer databases. **Education and Training:** Bachelor's degree. **Skills:** Math—High. English—Medium. Science—Medium. **Yearly Earnings:** $$$$$ **Job Growth:** ★★★★★ **Yearly Openings:** 🧍🧍

Mathematical Technicians. Apply mathematical formulas, principles, and methods to technological problems in engineering and physical sciences. This work is done in relation to specific industrial and research objectives, processes, equipment, and products. **Education and Training:** Bachelor's degree. **Skills:** Math—High. English—Medium. Science—High. **Yearly Earnings:** $$$ **Job Growth:** No data available. **Yearly Openings:** No data available.

Mathematicians. Conduct research in fundamental mathematics or in application of mathematical techniques to science, management, and other fields. Solve or direct solutions to problems in various fields by mathematical methods. **Education and Training:** Master's degree. **Skills:** Math—High. English—Medium. Science—Medium. **Yearly Earnings:** $$$$$ **Job Growth:** ★ **Yearly Openings:** 🚶

Network and Computer Systems Administrators. Install, configure, and support an organization's local area network (LAN), wide area network (WAN), and Internet system or a segment of a network system. Maintain network hardware and software. Monitor network to ensure network availability to all system users. Do maintenance to support network availability. May supervise other network support and client server specialists. May plan, coordinate, and implement network security measures. **Education and Training:** Bachelor's degree. **Skills:** Math—Medium. English—Medium. Science—Medium. **Yearly Earnings:** $$$$$ **Job Growth:** ★★★★★ **Yearly Openings:** 🚶🚶🚶

Network Systems and Data Communications Analysts. Analyze, design, test, and evaluate network systems, such as local area networks (LAN), wide area networks (WAN), Internet, intranet, and other data communications systems. Perform network modeling, analysis, and planning. Research and recommend network and data communications hardware and software. Includes telecommunications specialists who deal with the interfacing of computer and communications equipment. May supervise computer programmers. **Education and Training:** Bachelor's degree. **Skills:** Math—Medium. English—High. Science—High. **Yearly Earnings:** $$$$$ **Job Growth:** ★★★★★ **Yearly Openings:** 🚶🚶

Operations Research Analysts. Formulate and apply mathematical modeling and other optimizing methods using a computer to develop and interpret information that assists management with decision making, policy formulation, or other managerial functions. May develop related software, service, or products. Frequently concentrates on collecting and analyzing data and developing decision support software. May develop and supply optimal time, cost, or logistics networks for program evaluation, review, or implementation. **Education and Training:** Master's degree. **Skills:** Math—High. English—High. Science—High. **Yearly Earnings:** $$$$$ **Job Growth:** ★★ **Yearly Openings:** 🚶

Statistical Assistants. Compile and compute data according to statistical formulas for use in statistical studies. May perform actuarial computations and compile charts and graphs for use by actuaries. Includes actuarial clerks. **Education and Training:** Moderate-term on-the-job training. **Skills:** Math—High. English—Medium. Science—Medium. **Yearly Earnings:** $$ **Job Growth:** ★ **Yearly Openings:** 🚶

Statisticians. Engage in the development of mathematical theory. Apply statistical theory and methods to collect, organize, interpret, and summarize numerical data to provide usable information. May specialize in fields such as bio-statistics, agricultural

statistics, business statistics, or economic statistics. **Education and Training:** Master's degree. **Skills:** Math—High. English—High. Science—High. **Yearly Earnings:** $$$$$ **Job Growth:** ★ **Yearly Openings:** 🚶

ENGINEERING

These workers plan, design, and direct the development and construction of buildings, bridges, roads, airports, dams, sewage systems, air conditioning systems, mining machinery, and other structures and equipment. They utilize scientific principles to develop processes and techniques for generating and transmitting electrical power, for manufacturing chemicals, for extracting metals from ores, and for controlling the quality of products being made. Workers specialize in one or more kinds of engineering, such as civil, electrical, mechanical, mining, and safety. Some are hired by industrial plants, petroleum and mining companies, research laboratories, and construction companies. Others find employment with federal, state, and local governments.

Aerospace Engineers. Perform a variety of engineering work in designing, constructing, and testing aircraft, missiles, and spacecraft. May conduct basic and applied research to evaluate adaptability of materials and equipment to aircraft design and manufacture. May recommend improvements in testing equipment and techniques. **Education and Training:** Bachelor's degree. **Skills:** Math—High. English—High. Science—High. **Yearly Earnings:** $$$$$ **Job Growth:** ★★★ **Yearly Openings:** 🚶

Agricultural Engineers. Apply knowledge of engineering technology and biological science to agricultural problems concerned with power and machinery, electrification, structures, soil and water conservation, and processing of agricultural products. **Education and Training:** Bachelor's degree. **Skills:** Math—High. English—High. Science—High. **Yearly Earnings:** $$$$$ **Job Growth:** ★★★ **Yearly Openings:** 🚶

Architects, Except Landscape and Naval. Plan and design structures such as private residences, office buildings, theaters, factories, and other structural property. **Education and Training:** Bachelor's degree. **Skills:** Math—High. English—High. Science—Medium. **Yearly Earnings:** $$$$$ **Job Growth:** ★★★ **Yearly Openings:** 🚶

Biomedical Engineers. Apply knowledge of engineering, biology, and biomechanical principles to the design, development, and evaluation of biological and health systems and products, such as artificial organs, prostheses, instrumentation, medical information systems, and health management and care delivery systems. **Education and Training:** Bachelor's degree. **Skills:** Math—Medium. English—Medium. Science—Medium. **Yearly Earnings:** $$$$$ **Job Growth:** ★★★★ **Yearly Openings:** 🚶

Chemical Engineers. Design chemical plant equipment and devise processes for manufacturing chemicals and products, such as gasoline, synthetic rubber, plastics, detergents, cement, paper, and pulp, by applying principles and technology of chemistry, physics, and engineering. **Education and Training:** Bachelor's degree. **Skills:** Math—High. English—High. Science—High. **Yearly Earnings:** $$$$$ **Job Growth:** ★★ **Yearly Openings:** 🧍

Civil Engineers. Perform engineering duties in planning, designing, and overseeing construction and maintenance of building structures and facilities, such as roads, railroads, airports, bridges, harbors, channels, dams, irrigation projects, pipelines, power plants, water and sewage systems, and waste disposal units. Includes architectural, structural, traffic, ocean, and geo-technical engineers. **Education and Training:** Bachelor's degree. **Skills:** Math—High. English—High. Science—High. **Yearly Earnings:** $$$$$ **Job Growth:** ★★★ **Yearly Openings:** 🧍

Computer Hardware Engineers. Research, design, develop, and test computer or computer-related equipment for commercial, industrial, military, or scientific use. May supervise the manufacturing and installation of computer or computer-related equipment and components. **Education and Training:** Bachelor's degree. **Skills:** Math—High. English—High. Science—High. **Yearly Earnings:** $$$$$ **Job Growth:** ★★★★ **Yearly Openings:** 🧍

Computer Software Engineers, Applications. Develop, create, and modify general computer applications software or specialized utility programs. Analyze user needs and develop software solutions. Design software or customize software for client use with the aim of optimizing operational efficiency. May analyze and design databases within an application area. **Education and Training:** Bachelor's degree. **Skills:** Math—High. English—High. Science—High. **Yearly Earnings:** $$$$$ **Job Growth:** ★★★★★ **Yearly Openings:** 🧍🧍🧍

Computer Software Engineers, Systems Software. Research, design, develop, and test operating systems–level software, compilers, and network distribution software for medical, industrial, military, communications, aerospace, business, scientific, and general computing applications. Set operational specifications and formulate and analyze software requirements. Apply principles and techniques of computer science, engineering, and mathematical analysis. **Education and Training:** Bachelor's degree. **Skills:** Math—High. English—High. Science—High. **Yearly Earnings:** $$$$$ **Job Growth:** ★★★★★ **Yearly Openings:** 🧍🧍🧍

Electrical Engineers. Design, develop, test, or supervise the manufacturing and installation of electrical equipment, components, or systems for commercial, industrial, military, or scientific use. **Education and Training:** Bachelor's degree. **Skills:** Math—High. English—High. Science—High. **Yearly Earnings:** $$$$$ **Job Growth:** ★★★ **Yearly Openings:** 🧍🧍

Electronics Engineers, Except Computer. Research, design, develop, and test electronic components and systems for commercial, industrial, military, or scientific use. Use knowledge of electronic theory and materials properties. Design electronic circuits and components for use in fields such as telecommunications, aerospace guidance

and propulsion control, acoustics, or instruments and controls. **Education and Training:** Bachelor's degree. **Skills:** Math—High. English—High. Science—High. **Yearly Earnings:** $$$$$ **Job Growth:** ★★★ **Yearly Openings:** 🧍🧍

Environmental Engineers. Design, plan, or perform engineering duties in the prevention, control, and remediation of environmental health hazards, using various engineering disciplines. Work may include waste treatment, site remediation, or pollution control technology. **Education and Training:** Bachelor's degree. **Skills:** Math—Medium. English—Medium. Science—Medium. **Yearly Earnings:** $$$$$ **Job Growth:** ★★★★ **Yearly Openings:** 🧍

Fire-Prevention and Protection Engineers. Research causes of fires, determine fire protection methods, and design or recommend materials or equipment such as structural components or fire-detection equipment. This work assists organizations in safeguarding life and property against fire, explosion, and related hazards. **Education and Training:** Bachelor's degree. **Skills:** Math—Medium. English—Medium. Science—High. **Yearly Earnings:** $$$$$ **Job Growth:** ★★★ **Yearly Openings:** 🧍

Health and Safety Engineers, Except Mining Safety Engineers and Inspectors. Promote worksite or product safety by applying knowledge of industrial processes, mechanics, chemistry, psychology, and industrial health and safety laws. **Education and Training:** Bachelor's degree. **Skills:** Math—Medium. English—Medium. Science—Medium. **Yearly Earnings:** $$$$$ **Job Growth:** ★★★ **Yearly Openings:** 🧍

Industrial Engineers. Design, develop, test, and evaluate integrated systems for managing industrial production processes, including human work factors, quality control, inventory control, logistics and material flow, cost analysis, and production coordination. **Education and Training:** Bachelor's degree. **Skills:** Math—High. English—Medium. Science—High. **Yearly Earnings:** $$$$$ **Job Growth:** ★★ **Yearly Openings:** 🧍🧍

Industrial Safety and Health Engineers. Plan, implement, and coordinate safety programs requiring application of engineering principles and technology to prevent or correct unsafe environmental working conditions. **Education and Training:** Bachelor's degree. **Skills:** Math—High. English—Medium. Science—High. **Yearly Earnings:** $$$$$ **Job Growth:** ★★★ **Yearly Openings:** 🧍

Landscape Architects. Plan and design land areas for such projects as parks and other recreational facilities, airports, highways, hospitals, schools, land subdivisions, and commercial, industrial, and residential sites. **Education and Training:** Bachelor's degree. **Skills:** Math—High. English—High. Science—Medium. **Yearly Earnings:** $$$$ **Job Growth:** ★★★★ **Yearly Openings:** 🧍

Marine Architects. Design and oversee construction and repair of marine craft and floating structures, such as ships, barges, tugs, dredges, submarines, torpedoes, floats, and buoys. **Education and Training:** Bachelor's degree. **Skills:** Math—High. English—High. Science—High. **Yearly Earnings:** $$$$$ **Job Growth:** ★ **Yearly Openings:** 🧍

Marine Engineers. Design, develop, and take responsibility for the installation of ship machinery and related equipment, including propulsion machines and power supply systems. **Education and Training:** Bachelor's degree. **Skills:** Math—High. English—High. Science—High. **Yearly Earnings:** $$$$$ **Job Growth:** ★ **Yearly Openings:** 🧍

Marine Engineers and Naval Architects. Design, develop, and evaluate the operation of marine vessels, ship machinery, and related equipment, such as power supply and propulsion systems. **Education and Training:** Bachelor's degree. **Skills:** Math—Medium. English—Medium. Science—Medium. **Yearly Earnings:** $$$$$ **Job Growth:** ★ **Yearly Openings:** 🧍

Materials Engineers. Evaluate materials and develop machinery and processes to manufacture materials for use in products that must meet design and performance specifications. Develop new uses for known materials. Includes those working with composite materials or specializing in one type of material, such as graphite, metal and metal alloys, ceramics and glass, plastics and polymers, and naturally occurring materials. **Education and Training:** Bachelor's degree. **Skills:** Math—High. English—High. Science—High. **Yearly Earnings:** $$$$$ **Job Growth:** ★★ **Yearly Openings:** 🧍

Mechanical Engineers. Perform engineering duties in planning and designing tools, engines, machines, and other mechanically functioning equipment. Oversee installation, operation, maintenance, and repair of such equipment as centralized heat, gas, water, and steam systems. **Education and Training:** Bachelor's degree. **Skills:** Math—High. English—High. Science—High. **Yearly Earnings:** $$$$$ **Job Growth:** ★★★ **Yearly Openings:** 🧍🧍

Mining and Geological Engineers, Including Mining Safety Engineers. Determine the location and plan the extraction of coal, metallic ores, nonmetallic minerals, and building materials, such as stone and gravel. Work involves conducting preliminary surveys of deposits or undeveloped mines and planning their development; examining deposits or mines to determine whether they can be worked at a profit; making geological and topographical surveys; evolving methods of mining best suited to character, type, and size of deposits; and supervising mining operations. **Education and Training:** Bachelor's degree. **Skills:** Math—High. English—High. Science—High. **Yearly Earnings:** $$$$$ **Job Growth:** ★ **Yearly Openings:** 🧍

Nuclear Engineers. Conduct research on nuclear engineering problems or apply principles and theory of nuclear science to problems concerned with release, control, and utilization of nuclear energy and nuclear waste disposal. **Education and Training:** Bachelor's degree. **Skills:** Math—High. English—High. Science—High. **Yearly Earnings:** $$$$$ **Job Growth:** ★ **Yearly Openings:** 🧍

Petroleum Engineers. Devise methods to improve oil and gas well production and determine the need for new or modified tool designs. Oversee drilling and offer technical advice to achieve economical and satisfactory progress. **Education and Training:** Bachelor's degree. **Skills:** Math—High. English—High. Science—High. **Yearly Earnings:** $$$$$ **Job Growth:** ★ **Yearly Openings:** 🯅

Product Safety Engineers. Develop and conduct tests to evaluate product safety levels and recommend measures to reduce or eliminate hazards. **Education and Training:** Bachelor's degree. **Skills:** Math—High. English—Medium. Science—High. **Yearly Earnings:** $$$$$ **Job Growth:** ★★★ **Yearly Openings:** 🯅

Sales Engineers. Sell business goods or services, the selling of which requires a technical background equivalent to a bachelor's degree in engineering. **Education and Training:** Bachelor's degree. **Skills:** Math—High. English—Medium. Science—High. **Yearly Earnings:** $$$$$ **Job Growth:** ★★★ **Yearly Openings:** 🯅

ENGINEERING TECHNOLOGY

These workers perform a variety of technical tasks. They make detailed drawings and work plans; measure and prepare maps of land and water areas; operate complex communications equipment; inspect buildings and equipment for structural, mechanical, or electrical problems; and schedule and control production and transportation operations. Many work in industrial plants, oilfields and mines, research laboratories, and construction sites. Engineering firms, manufacturers, and federal, state, and local governments hire these workers.

Aerospace Engineering and Operations Technicians. Operate, install, calibrate, and maintain integrated computer/communications systems consoles, simulators, and other data acquisition, test, and measurement instruments and equipment to launch, track, position, and evaluate air and space vehicles. May record and interpret test data. **Education and Training:** Associate's degree. **Skills:** Math—High. English—Medium. Science—High. **Yearly Earnings:** $$$$ **Job Growth:** ★★ **Yearly Openings:** 🯅

Architectural and Civil Drafters. Prepare detailed drawings of architectural and structural features of buildings or drawings and topographical relief maps used in civil engineering projects, such as highways, bridges, and public works. Utilize knowledge of building materials, engineering practices, and mathematics to complete drawings. **Education and Training:** Postsecondary career and technical education. **Skills:** Math—Medium. English—Medium. Science—Medium. **Yearly Earnings:** $$$ **Job Growth:** ★★★ **Yearly Openings:** 🯅🯅🯅

Architectural Drafters. Prepare detailed drawings of architectural designs and plans for buildings and structures according to specifications provided by architect.

Education and Training: Associate's degree. **Skills:** Math—High. English—Medium. Science—Medium. **Yearly Earnings:** $$$ **Job Growth:** ★★★ **Yearly Openings:** 🧍🧍🧍

Calibration and Instrumentation Technicians. Develop, test, calibrate, operate, and repair electrical, mechanical, electromechanical, electrohydraulic, or electronic measuring and recording instruments, apparatus, and equipment. **Education and Training:** Associate's degree. **Skills:** Math—Medium. English—Medium. Science—Medium. **Yearly Earnings:** $$$$ **Job Growth:** ★★★ **Yearly Openings:** 🧍🧍🧍

Cartographers and Photogrammetrists. Collect, analyze, and interpret geographic information provided by geodetic surveys, aerial photographs, and satellite data. Research, study, and prepare maps and other spatial data in digital or graphic form for legal, social, political, educational, and design purposes. May work with Geographic Information Systems (GIS). May design and evaluate algorithms, data structures, and user interfaces for GIS and mapping systems. **Education and Training:** Bachelor's degree. **Skills:** Math—High. English—Medium. Science—Medium. **Yearly Earnings:** $$$ **Job Growth:** ★★★ **Yearly Openings:** 🧍

Civil Drafters. Prepare drawings and topographical and relief maps used in civil engineering projects, such as highways, bridges, pipelines, flood control projects, and water and sewage control systems. **Education and Training:** Postsecondary career and technical education. **Skills:** Math—High. English—Medium. Science—Medium. **Yearly Earnings:** $$$ **Job Growth:** ★★★ **Yearly Openings:** 🧍🧍🧍

Civil Engineering Technicians. Apply theory and principles of civil engineering in planning, designing, and overseeing construction and maintenance of structures and facilities under the direction of engineering staff or physical scientists. **Education and Training:** Associate's degree. **Skills:** Math—High. English—Medium. Science—High. **Yearly Earnings:** $$$ **Job Growth:** ★★★ **Yearly Openings:** 🧍🧍

Construction and Building Inspectors. Inspect structures, using engineering skills to determine structural soundness and compliance with specifications, building codes, and other regulations. Inspections may be general in nature or may be limited to a specific area, such as electrical systems or plumbing. **Education and Training:** Work experience in a related occupation. **Skills:** Math—Medium. English—Medium. Science—Medium. **Yearly Earnings:** $$$ **Job Growth:** ★★★ **Yearly Openings:** 🧍

Electrical and Electronic Engineering Technicians. Apply electrical and electronic theory and related knowledge, usually under the direction of engineering staff, to design, build, repair, calibrate, and modify electrical components, circuitry, controls, and machinery for use by engineering staff in making engineering design decisions. **Education and Training:** Associate's degree. **Skills:** Math—Medium. English—Medium. Science—Medium. **Yearly Earnings:** $$$$ **Job Growth:** ★★★ **Yearly Openings:** 🧍🧍🧍

Electrical and Electronics Drafters. Prepare wiring diagrams, circuit board assembly diagrams, and layout drawings used for manufacture, installation, and repair of electrical equipment in factories, power plants, and buildings. **Education and Training:** Associate's degree. **Skills:** Math—Medium. English—Medium. Science—Medium. **Yearly Earnings:** $$$ **Job Growth:** ★★★★ **Yearly Openings:** 🚶

Electrical Drafters. Develop specifications and instructions for installation of voltage transformers, overhead or underground cables, and related electrical equipment used to conduct electrical energy from transmission lines or high-voltage distribution lines to consumers. **Education and Training:** Associate's degree. **Skills:** Math—High. English—Medium. Science—Medium. **Yearly Earnings:** $$$ **Job Growth:** ★★★★ **Yearly Openings:** 🚶

Electrical Engineering Technicians. Apply electrical theory and related knowledge to test and modify developmental or operational electrical machinery and electrical control equipment and circuitry in industrial or commercial plants and laboratories. **Education and Training:** Associate's degree. **Skills:** Math—Medium. English—Medium. Science—Medium. **Yearly Earnings:** $$$$ **Job Growth:** ★★★ **Yearly Openings:** 🚶🚶🚶

Electro-Mechanical Technicians. Operate, test, and maintain unmanned, automated, servo-mechanical, or electro-mechanical equipment. May operate unmanned submarines, aircraft, or other equipment at worksites such as oil rigs, deep ocean exploration, or hazardous waste removal. May assist engineers in testing and designing robotics equipment. **Education and Training:** Associate's degree. **Skills:** Math—Medium. English—Medium. Science—Medium. **Yearly Earnings:** $$$ **Job Growth:** ★★★ **Yearly Openings:** 🚶

Electronic Drafters. Draw wiring diagrams, circuit board assembly diagrams, schematics, and layout drawings used for manufacture, installation, and repair of electronic equipment. **Education and Training:** Postsecondary career and technical education. **Skills:** Math—High. English—Medium. Science—High. **Yearly Earnings:** $$$ **Job Growth:** ★★★★ **Yearly Openings:** 🚶

Electronics Engineering Technicians. Lay out, build, test, troubleshoot, repair, and modify developmental and production electronic components, parts, equipment, and systems, such as computer equipment, missile control instrumentation, electron tubes, test equipment, and machine tool numerical controls. Apply principles and theories of electronics, electrical circuitry, engineering mathematics, electronic and electrical testing, and physics. **Education and Training:** Associate's degree. **Skills:** Math—High. English—Medium. Science—High. **Yearly Earnings:** $$$$ **Job Growth:** ★★★ **Yearly Openings:** 🚶🚶🚶

Environmental Engineering Technicians. Apply theory and principles of environmental engineering to modify, test, and operate equipment and devices used in the prevention, control, and remediation of environmental pollution, including waste

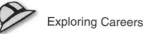

treatment and site remediation. May assist in the development of environmental pollution remediation devices under direction of engineer. **Education and Training:** Associate's degree. **Skills:** Math—Medium. English—Medium. Science—Medium. **Yearly Earnings:** $$$ **Job Growth:** ★★★★ **Yearly Openings:** 🚶

Industrial Engineering Technicians. Apply engineering theory and principles to problems of industrial layout or manufacturing production, usually under the direction of engineering staff. May study and record time, motion, method, and speed involved in performance of production, maintenance, clerical, and other worker operations for such purposes as establishing standard production rates or improving efficiency. **Education and Training:** Associate's degree. **Skills:** Math—High. English—High. Science—High. **Yearly Earnings:** $$$$ **Job Growth:** ★★★ **Yearly Openings:** 🚶

Mapping Technicians. Calculate mapmaking information from field notes and draw and verify accuracy of topographical maps. **Education and Training:** Moderate-term on-the-job training. **Skills:** Math—High. English—Medium. Science—Medium. **Yearly Earnings:** $$ **Job Growth:** ★★★★ **Yearly Openings:** 🚶🚶

Mechanical Drafters. Prepare detailed working diagrams of machinery and mechanical devices, including dimensions, fastening methods, and other engineering information. **Education and Training:** Postsecondary career and technical education. **Skills:** Math—High. English—Medium. Science—High. **Yearly Earnings:** $$$ **Job Growth:** ★★★ **Yearly Openings:** 🚶🚶

Mechanical Engineering Technicians. Apply theory and principles of mechanical engineering to modify, develop, and test machinery and equipment under direction of engineering staff or physical scientists. **Education and Training:** Associate's degree. **Skills:** Math—High. English—Medium. Science—High. **Yearly Earnings:** $$$ **Job Growth:** ★★★ **Yearly Openings:** 🚶

Numerical Tool and Process Control Programmers. Develop programs to control machining or processing of parts by automatic machine tools, equipment, or systems. **Education and Training:** Long-term on-the-job training. **Skills:** Math—High. English—Medium. Science—Medium. **Yearly Earnings:** $$$ **Job Growth:** ★★★ **Yearly Openings:** 🚶

Pressure Vessel Inspectors. Inspect pressure vessel equipment for conformance with safety laws and standards regulating their design, fabrication, installation, repair, and operation. **Education and Training:** Long-term on-the-job training. **Skills:** Math—Medium. English—Medium. Science—Medium. **Yearly Earnings:** $$$$ **Job Growth:** ★★ **Yearly Openings:** 🚶🚶

Surveying and Mapping Technicians. Perform surveying and mapping duties, usually under the direction of a surveyor, cartographer, or photogrammetrist. Obtain data used for construction, mapmaking, boundary location, mining, or other purposes. May calculate mapmaking information and create maps from source data, such as surveying notes, aerial photography, satellite data, or other maps to show topographical features,

political boundaries, and other features. May verify accuracy and completeness of topographical maps. **Education and Training:** Moderate-term on-the-job training. **Skills:** Math—Medium. English—Medium. Science—Medium. **Yearly Earnings:** $$ **Job Growth:** ★★★★ **Yearly Openings:** 🚶🚶

Surveying Technicians. Adjust and operate surveying instruments, such as theodolite and electronic distance-measuring equipment. Compile notes, make sketches, and enter data into computers. **Education and Training:** Long-term on-the-job training. **Skills:** Math—Medium. English—Medium. Science—Medium. **Yearly Earnings:** $$ **Job Growth:** ★★★★ **Yearly Openings:** 🚶🚶

Surveyors. Make exact measurements and determine property boundaries. Provide data relevant to the shape, contour, gravitation, location, elevation, or dimension of land or land features on or near the earth's surface for engineering, mapmaking, mining, land evaluation, construction, and other purposes. **Education and Training:** Bachelor's degree. **Skills:** Math—High. English—High. Science—High. **Yearly Earnings:** $$$ **Job Growth:** ★★ **Yearly Openings:** 🚶🚶

Exploring Careers: Plants and Animals

Start Your Journey Through Careers Related to

PLANTS AND ANIMALS

Careers in this area suit people interested in working with plants and animals, often outdoors.

EXPLORING CAREER CLUES

Your interests give important clues for exploring career options. Think about your interests to learn if jobs in the Plants and Animals interest area may be worth further exploration.

Do you like the school subjects related to the Plants and Animals interest area? Here are some examples of related subjects:

- Science
- Chemistry
- Biology
- Physics
- Math
- Business
- Physical education

Do you like the free-time activities related to the Plants and Animals interest area? Here are some examples of related activities:

- Growing flowers
- Raising vegetables
- Planting trees
- Mowing the lawn
- Trimming shrubs and hedges
- Identifying flowers, trees, and wildlife
- Belonging to a 4-H club or Future Farmers of America
- Participating in county and state fair events and competitions
- Raising, training, and caring for pets, livestock, or other animals
- Taking care of fish or an aquarium
- Camping, hiking, or doing other outdoor activities
- Fishing

EXPLORING JOB GROUPS

Jobs related to the Plants and Animals interest area fit into three groups. Read through the list to see which groups sound interesting to you.

- Managerial Work in Plants and Animals
- Animal Care and Training
- Hands-on Work in Plants and Animals

EXPLORING CAREER POSSIBILITIES

You can satisfy your interest in the Plants and Animals area by working in animal care, farming, landscaping, fishing, and several other related fields. Here are a few examples of career possibilities:

If you enjoy physical work and being outdoors, perhaps working as a farmer, rancher, or tree trimmer would appeal to you.

You may like animals. Perhaps you could train, breed, or take care of animals.

If you have management ability, you could own or oversee a fish hatchery, a landscaping business, or a greenhouse.

Turn the page to meet people working in the Plants and Animals interest area→

PROFILE

As a horseshoer, Jerome trims horses' hooves, prepares shoes, and nails those shoes to the hoof.

Jerome Newton—Horseshoer

Some of the world's largest athletes rely on the work of Jerome Newton. Jerome is a horseshoer, or farrier, a worker who makes and fits shoes for horses. Average horses, horses with foot problems, and equine Olympians have all worn his handiwork.

As a horseshoer, Jerome trims horses' hooves, prepares shoes, and nails those shoes to the hoof. "Hooves, like human fingernails, grow continuously. They must be trimmed, evened, and re-covered every six to eight weeks," Jerome said.

The shoes Jerome uses protect the hoof and keep it from wearing down too quickly. They also provide proper traction. Specially designed shoes alleviate foot and leg problems.

The Process of Fitting Horseshoes

Jerome begins his work with a horse by observing its gait. He determines if the horse is comfortable by watching how it distributes its weight when moving.

"An important part of being a good horseshoer," he said, "is knowing what's normal motion for a horse and what's not."

After becoming familiar with the horse, Jerome lifts its foot and carefully trims the hoof using a hoof knife and file. He maintains the hoof's natural shape during trimming. A hoof that is ragged, too long, or too short interferes with balance.

"An important part of being a good horseshoer is knowing what's normal motion for a horse and what's not."

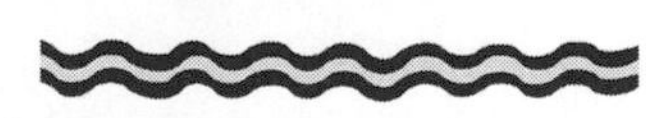

After trimming, Jerome measures the hoof and shapes a shoe or selects a ready-made shoe. "Ready-made shoes used to only come in small, medium, and large," said Jerome. "Now, shoes are available in almost every size and style." Shoes of varying weights and sizes are sold with or without prepunched nail holes.

This variety means that fewer shoes today are custom made. But knowing how to make a complete shoe is still important when working with hoof problems. Competition horses, like all athletes, need shoes tailored for their body and their event.

"Horses have wear and tear like other athletes," said Jerome. "Shoes can help." With racehorses, Jerome uses lightweight materials such as aluminum, titanium, and plastic. Standard shoes are steel. For a horse with a strained muscle, he might use a shoe that helps the horse to balance better.

To make a custom shoe, Jerome heats a piece of metal in his forge until it becomes flexible. He puts it on an anvil and beats it. He curves the metal to fit the hoof and punches nail holes.

Every shoe Jerome nails to a hoof is heated first. Heating creates a tighter fit for nailing. Nailing requires precision to avoid hitting the edge and the fleshy part of the hoof. After nailing, Jerome files the shoed hoof. He makes sure the horse moves with comfortable stability.

Conditions and Variety of Work

Horseshoers often travel for work. Jerome shoes competitive show horses at events in the United States and Europe. Sometimes he travels on short notice.

Once, he flew to Kentucky to reshoe a horse before a show. The job was difficult. He and another horseshoer worked on it until 2 a.m. Their long hours were rewarded: The horse not only made it through the show with its shoes on, but it won the event.

Most shoeing jobs don't require special care. But sometimes horses have a cracked hoof, punctured foot, or infection. Horseshoers use antibiotic creams, shock-absorbing pads, or other forms of protection to help these horses heal.

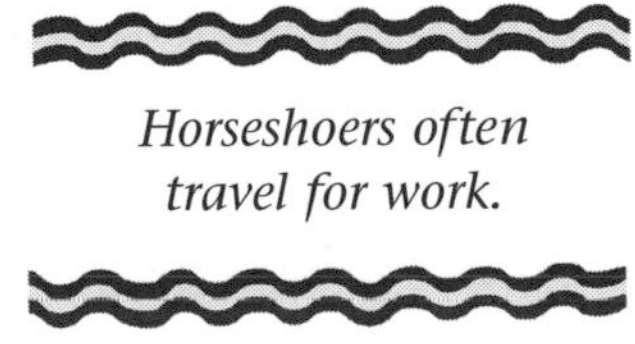

Horseshoers often travel for work.

Experienced horseshoers like Jerome often work with veterinarians to solve foot problems. Each week, Jerome visits equine patients in an animal hospital. There, he helps treat injured horses by creating prosthetics, castlike shoes for broken feet, or other devices. They allow an injured horse to continue competing or to stand and walk comfortably.

Jerome's work helps an injured horse to continue competing or to stand and walk comfortably.

Horseshoeing is hard work. Horseshoers often lift and hold a horse's hoof for fifteen minutes at a time. This is no small feat–horses often weigh at least 1,200 pounds.

In part because of the physical demands of the job, most horseshoers are men. The last decade has seen an increase in the number of women joining the ranks. The American Farrier's Association estimates that ten percent of today's horseshoers are women.

For both men and women horseshoers, experience lessens the physical demands. "Beginning horseshoers really struggle when shoeing a horse," said Jerome. "But soon they learn to work with the horse so it carries its own weight."

Over ninety percent of horseshoers are self-employed. Many work part time and have separate careers.

An Early Interest: Background and Education

Jerome's interest in horseshoeing began when he was young. He grew up around his family's horses and watched the horseshoer work.

At age fifteen, he started to think about a career as a horseshoer. He attended a horseshoer school after graduating from high school. The program he chose lasted six months. It introduced him to the basics of horse handling, anatomy, forge work, and hoof pathology.

After horseshoer school, Jerome apprenticed with an expert horseshoer. This experience was essential. "You need experience to develop the art and craft of shoeing," he said. "My advice is to work with an expert horseshoer. That is really the only way to learn. The longer you study, the better you'll be."

After his apprenticeship, Jerome spent one year doing independent shoeing. Then, he enrolled in a shoeing program at a university's veterinary school. He learned more about anatomy and specialty work there. That

knowledge helped him with the more complicated shoeing he performs today.

"My advice is to work with an expert horseshoer. That is really the only way to learn. The longer you study, the better you'll be."

Students researching the career should look up the job titles of farrier, horseshoer, and nonfarm animal caretaker.

Jerome has seen his patients grow from foals to champions to the happily retired. "I'm lucky," he said. "I make horses comfortable. It's very rewarding. I wouldn't want to do anything else."

PROFILE

Jeff Glickstein—Tree Doctor

Some trees in the neighborhood are dying. It's Jeff Glickstein's job to find out why. Jeff is a tree doctor, or *arborist.*

Jeff carefully cuts diseased or infected branches off a tree to save it.

After examining the trees and researching the diseases that affect them, he identifies the culprit: a fungus. Jeff injects the trees with a fungus killer and recommends a watering schedule.

"Tree doctors," Jeff explained, "diagnose and treat tree diseases, nutrient shortages, and structural problems.

"Trees are living organisms, like humans, constantly growing and changing. They need much the same care and attention as we do."

Jeff works as a consultant for a tree care company, helping people understand and care for their trees. "One of the things I like most is explaining how a tree works and how diseases affect trees," he said. "I help people understand that their trees are growing and need to be kept healthy."

"I help people understand that their trees are growing and need to be kept healthy."

A Tree Doctor's Day

Each working day, Jeff drives to customers' houses and examines their trees. He checks the bark for signs of rot or damage. Then, he checks the leaves for odd changes in color or texture. Sometimes, he removes dirt at the base of the tree to examine the root structure.

"I use binoculars to inspect the upper branches of the tree. Or I climb into the canopy of branches for a closer look," Jeff said.

When an illness is hard to diagnose, Jeff takes samples of leaves or small branches and sends the samples to arborist specialists for analysis.

If Jeff finds viruses, bacteria, fungi, or harmful insects, he recommends a course of action. He might spray the tree or inject medicine into its bark. After treatment, he might recommend special watering or fertilizer.

Often, he cuts diseased or infected branches off the tree to save the others, a process called pruning. He also prunes branches that rub together and those that are not well supported by the rest of the tree.

"Pruning a tree correctly takes skill," Jeff said. Tree doctors and tree trimmers climb onto a tree's branches using ropes and hanging seats called climbing saddles. They carefully remove branches with chainsaws, shears, and tiny clippers. If a branch is diseased, tree doctors sometimes dip their tools in disinfectant before cutting another branch to prevent the spread of infection.

Jeff uses math to analyze a tree's structure before he decides which branches to cut.

"I use equations to decide how structurally sound a tree is," said Jeff. "I measure the tree's circumference, and I can figure out a tree's height without climbing it." More and more, tree doctors are using computer programs to calculate information about a tree.

Jeff uses math to analyze a tree's structure before he decides which branches to cut.

If a tree limb is broken but can be saved, then Jeff will repair it. He binds it much the same as doctor binds a broken limb on a human. "I will do whatever it takes to save a tree that's worth saving."

Tree Care Matters to All of Us

"A tree's structure can be a matter of life and death for the people who live near it," Jeff stated. "Weak, diseased, or unsupported branches can crack and fall. They can crush cars, houses, or people beneath them."

Despite all the treatments, some trees cannot be saved. "People don't look up at their trees often enough," Jeff explained.

"It's not until a tree is screaming for attention that most people notice there's a problem. I can't always save trees that are very sick."

Removing a dead or dying tree can be tricky. To remove a poplar tree from a customer's yard, for example, Jeff needs a climbing saddle, ropes, chains and a 200-ton crane, along with the help of other tree doctors and landscape workers.

Avoiding injuries takes practice. And tree care can be strenuous. "You're carrying heavy wood," Jeff said, referring to the downed trees and branches. "This work can be hard on your back."

Tree Doctors Aren't Always in the Treetops

Not every tree doctor's job is so physically demanding. Some help clients decide which trees to buy and where to plant them. Conditions vary from region to region and even from one part of a back yard to another. Tree doctors understand which trees will thrive in which environment.

Tree doctors understand which trees will thrive in which environment.

Other tree doctors preserve trees growing on construction sites. They mark where roots begin and design temporary enclosures to protect them during building. A tree doctor can do this kind of work without ever climbing a tree.

Branching Out

Many tree doctors work for tree care companies. Others work for state and local governments, caring for trees on roadsides and other public properties. Some work for themselves as private consultants.

They may also pursue careers in landscape design, using their tree care knowledge as one way of serving clients. Other firms that employ tree doctors on an as-needed basis include landscape companies, tree nurseries, tree care contractors, and utility companies.

Earnings for tree doctors increase with experience and responsibility. Ground workers, who chop and carry away fallen branches, climbers, and crew leaders earn an hourly wage. Tree doctors who perform consulting services or who diagnose and treat specialty trees can earn more. Those who are employed by state or federal agencies earn an annual salary.

Becoming a Tree Doctor

Jeff became a tree doctor after realizing he wanted to work outdoors. "I was in college studying for a business degree, but at the same time I was working at a landscaping company," he said.

"I realized that with a business degree I might end up in a cubicle, watching the outdoors from a window. If I worked in landscaping, I could be outside all day in the natural environment." He stopped studying business and started working full time at a plant nursery.

Over time, Jeff's interest in trees grew. He took classes in tree anatomy, physiology, and disease treatment while working at the nursery. After gaining three years of field experience, he took a certification exam and became a certified arborist.

He still takes classes to maintain his certification and to keep up with advances in tree care. "We need people who are curious. There are always new things to learn about trees," he said.

"We need people who are curious. There are always new things to learn about trees."

Some tree doctors learn on the job. Others combine coursework with experience, as Jeff did, to enter the occupation.

Some enroll in formal degree programs, earning an associate's or bachelor's degree in horticulture, botany, or forestry. Still others continue their education, earning a master's or doctoral degree. Those with advanced degrees sometimes become researchers or expert witnesses in court cases involving trees.

When researching the career area, students should look up job titles such as these to find more information: arborists, tree doctors, tree trimmers, tree pruners, tree surgeons, landscaping and groundskeeping workers, foresters, and forester technicians.

Hands-on tree work is still the kind of tree care Jeff likes best. "It's an honor to work with these majestic living organisms," he said.

"To be able to understand what makes them strong and healthy is amazing."

PROFILE

Alicia Kovich—Veterinarian

"When I see a sick animal become healthy again, I wouldn't trade my veterinary license for anything."

"I wish horses could vomit!"

The waitress bringing Alicia Kovich's plate looked disgusted.

"Oh, excuse me!" said Alicia. "But at a veterinary school reunion, we're going to talk shop!

"I was just thinking how much horses suffer with stomach pain because they can't burp," she continued. "Did you know that?" The waitress shook her head and hurried to the next table.

Alicia turned to her friend and former classmate, Dr. Mark Keller. "Well, *you* know!" They both laughed.

Plenty of Patients

"I had to fly by helicopter into a canyon to free a mountain lion whose leg was caught in a hunter's illegal trap."

"Have you seen Dave Walsh?" Alicia asked Mark.

"Nope. I'd like to. We spent long hours together hitting the books over those four years studying veterinary medicine," Mark replied.

"Horses were his first love, weren't they? I'll bet he works with large animals like we do."

"I'm the only one in my practice who does," replied Mark. "Another doctor specializes in dogs and cats, and still another in reptiles, birds, and exotic animals."

"With a big clinic like yours, you must offer a wide range of services," Alicia said.

"You bet we do," Mark replied. "Obviously, we offer the same things most any vet does–diagnosis, treatment of illnesses and accidents, vaccinations, neutering, and so on.

"But we've added boarding, dentistry, and grooming. We even get involved with wildlife rescue programs. That's an interesting variation–and pretty exciting sometimes.

"I was once called to fly by helicopter into a remote mountain canyon to free a mountain lion whose leg was caught in a hunter's illegal trap."

"I've never done anything like that," Alicia said. "The most dangerous time I've had was with an angry stallion."

Trials and Triumphs

"Speaking of horses, yesterday was rough," Alicia said. "I had to put down Rocky, a dear old quarter horse. His owner sat up with him all night. He'd have done anything to save Rocky. But that horse was thirty years old. An operation would have been useless in the long run, and therefore cruel. Quality of life is of great importance."

"Days like that are hard," Mark said, "but think about how we're *always* needed–and about all the happier cases that are so rewarding."

Mark smiled as he told of a blind man who brought his guide dog, Ginger, to their clinic. "We discovered a liver problem that would kill her if left untreated.

"We were able to treat the sick guide dog, and she should live for a long time."

"This was terrible news for her owner, who depended on her for companionship as well as for her guide abilities. We were able to treat her, though–Ginger should live for a long time," Mark said.

"I wish we always worked with people like that, ones who appreciate their animals," Alicia said. Mark knew what she meant–the people who took their anger out on animals.

"It's tough to face abuse or neglect," Mark agreed. "And I also get frustrated when our clients don't have their pets neutered and they end up with unwanted litters. Sometimes they expect us to just 'put them to sleep.' It isn't right to do that to a healthy animal."

One Vet's Path

Alicia looked thoughtful. "When I was a girl, I worked for a wonderful vet–very kind and gentle, with a respect for his patients and for his staff. He'd take the time to explain things to me."

Mark smiled and said, "I think all people who want to be veterinarians should try to find work in animal hospitals, even if it's volunteer work."

"After I had my undergraduate degree, when I started applying to veterinary schools, I discovered that my grades weren't the only thing that mattered," Alicia said. "Having worked with animals as a teenager was considered important."

"All people who want to be veterinarians should try to find work in animal hospitals, even if it's volunteer work."

"Speaking of vet school," Mark said, "I remember that Dave and I agreed that it might be easier to be a 'people doctor' instead of a 'Doctor of Veterinary Medicine.' A 'people doctor' has to learn about the anatomy, illnesses, and treatments of humans, but vets have to learn all that about creatures from parrots to pot-bellied pigs–and none of *our* patients can tell us where it hurts."

A Hospital on Wheels

"Howdy, pardners," boomed a voice behind them. Alicia and Mark looked up and took a moment to recognize the man in cowboy boots.

"Dave Walsh!" they cried together.

"You remembered," the man laughed. "My card." He produced a small card that read:

WALSH'S ROLLING ANIMAL HOSPITAL
Large-Animal Care Our Specialty
"We Make Barn Calls!"

"What is this?" said Alicia.

"If you don't mind leaving your meal, I'll show you," said Dave. Mark and Alicia followed him to the parking lot, where a long vehicle with the hospital's name was printed on the side.

"It's wonderful!" Alicia exclaimed, as she stepped inside the well-equipped pet clinic on wheels. Dave had an X-ray machine, an examining table, a refrigerator, cabinets of medical supplies, and even a computer for keeping records.

"It works for me," Dave said with pride. "I have a technician who assists me, and we can go right to the sick animals."

Veterinary Variety

After singing "If I Could Talk to the Animals," it was time for the former classmates to take turns at the microphone. Each described where veterinary medicine had taken him or her.

One woman said, "I work with exotic birds. I have an avian hospital."

"I've heard of Jenelle's hospital," Alicia whispered to Mark. "It's one of the best. Parakeets are as important to their owners as poodles are to theirs, she says."

No one was surprised when Ron Green spoke. Always an animal activist, he'd traveled for awhile as resident veterinarian with a large circus. He later worked in a zoo, where he tried to improve the lives of the animals. He now works in wildlife management.

Then Alicia heard her name called. It was her turn to speak.

What am I going to say? she thought as she walked to the microphone. *I haven't done anything like work with cougars or other exotic animals.*

"Hello," she said, "I work outdoors on large farm animals. I've been scratched, bitten, and kicked. I can pick up fifty pounds if I have to. My hands often look like tree bark. I suffer from poison oak now and then.

"But all the same, when I see a sick animal become healthy again, I wouldn't trade my veterinary license for anything."

Alicia was relieved–and gratified–when her old classmates applauded loudly. Alicia looked with pride at her colleagues, who can diagnose the illnesses of patients who can't speak.

As she sat down again, she and Mark raised their glasses in a toast: "Here's to creatures large and small. And here's to the people who care for them all."

SKILL SAMPLER

John O'Quinn–Farmer

Even while he was studying agriculture at the University of Iowa, John O'Quinn came home almost every weekend to help his father run the family's farming operation. "The harvest is the best part of farming. It's what you spend months working toward."

John discussed the skills and knowledge a farmer needs. He offers you the following tips for deciding if you want to learn more about a career in farming.

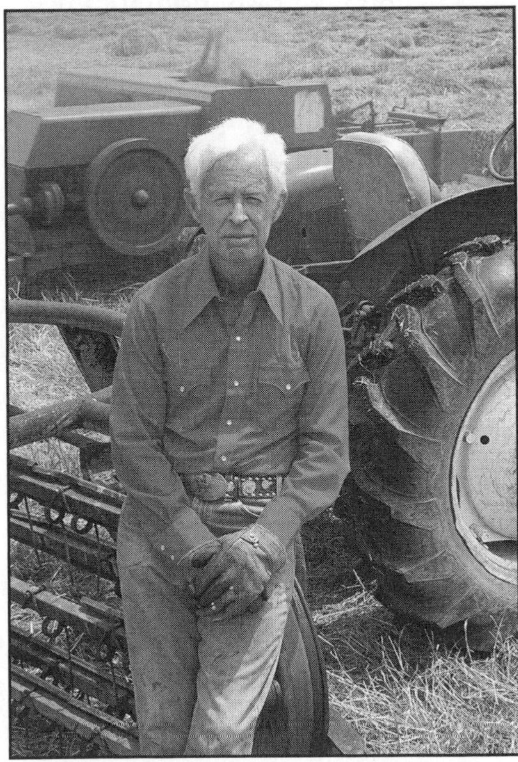

As a farmer, John O'Quinn loves the outdoors and enjoys the harvest season.

Farmers spend much of their time outdoors in all kinds of weather.

- Do you enjoy being outside?
- Do you like outdoor activities such as swimming, hiking, fishing, camping, and hunting?
- Do you like to work in the garden or mow lawns?
- Are you comfortable with extremes of heat and cold?

Farmers must have initiative and be self-starters. They are their own bosses.

- Do you get up in the morning by yourself?
- Do you do your homework and household chores without being prodded by your parents?
- Do you stick with projects until they are finished?
- Do you take responsibility for your family's pets?
- Do you get to class on time every day?

Farmers take on more planning and managerial duties as farming methods grow more complex.

- Do you always finish your homework on time?
- Do you keep a diary?
- Do you use an electronic or paper calendar to organize your time?
- Do you make lists of things to do?
- Are you good at long-range projects such as gardening that require organization?
- When you are in control of a project, can you inspire people to work without resenting you?

Farmers must respect the environment.

- Do you throw your trash in trash cans?
- Does it bother you when you see a polluted river?
- Have you ever e-mailed a politician about an environmental issue?
- Do you save cans, paper, and other materials for recycling?

Farmers must work with machinery and often maintain and repair their own equipment.

- Do you like to build and repair things?
- Do you like to work with your hands?
- Do you ever fix small household appliances?
- Are you handy with tools?
- Before you start working on something, do you think about how you will go about it?

Now learn about all major jobs in the Plants and Animals interest area→

Facts About All Major Jobs Related to

PLANTS AND ANIMALS

In addition to the jobs covered in the profiles and skill sampler, other careers in the Plants and Animals interest area may appeal to you. This section describes and gives facts about all major jobs in the Plants and Animals interest area. For an explanation of the $, ★, and 🚶 symbols, see page 6.

MANAGERIAL WORK IN PLANTS AND ANIMALS

These workers operate or manage farms, ranches, hatcheries, nurseries, forests, and other plant and animal businesses. Some breed specialty plants and animals. Others provide services to increase production or beautify land areas. Many work in rural areas or woodlands and on farms, ranches, and forest preserves. Others find employment with commercial nurseries, landscaping firms, business services, or government agencies located in large and small communities all over the country. Many of these workers are self-employed, operating their own large or small businesses.

Agricultural Crop Farm Managers. Direct and coordinate activities of workers engaged in agricultural crop production for corporations, cooperatives, or other owners. **Education and Training:** Work experience in a related occupation. **Skills:** Math—Medium. English—Medium. Science—Medium. **Yearly Earnings:** $$$ **Job Growth:** ★★ **Yearly Openings:** 🚶🚶🚶

Farm Labor Contractors. Recruit, hire, furnish, and supervise seasonal or temporary agricultural laborers for a fee. May transport, house, and provide meals for workers. **Education and Training:** Work experience in a related occupation. **Skills:** Math—Medium. English—Medium. Science—Medium. **Yearly Earnings:** $ **Job Growth:** No data available. **Yearly Openings:** No data available.

Farmers and Ranchers. On an ownership or rental basis, operate farms, ranches, greenhouses, nurseries, timber tracts, or other agricultural production establishments. These establishments produce crops, plant specialties, livestock, poultry, finfish, shellfish, or animal specialties. May plant, cultivate, harvest, perform post-harvest activities, and market crops and livestock. May hire, train, and supervise farm workers or supervise a farm labor contractor. May prepare cost, production, and other records. May maintain and operate machinery and perform physical work. **Education and Training:** Long-term on-the-job training. **Skills:** Math—Medium. English—Medium. Science—Medium. **Yearly Earnings:** No data available. **Job Growth:** ★ **Yearly Openings:** 🚶🚶🚶🚶🚶

First-Line Supervisors and Manager/Supervisors—Agricultural Crop Workers. Directly supervise and coordinate activities of agricultural crop workers. Manager/Supervisors are generally found in smaller establishments, where they perform both supervisory and management functions, such as accounting, marketing, and personnel work. They may also do the same agricultural work as the workers they supervise. **Education and Training:** Associate's degree. **Skills:** Math—Medium. English—Medium. Science—Medium. **Yearly Earnings:** No data available. **Job Growth:** ★★ **Yearly Openings:** 🧍 🧍 🧍

First-Line Supervisors and Manager/Supervisors—Animal Care Workers, Except Livestock. Directly supervise and coordinate activities of animal care workers. Manager/Supervisors are generally found in smaller establishments, where they perform both supervisory and management functions, such as accounting, marketing, and personnel work. They may also do the same animal care work as the workers they supervise. **Education and Training:** Associate's degree. **Skills:** Math—Medium. English—Medium. Science—Medium. **Yearly Earnings:** No data available. **Job Growth:** ★★ **Yearly Openings:** 🧍 🧍 🧍

First-Line Supervisors and Manager/Supervisors—Animal Husbandry Workers. Directly supervise and coordinate activities of animal husbandry workers. Manager/Supervisors are generally found in smaller establishments, where they perform both supervisory and management functions, such as accounting, marketing, and personnel work. They may also do the same animal husbandry work as the workers they supervise. **Education and Training:** Associate's degree. **Skills:** Math—Medium. English—Medium. Science—Medium. **Yearly Earnings:** No data available. **Job Growth:** ★★ **Yearly Openings:** 🧍 🧍 🧍

First-Line Supervisors and Manager/Supervisors—Fishery Workers. Directly supervise and coordinate activities of fishery workers. Manager/Supervisors are generally found in smaller establishments, where they perform both supervisory and management functions, such as accounting, marketing, and personnel work. They may also do the same fishery work as the workers they supervise. **Education and Training:** Associate's degree. **Skills:** Math—Medium. English—Medium. Science—Medium. **Yearly Earnings:** No data available. **Job Growth:** ★ **Yearly Openings:** 🧍

First-Line Supervisors and Manager/Supervisors—Horticultural Workers. Directly supervise and coordinate activities of horticultural workers. Manager/Supervisors are generally found in smaller establishments, where they perform both supervisory and management functions, such as accounting, marketing, and personnel work. They may also do the same horticultural work as the workers they supervise. **Education and Training:** Associate's degree. **Skills:** Math—Medium. English—Medium. Science—Medium. **Yearly Earnings:** No data available. **Job Growth:** ★★ **Yearly Openings:** 🧍 🧍 🧍

First-Line Supervisors and Manager/Supervisors—Landscaping Workers. Directly supervise and coordinate activities of landscaping workers. Manager/Supervisors are generally found in smaller establishments, where they perform both supervisory and management functions, such as accounting, marketing, and personnel work. They may also do the same landscaping work as the workers they supervise. **Education and Training:** Work experience in a related occupation. **Skills:** Math—Medium. English—Medium. Science—Medium. **Yearly Earnings:** $$$ **Job Growth:** ★★★ **Yearly Openings:** 🚶🚶

First-Line Supervisors and Manager/Supervisors—Logging Workers. Directly supervise and coordinate activities of logging workers. Manager/Supervisors are generally found in smaller establishments, where they perform both supervisory and management functions, such as accounting, marketing, and personnel work. They may also do the same logging work as the workers they supervise. **Education and Training:** Bachelor's degree. **Skills:** Math—Medium. English—Medium. Science—Medium. **Yearly Earnings:** No data available. **Job Growth:** ★★ **Yearly Openings:** 🚶🚶🚶

First-Line Supervisors/Managers of Farming, Fishing, and Forestry Workers. Directly supervise and coordinate the activities of agricultural, forestry, aquacultural, and related workers. **Education and Training:** Work experience in a related occupation. **Skills:** Math—Medium. English—Medium. Science—Medium. **Yearly Earnings:** $$ **Job Growth:** ★★★ **Yearly Openings:** 🚶🚶

First-Line Supervisors/Managers of Landscaping, Lawn Service, and Groundskeeping Workers. Plan, organize, direct, or coordinate activities of workers engaged in landscaping or groundskeeping activities, such as planting and maintaining ornamental trees, shrubs, flowers, and lawns and applying fertilizers, pesticides, and other chemicals. May coordinate activities of workers engaged in terracing hillsides, building retaining walls, constructing pathways, installing patios, and similar activities in following a landscape design plan. Work may involve reviewing contracts to determine service, machine, and workforce requirements; answering questions from potential customers regarding methods, material, and price ranges; and preparing estimates according to labor, material, and machine costs. **Education and Training:** Work experience in a related occupation. **Skills:** Math—Medium. English—Medium. Science—Medium. **Yearly Earnings:** $$$ **Job Growth:** ★★★ **Yearly Openings:** 🚶🚶

Fish Hatchery Managers. Direct and coordinate activities of workers engaged in fish hatchery production for corporations, cooperatives, or other owners. **Education and Training:** Work experience in a related occupation. **Skills:** Math—Medium. English—Medium. Science—Medium. **Yearly Earnings:** $$$ **Job Growth:** ★★ **Yearly Openings:** 🚶🚶🚶

Lawn Service Managers. Plan, direct, and coordinate activities of workers engaged in pruning trees and shrubs, cultivating lawns, and applying pesticides and other

chemicals. **Education and Training:** Work experience in a related occupation. **Skills:** Math—Medium. English—Medium. Science—Medium. **Yearly Earnings:** $$$ **Job Growth:** ★★★ **Yearly Openings:** 🚶🚶

Nursery and Greenhouse Managers. Plan, organize, direct, control, and coordinate activities of workers engaged in propagating, cultivating, and harvesting horticultural specialties, such as trees, shrubs, flowers, mushrooms, and other plants. **Education and Training:** Work experience in a related occupation. **Skills:** Math—Medium. English—Medium. Science—Medium. **Yearly Earnings:** $$$ **Job Growth:** ★★ **Yearly Openings:** 🚶🚶🚶

ANIMAL CARE AND TRAINING

These workers care for and train animals of many kinds. They work in pet shops, pet grooming parlors, testing laboratories, animal shelters, and veterinary offices. Some are employed by zoos, aquariums, circuses, and other places where animals are exhibited or used in entertainment acts. Others work for animal training or obedience schools, stables, kennels, racetracks, or riding academies.

Animal Breeders. Breed animals, including cattle, goats, horses, sheep, swine, poultry, dogs, cats, or pet birds. Select and breed animals according to their genealogy, characteristics, and offspring. May require knowledge of artificial insemination techniques and equipment use. May involve keeping records on heats, birth intervals, or pedigree. **Education and Training:** Associate's degree. **Skills:** Math—Medium. English—Medium. Science—Medium. **Yearly Earnings:** $$ **Job Growth:** No data available. **Yearly Openings:** No data available.

Animal Trainers. Train animals for riding, harness, security, performance, or obedience or for assisting persons with disabilities. Accustom animals to human voice and contact. Condition animals to respond to commands. Train animals according to standards for show or competition. May train animals to carry pack loads or work as part of pack team. **Education and Training:** Moderate-term on-the-job training. **Skills:** Math—Low. English—Medium. Science—Medium. **Yearly Earnings:** $$ **Job Growth:** ★★★ **Yearly Openings:** 🚶

Nonfarm Animal Caretakers. Feed, water, groom, bathe, exercise, or otherwise care for pets and other nonfarm animals, such as dogs, cats, ornamental fish or birds, zoo animals, and mice. Work in settings such as kennels, animal shelters, zoos, circuses, and aquariums. May keep records of feedings, treatments, and animals received or discharged. May clean and repair cages, pens, or fish tanks. **Education and Training:** Short-term on-the-job training. **Skills:** Math—Medium. English—Medium. Science—Medium. **Yearly Earnings:** $ **Job Growth:** ★★★★ **Yearly Openings:** 🚶🚶🚶

Veterinarians. Diagnose and treat diseases and dysfunctions of animals. Includes veterinarians who inspect livestock. **Education and Training:** Professional degree.

Skills: Math—High. English—High. Science—High. **Yearly Earnings:** $$$$$ **Job Growth:** ★★★★ **Yearly Openings:** 👤

Veterinary Assistants and Laboratory Animal Caretakers. Feed, water, and examine pets and other nonfarm animals for signs of illness, disease, or injury in laboratories and animal hospitals and clinics. Clean and disinfect cages and work areas. Sterilize laboratory and surgical equipment. May provide routine post-operative care, administer medication, or prepare samples for laboratory examination under the supervision of veterinary or laboratory animal technologists or technicians, veterinarians, or scientists. **Education and Training:** Short-term on-the-job training. **Skills:** Math—Medium. English—Medium. Science—Medium. **Yearly Earnings:** $ **Job Growth:** ★★★★★ **Yearly Openings:** 👤 👤

Veterinary Technologists and Technicians. Perform medical tests in a laboratory environment for use in the treatment and diagnosis of diseases in animals. Prepare vaccines and serums for prevention of diseases. Prepare tissue samples, take blood samples, and execute laboratory tests, such as urinalysis and blood counts. Clean and sterilize instruments and materials and maintain equipment and machines. **Education and Training:** Associate's degree. **Skills:** Math—Medium. English—Medium. Science—Medium. **Yearly Earnings:** $$ **Job Growth:** ★★★★★ **Yearly Openings:** 👤 👤

HANDS-ON WORK IN PLANTS AND ANIMALS

These workers perform strenuous tasks with plants or animals, usually outdoors in a non-factory setting. They work with their hands, use tools and equipment, or operate machinery. They work on farms or ranches; at logging camps or fish hatcheries; in forests or game preserves; or with commercial fishing businesses, onshore or in fishing boats. In cities and towns they usually work in parks, gardens, or nurseries.

Agricultural Equipment Operators. Drive and control farm equipment to till soil and to plant, cultivate, and harvest crops. May do crop baling or hay bucking. May operate stationary equipment to perform post-harvest tasks, such as husking, shelling, threshing, and ginning. **Education and Training:** Moderate-term on-the-job training. **Skills:** Math—Medium. English—Medium. Science—Medium. **Yearly Earnings:** $ **Job Growth:** ★★ **Yearly Openings:** 👤 👤 👤 👤 👤

Fallers. Use axes or chainsaws to fell trees, using knowledge of tree characteristics and cutting techniques to control direction of fall and minimize tree damage. **Education and Training:** Moderate-term on-the-job training. **Skills:** Math—Medium. English—Low. Science—Medium. **Yearly Earnings:** $$ **Job Growth:** ★ **Yearly Openings:** 👤

Farmworkers and Laborers, Crop, Nursery, and Greenhouse. Manually plant, cultivate, and harvest vegetables, fruits, nuts, plant specialties, and field crops. Use hand tools, such as shovels, trowels, hoes, tampers, pruning hooks, shears, and knives. Duties may include tilling soil and applying fertilizers; transplanting, weeding, thinning, or pruning crops; applying pesticides; cleaning, grading, sorting, packing and loading harvested products. May repair fences and farm buildings or participate in irrigation activities. **Education and Training:** Short-term on-the-job training. **Skills:** Math—Medium. English—Medium. Science—Medium. **Yearly Earnings:** $ **Job Growth:** ★★ **Yearly Openings:** 🯅🯅🯅🯅🯅

Farmworkers, Farm and Ranch Animals. Attend to live farm, ranch, or aquacultural animals that may include cattle, sheep, swine, goats, horses and other equines, poultry, finfish, shellfish, and bees. Attend to animals produced for animal products, such as meat, fur, skins, feathers, eggs, milk, and honey. Duties may include feeding, watering, herding, grazing, castrating, branding, de-beaking, weighing, catching, and loading animals. May maintain records on animals; examine animals to detect diseases and injuries; assist in birth deliveries; and administer medications, vaccinations, or insecticides. May clean and maintain animal housing areas. **Education and Training:** Short-term on-the-job training. **Skills:** Math—Low. English—Medium. Science—Medium. **Yearly Earnings:** $ **Job Growth:** ★★ **Yearly Openings:** 🯅🯅🯅🯅🯅

Fishers and Related Fishing Workers. Use nets, fishing rods, traps, or other equipment to catch and gather fish or other aquatic animals from rivers, lakes, or oceans for human consumption or other uses. May haul game onto ship. **Education and Training:** Short-term on-the-job training. **Skills:** Math—Medium. English—Medium. Science—Medium. **Yearly Earnings:** $$ **Job Growth:** ★ **Yearly Openings:** No data available.

Forest and Conservation Technicians. Compile data related to size, content, condition, and other characteristics of forest tracts under direction of foresters. Train and lead forest workers in forest propagation, fire prevention, and fire suppression. May assist conservation scientists in managing, improving, and protecting rangelands and wildlife habitats and help provide technical assistance on the conservation of soil, water, and related natural resources. **Education and Training:** Associate's degree. **Skills:** Math—Medium. English—Medium. Science—Medium. **Yearly Earnings:** $$ **Job Growth:** ★★ **Yearly Openings:** 🯅

Forest and Conservation Workers. Perform manual labor necessary to develop, maintain, or protect forest, forested areas, and woodlands through such activities as raising and transporting tree seedlings; combating insects, pests, and diseases harmful to trees; and building erosion and water control structures to prevent leaching of forest soil. Includes forester aides, seedling pullers, and tree planters. **Education and Training:** Moderate-term on-the-job training. **Skills:** Math—Medium. English—Medium. Science—Medium. **Yearly Earnings:** $ **Job Growth:** ★★ **Yearly Openings:** 🯅

General Farmworkers. Apply pesticides, herbicides, and fertilizer to crops and livestock. Plant, maintain, and harvest food crops. Tend livestock and poultry. Repair farm buildings and fences. Other duties may include operating milking machines and other dairy-processing equipment; supervising seasonal help; irrigating crops; and hauling livestock products to market. **Education and Training:** Short-term on-the-job training. **Skills:** Math—Low. English—Low. Science—Medium. **Yearly Earnings:** $ **Job Growth:** ★★ **Yearly Openings:** 🚹🚹🚹🚹🚹

Hunters and Trappers. Hunt and trap wild animals for human consumption, fur, feed, bait, or other purposes. **Education and Training:** Moderate-term on-the-job training. **Skills:** Math—Low. English—Low. Science—Medium. **Yearly Earnings:** $$ **Job Growth:** No data available. **Yearly Openings:** No data available.

Landscaping and Groundskeeping Workers. Landscape or maintain grounds of property using hand or power tools or equipment. Workers perform a variety of tasks, which may include the following: sod laying, mowing, trimming, planting, watering, fertilizing, digging, raking, and sprinkler installation. **Education and Training:** Short-term on-the-job training. **Skills:** Math—Medium. English—Low. Science—Medium. **Yearly Earnings:** $ **Job Growth:** ★★★★ **Yearly Openings:** 🚹🚹🚹🚹🚹

Logging Equipment Operators. Drive logging tractor or wheeled vehicle equipped with one or more accessories, such as bulldozer blade, frontal shear, grapple, logging arch, cable winches, hoisting rack, or crane boom, to fell tree; to skid, load, unload, or stack logs; or to pull stumps or clear brush. **Education and Training:** Moderate-term on-the-job training. **Skills:** Math—Medium. English—Medium. Science—Medium. **Yearly Earnings:** $$ **Job Growth:** ★ **Yearly Openings:** 🚹🚹

Logging Tractor Operators. Drive tractor equipped with one or more accessories, such as bulldozer blade, frontal hydraulic shear, grapple, logging arch, cable winches, hoisting rack, or crane boom, to fell tree; to skid, load, unload, or stack logs; or to pull stumps or clear brush. **Education and Training:** Moderate-term on-the-job training. **Skills:** Math—Low. English—Low. Science—Medium. **Yearly Earnings:** $$ **Job Growth:** ★ **Yearly Openings:** 🚹🚹

Nursery Workers. Work in nursery facilities or at customer location planting, cultivating, harvesting, and transplanting trees, shrubs, or plants. **Education and Training:** Short-term on-the-job training. **Skills:** Math—Low. English—Medium. Science—Medium. **Yearly Earnings:** $ **Job Growth:** ★★ **Yearly Openings:** 🚹🚹🚹🚹🚹

Pest Control Workers. Spray or release chemical solutions or toxic gases and set traps to kill pests and vermin, such as mice, termites, and roaches, that infest buildings and surrounding areas. **Education and Training:** Moderate-term on-the-job training. **Skills:** Math—Medium. English—Medium. Science—Medium. **Yearly Earnings:** $$ **Job Growth:** ★★★★ **Yearly Openings:** 🚹🚹

Pesticide Handlers, Sprayers, and Applicators, Vegetation. Mix or apply pesticides, herbicides, fungicides, or insecticides through sprays, dusts, vapors, soil incorporation, or chemical application on trees, shrubs, lawns, or botanical crops. Usually requires training and state or federal certification. **Education and Training:** Moderate-term on-the-job training. **Skills:** Math—Medium. English—Low. Science—Medium. **Yearly Earnings:** $$ **Job Growth:** ★★★ **Yearly Openings:** 🚶🚶

Tree Trimmers and Pruners. Cut away dead or excess branches from trees or shrubs to maintain right-of-way for roads, sidewalks, or utilities or to improve appearance, health, and value of tree. Prune or treat trees or shrubs using handsaws, pruning hooks, shears, and clippers. May use truck-mounted lifts and power pruners. May fill cavities in trees to promote healing and prevent deterioration. **Education and Training:** Short-term on-the-job training. **Skills:** Math—Low. English—Low. Science—Medium. **Yearly Earnings:** $$ **Job Growth:** ★★★ **Yearly Openings:** 🚶🚶🚶

Exploring Careers:

Law, Law Enforcement, and Public Safety

Start Your Journey Through Careers Related to

LAW, LAW ENFORCEMENT, AND PUBLIC SAFETY

Careers in this area suit people interested in upholding people's rights or in protecting people and property through authority, inspection, and monitoring.

EXPLORING CAREER CLUES

Your interests give important clues for exploring career options. Think about your interests to learn if jobs in the Law, Law Enforcement, and Public Safety interest area may be worth further exploration.

Do you like the school subjects related to the Law, Law Enforcement, and Public Safety interest area? Here are some examples of related subjects:

- English
- Speech
- History
- Government
- Social studies
- Sociology
- Psychology
- Science
- Chemistry
- Math
- Health
- Physical education

Do you like the free-time activities related to the Law, Law Enforcement, and Public Safety interest area? Here are some examples of related free-time activities:

- Being on the debate team
- Playing chess and other mentally challenging games
- Learning first aid and CPR
- Being a member of a school safety patrol
- Serving as an officer of the student council or other organization
- Persuading people to sign petitions or support a cause
- Researching things that sound interesting to you
- Doing strenuous activities such as dancing, climbing, backpacking, running, swimming, and skiing
- Reading stories and watching television shows about detectives, the police, and lawyers

EXPLORING JOB GROUPS

Jobs related to the Law, Law Enforcement, and Public Safety interest area fit into five groups. Read through the list to see which groups sound interesting to you.

- Managerial Work in Law, Law Enforcement, and Public Safety
- Law
- Law Enforcement
- Public Safety
- Military

EXPLORING CAREER POSSIBILITIES

You can satisfy your interest in the Law, Law Enforcement, and Public Safety area through jobs that protect people, their rights, and their property. Here are a few examples of career possibilities:

If you enjoy mental challenge and intrigue, you could investigate crimes or fires for a living. If you enjoy using verbal skills and research skills, you may want to defend citizens in court. If you want to help people in critical situations, you may want to fight fires, work as a police officer, or become a paramedic.

Or, if you want more routine work in public safety, perhaps a job in guarding, patrolling, or inspecting would appeal to you.

If you have management ability, you could seek a leadership position in law enforcement and the protective services. Work in the military gives you the chance to use technical and leadership skills while serving your country.

Turn the page to meet people working in the Law, Law Enforcement, and Public Safety interest area→

PROFILE

Rob DeCero—Fire Fighter

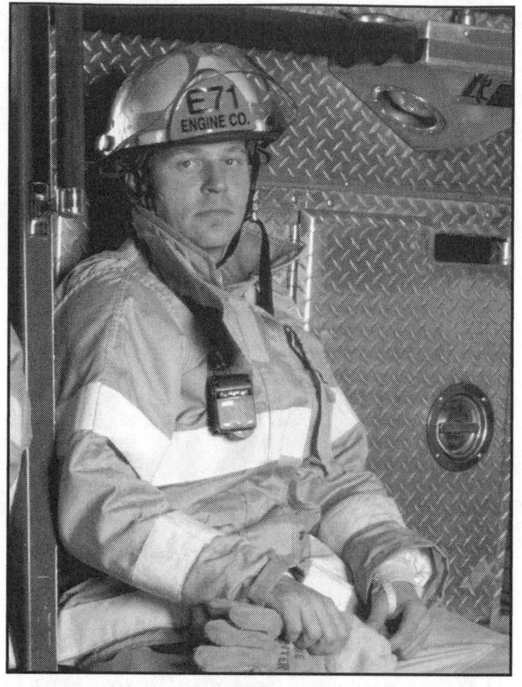

Fire fighters develop respect for each other through their dangerous work.

The alarm rang in the fire station just as the "designated cook" was starting dinner for the fire fighters on duty.

"Peak of rush-hour traffic!" said Rob DeCero, the shift commander with the fire department of a big suburb northwest of a major city. He has been shift commander for four years and a fire fighter for ten years.

One fire fighter was still damp from the shower as she pulled on her gear and jumped aboard the fire truck. When the alarm sounds, there's no time to waste.

Coordinating in a Crisis

The truck's sirens and flashing lights cleared traffic. The crew listened on headphones as information was relayed about the type of fire they would be facing. An apartment was on fire, but no one yet knew how dangerous the fire was.

As the first officer to arrive at the scene, Rob assumed the duties of incident commander. He quickly began assigning tasks to the units responding to the call. This coordination lessens confusion and promotes teamwork.

As the first officer to arrive at the scene, Rob assumed the duties of incident commander. He quickly began assigning tasks to the units responding to the call.

"Engine 4115, you take the third floor. The fire's reported to be in the northeast corner there. Be sure you have air packs. Some walls may also be on fire, so Engine 4113, you're in charge of the first

floor. Engine 4110, you handle the second. Truck 4130, I want your people on the roof."

Smoke, black and thick, was billowing from one apartment window. A neighbor said he believed a woman was still inside. Entering the building, the fire fighters from 4115 found the woman crouching on the first-floor landing, confused and coughing. The fire fighters carried her out of the building.

Smoke, black and thick, was billowing from one apartment window. A neighbor said he believed a woman was still inside.

The fire was brought under control. The units returned to their bases. Rob and the crew of Engine 4115 remained to keep watch on the situation.

"This was a pretty easy one," Rob said. "It's not always like this, you know."

Safety Is Priority One

Because fire fighting is dangerous work, safety standards are very strict. "For example," says Rob, "nobody can ride on the back step of a fire engine anymore.

"Newer trucks are fitted with headsets for everyone, so communication is constant. Fire engines must be equipped for the safety of the occupants.

"Helmets must meet standards, and air packs are required for anyone going into a hazardous site. Sometimes we look like creatures from another world. But we're a whole lot safer.

"Communications technology plays a part, too: laptop computers, portable fax machines, cell phones. Laptops, for example, make it possible for a commander to use a computer in his vehicle. With these devices, our efficiency goes up and our response time drops.

"Infrared technology is also helping us. At the fire we just came from, we used it to pinpoint the fire. It finds the hot spots even when we can't see a fire. That can be very important if the fire is hidden inside a wall."

"With this communication technology, our efficiency goes up and our response time drops dramatically."

Making the Grade

"You should first research the needs of the community in which you want to work. Requirements vary widely from area to area."

Being a fire fighter is not as glamorous as some people think. Nor is it easy to become one. "If you're interested, you should first research the needs of the community in which you want to work. Requirements vary widely from area to area," Rob said. "For example, many communities require their fire fighters to be paramedics, too. That's true in my own community.

"Typically, you first submit an application. If that's accepted, you'll be tested.

"When I took the physical tests, I thought I was in good shape. First I had to run a quarter mile. Next, I had to do a ladder 'up-down' carrying about fifty pounds of hose. I began to wonder if I had the stamina I thought I did. They measured my balance and coordination. They pay special attention to your back in these tests, because back injuries are common among fire fighters," Rob explained. "We have to do a lot of bending, lifting, and carrying, usually under urgent, difficult conditions.

"Once you've passed the physical tests, you'll usually be given written tests," Rob added.

Women candidates must pass the same tests as the men, including the physical ones, and put up with the same living conditions.

"The tests are tough. In our area, we recently accepted only about one hundred of more than a thousand applicants.

"Here's one of 'em right here!" Rob slapped a passing fire fighter on the back as he walked by.

"That's one reason why these positions are so desired, and why the loyalty and solidarity are so high among fire fighters. We have great respect for those who passed the tests and have proven themselves on the job.

"You have to be a caring person in this job. For example, we're a team. We depend on each other, sometimes literally for our lives.

"A caring attitude can help you and hurt you. It can motivate you to take action in the face of danger, but it can cause you pain you if you fail to rescue someone."

"The tests are tough. In our general area, we recently accepted only about one hundred of more than a thousand applicants."

Climbing the Ladder

Rob said that to become a fire fighter, you need a high school diploma. College–at least an associate's degree–is helpful if you want to climb up the ranks. If you want to work toward high levels, you may need a master's degree, particularly in big cities.

"The beginning level there is fire fighter. Then you can move up to fire fighter/EMT–that's emergency medical technician–and then to fire fighter/paramedic. From there you can work your way up to lieutenant, captain, and deputy chief and finally to fire chief. At these higher levels, you do more work in an office.

"A person starting out might do best in a larger city where there are often more jobs, benefits, and specialty training available."

To advance, Rob advises that before college, you look "up the ladder" to see what the requirements are for all the branches of fire service that might interest you: fire prevention, arson investigation, or community education, for example.

There are many fire-fighting specialties, too–airport, structural, chemical, and "wildland" fire fighting are examples. Other specialties are rescue and recovery, high-rise fire fighting, industrial fire fighting, paramedics, and hazardous materials handling.

"You can see why in advanced fire fighting, an advanced education is important. But there will always be a need for the basic fire fighter, too."

Rob's Recommendation

"Would I recommend this job to someone else? Of course! There's a big sense of achievement and personal reward when you know you've saved someone's life.

"And you often have the public's gratitude. We once saved a man by pulling him from his burning store. Now he brings a big turkey to the fire station every Thanksgiving for those of us who are working on the holiday.

"Of course, I also know what it takes. Fire fighting's not for just anybody. It's tough to *get* in and tough to *stay* in. But for me, it's a way of life I wouldn't want to give up."

PROFILE

Samuel Washington—Paralegal

Samuel Washington clicked the "Print" button on his word-processing program with a satisfied sigh. It had been a long but productive day.

Jane Ludden, the criminal defense attorney he worked for, was anxiously awaiting the printed document. It had to be filed at court first thing in the morning.

While the printer was doing its work, Samuel picked up the nameplate on his desk. The handsome object was engraved:

Samuel Washington
Legal Assistant

Samuel investigates the facts of a case and organizes the information that a lawyer uses.

"Jane had this made for me when she had my name put on the firm's letterhead paper. She felt it would give me more trust from the clients.

"It did. They no longer feel they have to hear everything directly from the attorney. That's a trend I'm glad to see," said Samuel.

"A good legal assistant does many of the jobs carried out by lawyers, except those that are considered the actual practice of law. That means we absolutely cannot give legal advice, set legal fees, or present cases in court."

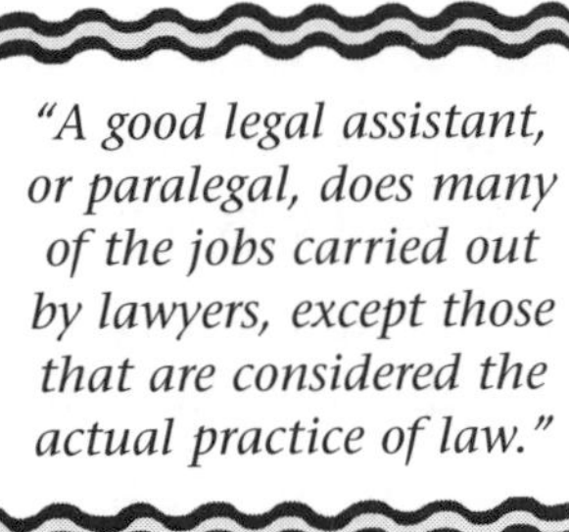
"A good legal assistant, or paralegal, does many of the jobs carried out by lawyers, except those that are considered the actual practice of law."

Samuel looked down at the nameplate again. "Actually the terms *legal assistant* and *paralegal* are used interchangeably. *Paralegal* is more widely used."

Winning a Tough One

Samuel retrieved the document from the printer just as Jane entered the room.

"Thanks for this, Samuel. And thanks for the great work you did on the Edgar case."

Samuel smiled and said, "Well, I was just doing my job."

"Don't be so modest. Your help made a big difference.

"We have a client," Jane explained, "who does body work on cars. He was charged with stealing and then selling an expensive car from a woman he'd once done some work for. Our client has a police record for grand theft. His record could be introduced into evidence only if he were to testify. Obviously, we wanted to keep him off the stand. He was out of town when that car was stolen, but he had no one who could testify to that.

"The stolen car had been recovered–repainted in an unusual shade that our client's business carried," Jane continued. "The man who was found driving the car claimed to have purchased it from our client."

Samuel finished the story. "That's when Jane decided we needed an expert witness, someone who could testify whether or not that paint was really an exact match.

"I had only one day to find that 'someone.' I located a chemist who testified that the paint on the car did not come from our client's paints."

Staying on Top of Things

Jane hurried off, but Samuel called out to her. "Do you have the continuance for the Reilly case?"

"Uh, Samuel, I forgot to tell you. It's on my desk," Jane called as she headed out the door.

Samuel shook his head, smiling. "I've got to stay on top of the work in every case. It's important for the attorney to give the paralegal any items or information received in court. If he or she doesn't do it, it's my job to remind the attorney. Communication is essential," said Samuel.

"Accuracy and organization are key in this profession. If you don't like detailed work, this definitely isn't the job for you."

Samuel motioned to a stack of papers on a table near his desk. "That represents a lot of preparation for cases getting ready for trial. Paralegals are responsible for most of the paperwork that is reviewed by the supervising attorney. They supply accurate information to the attorney for the trial.

"Accuracy and organization are key in this profession. If you don't like detailed work, this definitely isn't the job for you.

"The stakes can be high. If you forget to do something on time, it may result in legal malpractice action. In criminal defense cases, the clients could be looking at lengthy prison time. That doesn't leave much room for mistakes."

A Paralegal Prepares

Samuel has been in the legal field for nearly fifteen years. What made him decide to enter this field?

"I was in a work-study program in high school. Through my teacher, I found a part-time administrative assistant opening in a small law firm. After I graduated, I became a legal secretary there. The next logical step was to move up to legal assistant."

Samuel explained that paralegal training programs vary. Some schools offer a two-year associate's program. But many more now offer a four-year bachelor's degree program.

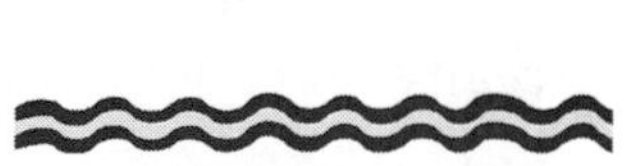

Samuel explained that paralegal training programs vary.

"I have also passed the two-day exam given by the National Board of Legal Assistants and am officially a Certified Legal Assistant, or CLA."

Samuel explained that the CLA designation is a sign of competence that can boost employment and advancement. The Paralegal Advanced Competency Exam offers similar recognition.

Samuel stresses that many professional organizations help keep paralegals updated on changes in the law. Some provide job leads. All are great places to network with others.

"Although paralegals are in demand, it's probably best to get that four-year degree," said Samuel. "Large law firms nearly always require an undergraduate degree, a degree from a certified paralegal program, and a couple of years of experience."

Other Skills Needed

"Knowing how to type well is essential. You must be familiar with computers and word processing. Paralegals do a lot of online research because so much legal information is stored in computer databases and on CD-ROM.

"Some people think that paralegals spend most of their time in the law library with their noses stuck in those heavy books. Not so!

"I deal with clients most of my working day. You have to be able to deal well with other people. Clients often have worrisome problems. I give them support and answers as best and as quickly as I can."

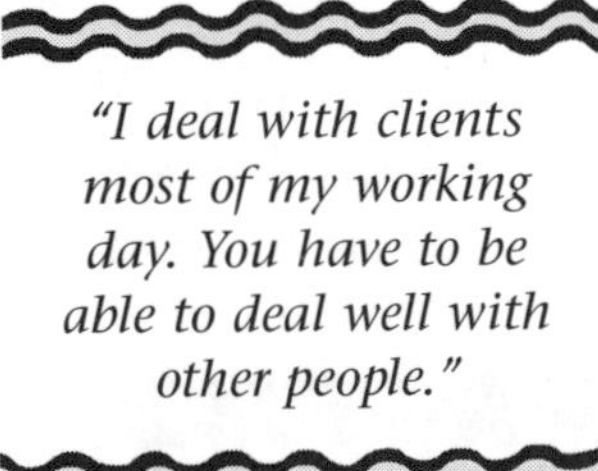

"I deal with clients most of my working day. You have to be able to deal well with other people."

A Wide-Open Field

Samuel sees the future looking bright for paralegals. "There's such a wide variety of legal areas to choose from–not just law firms," he said. "Paralegals find work in companies, perhaps specializing in employee benefit programs or in patent and copyright law.

"Large corporations almost always have a legal department where paralegals help with records and documents.

"The real estate industry, the medical profession, and the insurance industry also employ us. Banks and other financial institutions use paralegals to help with things like estate planning, contracts, mortgages, and trust documents.

"The government offers a large variety of positions for paralegals. For example, most communities have legal assistance organizations to help people who may not be able to afford to hire an attorney."

Behind-the-Scenes Bonuses

"Satisfaction comes from knowing that your efforts make the legal system run a little more smoothly."

"I'm hooked on this job," said Samuel. "This being a smaller firm, I get to involve myself in so many more aspects of the process. I get to research points of law and assist in jury selection and even the trial.

"I feel I really make a contribution. My hours are often long, but the rewards for the extra work are worth it.

"I like the feeling that there will always be a need for someone like me. There will always be disputes in civil cases, and there unfortunately doesn't seem to be any lack of criminals.

"Now, this is no glamour job. You're the behind-the-scenes person in this profession. My satisfaction comes from knowing that my efforts make the legal system run a little more smoothly for everyone concerned."

PROFILE

Dana Murphy—Paramedic

Robin Holland opened his eyes. He was staring straight up at the theater lobby's ceiling.

I'm on the floor! He tried to raise himself but was gently pushed down by the hands of someone he didn't recognize. She was wearing a dark blue uniform.

Her nametag read "Dana Murphy, Emergency Medical Services."

An Emergency Ride

Robin could see red lights through the doors. *It's an ambulance!* he thought.

Dana Murphy was taking his pulse while a man talked on a handheld radio.

"What's happened to me?" Robin croaked.

Dana gave his hand a gentle pat. She said that she was a paramedic and that he had lost consciousness for a short time. They were there to take him to the hospital.

"Mr. Holland, can you see how many fingers I'm holding up?" asked the other paramedic, Ed Smyth.

"Yes, five," he answered.

Things were happening so fast now. Robin felt himself being lifted gently. The cool night air was on his face as they wheeled him to the waiting ambulance.

The doors closed, and Ed got in the driver's seat. Dana sat next to Robin. As Ed drove, Dana chatted with the patient. She checked his blood pressure, heart rate, and pupils. She told him to expect a "little stick" and took blood to check his blood sugar.

When Dana wasn't talking to him, she was radioing reports of the tests to the hospital. When they got there, the paramedics took Robin into the emergency room, where the staff awaited him.

Dana and Ed reported their observations and what treatment Robin had received. Their job completed, they turned toward Robin. They wished him well and then hurried back to their ambulance. They needed to return to the station and restock its supplies.

The "Golden Hour"

In the station's break room, Dana sat down for a cup of coffee, although she was ready to leave again at any moment. She gestured around the room at the other paramedics drinking coffee and talking.

"Unlike paramedics in many communities, we're not fire fighters. We're not even city employees. We're specialists in emergency medical services who work for this private ambulance company.

> *"Paramedics transport a victim, administer emergency procedures, and radio information that will help the doctors and nurses be ready when the patient arrives."*

"Our emergency services are coordinated among the police department, fire department, and the other local private ambulance services," she explained.

"This is not an unusual arrangement," Dana continued, "although not all cities use private paramedic ambulance services. Each city structures its emergency services to fit its needs.

"Victims of severe trauma have only about an hour during which they can be treated and be expected to live. That's known as the 'Golden Hour.'

"That's where paramedics come in. We can transport a victim, administer emergency procedures, and radio information that will help the doctors and nurses be ready when the patient arrives."

Expect the Unexpected

Dana pointed to a young man who had just entered. "See Paul there? He's an EMT–or emergency medical technician–recently out of basic training, which he took at the community college. He could also have taken it at a high school education department or at some hospitals.

"Paul's going to be good. He's learned well, and he's very level-headed. He plans on getting additional training to become a paramedic, which will allow him to perform more difficult medical procedures."

Paul was shaking his head as he approached. "What's the matter, Paul?" quizzed Dana.

"Just got back from an accident on the expressway. The car was upside-down. We could see the guy was pinned in there pretty tight.

"He kept yelling, 'Sandy! Sandy!' We looked everywhere for 'Sandy' but saw no one. As far as we could see, he was the only one in the car. We thought perhaps he'd taken too much of a bang on the head, although he was wearing his seatbelt.

"After we determined it was okay to pull him out, we heard a low growl coming from underneath him.

"Sandy turned out to be one very angry dog. I think she would have taken a chunk out of the first hand that tried to get too close to her or her master.

"Good thing we carry animal tranquilizers on board, because pets are so often involved in accidents."

Total Training

Emergency medical technicians are trained in basic care and treatment. They take vital signs–heart rate, pulse, respiration, and so on–and stabilize fractures.

"Hey, Dana," Paul said. "Next week I'm going to begin my next level of training. That test to qualify for the school was tough. Good thing I took a lot of courses in science and math in high school."

Paul's next training will be the first real step on the road to becoming a paramedic–learning to start intravenous lines (IVs), give certain drugs, monitor the heart, and perform an intubation (placing a tube down a patient's windpipe to assist breathing).

Paul rose to leave. "I'm due for ambulance drivers' training in half an hour." He said, "It's not easy to drive an ambulance quickly and safely."

At that moment, Dana heard her name called over the loudspeaker. The supervisor wanted Dana and Ed to "post" for the rest of their shift in the northeast section of town.

Posting means the ambulance crew is not on a specific call but is assigned to be on alert in a specific area. If a call should come from nearby, they would be close to answer quickly.

On the Road with Dana and Ed

Approaching the river bridge on Main Street, Dana and Ed recalled posting in the area just the week before. A man had dragged another man–unconscious–from the river and was yelling for help.

"The satisfaction in being on the 'front lines' in saving someone's life is the greatest."

Ed and Dana had quickly determined that the unconscious man wasn't breathing and had no pulse. They successfully applied cardiopulmonary resuscitation (CPR) and took him to the hospital.

"The man who'd pulled that fellow from the river was really upset. 'I never bothered to learn CPR,' he said. 'Oh, I wish I had.'"

Dana said that onlookers like the "Good Samaritan" by the river are often a victim's first hope of rescue.

"They're usually the first ones on the scene. If they know a little first aid or CPR, they can do a lot of good before we get there."

But Dana cautioned that attempting a rescue could be very risky. Better to call for help immediately and then apply whatever knowledge you have about rescue. "We do not want someone who's not prepared to be placed in danger. That's what *we're* here for.

"Sometimes a paramedic's job is dangerous," Dana said. Still, she's encouraging about emergency medicine as a career choice.

"The technology keeps improving, allowing us to give more and better treatment. And it's a good point from which to go into other professions in medicine, such as working in an emergency room.

"As for me, though," said Dana, "I'll stay right here in this ambulance. The satisfaction in being on the 'front lines' in saving someone's life is the greatest."

SKILL SAMPLER

Earl Martinez–Police Officer

In his four years as a police officer, Earl Martinez has learned how important it is to talk to the people on his beat–especially the children. "In my line of work, you need all the friends you can get."

Earl talked about the skills that are important for police officers. He gives the following tips that can help you determine if you want to train to be a police officer.

Police officers uphold and enforce the law. They must have a deeply ingrained respect for law and order.

- Do you think it's important to obey a law even when you don't agree with it?
- Do you think it's important to be honest?
- Do you disapprove of cheating on exams or homework?
- Are you comfortable with the idea of people looking to you as an example?
- Are you conscious of your public responsibility when you are elected to the student council, chosen to be yearbook or newspaper editor, or asked to chair a club or committee?

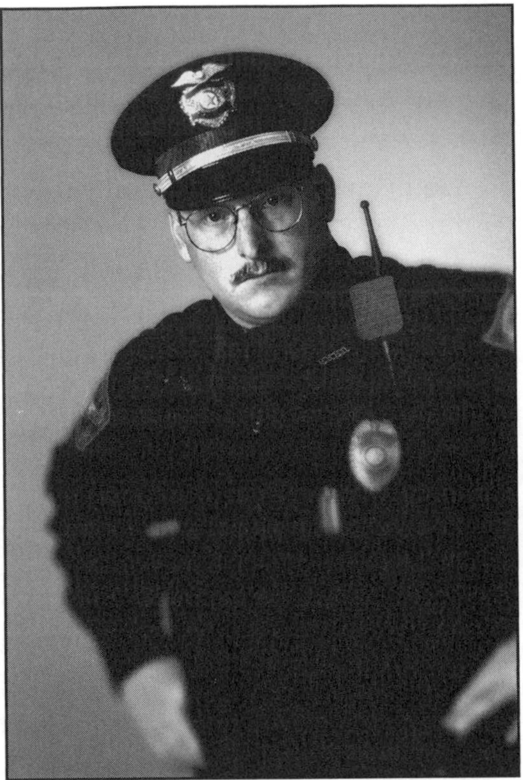

Earl has had a deep respect for law and order all his life.

Police officers spend much of their time educating the public about safety precautions.

- Do you obey traffic regulations when you cross a street or ride your bicycle?
- Do you have reflectors on your bicycle for riding at night?
- Do you check for oncoming traffic when you cross the street?
- Are you careful not to swim alone?
- Do you follow the instructions on the label when you use electric appliances?

Police officers must be able to think quickly and make decisions under pressure. They need excellent judgment to deal with such emergencies as family quarrels, highway accidents, or bank robberies.

- Could you keep calm and get help right away if your kitchen caught fire?
- Would you know what to do if an infant got hurt or stopped breathing while you were baby-sitting?
- Would you act sensibly if your brother or sister swallowed something poisonous?
- Would you know what to do if a friend injured himself or herself in the hall at school?

Police officers must be observant so they can recount details about people and events.

- When you are introduced to strangers, do you remember their names?
- Can you recall identifying characteristics about your friends–birthmarks, scars, eye color, hair color, height, and weight?
- Do you notice minor changes in television, radio, or stereo reception?
- Do you notice when the ink in a computer printer cartridge starts to fade?
- Do you enjoy identifying trees, leaves, or birds?
- Can you tell if something is missing from your room?
- Can you find a place on a road map quickly?

Police officers must be able to communicate effectively in different kinds of situations.

- Can you start conversations easily?
- Can you talk to a child without talking down to him or her?
- After listening to a friend, are you good at putting his or her situation into words?

- Are you good at expressing yourself verbally and in letters and e-mails?
- Are you good at speaking in front of a group?

Police officers must be good at giving orders, but they must be able to take orders as well.

- Are you good at supervising younger children?
- Have you ever been a camp counselor?
- Do you do what your parents or teachers ask without getting angry?
- Can you judge how far you can go when talking to a teacher about a grade you disagree with?

Police officers must keep accurate records.

- When you're the treasurer or secretary of a club, do you keep good records?
- Do people ask you to keep score in bowling or other activities?
- When you look back at the notes you take in class, are they clear?

Police officers must have stamina and be in top physical condition. They often handle emergencies in addition to the ordinary demands of their job.

- Do you enjoy strenuous activities such as dancing, hiking, climbing, backpacking, running, jogging, swimming, and skiing?
- Do you participate in sports at school?
- Do you like being active?

Now learn about all major jobs in the Law, Law Enforcement, and Public Safety interest area→

Facts About All Major Jobs Related to

LAW, LAW ENFORCEMENT, AND PUBLIC SAFETY

In addition to the jobs covered in the profiles and skill sampler, other careers in the Law, Law Enforcement, and Public Safety interest area may appeal to you. This section describes and gives facts about all major jobs in the Law, Law Enforcement, and Public Safety interest area. For an explanation of the $, ★, and 🚶 symbols, see page 6.

MANAGERIAL WORK IN LAW, LAW ENFORCEMENT, AND PUBLIC SAFETY

These workers manage fire and police departments. They set goals and policies, oversee financial and human resources, evaluate outcomes, and represent their departments to the public and the governments of the jurisdictions they serve. They work for cities and towns. Supervisors of forest fire fighters mostly work for the federal government.

Emergency Management Specialists. Coordinate disaster response or crisis management activities, provide disaster preparedness training, and prepare emergency plans and procedures for natural (for example, hurricanes, floods, earthquakes), wartime, or technological (for example, nuclear power plant emergencies, hazardous materials spills) disasters or hostage situations. **Education and Training:** Work experience in a related occupation. **Skills:** Math—Medium. English—Medium. Science—Medium. **Yearly Earnings:** $$$ **Job Growth:** ★★★ **Yearly Openings:** 🚶

First-Line Supervisors/Managers of Correctional Officers. Supervise and coordinate activities of correctional officers and jailers. **Education and Training:** Work experience in a related occupation. **Skills:** Math—Medium. English—Medium. Science—Medium. **Yearly Earnings:** $$$$ **Job Growth:** ★★★★ **Yearly Openings:** 🚶

First-Line Supervisors/Managers of Fire Fighting and Prevention Workers. Supervise and coordinate activities of workers engaged in fire fighting and fire prevention and control. **Education and Training:** Work experience in a related occupation. **Skills:** Math—Medium. English—Medium. Science—Medium. **Yearly Earnings:** $$$$$ **Job Growth:** ★★ **Yearly Openings:** 🚶

First-Line Supervisors/Managers of Police and Detectives. Supervise and coordinate activities of members of police force. **Education and Training:** Work experience in a related occupation. **Skills:** Math—Medium. English—Medium. Science—Medium. **Yearly Earnings:** $$$$$ **Job Growth:** ★★★ **Yearly Openings:** 🚹 🚹

Forest Fire Fighting and Prevention Supervisors. Supervise fire fighters who control and suppress fires in forests or vacant public land. **Education and Training:** Work experience in a related occupation. **Skills:** Math—Medium. English—Medium. Science—Medium. **Yearly Earnings:** $$$$$ **Job Growth:** ★★ **Yearly Openings:** 🚹

Municipal Fire Fighting and Prevention Supervisors. Supervise fire fighters who control and extinguish municipal fires, protect life and property, and conduct rescue efforts. **Education and Training:** Work experience in a related occupation. **Skills:** Math—Medium. English—High. Science—High. **Yearly Earnings:** $$$$$ **Job Growth:** ★★ **Yearly Openings:** 🚹

LAW

These workers provide legal advice and representation to clients, hear and make decisions on court cases, help individuals and groups reach agreements, and conduct investigations into legal matters. Although they specialize in many different fields, all of them apply knowledge of laws and regulations to the problems they must solve. They work for law firms, courts, businesses, government agencies, and legislators.

Administrative Law Judges, Adjudicators, and Hearing Officers. Conduct hearings to decide or recommend decisions on claims concerning government programs or government-related matters and prepare decisions. Determine penalties or the existence and the amount of liability, recommend the acceptance or rejection of claims, or compromise settlements. **Education and Training:** College degree, plus work experience. **Skills:** Math—Medium. English—High. Science—Medium. **Yearly Earnings:** $$$$$ **Job Growth:** ★ **Yearly Openings:** 🚹

Arbitrators, Mediators, and Conciliators. Bring about negotiation and conflict resolution through dialogue. Resolve conflicts outside of the court system by mutual consent of parties involved. **Education and Training:** College degree, plus work experience. **Skills:** Math—Medium. English—High. Science—Medium. **Yearly Earnings:** $$$$ **Job Growth:** ★★★★ **Yearly Openings:** 🚹

Judges, Magistrate Judges, and Magistrates. Arbitrate, advise, make rulings, or administer justice in a court of law. May sentence defendant in criminal cases according to government law. May determine liability of defendant in civil cases. May issue marriage licenses and perform wedding ceremonies. **Education and Training:** College degree, plus work experience. **Skills:** Math—Medium. English—High. Science—Medium. **Yearly Earnings:** $$$$$ **Job Growth:** ★ **Yearly Openings:** 🚹

Law Clerks. Assist lawyers or judges by researching or preparing legal documents. May meet with clients or assist lawyers and judges in court. **Education and Training:** Bachelor's degree. **Skills:** Math—Medium. English—High. Science—Medium. **Yearly Earnings:** $$ **Job Growth:** ★★★ **Yearly Openings:** 🚹

Lawyers. Represent clients in criminal and civil litigation and other legal proceedings, draw up legal documents, and manage or advise clients on legal transactions. May specialize in one area or may practice in many areas of law. **Education and Training:** Professional degree. **Skills:** Math—Medium. English—High. Science—Medium. **Yearly Earnings:** $$$$$ **Job Growth:** ★★★ **Yearly Openings:** 🚹 🚹 🚹

Paralegals and Legal Assistants. Assist lawyers by researching legal precedent, investigating facts, or preparing legal documents. Conduct research to support a legal proceeding, to formulate a defense, or to initiate legal action. **Education and Training:** Associate's degree. **Skills:** Math—Medium. English—High. Science—Medium. **Yearly Earnings:** $$$ **Job Growth:** ★★★★ **Yearly Openings:** 🚹 🚹 🚹

Title Examiners and Abstractors. *Title Examiners:* Search public records and examine titles to determine legal condition of property title. Copy or summarize (abstracts) recorded documents which affect the condition of title to property (for example, mortgages, trust deeds, and contracts). May prepare and issue policy that guarantees legality of title. *Abstractors:* Summarize relevant legal or insurance details or sections of statutes or case law from reference books for purpose of examination, proof, or ready reference. Search out titles to determine if title deed is correct. **Education and Training:** Long-term on-the-job training. **Skills:** Math—Medium. English—High. Science—Low. **Yearly Earnings:** $$ **Job Growth:** ★ **Yearly Openings:** 🚹

Title Examiners, Abstractors, and Searchers. Search real estate records, examine titles, or summarize relevant legal or insurance details for a variety of purposes. May compile lists of mortgages, contracts, and other instruments pertaining to titles by searching public and private records for law firms, real estate agencies, or title insurance companies. **Education and Training:** Moderate-term on-the-job training. **Skills:** Math—Medium. English—Medium. Science—Medium. **Yearly Earnings:** $$ **Job Growth:** ★ **Yearly Openings:** 🚹

Title Searchers. Compile list of mortgages, deeds, contracts, judgments, and other instruments pertaining to title by searching public and private records of real estate or title insurance company. **Education and Training:** Moderate-term on-the-job training. **Skills:** Math—Medium. English—Medium. Science—Low. **Yearly Earnings:** $$ **Job Growth:** ★ **Yearly Openings:** 🚹

LAW ENFORCEMENT

These workers enforce laws and regulations to protect people, animals, and property. They investigate suspicious persons and acts, prevent crimes, and identify the causes of fires. Many work for federal, state, and local governments. Some are hired by

private businesses and operate in a variety of settings, such as stores, office buildings, airports, railroads, hotels, lumberyards, industrial plants, and amusement establishments.

Animal Control Workers. Handle animals to investigate mistreatment or to control abandoned, dangerous, or unattended animals. **Education and Training:** Moderate-term on-the-job training. **Skills:** Math—Medium. English—Medium. Science—Medium. **Yearly Earnings:** $$ **Job Growth:** ★★★ **Yearly Openings:** 🚹

Bailiffs. Maintain order in courts of law. **Education and Training:** Moderate-term on-the-job training. **Skills:** Math—Low. English—Medium. Science—Low. **Yearly Earnings:** $$$ **Job Growth:** ★★★ **Yearly Openings:** 🚹

Child Support, Missing Persons, and Unemployment Insurance Fraud Investigators. Conduct investigations to locate missing persons and to locate, arrest, and return fugitives and persons wanted for nonpayment of support payments and unemployment insurance fraud. **Education and Training:** Work experience in a related occupation. **Skills:** Math—Medium. English—Medium. Science—Low. **Yearly Earnings:** $$$$ **Job Growth:** ★★★ **Yearly Openings:** 🚹

Correctional Officers and Jailers. Guard inmates in penal or rehabilitative institution in accordance with established regulations and procedures. May guard prisoners in transit between jail, courtroom, prison, or other point. Includes deputy sheriffs and police who spend the most of their time guarding prisoners in correctional institutions. **Education and Training:** Moderate-term on-the-job training. **Skills:** Math—Medium. English—Medium. Science—Medium. **Yearly Earnings:** $$$ **Job Growth:** ★★★★ **Yearly Openings:** 🚹 🚹 🚹

Criminal Investigators and Special Agents. Investigate possible criminal violations of federal, state, or local laws to determine if evidence is sufficient to recommend prosecution. **Education and Training:** Work experience in a related occupation. **Skills:** Math—Medium. English—Medium. Science—Medium. **Yearly Earnings:** $$$$ **Job Growth:** ★★★ **Yearly Openings:** 🚹

Crossing Guards. Guide or control traffic at streets, crosswalks, parking lots, schools, railroad crossings, and construction sites. **Education and Training:** Short-term on-the-job training. **Skills:** Math—Low. English—Low. Science—Low. **Yearly Earnings:** $ **Job Growth:** ★★ **Yearly Openings:** 🚹 🚹 🚹

Detectives and Criminal Investigators. Conduct investigations related to suspected violations of federal, state, or local laws to prevent or solve crimes. **Education and Training:** Work experience in a related occupation. **Skills:** Math—Medium. English—Medium. Science—Medium. **Yearly Earnings:** $$$$ **Job Growth:** ★★★ **Yearly Openings:** 🚹

Fire Investigators. Conduct investigations to determine causes of fires and explosions. **Education and Training:** Bachelor's degree. **Skills:** Math—Medium. English—Medium. Science—High. **Yearly Earnings:** $$$$ **Job Growth:** ★★★ **Yearly Openings:** 🧍

Fish and Game Wardens. Patrol assigned area to prevent fish and game law violations. Investigate reports of damage to crops or property by wildlife. Compile biological data. **Education and Training:** Long-term on-the-job training. **Skills:** Math—Medium. English—Medium. Science—Medium. **Yearly Earnings:** $$$ **Job Growth:** ★★★ **Yearly Openings:** 🧍

Forensic Science Technicians. Collect, identify, classify, and analyze physical evidence related to criminal investigations. Perform tests on weapons or substances, such as fiber, hair, and tissue, to determine significance to investigation. May testify as expert witnesses on evidence or crime laboratory techniques. May serve as specialists in area of expertise, such as ballistics, fingerprinting, handwriting, or biochemistry. **Education and Training:** Associate's degree. **Skills:** Math—Medium. English—Medium. Science—High. **Yearly Earnings:** $$$ **Job Growth:** ★★★ **Yearly Openings:** 🧍

Gaming Surveillance Officers and Gaming Investigators. Act as security agent for management and customers. Observe casino or casino hotel operation for irregular activities such as cheating or theft by employees or patrons. May use one-way mirrors above the casino floor and cashier's cage. Use of audio/video equipment is also common for observing operation of the business. **Education and Training:** Long-term on-the-job training. **Skills:** Math—Medium. English—Medium. Science—Medium. **Yearly Earnings:** $$ **Job Growth:** ★★★ **Yearly Openings:** 🧍

Highway Patrol Pilots. Pilot aircraft to patrol highway and enforce traffic laws. **Education and Training:** Long-term on-the-job training. **Skills:** Math—Low. English—Medium. Science—Medium. **Yearly Earnings:** $$$ **Job Growth:** ★★★★ **Yearly Openings:** 🧍🧍🧍

Immigration and Customs Inspectors. Investigate and inspect persons, vehicles, goods, and merchandise arriving in or departing from the United States or between states to detect violations of immigration and customs laws and regulations. **Education and Training:** Work experience in a related occupation. **Skills:** Math—Medium. English—Medium. Science—Medium. **Yearly Earnings:** $$$$ **Job Growth:** ★★★ **Yearly Openings:** 🧍

Lifeguards, Ski Patrol, and Other Recreational Protective Service Workers. Monitor recreational areas, such as pools, beaches, or ski slopes, to provide assistance and protection to participants. **Education and Training:** Short-term on-the-job training. **Skills:** Math—Medium. English—Medium. Science—Medium. **Yearly Earnings:** $ **Job Growth:** ★★★ **Yearly Openings:** 🧍🧍🧍

Parking Enforcement Workers. Patrol assigned area, such as public parking lot or section of city, to issue tickets to overtime parking violators and illegally parked vehicles. **Education and Training:** Short-term on-the-job training. **Skills:** Math—Low. English—Medium. Science—Medium. **Yearly Earnings:** $$ **Job Growth:** ★★★ **Yearly Openings:** 🧍

Police and Sheriff's Patrol Officers. Maintain order, enforce laws, and protect life and property in an assigned patrol district. Perform combination of following duties: Patrol a specific area on foot or in a vehicle, direct traffic, issue traffic summonses, investigate accidents, apprehend and arrest suspects. **Education and Training:** Long-term on-the-job training. **Skills:** Math—Medium. English—Medium. Science—Medium. **Yearly Earnings:** $$$ **Job Growth:** ★★★★ **Yearly Openings:** 🧍🧍🧍

Police Detectives. Conduct investigations to prevent crimes or solve criminal cases. **Education and Training:** Work experience in a related occupation. **Skills:** Math—Medium. English—Medium. Science—Medium. **Yearly Earnings:** $$$$ **Job Growth:** ★★★ **Yearly Openings:** 🧍

Police Identification and Records Officers. Collect evidence at crime scene, classify and identify fingerprints, and photograph evidence for use in criminal and civil cases. **Education and Training:** Work experience in a related occupation. **Skills:** Math—Low. English—Medium. Science—Medium. **Yearly Earnings:** $$$$ **Job Growth:** ★★★ **Yearly Openings:** 🧍

Police Patrol Officers. Patrol assigned area to enforce laws, regulate traffic, control crowds, prevent crime, and arrest violators. **Education and Training:** Long-term on-the-job training. **Skills:** Math—Medium. English—Medium. Science—Medium. **Yearly Earnings:** $$$ **Job Growth:** ★★★★ **Yearly Openings:** 🧍🧍🧍

Private Detectives and Investigators. Detect unlawful acts or infractions of rules in a private establishment or seek, examine, and compile information for client. **Education and Training:** Work experience in a related occupation. **Skills:** Math—Medium. English—Medium. Science—Medium. **Yearly Earnings:** $$ **Job Growth:** ★★★★ **Yearly Openings:** 🧍🧍

Security Guards. Guard, patrol, and monitor premises to prevent theft, violence, or violation of rules. **Education and Training:** Short-term on-the-job training. **Skills:** Math—Low. English—Medium. Science—Medium. **Yearly Earnings:** $ **Job Growth:** ★★★★ **Yearly Openings:** 🧍🧍🧍🧍🧍

Sheriffs and Deputy Sheriffs. Enforce law and order in rural or unincorporated districts or serve in legal processes of courts. May patrol courthouse, guard court or grand jury, and escort defendants. **Education and Training:** Long-term on-the-job training. **Skills:** Math—Medium. English—Medium. Science—Medium. **Yearly Earnings:** $$$ **Job Growth:** ★★★★ **Yearly Openings:** 🧍🧍🧍

Transit and Railroad Police. Protect and police railroad and transit property, employees, and passengers. **Education and Training:** Long-term on-the-job training. **Skills:** Math—Medium. English—Medium. Science—Medium. **Yearly Earnings:** $$$$ **Job Growth:** ★★★ **Yearly Openings:**

PUBLIC SAFETY

These workers protect the public by responding to emergencies and by assuring that people are not exposed to unsafe products or facilities. Some respond hastily to emergencies, stabilize sick or injured people, act quickly to put out fires, and evacuate people from buildings. Dealing with sudden crises requires them to have both technical skills and the ability to keep a cool head. Others investigate business practices, examine records, and inspect materials, products, workplaces, utilities, and transportation equipment for compliance with government regulations or conformance to company policies. They may seize records, close down businesses, or bring other pressures to bear against individuals or organizations which they find to be in violation of rules. Although they are not involved directly with construction, installation, or processing operations, they must know the technical principles to be able to measure and evaluate the quality of the materials and equipment they inspect.

Agricultural Inspectors. Inspect agricultural products, processing equipment, facilities, and fish and logging operations to ensure compliance with regulations and laws governing health, quality, and safety. **Education and Training:** Work experience in a related occupation. **Skills:** Math—Medium. English—Medium. Science—Medium. **Yearly Earnings:** $$ **Job Growth:** ★★ **Yearly Openings:**

Aviation Inspectors. Inspect aircraft, maintenance procedures, air navigational aids, air traffic controls, and communications equipment to ensure conformance with federal safety regulations. **Education and Training:** Work experience in a related occupation. **Skills:** Math—Medium. English—High. Science—High. **Yearly Earnings:** $$$$ **Job Growth:** ★★★ **Yearly Openings:**

Compliance Officers, Except Agriculture, Construction, Health and Safety, and Transportation. Examine, evaluate, and investigate eligibility for or conformity with laws and regulations governing contract compliance for licenses and permits. **Education and Training:** Long-term on-the-job training. **Skills:** Math—Medium. English—Medium. Science—Medium. **Yearly Earnings:** $$$$ **Job Growth:** ★★ **Yearly Openings:**

Emergency Medical Technicians and Paramedics. Assess injuries, administer emergency medical care, and free trapped individuals. Transport injured or sick persons to medical facilities. **Education and Training:** Postsecondary career and technical education. **Skills:** Math—Medium. English—Medium. Science—Medium. **Yearly Earnings:** $$ **Job Growth:** ★★★★ **Yearly Openings:**

Environmental Compliance Inspectors. Inspect and investigate sources of pollution to protect the public and environment and ensure conformance with federal, state, and local regulations and ordinances. **Education and Training:** Long-term on-the-job training. **Skills:** Math—Medium. English—High. Science—High. **Yearly Earnings:** $$$$ **Job Growth:** ★★ **Yearly Openings:** 🧍🧍

Equal Opportunity Representatives and Officers. Monitor and evaluate compliance with equal opportunity laws, guidelines, and policies to ensure that employment practices give equal opportunity without regard to race, religion, color, national origin, sex, age, or disability. **Education and Training:** Long-term on-the-job training. **Skills:** Math—Medium. English—High. Science—Medium. **Yearly Earnings:** $$$$ **Job Growth:** ★★ **Yearly Openings:** 🧍🧍

Financial Examiners. Enforce or ensure compliance with laws and regulations governing financial and securities institutions and financial and real estate transactions. May examine, verify correctness of, or establish authenticity of records. **Education and Training:** Bachelor's degree. **Skills:** Math—High. English—High. Science—Medium. **Yearly Earnings:** $$$$$ **Job Growth:** ★★★ **Yearly Openings:** 🧍

Fire Fighters. Control and extinguish fires or respond to emergency situations where life, property, or the environment is at risk. Duties may include fire prevention, emergency medical service, hazardous material response, search and rescue, and disaster management. **Education and Training:** Long-term on-the-job training. **Skills:** Math—Medium. English—Medium. Science—Medium. **Yearly Earnings:** $$$ **Job Growth:** ★★ **Yearly Openings:** 🧍🧍🧍

Fire Inspectors. Inspect buildings and equipment to detect fire hazards and enforce state and local regulations. **Education and Training:** Moderate-term on-the-job training. **Skills:** Math—Medium. English—Medium. Science—Medium. **Yearly Earnings:** $$$$ **Job Growth:** ★★★ **Yearly Openings:** 🧍

Fire Inspectors and Investigators. Inspect buildings to detect fire hazards and enforce local and state laws. Investigate and gather facts to determine cause of fires and explosions. **Education and Training:** Moderate-term on-the-job training. **Skills:** Math—Medium. English—Medium. Science—Medium. **Yearly Earnings:** $$$$ **Job Growth:** ★★★ **Yearly Openings:** 🧍

Forest Fire Fighters. Control and suppress fires in forests or vacant public land. **Education and Training:** Long-term on-the-job training. **Skills:** Math—Medium. English—Medium. Science—Medium. **Yearly Earnings:** $$$ **Job Growth:** ★★ **Yearly Openings:** 🧍🧍🧍

Forest Fire Inspectors and Prevention Specialists. Enforce fire regulations and inspect for forest fire hazards. Report forest fires and weather conditions. **Education and Training:** Moderate-term on-the-job training. **Skills:** Math—Medium. English—Medium. Science—Medium. **Yearly Earnings:** $$$$ **Job Growth:** ★★★ **Yearly Openings:** 🧍

Government Property Inspectors and Investigators. Investigate or inspect government property to ensure compliance with contract agreements and government regulations. **Education and Training:** Long-term on-the-job training. **Skills:** Math—Medium. English—High. Science—Medium. **Yearly Earnings:** $$$$ **Job Growth:** ★★ **Yearly Openings:** 👤👤

Licensing Examiners and Inspectors. Examine, evaluate, and investigate eligibility for, conformity with, or liability under licenses or permits. **Education and Training:** Long-term on-the-job training. **Skills:** Math—Medium. English—Medium. Science—Medium. **Yearly Earnings:** $$$$ **Job Growth:** ★★ **Yearly Openings:** 👤👤

Marine Cargo Inspectors. Inspect cargoes of seagoing vessels to certify compliance with health and safety regulations in cargo handling and stowage. **Education and Training:** Work experience in a related occupation. **Skills:** Math—High. English—Medium. Science—Medium. **Yearly Earnings:** $$$$ **Job Growth:** ★★★ **Yearly Openings:** 👤

Municipal Fire Fighters. Control and extinguish municipal fires, protect life and property, and conduct rescue efforts. **Education and Training:** Long-term on-the-job training. **Skills:** Math—Medium. English—Medium. Science—Medium. **Yearly Earnings:** $$$ **Job Growth:** ★★ **Yearly Openings:** 👤👤👤

Nuclear Monitoring Technicians. Collect and test samples to monitor results of nuclear experiments and contamination of humans, facilities, and the environment. **Education and Training:** Associate's degree. **Skills:** Math—High. English—Medium. Science—High. **Yearly Earnings:** $$$$$ **Job Growth:** ★★★ **Yearly Openings:** 👤

Occupational Health and Safety Specialists. Review, evaluate, and analyze work environments and design programs and procedures to control, eliminate, and prevent disease or injury caused by chemical, physical, and biological agents or ergonomic factors. May conduct inspections and enforce adherence to laws and regulations governing the health and safety of individuals. **Education and Training:** Master's degree. **Skills:** Math—High. English—High. Science—High. **Yearly Earnings:** $$$$ **Job Growth:** ★★★ **Yearly Openings:** 👤

Occupational Health and Safety Technicians. Collect data on work environments for analysis by occupational health and safety specialists. Implement and conduct evaluation of programs designed to limit chemical, physical, biological, and ergonomic risks to workers. **Education and Training:** Associate's degree. **Skills:** Math—Medium. English—Medium. Science—Medium. **Yearly Earnings:** $$$$ **Job Growth:** ★★★ **Yearly Openings:** 👤

Public Transportation Inspectors. Monitor operation of public transportation systems to ensure good service and compliance with regulations. Investigate accidents, equipment failures, and complaints. **Education and Training:** Work experience in a related occupation. **Skills:** Math—Medium. English—Medium. Science—Medium. **Yearly Earnings:** $$$$ **Job Growth:** ★★★ **Yearly Openings:** 👤

MILITARY

These workers serve in the armed forces of the United States: the Air Force, Army, Coast Guard, Marines, Navy, and National Guard. Although workers in the armed forces perform almost every occupation found in the civilian workforce, the occupations in this group are unique to the military and have no civilian match. The purpose of workers in the military is to ensure peace and protect the nation in times of war. In unusual cases, the military must assist in national emergencies or restore order in events of civil disobedience. ***Note:*** *For the jobs that follow, data is not available for yearly earnings, job growth, and yearly openings.*

Air Crew Members. Perform in-flight duties to ensure the successful completion of combat, reconnaissance, transport, and search and rescue missions. Duties involve operating aircraft communications and detection equipment, including establishing satellite linkages and jamming enemy communications capabilities; conducting pre-flight, in-flight, and post-flight inspections of onboard equipment; operating and maintaining aircraft weapons and defensive systems; operating and maintaining aircraft in-flight refueling systems; executing aircraft safety and emergency procedures; computing and verifying passenger, cargo, fuel, and emergency and special equipment weight and balance data; and conducting cargo and personnel drops. **Education and Training:** Moderate-term on-the-job training. **Skills:** Math—Medium. English—Medium. Science—Medium.

Air Crew Officers. Perform and direct in-flight duties to ensure the successful completion of combat, reconnaissance, transport, and search and rescue missions. Duties include operating aircraft communications and radar equipment, such as establishing satellite linkages and jamming enemy communications that operate aircraft weapons and defensive systems; conducting pre-flight, in-flight, and post-flight inspections of onboard equipment; and directing cargo and personnel drops. **Education and Training:** Long-term on-the-job training. **Skills:** Math—Medium. English—Medium. Science—Medium.

Aircraft Launch and Recovery Officers. Plan and direct the operation and maintenance of catapults, arresting gear, and associated mechanical, hydraulic, and control systems involved primarily in aircraft carrier takeoff and landing operations. Duties include supervision of readiness and safety of arresting gear, launching equipment, barricades, and visual landing aid systems; planning and coordinating the design, development, and testing of launch and recovery systems; preparing specifications for catapult and arresting gear installations; evaluating design proposals; determining handling equipment needed for new aircraft; preparing technical data and instructions for operation of landing aids; and training personnel in carrier takeoff and landing procedures. **Education and Training:** Long-term on-the-job training. **Skills:** Math—Medium. English—Medium. Science—Medium.

Aircraft Launch and Recovery Specialists. Operate and maintain catapults, arresting gear, and associated mechanical, hydraulic, and control systems involved primarily in aircraft carrier takeoff and landing operations. Duties include installing and maintaining visual landing aids; testing and maintaining launch and recovery equipment using electric and mechanical test equipment and hand tools; activating airfield arresting systems, such as crash barriers and cables, during emergency landing situations; directing aircraft launch and recovery operations using hand or light signals; and maintaining logs of airplane launches, recoveries, and equipment maintenance. **Education and Training:** Moderate-term on-the-job training. **Skills:** Math—Medium. English—Medium. Science—Medium.

Armored Assault Vehicle Crew Members. Operate tanks, light armor, and amphibious assault vehicles during combat situations on land or in aquatic environments. Duties include driving armored vehicles; operating and maintaining targeting and firing systems; operating and maintaining advanced onboard communications and navigation equipment; transporting personnel and equipment in a combat environment; and operating and maintaining auxiliary weapons, including machine guns and grenade launchers. **Education and Training:** Moderate-term on-the-job training. **Skills:** Math—Medium. English—Medium. Science—Medium.

Armored Assault Vehicle Officers. Direct the operation of tanks, light armor, and amphibious assault vehicle units during combat situations on land or in aquatic environments. Duties include directing crew members in the operation of targeting and firing systems; coordinating the operation of advanced onboard communications and navigation equipment; directing the transport of personnel and equipment during combat; formulating and implementing battle plans, including the tactical employment of armored vehicle units; and coordinating with infantry, artillery, and air support units. **Education and Training:** Long-term on-the-job training. **Skills:** Math—Medium. English—Medium. Science—Medium.

Artillery and Missile Crew Members. Target, fire, and maintain weapons used to destroy enemy positions, aircraft, and vessels. Field artillery crew members mainly use guns, cannons, and howitzers in ground combat operations, while air defense artillery crew members mainly use missiles and rockets. Naval artillery crew members mainly use torpedoes and missiles launched from a ship or submarine. Duties include testing, inspecting, and storing ammunition, missiles, and torpedoes; conducting preventive and routine maintenance on weapons and related equipment; establishing and maintaining radio and wire communications; and operating weapons targeting, firing, and launch computer systems. **Education and Training:** Moderate-term on-the-job training. **Skills:** Math—Medium. English—Medium. Science—Medium.

Artillery and Missile Officers. Manage personnel and weapons operations to destroy enemy positions, aircraft, and vessels. Duties include planning, targeting, and coordinating the tactical deployment of field artillery and air defense artillery missile systems units; directing the establishment and operation of fire control communications

systems; targeting and launching intercontinental ballistic missiles; directing the storage and handling of nuclear munitions and components; overseeing security of weapons storage and launch facilities; and managing maintenance of weapons systems. **Education and Training:** Long-term on-the-job training. **Skills:** Math—Medium. English—Medium. Science—Medium.

Command and Control Center Officers. Manage the operation of communications, detection, and weapons systems essential for controlling air, ground, and naval operations. Duties include managing critical communication links between air, naval, and ground forces; formulating and implementing emergency plans for natural and wartime disasters; coordinating emergency response teams and agencies; evaluating command center information and need for high-level military and government reporting; managing the operation of surveillance and detection systems; providing technical information and advice on capabilities and operational readiness; and directing operation of weapons targeting, firing, and launch computer systems. **Education and Training:** Long-term on-the-job training. **Skills:** Math—Medium. English—Medium. Science—Medium.

Command and Control Center Specialists. Operate and monitor communications, detection, and weapons systems essential for controlling air, ground, and naval operations. Duties include maintaining and relaying critical communications between air, naval, and ground forces; implementing emergency plans for natural and wartime disasters; relaying command center information to high-level military and government decision makers; monitoring surveillance and detection systems, such as air defense; interpreting and evaluating tactical situations and making recommendations to superiors; and operating weapons targeting, firing, and launch computer systems. **Education and Training:** Moderate-term on-the-job training. **Skills:** Math—Medium. English—Medium. Science—Medium.

First-Line Supervisors/Managers of Air Crew Members. Supervise and coordinate the activities of air crew members. Supervisors may also perform the same activities as the workers they supervise. **Education and Training:** Work experience in a related occupation. **Skills:** Math—Medium. English—Medium. Science—Medium.

First-Line Supervisors/Managers of All Other Tactical Operations Specialists. Supervise and coordinate the activities of all other tactical operations specialists not described separately above. Supervisors may also perform the same activities as the workers they supervise. **Education and Training:** Work experience in a related occupation. **Skills:** Math—Medium. English—Medium. Science—Medium.

First-Line Supervisors/Managers of Weapons Specialists/Crew Members. Supervise and coordinate the activities of weapons specialists/crew members. Supervisors may also perform the same activities as the workers they supervise. **Education and Training:** Work experience in a related occupation. **Skills:** Math—Medium. English—Medium. Science—Medium.

Infantry. Operate weapons and equipment in ground combat operations. Duties include operating and maintaining weapons, such as rifles, machine guns, mortars, and hand grenades; locating, constructing, and camouflaging infantry positions and equipment; evaluating terrain and recording topographical information; operating and maintaining field communications equipment; assessing need for and directing supporting fire; placing explosives and performing minesweeping activities on land; and participating in basic reconnaissance operations. **Education and Training:** Moderate-term on-the-job training. **Skills:** Math—Medium. English—Medium. Science—Medium.

Infantry Officers. Direct, train, and lead infantry units in ground combat operations. Duties include directing deployment of infantry weapons, vehicles, and equipment; directing location, construction, and camouflage of infantry positions and equipment; managing field communications operations; coordinating with armor, artillery, and air support units; performing strategic and tactical planning, including battle plan development; and leading basic reconnaissance operations. **Education and Training:** Long-term on-the-job training. **Skills:** Math—Medium. English—Medium. Science—Medium.

Radar and Sonar Technicians. Operate equipment using radio or sound wave technology to identify, track, and analyze objects or natural phenomena of military interest. Includes airborne, shipboard, and terrestrial positions. May perform minor maintenance. **Education and Training:** Moderate-term on-the-job training. **Skills:** Math—Medium. English—Medium. Science—Medium.

Special Forces. Implement unconventional operations by air, land, or sea during combat or peacetime as members of elite teams. These activities include offensive raids, demolitions, reconnaissance, search and rescue, and counterterrorism. In addition to their combat training, Special Forces members often have specialized training in swimming, diving, parachuting, survival, emergency medicine, and foreign languages. Duties include conducting advanced reconnaissance operations and collecting intelligence information; recruiting, training, and equipping friendly forces; conducting raids and invasions on enemy territories; laying and detonating explosives for demolition targets; locating, identifying, defusing, and disposing of ordnance; and operating and maintaining sophisticated communications equipment. **Education and Training:** Long-term on-the-job training. **Skills:** Math—Medium. English—Medium. Science—Medium.

Special Forces Officers. Lead elite teams that implement unconventional operations by air, land, or sea during combat or peacetime. These activities include offensive raids, demolitions, reconnaissance, search and rescue, and counterterrorism. In addition to their combat training, special forces officers often have specialized training in swimming, diving, parachuting, survival, emergency medicine, and foreign languages. Duties include directing advanced reconnaissance operations and evaluating intelligence information; recruiting, training, and equipping friendly forces; leading raids and invasions on enemy territories; training personnel to implement individual missions and contingency plans; performing strategic and tactical planning for politically sensitive missions; and operating sophisticated communications equipment. **Education and Training:** Long-term on-the-job training. **Skills:** Math—Medium. English—Medium. Science—Medium.

Exploring Careers: Mechanics, Installers, and Repairers

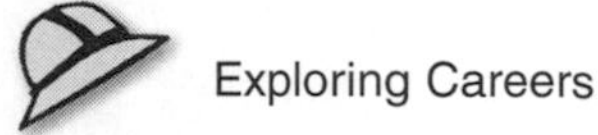

Start Your Journey Through Careers for

MECHANICS, INSTALLERS, AND REPAIRERS

Careers in this area suit people interested in applying mechanical and electrical/electronic principles to practical situations by use of machines or hand tools.

EXPLORING CAREER CLUES

Your interests give important clues for exploring career options. Think about your interests to learn if jobs in the Mechanics, Installers, and Repairers interest area may be worth further exploration.

Do you like the school subjects related to the Mechanics, Installers, and Repairers interest area? Here are some examples of related subjects:

- Math
- Algebra
- Computers
- Science
- Chemistry
- Physics
- Industrial or technology education
- Physical education

Do you like the free-time activities related to the Mechanics, Installers, and Repairers interest area? Here are some examples of related free-time activities:

- Installing, wiring, or repairing radios, TVs, stereos, personal computers, and other electronic or technical equipment
- Building model airplanes, cars, or boats
- Building robots, electronic devices, or working models
- Building stage sets for school or other amateur theater
- Building cabinets, furniture, and other items

- Helping friends and others with math
- Solving complex puzzles
- Upgrading hardware in personal computers
- Operating a CB or ham radio
- Working on bicycles, minibikes, lawn mowers, and cars
- Taking apart or repairing small appliances and devices
- Making sketches of machines or other mechanical equipment
- Reading about electronics, engines, computers, technology, or auto repair
- Operating model train layouts

EXPLORING JOB GROUPS

Jobs related to the Mechanics, Installers, and Repairers interest area fit into three groups. Read through the list to see which groups sound interesting to you.

- Managerial Work for Mechanics, Installers, and Repairers
- Electrical and Electronic Systems
- Mechanical Work

EXPLORING CAREER POSSIBILITIES

You can satisfy your interest in the Mechanics, Installers, and Repairers area through jobs that involve installation, maintenance, repair, and troubleshooting with a variety of equipment, tools, technologies, and materials. Here are a few examples of career possibilities:

If you enjoy making machines run efficiently or fixing them when they break down, you could seek a job installing or repairing such devices as copiers, aircraft engines, cars, or watches.

Or, if electricity and electronics interest you, you could install cables, troubleshoot phone networks, or repair electronic equipment.

If you prefer routine or physical work in settings other than factories, perhaps installing appliances or even repairing musical instruments would appeal to you.

Turn the page to meet people working in the Mechanics, Installers, and Repairers interest area→

PROFILE

Jackie Arnold— Data Processing Equipment Repairer

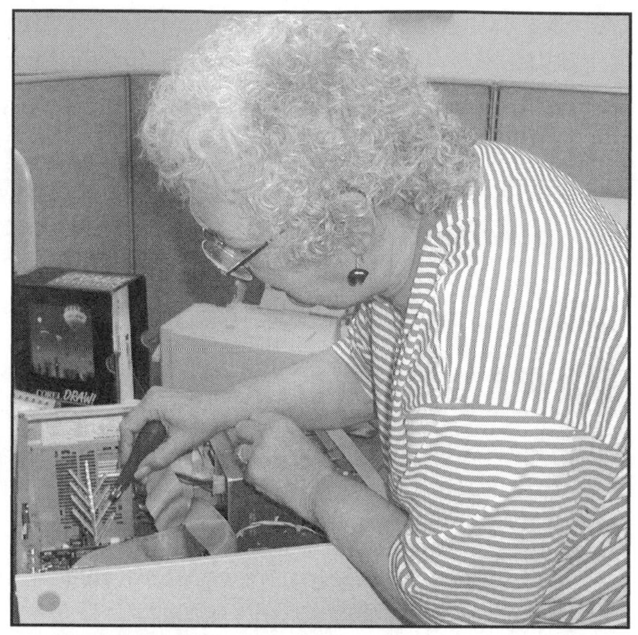
Jackie replaces a defective component for a client.

Jackie Arnold hung up the phone and grabbed her briefcase full of tools and manuals. She had left Commerce National Bank only a half hour before. Now, she was being called back to fix another problem right at noon.

Jackie is a data processing equipment repairer. "I do hands-on adjustment, repair, maintenance, and installation of computers and related equipment," Jackie said. She headed to her car.

She often replaces broken components instead of repairing them. Replacement is common because components are inexpensive. Businesses also don't like to shut down their computers for time-consuming repairs. Components commonly replaced include video cards, which transmit signals from the computer to the monitor; hard drives, which store data; and network cards, which allow communication over the network.

Jackie passes on defective components to bench technicians. They use software programs to diagnose the problem and may repair the components.

Soon Jackie pulled into a parking lot of Commerce National. She didn't have to take much with her because supplies were stored at the bank. Data Products, the company Jackie worked for, saw to that. The company

also sent parts and repair instructions directly to the bank's computer center. That way, Jackie and the other repairers didn't have to carry a lot of supplies or transport parts from the Data Products regional office.

In fact, Jackie sometimes worked for several weeks without going to the regional office at all. As she saw it, her job was taking care of the computer equipment at her three accounts–Commerce National Bank, County Hospital, and Wilson Manufacturing Company. So naturally she spent most of her time in those places, not at the Data Products office.

Making a Service Call

Jackie showed her Data Products identification card as she passed the bank's security guard and headed for the computer center. She quickly spotted Mr. Jimenez, who ran the office.

"Is it the sorter again?" she asked.

"Right," he replied.

Jackie went to the side room where the sorter was located. The cramped room also was used to store supplies. However, Jackie did not have to move the machine as she did in some offices.

The sorter was used to group bank documents in several ways. Twice during the past five days the sorter had failed to separate the papers correctly. From Mr. Jimenez's description of what had happened, Jackie got an idea of what the problem might be. She knew that equipment often requires several adjustments. She was used to visiting an office several times to fix a machine.

Jackie raised the metal cover on the front of the sorter and turned it on. She listened to the machine's hum and made a few adjustments. Jackie then ran the sorter while she watched and listened to it.

From High-School Hobby to Full-Time Career

Jackie had always been curious about how things worked. She began working with electrical equipment as a hobby.

She'd had a lot of experience with data processing equipment since then, and it confirmed her impression that machines could be as different as people. She'd taken electronics courses and other training courses at a technical school. Finally, her employer provided on-the-job training. It consisted of classroom instruction and work with an experienced repairer.

Job prospects are best for applicants with knowledge of electronics and with repair experience.

Job prospects are best for applicants with knowledge of electronics and with repair experience. Computer equipment continues to become less expensive and more reliable. However, malfunctions still occur and can cause severe problems for businesses. Computers are critical to most businesses today and will become even more so.

Documenting Her Work and Thinking Ahead

Jackie closed the machine cover and put away her tools. From her briefcase, she took a repair report form. She filled in the date, the machine model, the account's name, and the code for the type of breakdown and repair.

She made out a repair report for every service call. Data Products used the information to determine the kinds of problems with the equipment the company made. Engineers could then design machines that broke down less often and could be fixed more easily.

Jackie wrote the date and a brief description of the work she had done in the record book kept with the equipment. Others who worked on the machine would use the information in the book. Jackie also used the records to keep track of maintenance on the machines.

After putting the record book away, Jackie walked to Mr. Jimenez's office. "I think I've fixed it for good this time. But I'd like to be here the next time you use it, just to make sure that everything's okay. Will you be using it soon?"

"Not until tomorrow," said Mr. Jimenez.

"Hmm, I'm scheduled for training the rest of the week. My backup can handle any problem."

"Training again! I thought you already learned everything you need to know. Aren't you going to night school now?" said Mr. Jimenez.

“The training this week is for your new printers. Night school is for my future plans. I want to be an engineer. Then I’ll design these computers instead of fixing them.

“Well, I’d better run,” Jackie continued as she picked up her briefcase. “We’ve been busy the last two days, and I have to do some maintenance at Wilson Manufacturing this afternoon. If I don’t get it done, Ken Marcus will have problems.”

“Well, not everyone can be a nice guy like me,” said Mr. Jimenez with a laugh.

“True,” replied Jackie. “See you next week.”

Jackie called the office dispatcher from her cell phone to say that she had answered the Commerce National Bank call. To her surprise, there were no other repair calls.

Jackie looked at her watch. There was plenty of time to get to the Wilson account. She felt relaxed. “I guess I get to have lunch after all,” she thought as she headed for her car.

PROFILE

Kyle Picard—Electronic Home Entertainment Equipment Repairer

“When you’re in a service business and dealing with the public, you meet all kinds of people,” said electronic home entertainment equipment repairer Kyle Picard. The job is also called service technician or bench technician.

“The trend away from printed matter to video and audio gadgets continues. Stereos and TVs are here to stay. But they break down, and that’s where I come in.”

Kyle and his coworker, Brad Locke, worked for Fred Appleton, who owned and managed the shop. Behind the counter, one bench was piled high with papers, test equipment, and old parts. The sign over it said “Brad’s Place.” The other bench was neat and ordered. Kyle always cleaned off the debris from the last repair before moving on to the next challenge.

At the counter, Brad was taking in a defective TV, writing up the form about the problems the customer was having. After the customer left, he taped the form to the unit and stored it until its turn.

"A lot of folks try to analyze problems themselves. Or they'll tell us the set is dead when a button isn't working," Kyle said.

Kyle took the next unit to be fixed from the shelf. He read the customer's complaint. Then he unscrewed the chassis to see the receiver's innards and hooked it up to his test equipment. It showed that a blown output transistor must be replaced. As Kyle bent over the unit, the hot soldering iron sent fumes curling into the room.

"Technicians must think logically," Kyle said. "What part failure could cause these symptoms? If I replace it and the problem still exists, what else in the circuit should I test next? It's like solving puzzles."

Making Use of Resources

Replacing the blown transistor didn't improve the receiver's performance. Kyle checked the circuitry in the manual and disappeared into the back of the shop. There, he found two dozen file cabinets full of manuals.

He found the manual he needed and brought it to his bench. He pored over a yard-long map of the unit's circuitry to find the defect.

Ideally, anything that comes in to be fixed has a manual filed away. Sometimes they are on microfiche, laser disk, or CD-ROM. "These manuals are different from the ones that come with the unit. That manual gives instruction on how the controls work," Kyle said.

Although the shop never throws out a manual, it may not have one for every unit that comes in. If the manufacturer is small, it may not write manuals.

He pored over a yard-long map of the unit's circuitry to find the defect.

The equipment and tools on a TV/stereo repairer's bench are expensive, Kyle said. The manufacturer expects authorized service organizations to have

certain equipment. On Kyle's bench is an oscilloscope; a multimeter to test voltage, current, and resistance; a high-voltage probe; a DC power supply; an isolated AC power supply; multi-channel TV sound; and a color bar generator or NTS generator, among other things.

These mostly help solve electronic problems. A technician also needs other ordinary tools for fixing mechanical failures.

Avoiding Shocks and Hazards

Technology changes rapidly, but dangers don't go away. "Before I had training, I once grabbed the red cable in a TV while it was turned on. The voltage threw me across the room.

"Bad shocks make some technicians groggy. We often get shocked on the job. TVs have more voltage than other electronic devices. Even portable black-and-white TVs give a mean shock when they're off.

"There are other risks, but they won't kill you. For example, some of this equipment is heavy. Lifting it can hurt your back. But that's minor compared to high voltage."

What Is the Field's Future?

"I got into this business because I was interested in electronics. Have been since I was a kid. When I went to technical college, I put up fliers that I could repair stereos and TVs. It helped pay for my training.

"A successful small shop in today's market fixes almost everything–even telephones. It's a tough business, and I'm not sure there's a big future in it. No sense misleading anyone. All those TVs and stereos bought this year and last year and for the last ten years? I see them in landfills.

"Mostly this is because the cost of buying electronic equipment has come down so dramatically over the years that it doesn't pay to fix anything. There's potential in fixing computers and commercial quality electronics, though. And repairers will be needed for newer digital equipment like DVD players and digital TVs."

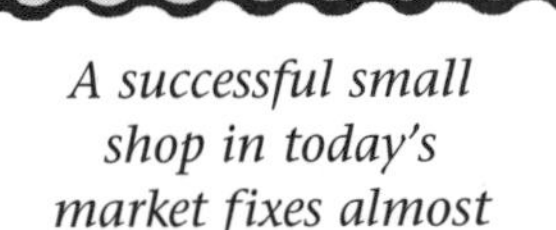

A successful small shop in today's market fixes almost everything–even telephones.

If something breaks down within the warranty period, the manufacturer pays for the repair. However, the manufacturer often pays less than half the going rate. Many technicians are not happy about these warranty rates.

Learning about electronics often starts when you're young.

"When customers come in, they sign an authorization. I estimate labor. Government regulations require us to come within ten percent of our estimate. Parts will cost close to half the labor charge.

"Customers approve this mix when they sign the repair authorization. I call them for approval if the parts will be more than the labor."

Training Starts Early

How can someone learn how to be a service technician? According to Kyle, learning about electronics often starts when you're young. "My uncle bought me a kit and I made a buzzer, a radio, a relay, and a crystal detector. The relay turned a light on and off.

"For years before I took training and became professional, I took apart my family's electronics. They usually didn't work when I put them back together. My folks still get nervous when I fix their TV. Though I have years of experience, they remember my failures.

"I read electronics technology and servicing magazines. If I didn't understand something, I read about it until I did.

"A student can attend a technical school or community college. The school starts the student out with hands-on work with the equipment, not lectures on theory.

"Technicians take courses to learn about new models. They study the latest in circuitry and gadgets. Ideally, they have a chance to work on what's current. Although it will be a while before they see these same models in the shop, I think this training is important," Kyle said.

Technicians take courses to learn about new models.

Repairs and Rewards

Returning to the receiver on the bench, Kyle replaced one small part, and everything tested okay. But when he put the chassis back on, it no longer worked. "Sometimes a screw in the wrong hole shorts something inside, especially if it's longer than the correct one," Kyle noted.

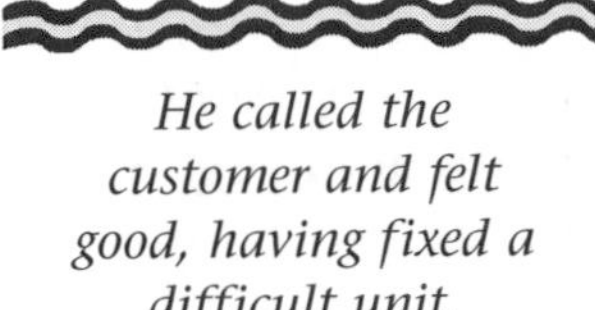

He called the customer and felt good, having fixed a difficult unit.

But that wasn't the problem. He found a hairline crack in the circuit board. Screwing the chassis tightly back together flexed the board and shorted a component. Kyle replaced the board. He called the customer and felt good, having fixed a difficult unit.

To fix electronics, a technician must be clever. A good technician is like a detective–smart, analytical, and able to study a problem from many different angles.

"It's not a job a tinkerer can jump into and expect to make a living. It takes training, continual study, a steady hand, and patience. A sense of humor helps, too," Kyle said.

PROFILE

Joseph Warren—Camera and Photographic Equipment Repairer

Click-click, ding-dong, whir-whir! The precise movements of gadgets such as clocks, cameras, and musical instruments have fascinated people for years.

Maintaining such small mechanical devices demands a level of skill and attention to detail that borders on an art. Highly skilled repairers keep precision equipment working.

Joseph Warren examines older cameras as well as digital ones.

Precision instrument and equipment repairers are a diverse group. They repair cameras, medical equipment, musical instruments, watches and clocks, and precision instruments. They also work on equipment used in manufacturing. These workers require attention to detail in fixing instruments and equipment. Their tasks vary according to specialty.

Details, Details, Details

"I disassemble the camera's numerous small parts to reach the source of the problem."

Joseph Warren is a camera and photographic equipment repairer. "When fixing a camera or photo equipment, I perform a series of steps," Joseph said as he looked up from his work.

"First, I diagnose the problem to determine whether a repair is profitable. I refer the most complicated and expensive problems back to the manufacturer. Inexpensive cameras cost more to repair than replace.

"Second, I disassemble the camera's or equipment's numerous small parts to reach the source of the problem.

"Next, I read an electrical schematic to work through possible electrical causes of a problem. I remove and replace broken or worn parts. Finally, I clean and lubricate gears and springs," Joseph said. "Many components and parts are quite small."

Close-Up Look at Duties and Skills

Frequently, older camera and photo equipment parts are no longer available. Joseph strips junked cameras and equipment. Sometimes he builds replacement parts. He uses metalworking tools such as a lathe and grinding wheel.

"Modern equipment requires some knowledge of computer and digital circuitry," said Joseph. "For example, most 35-millimeter cameras now have computerized circuit boards and computer programs. Older cameras have many small moving parts."

Joseph has to decide when a circuit board problem requires replacing a simple circuit, a transistor, or the whole board.

Digital cameras and photographic equipment require similar repairs to other modern cameras and photographic equipment. However, there is no film to wind in digital devices. The technology results in having fewer moving parts for repairers to fix or replace.

"I read an electrical schematic to work through possible electrical causes of a problem."

Joseph also tests and adjusts equipment and performs regular maintenance. He requests needed parts and supplies.

Joseph works for a company that does camera repair. He works standard daytime hours with little supervision. His repair area is quiet, air-conditioned, and well-lit. Camera repairers are sometimes self-employed.

Joseph's work requires good troubleshooting and problem-solving skills. He also needs patience, good vision, and fine motor skills.

Clicking with a Career

"When I was a boy, I enjoyed taking machines apart. I liked seeing how they worked," Joseph said. "As I got older, I began fixing things around the house and for neighbors." He enjoys moving methodically through the repair process.

Joseph enjoys moving methodically through the repair process.

Camera repairers need some background in electronics. They also need the ability to read an electrical schematic and comprehend other technical information.

When Joseph started in the field, he was trained on the job in two stages. First, he assisted a senior repairer for about six months. Then he refined his skills performing repairs on his own for an additional six months.

Some workers complete training after high school. They can get an associate's degree in camera and photographic equipment repair.

Joseph hones his skills by attending manufacturer-sponsored seminars for specific models.

A camera repairer's work is similar to that of electronic home entertainment equipment repairers. Both jobs work with consumer electronics that have circuit boards. They also involve numerous moving mechanical parts.

"With a mix of electronics, problem-solving, and detail work, this is the perfect job for me," Joseph said.

SKILL SAMPLER

Marty Romo—Auto Mechanic

Marty Romo started his own auto repair shop when he got out of the army. Business was slow at first, but now he has all the work he can handle. "You can learn a lot by helping friends fix cars. Being a mechanic has given me the opportunity to have my own business. I prefer working for myself."

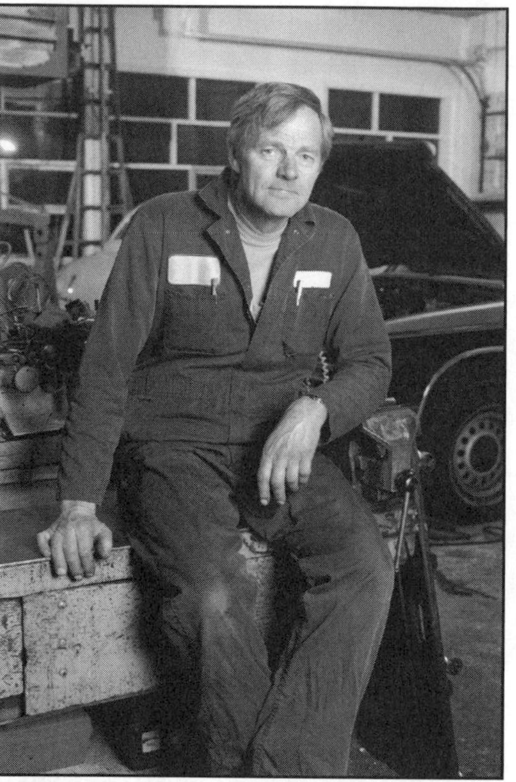

"Mechanics set their own work pace. A rushed job could cause more trouble later."

Marty talked about an auto mechanic's typical day. He offers the following tips to help you decide if you might enjoy working as an auto mechanic.

Auto mechanics repair and service cars.

- Are you interested in machines and the way they work?
- Do you like to read about cars, motorcycles, and other motor vehicles?
- Have you ever wondered how cars run or why they break down?

Auto mechanics work with their hands. They use tools and must do their work quickly and skillfully.

- Do you like to build models or repair things around your home?
- Do you ever help repair bicycles, minibikes, lawn mowers, or cars?

- Do you get a sense of accomplishment when you fix things?
- Are you handy with tools?
- Is it easy for you to learn how to use a tool you've never used before?

Auto mechanics sometimes must search for the cause of car trouble. They have to solve mechanical puzzles.

- Do you like to work on written mathematics problems?
- Do you like to do three-dimensional puzzles?
- Have you ever solved a problem with your computer?
- Are you persistent? Will you work on a problem until you solve it?

Auto mechanics use technical resources such as repair manuals.

- How well do you understand technical writing such as science and mathematics textbooks? Do you enjoy this kind of reading?
- Can you use charts, graphs, and diagrams?
- Have you ever used the Help feature on a computer to learn how to do something?
- Can you look at a drawing and picture the three-dimensional object in your mind?

Auto mechanics usually work alone. They must have confidence in themselves.

- Do you like to work by yourself?
- Do you do your homework by yourself?
- Do you like to make decisions?

Auto mechanics do strenuous work.

- Do you enjoy sports, hiking, dancing, or gardening?
- Do you like to be active most of the time?

Now learn about all major jobs in the Mechanics, Installers, and Repairers interest area→

Facts About All Major Jobs for

MECHANICS, INSTALLERS, AND REPAIRERS

In addition to the jobs covered in the profiles and skill sampler, other careers in the Mechanics, Installers, and Repairers interest area may appeal to you. This section describes and gives facts about all major jobs in the Mechanics, Installers, and Repairers interest area. For an explanation of the $, ★, and 🚶 symbols, see page 6.

MANAGERIAL WORK FOR MECHANICS, INSTALLERS, AND REPAIRERS

These workers directly supervise and coordinate activities of mechanics, repairers, and installers and their helpers. They are generally found in smaller establishments, where they perform both supervisory and management functions, such as accounting, marketing, and personnel work. They may also engage in the same repair and installation work as the workers they supervise.

First-Line Supervisors/Managers of Mechanics, Installers, and Repairers. Supervise and coordinate the activities of mechanics, installers, and repairers. **Education and Training:** Work experience in a related occupation. **Skills:** Math—Medium. English—Medium. Science—Medium. **Yearly Earnings:** $$$$ **Job Growth:** ★★★ **Yearly Openings:** 🚶🚶🚶

ELECTRICAL AND ELECTRONIC SYSTEMS

These workers repair and install electrical devices and systems such as motors, transformers, appliances, and power lines and electronic devices and systems such as radios, computers, and telephone networks. They work for manufacturers, utilities, and service companies. Since electrical and electronic equipment is used almost everywhere, they may work in almost any kind of location, as well as in repair shops.

Avionics Technicians. Install, inspect, test, adjust, or repair avionics equipment, such as radar, radio, navigation, and missile control systems in aircraft or space vehicles.

Education and Training: Postsecondary career and technical education. **Skills:** Math—Medium. English—Medium. Science—Medium. **Yearly Earnings:** $$$$ **Job Growth:** ★★ **Yearly Openings:** 🧍

Battery Repairers. Inspect, repair, recharge, and replace batteries. **Education and Training:** Moderate-term on-the-job training. **Skills:** Math—Medium. English—Medium. Science—Medium. **Yearly Earnings:** $$$ **Job Growth:** ★★ **Yearly Openings:** 🧍

Central Office and PBX Installers and Repairers. Test, analyze, and repair telephone or telegraph circuits and equipment at a central office location using test meters and hand tools. Analyze and repair defects in communications equipment on customers' premises using circuit diagrams, polarity probes, meters, and a telephone test set. May install equipment. **Education and Training:** Postsecondary career and technical education. **Skills:** Math—Medium. English—Medium. Science—Medium. **Yearly Earnings:** $$$$ **Job Growth:** ★ **Yearly Openings:** 🧍🧍

Communication Equipment Mechanics, Installers, and Repairers. Install, maintain, test, and repair communication cables and equipment. **Education and Training:** Postsecondary career and technical education. **Skills:** Math—Medium. English—Medium. Science—Medium. **Yearly Earnings:** $$$$ **Job Growth:** ★ **Yearly Openings:** 🧍🧍

Computer, Automated Teller, and Office Machine Repairers. Repair, maintain, or install computers, word processing systems, automated teller machines, and electronic office machines, such as duplicating and fax machines. **Education and Training:** Postsecondary career and technical education. **Skills:** Math—Medium. English—Medium. Science—Medium. **Yearly Earnings:** $$$ **Job Growth:** ★★★ **Yearly Openings:** 🧍🧍🧍

Data Processing Equipment Repairers. Repair, maintain, and install computer hardware, such as peripheral equipment and word-processing systems. **Education and Training:** Postsecondary career and technical education. **Skills:** Math—Medium. English—Medium. Science—High. **Yearly Earnings:** $$$ **Job Growth:** ★★★ **Yearly Openings:** 🧍🧍🧍

Electric Home Appliance and Power Tool Repairers. Repair, adjust, and install all types of electric household appliances. **Education and Training:** Long-term on-the-job training. **Skills:** Math—Medium. English—Medium. Science—Medium. **Yearly Earnings:** $$$ **Job Growth:** ★★ **Yearly Openings:** 🧍

Electric Meter Installers and Repairers. Install electric meters on customers' premises or on pole. Test meters and perform necessary repairs. Turn current on/off by connecting/disconnecting service drop. **Education and Training:** Moderate-term on-the-job training. **Skills:** Math—Medium. English—Medium. Science—Medium. **Yearly Earnings:** $$$$ **Job Growth:** ★ **Yearly Openings:** 🧍

Electric Motor and Switch Assemblers and Repairers. Test, repair, rebuild, and assemble electric motors, generators, and equipment. **Education and Training:** Long-term on-the-job training. **Skills:** Math—Medium. English—Medium. Science—High. **Yearly Earnings:** $$$ **Job Growth:** ★★ **Yearly Openings:** 🚹

Electric Motor, Power Tool, and Related Repairers. Repair, maintain, or install electric motors, wiring, or switches. **Education and Training:** Long-term on-the-job training. **Skills:** Math—Medium. English—Medium. Science—Medium. **Yearly Earnings:** $$$ **Job Growth:** ★★ **Yearly Openings:** 🚹

Electrical and Electronics Installers and Repairers, Transportation Equipment. Install, adjust, or maintain mobile electronics communication equipment, including sound, sonar, security, navigation, and surveillance systems on trains, watercraft, or other mobile equipment. **Education and Training:** Postsecondary career and technical education. **Skills:** Math—Medium. English—Medium. Science—Medium. **Yearly Earnings:** $$$ **Job Growth:** ★★★ **Yearly Openings:** 🚹

Electrical and Electronics Repairers, Commercial and Industrial Equipment. Repair, test, adjust, or install electronic equipment, such as industrial controls, transmitters, and antennas. **Education and Training:** Postsecondary career and technical education. **Skills:** Math—High. English—Medium. Science—High. **Yearly Earnings:** $$$ **Job Growth:** ★★ **Yearly Openings:** 🚹 🚹

Electrical and Electronics Repairers, Powerhouse, Substation, and Relay. Inspect, test, repair, or maintain electrical equipment in generating stations, substations, and in-service relays. **Education and Training:** Postsecondary career and technical education. **Skills:** Math—Medium. English—Medium. Science—High. **Yearly Earnings:** $$$$ **Job Growth:** ★ **Yearly Openings:** 🚹

Electrical Parts Reconditioners. Recondition and rebuild salvaged electrical parts of equipment and wind new coils on armatures of used generators and motors. **Education and Training:** Moderate-term on-the-job training. **Skills:** Math—Low. English—Low. Science—Medium. **Yearly Earnings:** $$$ **Job Growth:** ★★ **Yearly Openings:** 🚹

Electrical Power-Line Installers and Repairers. Install or repair cables or wires used in electrical power or distribution systems. May erect poles and light- or heavy-duty transmission towers. **Education and Training:** Long-term on-the-job training. **Skills:** Math—Medium. English—Medium. Science—Medium. **Yearly Earnings:** $$$$ **Job Growth:** ★★ **Yearly Openings:** 🚹

Electronic Equipment Installers and Repairers, Motor Vehicles. Install, diagnose, or repair communications, sound, security, or navigation equipment in motor vehicles. **Education and Training:** Postsecondary career and technical education. **Skills:** Math—Medium. English—Medium. Science—Medium. **Yearly Earnings:** $$ **Job Growth:** ★★★ **Yearly Openings:** 🚹

Electronic Home Entertainment Equipment Installers and Repairers. Repair, adjust, or install audio or television receivers, stereo systems, camcorders, video systems, or other electronic home entertainment equipment. **Education and Training:** Postsecondary career and technical education. **Skills:** Math—Medium. English—Medium. Science—High. **Yearly Earnings:** $$ **Job Growth:** ★ **Yearly Openings:** 🧍

Elevator Installers and Repairers. Assemble, install, repair, or maintain electric or hydraulic freight or passenger elevators, escalators, or dumbwaiters. **Education and Training:** Long-term on-the-job training. **Skills:** Math—Medium. English—Medium. Science—Medium. **Yearly Earnings:** $$$$ **Job Growth:** ★★★ **Yearly Openings:** 🧍

Frame Wirers, Central Office. Connect wires from telephone lines and cables to distributing frames in telephone company central office, using soldering iron and other hand tools. **Education and Training:** Postsecondary career and technical education. **Skills:** Math—Low. English—Low. Science—Medium. **Yearly Earnings:** $$$$ **Job Growth:** ★ **Yearly Openings:** 🧍🧍

Home Appliance Installers. Install household appliances, such as refrigerators, washing machines, and stoves, in customers' homes. **Education and Training:** Long-term on-the-job training. **Skills:** Math—Medium. English—Medium. Science—Medium. **Yearly Earnings:** $$ **Job Growth:** ★★ **Yearly Openings:** 🧍

Home Appliance Repairers. Repair, adjust, or install all types of electric or gas household appliances, such as refrigerators, washers, dryers, and ovens. **Education and Training:** Postsecondary career and technical education. **Skills:** Math—Medium. English—Medium. Science—Medium. **Yearly Earnings:** $$ **Job Growth:** ★★ **Yearly Openings:** 🧍

Office Machine and Cash Register Servicers. Repair and service office machines, such as adding, accounting, calculating, duplicating, and typewriting machines. Includes the repair of manual, electrical, and electronic office machines. **Education and Training:** Long-term on-the-job training. **Skills:** Math—Medium. English—Medium. Science—Medium. **Yearly Earnings:** $$$ **Job Growth:** ★★★ **Yearly Openings:** 🧍🧍🧍

Radio Mechanics. Test or repair mobile or stationary radio transmitting and receiving equipment and two-way radio communications systems used in ship-to-shore communications and found in service and emergency vehicles. **Education and Training:** Postsecondary career and technical education. **Skills:** Math—Low. English—Medium. Science—Medium. **Yearly Earnings:** $$$ **Job Growth:** ★ **Yearly Openings:** 🧍

Signal and Track Switch Repairers. Install, inspect, test, maintain, or repair electric gate crossings, signals, signal equipment, track switches, section lines, or intercommunications systems within a railroad system. **Education and Training:** Postsecondary career and technical education. **Skills:** Math—Medium. English—Medium. Science—Medium. **Yearly Earnings:** $$$$ **Job Growth:** ★★ **Yearly Openings:** No data available.

Station Installers and Repairers, Telephone. Install and repair telephone station equipment, such as telephones, coin collectors, telephone booths, and switching-key equipment. **Education and Training:** Postsecondary career and technical education. **Skills:** Math—Medium. English—Medium. Science—Medium. **Yearly Earnings:** $$$$ **Job Growth:** ★ **Yearly Openings:** 🧍🧍

Telecommunications Equipment Installers and Repairers, Except Line Installers. Set up, rearrange, or remove switching and dialing equipment used in central offices. Service or repair telephones and other communication equipment on customers' property. May install equipment in new locations or install wiring and telephone jacks in buildings under construction. **Education and Training:** Postsecondary career and technical education. **Skills:** Math—Medium. English—Medium. Science—Medium. **Yearly Earnings:** $$$$ **Job Growth:** ★ **Yearly Openings:** 🧍🧍

Telecommunications Facility Examiners. Examine telephone transmission facilities to determine equipment requirements for providing subscribers with new or additional telephone services. **Education and Training:** Long-term on-the-job training. **Skills:** Math—Medium. English—Medium. Science—Medium. **Yearly Earnings:** $$$$ **Job Growth:** ★ **Yearly Openings:** 🧍🧍

Telecommunications Line Installers and Repairers. String and repair telephone and television cable, including fiber optics and other equipment for transmitting messages or television programming. **Education and Training:** Long-term on-the-job training. **Skills:** Math—Medium. English—Medium. Science—Medium. **Yearly Earnings:** $$$ **Job Growth:** ★★★★ **Yearly Openings:** 🧍🧍

Transformer Repairers. Clean and repair electrical transformers. **Education and Training:** Long-term on-the-job training. **Skills:** Math—Low. English—Low. Science—Medium. **Yearly Earnings:** $$$ **Job Growth:** ★★ **Yearly Openings:** 🧍

MECHANICAL WORK

These workers install, service, and repair various kinds of machinery. Some machinery is large, such as the bodies and engines of cars, trucks, buses, airplanes, and ships; furnaces and air conditioners; office machines; and home appliances. Others are small, such as locks, watches, medical instruments, power tools, and musical instruments. These workers are hired by manufacturers, service companies, and businesses that use machines.

Aircraft Body and Bonded Structure Repairers. Repair body or structure of aircraft according to specifications. **Education and Training:** Postsecondary career and technical education. **Skills:** Math—Medium. English—Medium. Science—Medium. **Yearly Earnings:** $$$$ **Job Growth:** ★★★ **Yearly Openings:** 🧍🧍🧍

Aircraft Engine Specialists. Repair and maintain the operating condition of aircraft engines. Includes helicopter engine mechanics. **Education and Training:** Postsecondary career and technical education. **Skills:** Math—Medium. English—Medium. Science—Medium. **Yearly Earnings:** $$$$ **Job Growth:** ★★★ **Yearly Openings:** 🚶🚶🚶

Aircraft Mechanics and Service Technicians. Diagnose, adjust, repair, or overhaul aircraft engines and assemblies, such as hydraulic and pneumatic systems. **Education and Training:** Postsecondary career and technical education. **Skills:** Math—Medium. English—Medium. Science—Medium. **Yearly Earnings:** $$$$ **Job Growth:** ★★★ **Yearly Openings:** 🚶🚶🚶

Airframe-and-Power-Plant Mechanics. Inspect, test, repair, maintain, and service aircraft. **Education and Training:** Postsecondary career and technical education. **Skills:** Math—Medium. English—Medium. Science—Medium. **Yearly Earnings:** $$$$ **Job Growth:** ★★★ **Yearly Openings:** 🚶🚶🚶

Automotive Body and Related Repairers. Repair and refinish automotive vehicle bodies and straighten vehicle frames. **Education and Training:** Long-term on-the-job training. **Skills:** Math—Medium. English—Medium. Science—Medium. **Yearly Earnings:** $$$ **Job Growth:** ★★★ **Yearly Openings:** 🚶🚶🚶

Automotive Glass Installers and Repairers. Replace or repair broken windshields and window glass in motor vehicles. **Education and Training:** Long-term on-the-job training. **Skills:** Math—Medium. English—Medium. Science—Medium. **Yearly Earnings:** $$ **Job Growth:** ★★★ **Yearly Openings:** 🚶

Automotive Master Mechanics. Repair automobiles, trucks, buses, and other vehicles. Master mechanics repair almost any part on the vehicle or specialize in the transmission system. **Education and Training:** Postsecondary career and technical education. **Skills:** Math—Medium. English—Medium. Science—Medium. **Yearly Earnings:** $$ **Job Growth:** ★★★ **Yearly Openings:** 🚶🚶🚶🚶🚶

Automotive Service Technicians and Mechanics. Diagnose, adjust, repair, or overhaul automotive vehicles. **Education and Training:** Postsecondary career and technical education. **Skills:** Math—Medium. English—Medium. Science—Medium. **Yearly Earnings:** $$ **Job Growth:** ★★★ **Yearly Openings:** 🚶🚶🚶🚶🚶

Automotive Specialty Technicians. Repair only one system or component on a vehicle, such as brakes, suspension, or radiator. **Education and Training:** Postsecondary career and technical education. **Skills:** Math—Medium. English—Medium. Science—Medium. **Yearly Earnings:** $$ **Job Growth:** ★★★ **Yearly Openings:** 🚶🚶🚶🚶🚶

Bicycle Repairers. Repair and service bicycles. **Education and Training:** Moderate-term on-the-job training. **Skills:** Math—Low. English—Medium. Science—Low. **Yearly Earnings:** $ **Job Growth:** ★★★ **Yearly Openings:** 🚶

Bridge and Lock Tenders. Operate and tend bridges, canal locks, and lighthouses to permit marine passage on inland waterways, near shores, and at danger points in waterway passages. May supervise such operations. Includes drawbridge operators, lock tenders and operators, and slip bridge operators. **Education and Training:** Short-term on-the-job training. **Skills:** Math—Medium. English—Medium. Science—Medium. **Yearly Earnings:** $$$ **Job Growth:** ★ **Yearly Openings:** 🚶

Bus and Truck Mechanics and Diesel Engine Specialists. Diagnose, adjust, repair, or overhaul trucks, buses, and all types of diesel engines. Includes mechanics working primarily with automobile diesel engines. **Education and Training:** Postsecondary career and technical education. **Skills:** Math—Medium. English—Low. Science—Medium. **Yearly Earnings:** $$$ **Job Growth:** ★★★ **Yearly Openings:** 🚶🚶🚶

Camera and Photographic Equipment Repairers. Repair and adjust cameras and photographic equipment, including commercial video and motion picture camera equipment. **Education and Training:** Moderate-term on-the-job training. **Skills:** Math—Medium. English—Medium. Science—Medium. **Yearly Earnings:** $$ **Job Growth:** ★ **Yearly Openings:** 🚶

Coin, Vending, and Amusement Machine Servicers and Repairers. Install, service, adjust, or repair coin, vending, or amusement machines, including video games, jukeboxes, pinball machines, or slot machines. **Education and Training:** Moderate-term on-the-job training. **Skills:** Math—Medium. English—Medium. Science—Medium. **Yearly Earnings:** $$ **Job Growth:** ★★★ **Yearly Openings:** 🚶

Control and Valve Installers and Repairers, Except Mechanical Door. Install, repair, and maintain mechanical regulating and controlling devices, such as electric meters, gas regulators, thermostats, safety and flow valves, and other mechanical governors. **Education and Training:** Moderate-term on-the-job training. **Skills:** Math—Medium. English—Medium. Science—Medium. **Yearly Earnings:** $$$$ **Job Growth:** ★ **Yearly Openings:** 🚶

Farm Equipment Mechanics. Diagnose, adjust, repair, or overhaul farm machinery and vehicles, such as tractors, harvesters, dairy equipment, and irrigation systems. **Education and Training:** Postsecondary career and technical education. **Skills:** Math—Medium. English—Medium. Science—Medium. **Yearly Earnings:** $$ **Job Growth:** ★ **Yearly Openings:** 🚶

Gas Appliance Repairers. Repair and install gas appliances and equipment, such as ovens, dryers, and hot water heaters. **Education and Training:** Long-term on-the-job training. **Skills:** Math—Medium. English—Medium. Science—Medium. **Yearly Earnings:** $$ **Job Growth:** ★★ **Yearly Openings:** 🚶

Hand and Portable Power Tool Repairers. Repair and adjust hand and power tools. **Education and Training:** Moderate-term on-the-job training. **Skills:** Math—Low. English—Medium. Science—Medium. **Yearly Earnings:** $$$ **Job Growth:** ★★ **Yearly Openings:** 🚶

Heating and Air Conditioning Mechanics. Install, service, and repair heating and air conditioning systems in residences and commercial establishments. **Education and Training:** Long-term on-the-job training. **Skills:** Math—Medium. English—Medium. Science—Medium. **Yearly Earnings:** $$$ **Job Growth:** ★★★★ **Yearly Openings:** 🧍🧍🧍

Heating, Air Conditioning, and Refrigeration Mechanics and Installers. Install or repair heating, central air conditioning, or refrigeration systems, including oil burners, hot-air furnaces, and heating stoves. **Education and Training:** Long-term on-the-job training. **Skills:** Math—Medium. English—Medium. Science—Medium. **Yearly Earnings:** $$$ **Job Growth:** ★★★★ **Yearly Openings:** 🧍🧍🧍

Helpers—Electricians. Help electricians by performing duties of lesser skill. Duties include using, supplying, or holding materials or tools and cleaning work area and equipment. **Education and Training:** Short-term on-the-job training. **Skills:** Math—Medium. English—Low. Science—Medium. **Yearly Earnings:** $$ **Job Growth:** ★★★ **Yearly Openings:** 🧍🧍🧍

Helpers—Installation, Maintenance, and Repair Workers. Help installation, maintenance, and repair workers in maintenance, parts replacement, and repair of vehicles, industrial machinery, and electrical and electronic equipment. Perform duties such as furnishing tools, materials, and supplies to other workers; cleaning work area, machines, and tools; and holding materials or tools for other workers. **Education and Training:** Short-term on-the-job training. **Skills:** Math—Low. English—Low. Science—Medium. **Yearly Earnings:** $$ **Job Growth:** ★★★ **Yearly Openings:** 🧍🧍🧍

Industrial Machinery Mechanics. Repair, install, adjust, or maintain industrial production and processing machinery or refinery and pipeline distribution systems. **Education and Training:** Long-term on-the-job training. **Skills:** Math—Medium. English—Medium. Science—Medium. **Yearly Earnings:** $$$ **Job Growth:** ★★ **Yearly Openings:** 🧍🧍

Keyboard Instrument Repairers and Tuners. Repair, adjust, refinish, and tune musical keyboard instruments. **Education and Training:** Long-term on-the-job training. **Skills:** Math—Medium. English—Low. Science—Medium. **Yearly Earnings:** $$$ **Job Growth:** ★★ **Yearly Openings:** 🧍

Locksmiths and Safe Repairers. Repair and open locks, make keys, change locks and safe combinations, and install and repair safes. **Education and Training:** Moderate-term on-the-job training. **Skills:** Math—Low. English—Medium. Science—Medium. **Yearly Earnings:** $$ **Job Growth:** ★★ **Yearly Openings:** 🧍

Maintenance and Repair Workers, General. Perform work involving the skills of two or more maintenance or craft occupations to keep machines, mechanical equipment, or the structure of an establishment in repair. Duties may involve pipe fitting; boiler making; insulating; welding; machining; carpentry; repairing electrical or mechanical equipment; installing, aligning, and balancing new equipment; and repairing buildings, floors, or stairs. **Education and Training:** Long-term on-the-job training. **Skills:** Math—Medium. English—Medium. Science—Medium. **Yearly Earnings:** $$ **Job Growth:** ★★ **Yearly Openings:** 🧍🧍🧍🧍🧍

Maintenance Workers, Machinery. Lubricate machinery, change parts, or perform other routine machinery maintenance. **Education and Training:** Long-term on-the-job training. **Skills:** Math—Medium. English—Medium. Science—Medium. **Yearly Earnings:** $$$ **Job Growth:** ★★ **Yearly Openings:** 🧍

Mechanical Door Repairers. Install, service, or repair opening and closing mechanisms of automatic doors and hydraulic door closers. Includes garage door mechanics. **Education and Training:** Moderate-term on-the-job training. **Skills:** Math—Medium. English—Low. Science—Medium. **Yearly Earnings:** $$ **Job Growth:** ★★★ **Yearly Openings:** 🧍

Medical Appliance Technicians. Construct, fit, maintain, or repair medical supportive devices, such as braces, artificial limbs, joints, arch supports, and other surgical and medical appliances. **Education and Training:** Long-term on-the-job training. **Skills:** Math—Medium. English—Medium. Science—Medium. **Yearly Earnings:** $$ **Job Growth:** ★★★ **Yearly Openings:** 🧍

Medical Equipment Repairers. Test, adjust, or repair biomedical or electromedical equipment. **Education and Training:** Moderate-term on-the-job training. **Skills:** Math—Medium. English—Medium. Science—Medium. **Yearly Earnings:** $$$ **Job Growth:** ★★★ **Yearly Openings:** 🧍

Meter Mechanics. Test, adjust, and repair gas, water, and oil meters. **Education and Training:** Moderate-term on-the-job training. **Skills:** Math—Medium. English—Medium. Science—Medium. **Yearly Earnings:** $$$$ **Job Growth:** ★ **Yearly Openings:** 🧍

Millwrights. Install, dismantle, or move machinery and heavy equipment according to layout plans, blueprints, or other drawings. **Education and Training:** Long-term on-the-job training. **Skills:** Math—Medium. English—Medium. Science—Medium. **Yearly Earnings:** $$$$ **Job Growth:** ★★ **Yearly Openings:** 🧍🧍

Mobile Heavy Equipment Mechanics, Except Engines. Diagnose, adjust, repair, or overhaul mobile mechanical, hydraulic, and pneumatic equipment, such as cranes, bulldozers, graders, and conveyors, used in construction, logging, and surface mining. **Education and Training:** Postsecondary career and technical education. **Skills:** Math—Medium. English—Low. Science—Medium. **Yearly Earnings:** $$$ **Job Growth:** ★★★ **Yearly Openings:** 🧍🧍🧍

Motorboat Mechanics. Repair and adjust electrical and mechanical equipment of gasoline or diesel-powered inboard or inboard-outboard boat engines. **Education and Training:** Long-term on-the-job training. **Skills:** Math—Low. English—Medium. Science—Medium. **Yearly Earnings:** $$ **Job Growth:** ★★ **Yearly Openings:** 🧍

Motorcycle Mechanics. Diagnose, adjust, repair, or overhaul motorcycles, scooters, mopeds, dirt bikes, or similar motorized vehicles. **Education and Training:** Long-term on-the-job training. **Skills:** Math—Low. English—Medium. Science—Medium. **Yearly Earnings:** $$ **Job Growth:** ★★ **Yearly Openings:** 🧍

Musical Instrument Repairers and Tuners. Repair percussion, stringed, reed, or wind instruments. May specialize in one area, such as piano tuning. **Education and Training:** Long-term on-the-job training. **Skills:** Math—Medium. English—Medium. Science—Medium. **Yearly Earnings:** $$$ **Job Growth:** ★★ **Yearly Openings:** 🧍

Ophthalmic Laboratory Technicians. Cut, grind, and polish eyeglasses, contact lenses, or other precision optical elements. Assemble and mount lenses into frames or process other optical elements. **Education and Training:** Moderate-term on-the-job training. **Skills:** Math—Medium. English—Medium. Science—Medium. **Yearly Earnings:** $$ **Job Growth:** ★★ **Yearly Openings:** 🧍

Optical Instrument Assemblers. Assemble optical instruments, such as telescopes, level-transits, and gunsights. **Education and Training:** Moderate-term on-the-job training. **Skills:** Math—Medium. English—Medium. Science—Medium. **Yearly Earnings:** $$ **Job Growth:** ★★ **Yearly Openings:** 🧍

Outdoor Power Equipment and Other Small Engine Mechanics. Diagnose, adjust, repair, or overhaul small engines used to power lawn mowers, chain saws, and related equipment. **Education and Training:** Moderate-term on-the-job training. **Skills:** Math—Low. English—Medium. Science—Medium. **Yearly Earnings:** $$ **Job Growth:** ★★ **Yearly Openings:** 🧍🧍

Painters, Transportation Equipment. Operate or tend painting machines to paint surfaces of transportation equipment, such as automobiles, buses, trucks, trains, boats, and airplanes. **Education and Training:** Moderate-term on-the-job training. **Skills:** Math—Medium. English—Medium. Science—Medium. **Yearly Earnings:** $$$ **Job Growth:** ★★★ **Yearly Openings:** 🧍🧍

Percussion Instrument Repairers and Tuners. Repair and tune musical percussion instruments. **Education and Training:** Long-term on-the-job training. **Skills:** Math—Medium. English—Low. Science—Medium. **Yearly Earnings:** $$$ **Job Growth:** ★★ **Yearly Openings:** 🧍

Rail Car Repairers. Diagnose, adjust, repair, or overhaul railroad rolling stock, mine cars, or mass transit rail cars. **Education and Training:** Long-term on-the-job training. **Skills:** Math—Medium. English—Medium. Science—Medium. **Yearly Earnings:** $$$ **Job Growth:** ★ **Yearly Openings:** 🧍

Railroad Inspectors. Inspect railroad equipment, roadbed, and track to ensure safe transport of people or cargo. **Education and Training:** Work experience in a related occupation. **Skills:** Math—Medium. English—Medium. Science—Medium. **Yearly Earnings:** $$$$ **Job Growth:** ★★★ **Yearly Openings:** 🧍

Recreational Vehicle Service Technicians. Diagnose, inspect, adjust, repair, or overhaul recreational vehicles, including travel trailers. May specialize in maintaining gas, electrical, hydraulic, plumbing, or chassis/towing systems as well as repairing generators, appliances, and interior components. **Education and Training:** Long-term on-the-job training. **Skills:** Math—Medium. English—Medium. Science—Medium. **Yearly Earnings:** $$ **Job Growth:** ★★★★ **Yearly Openings:** 🚹

Reed or Wind Instrument Repairers and Tuners. Repair, adjust, refinish, and tune musical reed and wind instruments. **Education and Training:** Long-term on-the-job training. **Skills:** Math—Low. English—Low. Science—Medium. **Yearly Earnings:** $$$ **Job Growth:** ★★ **Yearly Openings:** 🚹

Refrigeration Mechanics. Install and repair industrial and commercial refrigerating systems. **Education and Training:** Long-term on-the-job training. **Skills:** Math—Medium. English—Medium. Science—Medium. **Yearly Earnings:** $$$ **Job Growth:** ★★★★ **Yearly Openings:** 🚹🚹🚹

Stringed Instrument Repairers and Tuners. Repair, adjust, refinish, and tune musical stringed instruments. **Education and Training:** Long-term on-the-job training. **Skills:** Math—Low. English—Medium. Science—Medium. **Yearly Earnings:** $$$ **Job Growth:** ★★ **Yearly Openings:** 🚹

Tire Repairers and Changers. Repair and replace tires. **Education and Training:** Short-term on-the-job training. **Skills:** Math—Low. English—Low. Science—Medium. **Yearly Earnings:** $ **Job Growth:** ★★ **Yearly Openings:** 🚹🚹🚹

Valve and Regulator Repairers. Test, repair, and adjust mechanical regulators and valves. **Education and Training:** Moderate-term on-the-job training. **Skills:** Math—Medium. English—Medium. Science—Medium. **Yearly Earnings:** $$$$ **Job Growth:** ★ **Yearly Openings:** 🚹

Watch Repairers. Repair, clean, and adjust mechanisms of timing instruments, such as watches and clocks. **Education and Training:** Long-term on-the-job training. **Skills:** Math—Medium. English—Medium. Science—Medium. **Yearly Earnings:** $$ **Job Growth:** ★★ **Yearly Openings:** 🚹

Exploring Careers:

Construction, Mining, and Drilling

Start Your Journey Through Careers Related to

CONSTRUCTION, MINING, AND DRILLING

Careers in this area suit people interested in assembling components of buildings and other structures or in using mechanical devices to drill or excavate.

EXPLORING CAREER CLUES

Your interests give important clues for exploring career options. Think about your interests to learn if jobs in the Construction, Mining, and Drilling interest area may be worth further exploration.

Do you like the school subjects related to the Construction, Mining, and Drilling interest area? Here are some examples of related subjects:

- Math
- Algebra
- Geometry
- Science
- Geology
- Physics
- Industrial or technology education
- Physical education

Do you like the free-time activities related to the Construction, Mining, and Drilling interest area? Here are some examples of related free-time activities:

- Building model airplanes, cars, or boats
- Building stage sets for school or other amateur theater
- Building cabinets, furniture, and other items
- Carving wood
- Building robots, electronic devices, or working models
- Helping with home repairs and home improvements
- Painting or refinishing furniture or other items
- Taking apart or repairing small appliances and devices

- Helping friends and others with math
- Reading about electronics, woodworking, construction, and home repair
- Watching television shows about do-it-yourself projects
- Collecting and studying rocks or minerals

EXPLORING JOB GROUPS

Jobs related to the Construction, Mining, and Drilling interest area fit into four groups. Read through the list to see which groups sound interesting to you.

- Managerial Work in Construction, Mining, and Drilling
- Construction
- Mining and Drilling
- Hands-on Work in Construction, Extraction, and Maintenance

EXPLORING CAREER POSSIBILITIES

You can satisfy your interest in the Construction, Mining, and Drilling area through jobs that involve working on buildings and other structures or that involve drilling and excavation. Here are a few examples of career possibilities:

If construction interests you, you can find fulfillment in the many building projects that are underway at all times. You can play a direct role in putting up and finishing buildings through working in plumbing, carpentry, masonry, painting, or roofing.

You may like working at a minefield or oil field, operating the powerful drilling or digging equipment.

Turn the page to meet people working in the Construction, Mining, and Drilling interest area→

PROFILE

Andy Jacobs–Brickmason

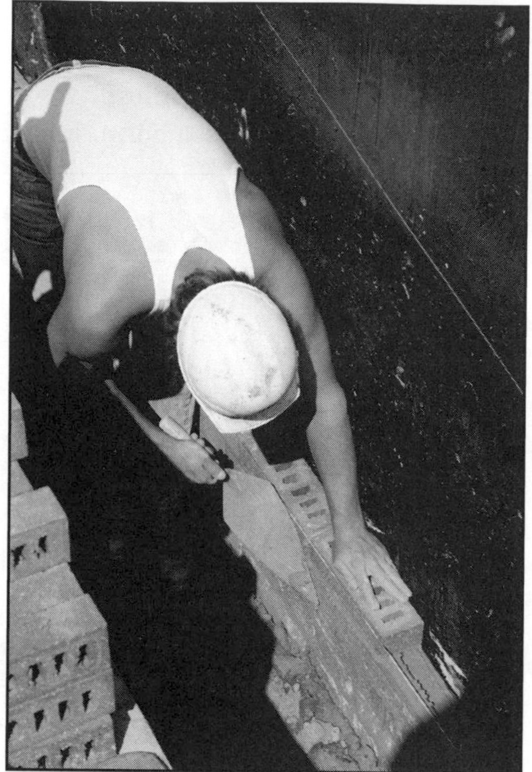
Using brick and mortar, Andy builds a wall according to a blueprint.

Andy Jacobs walked onto the site and saw Joe Lightfoot, the brickmason supervisor, examining some blueprints. "Good morning," Andy said.

The supervisor looked up, glanced at his watch, and said, "I'm glad you got here early. You can help me lay out these walls."

Andy is an apprentice brickmason. At twenty-two, he is more than halfway through his three-year apprenticeship program. The program has two parts: on-the-job training every day and classroom instruction two nights a week.

Brickmasons–who are often referred to simply as bricklayers–build and repair walls, floors, fireplaces, chimneys, and other structures with brick, precast masonry panels, concrete block, and other masonry materials.

Becoming an Apprentice

"I feel lucky to have been accepted for apprenticeship," Andy said. "First, I took an aptitude test. Then I interviewed with the union apprenticeship committee." The committee had asked about his school record and his interests. The last question had been the hardest: What makes you think you'd be a good bricklayer?

Andy told them he was a hard worker but also fast and careful. He said that he liked physical work, enjoyed building things, and wanted to learn

a trade. He also told the committee that he liked the idea that his bricklaying work would last for many years.

Andy had passed the interview with flying colors, but even then he had to wait nearly a year before there was an opening. "The apprenticeship committee accepts people into the program only a few at a time," Andy said. "It depends on the amount of construction activity in the area and the need to train more bricklayers. The committee tries to train only as many bricklayers as there are jobs."

Andy was pleased with the way things were going. "I am learning a skill and getting paid while learning," he said. Every six months since he had started, the apprenticeship committee had examined his progress.

Each time, they'd promoted him and raised his pay. When he had first started the program, he had been paid only about half the hourly wage for experienced bricklayers, but the amount had been increasing steadily.

"With the apprenticeship committee constantly reviewing my progress, I can't waste time on the job, skip classes, or be late for work," Andy said.

On the Job: Planning and Precision

That morning, Andy and the other bricklayers in the crew were to begin laying the exterior walls of a high-rise apartment building. Andy had learned long ago that there's more to being a bricklayer than just slapping bricks into place. "Bricklaying," he said, "is a precise activity. There is a lot of measuring to do before the first brick is laid."

The bricklayer supervisor must study the architect's blueprints and compare the dimensions indicated to the actual surface on which they're working. "The blueprints tell the length, width, and height of the walls to be built and the kinds of materials to be used," Andy said. Blueprints also show the size and locations of doors and windows, the pattern in which the bricks or blocks are to be placed (known as the pattern bond), the number of units needed for a row or "course" of brick or block, and the size of the joints between units.

"The bricklayers need all of this information before they can begin laying bricks or blocks," Andy explained.

Andy walked over to look at the architect's blueprints with Joe. Right away, he saw that the wall they were about to build was a composite wall.

This meant that the wall would be made of row upon row of cement block faced with rows of brick. The brick facing and block backing would be bonded with metal wall ties at regular intervals for added strength. The architect had specified exactly what types of brick, block, and wall ties to use.

The first step in laying out such walls is marking the dimensions on the foundation.

"The first step in laying out such walls is marking the dimensions on the foundation," said Andy. Andy and Joe began measuring in from one of the corners of the foundation. They checked the dimensions of the foundation against the dimensions in the blueprints.

"Let's start laying the bricks out dry," Joe said.

The two bricklayers laid a course of bricks without mortar in order to space them correctly. Then Joe marked spaces for doors and windows to make sure that the units would be placed properly around those openings to allow for a strong bond.

Andy got up from his kneeling position and looked at the layout. "It looks pretty good," he said. Joe nodded.

By now the other bricklayers had arrived. In addition to Andy and Joe, there were six bricklayers and eight helpers, called mason tenders or hod carriers.

"You'll be working with Fred Oberman," Joe told Andy. "He's been doing this for a long time, and he'll be able to help you out if you have any problems." Joe made sure that all the bricklayers saw the markings for the doors and windows.

Laying the Bricks

A mason tender brought a batch of freshly mixed mortar, and the bricklayers picked up their trowels. Fred moved to one of the corners. He cut into a pan of wet mortar with his trowel, spread the mortar thickly on the foundation surface, and then pressed a brick into place.

He picked up another brick, "buttered" one end of it with mortar, and pressed it into place next to the first brick. After placing each brick, he used his trowel to cut off the excess mortar that had been squeezed out from the brick joints.

Andy watched Fred, admiring the single flowing motion with which he loaded the trowel and spread the mortar. Then Andy stepped up and began helping Fred. Together, they built the outside corner of brick, and inside it they built another one of block. The other bricklayers had split up into smaller groups and had moved to other sections of the building. There, they were building corners just as Fred and Andy were doing.

The sight of the finished brickwork made him feel good.

It didn't take long for the crew to build the corners to the desired height. Then they began to lay the brick wall between the corners. First they stretched a line between the corner units at the top of the first course. The line was a guide for keeping the bricks all at an even height, as well as for keeping the row straight. Then they began laying the first course of bricks. On top of the first course they laid a second, then a third, and so on until the wall was six courses high.

The motions involved in laying brick are repetitive, and soon Andy was moving at a quick pace.

Proud of His Work

When they finished the sixth course of the brick wall, Andy stopped and examined the work he and Fred had done so far. "My arms and back are tired from stooping over and lifting the bricks," Andy said. "But I'm happy with our work on the wall."

The sight of the finished brickwork made him feel good. The mortar joints between courses still needed to be finished, so Andy picked up a tool called a jointer and ran it along the edge of each joint. The jointer left an indentation in the mortar that made the joints look much neater than before.

The sun was strong now. Andy's shirt was soaked with perspiration. Minutes later, Joe called out, "Let's break for lunch. You have half an hour."

He walked over to Andy and Fred and examined the work they had just completed. "When we get back," Fred said, "we'll lay the block backing inside the brickwork."

Andy nodded. Then he looked over at Fred, who said, "Let's find some shade. The way you've been working, you must be pretty hot and tired yourself. You're not so bad, you know."

"Thanks," Andy replied. The two bricklayers walked off to pick up their lunch bags.

PROFILE

Luis Garza—Carpenter

"Hey, get that other clamp over there, will you?" Luis called. He guided a panel of wood into place as the crane swung it toward him. Steve wedged another panel into place while Brenda brought the metal clamp, placed it on the form, and tightened it.

The column form they were building consisted of four wooden panels clamped together at opposite corners. They worked in silence for a few minutes, placing the clamps about a foot apart all the way to the top. At last, the form stood secure–a tall, boxlike structure about sixteen feet high and four feet square.

Luis has always liked building things. "In high school, I built the props and sets for plays."

From the Ground Up

Luis Garza and Steve MacPherson are carpenters. Brenda Patel is a carpenter's helper. The work they were doing–building concrete forms–is called rough carpentry. The forms are molds into which wet concrete can be poured to create the large concrete columns that will support the ceiling of a parking garage.

In another eight months, there would be a large office building here, with a two-level underground parking garage. Tall buildings require a lot of concrete, and wherever there's concrete to be poured, carpenters are on the job, building the forms that provide the shape for it.

Wherever there's concrete to be poured, carpenters are on the job, building the forms that provide the shape for it.

The other workers on the construction site that day were mostly cement masons or rodbusters. The rodbusters worked with the form carpenters, preparing for the pouring of the concrete. Their job is to install the steel rods that will give added strength to each column. When they finished, the spot would be ready for the carpenters to build the form around the rods.

Luis and his coworkers were working outside, in the center of the second level of the parking garage. Because there weren't any columns up yet in their area, there was no concrete slab above to serve as a roof. Luckily, it was a sunny spring day. In bad weather, however, carpenters may lose work time.

Moving Right Along

Luis, Steve, and Brenda would spend most of the day putting up column forms. The next day, they would be doing something different. The parking garage was in many different stages of construction, most of which needed some kind of rough carpentry.

At one end of the garage, the second level was just being started. Other carpenters were laying the plywood decking onto which the wet concrete would be poured to form the second-level slab floor.

At the other end, things were farther along. The slab floor for the second level had been laid, and columns were in place. Another crew of carpenters was busy putting up the lumber to support or brace the plywood decking for the floor. To do this, the carpenters nailed or braced pieces of lumber called jacks, ribs, and stringers to form an overhead frame on which they could nail the sheets of plywood.

Maybe we'll be working over there by the end of the week, Luis thought. It wasn't exactly his favorite task. Putting up ribs and stringers could be dangerous.

Putting up ribs and stringers could be dangerous. Carpenters have to be especially careful to avoid falling.

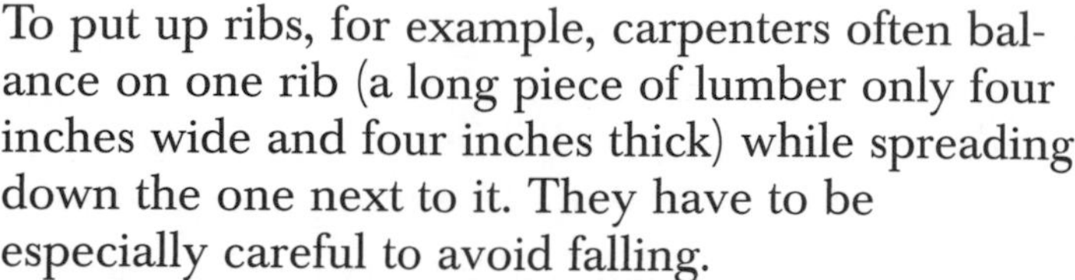

To put up ribs, for example, carpenters often balance on one rib (a long piece of lumber only four inches wide and four inches thick) while spreading down the one next to it. They have to be especially careful to avoid falling.

Luis imagined he'd likely spend most of the next day stripping column forms, which meant removing the forms from columns in which the concrete had begun to set. The wooden forms stuck tightly to the concrete that had hardened against them, and Luis would need to use leverage and strength to get them off. Once he had stripped a form, he would coat the inside with form oil. This would help the forms separate more easily from the hardened concrete the next time they were used.

As soon as he finished one form, Luis moved on and began building the next one. "I like to keep busy," Luis said. "And I know it keeps my supervisor happy." Even though there were plenty of job opportunities for carpenters, it sure couldn't hurt his job security to keep up a good pace.

How to Build a Career

Even though there were plenty of job opportunities for carpenters, it sure couldn't hurt his job security to keep up a good pace.

"Hey, you don't get tired very easily, do you?" said Steve. "Where'd you learn carpentry, anyway? You're good. I know you didn't go through a training program like I did."

Luis smiled at the compliment. Carpentry was something he'd always been good at and enjoyed doing.

"Well, I just picked it up," he began. "As a kid, I was always building things. Then, in high school, I built the props and the sets for school plays. The more carpentry work I did, the more I liked it.

"Right after high school I applied for a job with a small construction company that needed carpenters pretty badly. Since then I've gained experience and picked up new skills by working on different kinds of construction jobs."

Luis thought about that for a minute. Carpenters had been on the site almost since construction began. When the form work came to a finish, most of the form carpenters would move on to another site to begin the same type of work on another project. However, Luis wanted to stay on at the site and do some of the other necessary carpentry jobs: installing drywall, for example.

"As a kid, I was always building things. Then, in high school, I built the props and the sets for school plays. The more carpentry work I did, the more I liked it."

Luis knew that to stay employed year-round, he needed to be versatile. He had made it a point to learn to handle as many different kinds of carpentry work as possible. During the five years he had worked as a carpenter, he learned how to install acoustical tile and drywall and how to hang doors. These skills, he believed, would give him an advantage over some of the other carpenters.

"So, do you think you're going to stay on in construction?" Steve asked as they moved over to another column location.

"Are you reading my mind?" Luis laughed. "I sure will. Maybe someday I'll have a contracting business of my own."

"Great idea," said Steve. "Well, you know what you're doing, that's for sure."

"Thanks!"

Luis smiled, realizing that he had earned the respect of yet another fellow worker. As Steve walked away, Luis thought, *After all, doing a good job is what counts.*

PROFILE

Louis Sowinski—Electrician

Under a September sky, leaves are turning to colors like copper and brass. The building trade is rushing to finish its houses before winter.

Louis Sowinski, master electrician, heads to the union local for an assignment. He checks in first thing each day. "I've been a professional electrician for the union for twelve years," he said, filling out a referral slip.

"When times turn slow, the first electrician to get laid off is the first electrician hired when a job comes along. You can't take just any job you want.

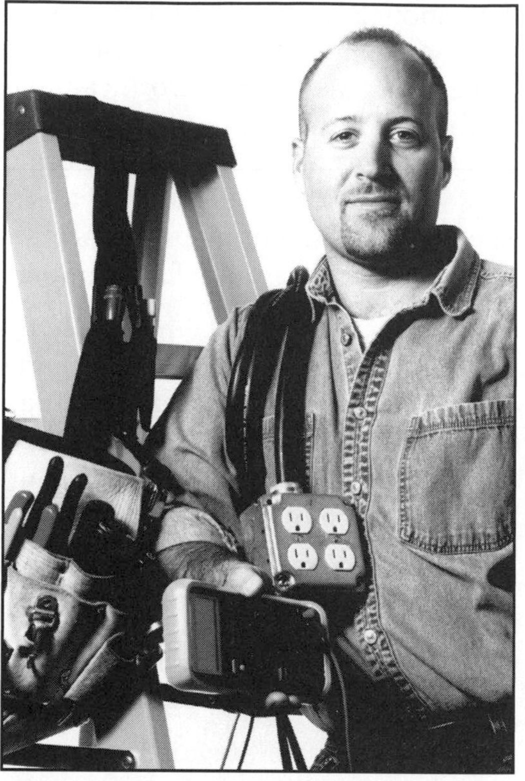

Louis becomes a detective when a switch, fixture, or outlet isn't working.

"But we do have the option to pass up a job if it will last only a few days and you want to hang in there and wait for a longer job."

Going Where the Work Is

A contractor estimates how long an electrical installation job will take and gives this information to the union.

One electrician can pipe an average-sized house in about a week, according to Louis. "The job includes turning the service on, installing a breaker box panel, piping through to all the outlets, pulling wire through, and hooking up circuitry to the plugs, receptacles, and switches."

The electrician adds the fixtures last. Finally, different agencies inspect the work for safety and compliance with local code.

The electrician brings only the necessary tools. It's up to the contractor to acquire all the materials–the pipe, boxes, and connectors.

"My tools aren't terribly expensive–some wires, pliers, fuse pullers. But the continuity and voltage testers get quite a workout and occasionally need replacing."

> *"The job includes turning the service on, installing a breaker box panel, piping through to all the outlets, pulling wire through, and hooking up circuitry."*

Louis gets an assignment today. In an established neighborhood, a new ranch house is going up. The construction workers on the site work at a steady pace, hoping to finish while the days remain warm.

Louis refers to the blueprint, which he needs to find out where the outlets go and what type of switches to install.

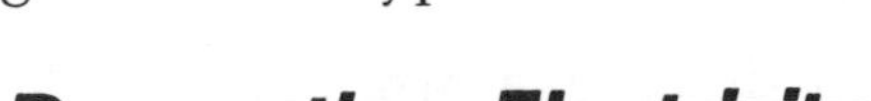

Respecting Electricity

Today, Louis sees that another electrician has already installed a receptacle. Is the circuit on? With a voltage tester, Louis checks the receptacle for power. Is the receptacle grounded? Louis inserts one probe of the voltage tester into the ground slot and the other into the thin slots, one after the other. The tester bulb should light up when the probe is in the "hot slot." If it doesn't, it's not grounded and Louis must correct it.

"You have to be careful in this business. Mistakes can be deadly," Louis said. "I always turn the power off if I'm standing in water or if my work area is wet. My tools have insulated handles. I work on wooden ladders. I wear rubber-soled tennis shoes. I handle only one wire at a time if I can.

"One time I asked my on-site supervisor–who wasn't an electrician–to turn off the switch so I could work on a malfunctioning conveyor. He said he would, but he didn't. When I touched the mechanism, 440 volts knocked me to the floor. That taught me *never* to trust anyone except myself to turn off the electricity.

"You've got to have a respectful attitude. If it's a complicated job, I'll sit back and study it first."

Louis pauses thoughtfully, raises his hard hat, and scratches his forehead with a heavily lined, leathery hand–a hand that's been hefting cable and pliers for years.

"I know some electricians who get lazy. They have to climb down a ladder to turn off the power. *The work will only take a moment,* they think. *Take a chance.*

"Well, not me. I'm down that ladder, turning off the power."

Coming in from the Cold

Louis prefers jobs on new construction. "It's cleaner," he said. "I like to work where the walls are wide open. On a remodeling job, we have to fish wires through existing walls, and that can be tricky. The wires can break inside the walls, and you don't know just where.

"On the other hand, working on new construction means working outside. Rain is no friend of the electrician. Around here, where the winters are cold, work on new construction slows and eventually stops. And even though I wear thermal clothing, I find that I can't do the work I need to while wearing gloves.

"When construction slows, you might find yourself doing repair or preventive maintenance in homes or companies, but you had better be prepared to get laid off," Louis advised.

"You might find yourself taking whatever work you can find. That happened to me, and I took a job with an oil company, repairing and maintaining its electrical equipment."

Detective and Troubleshooter

When something doesn't work, Louis becomes a detective. He tests the switch, fixture, and receptacle, isolating them. He may have to test each stretch of wire. By process of elimination, he finds the bad area.

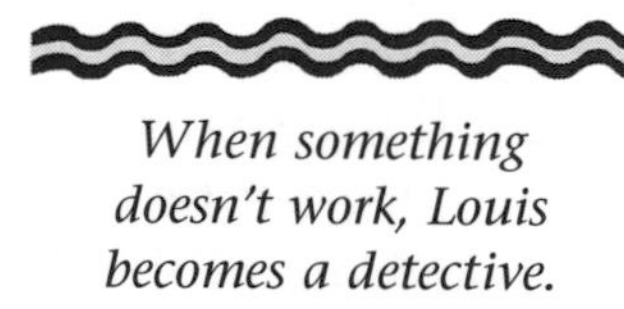
When something doesn't work, Louis becomes a detective.

Sometimes, Louis updates wiring in older houses. Adding or replacing wires in old structures can be difficult. "You never know what you're

getting into with an older house," Louis explained. "They may have all black wires instead of the usual color options. Then I have to test each wire to determine which is which and label it for future, safe work.

"Older houses also had primitive grounding systems that weren't completely reliable. That's one reason I do work in existing structures–updating the systems to make them safer."

Plugging into the Field

"In high school, it's a good idea to take a course in the theory of electricity," Louis advised. "That will teach you the basics. Coursework in science, math, and shop is also helpful. Then you should talk to a good vocational school that can teach you the practical techniques you will be required to know. Also, expect to put in four or five years as an apprentice. It's the best way to learn."

Those who do not enter a formal apprenticeship program can learn the trade informally by working as helpers for experienced electricians.

"Eventually," said Louis, "you'll probably work on everything–homes, offices, factories, commercial buildings. Beyond wiring a building, you might install phone systems, fiber optic cable for computers, or fire and security systems."

By taking courses through the union, Louis keeps up-to-date with changing techniques, new opportunities for electricians, and code.

Wired for Success

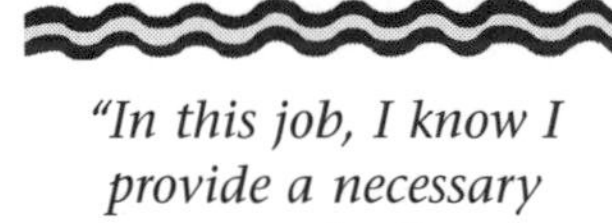

"In this job, I know I provide a necessary service."

At the end of the job, the city and the power company inspect Louis's work. They like what they find. All is neat and properly finished.

Louis's obviously pleased, and it's clear he takes pride in his work.

"In this job, I know I provide a necessary service. There will always be a need for someone like me. We can't imagine life without electricity," he said.

"That becomes vivid reality when the power goes out, usually in a major storm. Then people's thoughts turn to things like how long the refrigerator will stay cold or how to keep warm if the furnace can't run–basics that are impossible without electric current. No lights, no stove, no TV, no computer! A world without electric power seems pretty bleak."

Louis isn't the type to brag. But he knows it's important to bring electricity to people safely and professionally. "In this profession, there's no compromise on a job well done."

SKILL SAMPLER

Phillip Burnstein–Plumber

Phillip Burnstein is a plumber who works for an independent contractor. He is in charge of a crew of eight other plumbers. "My job gives me a broad view of all the phases of a construction project and how they fit together."

Phillip discussed the skills a plumber needs and offers the following suggestions to help you explore the possibility of becoming a plumber.

Plumbers work with their hands, using tools such as wrenches, hammers, chisels, and saws. Sometimes they use power tools and gas or acetylene torches.

- Do you enjoy activities that involve working with your hands, such as building or refinishing furniture, framing pictures, cooking, or making repairs around the house?
- Do you enjoy learning how to use a tool you've never used before?
- Do you enjoy computer work that involves using your mouse?
- Have you ever helped put up shelving, install screens or storm windows, fix loose boards or stair railings, or fix leaky faucets?
- Do you enjoy working on motorcycle or automobile engines?

Plumbers often have to search for the cause of a problem. They need to know mechanical principles and understand how things work.

- Are you curious about how things work?
- Have you ever taken a bicycle, alarm clock, or other item apart just to see how it's put together?
- Do you try to solve problems in an orderly and logical way?
- Are you persistent? Do you work on problems until you solve them?

Plumbers follow blueprints and diagrams.

- Can you read and understand graphs, diagrams, charts, and road maps?
- Can you read and follow computer manuals?
- Can you look at a drawing and picture the three-dimensional object in your mind?
- Do you understand football or basketball plays when they're written out?
- Can you follow the diagrams in the service booklet for a refrigerator, air conditioner, or dishwasher?

Plumbers need a working knowledge of mathematics and science.

- Do you enjoy mathematics and science courses?
- Do you know how to take measurements and calculate fractions, proportions, and percentages?

Plumbers find that each plumbing job is a little different.

- Do you like variety and change in your daily or weekly schedule?
- Do you like doing things you've never done before?

Plumbers do strenuous work. It involves a lot of standing, stooping, lifting, and squatting. Much of it is done outdoors.

- Are you in good physical condition?
- Do you like to be active most of the time?
- Do you enjoy outdoor sports and recreational activities?
- Do you like to mow lawns or work in a garden?

Now learn about all major jobs in the Construction, Mining, and Drilling interest area→

Facts About All Major Jobs Related to

CONSTRUCTION, MINING, AND DRILLING

In addition to the jobs covered in the profiles and skill sampler, other careers in the Construction, Mining, and Drilling interest area may appeal to you. This section describes and gives facts about all major jobs in the Construction, Mining, and Drilling interest area. For an explanation of the $, ★, and 🚶 symbols, see page 6.

MANAGERIAL WORK IN CONSTRUCTION, MINING, AND DRILLING

These workers directly supervise and coordinate activities of workers who construct buildings, roads, or other structures or who drill or dig for oil and minerals. They are responsible for setting and meeting goals and for bringing together the people and equipment needed to get the work done.

Construction Managers. Plan, direct, coordinate, or budget, usually through subordinate supervisory personnel, activities concerned with the construction and maintenance of structures, facilities, and systems. Participate in the conceptual development of a construction project and oversee its organization, scheduling, and implementation. **Education and Training:** Bachelor's degree. **Skills:** Math—High. English—Medium. Science—Medium. **Yearly Earnings:** $$$$$ **Job Growth:** ★★★ **Yearly Openings:** 🚶🚶🚶

First-Line Supervisors and Manager/Supervisors—Construction Trades Workers. Directly supervise and coordinate activities of construction trades workers and their helpers. Manager/Supervisors are generally found in smaller establishments, where they perform both supervisory and management functions, such as accounting, marketing, and personnel work. They may also engage in the same construction trades work as the workers they supervise. **Education and Training:** Work experience in a related occupation. **Skills:** Math—Medium. English—Medium. Science—Medium. **Yearly Earnings:** $$$$ **Job Growth:** ★★★ **Yearly Openings:** 🚶🚶🚶

First-Line Supervisors and Manager/Supervisors—Extractive Workers. Directly supervise and coordinate activities of extractive workers and their helpers. Manager/Supervisors are generally found in smaller establishments, where they perform both supervisory and management functions, such as accounting, marketing, and personnel work. They may also engage in the same extractive work as the

workers they supervise. **Education and Training:** Work experience in a related occupation. **Skills:** Math—Medium. English—Medium. Science—Medium. **Yearly Earnings:** $$$$ **Job Growth:** ★★★ **Yearly Openings:** 🚶🚶🚶

First-Line Supervisors/Managers of Construction Trades and Extraction Workers. Directly supervise and coordinate activities of construction or extraction workers. **Education and Training:** Work experience in a related occupation. **Skills:** Math—Medium. English—Medium. Science—Medium. **Yearly Earnings:** $$$$ **Job Growth:** ★★★ **Yearly Openings:** 🚶🚶🚶

CONSTRUCTION

These workers construct buildings and other large structures. Besides laying the foundations and putting up the framework, walls, floors, and roof, they also install plumbing and electric conduits, windows, and insulation and finish interior surfaces with paint, paper, and carpeting. Outside, they may install driveways, parking lots, fences, and swimming pools. They may also apply their skills to servicing or refurbishing components of buildings. General construction companies and specialized installation and service firms employ these workers.

Boat Builders and Shipwrights. Construct and repair ships or boats according to blueprints. **Education and Training:** Long-term on-the-job training. **Skills:** Math—Medium. English—Low. Science—Medium. **Yearly Earnings:** $$$ **Job Growth:** ★★ **Yearly Openings:** 🚶🚶🚶🚶🚶

Boilermakers. Construct, assemble, maintain, and repair stationary steam boilers and boiler house auxiliaries. Align structures or plate sections to assemble boiler frame tanks or vats, following blueprints. Work involves use of hand and power tools, plumb bobs, levels, wedges, dogs, or turnbuckles. Assist in testing assembled vessels. Direct cleaning of boilers and boiler furnaces. Inspect and repair boiler fittings, such as safety valves, regulators, automatic-control mechanisms, water columns, and auxiliary machines. **Education and Training:** Long-term on-the-job training. **Skills:** Math—Medium. English—Medium. Science—Medium. **Yearly Earnings:** $$$ **Job Growth:** ★ **Yearly Openings:** 🚶

Brattice Builders. Build doors or brattices (ventilation walls or partitions) in underground passageways to control the proper circulation of air through the passageways and to working places. **Education and Training:** Moderate-term on-the-job training. **Skills:** Math—Medium. English—Low. Science—Medium. **Yearly Earnings:** $$$ **Job Growth:** ★★ **Yearly Openings:** 🚶🚶🚶🚶🚶

Brickmasons and Blockmasons. Lay and bind building materials, such as brick, structural tile, concrete block, cinder block, glass block, and terra-cotta block, with mortar and other substances to construct or repair walls, partitions, arches, sewers, and other structures. **Education and Training:** Long-term on-the-job training.

Skills: Math—Medium. English—Low. Science—Medium. **Yearly Earnings:** $$$$ **Job Growth:** ★★★ **Yearly Openings:** 👤👤👤

Carpenters. Construct, erect, install, or repair structures and fixtures made of wood, such as concrete forms; building frameworks, including partitions, joists, studding, and rafters; wood stairways; window and door frames; and hardwood floors. May also install cabinets, siding, drywall, and batt or roll insulation. Includes brattice builders who build doors or brattices (ventilation walls or partitions) in underground passageways to control the proper circulation of air through the passageways and to working places. **Education and Training:** Long-term on-the-job training. **Skills:** Math—Medium. English—Medium. Science—Medium. **Yearly Earnings:** $$$ **Job Growth:** ★★ **Yearly Openings:** 👤👤👤👤👤

Carpet Installers. Lay and install carpet from rolls or blocks on floors. Install padding and trim flooring materials. **Education and Training:** Moderate-term on-the-job training. **Skills:** Math—Medium. English—Medium. Science—Medium. **Yearly Earnings:** $$$ **Job Growth:** ★★★ **Yearly Openings:** 👤👤

Ceiling Tile Installers. Apply plasterboard or other wallboard to ceilings or interior walls of buildings. Apply or mount acoustical tiles or blocks, strips, or sheets of shock-absorbing materials to ceilings and walls of buildings to reduce or reflect sound. Materials may be of decorative quality. Includes lathers who fasten wooden, metal, or rockboard lath to walls, ceilings, or partitions of buildings to provide support base for plaster, fire-proofing, or acoustical material. **Education and Training:** Moderate-term on-the-job training. **Skills:** Math—Medium. English—Low. Science—Medium. **Yearly Earnings:** $$$ **Job Growth:** ★★ **Yearly Openings:** 👤👤👤

Cement Masons and Concrete Finishers. Smooth and finish surfaces of poured concrete, such as floors, walks, sidewalks, roads, or curbs, using a variety of hand and power tools. Align forms for sidewalks, curbs, or gutters; patch voids; use saws to cut expansion joints. **Education and Training:** Long-term on-the-job training. **Skills:** Math—Medium. English—Low. Science—Medium. **Yearly Earnings:** $$ **Job Growth:** ★★ **Yearly Openings:** 👤

Commercial Divers. Work below surface of water, using scuba gear to inspect, repair, remove, or install equipment and structures. May use a variety of power and hand tools, such as drills, sledgehammers, torches, and welding equipment. May conduct tests or experiments, rig explosives, or photograph structures or marine life. **Education and Training:** Moderate-term on-the-job training. **Skills:** Math—Medium. English—Low. Science—Medium. **Yearly Earnings:** $$$ **Job Growth:** No data available. **Yearly Openings:** No data available.

Construction Carpenters. Construct, erect, install, and repair structures and fixtures of wood, plywood, and wallboard, using carpenter's hand tools and power tools. **Education and Training:** Long-term on-the-job training. **Skills:** Math—Medium.

English—Medium. Science—Medium. **Yearly Earnings:** $$$ **Job Growth:** ★★ **Yearly Openings:** 🚶🚶🚶🚶🚶

Drywall and Ceiling Tile Installers. Apply plasterboard or other wallboard to ceilings or interior walls of buildings. Apply or mount acoustical tiles or blocks, strips, or sheets of shock-absorbing materials to ceilings and walls of buildings to reduce or reflect sound. Materials may be of decorative quality. Includes lathers who fasten wooden, metal, or rockboard lath to walls, ceilings or partitions of buildings to provide support base for plaster, fire-proofing, or acoustical material. **Education and Training:** Moderate-term on-the-job training. **Skills:** Math—Medium. English—Medium. Science—Medium. **Yearly Earnings:** $$$ **Job Growth:** ★★ **Yearly Openings:** 🚶🚶🚶

Drywall Installers. Apply plasterboard or other wallboard to ceilings and interior walls of buildings. **Education and Training:** Moderate-term on-the-job training. **Skills:** Math—Medium. English—Low. Science—Medium. **Yearly Earnings:** $$$ **Job Growth:** ★★ **Yearly Openings:** 🚶🚶🚶

Electricians. Install, maintain, and repair electrical wiring, equipment, and fixtures. Ensure that work is in accordance with relevant codes. May install or service street lights, intercom systems, or electrical control systems. **Education and Training:** Long-term on-the-job training. **Skills:** Math—Medium. English—Medium. Science—Medium. **Yearly Earnings:** $$$$ **Job Growth:** ★★★ **Yearly Openings:** 🚶🚶🚶🚶

Explosives Workers, Ordnance Handling Experts, and Blasters. Place and detonate explosives to demolish structures or to loosen, remove, or displace earth, rock, or other materials. May perform specialized handling, storage, and accounting procedures. Includes seismograph shooters. **Education and Training:** Moderate-term on-the-job training. **Skills:** Math—Medium. English—Low. Science—Medium. **Yearly Earnings:** $$$ **Job Growth:** ★ **Yearly Openings:** 🚶

Fence Erectors. Erect and repair metal and wooden fences and fence gates around highways, industrial establishments, residences, or farms, using hand and power tools. **Education and Training:** Moderate-term on-the-job training. **Skills:** Math—Medium. English—Low. Science—Medium. **Yearly Earnings:** $$ **Job Growth:** ★★ **Yearly Openings:** 🚶

Floor Layers, Except Carpet, Wood, and Hard Tiles. Apply blocks, strips, or sheets of shock-absorbing, sound-deadening, or decorative coverings to floors. **Education and Training:** Moderate-term on-the-job training. **Skills:** Math—Medium. English—Low. Science—Medium. **Yearly Earnings:** $$$ **Job Growth:** ★★★ **Yearly Openings:** 🚶

Floor Sanders and Finishers. Scrape and sand wooden floors to smooth surfaces, using floor scraper and floor sanding machine, and apply coats of finish. **Education and Training:** Moderate-term on-the-job training. **Skills:** Math—Low. English—Low. Science—Medium. **Yearly Earnings:** $$ **Job Growth:** ★★★ **Yearly Openings:** 🚶

Glaziers. Install glass in windows, skylights, store fronts, and display cases or on surfaces such as building fronts, interior walls, ceilings, and tabletops. **Education and Training:** Long-term on-the-job training. **Skills:** Math—Medium. English—Medium. Science—Medium. **Yearly Earnings:** $$ **Job Growth:** ★★★ **Yearly Openings:** 🚶🚶

Grader, Bulldozer, and Scraper Operators. Operate machines or vehicles equipped with blades to remove, distribute, level, or grade earth. **Education and Training:** Moderate-term on-the-job training. **Skills:** Math—Medium. English—Low. Science—Medium. **Yearly Earnings:** $$$ **Job Growth:** ★★ **Yearly Openings:** 🚶🚶🚶

Hazardous Materials Removal Workers. Identify, remove, pack, transport, or dispose of hazardous materials, including asbestos, lead-based paint, waste oil, fuel, transmission fluid, radioactive materials, and contaminated soil. Specialized training and certification in hazardous materials handling or a confined entry permit are generally required. May operate earth-moving equipment or trucks. **Education and Training:** Moderate-term on-the-job training. **Skills:** Math—Medium. English—Medium. Science—Medium. **Yearly Earnings:** $$ **Job Growth:** ★★★★ **Yearly Openings:** 🚶🚶

Insulation Workers, Floor, Ceiling, and Wall. Line and cover structures with insulating materials. May work with batt, roll, or blown insulation materials. **Education and Training:** Moderate-term on-the-job training. **Skills:** Math—Medium. English—Low. Science—Medium. **Yearly Earnings:** $$ **Job Growth:** ★★ **Yearly Openings:** 🚶🚶

Insulation Workers, Mechanical. Apply insulating materials to pipes, ductwork, or other mechanical systems to help control and maintain temperature. **Education and Training:** Moderate-term on-the-job training. **Skills:** Math—Medium. English—Low. Science—Medium. **Yearly Earnings:** $$ **Job Growth:** ★★ **Yearly Openings:** 🚶🚶

Manufactured Building and Mobile Home Installers. Move or install mobile homes or prefabricated buildings. **Education and Training:** Moderate-term on-the-job training. **Skills:** Math—Medium. English—Medium. Science—Medium. **Yearly Earnings:** $$ **Job Growth:** ★★★ **Yearly Openings:** 🚶

Operating Engineers. Operate several types of power construction equipment, such as compressors, pumps, hoists, derricks, cranes, shovels, tractors, scrapers, or motor graders, to excavate, move, and grade earth; erect structures; or pour concrete or other hard surface pavement. May repair and maintain equipment in addition to other duties. **Education and Training:** Moderate-term on-the-job training. **Skills:** Math—Low. English—Low. Science—Medium. **Yearly Earnings:** $$$ **Job Growth:** ★★ **Yearly Openings:** 🚶🚶🚶

Operating Engineers and Other Construction Equipment Operators. Operate one or several types of power construction equipment, such as motor graders, bulldozers, scrapers, compressors, pumps, derricks, shovels, tractors, or front-end loaders, to

excavate, move, and grade earth; erect structures; or pour concrete or other hard surface pavement. May repair and maintain equipment. **Education and Training:** Moderate-term on-the-job training. **Skills:** Math—Medium. English—Medium. Science—Medium. **Yearly Earnings:** $$$ **Job Growth:** ★★ **Yearly Openings:** 🚹🚹🚹

Painters, Construction and Maintenance. Paint walls, equipment, buildings, bridges, and other structural surfaces, using brushes, rollers, and spray guns. May remove old paint to prepare surface prior to painting. May mix colors or oils to obtain desired color or consistency. **Education and Training:** Moderate-term on-the-job training. **Skills:** Math—Medium. English—Low. Science—Medium. **Yearly Earnings:** $$ **Job Growth:** ★★★ **Yearly Openings:** 🚹🚹🚹🚹

Paperhangers. Cover interior walls and ceilings of rooms with decorative wallpaper or fabric or attach advertising posters on surfaces such as walls and billboards. Duties include removing old materials from surface to be papered. **Education and Training:** Moderate-term on-the-job training. **Skills:** Math—Medium. English—Low. Science—Medium. **Yearly Earnings:** $$$ **Job Growth:** ★★★ **Yearly Openings:** 🚹

Paving, Surfacing, and Tamping Equipment Operators. Operate equipment used for applying concrete, asphalt, or other materials to road beds, parking lots, or airport runways and taxiways or operate equipment used for tamping gravel, dirt, or other materials. Includes concrete and asphalt paving machine operators, form tampers, tamping machine operators, and stone spreader operators. **Education and Training:** Moderate-term on-the-job training. **Skills:** Math—Low. English—Low. Science—Medium. **Yearly Earnings:** $$ **Job Growth:** ★★★ **Yearly Openings:** 🚹🚹

Pile-Driver Operators. Operate pile drivers mounted on skids, barges, crawler treads, or locomotive cranes to drive pilings for retaining walls, bulkheads, and foundations of structures such as buildings, bridges, and piers. **Education and Training:** Moderate-term on-the-job training. **Skills:** Math—Low. English—Low. Science—Medium. **Yearly Earnings:** $$$$ **Job Growth:** ★★★ **Yearly Openings:** 🚹

Pipe Fitters. Lay out, assemble, install, and maintain pipe systems, pipe supports, and related hydraulic and pneumatic equipment for steam, hot water, heating, cooling, lubricating, sprinkling, and industrial production and processing systems. **Education and Training:** Long-term on-the-job training. **Skills:** Math—Medium. English—Medium. Science—Medium. **Yearly Earnings:** $$$ **Job Growth:** ★★★ **Yearly Openings:** 🚹🚹🚹

Pipelayers. Lay pipe for storm or sanitation sewers, drains, and water mains. May grade trenches or culverts, position pipe, or seal joints. **Education and Training:** Moderate-term on-the-job training. **Skills:** Math—Medium. English—Low. Science—Medium. **Yearly Earnings:** $$ **Job Growth:** ★★★ **Yearly Openings:** 🚹🚹

Pipelaying Fitters. Align pipeline section in preparation of welding. Signal tractor driver for placement of pipeline sections in proper alignment. Insert steel spacer.

Education and Training: Moderate-term on-the-job training. **Skills:** Math—Medium. English—Low. Science—Medium. **Yearly Earnings:** $$$ **Job Growth:** ★★★ **Yearly Openings:** 🚶🚶🚶

Plasterers and Stucco Masons. Apply interior or exterior plaster, cement, stucco, or similar materials. May also set ornamental plaster. **Education and Training:** Long-term on-the-job training. **Skills:** Math—Low. English—Low. Science—Medium. **Yearly Earnings:** $$$ **Job Growth:** ★★★ **Yearly Openings:** 🚶🚶

Plumbers. Assemble, install, and repair pipes, fittings, and fixtures of heating, water, and drainage systems according to specifications and plumbing codes. **Education and Training:** Long-term on-the-job training. **Skills:** Math—Medium. English—Medium. Science—Medium. **Yearly Earnings:** $$$ **Job Growth:** ★★★ **Yearly Openings:** 🚶🚶🚶

Plumbers, Pipefitters, and Steamfitters. Assemble, install, alter, and repair pipelines or pipe systems that carry water, steam, air, or other liquids or gases. May install heating and cooling equipment and mechanical control systems. **Education and Training:** Long-term on-the-job training. **Skills:** Math—Medium. English—Medium. Science—Medium. **Yearly Earnings:** $$$ **Job Growth:** ★★★ **Yearly Openings:** 🚶🚶🚶

Rail-Track Laying and Maintenance Equipment Operators. Lay, repair, and maintain track for standard or narrow-gauge railroad equipment used in regular railroad service or in plant yards, quarries, sand and gravel pits, and mines. Includes ballast cleaning machine operators and road bed tamping machine operators. **Education and Training:** Moderate-term on-the-job training. **Skills:** Math—Low. English—Low. Science—Low. **Yearly Earnings:** $$$ **Job Growth:** ★ **Yearly Openings:** 🚶

Refractory Materials Repairers, Except Brickmasons. Build or repair furnaces, kilns, cupolas, boilers, converters, ladles, soaking pits, ovens, etc., using refractory materials. **Education and Training:** Short-term on-the-job training. **Skills:** Math—Medium. English—Medium. Science—Medium. **Yearly Earnings:** $$$ **Job Growth:** No data available. **Yearly Openings:** No data available.

Reinforcing Iron and Rebar Workers. Position and secure steel bars or mesh in concrete forms to reinforce concrete. Use a variety of fasteners, rod-bending machines, blowtorches, and hand tools. **Education and Training:** Long-term on-the-job training. **Skills:** Math—Medium. English—Low. Science—Medium. **Yearly Earnings:** $$$ **Job Growth:** ★★★ **Yearly Openings:** 🚶

Riggers. Set up or repair rigging for construction projects, manufacturing plants, logging yards, or ships and shipyards or for the entertainment industry. **Education and Training:** Short-term on-the-job training. **Skills:** Math—Medium. English—Medium. Science—Medium. **Yearly Earnings:** $$$ **Job Growth:** ★★★ **Yearly Openings:** 🚶

Roofers. Cover roofs of structures with shingles, slate, asphalt, aluminum, wood, and related materials. May spray roofs, sidings, and walls with material to bind, seal,

insulate, or soundproof sections of structures. **Education and Training:** Moderate-term on-the-job training. **Skills:** Math—Low. English—Low. Science—Medium. **Yearly Earnings:** $$ **Job Growth:** ★★★ **Yearly Openings:** 🚹🚹🚹

Rough Carpenters. Build rough wooden structures, such as concrete forms; scaffolds; tunnel, bridge, or sewer supports; billboard signs; and temporary frame shelters according to sketches, blueprints, or oral instructions. **Education and Training:** Moderate-term on-the-job training. **Skills:** Math—Medium. English—Low. Science—Medium. **Yearly Earnings:** $$$ **Job Growth:** ★★ **Yearly Openings:** 🚹🚹🚹🚹🚹

Security and Fire Alarm Systems Installers. Install, program, maintain, and repair security and fire alarm wiring and equipment. Ensure that work is in accordance with relevant codes. **Education and Training:** Postsecondary career and technical education. **Skills:** Math—Medium. English—Medium. Science—Medium. **Yearly Earnings:** $$$ **Job Growth:** ★★★★ **Yearly Openings:** 🚹

Segmental Pavers. Lay out, cut, and paste segmental paving units. Includes installers of bedding and restraining materials for the paving units. **Education and Training:** Moderate-term on-the-job training. **Skills:** Math—Medium. English—Medium. Science—Medium. **Yearly Earnings:** $$ **Job Growth:** ★★ **Yearly Openings:** 🚹🚹🚹

Sheet Metal Workers. Fabricate, assemble, install, and repair sheet metal products and equipment, such as ducts, control boxes, drainpipes, and furnace casings. Work may involve any of the following: setting up and operating fabricating machines to cut, bend, and straighten sheet metal; shaping metal over anvils, blocks, or forms using hammer operating soldering and welding equipment to join sheet metal parts; inspecting, assembling, and smoothing seams and joints of burred surfaces. **Education and Training:** Moderate-term on-the-job training. **Skills:** Math—Medium. English—Medium. Science—Medium. **Yearly Earnings:** $$$ **Job Growth:** ★★★★ **Yearly Openings:** 🚹🚹🚹

Ship Carpenters and Joiners. Fabricate, assemble, install, or repair wooden furnishings in ships or boats. **Education and Training:** Moderate-term on-the-job training. **Skills:** Math—Medium. English—Medium. Science—Medium. **Yearly Earnings:** $$$ **Job Growth:** ★★ **Yearly Openings:** 🚹🚹🚹🚹🚹

Stone Cutters and Carvers. Cut or carve stone according to diagrams and patterns. **Education and Training:** Moderate-term on-the-job training. **Skills:** Math—Medium. English—Low. Science—Medium. **Yearly Earnings:** $$ **Job Growth:** ★★ **Yearly Openings:** 🚹🚹

Stonemasons. Build stone structures, such as piers, walls, and abutments. Lay walks, curbstones, or special types of masonry for vats, tanks, and floors. **Education and Training:** Long-term on-the-job training. **Skills:** Math—Medium. English—Low. Science—Low. **Yearly Earnings:** $$$ **Job Growth:** ★★★ **Yearly Openings:** 🚹

Structural Iron and Steel Workers. Raise, place, and unite iron or steel girders, columns, and other structural members to form completed structures or structural frameworks. May erect metal storage tanks and assemble prefabricated metal buildings. **Education and Training:** Long-term on-the-job training. **Skills:** Math—Low. English—Low. Science—Medium. **Yearly Earnings:** $$$ **Job Growth:** ★★★ **Yearly Openings:** 🚶🚶🚶

Tapers. Seal joints between plasterboard or other wallboard to prepare wall surface for painting or papering. **Education and Training:** Moderate-term on-the-job training. **Skills:** Math—Low. English—Low. Science—Medium. **Yearly Earnings:** $$$ **Job Growth:** ★★ **Yearly Openings:** 🚶🚶

Terrazzo Workers and Finishers. Apply a mixture of cement, sand, pigment, or marble chips to floors, stairways, and cabinet fixtures to fashion durable and decorative surfaces. **Education and Training:** Long-term on-the-job training. **Skills:** Math—Medium. English—Low. Science—Medium. **Yearly Earnings:** $$$ **Job Growth:** ★ **Yearly Openings:** 🚶

Tile and Marble Setters. Apply hard tile, marble, and wood tile to walls, floors, ceilings, and roof decks. **Education and Training:** Long-term on-the-job training. **Skills:** Math—Medium. English—Low. Science—Medium. **Yearly Earnings:** $$$ **Job Growth:** ★★★ **Yearly Openings:** 🚶

MINING AND DRILLING

These workers operate drilling or other excavating and pumping equipment, usually in oil fields, quarries, or mines. They are hired by large energy or extractive companies or by small drilling contractors that do work for the large companies.

Construction Drillers. Operate machine to drill or bore through earth or rock. **Education and Training:** Moderate-term on-the-job training. **Skills:** Math—Low. English—Low. Science—Medium. **Yearly Earnings:** $$$ **Job Growth:** ★★★ **Yearly Openings:** 🚶

Continuous Mining Machine Operators. Operate self-propelled mining machines that rip coal, metal and nonmetal ores, rock, stone, or sand from the face and load it onto conveyors or into shuttle cars in a continuous operation. **Education and Training:** Moderate-term on-the-job training. **Skills:** Math—Low. English—Low. Science—Low. **Yearly Earnings:** $$$ **Job Growth:** ★ **Yearly Openings:** 🚶

Derrick Operators, Oil and Gas. Rig derrick equipment and operate pumps to circulate mud through drill hole. **Education and Training:** Moderate-term on-the-job training. **Skills:** Math—Medium. English—Low. Science—Medium. **Yearly Earnings:** $$ **Job Growth:** ★ **Yearly Openings:** 🚶

Earth Drillers, Except Oil and Gas. Operate a variety of drills—such as rotary, churn, and pneumatic—to tap sub-surface water and salt deposits, to remove core samples during mineral exploration or soil testing, and to facilitate the use of explosives in mining or construction. May use explosives. Includes horizontal and earth boring machine operators. **Education and Training:** Moderate-term on-the-job training. **Skills:** Math—Medium. English—Medium. Science—Medium. **Yearly Earnings:** $$$ **Job Growth:** ★★★ **Yearly Openings:** 🧍

Excavating and Loading Machine Operators. Operate machinery equipped with scoops, shovels, or buckets to excavate and load loose materials. **Education and Training:** Moderate-term on-the-job training. **Skills:** Math—Medium. English—Medium. Science—Medium. **Yearly Earnings:** $$$ **Job Growth:** ★★★ **Yearly Openings:** 🧍

Loading Machine Operators, Underground Mining. Operate underground loading machine to load coal, ore, or rock into shuttle or mine car or onto conveyors. Loading equipment may include power shovels, hoisting engines equipped with cable-drawn scraper or scoop, or machines equipped with gathering arms and conveyor. **Education and Training:** Moderate-term on-the-job training. **Skills:** Math—Low. English—Low. Science—Low. **Yearly Earnings:** $$ **Job Growth:** ★★★ **Yearly Openings:** No data available.

Mine Cutting and Channeling Machine Operators. Operate machinery—such as longwall shears, plows, and cutting machines—to cut or channel along the face or seams of coal mines, stone quarries, or other mining surfaces to facilitate blasting, separating, or removing minerals or materials from mines or from the earth's surface. **Education and Training:** Moderate-term on-the-job training. **Skills:** Math—Low. English—Low. Science—Medium. **Yearly Earnings:** $$$ **Job Growth:** No data available. **Yearly Openings:** No data available.

Rock Splitters, Quarry. Separate blocks of rough-dimension stone from quarry mass using jackhammer and wedges. **Education and Training:** Moderate-term on-the-job training. **Skills:** Math—Low. English—Low. Science—Medium. **Yearly Earnings:** $$ **Job Growth:** No data available. **Yearly Openings:** No data available.

Roof Bolters, Mining. Operate machinery to install roof support bolts in underground mine. **Education and Training:** Moderate-term on-the-job training. **Skills:** Math—Low. English—Low. Science—Medium. **Yearly Earnings:** $$$ **Job Growth:** No data available. **Yearly Openings:** No data available.

Rotary Drill Operators, Oil and Gas. Set up or operate a variety of drills to remove petroleum products from the earth and to find and remove core samples for testing during oil and gas exploration. **Education and Training:** Moderate-term on-the-job training. **Skills:** Math—Medium. English—Medium. Science—Medium. **Yearly Earnings:** $$$ **Job Growth:** ★ **Yearly Openings:** 🧍

Roustabouts, Oil and Gas. Assemble or repair oilfield equipment using hand and power tools. **Education and Training:** Short-term on-the-job training. **Skills:** Math—Low. English—Low. Science—Medium. **Yearly Earnings:** $$ **Job Growth:** ★ **Yearly Openings:** 🯅

Service Unit Operators, Oil, Gas, and Mining. Operate equipment to increase oil flow from producing wells or to remove stuck pipe, casing, tools, or other obstructions from drilling wells. May also perform similar services in mining exploration operations. **Education and Training:** Moderate-term on-the-job training. **Skills:** Math—Medium. English—Medium. Science—Medium. **Yearly Earnings:** $$ **Job Growth:** ★ **Yearly Openings:** 🯅

Shuttle Car Operators. Operate diesel or electric-powered shuttle car in underground mine to transport materials from working face to mine cars or conveyor. **Education and Training:** Moderate-term on-the-job training. **Skills:** Math—Low. English—Low. Science—Medium. **Yearly Earnings:** $$$ **Job Growth:** No data available. **Yearly Openings:** No data available.

Well and Core Drill Operators. Operate machine to drill wells and take samples or cores for analysis of strata. **Education and Training:** Long-term on-the-job training. **Skills:** Math—Medium. English—Medium. Science—Medium. **Yearly Earnings:** $$$ **Job Growth:** ★★★ **Yearly Openings:** 🯅

HANDS-ON WORK IN CONSTRUCTION, EXTRACTION, AND MAINTENANCE

These workers perform a variety of tasks requiring little skill, such as moving materials, cleaning work areas, doing routine installations, operating simple tools, and helping skilled workers. They work at construction sites, oilfields, quarries, and mines.

Carpenter Assemblers and Repairers. Perform a variety of tasks requiring a limited knowledge of carpentry, such as applying siding to building exteriors or assembling and erecting prefabricated buildings. **Education and Training:** Moderate-term on-the-job training. **Skills:** Math—Medium. English—Low. Science—Medium. **Yearly Earnings:** $$$ **Job Growth:** ★★ **Yearly Openings:** 🯅 🯅 🯅 🯅 🯅

Construction Laborers. Perform tasks involving physical labor at building, highway, and heavy construction projects, tunnel and shaft excavations, and demolition sites. May operate hand and power tools of all types: air hammers, earth tampers, cement mixers, small mechanical hoists, surveying and measuring equipment, and other equipment and instruments. May clean and prepare sites, dig trenches, set braces to support the sides of excavations, erect scaffolding, clean up rubble and debris, and remove asbestos, lead, and other hazardous waste materials. May assist other craft

workers. **Education and Training:** Moderate-term on-the-job training. **Skills:** Math—Medium. English—Low. Science—Medium. **Yearly Earnings:** $$ **Job Growth:** ★★★ **Yearly Openings:** 👤👤👤👤👤

Grips and Set-Up Workers, Motion Picture Sets, Studios, and Stages. Arrange equipment. Raise and lower scenery. Move dollies, cranes, and booms. Perform other duties for motion-picture, recording, or television industry. **Education and Training:** Short-term on-the-job training. **Skills:** Math—Low. English—Medium. Science—Medium. **Yearly Earnings:** $ **Job Growth:** ★★★ **Yearly Openings:** 👤👤👤👤👤

Helpers—Brickmasons, Blockmasons, Stonemasons, and Tile and Marble Setters. Help brickmasons, blockmasons, stonemasons, or tile and marble setters by performing duties of lesser skill. Duties include using, supplying, or holding materials or tools and cleaning work area and equipment. **Education and Training:** Short-term on-the-job training. **Skills:** Math—Medium. English—Low. Science—Low. **Yearly Earnings:** $$ **Job Growth:** ★★★ **Yearly Openings:** 👤👤👤

Helpers—Carpenters. Help carpenters by performing duties of lesser skill. Duties include using, supplying, or holding materials or tools and cleaning work area and equipment. **Education and Training:** Short-term on-the-job training. **Skills:** Math—Medium. English—Low. Science—Medium. **Yearly Earnings:** $$ **Job Growth:** ★★ **Yearly Openings:** 👤👤👤

Helpers—Extraction Workers. Help extraction craft workers, such as earth drillers, blasters and explosives workers, derrick operators, and mining machine operators, by performing duties of lesser skill. Duties include supplying equipment or cleaning work area. **Education and Training:** Short-term on-the-job training. **Skills:** Math—Low. English—Low. Science—Medium. **Yearly Earnings:** $$ **Job Growth:** ★ **Yearly Openings:** 👤👤

Helpers—Painters, Paperhangers, Plasterers, and Stucco Masons. Help painters, paperhangers, plasterers, or stucco masons by performing duties of lesser skill. Duties include using, supplying, or holding materials or tools and cleaning work area and equipment. **Education and Training:** Short-term on-the-job training. **Skills:** Math—Medium. English—Low. Science—Low. **Yearly Earnings:** $ **Job Growth:** ★★★ **Yearly Openings:** 👤👤

Helpers—Pipelayers, Plumbers, Pipefitters, and Steamfitters. Help plumbers, pipefitters, steamfitters, or pipelayers by performing duties of lesser skill. Duties include using, supplying, or holding materials or tools and cleaning work area and equipment. **Education and Training:** Short-term on-the-job training. **Skills:** Math—Medium. English—Low. Science—Medium. **Yearly Earnings:** $$ **Job Growth:** ★★★ **Yearly Openings:** 👤👤👤

Helpers—Roofers. Help roofers by performing duties of lesser skill. Duties include using, supplying, or holding materials or tools and cleaning work area and equipment.

Education and Training: Short-term on-the-job training. **Skills:** Math—Medium. English—Medium. Science—Medium. **Yearly Earnings:** $ **Job Growth:** ★★★ **Yearly Openings:** 🚹🚹

Highway Maintenance Workers. Maintain highways, municipal and rural roads, airport runways, and rights-of-way. Duties include patching broken or eroded pavement and repairing guard rails, highway markers, and snow fences. May also mow or clear brush from along road or plow snow. **Education and Training:** Moderate-term on-the-job training. **Skills:** Math—Medium. English—Low. Science—Low. **Yearly Earnings:** $$ **Job Growth:** ★★ **Yearly Openings:** 🚹🚹🚹

Septic Tank Servicers and Sewer Pipe Cleaners. Clean and repair septic tanks, sewer lines, or drains. May patch walls and partitions of tank, replace damaged drain tile, or repair breaks in underground piping. **Education and Training:** Moderate-term on-the-job training. **Skills:** Math—Medium. English—Medium. Science—Medium. **Yearly Earnings:** $$ **Job Growth:** ★★★ **Yearly Openings:** 🚹

Exploring Careers:

Transportation

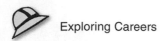

Start Your Journey Through Careers Related to

TRANSPORTATION

Careers in this area suit people interested in operations that move people or materials.

EXPLORING CAREER CLUES

Your interests give important clues for exploring career options. Think about your interests to learn if jobs in the Transportation interest area may be worth further exploration.

Do you like the school subjects related to the Transportation interest area? Here are some examples of related subjects:

- Math
- Computers
- English
- Science
- Geography
- Physics
- Industrial or technology education
- Driver's education
- Physical education

Do you like the free-time activities related to the Transportation interest area? Here are some examples of related free-time activities:

- Building model airplanes, cars, or boats
- Operating radio-controlled cars, trucks, planes, and boats
- Operating model train layouts
- Operating a CB or ham radio
- Operating flight and driving simulators on the computer
- Playing computer games that require quick and precise movements
- Working on bicycles, minibikes, lawn mowers, and cars
- Driving go-karts
- Driving a truck or tractor on a family farm
- Reading about airplanes, gliders, cars, boats, and trains

EXPLORING JOB GROUPS

Jobs related to the Transportation interest area fit into eight groups. Read through the list to see which groups sound interesting to you.

- Managerial Work in Transportation
- Vehicle Expediting and Coordinating
- Air Vehicle Operation
- Water Vehicle Operation
- Truck Driving
- Rail Vehicle Operation
- Other Services Requiring Driving
- Support Work

EXPLORING CAREER POSSIBILITIES

You can satisfy your interest in the Transportation area by managing a transportation service, by helping vehicles keep on their assigned schedules and routes, or by driving or piloting a vehicle. Here are a few examples of career possibilities:

If you enjoy taking responsibility, perhaps managing a rail line would appeal to you. If you work well with details and can take pressure on the job, you might consider being an air traffic controller.

Or would you rather get out on the highway, on the water, or up in the air? If so, then you could drive a truck from state to state, be employed on a ship, or fly a crop duster over a cornfield.

If you prefer to stay closer to home, you could drive a delivery van, taxi, or school bus.

You could use your physical strength to load freight and arrange it so it gets to its destination in one piece.

Turn the page to meet people working in the Transportation interest area→

PROFILE

Angela and Karen Wu—Air Traffic Controllers

Angela Wu became an air traffic controller at a time when few women entered the profession. Inspired, her daughter Karen decided that she too would become a controller.

Both now work in two different control centers for the same international airport. Karen works in the control tower at the airport. Angela works in another tower, miles away.

Happy Landings

Karen's sharp eyes detected something wrong in the distance. She had to act immediately.

One cloudy day, a small jet aircraft circled. The pilot had requested clearance to land. Aboard were executives of an oil company, flying in for a meeting.

In a tower with huge, tinted-glass windows, Karen scanned the sky. "Corporate 235, you're cleared to land on Runway 4," she said into her headset.

The pilot acknowledged her instructions and then lowered the jet's flaps and reduced speed. The jet bounced in the choppy air. Landing in a tricky breeze can be scary. Pilots and air traffic controllers worry about wind shear, a sudden downward gust that can force a plane into the ground.

Karen's sharp eyes detected something wrong in the distance. She had to act immediately. "Corporate 235! Your landing gear is not down! Repeat–Your landing gear is not down!"

Karen heard the pilot gasp. She saw the wheels lock in place in the nick of time. Karen had just saved lives, not to mention a million-dollar airplane.

High Action or No Action, Karen Is There

Karen instructs pilots when and where to land. As incoming and outgoing planes occupy the airspace, she must keep them away from each other. Sometimes the air is filled with planes. Other times, nothing's happening.

Karen works a staggered shift, which can be disorienting to some people. She starts at 3 p.m. on Monday, 2 p.m. on Tuesday, and 1 p.m. on Wednesday, working eight-hour shifts.

"These changing schedules organize themselves into a seven-week rotation. Afternoon shifts become night shifts," explained Karen.

"I can't say I like the night shifts. They're pretty uneventful. Of course, the day work is a different story, with many flights to monitor and direct. *Then* there's a lot of responsibility on the shoulders of the controllers.

"A controller has to develop ways of coping with pressure. Breaks top the list. After an hour on duty during busy air traffic times, a controller can use a break and a bite to eat."

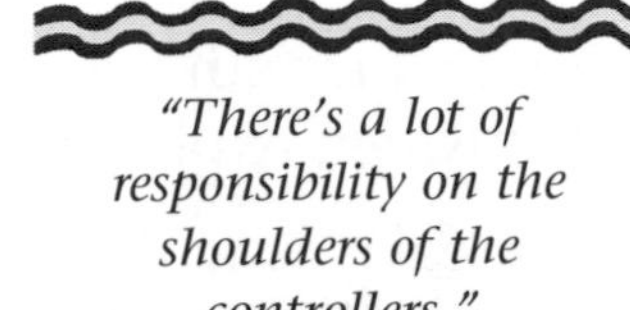

"There's a lot of responsibility on the shoulders of the controllers."

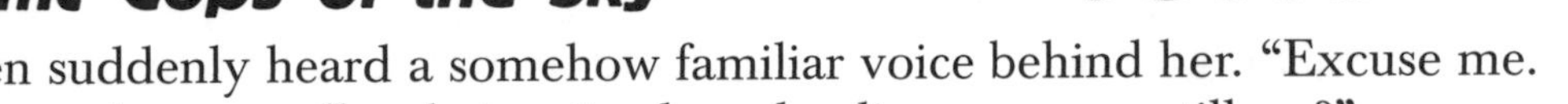

Traffic Cops of the Sky

Karen suddenly heard a somehow familiar voice behind her. "Excuse me. Are you the controller that noticed my landing gear was still up?"

"Sure am."

Karen checked her monitor. All the planes in her area of responsibility remained more than five miles apart. She could safely look away for a moment. With wires flowing from her headset to the monitor, keyboard, and radar screen, she glanced up at the pilot while remaining hooked to the Instrument Landing System.

"My name is Gibbs, ma'am. I just wanted to thank you. I can't imagine where my head was. You saved my plane and maybe my life."

Karen smiled at the pilot. "Thanks! I was just doing my job. But I really appreciate your coming up here. It's nice to hear your kind words."

Karen has rarely met any of the pilots she's talked to and joked with for the last six years. She's helped some of them out of tight spots. But just like a traffic police officer, she seldom gets to know the people she serves.

The Flight Stuff

"Some controllers are naturals," said Karen. "They seem born to it, calm and focused even in the midst of hair-raising episodes. The Federal

Aviation Administration seeks mature people who can deal well with boredom one moment and sudden stress the next."

"The Federal Aviation Administration seeks mature people who can deal well with boredom one moment and sudden stress the next."

Before he or she starts, a trainee must have several years of college or work experience. "As an applicant, I had to first take an FAA civil-service test. Afterward, a supervisor interviewed me, and I had to have a physical. After that? Three months of training.

"My first month was in a classroom environment, and then we moved to a lab," Karen explained.

"There we assigned 'flight strips' to simulated planes. Flight strips are their identifying labels. From looking at the flight strips on the screen, I could say 'That one is American Flight 101,' or 'That one is Delta 409.'

"During training we worked manually, without radar, visualizing planes flying. After training, our supervisor certified us as ready for radar instruction."

From the Ground Up

Even then, trainees at that level aren't fully responsible for keeping planes apart. Karen sat with an instructor for a couple of years, mastering her skills.

"Each air traffic controller gets lots of experience before handling a huge air space," Karen said.

Karen used to be stationed on the ground level of the tower in a windowless room where she worked only with high-altitude planes, which she tracked on radar.

"I prefer being in the tower, where I can see the planes and deal with takeoffs and landings. On the other hand, working on the ground is still a major responsibility.

"Each air traffic controller gets lots of experience before handling a huge air space."

"On a radar screen, planes flying a couple of thousand feet above or below each other seem

almost to occupy the same space. Since pilots can't see other planes beyond that limit, especially from above and below, the controller has to make sure that the air space a pilot wants to move into is really empty."

Wide Open Spaces

Karen's mother, Angela, first worked at the airport, but now she works in a center that operates thirty miles outside its boundaries. She sees ten times the number of planes her daughter does, and she works with a great many more controllers.

Air traffic controllers earn every cent of their pay when the weather turns very bad.

Today's big jetliners can usually fly safely through snow and rain, but air traffic controllers earn every cent of their pay when the weather turns very bad.

"Pilots won't fly through thunderstorms, which have strong up and down drafts," said Angela. "Air traffic controllers constantly monitor weather, paying particular attention to storms.

"Because the radar screen won't show fog, it isn't our main source for making us aware of bad flying weather."

On her computer readout device screen, Angela can monitor weather all along the Mississippi River. It will tell her whether there is fog. She can also call other centers on the "holler lines" by simply pushing a button.

When storms arise quickly, as they often do in Angela's part of the country, planes in the air must be diverted to other airports or circle in a holding pattern until the storm ends.

"It can get tense when your sector has the only good weather for a hundred miles.

"Every pilot asks us for a change from his or her set course. It can be difficult to coordinate them all safely. Just saying 'Twenty degrees north of course' may not be specific enough. There's only so much time and airspace.

"Some people joke about controllers and how intense they are because of stressful situations like that. But I love the job.

"I consider the pay excellent and the benefits super. And airlines sometimes offer controllers special deals on airfares," she added.

"If you can stand up to the competition for this kind of job, which is intense, I'd highly recommend it."

PROFILE

Harrison Moore–Airline Pilot

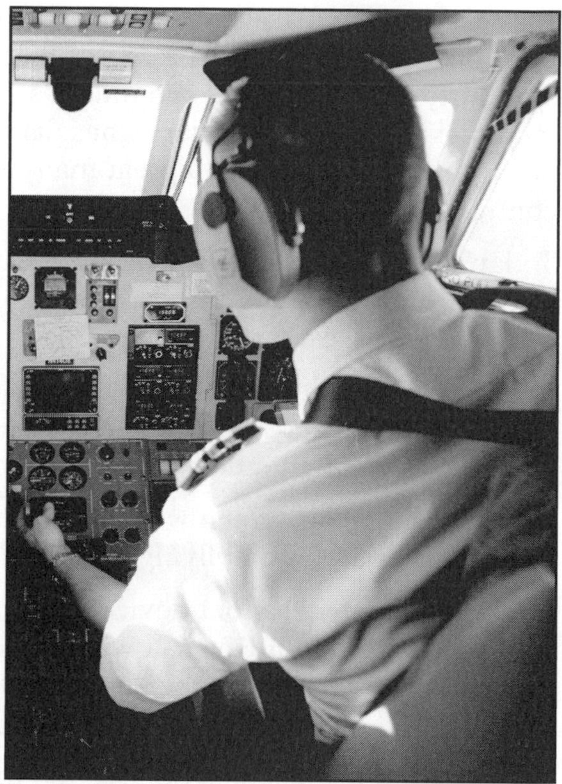

Pilots need the personal qualities of determination and commitment.

The sky was blue, the weather report was great, and piloting the big commercial airplane was almost relaxing. At 22,000 feet, First Officer Harrison Moore glanced down at the sparkling bay.

His thoughts drifted to the day ahead–one stop in Denver, another in Albuquerque, then back to the coast.

His thoughts were brought back to the present by a piercing alarm. The fire warning! He quickly checked the instrument panel. Though the fire warning flashed red, the heat gauge and other instruments appeared normal. There was no way of knowing whether this was a false alarm.

With Flying Colors

Harrison immediately discharged the fire-extinguishing system to put out any flames around the engines. Nevertheless, the light still flashed, and the alarm continued.

"Take the radio," Captain Roberts ordered. "We've got a fire in engine number two."

"Much of a pilot's training is drilling on emergency procedures. Doing what needs to be done becomes automatic."

Harrison radioed the tower. "Oakland Center, this is Flight 5-0-5. We have an engine fire."

The air traffic controller responded immediately, giving Harrison the coordinates for the nearest airport and working to clear a runway for the plane.

Harrison called a flight attendant to prepare the cabin for emergency landing. "I'll address the passengers first," he said.

"Ladies and gentlemen, this is First Officer Moore," he said calmly over the intercom. "We have a warning light that requires an unscheduled landing. Remain in your seats, and listen closely to the flight attendants for emergency landing procedures. Please give them your cooperation."

After that, he let the attendants deal with the passengers. He and Captain Roberts had much to do to make a clean landing. As they approached the airport, Harrison contacted the tower to see that the runway was clear.

They landed the big jet safely in Monterey, only to find it had been a false alarm.

"In a situation like that, we have to assume the alarm is real," said Harrison. "Much of a pilot's training is drilling on emergency procedures. Doing what needs to be done becomes automatic."

A Pilot's Personality

Pilots must be skilled in technology and mathematics. They must have mechanical ability. And they must maintain their health.

Harrison is a fit, no-nonsense man. It's hard to imagine him being nervous about anything.

"Oh, I've had my moments," he said. "But confidence is a key to success in an emergency."

A pilot also needs the personal qualities of determination and commitment, Harrison said.

"The fact is, training is repetitious. You do the same thing over and over. It can take years to acquire all your flight time and licenses."

Pilots must also be skilled in technology and mathematics. They must have mechanical ability. And, of course, pilots must maintain their health, and their vision must be correctable to 20/20.

They must also be able to deal with passengers effectively. "Many people have always been afraid of flying. And many more have become that way since the tragedy of September 11, 2001." Harrison said quietly.

"I certainly understand that. But air travel is a fact of life. Part of my job is to help passengers understand we're keeping them safe and secure."

Getting Off the Ground

"Anyone willing to commit to the training can fly."

"Flying wasn't my lifelong dream. It was something I just fell into," Harrison recalled.

His first job was with Air France as part of the ground crew. "I fell in love with the industry. I saw that pilots had the best jobs. I learned that anyone willing to commit to the training could fly."

The industry demands a bachelor's degree and plenty of flight time. Candidates may learn to fly through private schools or the military.

After candidates earn a private pilot's license, they must earn several other licenses if they want a job like Harrison's. Even then, a candidate may have accumulated only a fraction of the 1,500 hours required to earn the necessary Airline Transport Pilot's License.

Harrison became a flight instructor, as many pilots do, to gain his needed flight hours. Others may fly commuter or corporate aircraft, fly charter or cargo flights, or earn flight time while serving their country in the military.

Regardless of the method they choose, all commercial pilots must be very experienced flyers before taking the controls of a commercial aircraft.

Pilots are constantly tested to keep them alert and current. Once every year, pilots must go through more training, oral and written tests, and *check rides,* or simulator training. Every six months, pilots must pass take-home tests.

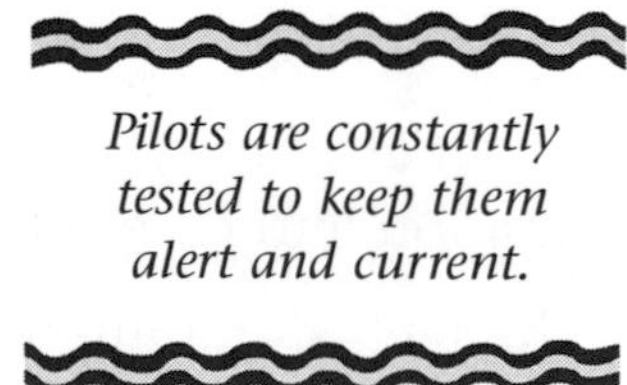
Pilots are constantly tested to keep them alert and current.

"I like the challenge of that," said Harrison. "Some people resent testing. But let's face it, you have a lot of responsibility up there."

A Long-Distance Day

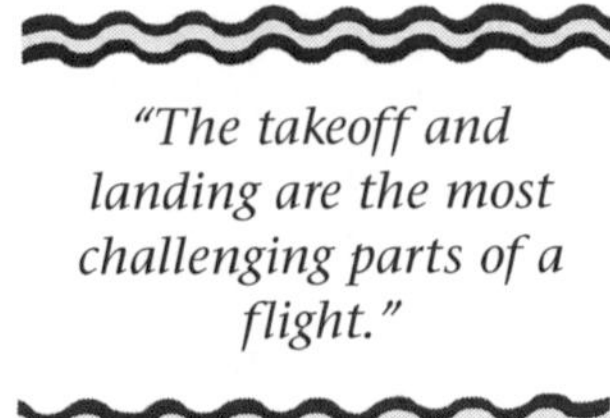

"The takeoff and landing are the most challenging parts of a flight."

Harrison's workday is actually a one- to four-day trip that includes many destinations, or *legs*. He arrives at the airline well before departure to meet the captain and be briefed. They then discuss the amount of fuel assigned to the aircraft and strategies for changing weather conditions.

Next, they meet the flight attendants and determine security measures for that flight. They alert the crew to any difficult weather conditions. A *cockpit prep* tests all aircraft systems. There is a visual inspection of the exterior.

While passengers board, the pilots run through a checklist and meet with the airline's customer service representative about final passenger count. This count helps establish the weight of the aircraft and therefore its speed, engine thrust, and fuel needs.

After the craft's door is locked, a tractor driver maneuvers the craft away from the ramp. The pilots start their engines.

Air traffic control radios clearance for the pilots to move out to the runway. Another clearance for takeoff, and the pilots ready the flight crew. Passenger count is confirmed. The pilots make a final check of flight calculations.

Then, and only then, do the pilots engage the plane's engines at full throttle, speeding down the long runway and into the sky.

When the plane reaches its assigned altitude, the pilot usually switches to autopilot, which helps maintain a constant course and altitude.

If good conditions persist, the rest of the flight prior to landing mostly involves navigating and holding speed.

"The takeoff and landing are the most challenging parts of a flight," said Harrison. "I prefer short hauls because it's real flying. Those are more hands-on, and you have a bit more control of your schedule."

A Pilot's Ups and Downs

"I love flying. And I get to travel, see the world, and meet all kinds of people."

It isn't easy to become a successful pilot.

"Besides requiring so much training, it's a highly competitive field," said Harrison. "And the industry has suffered financially in recent years. The events of September 2001 only made matters worse."

Harrison said that a downside of his job is that his work schedule makes planning a personal life tricky. "You're away from home a lot. You also work long hours. You have little control over the days you get off. And jet lag can be difficult, too."

But if you stick with a company long enough, he said, the pay and benefits can be well worth it.

"That's not all, of course. I love flying. And I get to travel, see the world, meet all kinds of people," said Harrison. "It's just right for the independent sort of person I am."

PROFILE

Betsy Hanrahan—Bus Driver

A pleasant smile appeared on Betsy Hanrahan's face as she greeted Dan Martin. Dan was a regular passenger on the X-2 bus that ran from the town of Hillside into the big city each morning.

"Looks like it's going to be a beautiful weekend," Dan remarked as he dropped $1.50 into the fare box. Behind Dan, a half-dozen passengers followed, many of them on their way to work. Some dropped coins and bills into the box. Others used their prepaid electronic transit cards.

Once all the riders were safely aboard, Betsy pulled the door handle toward her. Out of habit, she glanced up at the rearview mirror that gave her a full view of the inside of the bus. Next, Betsy checked both side mirrors and turned her head to take a quick look at the traffic before she felt confident pulling away from the curb.

Light chatter could be heard throughout the bus, which was about one-third full. Many passengers, however, settled back and read the morning newspaper or a book.

Betsy checked both side mirrors and turned her head to take a quick look at the traffic before she felt confident pulling away from the curb.

Betsy continued on her way, stopping every few blocks to pick up passengers. The morning rush-hour traffic was heavy, as usual, but moved steadily. The bus quickly filled after passengers boarded from the Park 'n' Ride, where business commuters left their cars during the workday. The early-morning mist had lifted and the sun was shining. It was a good day to be a bus driver.

Information, Please

A young woman with two small children stepped onto the bus. "Does this bus go to Greenwich?" she asked.

"No, ma'am," Betsy responded. "The X-2 goes only as far as Cedar Crossroads. If you take this bus, you'll have to transfer there to get to Greenwich. If you'd rather wait, the X-18 will be by in about twenty minutes. That one goes all the way to Greenwich."

"This doesn't go to Greenwich? My sister told me to catch this one."

"I'm sorry, ma'am, but no. You can ride this bus if you'd like, and the transfer to Greenwich would cost you an extra thirty cents."

"But I thought my sister *must* be right. She rides the bus all the time."

"I'm sorry, but she was mistaken. Did you know you can telephone for bus information–or even find it on the Internet? That way you're sure to get the correct routes and schedules."

The woman hesitated and then opened her purse and took out some money. "I'll take this bus, I guess. How much is the children's fare?"

"Seventy-five cents apiece, plus fifteen cents for each transfer." Betsy looked down at the children. "How old is the little boy?"

"He just turned six."

"Good news! He rides free."

"How much is it all together?" the woman asked, still looking confused.

"That would be $2.70, ma'am," Betsy replied promptly.

"When I started this job, I figured that the traffic would take the most patience. But sometimes it's dealing with people."

As the woman deposited the fare, Betsy tore three transfers from a booklet. The family moved to the back of the bus and Betsy breathed a small sigh of relief. After four years, she had learned to be calm and courteous, polite but firm in dealing with passengers. *It's funny,* she thought, *when I started this job, I figured that the traffic would take the most patience. But sometimes it's dealing with people.*

Strategic Driving

The road became more crowded as the X-2 approached the city, and the traffic slowed. Betsy automatically became more cautious about her driving. Too many times, she had seen drivers make a last-minute decision to turn–not paying any attention to the fact that they were in the wrong lane or that the traffic light was red. Betsy felt that a good driver must be a defensive one. She took pride in her own fine driving record.

The bell rang often between stops, signaling that a passenger wanted to get off the bus. Sometimes Betsy glanced at her watch to make sure she was on schedule. Betsy valued safety first, but she also valued being on time.

Up ahead, Betsy saw that a truck whose driver was making a delivery was stopped in the right lane, lights flashing. Because she sat higher above the ground than most of the drivers around her, she could see such "trouble spots" in plenty of time. Whenever she could, Betsy planned ahead to minimize her delays, so she changed lanes to avoid getting stopped behind the truck.

Old Friends and New Faces

"Good morning, Mrs. Godfrey," Betsy greeted the elderly woman boarding the bus. Mrs. Godfrey was one of the patrons who rode the morning bus regularly on its return from the city out to Hillside.

She remembered proudly that she'd had the best scores on both the written and driving portions of her licensing exam.

"Hello, Betsy. Fine morning, isn't it?" the woman replied as she rummaged in her purse for the bus fare. "Oh, dear, I've forgotten my change purse. What shall I do?"

"Don't worry," Betsy replied kindly. She took some change from her pocket, deposited it in the box, and said, "You can bring me the money on Monday."

"You're a real lifesaver! You can trust me not to forget it on Monday."

The return run from the city to Hillside went quickly because Betsy passed by many stops where no one stood waiting. At one stop, a man leaned in through the door. "Ma'am, does this bus go by St. John's Hospital? It's on the corner of Fourth and Pine."

"Yes, it does, sir. If you'd like, I'll call out that stop as we get to it," Betsy replied.

"That would be very helpful, thank you," he said as he paid his fare. He looked at her curiously. "I think you're the youngest lady bus driver I've ever met."

"Maybe so, but I guarantee that you're safe with me, sir. I can handle this bus just fine," Betsy replied with good humor.

In fact, she thought to herself as she watched the man take his seat, *I can handle it better than most.* After all, when she'd applied for the job, she'd had more than three years of experience driving delivery vans and small delivery trucks.

Betsy, a high school graduate, remembered proudly that she'd had the best scores on both the written and driving portions of her licensing exam. Betsy also had to pass a physical exam and undergo a background check for a criminal record. Finally, the city bus system gave her several months of classroom and "behind the wheel" instruction after being hired.

End of the Line

The rest of the trip went smoothly, with no major problems or delays. In fact, at one point Betsy had to make an effort to pace her driving so as not to get ahead of her schedule. She didn't want to pass any of the bus stops early and risk leaving a passenger behind.

After this run was finished, Betsy drove to the garage, where she checked in with the dispatcher. She reported the runs she'd made that morning, added the fares collected, and turned in her booklet of transfer slips after recording the number of transfers she had sold. At this point she'd normally report any problems or delays she'd had, but this morning's trips had gone like clockwork.

Betsy worked a split shift–from 5:30 to 9:30 a.m. and then from 4 to 8 p.m. It was time to go home and get some rest before coming back in the evening.

She returned to the garage and boarded the X-5 bus, which was driven by her friend Sam. He grinned as she got on.

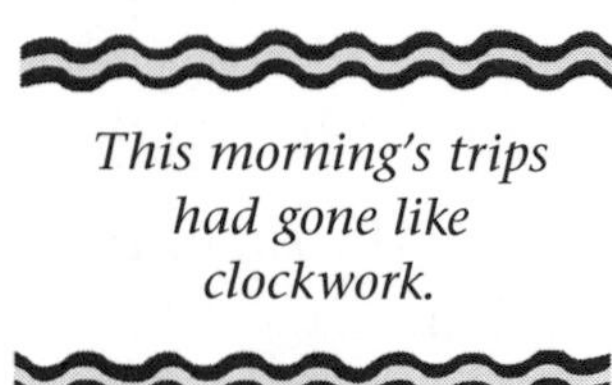
This morning's trips had gone like clockwork.

"Pick any seat you like, ma'am! And enjoy the ride!"

SKILL SAMPLER

Dan Walker–Taxi Driver

For the past ten years, Dan Walker has been a taxi driver in New York City. "When I first started driving, I figured that being in traffic all day would take the most patience. But hectic traffic is nothing compared to some of the people I meet."

Dan described some of the skills that are important to taxi drivers. He offers the following tips for deciding if you will pursue a career as a taxi driver.

Taxi drivers must be easygoing and even-tempered to be able to deal with all kinds of passengers, weather conditions, and traffic problems.

- Can you control your emotions when everything seems to go wrong?
- Can you maintain control of your temper when an umpire calls you out and you think you are safe?

- Can you remain calm and courteous, even when people irritate you or something troubles you?
- Can you make your case calmly when a teacher gives you a grade that you think is unfair?

Dan Walker feels that a good driver is a defensive one. He takes pride in his good driving record.

Taxi drivers must be safety conscious and follow traffic regulations in delivering passengers safely to their destinations.

- Do you look both ways before you cross the street?
- Do you obey traffic regulations such as riding your bicycle with the traffic and only crossing at a crosswalk?
- When you are baby-sitting, do you pay close attention to things that might hurt a child?

Taxi drivers are generally free from close supervision while at work. They must be able to pick up customers and get them to their destinations safely and on time. They must be able to handle emergencies on their own.

- Do you do your homework without being told to?
- Do you clean your room or help with chores around the house without being told to?
- Are you generally on time for class or for meetings?

- Are you sometimes able to correct problems with your computer or printer without involving anyone else?
- Would you know what to do in case of a fire or other emergency at home?

Taxi drivers must have good driving ability to maneuver the taxi in heavy traffic. This includes good eye-foot-hand coordination, quick reflexes, and good depth perception.

- Can you play the piano or organ?
- Are you a good bowler or ice-skater?
- Can you pitch, hit, and catch a softball?
- Do you enjoy computer games that require quick hand movements?

Now learn about all major jobs in the Transportation interest area→

Facts About All Major Jobs Related to

TRANSPORTATION

In addition to the jobs covered in the profiles and skill sampler, other careers in the Transportation area may appeal to you. This section describes and gives facts about all major jobs in the Transportation interest area. For an explanation of the $, ★, and 🚹 symbols, see page 6.

MANAGERIAL WORK IN TRANSPORTATION

These workers manage transportation services. They may be responsible for a whole airline, rail line, bus line, or subway system; oversee a fleet of trucks or cargo vessels; or coordinate the activities of the crew on one large train. They have a good knowledge of the transportation equipment for which they are responsible. They understand how to plan for and react to factors that might affect whether the vehicles complete their routes safely, on schedule, and within budget.

First-Line Supervisors/Managers of Transportation and Material-Moving Machine and Vehicle Operators. Directly supervise and coordinate activities of transportation and material-moving machine and vehicle operators and helpers. **Education and Training:** Work experience in a related occupation. **Skills:** Math—Medium. English—Medium. Science—Medium. **Yearly Earnings:** $$$$ **Job Growth:** ★★★ **Yearly Openings:** 🚹🚹🚹

Railroad Conductors and Yardmasters. Conductors coordinate activities of train crew on passenger or freight train. Coordinate activities of switch-engine crew within yard of railroad, industrial plant, or similar location. Yardmasters coordinate activities of workers engaged in railroad traffic operations, such as the makeup or breakup of trains and yard switching, and review train schedules and switching orders. **Education and Training:** Work experience in a related occupation. **Skills:** Math—Medium. English—Medium. Science—Medium. **Yearly Earnings:** $$$ **Job Growth:** ★ **Yearly Openings:** 🚹

Transportation Managers. Plan, direct, and coordinate the transportation operations within an organization or the activities of organizations that provide transportation services. **Education and Training:** Work experience in a related occupation. **Skills:** Math—Medium. English—Medium. Science—Medium. **Yearly Earnings:** $$$$$ **Job Growth:** ★★★ **Yearly Openings:** 🚹🚹🚹

VEHICLE EXPEDITING AND COORDINATING

These workers monitor and control the movements of vehicles. They work at airports or along rail lines, routing vehicles so they keep on schedule but keep a safe distance from other vehicles. Traffic technicians work under the direction of a traffic engineer to conduct field studies of traffic volume, signals, lighting, and other factors that influence the flow of vehicles.

Air Traffic Controllers. Control air traffic on and within vicinity of airport and movement of air traffic between altitude sectors and control centers according to established procedures and policies. Authorize, regulate, and control commercial airline flights according to government or company regulations to expedite and ensure flight safety. **Education and Training:** Long-term on-the-job training. **Skills:** Math—Medium. English—Medium. Science—Medium. **Yearly Earnings:** $$$$$ **Job Growth:** ★★ **Yearly Openings:** 🚶

Airfield Operations Specialists. Ensure the safe takeoff and landing of commercial and military aircraft. Duties include coordination between air-traffic control and maintenance personnel, dispatching, using airfield landing and navigational aids, implementing airfield safety procedures, monitoring and maintaining flight records, and applying knowledge of weather information. **Education and Training:** Short-term on-the-job training. **Skills:** Math—Medium. English—Medium. Science—Medium. **Yearly Earnings:** $$$ **Job Growth:** ★★★★ **Yearly Openings:** 🚶

Railroad Brake, Signal, and Switch Operators. Operate railroad track switches. Couple or uncouple rolling stock to make up or break up trains. Signal engineers by hand or flagging. May inspect couplings, air hoses, journal boxes, and hand brakes. **Education and Training:** Moderate-term on-the-job training. **Skills:** Math—Medium. English—Medium. Science—Medium. **Yearly Earnings:** $$$ **Job Growth:** ★ **Yearly Openings:** 🚶

Traffic Technicians. Conduct field studies to determine traffic volume, speed, effectiveness of signals, adequacy of lighting, and other factors influencing traffic conditions, under direction of traffic engineer. **Education and Training:** Short-term on-the-job training. **Skills:** Math—High. English—Medium. Science—Medium. **Yearly Earnings:** $$$ **Job Growth:** ★★★ **Yearly Openings:** 🚶

AIR VEHICLE OPERATION

These workers pilot airplanes or helicopters or train or supervise pilots. Most are hired by commercial airlines. Some find jobs piloting planes for private companies, such as package delivery services or crop-dusting services, or for individuals.

Airline Pilots, Copilots, and Flight Engineers. Pilot and navigate the flight of multi-engine aircraft in regularly scheduled service for the transport of passengers and cargo. Requires Federal Air Transport rating and certification in specific aircraft type used. **Education and Training:** Bachelor's degree. **Skills:** Math—Medium. English—Medium. Science—High. **Yearly Earnings:** $$$$$ **Job Growth:** ★★ **Yearly Openings:** 🧍

Commercial Pilots. Pilot and navigate the flight of small fixed or rotary winged aircraft, primarily for the transport of cargo and passengers. Requires Commercial Rating. **Education and Training:** Postsecondary career and technical education. **Skills:** Math—Medium. English—Medium. Science—High. **Yearly Earnings:** $$$$ **Job Growth:** ★★★★ **Yearly Openings:** 🧍

WATER VEHICLE OPERATION

These workers operate ships, boats, and barges. They steer them, operate motor equipment, maintain the vessel, and see that passengers and/or cargo are handled well. Most are hired by freight shipping companies, although some work for cruise lines, fishing fleets, or individuals.

Able Seamen. Stand watch at bow or on wing of bridge to look for obstructions in path of vessel. Measure water depth. Turn wheel on bridge or use emergency equipment as directed by mate. Break out, rig, overhaul, and store cargo-handling gear, stationary rigging, and running gear. Chip rust from and paint deck or ship's structure. Must hold government-issued certification. Must hold certification when working aboard liquid-carrying vessels. **Education and Training:** Short-term on-the-job training. **Skills:** Math—Medium. English—Medium. Science—Medium. **Yearly Earnings:** $$ **Job Growth:** ★★ **Yearly Openings:** 🧍

Captains, Mates, and Pilots of Water Vessels. Command or supervise operations of ships and water vessels, such as tugboats and ferryboats, that travel into and out of harbors, estuaries, straits, and sounds and on rivers, lakes, bays, and oceans. Required to hold license issued by U.S. Coast Guard. **Education and Training:** Long-term on-the-job training. **Skills:** Math—Medium. English—Medium. Science—Medium. **Yearly Earnings:** $$$$ **Job Growth:** ★★ **Yearly Openings:** 🧍

Dredge Operators. Operate dredge to remove sand, gravel, or other materials from lakes, rivers, or streams and to excavate and maintain navigable channels in waterways. **Education and Training:** Moderate-term on-the-job training. **Skills:** Math—Low. English—Low. Science—Medium. **Yearly Earnings:** $$ **Job Growth:** No data available. **Yearly Openings:** No data available.

Mates—Ship, Boat, and Barge. Supervise and coordinate activities of crew aboard ships, boats, barges, or dredges. **Education and Training:** Work experience in a related occupation. **Skills:** Math—Medium. English—Medium. Science—Medium. **Yearly Earnings:** $$$$ **Job Growth:** ★★ **Yearly Openings:** 🧍

Motorboat Operators. Operate small motor-driven boats to carry passengers and freight between ships or from ship to shore. May patrol harbors and beach areas. May assist in navigational activities. **Education and Training:** Moderate-term on-the-job training. **Skills:** Math—Low. English—Low. Science—Low. **Yearly Earnings:** $$$$ **Job Growth:** ★★ **Yearly Openings:** 🚶

Ordinary Seamen and Marine Oilers. Stand deck department watches and perform a variety of tasks to preserve the painted surface of the ship and to maintain lines and ship equipment, such as running and cargo-handling gear. May oil and grease moving parts of engines and auxiliary equipment. Must hold government-issued certification. Must hold certification when working aboard liquid-carrying vessels. **Education and Training:** Short-term on-the-job training. **Skills:** Math—Low. English—Medium. Science—Medium. **Yearly Earnings:** $$ **Job Growth:** ★★ **Yearly Openings:** 🚶

Pilots, Ship. Command ships to steer them into and out of harbors, estuaries, straits, and sounds and on rivers, lakes, and bays. Must be licensed by U.S. Coast Guard with limitations indicating class and tonnage of vessels for which license is valid and route and waters that may be piloted. **Education and Training:** College degree plus work experience. **Skills:** Math—Medium. English—Medium. Science—Medium. **Yearly Earnings:** $$$$ **Job Growth:** ★★ **Yearly Openings:** 🚶

Sailors and Marine Oilers. Stand watch to look for obstructions in path of vessel, measure water depth, turn wheel on bridge, or use emergency equipment as directed by captain, mate, or pilot. Break out, rig, overhaul, and store cargo-handling gear, stationary rigging, and running gear. Perform a variety of maintenance tasks to preserve the painted surface of the ship and to maintain line and ship equipment. Must hold government-issued certification and tankerman certification when working aboard liquid-carrying vessels. **Education and Training:** Short-term on-the-job training. **Skills:** Math—Medium. English—Medium. Science—Medium. **Yearly Earnings:** $$ **Job Growth:** ★★ **Yearly Openings:** 🚶

Ship and Boat Captains. Command vessels in oceans, bays, lakes, rivers, and coastal waters. **Education and Training:** Long-term on-the-job training. **Skills:** Math—Medium. English—Medium. Science—Medium. **Yearly Earnings:** $$$$ **Job Growth:** ★★ **Yearly Openings:** 🚶

TRUCK DRIVING

These workers drive large trucks, small trucks, or delivery vans. They may cover long distances or a familiar local route. Most of these jobs are found with trucking companies or with wholesale and retail companies that do deliveries.

Tractor-Trailer Truck Drivers. Drive tractor-trailer truck to transport products, livestock, or materials to specified destinations. **Education and Training:** Moderate-term on-the-job training. **Skills:** Math—Medium. English—Medium. Science—Medium. **Yearly Earnings:** $$$ **Job Growth:** ★★★ **Yearly Openings:** 🚶🚶🚶🚶🚶

Truck Drivers, Heavy. Drive truck with capacity of more than three tons to transport materials to specified destinations. **Education and Training:** Short-term on-the-job training. **Skills:** Math—Medium. English—Medium. Science—Medium. **Yearly Earnings:** $$$ **Job Growth:** ★★★ **Yearly Openings:** 🚶🚶🚶🚶🚶

Truck Drivers, Heavy and Tractor-Trailer. Drive a tractor-trailer combination or a truck with a capacity of at least 26,000 GVW to transport and deliver goods, livestock, or materials in liquid, loose, or packaged form. May be required to unload truck. May require use of automated routing equipment. Requires commercial driver's license. **Education and Training:** Moderate-term on-the-job training. **Skills:** Math—Medium. English—Medium. Science—Medium. **Yearly Earnings:** $$$ **Job Growth:** ★★★ **Yearly Openings:** 🚶🚶🚶🚶🚶

Truck Drivers, Light or Delivery Services. Drive a truck or van with a capacity of under 26,000 GVW primarily to deliver or pick up merchandise or to deliver packages within a specified area. May require use of automatic routing or location software. May load and unload truck. **Education and Training:** Short-term on-the-job training. **Skills:** Math—Medium. English—Medium. Science—Medium. **Yearly Earnings:** $$ **Job Growth:** ★★★ **Yearly Openings:** 🚶🚶🚶🚶🚶

RAIL VEHICLE OPERATION

These workers drive locomotives, subways, and streetcars. Most of these jobs are found with railroads and city transit authorities.

Locomotive Engineers. Drive electric, diesel-electric, steam, or gas-turbine-electric locomotives to transport passengers or freight. Interpret train orders, electronic or manual signals, and railroad rules and regulations. **Education and Training:** Work experience in a related occupation. **Skills:** Math—Low. English—Medium. Science—Medium. **Yearly Earnings:** $$$$ **Job Growth:** ★ **Yearly Openings:** 🚶

Locomotive Firers. Monitor locomotive instruments and watch for dragging equipment, obstacles on rights-of-way, and train signals during run. Watch for and relay traffic signals from yard workers to yard engineer in railroad yard. **Education and Training:** Postsecondary career and technical education. **Skills:** Math—Medium. English—Medium. Science—Medium. **Yearly Earnings:** $$$$ **Job Growth:** ★ **Yearly Openings:** 🚶

Rail Yard Engineers, Dinkey Operators, and Hostlers. Drive switching or other locomotive or dinkey engines within railroad yard, industrial plant, quarry, construction project, or similar location. **Education and Training:** Work experience in a related occupation. **Skills:** Math—Medium. English—Medium. Science—Medium. **Yearly Earnings:** $$$ **Job Growth:** ★ **Yearly Openings:** 🚶

Subway and Streetcar Operators. Operate subway or elevated suburban train with no separate locomotive or operate electric-powered streetcar to transport passengers.

May handle fares. **Education and Training:** Moderate-term on-the-job training. **Skills:** Math—Medium. English—Medium. Science—Low. **Yearly Earnings:** $$$$ **Job Growth:** ★★ **Yearly Openings:** 🚶

OTHER SERVICES REQUIRING DRIVING

These workers drive ambulances, taxis, buses (city, intercity, or school), or other small vehicles, mostly to take people from place to place. Some drive a route to sell or deliver items, such as ice cream bars, take-out food, or newspapers. Some park cars in parking lots.

Ambulance Drivers and Attendants, Except Emergency Medical Technicians. Drive ambulance or assist ambulance driver in transporting sick, injured, or convalescent persons. Assist in lifting patients. **Education and Training:** Moderate-term on-the-job training. **Skills:** Math—Low. English—Medium. Science—Medium. **Yearly Earnings:** $ **Job Growth:** ★★★★ **Yearly Openings:** 🚶

Bus Drivers, School. Transport students or special clients, such as the elderly or persons with disabilities. Ensure adherence to safety rules. May assist passengers in boarding or exiting. **Education and Training:** Short-term on-the-job training. **Skills:** Math—Low. English—Medium. Science—Low. **Yearly Earnings:** $$ **Job Growth:** ★★★ **Yearly Openings:** 🚶🚶🚶🚶

Bus Drivers, Transit and Intercity. Drive bus or motor coach, including regular route operations, charters, and private carriage. May assist passengers with baggage. May collect fares or tickets. **Education and Training:** Moderate-term on-the-job training. **Skills:** Math—Medium. English—Medium. Science—Medium. **Yearly Earnings:** $$ **Job Growth:** ★★★ **Yearly Openings:** 🚶🚶🚶

Driver/Sales Workers. Drive truck or other vehicle over established routes or within an established territory and sell goods, such as food products, including restaurant take-out items, or pick up and deliver items such as laundry. May also take orders and collect payments. Includes newspaper delivery drivers. **Education and Training:** Short-term on-the-job training. **Skills:** Math—Medium. English—Medium. Science—Medium. **Yearly Earnings:** $$ **Job Growth:** ★★ **Yearly Openings:** 🚶🚶🚶🚶

Parking Lot Attendants. Park automobiles or issue tickets for customers in a parking lot or garage. May collect fee. **Education and Training:** Short-term on-the-job training. **Skills:** Math—Medium. English—Medium. Science—Medium. **Yearly Earnings:** $ **Job Growth:** ★★★ **Yearly Openings:** 🚶🚶🚶

Taxi Drivers and Chauffeurs. Drive automobiles, vans, or limousines to transport passengers. May carry cargo. **Education and Training:** Short-term on-the-job training. **Skills:** Math—Medium. English—Medium. Science—Low. **Yearly Earnings:** $ **Job Growth:** ★★★★ **Yearly Openings:** 🚶🚶🚶

SUPPORT WORK

These workers provide support for routine operations at airports, railroads, and docks. They load and unload cargo, secure cargo inside vehicles, and refuel and clean vehicles.

Freight Inspectors. Inspect freight for proper storage according to specifications. **Education and Training:** Work experience in a related occupation. **Skills:** Math—Medium. English—Medium. Science—Medium. **Yearly Earnings:** $$$$ **Job Growth:** ★★★ **Yearly Openings:** 🧍

Railroad Yard Workers. Perform a variety of activities such as coupling railcars and operating railroad track switches in railroad yard to facilitate the movement of railcars within the yard. **Education and Training:** Work experience in a related occupation. **Skills:** Math—Low. English—Low. Science—Low. **Yearly Earnings:** $$$ **Job Growth:** ★ **Yearly Openings:** 🧍

Stevedores, Except Equipment Operators. Manually load and unload ship cargo. Stack cargo in transit shed or in hold of ship using pallet or cargo board. Attach and move slings to lift cargo. Guide load lift. **Education and Training:** Short-term on-the-job training. **Skills:** Math—Low. English—Low. Science—Low. **Yearly Earnings:** $ **Job Growth:** ★★★ **Yearly Openings:** 🧍🧍🧍🧍🧍

Train Crew Members. Inspect couplings, airhoses, journal boxes, and handbrakes on trains to ensure that they function properly. **Education and Training:** Work experience in a related occupation. **Skills:** Math—Medium. English—Low. Science—Medium. **Yearly Earnings:** $$$ **Job Growth:** ★ **Yearly Openings:** 🧍

Transportation Inspectors. Inspect equipment or goods in connection with the safe transport of cargo or people. Includes rail transport inspectors, such as freight inspectors, car inspectors, rail inspectors, and other nonprecision inspectors of other types of transportation vehicles. **Education and Training:** Work experience in a related occupation. **Skills:** Math—Medium. English—Medium. Science—Medium. **Yearly Earnings:** $$$$ **Job Growth:** ★★★ **Yearly Openings:** 🧍

Exploring Careers:

Industrial Production

Start Your Journey Through Careers Related to

INDUSTRIAL PRODUCTION

Careers in this area suit people interested in concrete, organized, and repetitive activities, often in an industrial or factory setting.

EXPLORING CAREER CLUES

Your interests give important clues for exploring career options. Think about your interests to learn if jobs in the Industrial Production interest area may be worth further exploration.

Do you like the school subjects related to the Industrial Production interest area? Here are some examples of related subjects:

- Math
- Computers
- Science
- Chemistry
- Physics
- English
- Art
- Industrial or technology education
- Physical education

Do you like the free-time activities related to the Industrial Production interest area? Here are some examples of related free-time activities:

- Building model airplanes, cars, or boats
- Building cabinets, furniture, and other items
- Carving wood
- Setting up and installing stereos, personal computers, and other electronic or technical equipment
- Taking apart or repairing small appliances and devices
- Assembling or working on bicycles, minibikes, lawn mowers, and cars
- Assembling radios and other devices from kits
- Assembling toys, shelving, furniture, and other items around the house
- Studying diagrams and sketches of machines, football plays, or other things that interest you
- Sewing, knitting, or doing needlework
- Making jewelry or stringing beads

EXPLORING JOB GROUPS

Jobs related to the Industrial Production interest area fit into seven groups. Read through the list to see which groups sound interesting to you.

- Managerial Work in Industrial Production
- Production Technology
- Production Work
- Metal and Plastics Machining Technology
- Woodworking Technology
- Systems Operation
- Hands-on Work: Loading, Moving, Hoisting, and Conveying

EXPLORING CAREER POSSIBILITIES

You can satisfy your interest in the Industrial Production area by working in one of many industries that mass-produce goods or by working for a utility that distributes electric power or other resources. Here are a few examples of career possibilities:

You may enjoy manual work using your hands or hand tools in highly skilled jobs such as engine assembly or electronic equipment assembly. Perhaps you prefer to set up or operate machines that are used to manufacture products made of food, glass, or paper. You may enjoy cutting and grinding metal and plastic parts to desired shapes and measurements.

Or you may wish to operate equipment in systems that provide water and process wastewater. You may like inspecting, counting, or weighing products. Another option is to work with your hands and machinery to move boxes and freight in a warehouse.

Turn the page to meet people working in the Industrial Production interest area→

PROFILE

Galen Anthony—Jeweler

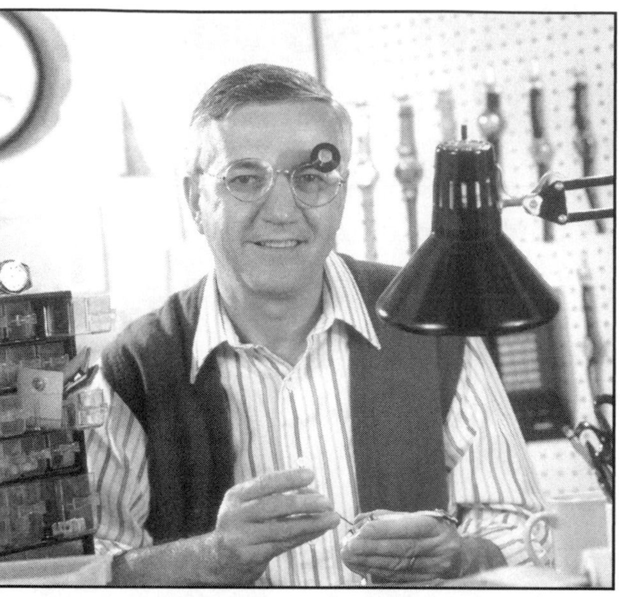

Galen performs detailed repairs as well as making new pieces.

Galen Anthony sat under a single bright light at his workbench. Scattered across it were tweezers and pliers, small brown envelopes, and gold wire. He placed the eyeglasses that he had just repaired in a small case and then sat up straight and stretched.

Glancing at his watch, he thought, *Less than an hour until we open.* He decided against beginning to make Ms. Sturgis's earrings. There would be too many interruptions for such a difficult job once the store was open. Galen's power of concentration was excellent, but even the best jewelers need quiet time to work.

Under the Magnifying Glass

He looked over the envelopes and chose the one marked "Repair ring setting." Removing the ring, he slipped on his magnifying glasses to examine it.

Two small loops of gold held an emerald in place, but one of the loops had broken at the bottom. To fix the ring, Galen would have to first remove the stone. He would then have to melt metal to rejoin the broken ends. This was called soldering.

The work would be delicate–a slip of the pliers, and the valuable stone could be chipped and ruined. However, Galen had fixed hundreds of rings in his life as a jeweler. He could fix the ring between handling customer problems and questions.

Using pliers, he bent back both loops. As he worked the stone loose from its small gold mounting plate, he heard the front door open.

"Galen, what are you doing?" called Deb Rothstein, the salesclerk. "Have you been here long?"

"Only a few hours," he said with a laugh. "With the holidays coming up, I can't work undisturbed during business hours."

"I know, but you really should take it easy," Deb said softly.

"Please don't worry about me so much," said Galen. "Go ahead and set the jewelry in the display cases and get ready to open the store."

Deb quickly returned to the front of the store. Deb was a first-class salesperson. More than that, she was a good friend. *Funny how people you work with every day can become like family,* he thought. He put aside the thought for the moment and returned to his work.

Handle with Care

The gold wire had to be filed to lie flat on the ring. That took no time at all. Then, using the pliers, Galen bent the wire down so it touched the top of the ring. He moved to his soldering equipment.

Using tweezers, he dipped the ring in an acid solution that would keep the metal from turning black under the torch's flame. He placed the ring in a soldering clamp and brought out a packet of gold solder.

"Excuse me," called Deb from the sales floor. "Did the gift boxes come in yesterday?"

"No, and we're almost out. If they don't come in by noon, please call Schmidt's."

Galen took a piece of solder from the packet. From this piece he clipped a speck of solder–small as a grain of sand.

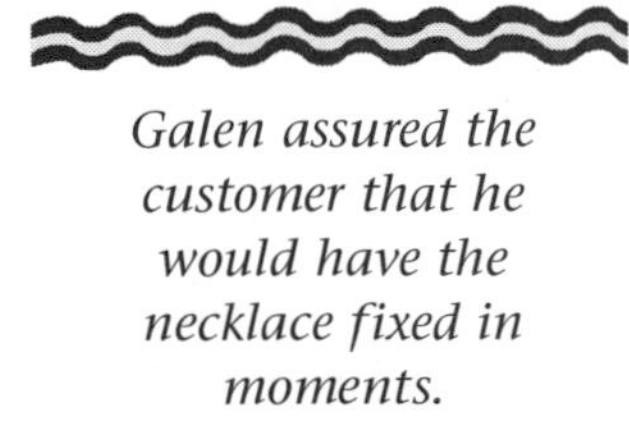

Galen assured the customer that he would have the necklace fixed in moments.

He lit the torch and adjusted the flame to a fine line. With the tip of an old file, he held the speck of solder to the break in the ring. He then carefully but quickly applied the flame.

In seconds the solder had melted in place. Galen made sure to turn off the torch and replace it in the stand before inspecting the ring. He heard the door open, and Deb called out again.

"Galen, could you come here for a moment? It's Mr. Johnson." Galen went to the counter.

"How can I help you?" he asked his customer.

"You can help me by giving me my wife's necklace," said the man a bit sharply. "I brought it in yesterday to have the clasp fixed, and my wife wants to wear it to a party tonight."

Galen assured the man that he would have the necklace fixed in moments. He stepped back to his bench and quickly replaced the clasp. When he was finished, Galen said, "No charge, sir. To make up for any inconvenience."

"Oh!" Mr. Johnson looked surprised. "Well, thank you," he said as he left quickly.

Finishing Touches

Galen retrieved the unfinished ring and took it to his polishing machine in the back room. To this he attached a wheel with bristles and turned it on. He touched the edges of the spinning bristles with a lump of abrasive clay called tripoli, which quickly covered the bristles' edges.

If the stone were not set exactly, it would look lopsided.

Then he ran the soldered joint under the bristles. When he pulled the ring away, the lump of solder was smooth.

Galen slipped on a different wheel on the machine and applied a red, iron oxide clay–jeweler's rouge–to its bristles. This time he polished the entire ring, which he then placed in an ultrasonic cleaner. The cleaner used air bubbles to remove tiny particles of dirt.

After a few minutes, the ring sparkled, showing hardly a trace of the soldered joint. Still, the jeweler's trained eye saw that the solder was a different color than the gold.

"One more step," Galen said quietly. Many jewelers would reset the stone at this point, but not Galen. He wouldn't do a job that didn't satisfy him.

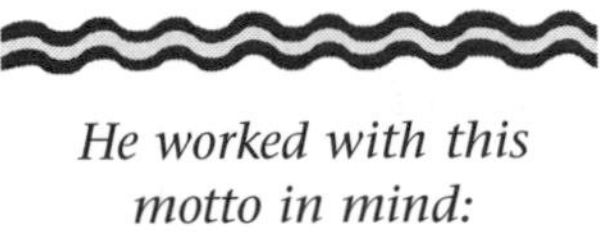

He worked with this motto in mind: "Do it right."

He would goldplate the ring to hide the joint. The process would take several minutes, so he leaned against the wall and relaxed.

He remembered Mr. Wisniewski's motto: "Do it right." At age seventeen, he had gone to Mr. Wisniewski's jewelry repair shop as an apprentice and had stayed there four years. He had learned all types of jewelry work: stone setting, watch repair, jewelry-making and repair, and model-making.

These days, only a few shop owners hire apprentices, he reflected. *Most jewelers now learn their trade in factories so specialized that a person usually learns only one or two skills.*

The buzz of the timer interrupted Galen's thoughts. The ring was now covered with a new layer of gold, completely hiding the solder.

All that remained was to reset the stone, but this was no simple task. If the stone were not set exactly, it would look lopsided. Furthermore, when he set the prongs, he could easily damage the emerald.

Galen's Golden Moment

The door opened yet again, and a well-dressed woman entered. "Good morning, Mrs. Banks. You've come for your ring?" said Deb.

"Yes, I'm anxious to see it."

"It's in the safe," said Galen. "I'll get it."

He soon returned with a small black box, which he opened under a fluorescent lamp on the counter. Three diamonds surrounding a ruby in a fine gold setting sparkled and flashed.

Mrs. Banks gasped and then said, "Beautiful, truly beautiful."

"I'm glad you like it," Galen said.

He had made this ring by hand from a design Mrs. Banks had given him. It had been a long and difficult job but well worth it. The ring was a work of art in metal and stones. "Deb will wrap the ring and make out your receipt," said Galen.

"Thank you again. You've done a magnificent job," said Mrs. Banks.

Galen smiled for a moment and then hurried back to his bench.

PROFILE

Michael Von Braun—Machinist

Michael Von Braun can't wait to get up every morning. Most days he wakes up before the alarm goes off. The reason is his job, which he finds interesting and challenging.

As a machinist, Michael makes a variety of metal parts for appliances and machines.

"I work in a machine shop that makes replacement parts for water pumps, electric generators, sometimes cars. Well, anything, really. We'll make almost anything from metal," Michael explained.

"Usually I work from a blueprint the boss gives me. A blueprint is a drawing of the part I have to make. By looking at it I know what the final product will look like.

"The blueprint also has the specifications. They tell me how long and wide to make the part and what kind of metal to use. Usually the specifications also give an estimate of how much time I have to make the part."

How Does a Machinist Do the Job?

"First I gather the metal stock, all the different pieces of metal I'll be working with: Steel rods, brass tubing, bars of aluminum, whatever. Then I mark the metal to show where I should cut it, put holes in it, or shape it.

"There are all kinds of machines specially designed to work metal," Michael said. "Lathes, milling machines, drill presses, planers, and grinders, for example.

"I use saws to cut metal to the right length; drills to put holes in it; planers to shape it; and grinders to smooth its surface. The milling machine and the lathe are the most versatile of all. They can do almost any job.

"For some jobs I have to use a certain size lathe or a milling machine. For others I can choose how I do the job. Take drilling a hole. I can use a drill press or a milling machine. The drill is a little faster, but the milling machine is more accurate.

"After I've cut the metal, I measure it to make sure it meets the specifications. Sometimes I can do it with a ruler, but most jobs require more precision. A workpiece may have to be between 5.999 and 6.001 inches long. I use a micrometer to make really precise measurements.

"The precision is necessary because the part I make usually goes into a larger machine. I have to make it just the right size, so it fits.

"The precision is necessary because the part I make usually goes into a larger machine. I have to make it just the right size, so it fits."

"When I'm sure all the pieces are acceptable, I can assemble the part. That means a lot of hand work with files, hammers, and screwdrivers–more measuring. And that's it," concluded Michael.

In the Machine Shop

Some machinists make the same part over and over again. This repetitive activity can lead to injuries like carpal tunnel syndrome, which most people think of as a problem for those who use computers all day. But anyone who repeats the same physical movements throughout the day can develop the problem.

In some modern machine shops, industrial robots do that kind of repetitive job, while the machinists perform specialized tasks.

The shops can be noisy places to work, so it's important to wear hearing protection. Just as your hands and wrists can be injured, so can your eardrums.

Anytime you work with machinery there is the risk of injury. "Fortunately, you are taught how to handle the risks when you learn how to work the machines," Michael stated. "Statistics show that it's usually the amateur who gets hurt operating his drill or other machines, not the professional."

"Machinists are among the most highly skilled and versatile manual workers. You have to like machines and tools."

A Machinist's Skills

"Machinists may make many different kinds of parts. That's what I do. It's interesting and challenging most of the time. You might also work in a factory repairing production machinery," Michael pointed out. "Machinists are among the most highly skilled and versatile manual workers.

"You have to like machines and tools. It's dirty, hard work a lot of the time. You're on your feet most of the day, and it's not just physical work.

"You have to be able to plan. You have to be good at math to calculate the measurements, machine speeds, and such. You can't escape the need to make calculations when you're building a machine. Even a computer can't do it all.

"You have to be able to concentrate and have the patience to do really precise work.

"Besides all that, you need a bit of imagination. Not everyone can make a three-dimensional object from a flat drawing."

"You need a bit of imagination. Not everyone can make a three-dimensional object from a flat drawing."

Good communication skills are definitely important, Michael said. You must be able to understand what is needed. "You must be able to tell your boss or client or the designer if it won't work and why."

Along with communication is the ability to solve problems, according to Michael. "You may think something won't work, but your boss insists you make it work. That's when your problem-solving has to kick in. You'll be amazed at what you can do when you have to."

"As for teamwork, I never knew of a machinist who could do it all alone. Whether you need to consult your boss for direction or talk over a difficult project with a colleague, it's all about working together to get results."

How to Learn the Trade

Typically, machinists train through apprenticeships either on the job or in high school, vocational schools, or community or technical colleges. "Most of the programs work the same way," Michael continued.

"You learn by working alongside more experienced workers. And by studying. After I graduated from high school, I was accepted in an apprenticeship program. I learned to run the machines on the job and studied math, blueprint reading, and the characteristics of metals in evening classes."

It is helpful to have some experience with machines before you begin a program. In fact, many machinists start out as machine setters, operators, or tenders.

"If you can," Michael said, "take courses in math, blueprint reading, metalworking, and drafting in high school. It will give you a good start once you get to the apprenticeship program."

"Take math, blueprint reading, metalworking, and drafting in high school. It will give you a good start once you get to the apprenticeship program."

"One way to increase your income is to specialize," Michael said. "If you become a computer-control programmer or operator, you will definitely earn more. As in many other professions, computers are the wave of the future.

"You might also consider opening a machinist's shop of your own. Like any other business, it takes time and commitment to get it off the ground. But those who do say there's nothing like the freedom of owning your own place."

How Does the Future Look?

"Some people say that computers will replace machinists sooner than we think. Others say there will always be a need for skilled machinists," Michael said.

"I believe we will always need machinists. I have talked to others in the industry who say that there aren't that many well-trained machinists out there.

"I would say that if you have the desire to become a machinist, and your skills are compatible with what it takes to do the work, go for it."

PROFILE

Nancy Jamison—Semiconductor Processor

Nancy Jamison is a semiconductor processor. "I work in a bunny suit," she said with a laugh. "But it's not the kind with long ears, whiskers, tail, and fur."

It is a lightweight outer suit that fits over clothing. It prevents lint and particles from contaminating semiconductor processing worksites. A sterile environment is essential for Nancy's work. She manufactures a high-tech component called the semiconductor.

Semiconductors are also known as computer chips, microchips, or integrated chips. They are tiny aluminum wires and electric switches that manipulate the flow of electrical current. "The process of manufacturing a semiconductor involves several hundred steps. Each is controlled by a semiconductor processor," Nancy said.

Precision on the Job

Semiconductor processors manufacture semiconductors in disks about the size of dinner plates. These disks are called wafers. They are thin slices of silicon on which the semiconductor wiring is layered. Machines cut each wafer into dozens of semiconductors.

Semiconductors are also known as computer chips, microchips, or integrated chips.

"I make wafers using photolithography. It's a printing process for creating plates from photographic images," Nancy explained. Operating automated equipment, Nancy imprints precise microscopic patterns of wiring on the wafers. She etches the patterns with acids. She then replaces them with silicon and other materials.

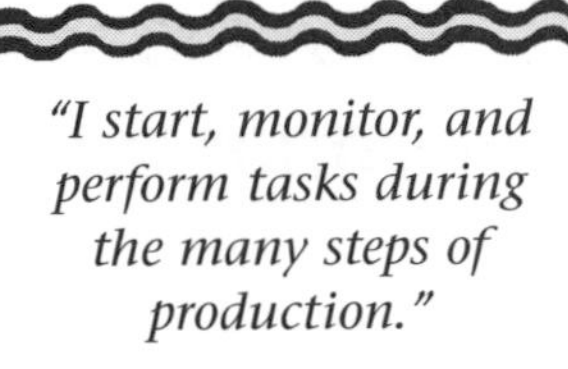

"I start, monitor, and perform tasks during the many steps of production."

The wafers get a chemical bath to make them smooth. The imprint process starts again on a new layer with the next pattern. Typically, wafers have eight to twenty layers of microscopic three-dimensional wiring.

The manufacturing process happens in "clean rooms." Clean rooms are production areas that are free of airborne matter. The least bit of dirt can ruin a semiconductor. "All semiconductor processors working in clean rooms wear bunny suits," said Nancy.

Two types of semiconductor processors work in clean rooms: operators and technicians.

Operators like Nancy are the majority of workers in clean rooms. "I start, monitor, and perform tasks during the many steps of production," Nancy explained.

She monitors the equipment at computer terminals. She also transfers wafer carriers from one development station to the next. Because she is responsible for maintaining continuous production, Nancy keeps the machinery at proper operating parameters.

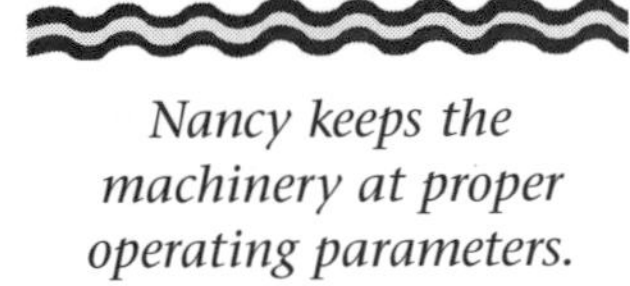

Nancy keeps the machinery at proper operating parameters.

Technicians are a smaller percentage of the work force in clean rooms. They troubleshoot production problems. They also make equipment adjustments and repairs. They take the lead in quality control and equipment maintenance. To cut down on repairs, technicians perform diagnostics and run computations. For example, a technician might analyze a semiconductor's flaw by determining its source. Is the flaw due to contamination in that wafer, or is it in the manufacturing process?

A Very Clean and Safe Work Environment

"The work environment of semiconductor fabricating plants is one of the safest in any industry."

"The work pace in clean rooms is deliberately slow," Nancy said. "Limited movement keeps the air as free as possible of dust and other particles, which can destroy semiconductors during production."

Because machinery sets operators' rate of work in the production process, workers keep an easy-going pace as well. Workers spend some time alone monitoring equipment. Operators and technicians spend much of their time working in teams.

Technicians are on their feet most of the day. They walk through the clean room to oversee production activities. Operators spend a great deal of time sitting or standing at work stations, monitoring computer readouts and gauges. Sometimes they take wafers from one station to another. To minimize the risk of dropping expensive wafers and semiconductors, machines do the lifting.

"The clean room temperature must be kept within narrow ranges, usually a comfortable 72 degrees Fahrenheit," Nancy said. "The temperature inside bunny suits stays fairly constant as well." Workers in bunny suits face some restrictions because entry and exit from each clean room is controlled to minimize contamination.

"The work environment of semiconductor fabricating plants is one of the safest in any industry," Nancy stated. "Measures taken to avoid contamination of the wafers result in a work environment that has one of the lowest rates of illnesses and accidents." Air in clean rooms is much purer than normal household air.

Semiconductor fabricating plants operate around the clock. Night and weekend work is common. In Nancy's plant, workers maintain standard eight-hour shifts five days a week. In other plants, employees work twelve-hour shifts to minimize the disruption of clean room operations brought about by shift changes. Managers in some plants allow workers to alternate schedules.

Industry Changes and Job Prospects

The number of electronic semiconductor processor jobs is projected to increase over the next few years. Growing need for semiconductor processors will stem from applications for semiconductors in appliances, vehicles, computers, and other equipment.

Development of semiconductors made from better material for transmitting electricity means that semiconductors will become even smaller and more powerful. This development will lead to new applications, resulting in employment growth in the industry.

Job prospects should be best for people with postsecondary education in electronics or semiconductor technology. Prospects should also be good for high school graduates with a strong science background, especially for those working toward a postsecondary degree while employed.

Solid Math and Science Background Needed

People interested in becoming operators or technicians need a solid background in math and physical sciences. "I always enjoyed and did well in math and science in school," Nancy said.

Math and science knowledge are essentials for pursuing higher education in semiconductor technology–and knowledge of both subjects is one of the best ways to advance.

"Semiconductor processor workers must think analytically and critically to anticipate problems and avoid costly mistakes," said Nancy. "Oral and written communication skills are also vital."

A high school diploma is the minimum requirement for entry-level operator jobs. Technicians must have at least an associate's degree in electronics technology or a related field. Some community colleges offer a one-year certificate program in semiconductor technology. Employers prefer to hire people with an associate's degree.

In some plants, high school students with strong math and science skills are hired to work during the summer.

Degree or certificate candidates who get hands-on training while attending school are attractive to employers. Semiconductor processing programs in community colleges include an internship at a semiconductor fabricating plant.

Nancy and her coworkers attend forty hours of formal training per year financed by their employer.

Getting postsecondary training is perhaps the easiest route for most people to enter the field. In some plants, high school students with strong math and science skills are hired to work during the summer. That's how Nancy got started in her job.

"I really enjoy this work and plan to continue it for a long time," Nancy said. "The job and the bunny suit fit me just right."

SKILL SAMPLER

Kevin Bagwell—Electronic Equipment Assembler

Kevin Bagwell is an electronic equipment assembler. He assembles circuit boards for television sets and other electronic equipment. "You don't need a great deal of education and experience to do what I do, but you have to be good with your hands."

Kevin discussed the skills needed by an electronic equipment assembler. He offers several tips to help you determine if this is a career you want to pursue.

Electronic equipment assemblers must be good at working with their hands.

- Are you good at fixing things?
- Are you handy with tools?
- Can you repair a bicycle?
- Do you enjoy sewing, stringing beads, building models, refinishing furniture, or doing other activities that involve working with your hands?

Electronic equipment assemblers do work that involves a lot of repetition.

- Do you enjoy needlework such as knitting, crocheting, or quilting?

- Can you put up with the repetition involved in mowing grass, shoveling snow, painting a house, or putting down tile?

Electronic equipment assemblers must be able to do detailed work quickly.

- Are you good at activities such as playing jacks, shuffling and dealing cards, or doing other activities that require finger dexterity?
- Do you enjoy computer games that involve doing something within a short amount of time?

Electronic equipment assemblers must be able to follow diagrams and written directions.

- Are you good at following a recipe, sewing or doing needlepoint from a pattern, building a model from written instructions, or assembling a radio from a kit?
- Are you good at reading maps?
- Do you understand football plays when they are written out?

Electronic equipment assemblers work indoors. They stay in a small work area while they do their jobs.

- Can you sit still through your classes?
- Can you concentrate without feeling the need to move around all the time?

Now learn about all major jobs in the Industrial Production interest area→

Facts About All Major Jobs Related to

INDUSTRIAL PRODUCTION

In addition to the jobs covered in the profiles and skill sampler, other careers in the Industrial Production interest area may appeal to you. This section describes and gives facts about all major jobs in the Industrial Production interest area. For an explanation of the $, ★, and 🚶 symbols, see page 6.

MANAGERIAL WORK IN INDUSTRIAL PRODUCTION

These workers manage industrial processing and manufacturing plants. They make decisions about policy and operation in line with company policy and goals. They must have working knowledge of the equipment and methods for the activity that they direct.

First-Line Supervisors/Managers of Helpers, Laborers, and Material Movers, Hand. Supervise and coordinate the activities of helpers, laborers, or material movers. **Education and Training:** Work experience in a related occupation. **Skills:** Math—Medium. English—Medium. Science—Medium. **Yearly Earnings:** $$$ **Job Growth:** ★★★ **Yearly Openings:** 🚶🚶🚶

First-Line Supervisors/Managers of Production and Operating Workers. Supervise and coordinate the activities of production and operating workers, such as inspectors, precision workers, machine setters and operators, assemblers, fabricators, and plant and system operators. **Education and Training:** Work experience in a related occupation. **Skills:** Math—Medium. English—Medium. Science—Medium. **Yearly Earnings:** $$$$ **Job Growth:** ★ **Yearly Openings:** 🚶🚶🚶🚶

Industrial Production Managers. Plan, direct, or coordinate the work activities and resources necessary for manufacturing products according to cost, quality, and quantity specifications. **Education and Training:** Bachelor's degree. **Skills:** Math—Medium. English—Medium. Science—Medium. **Yearly Earnings:** $$$$$ **Job Growth:** ★★ **Yearly Openings:** 🚶🚶🚶

PRODUCTION TECHNOLOGY

These workers perform highly skilled hand and/or machine work requiring special techniques, training, and experience. Some set up machines for others to operate, or they set up and perform a variety of machine operations on their own. Some do

precision handwork. Some inspect and test the work of others to make sure it meets standards of quality. Production technology workers mostly are employed on assembly lines, but the materials they work with may be as big as airplane bodies or as small as gemstones.

Aircraft Rigging Assemblers. Fabricate and assemble aircraft tubing or cable components or assemblies. **Education and Training:** Long-term on-the-job training. **Skills:** Math—Medium. English—Medium. Science—Medium. **Yearly Earnings:** $$$$ **Job Growth:** ★★★ **Yearly Openings:** 🧍

Aircraft Structure Assemblers, Precision. Assemble tail, wing, fuselage, or other structural section of aircraft, space vehicles, and missiles from parts, subassemblies, and components and install functional units, parts, or equipment, such as landing gear, control surfaces, doors, and floorboards. **Education and Training:** Long-term on-the-job training. **Skills:** Math—Medium. English—Medium. Science—Medium. **Yearly Earnings:** $$$$ **Job Growth:** ★★★ **Yearly Openings:** 🧍

Aircraft Structure, Surfaces, Rigging, and Systems Assemblers. Assemble, fit, fasten, and install parts of airplanes, space vehicles, or missiles, such as tails, wings, fuselage, bulkheads, stabilizers, landing gear, rigging and control equipment, or heating and ventilating systems. **Education and Training:** Long-term on-the-job training. **Skills:** Math—Medium. English—Medium. Science—Medium. **Yearly Earnings:** $$$$ **Job Growth:** ★★★ **Yearly Openings:** 🧍

Aircraft Systems Assemblers, Precision. Lay out, assemble, install, and test aircraft systems, such as armament, environmental control, plumbing, and hydraulic. **Education and Training:** Long-term on-the-job training. **Skills:** Math—Medium. English—Medium. Science—Medium. **Yearly Earnings:** $$$$ **Job Growth:** ★★★ **Yearly Openings:** 🧍

Bench Workers, Jewelry. Cut, file, form, and solder parts for jewelry. **Education and Training:** Long-term on-the-job training. **Skills:** Math—Medium. English—Medium. Science—Medium. **Yearly Earnings:** $$ **Job Growth:** ★ **Yearly Openings:** 🧍

Bindery Machine Setters and Set-Up Operators. Set up or set up and operate machines that perform some or all of the following functions to produce books, magazines, catalogs, and other printed materials: gathering, folding, cutting, stitching, rounding and backing, supering, casing in, lining, pressing, and trimming. **Education and Training:** Moderate-term on-the-job training. **Skills:** Math—Low. English—Medium. Science—Medium. **Yearly Earnings:** $$ **Job Growth:** ★★ **Yearly Openings:** 🧍🧍🧍

Bindery Workers. Set up or operate binding machines that produce books and other printed materials. **Education and Training:** Moderate-term on-the-job training. **Skills:** Math—Medium. English—Medium. Science—Medium. **Yearly Earnings:** $$ **Job Growth:** ★★ **Yearly Openings:** 🧍🧍🧍

Bookbinders. Perform highly skilled hand finishing operations, such as grooving and lettering, to bind books. **Education and Training:** Moderate-term on-the-job training. **Skills:** Math—Low. English—Medium. Science—Low. **Yearly Earnings:** $$ **Job Growth:** ★★ **Yearly Openings:** 🯅

Buffing and Polishing Set-Up Operators. Set up and operate buffing or polishing machine. **Education and Training:** Moderate-term on-the-job training. **Skills:** Math—Low. English—Low. Science—Medium. **Yearly Earnings:** $$ **Job Growth:** ★★ **Yearly Openings:** 🯅 🯅 🯅

Casting Machine Set-Up Operators. Set up and operate machines to cast and assemble printing type. **Education and Training:** Postsecondary career and technical education. **Skills:** Math—Low. English—Low. Science—Medium. **Yearly Earnings:** $$ **Job Growth:** ★★ **Yearly Openings:** 🯅 🯅 🯅

Coating, Painting, and Spraying Machine Setters and Set-Up Operators. Set up or set up and operate machines to coat or paint any of a wide variety of products, such as food products; glassware; and cloth, ceramic, metal, plastic, paper, and wood products. Products are coated or painted with lacquer, silver and copper solution, rubber, paint, varnish, glaze, enamel, oil, or rust-proofing materials. **Education and Training:** Moderate-term on-the-job training. **Skills:** Math—Medium. English—Medium. Science—Medium. **Yearly Earnings:** $$ **Job Growth:** ★★★ **Yearly Openings:** 🯅 🯅 🯅

Coating, Painting, and Spraying Machine Setters, Operators, and Tenders. Set up, operate, or tend machines to coat or paint any of a wide variety of products, including food, glassware, cloth, ceramics, metal, plastic, paper, or wood. Products are coated or painted with lacquer, silver, copper, rubber, varnish, glaze, enamel, oil, or rust-proofing materials. **Education and Training:** Short-term on-the-job training. **Skills:** Math—Medium. English—Medium. Science—Medium. **Yearly Earnings:** $$ **Job Growth:** ★★★ **Yearly Openings:** 🯅 🯅 🯅

Combination Machine Tool Setters and Set-Up Operators, Metal and Plastic. Set up or set up and operate more than one type of cutting or forming machine tool, such as gear hobbers, lathes, press brakes, shearing, and boring machines. **Education and Training:** Moderate-term on-the-job training. **Skills:** Math—Medium. English—Medium. Science—Medium. **Yearly Earnings:** $$ **Job Growth:** ★★★ **Yearly Openings:** 🯅 🯅 🯅

Cutting, Punching, and Press Machine Setters, Operators, and Tenders, Metal and Plastic. Set up, operate, or tend machines to saw, cut, shear, slit, punch, crimp, notch, bend, or straighten metal or plastic material. **Education and Training:** Moderate-term on-the-job training. **Skills:** Math—Medium. English—Medium. Science—Medium. **Yearly Earnings:** $$ **Job Growth:** ★ **Yearly Openings:** 🯅 🯅 🯅

Dental Laboratory Technicians. Construct and repair full or partial dentures or dental appliances. **Education and Training:** Long-term on-the-job training. **Skills:** Math—Medium. English—Medium. Science—High. **Yearly Earnings:** $$ **Job Growth:** ★★ **Yearly Openings:** 🚶

Drilling and Boring Machine Tool Setters, Operators, and Tenders, Metal and Plastic. Set up, operate, or tend drilling machines to drill, bore, ream, mill, or countersink metal or plastic work pieces. **Education and Training:** Moderate-term on-the-job training. **Skills:** Math—Medium. English—Medium. Science—Medium. **Yearly Earnings:** $$ **Job Growth:** ★ **Yearly Openings:** 🚶🚶

Electrical and Electronic Equipment Assemblers. Assemble or modify electrical or electronic equipment, such as computers, test equipment telemetering systems, electric motors, and batteries. **Education and Training:** Short-term on-the-job training. **Skills:** Math—Medium. English—Medium. Science—High. **Yearly Earnings:** $$ **Job Growth:** ★ **Yearly Openings:** 🚶🚶🚶🚶

Electrical and Electronic Inspectors and Testers. Inspect and test electrical and electronic systems, such as radar navigational equipment, computer memory units, and television and radio transmitters, using precision measuring instruments. **Education and Training:** Moderate-term on-the-job training. **Skills:** Math—High. English—Medium. Science—High. **Yearly Earnings:** $$ **Job Growth:** ★ **Yearly Openings:** 🚶🚶🚶🚶

Electromechanical Equipment Assemblers. Assemble or modify electromechanical equipment or devices, such as servomechanisms, gyros, dynamometers, magnetic drums, tape drives, brakes, control linkage, actuators, and appliances. **Education and Training:** Short-term on-the-job training. **Skills:** Math—Medium. English—Medium. Science—Medium. **Yearly Earnings:** $$ **Job Growth:** ★★ **Yearly Openings:** 🚶🚶🚶

Engine and Other Machine Assemblers. Construct, assemble, or rebuild machines, such as engines, turbines, and similar equipment, used in such industries as construction, extraction, textiles, and paper manufacturing. **Education and Training:** Short-term on-the-job training. **Skills:** Math—Medium. English—Medium. Science—Medium. **Yearly Earnings:** $$ **Job Growth:** ★★ **Yearly Openings:** 🚶🚶🚶

Extruding and Drawing Machine Setters, Operators, and Tenders, Metal and Plastic. Set up, operate, or tend machines to extrude or draw thermoplastic or metal materials into tubes, rods, hoses, wire, bars, or structural shapes. **Education and Training:** Moderate-term on-the-job training. **Skills:** Math—Medium. English—Medium. Science—Medium. **Yearly Earnings:** $$ **Job Growth:** ★★★ **Yearly Openings:** 🚶🚶🚶

Extruding, Forming, Pressing, and Compacting Machine Setters and Set-Up Operators. Set up or set up and operate machines, such as glass forming machines, plodder machines, and tuber machines, to manufacture any of a wide variety of products, such as soap bars, formed rubber, glassware, food, brick, and tile, by means of extruding, compressing, or compacting. **Education and Training:** Moderate-term on-the-job training. **Skills:** Math—Medium. English—Medium. Science—Medium. **Yearly Earnings:** $$ **Job Growth:** ★★ **Yearly Openings:** 🚹🚹🚹

Extruding, Forming, Pressing, and Compacting Machine Setters, Operators, and Tenders. Set up, operate, or tend machines, such as glass forming machines, plodder machines, and tuber machines, to shape and form products such as glassware, food, rubber, soap, brick, tile, clay, wax, tobacco, or cosmetics. **Education and Training:** Short-term on-the-job training. **Skills:** Math—Medium. English—Medium. Science—Medium. **Yearly Earnings:** $$ **Job Growth:** ★★ **Yearly Openings:** 🚹🚹🚹

Forging Machine Setters, Operators, and Tenders, Metal and Plastic. Set up, operate, or tend forging machines to taper, shape, or form metal or plastic parts. **Education and Training:** Moderate-term on-the-job training. **Skills:** Math—Medium. English—Medium. Science—Medium. **Yearly Earnings:** $$ **Job Growth:** ★★ **Yearly Openings:** 🚹🚹

Foundry Mold and Coremakers. Make or form wax or sand cores or molds used in the production of metal castings in foundries. **Education and Training:** Moderate-term on-the-job training. **Skills:** Math—Medium. English—Low. Science—Medium. **Yearly Earnings:** $$ **Job Growth:** ★ **Yearly Openings:** 🚹🚹🚹

Gem and Diamond Workers. Split, saw, cut, shape, polish, or drill gems and diamonds used in jewelry or industrial tools. **Education and Training:** Moderate-term on-the-job training. **Skills:** Math—Medium. English—Low. Science—Medium. **Yearly Earnings:** $$ **Job Growth:** ★ **Yearly Openings:** 🚹

Grinding, Honing, Lapping, and Deburring Machine Set-Up Operators. Set up and operate grinding, honing, lapping, or deburring machines to remove excess materials or burrs from internal and external surfaces. **Education and Training:** Moderate-term on-the-job training. **Skills:** Math—Medium. English—Low. Science—Medium. **Yearly Earnings:** $$ **Job Growth:** ★★ **Yearly Openings:** 🚹🚹🚹

Grinding, Lapping, Polishing, and Buffing Machine Tool Setters, Operators, and Tenders, Metal and Plastic. Set up, operate, or tend grinding and related tools that remove excess material or burrs from surfaces; sharpen edges or corners; or buff, hone, or polish metal or plastic work pieces. **Education and Training:** Moderate-term on-the-job training. **Skills:** Math—Medium. English—Medium. Science—Medium. **Yearly Earnings:** $$ **Job Growth:** ★★ **Yearly Openings:** 🚹🚹🚹

Heat Treating Equipment Setters, Operators, and Tenders, Metal and Plastic. Set up, operate, or tend heating equipment, such as heat-treating furnaces, flame-hardening machines, induction machines, soaking pits, or vacuum equipment, to temper, harden, anneal, or heat-treat metal or plastic objects. **Education and Training:** Moderate-term on-the-job training. **Skills:** Math—Medium. English—Medium. Science—Medium. **Yearly Earnings:** $$ **Job Growth:** ★★★ **Yearly Openings:** 🚹🚹

Heat Treating, Annealing, and Tempering Machine Operators and Tenders, Metal and Plastic. Operate or tend machines, such as furnaces, baths, flame-hardening machines, and electronic induction machines, to harden, anneal, and heat-treat metal products or metal parts. **Education and Training:** Moderate-term on-the-job training. **Skills:** Math—Medium. English—Medium. Science—Medium. **Yearly Earnings:** $$ **Job Growth:** ★★★ **Yearly Openings:** 🧍🧍

Heating Equipment Setters and Set-Up Operators, Metal and Plastic. Set up or set up and operate heating equipment, such as heat-treating furnaces, flame-hardening machines, and induction machines, that anneal or heat-treat metal objects. **Education and Training:** Postsecondary career and technical education. **Skills:** Math—Medium. English—Medium. Science—Medium. **Yearly Earnings:** $$ **Job Growth:** ★★★ **Yearly Openings:** 🧍🧍

Inspectors, Testers, Sorters, Samplers, and Weighers. Inspect, test, sort, sample, or weigh nonagricultural raw materials or processed, machined, fabricated, or assembled parts or products for defects, wear, and deviations from specifications. May use precision measuring instruments and complex test equipment. **Education and Training:** Postsecondary career and technical education. **Skills:** Math—Medium. English—Medium. Science—Medium. **Yearly Earnings:** $$ **Job Growth:** ★ **Yearly Openings:** 🧍🧍🧍🧍

Jewelers. Fabricate and repair jewelry articles. **Education and Training:** Postsecondary career and technical education. **Skills:** Math—Medium. English—Medium. Science—Medium. **Yearly Earnings:** $$ **Job Growth:** ★ **Yearly Openings:** 🧍

Jewelers and Precious Stone and Metal Workers. Design, fabricate, adjust, repair, or appraise jewelry, gold, silver, other precious metals, or gems. Includes diamond polishers and gem cutters and persons who perform precision casting and modeling of molds, casting metal in molds, or setting precious and semi-precious stones for jewelry and related products. **Education and Training:** Long-term on-the-job training. **Skills:** Math—Medium. English—Medium. Science—Medium. **Yearly Earnings:** $$ **Job Growth:** ★ **Yearly Openings:** 🧍

Lathe and Turning Machine Tool Setters, Operators, and Tenders, Metal and Plastic. Set up, operate, or tend lathe and turning machines to turn, bore, thread, form, or face metal or plastic materials, such as wire, rod, or bar stock. **Education and Training:** Moderate-term on-the-job training. **Skills:** Math—Medium. English—Low. Science—Medium. **Yearly Earnings:** $$ **Job Growth:** ★ **Yearly Openings:** 🧍🧍🧍

Log Graders and Scalers. Grade logs or estimate the marketable content or value of logs or pulpwood in sorting yards, millpond, log deck, or similar locations. Inspect logs for defects or measure logs to determine volume. **Education and Training:** Moderate-term on-the-job training. **Skills:** Math—Medium. English—Medium. Science—Medium. **Yearly Earnings:** $$ **Job Growth:** ★ **Yearly Openings:** 🧍

Materials Inspectors. Examine and inspect materials and finished parts and products for defects and wear and to ensure conformance with work orders, diagrams, blueprints, and specifications. Usually specialize in a single phase of inspection. **Education and Training:** Moderate-term on-the-job training. **Skills:** Math—Medium. English—Medium. Science—Medium. **Yearly Earnings:** $$ **Job Growth:** ★ **Yearly Openings:** 🚶🚶🚶🚶

Mechanical Inspectors. Inspect and test mechanical assemblies and systems, such as motors, vehicles, and transportation equipment, for defects and wear to ensure compliance with specifications. **Education and Training:** Long-term on-the-job training. **Skills:** Math—Medium. English—Medium. Science—High. **Yearly Earnings:** $$ **Job Growth:** ★ **Yearly Openings:** 🚶🚶🚶🚶

Metal Molding, Coremaking, and Casting Machine Operators and Tenders. Operate or tend metal molding, casting, or coremaking machines to mold or cast metal products, such as pipes, brake drums, and rods, and metal parts, such as automobile trim, carburetor housings, and motor parts. Machines include centrifugal casting machines, vacuum casting machines, turnover draw-type coremaking machines, conveyor-screw coremaking machines, and die casting machines. **Education and Training:** Short-term on-the-job training. **Skills:** Math—Medium. English—Medium. Science—Medium. **Yearly Earnings:** $$ **Job Growth:** ★★ **Yearly Openings:** 🚶🚶🚶

Metal Molding, Coremaking, and Casting Machine Setters and Set-Up Operators. Set up or set up and operate metal casting, molding, and coremaking machines to mold or cast metal parts and products, such as tubes, rods, automobile trim, carburetor housings, and motor parts. Machines include die casting and continuous casting machines and roll-over, squeeze, and shell molding machines. **Education and Training:** Moderate-term on-the-job training. **Skills:** Math—Medium. English—Medium. Science—Medium. **Yearly Earnings:** $$ **Job Growth:** ★★ **Yearly Openings:** 🚶🚶🚶

Milling and Planing Machine Setters, Operators, and Tenders, Metal and Plastic. Set up, operate, or tend milling or planing machines to mill, plane, shape, groove, or profile metal or plastic work pieces. **Education and Training:** Moderate-term on-the-job training. **Skills:** Math—Medium. English—Low. Science—Medium. **Yearly Earnings:** $$ **Job Growth:** ★ **Yearly Openings:** 🚶

Model and Mold Makers, Jewelry. Make models or molds to create jewelry items. **Education and Training:** Long-term on-the-job training. **Skills:** Math—Medium. English—Medium. Science—Medium. **Yearly Earnings:** $$ **Job Growth:** ★ **Yearly Openings:** 🚶

Molders, Shapers, and Casters, Except Metal and Plastic. Mold, shape, form, cast, or carve products such as food products, figurines, tile, pipes, and candles consisting of clay, glass, plaster, concrete, stone, or combinations of materials. **Education and Training:** Postsecondary career and technical education. **Skills:** Math—Medium.

English—Medium. Science—Medium. **Yearly Earnings:** $$ **Job Growth:** ★★ **Yearly Openings:** 🚶🚶

Molding, Coremaking, and Casting Machine Setters, Operators, and Tenders, Metal and Plastic. Set up, operate, or tend metal or plastic molding, casting, or coremaking machines to mold or cast metal or thermoplastic parts or products. **Education and Training:** Moderate-term on-the-job training. **Skills:** Math—Medium. English—Medium. Science—Medium. **Yearly Earnings:** $$ **Job Growth:** ★★ **Yearly Openings:** 🚶🚶🚶

Motor Vehicle Inspectors. Inspect automotive vehicles to ensure compliance with governmental regulations and safety standards. **Education and Training:** Work experience in a related occupation. **Skills:** Math—Low. English—Medium. Science—Medium. **Yearly Earnings:** $$$$ **Job Growth:** ★★★ **Yearly Openings:** 🚶

Multiple Machine Tool Setters, Operators, and Tenders, Metal and Plastic. Set up, operate, or tend more than one type of cutting or forming machine tool or robot. **Education and Training:** Postsecondary career and technical education. **Skills:** Math—Medium. English—Medium. Science—Medium. **Yearly Earnings:** $$ **Job Growth:** ★★★ **Yearly Openings:** 🚶🚶🚶

Paper Goods Machine Setters, Operators, and Tenders. Set up, operate, or tend paper goods machines that perform a variety of functions, such as converting, sawing, corrugating, banding, wrapping, boxing, stitching, forming, or sealing paper or paperboard sheets into products. **Education and Training:** Moderate-term on-the-job training. **Skills:** Math—Medium. English—Low. Science—Medium. **Yearly Earnings:** $$ **Job Growth:** ★ **Yearly Openings:** 🚶🚶🚶

Pewter Casters and Finishers. Cast and finish pewter alloy to form parts for goblets, candlesticks, and other pewterware. **Education and Training:** Postsecondary career and technical education. **Skills:** Math—Medium. English—Medium. Science—Medium. **Yearly Earnings:** $$ **Job Growth:** ★ **Yearly Openings:** 🚶

Plastic Molding and Casting Machine Operators and Tenders. Operate or tend plastic molding machines, such as compression or injection molding machines, to mold, form, or cast thermoplastic materials to specified shape. **Education and Training:** Short-term on-the-job training. **Skills:** Math—Medium. English—Medium. Science—Medium. **Yearly Earnings:** $$ **Job Growth:** ★★ **Yearly Openings:** 🚶🚶🚶

Plastic Molding and Casting Machine Setters and Set-Up Operators. Set up or set up and operate plastic molding machines, such as compression or injection molding machines, to mold, form, or cast thermoplastic materials to specified shape. **Education and Training:** Moderate-term on-the-job training. **Skills:** Math—Medium. English—Medium. Science—Medium. **Yearly Earnings:** $$ **Job Growth:** ★★ **Yearly Openings:** 🚶🚶🚶

Precision Devices Inspectors and Testers. Verify accuracy of and adjust precision devices, such as meters and gauges, testing instruments, and clock and watch mechanisms, to ensure operation of device matches design specifications. **Education and Training:** Moderate-term on-the-job training. **Skills:** Math—Medium. English—Medium. Science—High. **Yearly Earnings:** $$ **Job Growth:** ★ **Yearly Openings:** 🧍🧍🧍🧍

Precision Lens Grinders and Polishers. Set up and operate variety of machines and equipment to grind and polish lens and other optical elements. **Education and Training:** Moderate-term on-the-job training. **Skills:** Math—Medium. English—Medium. Science—Medium. **Yearly Earnings:** $$ **Job Growth:** ★★ **Yearly Openings:** 🧍

Precision Mold and Pattern Casters, Except Nonferrous Metals. Cast molds and patterns from a variety of materials, except nonferrous metals, according to blueprints and specifications. **Education and Training:** Moderate-term on-the-job training. **Skills:** Math—Medium. English—Low. Science—Medium. **Yearly Earnings:** $$ **Job Growth:** ★★ **Yearly Openings:** 🧍🧍

Precision Pattern and Die Casters, Nonferrous Metals. Cast metal patterns and dies, according to specifications, from a variety of nonferrous metals, such as aluminum or bronze. **Education and Training:** Long-term on-the-job training. **Skills:** Math—Low. English—Low. Science—Medium. **Yearly Earnings:** $$ **Job Growth:** ★★ **Yearly Openings:** 🧍🧍

Press and Press Brake Machine Setters and Set-Up Operators, Metal and Plastic. Set up or set up and operate power-press machines or power-brake machines to bend, form, stretch, notch, punch, or straighten metal or plastic plate and structural shapes as specified by work order, blueprints, drawing, templates, or layout. **Education and Training:** Moderate-term on-the-job training. **Skills:** Math—Medium. English—Medium. Science—High. **Yearly Earnings:** $$ **Job Growth:** ★ **Yearly Openings:** 🧍🧍🧍

Production Inspectors, Testers, Graders, Sorters, Samplers, Weighers. Inspect, test, grade, sort, sample, or weigh nonagricultural raw materials or processed, machined, fabricated, or assembled parts or products. Work may be performed before, during, or after processing. **Education and Training:** Short-term on-the-job training. **Skills:** Math—Medium. English—Medium. Science—Medium. **Yearly Earnings:** $$ **Job Growth:** ★ **Yearly Openings:** 🧍🧍🧍🧍

Punching Machine Setters and Set-Up Operators, Metal and Plastic. Set up or set up and operate machines to punch, crimp, cut blanks, or notch metal or plastic workpieces between preset dies according to specifications. **Education and Training:** Moderate-term on-the-job training. **Skills:** Math—Medium. English—Low. Science—Medium. **Yearly Earnings:** $$ **Job Growth:** ★ **Yearly Openings:** 🧍🧍🧍

Rolling Machine Setters, Operators, and Tenders, Metal and Plastic. Set up, operate, or tend machines to roll steel or plastic, forming bends, beads, knurls, rolls, or plate or to flatten, temper, or reduce gauge of material. **Education and Training:** Moderate-term on-the-job training. **Skills:** Math—Medium. English—Medium. Science—Medium. **Yearly Earnings:** $$ **Job Growth:** ★ **Yearly Openings:** 🧍🧍

Sawing Machine Tool Setters and Set-Up Operators, Metal and Plastic. Set up or set up and operate metal or plastic sawing machines to cut straight, curved, irregular, or internal patterns in metal or plastic stock or to trim edges of metal or plastic objects. Involves the use of such machines as band saws, circular saws, friction saws, hacksawing machines, and jigsaws. **Education and Training:** Moderate-term on-the-job training. **Skills:** Math—Medium. English—Medium. Science—Medium. **Yearly Earnings:** $$ **Job Growth:** ★ **Yearly Openings:** 🧍🧍🧍

Screen Printing Machine Setters and Set-Up Operators. Set up or set up and operate screen printing machines to print designs onto articles and materials such as glass or plasticware, cloth, and paper. **Education and Training:** Moderate-term on-the-job training. **Skills:** Math—Medium. English—Medium. Science—Medium. **Yearly Earnings:** $$ **Job Growth:** ★★ **Yearly Openings:** 🧍🧍🧍

Shear and Slitter Machine Setters and Set-Up Operators, Metal and Plastic. Set up or set up and operate power-shear or slitting machines to cut metal or plastic material, such as plates, sheets, slabs, billets or bars, to specified dimensions and angles. **Education and Training:** Moderate-term on-the-job training. **Skills:** Math—Medium. English—Medium. Science—Medium. **Yearly Earnings:** $$ **Job Growth:** ★ **Yearly Openings:** 🧍🧍🧍

Silversmiths. Anneal, solder, hammer, shape, and glue silver articles. **Education and Training:** Long-term on-the-job training. **Skills:** Math—Medium. English—Low. Science—Medium. **Yearly Earnings:** $$ **Job Growth:** ★ **Yearly Openings:** 🧍

Soldering and Brazing Machine Setters and Set-Up Operators. Set up or set up and operate soldering or brazing machines to braze, solder, heat treat, or spot weld fabricated metal products or components as specified by work orders, blueprints, and layout specifications. **Education and Training:** Moderate-term on-the-job training. **Skills:** Math—Medium. English—Medium. Science—Medium. **Yearly Earnings:** $$ **Job Growth:** ★★★ **Yearly Openings:** 🧍🧍

Textile Cutting Machine Setters, Operators, and Tenders. Set up, operate, or tend machines that cut textiles. **Education and Training:** Moderate-term on-the-job training. **Skills:** Math—Medium. English—Medium. Science—Medium. **Yearly Earnings:** $ **Job Growth:** ★ **Yearly Openings:** 🧍🧍

Textile Knitting and Weaving Machine Setters, Operators, and Tenders. Set up, operate, or tend machines that knit, loop, weave, or draw in textiles. **Education and Training:** Long-term on-the-job training. **Skills:** Math—Medium. English—Medium. Science—Medium. **Yearly Earnings:** $$ **Job Growth:** ★ **Yearly Openings:** 🧍🧍🧍

Textile Winding, Twisting, and Drawing Out Machine Setters, Operators, and Tenders. Set up, operate, or tend machines that wind or twist textiles or draw out and combine sliver, such as wool, hemp, or synthetic fibers. **Education and Training:** Moderate-term on-the-job training. **Skills:** Math—Medium. English—Medium. Science—Medium. **Yearly Earnings:** $$ **Job Growth:** ★ **Yearly Openings:** 🚶🚶🚶

Timing Device Assemblers, Adjusters, and Calibrators. Perform precision assembling or adjusting, within narrow tolerances, of timing devices, such as watches, clocks, or chronometers. **Education and Training:** Moderate-term on-the-job training. **Skills:** Math—Medium. English—Medium. Science—Medium. **Yearly Earnings:** $$ **Job Growth:** ★ **Yearly Openings:** 🚶

Welding Machine Setters and Set-Up Operators. Set up or set up and operate welding machines that join or bond together components to fabricate metal products or assemblies according to specifications and blueprints. **Education and Training:** Postsecondary career and technical education. **Skills:** Math—Medium. English—Medium. Science—Medium. **Yearly Earnings:** $$ **Job Growth:** ★★★ **Yearly Openings:** 🚶🚶

Welding, Soldering, and Brazing Machine Setters, Operators, and Tenders. Set up, operate, or tend welding, soldering, or brazing machines or robots that weld, braze, solder, or heat treat metal products, components, or assemblies. **Education and Training:** Moderate-term on-the-job training. **Skills:** Math—Medium. English—Medium. Science—Medium. **Yearly Earnings:** $$ **Job Growth:** ★★★ **Yearly Openings:** 🚶🚶

Woodworking Machine Setters and Set-Up Operators, Except Sawing. Set up or set up and operate woodworking machines, such as lathes, drill presses, sanders, shapers, and planing machines, to perform woodworking operations. **Education and Training:** Moderate-term on-the-job training. **Skills:** Math—Low. English—Medium. Science—Medium. **Yearly Earnings:** $$ **Job Growth:** ★★ **Yearly Openings:** 🚶🚶🚶

Woodworking Machine Setters, Operators, and Tenders, Except Sawing. Set up, operate, or tend woodworking machines, such as drill presses, lathes, shapers, routers, sanders, planers, and wood nailing machines. **Education and Training:** Moderate-term on-the-job training. **Skills:** Math—Medium. English—Medium. Science—Medium. **Yearly Earnings:** $$ **Job Growth:** ★★ **Yearly Openings:** 🚶🚶🚶

PRODUCTION WORK

These workers use hands and hand tools with skill to make or process materials, products, and parts. They follow established procedures and techniques. Although their jobs are found most often in manufacturing plants, they are also found in places we might not ordinarily think of as factories, such as printing and publishing companies, slaughterhouses, and canneries.

Bakers, Manufacturing. Mix and bake ingredients according to recipes to produce breads, pastries, and other baked goods. Goods are produced in large quantities for sale through establishments such as grocery stores. Generally, high-volume production equipment is used. **Education and Training:** Long-term on-the-job training. **Skills:** Math—Medium. English—Medium. Science—Medium. **Yearly Earnings:** $ **Job Growth:** ★★★ **Yearly Openings:** 🚶🚶🚶

Bindery Machine Operators and Tenders. Operate or tend binding machines that round, back, case, line stitch, press, fold, trim, or perform other binding operations on books and related articles. **Education and Training:** Short-term on-the-job training. **Skills:** Math—Medium. English—Low. Science—Medium. **Yearly Earnings:** $$ **Job Growth:** ★★ **Yearly Openings:** 🚶🚶🚶

Brazers. Braze together components to assemble fabricated metal parts, using torch or welding machine and flux. **Education and Training:** Short-term on-the-job training. **Skills:** Math—Medium. English—Medium. Science—Medium. **Yearly Earnings:** $$ **Job Growth:** ★★★ **Yearly Openings:** 🚶🚶🚶🚶

Cementing and Gluing Machine Operators and Tenders. Operate or tend cementing and gluing machines to join items for further processing or to form a completed product. Processes include joining veneer sheets into plywood; gluing paper; and joining rubber and rubberized fabric parts, plastic, simulated leather, or other materials. **Education and Training:** Moderate-term on-the-job training. **Skills:** Math—Medium. English—Medium. Science—Medium. **Yearly Earnings:** $$ **Job Growth:** ★★ **Yearly Openings:** 🚶

Chemical Equipment Controllers and Operators. Control or operate equipment to control chemical changes or reactions in the processing of industrial or consumer products. Typical equipment used are reaction kettles, catalytic converters, continuous or batch treating equipment, saturator tanks, electrolytic cells, reactor vessels, recovery units, and fermentation chambers. **Education and Training:** Moderate-term on-the-job training. **Skills:** Math—Medium. English—Medium. Science—High. **Yearly Earnings:** $$$ **Job Growth:** ★★★ **Yearly Openings:** 🚶🚶

Chemical Equipment Operators and Tenders. Operate or tend equipment to control chemical changes or reactions in the processing of industrial or consumer products. Equipment used includes devulcanizers, steam-jacketed kettles, and reactor vessels. **Education and Training:** Moderate-term on-the-job training. **Skills:** Math—Medium. English—Medium. Science—Medium. **Yearly Earnings:** $$$ **Job Growth:** ★★★ **Yearly Openings:** 🚶🚶

Chemical Equipment Tenders. Tend equipment in which a chemical change or reaction takes place in the processing of industrial or consumer products. Typical equipment used are devulcanizers, batch stills, fermenting tanks, steam-jacketed kettles, and reactor vessels. **Education and Training:** Moderate-term on-the-job training. **Skills:** Math—Medium. English—Medium. Science—Medium. **Yearly Earnings:** $$$ **Job Growth:** ★★★ **Yearly Openings:** 🚶🚶

Cleaning, Washing, and Metal Pickling Equipment Operators and Tenders. Operate or tend machines to wash or clean products, such as barrels or kegs, glass items, tin plate, food, pulp, coal, plastic, or rubber, to remove impurities. **Education and Training:** Moderate-term on-the-job training. **Skills:** Math—Medium. English—Medium. Science—Medium. **Yearly Earnings:** $$ **Job Growth:** ★ **Yearly Openings:** 🧍

Coating, Painting, and Spraying Machine Operators and Tenders. *Coating Machine Operators and Tenders:* Operate or tend machines to coat any of a wide variety of items: Coat food products with sugar, chocolate, or butter; coat paper and paper products with chemical solutions, wax, or glazes; or coat fabric with rubber or plastic. *Painting and Spraying Machine Operators and Tenders:* Operate or tend machines to spray or paint decorative, protective, or other coating or finish, such as adhesive, lacquer, paint, stain, latex, preservative, oil, or other solutions. May apply coating or finish to any of a wide variety of items or materials, such as wood and wood products, ceramics, and glass. Includes workers who apply coating or finish to materials before further processing. **Education and Training:** Moderate-term on-the-job training. **Skills:** Math—Medium. English—Medium. Science—Medium. **Yearly Earnings:** $$ **Job Growth:** ★★★ **Yearly Openings:** 🧍🧍🧍

Coil Winders, Tapers, and Finishers. Wind wire coils used in electrical components, such as resistors and transformers, and in electrical equipment and instruments, such as field cores, bobbins, armature cores, electrical motors, generators, and control equipment. **Education and Training:** Short-term on-the-job training. **Skills:** Math—Medium. English—Medium. Science—Medium. **Yearly Earnings:** $$ **Job Growth:** ★★ **Yearly Openings:** 🧍🧍

Combination Machine Tool Operators and Tenders, Metal and Plastic. Operate or tend more than one type of cutting or forming machine tool which has been previously set up. Includes such machine tools as band saws, press brakes, slitting machines, drills, lathes, and boring machines. **Education and Training:** Moderate-term on-the-job training. **Skills:** Math—Medium. English—Medium. Science—Medium. **Yearly Earnings:** $$ **Job Growth:** ★★★ **Yearly Openings:** 🧍🧍🧍

Computer-Controlled Machine Tool Operators, Metal and Plastic. Operate computer-controlled machines or robots to perform one or more machine functions on metal or plastic work pieces. **Education and Training:** Moderate-term on-the-job training. **Skills:** Math—Medium. English—Medium. Science—Medium. **Yearly Earnings:** $$ **Job Growth:** ★★★ **Yearly Openings:** 🧍🧍🧍

Cooling and Freezing Equipment Operators and Tenders. Operate or tend equipment, such as cooling and freezing units, refrigerators, batch freezers, and freezing tunnels, to cool or freeze products, food, blood plasma, and chemicals. **Education and Training:** Moderate-term on-the-job training. **Skills:** Math—Medium. English—Medium. Science—Medium. **Yearly Earnings:** $$ **Job Growth:** ★ **Yearly Openings:** 🧍

Crushing, Grinding, and Polishing Machine Setters, Operators, and Tenders. Set up, operate, or tend machines to crush, grind, or polish materials such as coal, glass, grain, stone, food, or rubber. **Education and Training:** Moderate-term on-the-job training. **Skills:** Math—Medium. English—Medium. Science—Medium. **Yearly Earnings:** $$ **Job Growth:** ★★ **Yearly Openings:** 🚹

Cutters and Trimmers, Hand. Use hand tools or hand-held power tools to cut and trim a variety of manufactured items, such as carpet, fabric, stone, glass, or rubber. **Education and Training:** Short-term on-the-job training. **Skills:** Math—Medium. English—Medium. Science—Low. **Yearly Earnings:** $$ **Job Growth:** ★ **Yearly Openings:** 🚹🚹

Cutting and Slicing Machine Operators and Tenders. Operate or tend machines to cut or slice any of a wide variety of products or materials, such as tobacco, food, paper, roofing slate, glass, stone, rubber, cork, and insulating material. **Education and Training:** Short-term on-the-job training. **Skills:** Math—Medium. English—Medium. Science—Medium. **Yearly Earnings:** $$ **Job Growth:** ★ **Yearly Openings:** 🚹🚹🚹

Cutting and Slicing Machine Setters, Operators, and Tenders. Set up, operate, or tend machines that cut or slice materials such as glass, stone, cork, rubber, tobacco, food, paper, or insulating material. **Education and Training:** Moderate-term on-the-job training. **Skills:** Math—Medium. English—Medium. Science—Medium. **Yearly Earnings:** $$ **Job Growth:** ★ **Yearly Openings:** 🚹🚹🚹

Design Printing Machine Setters and Set-Up Operators. Set up or set up and operate machines to print designs on materials. **Education and Training:** Postsecondary career and technical education. **Skills:** Math—Medium. English—Medium. Science—Medium. **Yearly Earnings:** $$ **Job Growth:** ★★ **Yearly Openings:** 🚹🚹🚹

Electrolytic Plating and Coating Machine Operators and Tenders, Metal and Plastic. Operate or tend electrolytic plating or coating machines, such as zinc-plating machines and anodizing machines, to coat metal or plastic products electrolytically with chromium, zinc, copper, cadmium, or other metal to provide protective or decorative surfaces or to build up worn surfaces. **Education and Training:** Moderate-term on-the-job training. **Skills:** Math—Medium. English—Low. Science—Medium. **Yearly Earnings:** $$ **Job Growth:** ★★★ **Yearly Openings:** 🚹🚹🚹

Electrolytic Plating and Coating Machine Setters and Set-Up Operators, Metal and Plastic. Set up or set up and operate electrolytic plating or coating machines, such as continuous multistrand electrogalvanizing machines, to coat metal or plastic products electrolytically with chromium, copper, cadmium, or other metal to provide protective or decorative surfaces or to build up worn surfaces. **Education and Training:** Postsecondary career and technical education. **Skills:** Math—Medium. English—Low. Science—Medium. **Yearly Earnings:** $$ **Job Growth:** ★★★ **Yearly Openings:** 🚹🚹🚹

Electrotypers and Stereotypers. Fabricate and finish electrotype and stereotype printing plates. **Education and Training:** Long-term on-the-job training. **Skills:** Math—Medium. English—Low. Science—Medium. **Yearly Earnings:** $$$ **Job Growth:** ★ **Yearly Openings:** 🧍🧍🧍

Embossing Machine Set-Up Operators. Set up and operate embossing machines. **Education and Training:** Postsecondary career and technical education. **Skills:** Math—Low. English—Low. Science—Medium. **Yearly Earnings:** $$ **Job Growth:** ★★ **Yearly Openings:** 🧍🧍🧍

Engraver Set-Up Operators. Set up and operate machines to transfer printing designs. **Education and Training:** Long-term on-the-job training. **Skills:** Math—Medium. English—Low. Science—Medium. **Yearly Earnings:** $$ **Job Growth:** ★★ **Yearly Openings:** 🧍🧍🧍

Extruding and Forming Machine Operators and Tenders, Synthetic or Glass Fibers. Operate or tend machines that extrude and form continuous filaments from synthetic materials, such as liquid polymer, rayon, and fiberglass, preparatory to further processing. **Education and Training:** Moderate-term on-the-job training. **Skills:** Math—Medium. English—Medium. Science—Medium. **Yearly Earnings:** $$ **Job Growth:** ★★ **Yearly Openings:** 🧍🧍

Extruding and Forming Machine Setters, Operators, and Tenders, Synthetic and Glass Fibers. Set up, operate, or tend machines that extrude and form continuous filaments from synthetic materials, such as liquid polymer, rayon, and fiberglass. **Education and Training:** Moderate-term on-the-job training. **Skills:** Math—Medium. English—Medium. Science—Medium. **Yearly Earnings:** $$ **Job Growth:** ★★ **Yearly Openings:** 🧍🧍

Extruding, Forming, Pressing, and Compacting Machine Operators and Tenders. Operate or tend machines to shape and form any of a wide variety of manufactured products, such as glass bulbs, molded food and candy, rubber goods, clay products, wax products, tobacco plugs, cosmetics, or paper products, by means of extruding, compressing or compacting. **Education and Training:** Short-term on-the-job training. **Skills:** Math—Medium. English—Medium. Science—Medium. **Yearly Earnings:** $$ **Job Growth:** ★★ **Yearly Openings:** 🧍🧍🧍

Fabric and Apparel Patternmakers. Draw and construct sets of precision master fabric patterns or layouts. May also mark and cut fabrics and apparel. **Education and Training:** Long-term on-the-job training. **Skills:** Math—Medium. English—Medium. Science—Medium. **Yearly Earnings:** $$ **Job Growth:** ★ **Yearly Openings:** 🧍

Fiber Product Cutting Machine Setters and Set-Up Operators. Set up and operate machine to cut or slice fiber material, such as paper, wallboard, and insulation material. **Education and Training:** Moderate-term on-the-job training. **Skills:** Math—Medium. English—Medium. Science—Medium. **Yearly Earnings:** $$ **Job Growth:** ★ **Yearly Openings:** 🧍🧍🧍

Fiberglass Laminators and Fabricators. Laminate layers of fiberglass on molds to form boat decks and hulls, bodies for golf carts, automobiles, or other products. **Education and Training:** Moderate-term on-the-job training. **Skills:** Math—Medium. English—Medium. Science—Medium. **Yearly Earnings:** $$ **Job Growth:** ★★★ **Yearly Openings:** 🚶 🚶

Film Laboratory Technicians. Evaluate motion picture film to determine characteristics such as sensitivity to light, density, and exposure time required for printing. **Education and Training:** Moderate-term on-the-job training. **Skills:** Math—Medium. English—Medium. Science—Medium. **Yearly Earnings:** $ **Job Growth:** ★ **Yearly Openings:** 🚶

Fitters, Structural Metal—Precision. Lay out, position, align, and fit together fabricated parts of structural metal products preparatory to welding or riveting. **Education and Training:** Moderate-term on-the-job training. **Skills:** Math—High. English—Medium. Science—Medium. **Yearly Earnings:** $$ **Job Growth:** ★★★ **Yearly Openings:** 🚶 🚶 🚶

Food and Tobacco Roasting, Baking, and Drying Machine Operators and Tenders. Operate or tend food or tobacco roasting, baking, or drying equipment, including hearth ovens, kiln driers, roasters, char kilns, and vacuum drying equipment. **Education and Training:** Short-term on-the-job training. **Skills:** Math—Medium. English—Medium. Science—Medium. **Yearly Earnings:** $$ **Job Growth:** ★ **Yearly Openings:** 🚶

Food Batchmakers. Set up and operate equipment that mixes or blends ingredients used in the manufacturing of food products. Includes candy makers and cheese makers. **Education and Training:** Short-term on-the-job training. **Skills:** Math—Medium. English—Medium. Science—Medium. **Yearly Earnings:** $$ **Job Growth:** ★ **Yearly Openings:** 🚶 🚶

Food Cooking Machine Operators and Tenders. Operate or tend cooking equipment, such as steam cooking vats, deep fry cookers, pressure cookers, kettles, and boilers, to prepare food products. **Education and Training:** Short-term on-the-job training. **Skills:** Math—Medium. English—Medium. Science—Medium. **Yearly Earnings:** $$ **Job Growth:** ★ **Yearly Openings:** 🚶 🚶

Furnace, Kiln, Oven, Drier, and Kettle Operators and Tenders. Operate or tend heating equipment other than basic metal, plastic, or food processing equipment. Includes activities such as annealing glass, drying lumber, curing rubber, removing moisture from materials, or boiling soap. **Education and Training:** Moderate-term on-the-job training. **Skills:** Math—Medium. English—Medium. Science—Medium. **Yearly Earnings:** $$ **Job Growth:** ★★ **Yearly Openings:** 🚶

Glass Cutting Machine Setters and Set-Up Operators. Set up and operate machines to cut glass. **Education and Training:** Short-term on-the-job training.

Skills: Math—Medium. English—Medium. Science—Medium. **Yearly Earnings:** $$ **Job Growth:** ★ **Yearly Openings:** 🧍🧍🧍

Graders and Sorters, Agricultural Products. Grade, sort, or classify unprocessed food and other agricultural products by size, weight, color, or condition. **Education and Training:** Work experience in a related occupation. **Skills:** Math—Low. English—Low. Science—Medium. **Yearly Earnings:** $ **Job Growth:** ★★ **Yearly Openings:** 🧍🧍🧍

Grinding and Polishing Workers, Hand. Grind, sand, or polish a variety of metal, wood, stone, clay, plastic, or glass objects, using hand tools or hand-held power tools. **Education and Training:** Moderate-term on-the-job training. **Skills:** Math—Low. English—Low. Science—Medium. **Yearly Earnings:** $$ **Job Growth:** ★★★ **Yearly Openings:** 🧍

Hand Compositors and Typesetters. Set up and arrange type by hand. Assemble and lock setup of type, cuts, and headings. Pull proofs. **Education and Training:** Long-term on-the-job training. **Skills:** Math—Medium. English—Medium. Science—Low. **Yearly Earnings:** $$$ **Job Growth:** ★ **Yearly Openings:** 🧍🧍🧍

Heaters, Metal and Plastic. Operate or tend heating equipment, such as soaking pits, reheating furnaces, and heating and vacuum equipment, to heat metal sheets, blooms, billets, bars, plate, and rods to a specified temperature for rolling or processing or to heat and cure preformed plastic parts. **Education and Training:** Moderate-term on-the-job training. **Skills:** Math—Low. English—Medium. Science—Medium. **Yearly Earnings:** $$ **Job Growth:** ★★★ **Yearly Openings:** 🧍🧍

Helpers—Production Workers. Help production workers by performing duties of lesser skill. Duties include supplying or holding materials or tools and cleaning work area and equipment. **Education and Training:** Short-term on-the-job training. **Skills:** Math—Medium. English—Medium. Science—Medium. **Yearly Earnings:** $ **Job Growth:** ★★★ **Yearly Openings:** 🧍🧍🧍🧍🧍

Job Printers. Set type according to copy. Operate press to print job order. Read proof for errors and clarity of impression and correct imperfections. Job printers are often found in small establishments where work combines several job skills. **Education and Training:** Long-term on-the-job training. **Skills:** Math—Low. English—Medium. Science—Low. **Yearly Earnings:** $$ **Job Growth:** ★★ **Yearly Openings:** 🧍🧍

Letterpress Setters and Set-Up Operators. Set up or set up and operate direct relief letterpresses, either sheet or roll (web) fed, to produce single- or multicolor printed material, such as newspapers, books, and periodicals. **Education and Training:** Moderate-term on-the-job training. **Skills:** Math—Medium. English—Medium. Science—Medium. **Yearly Earnings:** $$ **Job Growth:** ★★ **Yearly Openings:** 🧍🧍🧍

Marking and Identification Printing Machine Setters and Set-Up Operators. Set up or set up and operate machines to print trademarks, labels, or multicolored

identification symbols on materials. **Education and Training:** Short-term on-the-job training. **Skills:** Math—Low. English—Medium. Science—Medium. **Yearly Earnings:** $$ **Job Growth:** ★★ **Yearly Openings:** 🚹🚹🚹

Meat, Poultry, and Fish Cutters and Trimmers. Use hand tools to perform routine cutting and trimming of meat, poultry, and fish. **Education and Training:** Short-term on-the-job training. **Skills:** Math—Low. English—Low. Science—Medium. **Yearly Earnings:** $ **Job Growth:** ★★ **Yearly Openings:** 🚹🚹🚹

Metal Fabricators, Structural Metal Products. Fabricate and assemble structural metal products, such as frameworks or shells for machinery, ovens, tanks, and stacks, and metal parts for buildings and bridges, according to job order or blueprints. **Education and Training:** Moderate-term on-the-job training. **Skills:** Math—High. English—Medium. Science—Medium. **Yearly Earnings:** $$ **Job Growth:** ★★★ **Yearly Openings:** 🚹🚹🚹

Metal-Refining Furnace Operators and Tenders. Operate or tend furnaces, such as gas, oil, coal, electric-arc or electric induction, open-hearth, or oxygen furnaces, to melt and refine metal before casting or to produce specified types of steel. **Education and Training:** Moderate-term on-the-job training. **Skills:** Math—Medium. English—Low. Science—Medium. **Yearly Earnings:** $$ **Job Growth:** ★★ **Yearly Openings:** 🚹

Mixing and Blending Machine Setters, Operators, and Tenders. Set up, operate, or tend machines to mix or blend materials, such as chemicals, tobacco, liquids, color pigments, or explosive ingredients. **Education and Training:** Moderate-term on-the-job training. **Skills:** Math—Medium. English—Medium. Science—Medium. **Yearly Earnings:** $$ **Job Growth:** ★★ **Yearly Openings:** 🚹🚹🚹

Mold Makers, Hand. Construct or form molds from existing forms for use in casting objects. **Education and Training:** Moderate-term on-the-job training. **Skills:** Math—Medium. English—Low. Science—Medium. **Yearly Earnings:** $$ **Job Growth:** ★★ **Yearly Openings:** 🚹🚹

Molding and Casting Workers. Perform a variety of duties such as mixing materials, assembling mold parts, filling molds, and stacking molds to mold and cast a wide range of products. **Education and Training:** Moderate-term on-the-job training. **Skills:** Math—Medium. English—Medium. Science—Medium. **Yearly Earnings:** $$ **Job Growth:** ★★ **Yearly Openings:** 🚹🚹

Nonelectrolytic Plating and Coating Machine Operators and Tenders, Metal and Plastic. Operate or tend nonelectrolytic plating or coating machines, such as metal-spraying machines and vacuum metalizing machines, to coat metal or plastic products or parts with metal. **Education and Training:** Short-term on-the-job training. **Skills:** Math—Medium. English—Low. Science—Medium. **Yearly Earnings:** $$ **Job Growth:** ★★★ **Yearly Openings:** 🚹🚹🚹

Nonelectrolytic Plating and Coating Machine Setters and Set-Up Operators, Metal and Plastic. Set up or set up and operate nonelectrolytic plating or coating machines, such as hot-dip lines and metal-spraying machines, to coat metal or plastic products or parts with metal. **Education and Training:** Postsecondary career and technical education. **Skills:** Math—Medium. English—Medium. Science—Medium. **Yearly Earnings:** $$ **Job Growth:** ★★★ **Yearly Openings:** 🚹🚹🚹

Numerical Control Machine Tool Operators and Tenders, Metal and Plastic. Set up and operate numerical control (magnetic- or punched-tape–controlled) machine tools that automatically mill, drill, broach, and ream metal and plastic parts. May adjust machine feed and speed, change cutting tools, or adjust machine controls when automatic programming is faulty or if machine malfunctions. **Education and Training:** Long-term on-the-job training. **Skills:** Math—Medium. English—Medium. Science—Medium. **Yearly Earnings:** $$ **Job Growth:** ★★★ **Yearly Openings:** 🚹🚹🚹

Offset Lithographic Press Setters and Set-Up Operators. Set up or set up and operate offset printing press, either sheet or web fed, to print single- and multicolor copy from lithographic plates. Examine job order to determine press operating time, quantity to be printed, and stock specifications. **Education and Training:** Long-term on-the-job training. **Skills:** Math—Medium. English—Low. Science—Medium. **Yearly Earnings:** $$ **Job Growth:** ★★ **Yearly Openings:** 🚹🚹🚹

Packaging and Filling Machine Operators and Tenders. Operate or tend machines to prepare industrial or consumer products for storage or shipment. Includes cannery workers who pack food products. **Education and Training:** Short-term on-the-job training. **Skills:** Math—Medium. English—Low. Science—Medium. **Yearly Earnings:** $ **Job Growth:** ★★★ **Yearly Openings:** 🚹🚹🚹🚹

Painting, Coating, and Decorating Workers. Paint, coat, or decorate articles such as furniture, glass, plateware, pottery, jewelry, cakes, toys, books, or leather. **Education and Training:** Short-term on-the-job training. **Skills:** Math—Low. English—Low. Science—Medium. **Yearly Earnings:** $ **Job Growth:** ★★★ **Yearly Openings:** 🚹🚹

Photoengraving and Lithographing Machine Operators and Tenders. Operate or tend photoengraving and lithographing equipment, such as plate graining, pantograph, roll varnishing, and routing machines. **Education and Training:** Moderate-term on-the-job training. **Skills:** Math—Low. English—Low. Science—Medium. **Yearly Earnings:** $$$ **Job Growth:** ★ **Yearly Openings:** 🚹🚹🚹

Photographic Hand Developers. Develop exposed photographic film or sensitized paper in series of chemical and water baths to produce negative or positive prints. **Education and Training:** Moderate-term on-the-job training. **Skills:** Math—Medium. English—Medium. Science—Medium. **Yearly Earnings:** $ **Job Growth:** ★ **Yearly Openings:** 🚹

Photographic Process Workers. Perform precision work involved in photographic processing, such as editing photographic negatives and prints, using photo-mechanical, chemical, or computerized methods. **Education and Training:** Moderate-term on-the-job training. **Skills:** Math—Medium. English—Medium. Science—Medium. **Yearly Earnings:** $ **Job Growth:** ★ **Yearly Openings:** 🚹

Photographic Processing Machine Operators. Operate photographic processing machines, such as photographic printing machines, film developing machines, and mounting presses. **Education and Training:** Short-term on-the-job training. **Skills:** Math—Medium. English—Medium. Science—Medium. **Yearly Earnings:** $ **Job Growth:** ★★ **Yearly Openings:** 🚹🚹

Photographic Reproduction Technicians. Duplicate materials to produce prints on sensitized paper, cloth, or film, using photographic equipment. **Education and Training:** Moderate-term on-the-job training. **Skills:** Math—Medium. English—Medium. Science—Medium. **Yearly Earnings:** $ **Job Growth:** ★ **Yearly Openings:** 🚹

Photographic Retouchers and Restorers. Retouch or restore photographic negatives and prints to accentuate desirable features of subject, using pencils, watercolors, or airbrushes. **Education and Training:** Moderate-term on-the-job training. **Skills:** Math—Low. English—Low. Science—Medium. **Yearly Earnings:** $ **Job Growth:** ★ **Yearly Openings:** 🚹

Plate Finishers. Set up and operate equipment to trim and mount electrotype or stereotype plates. **Education and Training:** Long-term on-the-job training. **Skills:** Math—Low. English—Low. Science—Medium. **Yearly Earnings:** $$$ **Job Growth:** ★ **Yearly Openings:** 🚹🚹🚹

Platemakers. Produce printing plates by exposing sensitized metal sheets to special light through a photographic negative. May operate machines that process plates automatically. **Education and Training:** Long-term on-the-job training. **Skills:** Math—Low. English—Low. Science—Medium. **Yearly Earnings:** $$$ **Job Growth:** ★ **Yearly Openings:** 🚹🚹🚹

Plating and Coating Machine Setters, Operators, and Tenders, Metal and Plastic. Set up, operate, or tend plating or coating machines to coat metal or plastic products with chromium, zinc, copper, cadmium, nickel, or other metal to protect or decorate surfaces. Includes electrolytic processes. **Education and Training:** Moderate-term on-the-job training. **Skills:** Math—Medium. English—Medium. Science—Medium. **Yearly Earnings:** $$ **Job Growth:** ★★★ **Yearly Openings:** 🚹🚹🚹

Pourers and Casters, Metal. Operate hand-controlled mechanisms to pour and regulate the flow of molten metal into molds to produce castings or ingots. **Education and Training:** Moderate-term on-the-job training. **Skills:** Math—Medium. English—Low. Science—Medium. **Yearly Earnings:** $$ **Job Growth:** ★★ **Yearly Openings:** 🚹

Precision Printing Workers. Perform variety of precision printing activities, such as duplication of microfilm and reproduction of graphic arts materials. **Education and Training:** Moderate-term on-the-job training. **Skills:** Math—Medium. English—Medium. Science—Medium. **Yearly Earnings:** $$ **Job Growth:** ★★ **Yearly Openings:** 🯅🯅🯅

Prepress Technicians and Workers. Set up and prepare material for printing presses. **Education and Training:** Long-term on-the-job training. **Skills:** Math—Medium. English—Medium. Science—Medium. **Yearly Earnings:** $$$ **Job Growth:** ★ **Yearly Openings:** 🯅🯅🯅

Pressing Machine Operators and Tenders—Textile, Garment, and Related Materials. Operate or tend pressing machines, such as hot-head pressing, steam pressing, automatic pressing, ironing, plunger pressing, and hydraulic pressing machines, to press and shape articles such as leather, fur, and cloth garments, drapes, slipcovers, handkerchiefs, and millinery. **Education and Training:** Short-term on-the-job training. **Skills:** Math—Medium. English—Medium. Science—Medium. **Yearly Earnings:** $ **Job Growth:** ★ **Yearly Openings:** 🯅🯅🯅

Printing Machine Operators. Set up or operate various types of printing machines, such as offset, letterset, intaglio, or gravure presses or screen printers, to produce print on paper or other materials. **Education and Training:** Moderate-term on-the-job training. **Skills:** Math—Medium. English—Medium. Science—Medium. **Yearly Earnings:** $$ **Job Growth:** ★★ **Yearly Openings:** 🯅🯅🯅

Printing Press Machine Operators and Tenders. Operate or tend various types of printing machines, such as offset lithographic presses, letter or letterset presses, or flexographic or gravure presses, to produce print on paper or other materials, such as plastic, cloth, or rubber. **Education and Training:** Short-term on-the-job training. **Skills:** Math—Medium. English—Medium. Science—Medium. **Yearly Earnings:** $$ **Job Growth:** ★★ **Yearly Openings:** 🯅🯅🯅

Production Helpers. Perform variety of tasks requiring limited knowledge of production processes in support of skilled production workers. **Education and Training:** Short-term on-the-job training. **Skills:** Math—Medium. English—Low. Science—Medium. **Yearly Earnings:** $ **Job Growth:** ★★★ **Yearly Openings:** 🯅🯅🯅🯅🯅

Production Laborers. Perform variety of routine tasks to assist in production activities. **Education and Training:** Short-term on-the-job training. **Skills:** Math—Medium. English—Medium. Science—Medium. **Yearly Earnings:** $ **Job Growth:** ★★★ **Yearly Openings:** 🯅🯅🯅🯅🯅

Sawing Machine Operators and Tenders. Operate or tend wood-sawing machines, such as circular saws, band saws, multiple blade sawing machines, scroll saws, rip-saws, equalizer saws, power saws, and crozer machines. Duties include sawing logs to specifications; cutting lumber to specified dimensions; sawing curved or irregular designs; trimming edges and removing defects from lumber; or cutting grooves, bevel,

and miter according to specifications or work orders. **Education and Training:** Moderate-term on-the-job training. **Skills:** Math—Medium. English—Low. Science—Medium. **Yearly Earnings:** $$ **Job Growth:** ★★★ **Yearly Openings:** 🚹🚹

Sawing Machine Setters and Set-Up Operators. Set up or set up and operate wood-sawing machines. Examine blueprints, drawings, work orders, and patterns to determine size and shape of items to be sawed, sawing machines to set up, and sequence of sawing operations. **Education and Training:** Moderate-term on-the-job training. **Skills:** Math—Medium. English—Low. Science—Low. **Yearly Earnings:** $$ **Job Growth:** ★★★ **Yearly Openings:** 🚹🚹

Sawing Machine Setters, Operators, and Tenders, Wood. Set up, operate, or tend wood sawing machines. Includes head sawyers. **Education and Training:** Moderate-term on-the-job training. **Skills:** Math—Medium. English—Medium. Science—Medium. **Yearly Earnings:** $$ **Job Growth:** ★★★ **Yearly Openings:** 🚹🚹

Scanner Operators. Operate electronic or computerized scanning equipment to produce and screen film separations of photographs or art for use in producing lithographic printing plates. Evaluate and correct for deficiencies in the film. **Education and Training:** Long-term on-the-job training. **Skills:** Math—Low. English—Medium. Science—Medium. **Yearly Earnings:** $$$ **Job Growth:** ★ **Yearly Openings:** 🚹🚹🚹

Semiconductor Processors. Perform any or all of the following functions in the manufacture of electronic semiconductors: Load semiconductor material into furnace; saw formed ingots into segments; load individual segment into crystal growing chamber and monitor controls; locate crystal axis in ingot using X-ray equipment and saw ingots into wafers; clean, polish, and load wafers into series of special-purpose furnaces, chemical baths, and equipment used to form circuitry and change conductive properties. **Education and Training:** Associate's degree. **Skills:** Math—Medium. English—Medium. Science—High. **Yearly Earnings:** $$ **Job Growth:** ★★★★ **Yearly Openings:** 🚹🚹

Separating, Filtering, Clarifying, Precipitating, and Still Machine Setters, Operators, and Tenders. Set up, operate, or tend continuous flow or vat-type equipment; filter presses; shaker screens; centrifuges; condenser tubes; precipitating, fermenting, or evaporating tanks; scrubbing towers; or batch stills. These machines extract, sort, or separate liquids, gases, or solids from other materials to recover a refined product. Includes dairy processing equipment operators. **Education and Training:** Moderate-term on-the-job training. **Skills:** Math—Medium. English—Medium. Science—Medium. **Yearly Earnings:** $$ **Job Growth:** ★ **Yearly Openings:** 🚹

Sewers, Hand. Sew, join, reinforce, or finish, usually with needle and thread, a variety of manufactured items. Includes weavers and stitchers. **Education and Training:** Short-term on-the-job training. **Skills:** Math—Medium. English—Low. Science—Low. **Yearly Earnings:** $ **Job Growth:** ★ **Yearly Openings:** 🚹🚹

Sewing Machine Operators. Operate or tend sewing machines to join, reinforce, decorate, or perform related sewing operations in the manufacture of garment or non-garment products. **Education and Training:** Moderate-term on-the-job training. **Skills:** Math—Medium. English—Medium. Science—Medium. **Yearly Earnings:** $ **Job Growth:** ★ **Yearly Openings:** 🧍🧍🧍🧍

Sewing Machine Operators, Garment. Operate or tend sewing machines to perform garment sewing operations, such as joining, reinforcing, or decorating garments or garment parts. **Education and Training:** Moderate-term on-the-job training. **Skills:** Math—Medium. English—Low. Science—Medium. **Yearly Earnings:** $ **Job Growth:** ★ **Yearly Openings:** 🧍🧍🧍🧍

Sewing Machine Operators, Non-Garment. Operate or tend sewing machines to join together, reinforce, decorate, or perform related sewing operations in the manufacture of nongarment products, such as upholstery, draperies, linens, carpets, and mattresses. **Education and Training:** Moderate-term on-the-job training. **Skills:** Math—Medium. English—Low. Science—Medium. **Yearly Earnings:** $ **Job Growth:** ★ **Yearly Openings:** 🧍🧍🧍🧍

Shoe Machine Operators and Tenders. Operate or tend a variety of machines to join, decorate, reinforce, or finish shoes and shoe parts. **Education and Training:** Moderate-term on-the-job training. **Skills:** Math—Low. English—Medium. Science—Low. **Yearly Earnings:** $ **Job Growth:** ★ **Yearly Openings:** 🧍

Slaughterers and Meat Packers. Work in slaughtering, meat packing, or wholesale establishments performing precision functions involving the preparation of meat. Work may include specialized slaughtering tasks, cutting standard or premium cuts of meat for marketing, making sausage, or wrapping meats. **Education and Training:** Moderate-term on-the-job training. **Skills:** Math—Low. English—Low. Science—Medium. **Yearly Earnings:** $ **Job Growth:** ★ **Yearly Openings:** 🧍🧍🧍

Solderers. Solder together components to assemble fabricated metal products, using soldering iron. **Education and Training:** Short-term on-the-job training. **Skills:** Math—Medium. English—Low. Science—Medium. **Yearly Earnings:** $$ **Job Growth:** ★★★ **Yearly Openings:** 🧍🧍🧍🧍

Soldering and Brazing Machine Operators and Tenders. Operate or tend soldering and brazing machines that braze, solder, or spot weld fabricated metal products or components as specified by work orders, blueprints, and layout specifications. **Education and Training:** Short-term on-the-job training. **Skills:** Math—Medium. English—Medium. Science—Medium. **Yearly Earnings:** $$ **Job Growth:** ★★★ **Yearly Openings:** 🧍🧍

Stone Sawyers. Set up and operate gang saws, reciprocating saws, circular saws, or wire saws to cut blocks of stone into specified dimensions. **Education and Training:** Moderate-term on-the-job training. **Skills:** Math—Medium. English—Low. Science—Medium. **Yearly Earnings:** $$ **Job Growth:** ★ **Yearly Openings:** 🧍🧍🧍

Strippers. Cut and arrange film into flats (layout sheets resembling a film negative of text in its final form), which are used to make plates. Prepare separate flat for each color. **Education and Training:** Long-term on-the-job training. **Skills:** Math—Medium. English—Medium. Science—Medium. **Yearly Earnings:** $$$ **Job Growth:** ★ **Yearly Openings:** 👤👤👤

Structural Metal Fabricators and Fitters. Fabricate, lay out, position, align, and fit parts of structural metal products. **Education and Training:** Moderate-term on-the-job training. **Skills:** Math—Medium. English—Medium. Science—Medium. **Yearly Earnings:** $$ **Job Growth:** ★★★ **Yearly Openings:** 👤👤👤

Team Assemblers. Work as part of a team having responsibility for assembling an entire product or component of a product. Team assemblers can perform all tasks conducted by the team in the assembly process and rotate through all or most of them rather than being assigned to a specific task on a permanent basis. **Education and Training:** Moderate-term on-the-job training. **Skills:** Math—Medium. English—Medium. Science—Medium. **Yearly Earnings:** $$ **Job Growth:** ★★ **Yearly Openings:** 👤👤👤👤👤

Textile Bleaching and Dyeing Machine Operators and Tenders. Operate or tend machines to bleach, shrink, wash, dye, or finish textiles or synthetic or glass fibers. **Education and Training:** Moderate-term on-the-job training. **Skills:** Math—Medium. English—Medium. Science—Medium. **Yearly Earnings:** $ **Job Growth:** ★★★ **Yearly Openings:** 👤

Tire Builders. Operate machines to build tires from rubber components. **Education and Training:** Moderate-term on-the-job training. **Skills:** Math—Low. English—Low. Science—Low. **Yearly Earnings:** $$$ **Job Growth:** ★★ **Yearly Openings:** 👤

Welder-Fitters. Lay out, fit, and fabricate metal components to assemble structural forms, such as machinery frames, bridge parts, and pressure vessels, using knowledge of welding techniques, metallurgy, and engineering requirements. Includes experimental welders who analyze engineering drawings and specifications to plan welding operations where procedural information is unavailable. **Education and Training:** Long-term on-the-job training. **Skills:** Math—Medium. English—Medium. Science—Medium. **Yearly Earnings:** $$ **Job Growth:** ★★★ **Yearly Openings:** 👤👤👤👤

Welders and Cutters. Use hand welding and flame-cutting equipment to weld together metal components and parts or to cut, trim, or scarf metal objects to dimensions as specified by layouts, work orders, or blueprints. **Education and Training:** Long-term on-the-job training. **Skills:** Math—Medium. English—Low. Science—Medium. **Yearly Earnings:** $$ **Job Growth:** ★★★ **Yearly Openings:** 👤👤👤👤

Welders, Cutters, Solderers, and Brazers. Use hand-welding, flame-cutting, hand soldering, or brazing equipment to weld or join metal components or to fill holes, indentations, or seams of fabricated metal products. **Education and Training:** Long-term on-the-job training. **Skills:** Math—Medium. English—Medium. Science—Medium. **Yearly Earnings:** $$ **Job Growth:** ★★★ **Yearly Openings:** 🚶🚶🚶🚶

Welders, Production. Assemble and weld metal parts on production line, using welding equipment. Requires only a limited knowledge of welding techniques. **Education and Training:** Short-term on-the-job training. **Skills:** Math—Medium. English—Low. Science—Medium. **Yearly Earnings:** $$ **Job Growth:** ★★★ **Yearly Openings:** 🚶🚶🚶🚶

Welding Machine Operators and Tenders. Operate or tend welding machines that join or bond together components to fabricate metal products and assemblies according to specifications and blueprints. **Education and Training:** Moderate-term on-the-job training. **Skills:** Math—Medium. English—Medium. Science—Medium. **Yearly Earnings:** $$ **Job Growth:** ★★★ **Yearly Openings:** 🚶🚶

Woodworking Machine Operators and Tenders, Except Sawing. Operate or tend woodworking machines, such as drill presses, lathes, shapers, routers, sanders, planers, and wood-nailing machines, to perform woodworking operations. **Education and Training:** Moderate-term on-the-job training. **Skills:** Math—Medium. English—Medium. Science—Medium. **Yearly Earnings:** $$ **Job Growth:** ★★ **Yearly Openings:** 🚶🚶🚶

METAL AND PLASTICS MACHINING TECHNOLOGY

These workers cut and grind metal and plastic parts to desired shapes and measurements, usually following specifications that require very precise work. They create the patterns, molds, and models that manufacturers then use to mass-produce products of all kinds. Most work in machine shops of manufacturing plants.

Lay-Out Workers, Metal and Plastic. Lay out reference points and dimensions on metal or plastic stock or workpieces, such as sheets, plates, tubes, structural shapes, castings, or machine parts, for further processing. Includes shipfitters. **Education and Training:** Postsecondary career and technical education. **Skills:** Math—High. English—Medium. Science—Medium. **Yearly Earnings:** $$ **Job Growth:** ★ **Yearly Openings:** 🚶

Machinists. Set up and operate a variety of machine tools to produce precision parts and instruments. Includes precision instrument makers who fabricate, modify, or repair mechanical instruments. May also fabricate and modify parts to make or repair machine tools or maintain industrial machines, applying knowledge of mechanics, shop mathematics, metal properties, layout, and machining procedures. **Education and Training:** Long-term on-the-job training. **Skills:** Math—High. English—Medium. Science—High. **Yearly Earnings:** $$$ **Job Growth:** ★★ **Yearly Openings:** 🚶🚶🚶

Model Makers, Metal and Plastic. Set up and operate machines, such as lathes, milling and engraving machines, and jig borers, to make working models of metal or plastic objects. **Education and Training:** Moderate-term on-the-job training. **Skills:** Math—Medium. English—Medium. Science—Medium. **Yearly Earnings:** $$$ **Job Growth:** ★ **Yearly Openings:** 🧍

Patternmakers, Metal and Plastic. Lay out, machine, fit, and assemble castings and parts to metal or plastic foundry patterns, core boxes, or match plates. **Education and Training:** Moderate-term on-the-job training. **Skills:** Math—Medium. English—Medium. Science—Medium. **Yearly Earnings:** $$$ **Job Growth:** ★ **Yearly Openings:** 🧍

Tool and Die Makers. Analyze specifications, lay out metal stock, set up and operate machine tools, and fit and assemble parts to make and repair dies, cutting tools, jigs, fixtures, gauges, and machinists' hand tools. **Education and Training:** Long-term on-the-job training. **Skills:** Math—Medium. English—Low. Science—Medium. **Yearly Earnings:** $$$$ **Job Growth:** ★ **Yearly Openings:** 🧍🧍

Tool Grinders, Filers, and Sharpeners. Perform precision smoothing, sharpening, polishing, or grinding of metal objects. **Education and Training:** Moderate-term on-the-job training. **Skills:** Math—Medium. English—Medium. Science—Medium. **Yearly Earnings:** $$ **Job Growth:** ★ **Yearly Openings:** 🧍

WOODWORKING TECHNOLOGY

These workers follow specifications as they cut, shape, and finish wood products such as furniture and cabinets. Some create wooden models of products that will be mass-produced out of wood, metal, or plastic. Although most work in manufacturing plants, some work in homes and offices to custom-make cabinets.

Cabinetmakers and Bench Carpenters. Cut, shape, and assemble wooden articles or set up and operate a variety of woodworking machines, such as power saws, jointers, and mortisers, to surface, cut, or shape lumber or to fabricate parts for wood products. **Education and Training:** Long-term on-the-job training. **Skills:** Math—Medium. English—Low. Science—Medium. **Yearly Earnings:** $$ **Job Growth:** ★★ **Yearly Openings:** 🧍🧍

Furniture Finishers. Shape, finish, and refinish damaged, worn, or used furniture or new high-grade furniture to specified color or finish. **Education and Training:** Long-term on-the-job training. **Skills:** Math—Low. English—Low. Science—Medium. **Yearly Earnings:** $$ **Job Growth:** ★★ **Yearly Openings:** 🧍

Model Makers, Wood. Construct full-size and scale wooden precision models of products. Includes wood jig builders and loft workers. **Education and Training:** Long-term on-the-job training. **Skills:** Math—Medium. English—Medium. Science—Medium. **Yearly Earnings:** $$ **Job Growth:** ★★★ **Yearly Openings:** 🧍

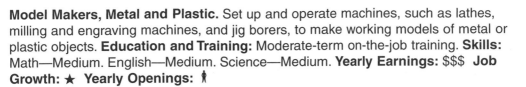

Patternmakers, Wood. Plan, lay out, and construct wooden unit or sectional patterns used in forming sand molds for castings. **Education and Training:** Long-term on-the-job training. **Skills:** Math—Medium. English—Medium. Science—Medium. **Yearly Earnings:** $$ **Job Growth:** ★★★ **Yearly Openings:** 🚶

SYSTEMS OPERATION

These workers operate and maintain equipment in systems that generate and distribute electricity, provide water and process wastewater, and pump oil and gas from oil fields to storage tanks. These jobs are found in utility companies, refineries, ships, industrial plants, and large apartment houses.

Auxiliary Equipment Operators, Power. Control and maintain auxiliary equipment, such as pumps, fans, compressors, condensers, feedwater heaters, filters, and chlorinators, that supply water, fuel, lubricants, air, and auxiliary power for turbines, generators, boilers, and other power-generating plant facilities. **Education and Training:** Long-term on-the-job training. **Skills:** Math—Low. English—Low. Science—Medium. **Yearly Earnings:** $$$$ **Job Growth:** ★ **Yearly Openings:** 🚶

Boiler Operators and Tenders, Low Pressure. Operate or tend low-pressure stationary steam boilers and auxiliary steam equipment, such as pumps, compressors, and air conditioning equipment, to supply steam heat for office buildings, apartment houses, or industrial establishments; to maintain steam at specified pressure aboard marine vessels; or to generate and supply compressed air for operation of pneumatic tools, hoists, and air lances. **Education and Training:** Moderate-term on-the-job training. **Skills:** Math—Medium. English—Medium. Science—Medium. **Yearly Earnings:** $$$$ **Job Growth:** ★ **Yearly Openings:** 🚶

Chemical Plant and System Operators. Control or operate an entire chemical process or system of machines. **Education and Training:** Long-term on-the-job training. **Skills:** Math—Medium. English—Medium. Science—High. **Yearly Earnings:** $$$$ **Job Growth:** ★ **Yearly Openings:** 🚶

Gas Compressor and Gas Pumping Station Operators. Operate steam, gas, electric motor, or internal combustion engine–driven compressors. Transmit, compress, or recover gases, such as butane, nitrogen, hydrogen, and natural gas. **Education and Training:** Moderate-term on-the-job training. **Skills:** Math—Medium. English—Medium. Science—Medium. **Yearly Earnings:** $$$$ **Job Growth:** ★★ **Yearly Openings:** 🚶

Gas Compressor Operators. Operate steam or internal combustion engines to transmit, compress, or recover gases, such as butane, nitrogen, hydrogen, and natural gas, in various production processes. **Education and Training:** Moderate-term on-the-job training. **Skills:** Math—Medium. English—Medium. Science—Medium. **Yearly Earnings:** $$$$ **Job Growth:** ★★ **Yearly Openings:** 🚶

Gas Distribution Plant Operators. Control equipment to regulate flow and pressure of gas for utility companies and industrial use. May control distribution of gas for a municipal or industrial plant or a single process in an industrial plant. **Education and Training:** Long-term on-the-job training. **Skills:** Math—Medium. English—Medium. Science—Medium. **Yearly Earnings:** $$$$ **Job Growth:** ★ **Yearly Openings:** 🚹

Gas Plant Operators. Distribute or process gas for utility companies and others by controlling compressors to maintain specified pressures on main pipelines. **Education and Training:** Long-term on-the-job training. **Skills:** Math—Medium. English—Medium. Science—Medium. **Yearly Earnings:** $$$$ **Job Growth:** ★ **Yearly Openings:** 🚹

Gas Processing Plant Operators. Control equipment such as compressors, evaporators, heat exchangers, and refrigeration equipment to process gas for utility companies and for industrial use. **Education and Training:** Long-term on-the-job training. **Skills:** Math—Medium. English—Medium. Science—Medium. **Yearly Earnings:** $$$$ **Job Growth:** ★ **Yearly Openings:** 🚹

Gas Pumping Station Operators. Control the operation of steam, gas, or electric-motor-driven compressor to maintain specified pressures on high- and low-pressure mains dispensing gas from gasholders. **Education and Training:** Moderate-term on-the-job training. **Skills:** Math—Medium. English—Low. Science—Medium. **Yearly Earnings:** $$$$ **Job Growth:** ★★ **Yearly Openings:** 🚹

Gaugers. Gauge and test oil in storage tanks. Regulate flow of oil into pipelines at wells, tank farms, refineries, and marine and rail terminals, following prescribed standards and regulations. **Education and Training:** Long-term on-the-job training. **Skills:** Math—High. English—Medium. Science—High. **Yearly Earnings:** $$$$ **Job Growth:** ★ **Yearly Openings:** 🚹

Nuclear Power Reactor Operators. Control nuclear reactors. **Education and Training:** Long-term on-the-job training. **Skills:** Math—Medium. English—Medium. Science—Medium. **Yearly Earnings:** $$$$$ **Job Growth:** ★ **Yearly Openings:** 🚹

Petroleum Pump System Operators. Control or operate manifold and pumping systems to circulate liquids through a petroleum refinery. **Education and Training:** Long-term on-the-job training. **Skills:** Math—Medium. English—Medium. Science—Medium. **Yearly Earnings:** $$$$ **Job Growth:** ★ **Yearly Openings:** 🚹

Petroleum Pump System Operators, Refinery Operators, and Gaugers. Control the operation of petroleum refining or processing units. May specialize in controlling manifold and pumping systems, gauging or testing oil in storage tanks, or regulating the flow of oil into pipelines. **Education and Training:** Long-term on-the-job training. **Skills:** Math—Medium. English—Medium. Science—Medium. **Yearly Earnings:** $$$$ **Job Growth:** ★ **Yearly Openings:** 🚹

Petroleum Refinery and Control Panel Operators. Analyze specifications and control continuous operation of petroleum refining and processing units. Operate control panel to regulate temperature, pressure, rate of flow, and tank level in petroleum refining unit according to process schedules. **Education and Training:** Long-term on-the-job training. **Skills:** Math—Medium. English—Medium. Science—Medium. **Yearly Earnings:** $$$$ **Job Growth:** ★ **Yearly Openings:** 🚶

Power Distributors and Dispatchers. Coordinate, regulate, or distribute electricity or steam. **Education and Training:** Long-term on-the-job training. **Skills:** Math—Medium. English—Medium. Science—Medium. **Yearly Earnings:** $$$$ **Job Growth:** ★ **Yearly Openings:** 🚶

Power Generating Plant Operators, Except Auxiliary Equipment Operators. Control or operate machinery, such as steam-driven turbogenerators, to generate electric power, often through the use of panelboards, control boards, or semi-automatic equipment. **Education and Training:** Long-term on-the-job training. **Skills:** Math—Medium. English—Medium. Science—Medium. **Yearly Earnings:** $$$$ **Job Growth:** ★ **Yearly Openings:** 🚶

Power Plant Operators. Control, operate, or maintain machinery to generate electric power. Includes auxiliary equipment operators. **Education and Training:** Long-term on-the-job training. **Skills:** Math—Medium. English—Medium. Science—Medium. **Yearly Earnings:** $$$$ **Job Growth:** ★ **Yearly Openings:** 🚶

Ship Engineers. Supervise and coordinate activities of crew engaged in operating and maintaining engines, boilers, deck machinery, and electrical, sanitary, and refrigeration equipment aboard ship. **Education and Training:** Postsecondary career and technical education. **Skills:** Math—Medium. English—Medium. Science—Medium. **Yearly Earnings:** $$$$ **Job Growth:** ★★ **Yearly Openings:** 🚶

Stationary Engineers. Operate and maintain stationary engines and mechanical equipment to provide utilities for buildings or industrial processes. Operate equipment such as steam engines, generators, motors, turbines, and steam boilers. **Education and Training:** Long-term on-the-job training. **Skills:** Math—Medium. English—Medium. Science—Medium. **Yearly Earnings:** $$$$ **Job Growth:** ★ **Yearly Openings:** 🚶

Stationary Engineers and Boiler Operators. Operate or maintain stationary engines, boilers, or other mechanical equipment to provide utilities for buildings or industrial processes. Operate equipment such as steam engines, generators, motors, turbines, and steam boilers. **Education and Training:** Moderate-term on-the-job training. **Skills:** Math—Medium. English—Medium. Science—Medium. **Yearly Earnings:** $$$$ **Job Growth:** ★ **Yearly Openings:** 🚶

Water and Liquid Waste Treatment Plant and System Operators. Operate or control an entire process or system of machines, often through the use of control boards,

to transfer or treat water or liquid waste. **Education and Training:** Long-term on-the-job training. **Skills:** Math—Medium. English—Medium. Science—High. **Yearly Earnings:** $$$ **Job Growth:** ★★★ **Yearly Openings:** 🧍🧍

Wellhead Pumpers. Operate power pumps and auxiliary equipment to produce flow of oil or gas from wells in oil field. **Education and Training:** Moderate-term on-the-job training. **Skills:** Math—Medium. English—Medium. Science—Medium. **Yearly Earnings:** $$$ **Job Growth:** ★ **Yearly Openings:** 🧍

HANDS-ON WORK: LOADING, MOVING, HOISTING, AND CONVEYING

These workers use their hands, machinery, tools, and other equipment to package or move products or materials. They work in a variety of settings, including offices, mailrooms, manufacturing plants, water treatment plants, and construction sites. They may work with small packages or computer chips or with huge containers or structural components of buildings.

Conveyor Operators and Tenders. Control or tend conveyors or conveyor systems that move materials or products to and from stockpiles, processing stations, departments, or vehicles. May control speed and routing of materials or products. **Education and Training:** Short-term on-the-job training. **Skills:** Math—Medium. English—Medium. Science—Medium. **Yearly Earnings:** $$ **Job Growth:** ★★★ **Yearly Openings:** 🧍🧍

Crane and Tower Operators. Operate mechanical boom and cable or tower and cable equipment to lift and move materials, machines, or products in many directions. **Education and Training:** Moderate-term on-the-job training. **Skills:** Math—Medium. English—Medium. Science—Medium. **Yearly Earnings:** $$$ **Job Growth:** ★★ **Yearly Openings:** 🧍

Dragline Operators. Operate power-driven crane equipment with dragline bucket to excavate or move sand, gravel, mud, or other materials. **Education and Training:** Moderate-term on-the-job training. **Skills:** Math—Low. English—Low. Science—Medium. **Yearly Earnings:** $$$ **Job Growth:** ★★★ **Yearly Openings:** 🧍

Excavating and Loading Machine and Dragline Operators. Operate or tend machinery equipped with scoops, shovels, or buckets to excavate and load loose materials. **Education and Training:** Moderate-term on-the-job training. **Skills:** Math—Medium. English—Medium. Science—Medium. **Yearly Earnings:** $$$ **Job Growth:** ★★★ **Yearly Openings:** 🧍

Freight, Stock, and Material Movers, Hand. Load, unload and move materials at plant, yard, or other work site. **Education and Training:** Short-term on-the-job training. **Skills:** Math—Low. English—Medium. Science—Medium. **Yearly Earnings:** $ **Job Growth:** ★★★ **Yearly Openings:** 🚶🚶🚶🚶🚶

Hoist and Winch Operators. Operate or tend hoists or winches to lift and pull loads using power-operated cable equipment. **Education and Training:** Moderate-term on-the-job training. **Skills:** Math—Medium. English—Medium. Science—Medium. **Yearly Earnings:** $$ **Job Growth:** ★★ **Yearly Openings:** 🚶

Industrial Truck and Tractor Operators. Operate industrial trucks or tractors equipped to move materials around a warehouse, storage yard, factory, construction site, or similar location. **Education and Training:** Short-term on-the-job training. **Skills:** Math—Medium. English—Low. Science—Medium. **Yearly Earnings:** $$ **Job Growth:** ★★★ **Yearly Openings:** 🚶🚶🚶🚶

Irradiated-Fuel Handlers. Package, store, and convey irradiated fuels and wastes, using hoists, mechanical arms, shovels, and industrial truck. **Education and Training:** Moderate-term on-the-job training. **Skills:** Math—Medium. English—Medium. Science—Medium. **Yearly Earnings:** $$ **Job Growth:** ★★★★ **Yearly Openings:** 🚶🚶

Laborers and Freight, Stock, and Material Movers, Hand. Manually move freight, stock, or other materials or perform other unskilled general labor. **Education and Training:** Short-term on-the-job training. **Skills:** Math—Medium. English—Medium. Science—Medium. **Yearly Earnings:** $ **Job Growth:** ★★★ **Yearly Openings:** 🚶🚶🚶🚶🚶

Machine Feeders and Offbearers. Feed materials into or remove materials from machines or equipment that is automatic or tended by other workers. **Education and Training:** Short-term on-the-job training. **Skills:** Math—Medium. English—Medium. Science—Medium. **Yearly Earnings:** $$ **Job Growth:** ★ **Yearly Openings:** 🚶🚶🚶

Packers and Packagers, Hand. Pack or package by hand a wide variety of products and materials. **Education and Training:** Short-term on-the-job training. **Skills:** Math—Medium. English—Medium. Science—Low. **Yearly Earnings:** $ **Job Growth:** ★★★ **Yearly Openings:** 🚶🚶🚶🚶🚶

Pump Operators, Except Wellhead Pumpers. Tend, control, or operate power-driven, stationary, or portable pumps and manifold systems to transfer gases, oil, other liquids, slurries, or powdered materials to and from various vessels and processes. **Education and Training:** Moderate-term on-the-job training. **Skills:** Math—Medium. English—Medium. Science—Medium. **Yearly Earnings:** $$$ **Job Growth:** ★★ **Yearly Openings:** 🚶

Refuse and Recyclable Material Collectors. Collect and dump refuse or recyclable materials from containers into truck. May drive truck. **Education and Training:** Short-term on-the-job training. **Skills:** Math—Low. English—Low. Science—Low. **Yearly Earnings:** $$ **Job Growth:** ★★★ **Yearly Openings:** 🚶🚶🚶

Tank Car, Truck, and Ship Loaders. Load and unload chemicals and bulk solids, such as coal, sand, and grain, into or from tank cars, trucks, or ships, using material moving equipment. May perform a variety of other tasks relating to shipment of products. May gauge or sample shipping tanks and test them for leaks. **Education and Training:** Moderate-term on-the-job training. **Skills:** Math—Medium. English—Medium. Science—Medium. **Yearly Earnings:** $$ **Job Growth:** ★★★ **Yearly Openings:** 🚶

Exploring Careers:

Business Detail

Start Your Journey Through Careers Related to

BUSINESS DETAIL

Careers in this area suit people interested in organized, clearly defined activities requiring accuracy and attention to detail, primarily in an office setting.

EXPLORING CAREER CLUES

Your interests give important clues for exploring career options. Think about your interests to learn if jobs in the Business Detail interest area may be worth further exploration.

Do you like the school subjects related to the Business Detail interest area? Here are some examples of related subjects:

- English
- Composition and writing
- Speech
- Math
- Computers
- Business
- Keyboarding

Do you like the free-time activities related to the Business Detail interest area? Here are some examples of related free-time activities:

- Writing letters and e-mails to friends and family
- Keeping a journal or diary
- Helping to organize and run school or community events
- Planning parties and outings
- Helping to keep things running smoothly at home, including making shopping lists, taking phone messages, sorting mail, checking e-mail, budgeting, or updating calendars
- Talking on the phone
- Learning to use extra features of word-processing and other computer programs
- Keyboarding papers and letters for others
- Doing desktop publishing or Web pages for a school or community publication
- Keeping score for athletic events

- Helping friends and others with math or homework
- Organizing your room, CDs, DVDs, tools, closets, books, desks, or other items and areas
- Collecting and arranging stamps, coins, or other items
- Volunteering at the library
- Serving as an officer of a club or other organization

EXPLORING JOB GROUPS

Jobs related to the Business Detail interest area fit into nine groups. Read through the list to see which groups sound interesting to you.

- Managerial Work in Business Detail
- Administrative Detail
- Bookkeeping, Auditing, and Accounting
- Material Control
- Customer Service
- Communications
- Records Processing
- Records and Materials Processing
- Clerical Machine Operation

EXPLORING CAREER POSSIBILITIES

You can satisfy your interest in the Business Detail area in a variety of jobs where you take care of the details of a business operation. Here are a few examples of career possibilities:

If you have good math skills, perhaps a job in billing, computing, or financial record-keeping would satisfy you. If you prefer to deal with and help people, you may want a job in customer service. If you like speaking on the phone, you may wish to work as a dispatcher or telephone operator.

A job as an office manager may interest you if you like a variety of work in a busy environment. If you are good with details and word processing, you may enjoy a job as an administrative assistant or data entry keyer.

Turn the page to meet people working in the Business Detail interest area→

PROFILE

Beverly McClain-Petri—Bill Collector

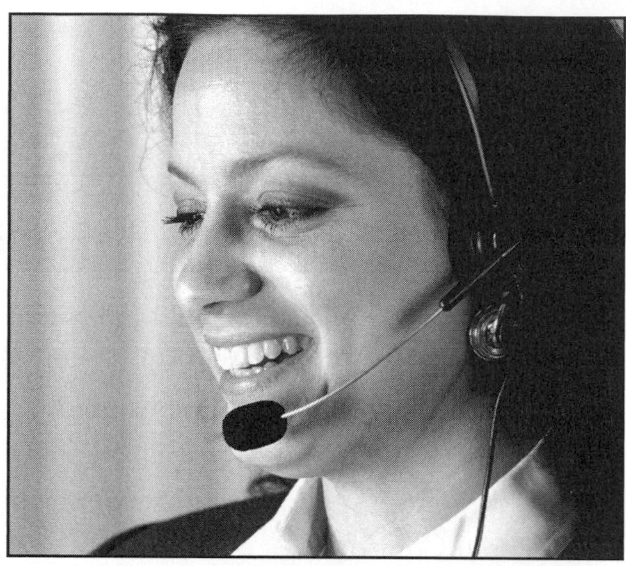
Beverly works with debtors to establish a payment plan.

Beverly McClain-Petri has a calling. She's a salesperson making the hardest sale of all. She sells debtors (people who owe money) on the idea of paying their debts. She's a bill collector with a collection agency.

Her work starts with a common story. Debtors owe money to creditors, but some of them don't pay. Creditors ask Beverly to collect the money. They offer a commission as a reward. Each creditor provides contact information for nonpaying debtors.

"You call and call–and call some more," Beverly said. "The more contacts you make, the higher your success rate. That means more money for you."

Searching for the Debtor

In some cases, Beverly has no current address, so she begins by finding the debtor, a task called skip tracing. "One of the best places to start is with relatives," she said. "Usually, you can find people with the same last name. You use the phone book, the Internet, or other resources. Then, you hope someone knows the person you're looking for."

Beverly might check credit records or use an online service to locate people. She finds the phone book more effective than Web searches when looking in remote areas. Cyber-tracing works better for searching in big cities.

Contacting Debtors in a Professional Way

When Beverly knows a debtor's whereabouts, she sends a letter. She then follows up with a phone call. "If you do that first phone contact properly," she said, "you often get all the information you need." Beverly verifies address, phone, and employment information. She finds out if the debtor has disputed the account. She also asks if any insurance claim is pending, if appropriate. She then tries to "close the sale," or convince the debtor to pay in full or agree to a payment schedule.

Of course, most debtors don't like hearing from a bill collector. But Beverly likes the challenge of keeping them on the phone. She assumes a professional, helpful attitude and lets people know their options.

"If they pay within thirty-one days, we don't charge interest," she said. "Nothing bad goes onto their credit record, either. If they have an insurance problem, I help them solve it, if possible.

"You don't want to talk down to them," Beverly said. "People need to be respected. I believe that if I treat people with dignity, they're more likely to pay each month." Excluding cases with pending insurance claims, Beverly gets payment about forty percent of the time with the first phone call.

When People Can't Pay

"You don't want to talk down to them. People need to be respected."

Despite Beverly's best phone manner, some people can't or won't put the check in the mail. In that case, Beverly investigates their ability to pay. She tries to discover any cash or other property a debtor has. She contacts the bureau of motor vehicles to see if the debtor owns cars. She calls the county treasurer to check whether the person owns real estate.

Beverly relies on intuition, too. "After years of being on the phone," she said, "you learn to read people. You can tell if they're telling the truth most of the time."

When debtors can't pay, some creditors write off debts to charity. For example, they sometimes write off medical bills in cases of extreme illness. In these cases, Beverly explains how to apply for charity care.

More often, though, debtors have the means to pay. In those cases, Beverly follows up with more calls. She can also "go legal," sending the case to a lawyer.

"After years of being on the phone, you learn to read people."

Sometimes debtors tell her, "Don't ever call me again!" By law, Beverly may make only one more contact. She usually sends a letter telling what legal action will be taken.

Collecting Experience on the Job

Beverly began collecting small accounts for her parents' business at age seventeen. She continued to work there after graduating from high school and eventually went to work for the collection agency. She learned on the job, like all collectors.

Today, new employees at the collection agency where Beverly works spend their first days on the job reading about policies and procedures. They also learn about the computer system used for tracking cases.

"After a couple of weeks of on-the-job training," said Beverly, "they make calls with a manager sitting next to them." The manager and collector wear headsets. The manager listens in and prompts the new employee. Both collector and manager can hear the manager. The debtor on the other end cannot. At Beverly's company, the computer dials the phone automatically. The collector speaks only when a connection is made, which saves time spent calling busy or unanswered numbers.

New collectors make their own calls after a few days of supervised practice. Experience makes them better speakers and persuaders.

Communication and Confidence Are Key

"The biggest thing in this field," said Beverly, "is communication skills, both verbal and written. You have to inspire confidence that you know what you're doing and communicate clearly."

Experience with accounts receivable for a credit bureau, a bank, or any other business helps beginning collectors. Experienced collectors may study advanced collection techniques. They can take courses sponsored by the American Collectors Association.

At entry level, collectors need a high school education. College isn't required, but it helps collectors who want to advance into management. Courses relating to business or communication at any level are helpful.

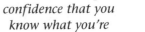

"You have to inspire confidence that you know what you're doing and communicate clearly."

Students interested in the field should do further research on the following job titles: collector, bill and account collector, payment collector, collection clerk, installment agent, and repossessor.

"One of the toughest things is accepting rejection," Beverly said. "People tell you they don't want to pay. They say 'no' a lot. You have to make another call anyway. That takes some confidence." At that, Beverly turned to make another call.

PROFILE

Charlie Edwards—Counter Clerk

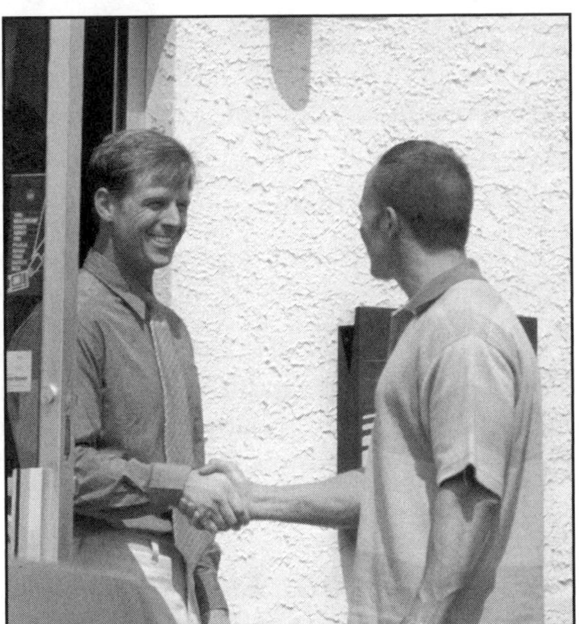

Charlie helps customers obtain the parts they need.

Charlie Edwards stood behind the counter of Southeast Auto Parts. Behind him were about twenty metal shelves, each seven feet high and about thirty feet long. These shelves contained thousands and thousands of automobile parts.

Directly in front of Charlie was the big picture window that overlooked the parking lot of the store. Past the battery and tool displays at the front of Southeast Auto Parts, he watched customers come and go as well as the traffic on the busy street.

Finding the Right Part

At 8:30 a.m., the telephone rang for at least the tenth time since the store opened at 8 a.m. "Southeast Auto Parts, may I help you?" Charlie said as he pulled a notepad closer to the phone.

"I hope so," said the caller. "This is Jerry over at Collins Auto Repair. Do you have brake shoes for a 1995 Chevy Monte Carlo?"

"I think so, Jerry, but let me check," said Charlie as he quickly entered the name of the part into the computer inventory software. Next to the computer was a catalog that listed many older or obsolete parts that the store stocked in limited quantities.

This parts catalog was actually a loosely bound collection of various manufacturers' catalogs. Sometimes, Charlie was amazed that he worked for so many years using just the bulky catalog.

The computer displayed the part number, its location, and the available quantity in inventory. Charlie wrote down the part number and its price. "We have the part in stock, Jerry. I'll have Susan deliver it in just a few minutes. Do you need anything else?"

"Not right now, thanks," Jerry replied.

Charlie hung up the phone and turned to a young woman who was stocking shelves behind the counter. "Susan, would you get some brake shoes, number 5329, and deliver them to Jerry at Collins Auto Repair?"

"Sure," Susan said. Susan Schafer was the driver who delivered parts to customers, picked up parts at the warehouse, and helped stock parts on the shelves. Sometimes she helped wait on customers when Charlie was very busy.

Getting in the Driver's Seat

Charlie himself started out as a driver while he was still in high school and learned the auto parts business that way. When he finished high school, with good grades in math and customer service skills learned on the job, he was hired full time. The boss often complimented him on being so

Charlie quickly entered the name of the part into the computer inventory software.

reliable. When he became familiar enough with the business, he was promoted to parts counter worker.

The boss often complimented him on being so reliable.

Students curious about the field should research the following job titles: cashier, counter and rental clerk, parts clerk, parts salesperson, auto parts salesperson, and retail salesperson.

Charlie handed Susan a printout of parts that were not currently in stock, the result of Charlie's early morning inventory as well as customer orders from late the day before. "While you're out, please pick these up at the warehouse. I promised we would have them by noon," he explained.

Juggling Customers and Calls

Just after Susan left, three customers walked into the store at the same time "That's how this business is," Charlie said. "It comes in spurts." Charlie waited on the customers one by one, first come, first served.

The first wanted a radiator hose for a 1997 Camaro. Charlie pulled the part off the shelf, generated the receipt on the computer/cash register, and took payment. Without any further action on Charlie's part, the computer adjusted the parts inventory to reflect this sale.

Charlie's next customer had a different problem. Her van had a difficult time starting in very cold weather. She wondered if Charlie had any ideas for improving this situation.

"What kind of oil are you using in your van now?" Charlie asked.

"I believe it's 10W-30, but I'm not sure," the customer responded.

"That could be the problem, then," Charlie said. "Why don't you try this 5W-30? It just might solve your problem because it's a lighter oil." The customer bought five quarts of 5W-30, enough to change the oil in her van.

Charlie waited on the customers one by one, first come, first served.

Charlie's next customer was not so easy to please. He wanted a part that was stocked only by auto dealers, not independent parts stores such as the one where Charlie worked. Charlie explained this to the customer, apologizing that he was sorry he couldn't help this time.

"Check with me again if you need any other parts in the future," Charlie said politely.

"Check with me again if you need any other parts in the future," Charlie said politely. He then referred the customer to a local Ford dealer whom Charlie knew would have the part.

During the time Charlie waited on the walk-in customers, he also helped customers over the phone. As he spoke, he checked for the parts on the computer and wrote orders on the notepad beside him. After the phone calls slowed down, he would complete the more thorough paper and computer work for the orders.

About 10:30 a.m., Jane Bregan walked into the store, greeted Charlie, and moved to the shelves behind the counter. Jane was a manufacturer's representative and was in the store to be sure that there was an adequate stock of all her company's parts. She was there for a couple of hours, taking inventory on her line of parts and ordering those the store needed.

While Jane was in the back of the store, Charlie continued waiting on customers. He knew many of the customers by name. When business slowed, he sometimes stopped and talked for a short time with them. But lulls didn't occur very often and never lasted long.

Service with a Smile, Always

A little after noon, Susan returned, bringing sandwiches from a local carryout for them both. Charlie always ate in the store, grabbing a bite when he could. Charlie was just about to eat his sandwich when a customer walked into the store.

"May I help you?" Charlie asked.

"Yes, I need new piston rings for my car. Do you have any in stock?"

"We sure do," said Charlie. "What kind of car do you have?"

Lulls didn't occur very often and never lasted long.

"It's a 1998 Ford Contour."

"What size engine?" asked Charlie.

"I don't know," said the customer.

"Sorry," said Charlie, "but I can't get the part unless I know what size engine your car has. I could sell you piston rings right now, but there is no way of being sure they would be the right ones without knowing the size of your car's engine."

"Well, can I take the different piston rings and return the ones that don't work?" asked the customer.

"Sure," Charlie agreed, "but you'll have to buy both options. I'll give you a refund when you return the ones that don't work."

"It sounds like you don't trust me," the customer said. "I'll just take my business elsewhere," he added as he stomped out of the store.

Charlie was sorry to lose the sale but somewhat relieved that the customer had left. When he first started in the business, customers like that one had given him severe indigestion.

But now he was more philosophical. "Unreasonable customers are an unavoidable part of dealing with the public. I'm always polite and try to help, but it no longer bothers me if a difficult customer goes away angry."

Just then, another person walked into the store. Without hesitation, Charlie smiled and asked, "May I help you?"

PROFILE

Paula Ann Linstrom—Police, Fire, and Ambulance Dispatcher

According to Paula Ann Linstrom, it takes a special kind of person to handle the pressures of 911.

"You rarely know the outcome of the incidents you've handled. Your job is to control the situation at hand. Communication skills and the ability to work under pressure are key," Paula Ann said.

Paula Ann has had ten years as a dispatcher in a large metropolitan area's 911 facility. "You must be able to identify and be satisfied with your niche in a very complex and lengthy process," she said. "You can control only what is directly in front of you."

Many Roles with One Result

"The person on the other end of the phone is depending on me for help."

In large metropolitan areas, the dispatcher role may be broken down into four separate positions. Paula has done all of these jobs.

The first position is the call taker. "The call taker answers the call and deals with the public," Paula Ann said. "The call taker collects the information, makes referrals when necessary, and translates the information to law enforcement officials."

The call taker almost always speaks to distraught, frightened, angry, or just plain unhappy people, usually victims or close associates of victims. The call taker must do so as pleasantly, calmly, and effectively as possible.

The call taker must talk with upset people as pleasantly, calmly, and effectively as possible.

A second position is the radio dispatcher. The call taker inputs all pertinent information into the computer and then sends it to the screen of the radio dispatcher. In a large facility, radio dispatchers rarely talk to the public. Dispatchers are the voices heard over police radios and are the trusted guides that inform and direct law enforcement officials.

Another emergency dispatcher role is that of fire station dispatcher. "It is a much more procedural position compared to the others," stated Paula Ann. "Either something's on fire or it isn't."

The do-it-all dispatcher, the final dispatcher role, is by far the toughest. This dispatcher is acting as call taker, radio dispatcher, and fire station dispatcher all at once.

"Most facilities in the country require that the dispatchers do it all," said Paula Ann. "That can create anxiety for those ready and willing to answer the call."

"Most facilities in the country require that the dispatchers fill three roles."

A Dispatcher's "Day" May Start at Night

Paula Ann's emergency communications operation is set in a calm, carpeted section of City Hall, bunkered in the basement. It has subdued lighting and spacious rooms. This is a pretty standard setup, she said.

Dispatchers sit together around large, L-shaped desks outfitted with radio scanners, switchboards, and computers. A kitchen and restrooms are nearby.

Dispatchers may rarely leave their posts during a typical eight-hour shift. Such facilities may be connected to law enforcement offices, or they may be separate community-based services.

A dispatcher may be required to work five shifts per week, eight hours per shift, with only forty minutes of break time. Hours vary from facility to facility. Newcomers should expect the graveyard shift–working late at night through the wee morning hours.

"Whoever looks into a job as a dispatcher must be able to handle shift work," said Paula Ann. "Working 10 p.m. to 6 a.m. can be physically difficult. You may become somewhat isolated from family and friends. And 911 does not recognize Christmas or the Fourth of July."

Stress Leads to Improvement

"Whoever looks into a job as a dispatcher must be able to handle shift work."

All transactions made by dispatchers are recorded and reviewed to enforce quality control. "The average dispatcher responds to roughly twenty calls per hour on an eight-hour shift," said Paula Ann.

"It adds to the stress, knowing you're being monitored. But it's also a learning device. We don't expect perfection. Transactions can be re-created down to the nanosecond. We can trace what went wrong and how it could have been handled better.

"Dispatchers are expected to make mistakes, to learn from and acknowledge those mistakes, and to move on. We reward the process, not the outcome."

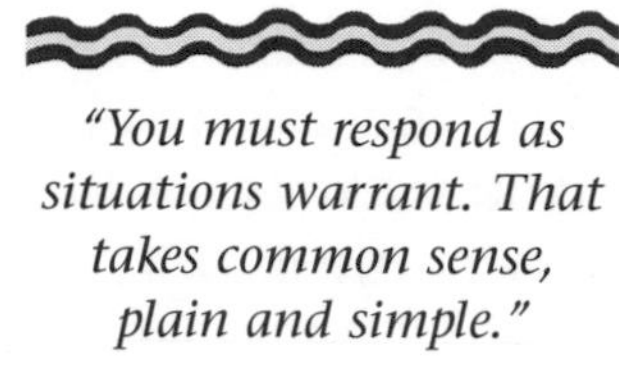
"You must respond as situations warrant. That takes common sense, plain and simple."

The First to Know

A dispatcher is the link who communicates events as they happen and is usually the first person to hear of those events. This "need to know" combined with a "need to be needed" helps dispatchers feel that they are performing a valuable service.

"Knowing that the person on the other end of every call is depending on you for help–that's a powerful attraction for most people," Paula Ann said.

Technology improvements are helping dispatchers do a better job. Dispatchers are being linked to a Global Positioning System designed to pinpoint the location of a wired or wireless phone caller. Through this technology, dispatchers can give emergency service workers an exact address or intersection.

"Also, the camaraderie in the emergency services is unlike anything you've ever experienced. Anyone who works in the emergency services area has a kind of extended family with everyone else in the profession."

What It Takes to Succeed

Topping her list of personal qualifications important in a proficient dispatcher is common sense. "You have to be levelheaded and good at interpreting events," said Paula Ann. "You must respond as situations warrant. That takes common sense, plain and simple."

Dispatchers must also be strong oral communicators, good listeners, and have good spatial relationship skills when directing officers to geographic locations. Computerization of the 911 system requires that dispatchers type at least thirty-five words per minute.

The vast majority of dispatchers today are civilians, though many of those enter the dispatch profession as a vehicle to law enforcement careers. "I suggest to new trainees that they get a job first in a larger city, if possible. There are more resources available to them for extensive training," she said. "Later they can move to smaller regions if they like, and bring with them the big city perspective."

After that, 911 trainees are assigned to a dispatching "coach" for up to twenty weeks before they are allowed to operate the phone lines. In addition, new dispatchers must pass a skills qualifications test. If they fail, they are placed on probation until the facility director feels confident that the trainee can handle the job.

"But if you train properly, you'll find that the training has conditioned you to respond appropriately and automatically. You learn to rely on the training for the basics and your judgment for the rest."

Students should research the following related job titles: 911 operator, dispatcher, emergency operator, public safety dispatcher, security dispatcher, truck dispatcher, and service dispatcher.

Some states and organizations offer certification programs, which improve prospects for career advancement. Paula Ann suggested that those interested in moving up to management positions should obtain a college degree.

Finally, Paula Ann summed it all up. "Sometimes I can prevent harm or save lives. Other times, help can't get to a scene fast enough. As a 911 dispatcher, you must be emotionally and psychologically prepared and able to cope with that."

PROFILE

Stephanie Kruthers—Word Processor

Stephanie Kruthers's work day starts after her husband gets home from his day job. Stephanie works for an insurance company. She is a word processor and types for her entire shift.

Because she works at night, her employer has no dress code. Stephanie usually wears jeans and a long-sleeved shirt. Her office is a sea of desks, all uniformly positioned in the room.

Nineteen other people share her shift. Stephanie works twenty hours a week for an insurance company. She may put in four hours for five days or five hours for four days. Some of her coworkers start earlier. These are flexible shifts.

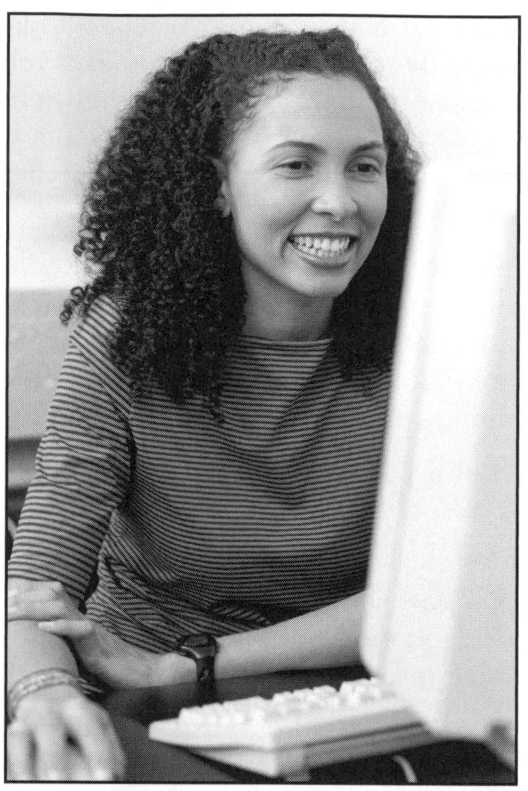

Stephanie looks over a letter she typed to make sure it doesn't have any errors.

Her Type of Work

Stephanie shares a desk with a day person. Her desk holds a computer with keyboard and monitor. Stephanie searches the computer for the file she wants. When it comes up on the screen, Stephanie listens to a tape of a client's conversation with the insurance company. She usually has no direct contact with clients. Stephanie types furiously to document the discussion in text form.

She hears that two cars backed into each other in a parking lot. There was $2,000 worth of damage to a newer car, which now has a large dent in the rear quarter panel. The other car was so dilapidated that the client couldn't find where he'd smacked it.

Stephanie's computer automatically saves her work every few minutes. The computer also keeps track of the date, word count, and number of minutes spent editing.

"I type all the various kinds of letters the insurance company sends."

Stephanie spell-checks the document and saves the final, revised copy. She turns on her printer and checks that the paper is properly positioned.

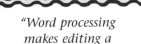

"Word processing makes editing a breeze."

"I also type all the various kinds of letters the insurance company sends," she said. "Often they are form letters that contain the same general message but change in details. On a separate screen, I enter the name, date, address, unique amounts, and other personal data. Then I instruct the computer to merge the information into each form letter."

Stephanie inserts a blank CD and writes her night's work to it. "It's a good policy to back up files in case the computer fails. So I back up my work." Stephanie said.

Technology Equals Efficiency

"I prefer word processing to typewriter typing. In the old way, I had to shift a lever to change lines, which tired my arm after five hours. When I made a mistake on the typewriter, I whited it out with liquid. That took time to dry and the result often looked messy. Worse, the carbon copy retained the error.

"Editing used to be difficult. I had to type a new page with every single wording change. Sometimes I accepted awkward phrases rather than change to a clearer wording.

"Word processing makes editing a breeze. With the word processor, I move paragraphs, insert phrases, and take out words with a couple of keystrokes. Spelling and grammar checks are a snap. I edit before I print.

"There are no typos unless I missed them when editing. Tell the computer to print ten copies and it's all the same to the printer. If you'd asked me to type ten letters when I used a typewriter, I would have headed for the copy machine. Imagine the way it was before copying machines!

"I didn't have to re-learn everything when I learned word processing. Much is done the same way–tabs and margins, for example," Stephanie said.

As the moon comes up, Stephanie finishes tape after tape and types letter after letter, document after document.

"I don't think typists are productive after much more than five hours of typing. We compare our productivity with people who work eight hours a day. They type to fill the time, stretching the work to end with the day. We are as productive as they are. The human hand gets tired. Five hours is a sensible limit."

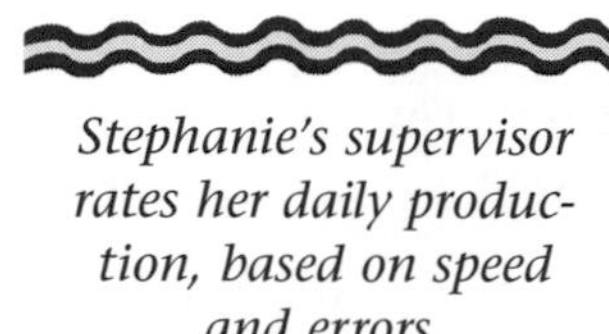

Stephanie's supervisor rates her daily production, based on speed and errors.

Avoiding a Few Hazards

"I don't want to get carpal tunnel syndrome or a repetitive stress disorder. I've typed insurance claims for people who need that surgery.

"Sometimes my hands get numb, especially if I put in extra hours. My back and shoulders ache after an hour or so. After a while, I must rest my eyes. My eye doctor recommends that I look up and focus far away often. We get two breaks. It's important to take them.

"When I started word processing, we typed with the computer on top of the desk. The height wasn't the best. The keyboard should be lower than my elbow. That prevents fatigue. Now the company purchases proper computer desks as well as other quality equipment. Even the printers rarely jam any more," said Stephanie.

Daily Production Is Critical

Stephanie types constantly, finishing nearly fifty letters. In a night, she finishes seven or eight tapes. Each tape holds five or six letters. She learns of burglaries, fires, and accidents.

Stephanie's supervisor rates her daily production, based on speed and errors. "She counts the work in a regimented way. How many pages typed per hour? What is the frequency of errors?"

The company tries to maintain standards. With a garbled tape or illegible penmanship, Stephanie makes her best guess. She can't always be correct.

"Nowadays, people in word processing aren't highly trained. It's an entry-level job. With today's systems, you can learn all you need for minimum production with a short amount of practice. It's a good way to get your foot in the door."

But the job suits Stephanie. She enjoys and takes pride in her work. "I like being productive and getting things done."

"It's a flexible job for people with complicated personal lives."

Where to Begin

In high school, Stephanie excelled in language and learned to type. The computer keyboard uses mainly the same arrangement of letters. "When I learned to use a mainframe system, I needed six months of training and on-the-job practice to become proficient.

"When my insurance company adopted the current word-processing system, I typed the wrong keys for a little while. I quickly mastered the new program by studying the reference manual and a tutorial.

"Someone starting today might choose to earn a certificate with a specialty in word processing.

"It's a flexible job for people with complicated personal lives. If you perform well, with intelligence, your supervisor may promote you. You can study for tests in office management and advance. It's a good, solid beginning.

"I know my job is important. When people meet misfortune and require the help their insurance provides, what I do is important in bringing assistance to them as quickly as possible. I feel I've done worthwhile work at the end of the day," Stephanie said.

SKILL SAMPLER

Matt Trudeau—Medical Transcriptionist

Matt Trudeau is a medical transcriptionist in the office of a heart physician. "I enjoy the quick, steady pace of my work, and I like seeing the tangible results of my efforts."

Matt shared some ideas about what skills are required to be a medical transcriptionist. He offers the following tips to help you decide if you might enjoy this kind of work.

Medical transcriptionists must be experts in the language of medicine. They must be able to recognize and spell the names of bones, muscles, procedures, and prescriptions.

- Are you interested in medical treatments and diagnoses?
- Do you enjoy reading about new medical procedures and discoveries?
- Do you take time to learn the scientific names of plants and animals?
- Is it important to you to find out the correct way of pronouncing the first and last names of people you meet?

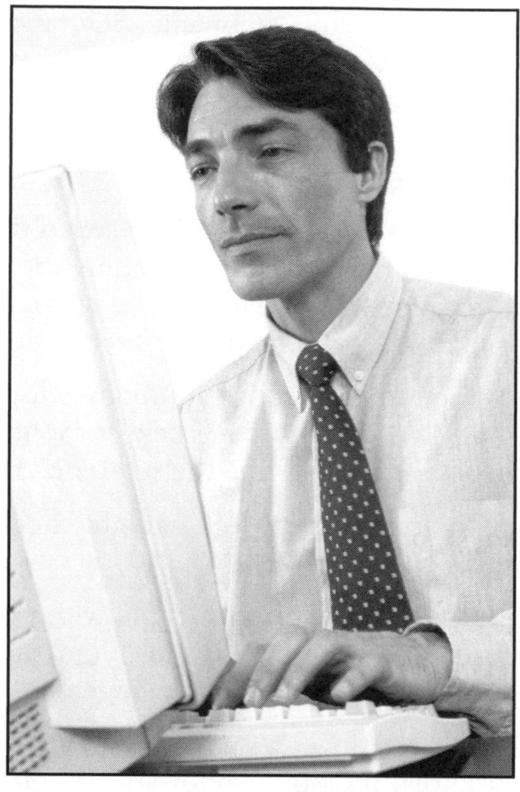

Matt types notes for healthcare providers.

Medical transcriptionists must be able to turn healthcare providers' spoken notes into well-edited, typed reports.

- Do you have a keen ear for interpreting the sounds you hear?
- Do your friends say you have good ears because you often hear ringing cell phones or approaching trains before other people do?
- Do you enjoy talking to people from other countries?
- Do you have good grammar skills?
- Do you like to keyboard your school assignments and take pride in turning in accurate, neat reports?

Medical transcriptionists must follow strict legal and ethical guidelines when transmitting or storing confidential medical records.

- Can you keep a secret?

- Do you enjoy sports or computer games that require you to follow set rules and guidelines?
- Do you obey laws protecting the use of audio or video materials?

Medical transcriptionists sit indoors in the same position for long periods and must often meet tight deadlines.

- Are you content to be indoors?
- Can you sit at your computer until you finish a homework assignment?
- Do you turn in your school assignments on time?
- Can you remain calm in pressure situations?

Now learn about all major jobs in the Business Detail interest area→

Facts About All Major Jobs Related to

BUSINESS DETAIL

In addition to the jobs covered in the profiles and skill sampler, other careers in the Business Detail interest area may appeal to you. This section describes and gives facts about all major jobs in the Business Detail interest area. For an explanation of the $, ★, and 🚹 symbols, see page 6.

MANAGERIAL WORK IN BUSINESS DETAIL

These workers supervise and coordinate certain high-level business activities: contracts for buying or selling goods and services, office support services, facilities planning and maintenance, customer service, administrative support. Within the general policies and goals of their organization, they make plans, oversee financial and technical resources, and evaluate outcomes. They work in the offices of every kind of business, government agency, and school.

Administrative Services Managers. Plan, direct, or coordinate supportive services of an organization, such as recordkeeping, mail distribution, telephone operator/receptionist, and other office support services. May oversee facilities planning and maintenance and custodial operations. **Education and Training:** College degree plus work experience. **Skills:** Math—Medium. English—High. Science—Low. **Yearly Earnings:** $$$$ **Job Growth:** ★★★ **Yearly Openings:** 🚹🚹🚹

First-Line Supervisors, Administrative Support. Supervise and coordinate activities of workers involved in providing administrative support. **Education and Training:** Work experience in a related occupation. **Skills:** Math—Medium. English—Medium. Science—Medium. **Yearly Earnings:** $$$ **Job Growth:** ★★ **Yearly Openings:** 🚹🚹🚹🚹🚹

First-Line Supervisors, Customer Service. Supervise and coordinate activities of workers involved in providing customer service. **Education and Training:** Work experience in a related occupation. **Skills:** Math—Medium. English—Medium. Science—Low. **Yearly Earnings:** $$$ **Job Growth:** ★★ **Yearly Openings:** 🚹🚹🚹🚹🚹

First-Line Supervisors/Managers of Office and Administrative Support Workers. Supervise and coordinate the activities of clerical and administrative support workers. **Education and Training:** Work experience in a related occupation. **Skills:** Math—Medium. English—Medium. Science—Medium. **Yearly Earnings:** $$$ **Job Growth:** ★★ **Yearly Openings:** 🚹🚹🚹🚹🚹

ADMINISTRATIVE DETAIL

These workers do high-level clerical work requiring special skills and knowledge, as well as some lower-level managerial work. They work in the offices of businesses, industries, courts of law, and government agencies, as well as in medicine, law, and other professions.

Claims Takers, Unemployment Benefits. Interview unemployed workers and compile data to determine eligibility for unemployment benefits. **Education and Training:** Moderate-term on-the-job training. **Skills:** Math—Low. English—Medium. Science—Low. **Yearly Earnings:** $$ **Job Growth:** ★ **Yearly Openings:** 🧍🧍🧍

Court Clerks. Perform clerical duties in court of law; prepare docket of cases to be called; secure information for judges; and contact witnesses, attorneys, and litigants to obtain information for court. **Education and Training:** Short-term on-the-job training. **Skills:** Math—Medium. English—Medium. Science—Medium. **Yearly Earnings:** $$ **Job Growth:** ★★★ **Yearly Openings:** 🧍🧍🧍

Court, Municipal, and License Clerks. Perform clerical duties in courts of law, municipalities, and governmental licensing agencies and bureaus. May prepare docket of cases to be called; secure information for judges and court; prepare draft agendas or bylaws for town or city council; answer official correspondence; keep fiscal records and accounts; issue licenses or permits; and record data, administer tests, or collect fees. **Education and Training:** Short-term on-the-job training. **Skills:** Math—Medium. English—Medium. Science—Medium. **Yearly Earnings:** $$ **Job Growth:** ★★★ **Yearly Openings:** 🧍🧍🧍

Eligibility Interviewers, Government Programs. Determine eligibility of persons applying to receive assistance from government programs and agency resources, such as welfare, unemployment benefits, social security, and public housing. **Education and Training:** Moderate-term on-the-job training. **Skills:** Math—Medium. English—Medium. Science—Medium. **Yearly Earnings:** $$ **Job Growth:** ★ **Yearly Openings:** 🧍🧍🧍

Executive Secretaries and Administrative Assistants. Provide high-level administrative support by conducting research, preparing statistical reports, handling information requests, and performing clerical functions. Clerical functions include preparing correspondence, receiving visitors, arranging conference calls, and scheduling meetings. May also train and supervise lower-level clerical staff. **Education and Training:** Moderate-term on-the-job training. **Skills:** Math—Medium. English—Medium. Science—Medium. **Yearly Earnings:** $$$ **Job Growth:** ★★★ **Yearly Openings:** 🧍🧍🧍🧍🧍

Interviewers, Except Eligibility and Loan. Interview persons by telephone, by mail, in person, or by other means for the purpose of completing forms, applications, or questionnaires. Ask specific questions, record answers, and assist persons with completing form. May sort, classify, and file forms. **Education and Training:** Short-term on-the-job training. **Skills:** Math—Low. English—Medium. Science—Medium. **Yearly Earnings:** $$ **Job Growth:** ★★★★ **Yearly Openings:** 🯅🯅🯅🯅

Legal Secretaries. Perform secretarial duties utilizing legal terminology, procedures, and documents. Prepare legal papers and correspondence, such as summonses, complaints, motions, and subpoenas. May also assist with legal research. **Education and Training:** Postsecondary career and technical education. **Skills:** Math—Medium. English—High. Science—Medium. **Yearly Earnings:** $$$ **Job Growth:** ★★★ **Yearly Openings:** 🯅🯅🯅

License Clerks. Issue licenses or permits to qualified applicants. Obtain necessary information, record data, advise applicants on requirements, collect fees, and issue licenses. May conduct oral, written, visual, or performance testing. **Education and Training:** Short-term on-the-job training. **Skills:** Math—Medium. English—Medium. Science—Low. **Yearly Earnings:** $$ **Job Growth:** ★★★ **Yearly Openings:** 🯅🯅🯅

Loan Interviewers and Clerks. Interview loan applicants to elicit information; investigate applicants' backgrounds and verify references; prepare loan request papers; and forward findings, reports, and documents to appraisal department. Review loan papers to ensure completeness. Complete transactions between loan establishment, borrowers, and sellers upon approval of loan. **Education and Training:** Short-term on-the-job training. **Skills:** Math—Medium. English—Medium. Science—Low. **Yearly Earnings:** $$ **Job Growth:** ★ **Yearly Openings:** 🯅🯅🯅

Medical Secretaries. Perform secretarial duties using specific knowledge of medical terminology and hospital, clinic, or laboratory procedures. Duties include scheduling appointments; billing patients; and compiling and recording medical charts, reports, and correspondence. **Education and Training:** Postsecondary career and technical education. **Skills:** Math—Medium. English—Medium. Science—Medium. **Yearly Earnings:** $$ **Job Growth:** ★★★ **Yearly Openings:** 🯅🯅🯅

Municipal Clerks. Draft agendas and bylaws for town or city council, record minutes of council meetings, answer official correspondence, keep fiscal records and accounts, and prepare reports on civic needs. **Education and Training:** Short-term on-the-job training. **Skills:** Math—Medium. English—Medium. Science—Low. **Yearly Earnings:** $$ **Job Growth:** ★★★ **Yearly Openings:** 🯅🯅🯅

Secretaries, Except Legal, Medical, and Executive. Perform routine clerical and administrative functions, such as drafting correspondence, scheduling appointments, organizing and maintaining paper and electronic files, or providing information to callers. **Education and Training:** Moderate-term on-the-job training. **Skills:** Math—Medium. English—Medium. Science—Low. **Yearly Earnings:** $$ **Job Growth:** ★ **Yearly Openings:** 🯅🯅🯅🯅🯅

Welfare Eligibility Workers and Interviewers. Interview and investigate applicants and recipients to determine eligibility for use of social programs and agency

resources. Duties include recording and evaluating personal and financial data obtained from individuals; initiating procedures to grant, modify, deny, or terminate eligibility for various aid programs; authorizing grant amounts; and preparing reports. These workers generally receive specialized training and assist social service caseworkers. **Education and Training:** Moderate-term on-the-job training. **Skills:** Math—Medium. English—Medium. Science—Low. **Yearly Earnings:** $$ **Job Growth:** ★ **Yearly Openings:** 🚶🚶🚶

BOOKKEEPING, AUDITING, AND ACCOUNTING

These workers collect, organize, compute, and record the numerical information used in business and financial transactions. They use both clerical and math skills, and some use machines. They work in banks, finance companies, accounting firms, payroll and inventory control departments in business and government agencies, and other places.

Billing and Posting Clerks and Machine Operators. Compile, compute, and record billing, accounting, statistical, and other numerical data for billing purposes. Prepare billing invoices for services rendered or for delivery or shipment of goods. **Education and Training:** Moderate-term on-the-job training. **Skills:** Math—Medium. English—Medium. Science—Medium. **Yearly Earnings:** $$ **Job Growth:** ★★ **Yearly Openings:** 🚶🚶🚶🚶

Billing, Cost, and Rate Clerks. Compile data, compute fees and charges, and prepare invoices for billing purposes. Duties include computing costs and calculating rates for goods, services, and shipment of goods; posting data; and keeping other records. May involve use of computer, calculator, and adding and bookkeeping machines. **Education and Training:** Short-term on-the-job training. **Skills:** Math—Medium. English—Medium. Science—Medium. **Yearly Earnings:** $$ **Job Growth:** ★★ **Yearly Openings:** 🚶🚶🚶🚶

Bookkeeping, Accounting, and Auditing Clerks. Compute, classify, and record numerical data to keep financial records complete. Perform any combination of routine calculating, posting, and verifying duties to obtain primary financial data for maintaining accounting records. May also check the accuracy of figures, calculations, and postings pertaining to business transactions recorded by other workers. **Education and Training:** Moderate-term on-the-job training. **Skills:** Math—High. English—Medium. Science—Low. **Yearly Earnings:** $$ **Job Growth:** ★ **Yearly Openings:** 🚶🚶🚶🚶🚶

Brokerage Clerks. Perform clerical duties involving the purchase or sale of securities. Duties include writing orders for stock purchases and sales, computing transfer taxes, verifying stock transactions, accepting and delivering securities, tracking stock price fluctuations, computing equity, distributing dividends, and keeping records of daily transactions and holdings. **Education and Training:** Moderate-term on-the-job training. **Skills:** Math—Medium. English—Medium. Science—Low. **Yearly Earnings:** $$$ **Job Growth:** ★ **Yearly Openings:** 🚹🚹

Payroll and Timekeeping Clerks. Compile and post employee time and payroll data. May compute employees' time worked, production, and commission. May compute and post wages and deductions. May prepare paychecks. **Education and Training:** Short-term on-the-job training. **Skills:** Math—Medium. English—Medium. Science—Low. **Yearly Earnings:** $$ **Job Growth:** ★ **Yearly Openings:** 🚹🚹🚹

Statement Clerks. Prepare and distribute bank statements to customers, answer inquiries, and reconcile discrepancies in records and accounts. **Education and Training:** Short-term on-the-job training. **Skills:** Math—Medium. English—Medium. Science—Low. **Yearly Earnings:** $$ **Job Growth:** ★★ **Yearly Openings:** 🚹🚹🚹🚹

Tax Preparers. Prepare tax returns for individuals or small businesses, but do not have the background or responsibilities of an accredited or certified public accountant. **Education and Training:** Moderate-term on-the-job training. **Skills:** Math—High. English—Medium. Science—Medium. **Yearly Earnings:** $$ **Job Growth:** ★★★ **Yearly Openings:** 🚹🚹

MATERIAL CONTROL

These workers monitor the production of a business or the use of utilities. They examine documents or meters and maintain records of consumption or production. Some order raw materials and supplies and arrange for shipping of output. Workers find jobs for water works, electricity and gas suppliers, institutions, industrial plants, government agencies, factories, transportation companies, department stores, hotels, restaurants, hospitals, laundries, and dry-cleaning plants.

Meter Readers, Utilities. Read meter and record consumption of electricity, gas, water, or steam. **Education and Training:** Short-term on-the-job training. **Skills:** Math—Medium. English—Medium. Science—Medium. **Yearly Earnings:** $$ **Job Growth:** ★ **Yearly Openings:** 🚹🚹

Production, Planning, and Expediting Clerks. Coordinate and expedite the flow of work and materials within or between departments of an establishment according to production schedule. Duties include reviewing and distributing production, work, and shipment schedules; conferring with department supervisors to determine progress of work and completion dates; and compiling reports on progress of work, inventory levels, costs, and production problems. **Education and Training:** Short-term on-the-job training. **Skills:** Math—Medium. English—Medium. Science—Medium. **Yearly Earnings:** $$$ **Job Growth:** ★★★ **Yearly Openings:** 🚹🚹🚹

CUSTOMER SERVICE

These workers deal with people in person, often standing behind a window or in a booth. They may receive payment; collect information; give out change, cash, or merchandise; provide information in answer to questions; or help customers fill out forms. Many keep written records of the information or money they receive or perform other clerical duties. Private businesses, banks, institutions such as schools and hospitals, and government agencies hire them to work in offices and reception areas.

Adjustment Clerks. Investigate and resolve customers' inquiries concerning merchandise, service, billing, or credit rating. Examine pertinent information to determine accuracy of customers' complaints and responsibility for errors. Notify customers and appropriate personnel of findings, adjustments, and recommendations, such as exchange of merchandise, refund of money, credit to customers' accounts, or adjustment to customers' bills. **Education and Training:** Moderate-term on-the-job training. **Skills:** Math—Medium. English—Medium. Science—Medium. **Yearly Earnings:** $$ **Job Growth:** ★★★★ **Yearly Openings:** 🚶🚶🚶🚶🚶

Bill and Account Collectors. Locate and notify customers of delinquent accounts by mail, telephone, or personal visit to solicit payment. Duties include receiving payment and posting amount to customer's account, preparing statements to credit department if customer fails to respond, initiating repossession proceedings or service disconnection, and keeping records of collection and status of accounts. **Education and Training:** Short-term on-the-job training. **Skills:** Math—Medium. English—Medium. Science—Low. **Yearly Earnings:** $$ **Job Growth:** ★★★★ **Yearly Openings:** 🚶🚶🚶🚶

Cashiers. Receive and disburse money in establishments other than financial institutions. Usually involves use of electronic scanners, cash registers, or related equipment. Often involved in processing credit or debit card transactions and validating checks. **Education and Training:** Short-term on-the-job training. **Skills:** Math—Medium. English—Medium. Science—Medium. **Yearly Earnings:** $ **Job Growth:** ★★★ **Yearly Openings:** 🚶🚶🚶🚶🚶

Counter and Rental Clerks. Receive orders for repairs, rentals, and services. May describe available options, compute cost, and accept payment. **Education and Training:** Short-term on-the-job training. **Skills:** Math—Medium. English—Medium. Science—Medium. **Yearly Earnings:** $ **Job Growth:** ★★★ **Yearly Openings:** 🚶🚶🚶🚶🚶

Customer Service Representatives. Interact with customers to provide information in response to inquiries about products and services and to handle and resolve complaints. **Education and Training:** Moderate-term on-the-job training. **Skills:** Math—Medium. English—Medium. Science—Medium. **Yearly Earnings:** $$ **Job Growth:** ★★★★ **Yearly Openings:** 🚶🚶🚶🚶🚶

Customer Service Representatives, Utilities. Interview applicants for water, gas, electric, or telephone service. Talk with customer by phone or in person and receive orders for installation, turn-on, discontinuance, or change in services. **Education and Training:** Moderate-term on-the-job training. **Skills:** Math—Medium. English—Medium. Science—Low. **Yearly Earnings:** $$ **Job Growth:** ★★★★ **Yearly Openings:** 🧍🧍🧍🧍🧍

Gaming Cage Workers. In a gaming establishment, conduct financial transactions for patrons. May reconcile daily summaries of transactions to balance books. Accept patron's credit application and verify credit references to provide check-cashing authorization or to establish house credit accounts. May sell gambling chips, tokens, or tickets to patrons or to other workers for resale to patrons. May convert gaming chips, tokens, or tickets to currency upon patrons' request. May use a cash register or computer to record transaction. **Education and Training:** Moderate-term on-the-job training. **Skills:** Math—Medium. English—Medium. Science—Medium. **Yearly Earnings:** $$ **Job Growth:** ★★★★ **Yearly Openings:** 🧍🧍

Gaming Change Persons and Booth Cashiers. Exchange coins and tokens for patrons' money. May issue payoffs and obtain customer's signature on receipt when winnings exceed the amount held in the slot machine. May operate a booth in the slot machine area and furnish change persons with money bank at the start of the shift or count and audit money in drawers. **Education and Training:** Short-term on-the-job training. **Skills:** Math—Medium. English—Medium. Science—Medium. **Yearly Earnings:** $ **Job Growth:** ★★★★★ **Yearly Openings:** 🧍🧍🧍

New Accounts Clerks. Interview persons desiring to open bank accounts. Explain banking services available to prospective customers and assist them in preparing application form. **Education and Training:** Work experience in a related occupation. **Skills:** Math—Medium. English—Medium. Science—Low. **Yearly Earnings:** $$ **Job Growth:** ★ **Yearly Openings:** 🧍🧍🧍

Order Clerks. Receive and process incoming orders for materials, merchandise, classified ads, or services such as repairs, installations, or rental of facilities. Duties include informing customers of receipt, prices, shipping dates, and delays; preparing contracts; and handling complaints. **Education and Training:** Short-term on-the-job training. **Skills:** Math—Medium. English—Medium. Science—Low. **Yearly Earnings:** $$ **Job Growth:** ★ **Yearly Openings:** 🧍🧍🧍

Receptionists and Information Clerks. Answer inquiries and obtain information for general public, customers, visitors, and other interested parties. Provide information regarding activities conducted at establishment and location of departments, offices, and employees within organization. **Education and Training:** Short-term on-the-job training. **Skills:** Math—Medium. English—Medium. Science—Medium. **Yearly Earnings:** $$ **Job Growth:** ★★★★ **Yearly Openings:** 🧍🧍🧍🧍🧍

Tellers. Receive and pay out money. Keep records of money and negotiable instruments involved in a financial institution's various transactions. **Education and**

Training: Short-term on-the-job training. **Skills:** Math—Medium. English—Medium. Science—Low. **Yearly Earnings:** $ **Job Growth:** ★ **Yearly Openings:** 🚶🚶🚶🚶

Travel Clerks. Provide tourists with travel information, such as points of interest, restaurants, rates, and emergency service. Duties include answering inquiries, offering suggestions, and providing literature pertaining to trips, excursions, sporting events, concerts, and plays. May make reservations, deliver tickets, arrange for visas, or contact individuals and groups to inform them of package tours. **Education and Training:** Short-term on-the-job training. **Skills:** Math—Medium. English—Medium. Science—Medium. **Yearly Earnings:** $$ **Job Growth:** ★★★ **Yearly Openings:** 🚶🚶🚶

COMMUNICATIONS

These workers talk with people by telephone or using other communication equipment to give and receive information. Some deal with the public. Some interact only with fellow workers. Many keep written records of the information they receive or perform other clerical duties. Private businesses, hotels, telephone companies, institutions such as schools and hospitals, and government agencies hire them to work in offices.

Central Office Operators. Operate telephone switchboard to establish or assist customers in establishing local or long-distance telephone connections. **Education and Training:** Short-term on-the-job training. **Skills:** Math—Medium. English—Medium. Science—Medium. **Yearly Earnings:** $$ **Job Growth:** ★ **Yearly Openings:** 🚶🚶

Directory Assistance Operators. Provide telephone information from central office switchboard. Refer to alphabetical or geographical reels or directories to answer questions or suggest answer sources. **Education and Training:** Short-term on-the-job training. **Skills:** Math—Low. English—Medium. Science—Low. **Yearly Earnings:** $$ **Job Growth:** ★ **Yearly Openings:** 🚶🚶

Dispatchers, Except Police, Fire, and Ambulance. Schedule and dispatch workers, work crews, equipment, or service vehicles for conveyance of materials, freight, or passengers or for normal installation, service, or emergency repairs rendered outside the place of business. Duties may include using radio, telephone, or computer to transmit assignments and compiling statistics and reports on work progress. **Education and Training:** Moderate-term on-the-job training. **Skills:** Math—Medium. English—Medium. Science—Medium. **Yearly Earnings:** $$ **Job Growth:** ★★★★ **Yearly Openings:** 🚶🚶

Police, Fire, and Ambulance Dispatchers. Receive complaints from public concerning crimes and police emergencies. Broadcast orders to police patrol units in vicinity of complaint to investigate. Operate radio, telephone, or computer equipment to receive reports of fires and medical emergencies and relay information or orders to proper officials. **Education and Training:** Moderate-term on-the-job training. **Skills:** Math—Medium. English—Medium. Science—Medium. **Yearly Earnings:** $$ **Job Growth:** ★★★ **Yearly Openings:** 🚶

Switchboard Operators, Including Answering Service. Operate telephone business systems equipment or switchboards to relay incoming, outgoing, and interoffice calls. May supply information to callers and record messages. **Education and Training:** Short-term on-the-job training. **Skills:** Math—Low. English—Medium. Science—Low. **Yearly Earnings:** $$ **Job Growth:** ★ **Yearly Openings:** 🧍🧍🧍

Telephone Operators. Provide information by accessing alphabetical and geographical directories. Assist customers with special billing requests, such as charges to a third party and credits or refunds for incorrectly dialed numbers or bad connections. May handle emergency calls and assist children or people with physical disabilities to make telephone calls. **Education and Training:** Short-term on-the-job training. **Skills:** Math—Medium. English—Medium. Science—Medium. **Yearly Earnings:** $$ **Job Growth:** ★ **Yearly Openings:** 🧍🧍

RECORDS PROCESSING

These workers prepare, review, file, and coordinate recorded information. Some check records and schedules for accuracy. Some schedule the activities of people or the use of equipment. Jobs in this group are found in most businesses, institutions, and government agencies.

Correspondence Clerks. Compose letters in reply to requests for merchandise, damage claims, credit and other information, delinquent accounts, incorrect billings, or unsatisfactory services. Duties may include gathering data to formulate reply and typing correspondence. **Education and Training:** Short-term on-the-job training. **Skills:** Math—Medium. English—Medium. Science—Medium. **Yearly Earnings:** $$ **Job Growth:** ★★ **Yearly Openings:** 🧍

Court Reporters. Use verbatim methods and equipment to capture, store, retrieve, and transcribe pretrial and trial proceedings or other information. Includes stenocaptioners who operate computerized stenographic captioning equipment to provide captions of live or prerecorded broadcasts for hearing-impaired viewers. **Education and Training:** Postsecondary career and technical education. **Skills:** Math—Medium. English—Medium. Science—Medium. **Yearly Earnings:** $$$ **Job Growth:** ★★★ **Yearly Openings:** 🧍

Credit Authorizers. Authorize credit charges against customers' accounts. **Education and Training:** Short-term on-the-job training. **Skills:** Math—Medium. English—Medium. Science—Low. **Yearly Earnings:** $$ **Job Growth:** ★★ **Yearly Openings:** 🧍🧍🧍

Credit Authorizers, Checkers, and Clerks. Authorize credit charges against customers' accounts. Investigate history and credit standing of individuals or business establishments applying for credit. May interview applicants to obtain personal and financial data, determine creditworthiness, process applications, and notify customers

of acceptance or rejection of credit. **Education and Training:** Short-term on-the-job training. **Skills:** Math—Medium. English—Medium. Science—Medium. **Yearly Earnings:** $$ **Job Growth:** ★★ **Yearly Openings:** 🯅🯅🯅

Credit Checkers. Investigate history and credit standing of individuals or business establishments applying for credit. Telephone or write to credit departments of business and service establishments to obtain information about applicant's credit standing. **Education and Training:** Short-term on-the-job training. **Skills:** Math—Medium. English—Medium. Science—Low. **Yearly Earnings:** $$ **Job Growth:** ★★ **Yearly Openings:** 🯅🯅🯅

File Clerks. File correspondence, cards, invoices, receipts, and other records in alphabetical or numerical order or according to the filing system used. Locate and remove material from file when requested. **Education and Training:** Short-term on-the-job training. **Skills:** Math—Medium. English—Medium. Science—Medium. **Yearly Earnings:** $ **Job Growth:** ★★ **Yearly Openings:** 🯅🯅🯅

Human Resources Assistants, Except Payroll and Timekeeping. Compile and keep personnel records. Record data for each employee, such as address, weekly earnings, absences, amount of sales or production, supervisory reports on ability, and date of and reason for termination. Compile and type reports from employment records. File employment records. Search employee files and furnish information to authorized persons. **Education and Training:** Short-term on-the-job training. **Skills:** Math—Medium. English—Medium. Science—Medium. **Yearly Earnings:** $$ **Job Growth:** ★★★ **Yearly Openings:** 🯅🯅🯅

Insurance Claims and Policy Processing Clerks. Process new insurance policies, modifications to existing policies, and claims forms. Obtain information from policyholders to verify the accuracy and completeness of information on claims forms, applications and related documents, and company records. Update existing policies and company records to reflect changes requested by policyholders and insurance company representatives. **Education and Training:** Short-term on-the-job training. **Skills:** Math—Medium. English—Medium. Science—Medium. **Yearly Earnings:** $$ **Job Growth:** ★ **Yearly Openings:** 🯅🯅🯅

Insurance Claims Clerks. Obtain information from insured or designated persons for purpose of settling claim with insurance carrier. **Education and Training:** Moderate-term on-the-job training. **Skills:** Math—Medium. English—Medium. Science—Medium. **Yearly Earnings:** $$ **Job Growth:** ★ **Yearly Openings:** 🯅🯅🯅

Insurance Policy Processing Clerks. Process applications for, changes to, reinstatement of, and cancellation of insurance policies. Duties include reviewing insurance applications to ensure that all questions have been answered, compiling data on insurance policy changes, changing policy records to conform to insured party's specifications, compiling data on lapsed insurance policies to determine automatic reinstatement according to company policies, canceling insurance policies as requested by agents, and verifying the accuracy of insurance company records. **Education and Training:** Moderate-term on-the-job training. **Skills:** Math—Medium. English—Medium. Science—Low. **Yearly Earnings:** $$ **Job Growth:** ★ **Yearly Openings:** 🚹🚹🚹

Medical Records and Health Information Technicians. Compile, process, and maintain medical records of hospital and clinic patients in a manner consistent with medical, administrative, ethical, legal, and regulatory requirements of the health care system. Process, maintain, compile, and report patient information for health requirements and standards. **Education and Training:** Associate's degree. **Skills:** Math—Medium. English—Medium. Science—Medium. **Yearly Earnings:** $$ **Job Growth:** ★★★★★ **Yearly Openings:** 🚹🚹🚹

Medical Transcriptionists. Use transcribing machines with headset and foot pedal to listen to recordings by physicians and other healthcare professionals dictating a variety of medical reports, such as emergency room visits, diagnostic imaging studies, operations, chart reviews, and final summaries. Transcribe dictated reports and translate medical jargon and abbreviations into their expanded forms. Edit and return reports in either printed or electronic form to the dictator for review and signature or correction. **Education and Training:** Associate's degree. **Skills:** Math—Medium. English—Medium. Science—Medium. **Yearly Earnings:** $$ **Job Growth:** ★★★★ **Yearly Openings:** 🚹🚹🚹

Office Clerks, General. Perform varied and diverse duties, including answering phones, bookkeeping, word processing, stenography, office machine operation, and filing. **Education and Training:** Short-term on-the-job training. **Skills:** Math—Medium. English—Medium. Science—Low. **Yearly Earnings:** $$ **Job Growth:** ★★★ **Yearly Openings:** 🚹🚹🚹🚹🚹

Procurement Clerks. Compile information and records to draw up purchase orders for procurement of materials and services. **Education and Training:** Short-term on-the-job training. **Skills:** Math—Medium. English—Medium. Science—Low. **Yearly Earnings:** $$ **Job Growth:** ★ **Yearly Openings:** 🚹🚹🚹

Proofreaders and Copy Markers. Read transcript or proof type setup to detect and mark for correction any grammatical, typographical, or compositional errors. **Education and Training:** Short-term on-the-job training. **Skills:** Math—Medium. English—Medium. Science—Medium. **Yearly Earnings:** $$ **Job Growth:** ★ **Yearly Openings:** 🚹🚹

RECORDS AND MATERIALS PROCESSING

These workers routinely file, sort, route, or deliver items such as letters, packages, or messages. Some of their work may be done with machines and computer terminals. Their jobs are found in most businesses, factories, and government agencies and in the U.S. Postal Service and various private courier services.

Cargo and Freight Agents. Expedite and route movement of incoming and outgoing cargo and freight shipments in airline, train, and trucking terminals and shipping docks. Take orders from customers and arrange pickup of freight and cargo for delivery to loading platform. Prepare and examine bills of lading to determine shipping charges and tariffs. **Education and Training:** Moderate-term on-the-job training. **Skills:** Math—Medium. English—Medium. Science—Medium. **Yearly Earnings:** $$ **Job Growth:** ★★ **Yearly Openings:** 🚶🚶

Couriers and Messengers. Pick up and carry messages, documents, packages, and other items between offices or departments within an establishment or to other business concerns. Travel by foot, bicycle, motorcycle, automobile, or public transportation. **Education and Training:** Short-term on-the-job training. **Skills:** Math—Low. English—Medium. Science—Medium. **Yearly Earnings:** $ **Job Growth:** ★ **Yearly Openings:** 🚶🚶🚶

Mail Clerks, Except Mail Machine Operators and Postal Service. Prepare incoming and outgoing mail for distribution. Duties include time stamping, opening, reading, sorting, and routing incoming mail; sealing, stamping, and affixing postage to outgoing mail or packages; and keeping records and completed forms. **Education and Training:** Short-term on-the-job training. **Skills:** Math—Medium. English—Medium. Science—Medium. **Yearly Earnings:** $ **Job Growth:** ★★ **Yearly Openings:** 🚶🚶🚶

Marking Clerks. Print and attach price tickets to articles of merchandise using one or several methods, such as marking price on tickets by hand or using ticket-printing machine. **Education and Training:** Short-term on-the-job training. **Skills:** Math—Medium. English—Medium. Science—Medium. **Yearly Earnings:** $ **Job Growth:** ★★ **Yearly Openings:** 🚶🚶🚶🚶🚶

Order Fillers, Wholesale and Retail Sales. Fill customers' mail and telephone orders from stored merchandise according to information on sales slips or order forms. Duties include computing prices of items; completing order receipts; keeping records of outgoing orders; and requisitioning materials, supplies, and equipment. **Education and Training:** Moderate-term on-the-job training. **Skills:** Math—Medium. English—Medium. Science—Low. **Yearly Earnings:** $ **Job Growth:** ★★ **Yearly Openings:** 🚶🚶🚶🚶🚶

Postal Service Mail Carriers. Sort mail for delivery. Deliver mail on established route by vehicle or on foot. **Education and Training:** Short-term on-the-job training. **Skills:** Math—Medium. English—Medium. Science—Low. **Yearly Earnings:** $$$ **Job Growth:** ★ **Yearly Openings:** 🧍🧍🧍

Postal Service Mail Sorters, Processors, and Processing Machine Operators. Prepare incoming and outgoing mail for distribution. Examine, sort, and route mail by state, type of mail, or other scheme. Load, operate, and occasionally adjust and repair mail processing, sorting, and canceling machinery. Keep records of shipments, pouches, and sacks and other duties related to mail handling within the postal service. Must complete a competitive exam. **Education and Training:** Short-term on-the-job training. **Skills:** Math—Medium. English—Medium. Science—Medium. **Yearly Earnings:** $$$ **Job Growth:** ★ **Yearly Openings:** 🧍🧍🧍

Shipping, Receiving, and Traffic Clerks. Verify and keep records on incoming and outgoing shipments. Prepare items for shipment. Duties include assembling, addressing, stamping, and shipping merchandise or material; receiving, unpacking, verifying, and recording incoming merchandise or material; and arranging for the transportation of products. **Education and Training:** Short-term on-the-job training. **Skills:** Math—Medium. English—Medium. Science—Medium. **Yearly Earnings:** $$ **Job Growth:** ★★ **Yearly Openings:** 🧍🧍🧍🧍🧍

Stock Clerks and Order Fillers. Receive, store, and issue sales floor merchandise, materials, equipment, and other items from stockroom, warehouse, or storage yard to fill shelves, racks, tables, or customers' orders. May mark prices on merchandise and set up sales displays. **Education and Training:** Short-term on-the-job training. **Skills:** Math—Medium. English—Medium. Science—Medium. **Yearly Earnings:** $ **Job Growth:** ★★ **Yearly Openings:** 🧍🧍🧍🧍🧍

Stock Clerks—Stockroom, Warehouse, or Storage Yard. Receive, store, and issue materials, equipment, and other items from stockroom, warehouse, or storage yard. Keep records and compile stock reports. **Education and Training:** Moderate-term on-the-job training. **Skills:** Math—Medium. English—Medium. Science—Medium. **Yearly Earnings:** $ **Job Growth:** ★★ **Yearly Openings:** 🧍🧍🧍🧍🧍

Weighers, Measurers, Checkers, and Samplers, Recordkeeping. Weigh, measure, and check materials, supplies, and equipment for the purpose of keeping relevant records. **Education and Training:** Short-term on-the-job training. **Skills:** Math—Medium. English—Medium. Science—Medium. **Yearly Earnings:** $$ **Job Growth:** ★★★ **Yearly Openings:** 🧍🧍🧍

CLERICAL MACHINE OPERATION

These workers use business machines to record or process data. They operate machines that type, print, sort, compute, send, or receive information. Their jobs are found in businesses, factories, and government agencies and wherever else large amounts of data are handled.

Automatic Teller Machine Servicers. Collect deposits and replenish automatic teller machines with cash and supplies. **Education and Training:** Long-term on-the-job training. **Skills:** Math—Medium. English—Medium. Science—Medium. **Yearly Earnings:** $$$ **Job Growth:** ★★★ **Yearly Openings:** 🚹🚹🚹

Billing, Posting, and Calculating Machine Operators. Operate machines that automatically perform mathematical processes, such as addition, subtraction, multiplication, and division, to calculate and record billing, accounting, statistical, and other numerical data. Duties include operating special billing machines to prepare statements, bills, and invoices and operating bookkeeping machines to copy and post data, make computations, and compile records of transactions. **Education and Training:** Short-term on-the-job training. **Skills:** Math—Medium. English—Medium. Science—Medium. **Yearly Earnings:** $$ **Job Growth:** ★★ **Yearly Openings:** 🚹🚹🚹🚹

Computer Operators. Monitor and control electronic computer and peripheral electronic data processing equipment to process business, scientific, engineering, and other data. May enter commands at a computer terminal and set controls on computer and peripheral devices. Monitor and respond to operating and error messages. **Education and Training:** Moderate-term on-the-job training. **Skills:** Math—Medium. English—Medium. Science—Medium. **Yearly Earnings:** $$ **Job Growth:** ★ **Yearly Openings:** 🚹🚹🚹

Data Entry Keyers. Operate data entry device, such as keyboard or photo composing perforator. Duties may include verifying data and preparing materials for printing. **Education and Training:** Moderate-term on-the-job training. **Skills:** Math—Medium. English—Medium. Science—Medium. **Yearly Earnings:** $$ **Job Growth:** ★★ **Yearly Openings:** 🚹🚹🚹🚹

Duplicating Machine Operators. Operate a variety of office machines, such as photocopying, photographic, and duplicating machines, to make copies. **Education and Training:** Short-term on-the-job training. **Skills:** Math—Medium. English—Low. Science—Low. **Yearly Earnings:** $$ **Job Growth:** ★ **Yearly Openings:** 🚹🚹🚹

Mail Clerks and Mail Machine Operators, Except Postal Service. Prepare incoming and outgoing mail for distribution. Use hand or mail handling machines to time stamp, open, read, sort, and route incoming mail and address, seal, stamp, fold, stuff, and affix postage to outgoing mail or packages. Duties may also include keeping records and completed forms. **Education and Training:** Short-term on-the-job training. **Skills:** Math—Medium. English—Medium. Science—Medium. **Yearly Earnings:** $ **Job Growth:** ★★ **Yearly Openings:** 🯅🯅🯅

Mail Machine Operators, Preparation and Handling. Operate machines that emboss names, addresses, and other matter onto metal plates for use in addressing machines; print names, addresses, and similar information onto items such as envelopes, accounting forms, and advertising literature; address, fold, stuff, seal, and stamp mail; and open envelopes. **Education and Training:** Short-term on-the-job training. **Skills:** Math—Medium. English—Medium. Science—Medium. **Yearly Earnings:** $ **Job Growth:** ★★ **Yearly Openings:** 🯅🯅🯅

Office Machine Operators, Except Computer. Operate a variety of office machines, such as photocopying, photographic, and duplicating machines, or other office machines. **Education and Training:** Short-term on-the-job training. **Skills:** Math—Medium. English—Medium. Science—Medium. **Yearly Earnings:** $$ **Job Growth:** ★ **Yearly Openings:** 🯅🯅🯅

Postal Service Clerks. Perform any combination of tasks in a post office, such as receive letters and parcels; sell postage and revenue stamps, postal cards, and stamped envelopes; fill out and sell money orders; place mail in pigeon holes of mail rack or in bags according to state, address, or other scheme; and examine mail for correct postage. **Education and Training:** Short-term on-the-job training. **Skills:** Math—Medium. English—Medium. Science—Low. **Yearly Earnings:** $$$ **Job Growth:** ★ **Yearly Openings:** 🯅

Typesetting and Composing Machine Operators and Tenders. Operate or tend typesetting and composing equipment, such as phototypesetters, linotype or monotype keyboard machines, photocomposers, linocasters, and photoletterers. **Education and Training:** Moderate-term on-the-job training. **Skills:** Math—Low. English—Medium. Science—Medium. **Yearly Earnings:** $$$ **Job Growth:** ★ **Yearly Openings:** 🯅🯅🯅

Word Processors and Typists. Use word processor/computer or typewriter to type letters, reports, forms, or other material from rough draft, corrected copy, or voice recording. May perform other clerical duties. **Education and Training:** Moderate-term on-the-job training. **Skills:** Math—Medium. English—Medium. Science—Low. **Yearly Earnings:** $$ **Job Growth:** ★ **Yearly Openings:** 🯅🯅🯅

Exploring Careers:

Sales and Marketing

Start Your Journey Through Careers Related to

SALES AND MARKETING

Careers in this area suit people interested bringing others to a particular point of view by personal persuasion and by sales and promotional techniques.

EXPLORING CAREER CLUES

Your interests give important clues for exploring career options. Think about your interests to learn if jobs in the Sales and Marketing interest area may be worth further exploration.

Do you like the school subjects related to the Sales and Marketing interest area? Here are some examples of related subjects:

- English
- Speech
- Composition and writing
- Foreign language
- Math
- Accounting
- Science
- Psychology
- Economics
- Business
- Marketing
- Computers

Do you like the free-time activities related to the Sales and Marketing interest area? Here are some examples of related free-time activities:

- Being on the debate team
- Persuading people to sign petitions or support a cause
- Collecting clothes, food, and supplies for needy people
- Talking on the phone
- Doing fundraising for school groups, sports teams, or other organizations
- Doing errands and odd jobs to earn cash
- Entering contests and playing competitive games
- Creating publicity flyers for school or community events
- Selling ad space for your school newspaper or yearbook
- Recruiting members for a club or other organization
- Serving as an officer of a club or other organization

EXPLORING JOB GROUPS

Jobs related to the Sales and Marketing interest area fit into four groups. Read through the list to see which groups sound interesting to you.

- Managerial Work in Sales and Marketing
- Sales Technology
- General Sales
- Personal Soliciting

EXPLORING CAREER POSSIBILITIES

You can satisfy your interest in the Sales and Marketing area in a variety of jobs that involve persuasion and selling. Here are a few examples of career possibilities:

If you like using knowledge of science, you may enjoy selling pharmaceutical, medical, or electronic products or services. Or perhaps you would be more interested in selling business-related services such as insurance coverage, advertising space, or investment opportunities. Real estate offers several kinds of sales jobs as well.

If you like speaking on the phone, you could work as a telemarketer. Or you may enjoy selling apparel and other merchandise in a retail setting.

Turn the page to meet people working in the Sales and Marketing interest area→

PROFILE

James Youngs— Insurance Sales Agent

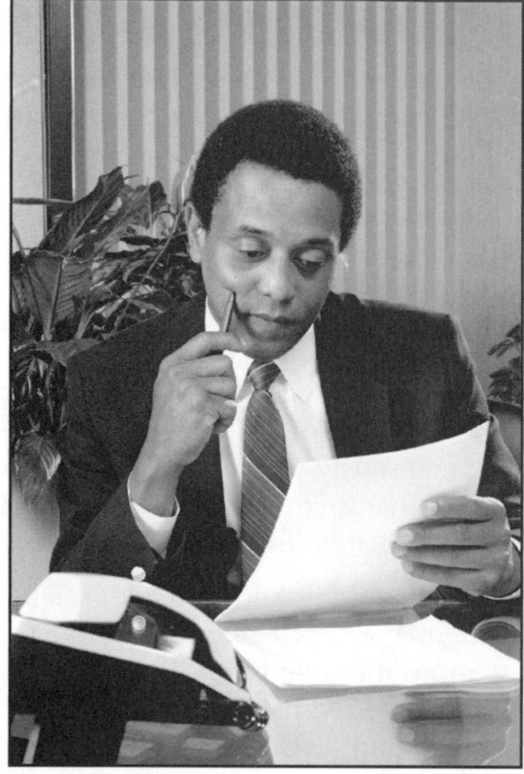

To serve his clients well, James keeps up with changes in the law, new procedures, and related insurance matters.

On their return from a vacation at the shore, Carlos and Rosita Vargas found a different "sea" back home. While they were away, heavy rains had flooded their basement with water. The beautiful recreation room they had recently built there was ruined.

Shortly afterward, James Youngs received their phone call and agreed to meet the stunned couple. "When I met them," said James, "they were in tears. Even when I assured them that they had adequate insurance, they were feeling very down.

"Last week, though, we all watched the basketball game on the new couch in their restored room. It was a great feeling to see all around us the result of being adequately insured."

James, an independent contractor with a major insurance company, explained, "When a client has adequate coverage, he or she avoids a financial crisis.

"The policy will pay whatever is needed to restore a damaged house or, for another example, to replace a car that was totaled.

"Applying for insurance protection on a car or home is not an exciting activity for most people. But for some insurance buyers, it is one of the smartest things they'll ever do."

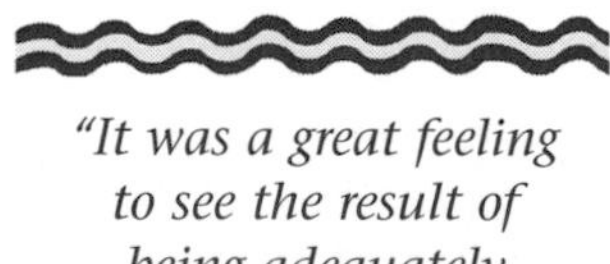

"It was a great feeling to see the result of being adequately insured."

Career Foundations

James's company requires a college degree. "The company wants to know that you pursued a goal and reached it. That's more important than the subject you majored in. However, courses in business, finance, law, and at some schools, in insurance itself, are useful.

"Courses in insurance are required for certification and licensing no matter how a person gets started in insurance."

After completing all required courses, a trainee becomes an agent, perhaps in a regional office or working for a contractor or broker.

The contractor works just for the insurance company he or she represents. The broker sells the products of a number of companies. There are also agents who work directly for an insurance company.

Many people change from a previous career to one in the insurance industry, according to James. "I became a claims adjuster after having a career in sales in another field," said James. I answered an ad. I didn't know a thing about it. As a claims adjuster, I gathered facts and ensured that clients' claims were paid promptly.

"I received training through the company and did claims adjusting for three years. Then I decided that agency work looked more attractive."

James's track record was very good. He moved from claims adjuster to an independent contractor for the same large insurer.

"I don't think I would have made it if I hadn't had adjusting experience," he said. "Going into the field and handling claims is an important part of an agent's responsibility."

Ensuring Career Success

"We encourage agents to move into agency management positions as employees of the company who head a group of agents," explained James. "The agency manager trains his staff and keeps them enthusiastic. Many agents find this path satisfying."

"I manage our daily routines, control expenses, schedule our time, and most important, give good service to my clients."

Although James's business consists of himself and an assistant, he too needs management skills. "I manage our daily routines, control expenses, schedule our time, and most important, give good service to my clients," said James.

James is required by the state to continue his insurance education. An agent needs to keep up with tax law changes, new procedures, and related matters. James's company reimburses agents for the cost of training programs, provided they pass the courses.

James completes many more hours of training than are required. "I take advantage of the opportunities. I feel it's another way to ensure that my clients get top service."

James pointed to framed certificates on his office wall. "Those signify that I'm at the top of my field in experience and training."

In the Office or On the Go

"When I started, I began each day at 7 a.m. and got home about 9 p.m.," James said. "Now, I try to work 9 to 5 on weekdays, but I'm available at all times. I meet with clients to review their coverage and make suggestions. The phone rings all day.

"Often, I have to be where my clients are. I go out on location for fire and other casualty claims."

"Some people come in for advice. Some even come in about matters unrelated to insurance. Maybe it's because I'm easier to get a hold of than their attorney, doctor, or mechanic," James said.

"Often, I have to be where my clients are. I go out on location for fire and other casualty claims. This means I have to stay physically fit. It's difficult and sometimes almost impossible to climb around a home that's been badly fire-damaged."

The Highs and the Lows

"Denying a claim is the toughest part of my job," James stated. "About six months ago, customers of mine requested coverage on an older car they were giving to their son. They didn't want to spend too much on insurance because of the car's age.

"I explained what type of coverage they really needed, but they'd made up their minds," recalled James. "During last week's ice storm, the son had an accident.

"Many people find price quotes on the Internet now, but they still value the personal services of an agent."

"Fortunately, nobody was hurt. But because they had turned down the collision coverage I'd recommended, their policy didn't cover the damages.

"The flip side is this: About a year ago, I had a meeting with a young couple with two children. They were on a tight budget. So they were reluctant to raise their auto insurance liability limits–what the insurance covers if they must pay because they are at fault in an accident.

"However, I did convince them, and about six months later, they were found at fault in a serious-injury accident. Because they increased their coverage, they were protected financially."

Times Change, But Rewards Remain

"Dramatic changes have happened over the past ten years, thanks to communications technology. The result has been improved service.

"Today, an insurance agent can get almost instant approval on applications. About ninety percent of business transactions are handled electronically now, and more positive changes are on the way."

The insurance industry isn't growing as quickly as other occupations. But there are still opportunities for the right people, according to James. "Many people find price quotes on the Internet now, but they still value the personal services of an agent.

"To succeed in this business, you have to like to sell, and you have to like people. An agent has to relate to his company, his clients, and his staff.

"Staff problems can arise. Clients sometimes want something the company doesn't provide. It takes positive relations with clients to build trust. Part of an agent's reward is the good word-of-mouth advertising he gets from satisfied clients.

"To succeed in this business, you have to like to sell, and you have to like people."

"I value the time I spent as an adjuster, too. I'd already handled about every kind of claim there is. I knew how to comfort people who are hurting and scared.

"I think this business is fun. It's a service that benefits society.

"Plus, I like living in a small town, meeting people, and earning a comfortable income, while having freedom to set my hours and manage things as I like. I wouldn't have it any other way."

PROFILE

Tracy Brunetti—Retail Sales Manager

Tracy Brunetti pulled into the parking area of the mall to start her workday at the retail store she managed. She walked quickly to her office at the back of the store and settled in front of the computer.

Tracy enjoys all aspects of managing a store, from training staff to helping customers to keeping the merchandise neatly organized.

"This is my first priority," she explained. "This is the information from the corporate office: promotions, price changes, and sign changes. Once it's printed, I'll work it into the day's agenda."

With an hour to go before opening, Tracy headed out on the sales floor for what she refers to as her "housekeeping patrol."

"I want to have the cleanest store in the mall because that attracts customers. People react in a positive or negative way within moments of entering a store, depending on layout and appearance," said Tracy as she straightened a display of sweaters.

"Customers come in. They like the store. They like the merchandise. They buy!"

> *"I want to have the cleanest store in the mall because that attracts customers. People react in a positive or negative way within moments of entering a store."*

The daily merchandise delivery arrived with loud thumps from the area of the stockroom. Tracy hurried through the double doors to receive the paperwork and direct one of the store staff to begin steam pressing the merchandise to display.

"If the merchandise isn't out there, we can't sell it," explained Tracy. "We also try to place the merchandise in groupings that are attractive and flow logically, like sweaters near other outerwear.

"In a national chain such as this, stores are arranged in a specific manner. Not all retailers do this, but we feel it's important for customers to find that the store is familiar to them, wherever it's located.

"It's good to make the buying experience for the customer as easy and pleasant as possible," Tracy said.

It's Not the Corner Store Anymore

"Things have changed from the old days," Tracy said. "There used to be the friendly shopkeeper who knew every customer, shared the neighborhood gossip, and gave credit in time of need. No one would think of stealing from that store.

"Now there are chain stores like this one, and we face daily shoplifting and internal theft, which we call 'shrinkage.' This is the unpleasant side of being a retail manager, like it or not. Our company, like most, has a firm policy of prosecuting shoplifters. Sometimes I have to go to court to testify."

On Her Feet

"If the job sounds taxing, that's because it is, to a certain extent," Tracy said. "Mental and physical stress are part of the retail business. But the physical effort is a surprise to people new to the business.

"Being on your feet for nine or ten hours a day is hard work. There can be a lot of lifting involved–stocking and arranging the shelves and displays."

"Being on your feet for nine or ten hours a day is hard work. There can be a lot of lifting involved–stocking and arranging the shelves and displays."

According to Tracy, the average retail workweek is somewhere between forty and fifty hours. During the holidays, that number increases greatly.

"If there's one thing I would change about my job, it's the hours," Tracy confided. "I have to work two nights a week and at least one day on weekends. Holidays can be the hardest of all. Being in retail means fewer days off than with a typical corporate job.

"I've found ways to deal with stress. I love to walk and I love to have a good laugh. Daily walking keeps my head straight. Having a good laugh and a sense of humor keeps everything else in perspective.

"But I can't deny that I love this business," Tracy said. "Because of that, I'm able to keep an upbeat, positive attitude, which is always contagious, from me to the sales staff to the customer. That keeps our customers coming back."

Getting Sold on a Retail Sales Career

"Store managers or assistant managers are paid an annual salary. Sales people are paid an hourly wage or a smaller hourly amount with sales commissions. With many large retailers, store managers earn bonuses if the store consistently meets or exceeds its sales goals.

"You begin in sales. If you already have some work experience, you may start as a manager trainee and then move up to assistant manager. That's only one step away from having your own store to manage."

"You have to be patient when waiting for the opportunities to open up, but they do," Tracy said.

Do You Need to Go to Retail School?

There are two ways to get the right "education" to become a retail sales manager: by obtaining a college degree or working up through the ranks, starting at the sales associate level.

"There is heavy recruitment of people from colleges," Tracy said. "And many stores list having a degree as one of their requirements.

"But there are just as many retailers who prefer people with a proven sales record. For instance, you may need five years or more experience, with sales results that they can verify, rather than a degree."

Tracy pointed out that more colleges are offering a retailing major. That could make the competition for store manager and higher positions more intense in the future.

Students interested in the field should research job titles such as first-line supervisor/manager of retail sales workers; department manager; supervisor of cashiers; manager, retail store; and sales worker supervisor.

"Many retailers prefer people with a proven sales record."

Two Key Responsibilities: Hiring and Training

Tracy stresses that her most important task is to interview and hire staff. "I must fill my store with the best people I can, on my sales floor, at the registers, at the wrap desk, and in the stock room. I look for people who are energetic, are aggressive, are personable, and have excellent customer service skills."

Retail training is a hands-on experience, according to Tracy. With the exception of two or three days of becoming familiar with store policies and procedures, you learn almost entirely on the job.

"I look for people who are energetic, aggressive, personable, and have excellent customer service skills."

"As store manager, I train the sales staff. I'm very serious about good sales training, so I delegate a lot of other tasks to my assistant manager, Gail," she said as Gail approached. "She's not afraid to ask plenty of questions, and she's really shown a lot of initiative."

"Thanks," Gail said as she continued to the rear of the store, straightening merchandise as she went.

Tracy said, "An extra bonus is that I can still sell. I love that. When I make a big sale or when I see big sales results for my store, I know this job is worth it.

"My other big 'love' is to train a new sales associate. Watching one of my staff use what I taught to make a sale is terrific. They feel great, I feel great, and of course the company loves it."

PROFILE

Virginia Dossey—Telemarketer

During the day, Virginia Dossey works as a telemarketer, selling products to businesses by phone. At night, she earns a second paycheck playing violin. Her two callings form a curious counterpoint.

Virginia Dossey sells subscriptions to businesses over the phone.

By day, she works at the Schroeder Call Center, a teleservices firm. She sells subscriptions to a major business publication. "I prefer music," she said, "but I've been successful in sales. I know I can sell."

Engaging an Audience

Virginia sits at a workstation in a semicircular cubicle, or pod, along with three to five colleagues. She uses a computer, a phone line, an automated dialing system, and an electronic list of prospective customers and phone

numbers. Her prospects include office managers, small business owners, and other financially savvy people.

Virginia strives to captivate an audience.

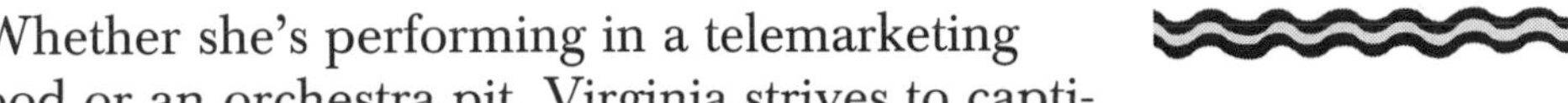

Whether she's performing in a telemarketing pod or an orchestra pit, Virginia strives to captivate an audience. When someone answers her call, Virginia has only seconds to make an impression.

She introduces herself and explains the purpose of her call in a professional, upbeat tone. Reading from an approved sales script, she begins to establish a rapport with her audience of one.

"There are questions you can ask to generate and keep interest," Virginia said. "I might ask if they've ever read or heard of the publication to get them involved in a conversation."

Often, her audience has read the publication. Virginia asks about the value they found in it. Although Virginia must memorize a musical score for some of her violin recitals, she doesn't need to take such careful note of her sales script.

She often improvises, choosing variations to suit the audience. "I try to customize my presentation so people feel like I'm just talking instead of reading from a script," she said.

"I try to customize my presentation so people feel like I'm just talking instead of reading from a script."

As Virginia speaks, voices of other telemarketers accompany her indistinctly in the background. She must focus on her own performance.

It's not easy for telemarketers to win over an audience and make a sale. Virginia's business customers have work to do, deals to make, and deadlines to meet. These busy people often see Virginia as a distraction from work. She must fine-tune her pitch to the needs of each individual.

"If they say they're not interested," said Virginia, "I try to figure out why. I present the product in a way that shows how it would meet individual needs."

Potential customers often object, saying they don't have time to talk to a telemarketer or to read the publication even if they were to receive it.

Virginia answers their objections. She explains how the product provides important information that will increase their effectiveness, saving them time in the long run.

"You just focus on the next call being successful."

But more often than not, even a virtuoso sales performance leads to no sale. Some potential customers react rudely to Virginia's persistence. They make nasty comments and hang up. Virginia must maintain her composure and move on. "You can't let a string of no sales or hangups bother you," Virginia said. "You just focus on the next call being successful."

Virginia's sales manager supervises telemarketers on the sales floor. He also helps keep morale high. When telemarketers make a sale, they summon the sales manager, who gets on the line to confirm necessary details.

The manager announces the sale after completing the call. The other telemarketers applaud or offer a congratulatory wave if they are on the line with a customer. "I thought this would be distracting when I started, but it's not," Virginia said. "It gives everyone a boost."

Opportunity Is Calling

Telemarketing offers many opportunities for part-time and temporary work, as well as full-time employment. Virginia began working at the call center a year ago to supplement her music earnings. She officially works for a temporary help firm that supplies telemarketing workers as needed for the center.

Many companies hire telemarketers for in-house call centers.

In the future, she plans to telemarket for thirty to thirty-five hours per week during the summer. It is the slow season for her musical career. She'll decrease her hours when her musical pursuits pick up in the fall.

Many companies hire telemarketers for in-house call centers. These workers sell the services or products produced by their employers. Other telemarketers, like Virginia, work at independent call centers. They sell on behalf of other companies for a fee.

A Short Training Period

Whereas playing a violin concerto takes years of practice, telemarketers usually need only a few days of on-the-job training before making their first live telephone sales performance. The length of training for telemarketers depends on the number and type of products being sold.

Like all new workers at the Schroeder Call Center, Virginia had three days of training. She learned about phone sales techniques, telemarketing laws and guidelines, and the product she would be selling. She also listened in on live calls initiated by experienced telemarketers. Then she made practice calls, with another worker playing the role of the customer.

Virginia has had more formal education and training than the average telemarketer. Many firms prefer, but do not require, a high school diploma for telemarketing work. Some employers may find college education desirable, but most do not require a college degree. It often depends on the products sold.

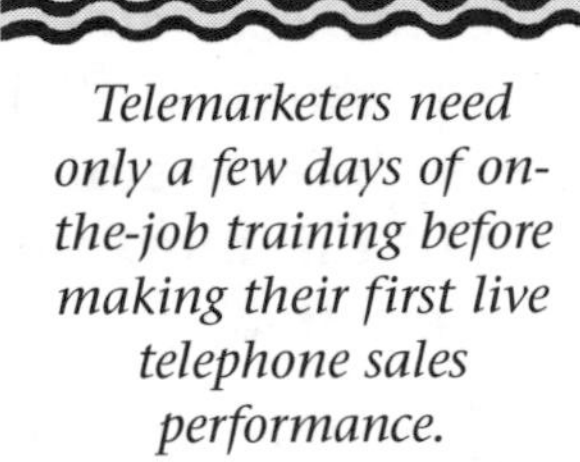

Telemarketers need only a few days of on-the-job training before making their first live telephone sales performance.

Virginia has a bachelor's degree in music education and completed advanced sales training before working at the call center. Virginia also had years of previous sales experience. While working for an adult education school, she moved into sales and marketing. She started promoting the school to new students. She spent three years in her next job, selling memberships for the local chamber of commerce.

After selling subscriptions all day, Virginia pulls off her telephone headset and reaches for her violin case. She lets go of one performance and turns her thoughts to another.

SKILL SAMPLER

Lisa Whitely—Stockbroker

Lisa Whitely sells stocks and bonds for a large brokerage firm. "Keeping up with what is happening in the business world has helped me build up a following of repeat investors."

Lisa discussed the skills and knowledge a stockbroker must have. She offers the following tips to help you decide if you will pursue a career as a stockbroker.

In addition, she said that students interested in the career should research job titles such as broker; sales agent, securities and commodities; securities, commodities, and financial services sales agent; registered representative; account executive; financial consultant; floor broker; stock trader; securities trader; and sales agent, financial services.

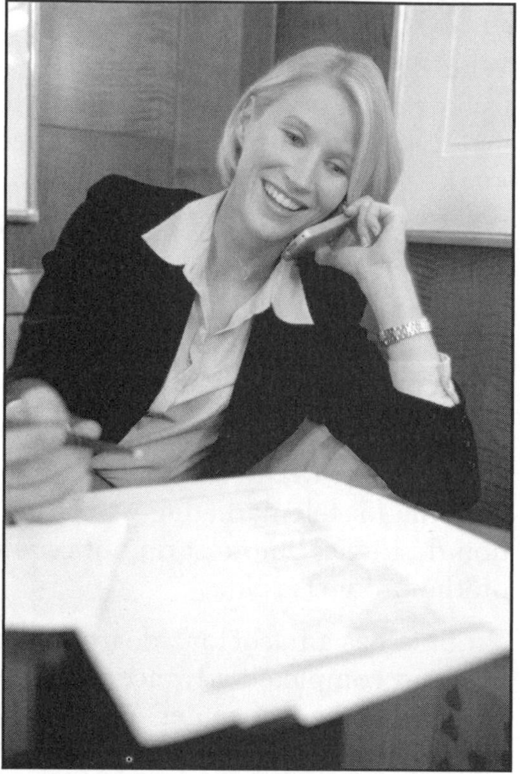

Lisa talks with a customer who wants to sell some stock.

Stockbrokers must be articulate and persuasive. Persuading people to buy or sell securities is one of the most important parts of the job.

- Are you a good listener?
- Do you remember what people tell you about themselves?
- Can you tell how people feel about things by talking to them?
- Do you like to campaign for a school office?
- Are you often chosen for group activities?
- Do you like to debate?
- Do you like to speak in front of your class?

Stockbrokers often work for commissions. They must be able to take the initiative and be self-starters.

- Have you ever organized and started a club such as a computer or football club?

- Do you get up in the morning by yourself?
- Do you do your homework and household chores without being prodded by your parents?
- Do you stick with projects until they are finished?

Stockbrokers must perform well in a highly competitive situation.

- Do you like being the best at the things you do?
- Do you like entering contests and playing competitive games?
- Do you want to be at the top of your class?

Stockbrokers must be optimistic to face slow sales periods and downturns in the stock market.

- Are you persistent?
- Do you always assume things will get better?
- When your team loses, do you still look forward to the next game?
- Are you good at cheering up your friends when they are depressed?
- Does failure make you want to try harder?

Stockbrokers, unlike people in many other jobs, can measure their success directly by the amount of money they make.

- Is making money important to you?
- Do you like having your performance measured?
- Do you like to be recognized when you do something well?

Now learn about all major jobs in the Sales and Marketing interest area→

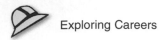

Facts About All Major Jobs Related to

SALES AND MARKETING

In addition to the jobs covered in the profiles and skill sampler, other careers in the Sales and Marketing interest area may appeal to you. This section describes and gives facts about all major jobs in the Sales and Marketing interest area. For an explanation of the $, ★, and 🚶 symbols, see page 6.

 *MANAGERIAL WORK IN SALES AND MARKETING*

These workers direct or manage various kinds of selling and/or advertising operations—either a department within a business or a specialized business firm that contracts to provide selling and/or advertising services. These workers usually carry out their activities according to policies and procedures determined by owners, boards of directors, administrators, and other persons with higher authority.

Advertising and Promotions Managers. Plan and direct advertising policies and programs or produce collateral materials, such as posters, contests, coupons, or give-aways, to create extra interest in the purchase of a product or service for a department, for an entire organization, or on an account basis. **Education and Training:** College degree plus work experience. **Skills:** Math—Medium. English—High. Science—Low. **Yearly Earnings:** $$$$$ **Job Growth:** ★★★★ **Yearly Openings:** 🚶🚶

First-Line Supervisors/Managers of Non-Retail Sales Workers. Directly supervise and coordinate activities of sales workers other than retail sales workers. May perform duties such as budgeting, accounting, and personnel work in addition to supervisory duties. **Education and Training:** Work experience in a related occupation. **Skills:** Math—Medium. English—Medium. Science—Medium. **Yearly Earnings:** $$$$ **Job Growth:** ★★ **Yearly Openings:** 🚶🚶🚶

First-Line Supervisors/Managers of Retail Sales Workers. Directly supervise sales workers in a retail establishment or department. Duties may include management functions, such as purchasing, budgeting, accounting, and personnel work, in addition to supervisory duties. **Education and Training:** Work experience in a related occupation. **Skills:** Math—Medium. English—Medium. Science—Medium. **Yearly Earnings:** $$ **Job Growth:** ★★ **Yearly Openings:** 🚶🚶🚶🚶🚶

Marketing Managers. Determine the demand for products and services offered by a firm and its competitors and identify potential customers. Develop pricing strategies with the goal of maximizing the firm's profits or share of the market while ensuring that

the firm's customers are satisfied. Oversee product development or monitor trends that indicate the need for new products and services. **Education and Training:** College degree plus work experience. **Skills:** Math—Medium. English—High. Science—Medium. **Yearly Earnings:** $$$$$ **Job Growth:** ★★★★ **Yearly Openings:** 🧍🧍🧍

Sales Managers. Direct the actual distribution or movement of a product or service to the customer. Coordinate sales distribution by establishing sales territories, quotas, and goals and establish training programs for sales representatives. Analyze sales statistics gathered by staff to determine sales potential and inventory requirements and monitor the preferences of customers. **Education and Training:** College degree plus work experience. **Skills:** Math—Medium. English—Medium. Science—Medium. **Yearly Earnings:** $$$$$ **Job Growth:** ★★★★ **Yearly Openings:** 🧍🧍🧍

SALES TECHNOLOGY

These workers sell products such as industrial machinery, data processing equipment, and pharmaceuticals, plus services such as investment counseling, insurance, and advertising. They advise customers of the capabilities, uses, and other important features of these products and services and help customers choose those best suited to their needs. They work for manufacturers, wholesalers, insurance companies, financial institutions, and business service establishments. Some are self-employed.

Advertising Sales Agents. Sell or solicit advertising, including graphic art, advertising space in publications, custom-made signs, or TV and radio advertising time. May obtain leases for outdoor advertising sites or persuade retailer to use sales promotion display items. **Education and Training:** Moderate-term on-the-job training. **Skills:** Math—Medium. English—High. Science—Low. **Yearly Earnings:** $$$ **Job Growth:** ★★★★ **Yearly Openings:** 🧍🧍🧍

Insurance Sales Agents. Sell life, property, casualty, health, automotive, or other types of insurance. May refer clients to independent brokers, work as independent broker, or be employed by an insurance company. **Education and Training:** Bachelor's degree. **Skills:** Math—Medium. English—Medium. Science—Low. **Yearly Earnings:** $$$ **Job Growth:** ★★ **Yearly Openings:** 🧍🧍🧍

Sales Agents, Financial Services. Sell financial services, such as loan, tax, and securities counseling, to customers of financial institutions and business establishments. **Education and Training:** Bachelor's degree. **Skills:** Math—High. English—Medium. Science—Medium. **Yearly Earnings:** $$$$$ **Job Growth:** ★★★★ **Yearly Openings:** 🧍🧍🧍🧍

Sales Agents, Securities and Commodities. Buy and sell securities in investment and trading firms and develop and implement financial plans for individuals, businesses, and organizations. **Education and Training:** Bachelor's degree. **Skills:** Math—High. English—High. Science—Medium. **Yearly Earnings:** $$$$$ **Job Growth:** ★★★★ **Yearly Openings:** 🧍🧍🧍🧍

Sales Representatives, Agricultural. Sell agricultural products and services, such as animal feeds; farm and garden equipment; and dairy, poultry, and veterinarian supplies. **Education and Training:** Moderate-term on-the-job training. **Skills:** Math—Medium. English—Medium. Science—Medium. **Yearly Earnings:** $$$$$ **Job Growth:** ★★ **Yearly Openings:** 🧍🧍🧍

Sales Representatives, Chemical and Pharmaceutical. Sell chemical or pharmaceutical products or services, such as acids, industrial chemicals, agricultural chemicals, medicines, drugs, and water treatment supplies. **Education and Training:** Moderate-term on-the-job training. **Skills:** Math—Medium. English—Medium. Science—Medium. **Yearly Earnings:** $$$$$ **Job Growth:** ★★ **Yearly Openings:** 🧍🧍🧍

Sales Representatives, Electrical/Electronic. Sell electrical, electronic, or related products or services, such as communication equipment, radiographic-inspection equipment and services, ultrasonic equipment, electronics parts, computers, and EDP systems. **Education and Training:** Moderate-term on-the-job training. **Skills:** Math—Medium. English—Medium. Science—Medium. **Yearly Earnings:** $$$$$ **Job Growth:** ★★ **Yearly Openings:** 🧍🧍🧍

Sales Representatives, Instruments. Sell precision instruments, such as dynamometers and spring scales, and laboratory, navigation, and surveying instruments. **Education and Training:** Moderate-term on-the-job training. **Skills:** Math—Medium. English—Medium. Science—Medium. **Yearly Earnings:** $$$$$ **Job Growth:** ★★ **Yearly Openings:** 🧍🧍🧍

Sales Representatives, Mechanical Equipment and Supplies. Sell mechanical equipment, machinery, materials, and supplies, such as aircraft and railroad equipment and parts, construction machinery, material-handling equipment, industrial machinery, and welding equipment. **Education and Training:** Moderate-term on-the-job training. **Skills:** Math—Medium. English—Medium. Science—Medium. **Yearly Earnings:** $$$$$ **Job Growth:** ★★ **Yearly Openings:** 🧍🧍🧍

Sales Representatives, Medical. Sell medical equipment, products, and services. **Education and Training:** Moderate-term on-the-job training. **Skills:** Math—Medium. English—Medium. Science—Medium. **Yearly Earnings:** $$$$$ **Job Growth:** ★★ **Yearly Openings:** 🧍🧍🧍

Sales Representatives, Wholesale and Manufacturing, Technical and Scientific Products. Sell goods for wholesalers or manufacturers where technical or scientific knowledge is required in such areas as biology, engineering, chemistry, and electronics and is normally obtained from at least two years of postsecondary education. **Education and Training:** Moderate-term on-the-job training. **Skills:** Math—Medium. English—Medium. Science—Medium. **Yearly Earnings:** $$$$$ **Job Growth:** ★★ **Yearly Openings:** 🧍🧍🧍

Securities, Commodities, and Financial Services Sales Agents. Buy and sell securities in investment and trading firms or call upon businesses and individuals to sell financial services. Provide financial services, such as loan, tax, and securities counseling. May advise securities customers about such things as stocks, bonds, and market conditions. **Education and Training:** Bachelor's degree. **Skills:** Math—Medium. English—Medium. Science—Medium. **Yearly Earnings:** $$$$$ **Job Growth:** ★★★★ **Yearly Openings:** 🚶🚶🚶🚶

GENERAL SALES

These workers sell, demonstrate, and solicit orders for products and services of many kinds. They are hired by retail and wholesale firms, manufacturers and distributors, business services, and nonprofit organizations. Some spend all their time in a single location, such as a department store or automobile agency. Others call on businesses or individuals to sell products or services or follow up on earlier sales.

Parts Salespersons. Sell spare and replacement parts and equipment in repair shop or parts store. **Education and Training:** Moderate-term on-the-job training. **Skills:** Math—Medium. English—Medium. Science—Medium. **Yearly Earnings:** $$ **Job Growth:** ★ **Yearly Openings:** 🚶🚶🚶

Real Estate Brokers. Operate real estate office or work for commercial real estate firm, overseeing real estate transactions. Other duties usually include selling real estate or renting properties and arranging loans. **Education and Training:** Work experience in a related occupation. **Skills:** Math—Medium. English—Medium. Science—Medium. **Yearly Earnings:** $$$$ **Job Growth:** ★★ **Yearly Openings:** 🚶🚶

Real Estate Sales Agents. Rent, buy, or sell property for clients. Perform duties such as studying property listings, interviewing prospective clients, accompanying clients to property site, discussing conditions of sale, and drawing up real estate contracts. Includes agents who represent buyers. **Education and Training:** Postsecondary career and technical education. **Skills:** Math—Medium. English—Medium. Science—Medium. **Yearly Earnings:** $$ **Job Growth:** ★★ **Yearly Openings:** 🚶🚶🚶

Retail Salespersons. Sell merchandise such as furniture, motor vehicles, appliances, or apparel in a retail establishment. **Education and Training:** Short-term on-the-job training. **Skills:** Math—Medium. English—Medium. Science—Medium. **Yearly Earnings:** $ **Job Growth:** ★★★ **Yearly Openings:** 🚶🚶🚶🚶🚶

Sales Representatives, Wholesale and Manufacturing, Except Technical and Scientific Products. Sell goods for wholesalers or manufacturers to businesses or groups of individuals. Work requires substantial knowledge of items sold. **Education and Training:** Moderate-term on-the-job training. **Skills:** Math—Medium. English—Medium. Science—Low. **Yearly Earnings:** $$$$ **Job Growth:** ★★ **Yearly Openings:** 🚶🚶🚶🚶

Service Station Attendants. Service automobiles, buses, trucks, boats, and other automotive or marine vehicles with fuel, lubricants, and accessories. Collect payment for services and supplies. May lubricate vehicle, change motor oil, install antifreeze, or replace lights or other accessories, such as windshield wiper blades or fan belts. May repair or replace tires. **Education and Training:** Short-term on-the-job training. **Skills:** Math—Medium. English—Medium. Science—Medium. **Yearly Earnings:** $ **Job Growth:** ★ **Yearly Openings:** 🚶🚶🚶

Stock Clerks, Sales Floor. Receive, store, and issue sales floor merchandise. Stock shelves, racks, cases, bins, and tables with merchandise and arrange merchandise displays to attract customers. May periodically take physical count of stock or check and mark merchandise. **Education and Training:** Short-term on-the-job training. **Skills:** Math—Medium. English—Medium. Science—Medium. **Yearly Earnings:** $ **Job Growth:** ★★ **Yearly Openings:** 🚶🚶🚶🚶🚶

Travel Agents. Plan and sell transportation and accommodations for travel agency customers. Determine destination, modes of transportation, travel dates, costs, and accommodations required. **Education and Training:** Postsecondary career and technical education. **Skills:** Math—Medium. English—Medium. Science—Medium. **Yearly Earnings:** $$ **Job Growth:** ★★ **Yearly Openings:** 🚶🚶🚶

PERSONAL SOLICITING

These workers appeal to people directly and sell them merchandise or services. In most cases, they do not build a long-term relationship with the buyer. They may sell products on the street, staying in one location or moving through business and residential areas. They may call potential buyers by telephone. They may demonstrate a product in a mall or other place with a lot of foot traffic.

Demonstrators and Product Promoters. Demonstrate merchandise and answer questions for the purpose of creating public interest in buying the product. May sell demonstrated merchandise. **Education and Training:** Moderate-term on-the-job training. **Skills:** Math—Medium. English—Medium. Science—Low. **Yearly Earnings:** $ **Job Growth:** ★★★★ **Yearly Openings:** 🚶🚶🚶

Door-To-Door Sales Workers, News and Street Vendors, and Related Workers. Sell goods or services door-to-door or on the street. **Education and Training:** Short-term on-the-job training. **Skills:** Math—Medium. English—Medium. Science—Low. **Yearly Earnings:** $$ **Job Growth:** ★ **Yearly Openings:** 🚶🚶🚶

Telemarketers. Solicit orders for goods or services over the telephone. **Education and Training:** Short-term on-the-job training. **Skills:** Math—Medium. English—Medium. Science—Low. **Yearly Earnings:** $ **Job Growth:** ★★★★ **Yearly Openings:** 🚶🚶🚶🚶🚶

Exploring Careers:

Recreation, Travel, and Other Personal Services

Start Your Journey Through Careers Related to

RECREATION, TRAVEL, AND OTHER PERSONAL SERVICES

Careers in this area suit people interested in meeting the personal needs and wishes of others so that they may enjoy a clean environment, an attractive appearance, good food and drink, comfortable lodging away from home, and recreation.

EXPLORING CAREER CLUES

Your interests give important clues for exploring career options. Think about your interests to learn if jobs in the Recreation, Travel, and Other Personal Services interest area may be worth further exploration.

Do you like the school subjects related to the Recreation, Travel, and Other Personal Services interest area? Here are some examples of related subjects:

- English
- Math
- Family and consumer sciences
- Health
- Business
- Computers
- Industrial or technology education
- Driver's education
- Physical education

Do you like the free-time activities related to the Recreation, Travel, and Other Personal Services interest area? Here are some examples of related free-time activities:

- Cutting hair for family and friends
- Doing makeup, hair, and nails for school plays, for friends, and for family
- Planning meals
- Planning parties and outings
- Taking trips
- Cooking and baking
- Helping in the kitchen and at meals
- Helping to organize and run school or community events
- Baby-sitting or caring for children

- Cleaning and organizing your room and the house
- Helping with home repairs and home maintenance
- Making costumes or clothes
- Doing crafts
- Sewing, knitting, or doing needlework
- Serving as a volunteer in a hospital, nursing home, or retirement home
- Helping sick relatives, friends, and neighbors

EXPLORING JOB GROUPS

Jobs related to the Recreation, Travel, and Other Personal Services interest area fit into eight groups. Read through the list to see which groups sound interesting to you.

- Managerial Work in Recreation, Travel, and Other Personal Services
- Recreational Services
- Transportation and Lodging Services
- Barber and Beauty Services
- Food and Beverage Services
- Apparel, Shoes, Leather, and Fabric Care
- Cleaning and Building Services
- Other Personal Services

EXPLORING CAREER POSSIBILITIES

You can satisfy your interest in the Recreation, Travel, and Other Personal Services by providing services for the convenience, care, and pampering of others in hotels, in restaurants, on airplanes, and so on. Here are a few examples of career possibilities:

If you enjoy improving the appearance of others, perhaps working in the hair and beauty care field would satisfy you. You may wish to use your love of cooking as a chef. If you like people, you may wish to provide personal services by being a travel guide, a flight attendant, a concierge, or a waiter.

If you like sewing for others, you may enjoy a job as a tailor. You may wish to work in cleaning and building services if you like a clean environment.

Turn the page to meet people working in the Recreation, Travel, and Other Personal Services interest area→

PROFILE

Kareem Newsome—Chef

Kareem helps the restaurant keep its reputation for good food.

Every Wednesday morning, chef Kareem Newsome prepares the weekly schedule for the kitchen staff at Peterson's Restaurant. It takes peace and quiet to juggle the schedules of fourteen people, even though only four or five of them are at work in the kitchen at any one time.

"I have to plan two shifts a day, seven days a week, and that's a challenge," Kareem said. "Some of the kitchen staff work full time and others work part time. Some prefer to work nights so that they can go to school during the day. Others like to work days so they can be with their families at night."

He also works on the food budget and notes any problems. This month, for example, the price of romaine lettuce is very high, so Kareem plans to hold down food costs by substituting other kinds of lettuce on the salad bar.

Kareem sets his paperwork aside to spend a little extra time in the kitchen. Ellen Radner, his most experienced line cook, called in sick earlier this morning.

"I have to solve problems and handle the unexpected every day," Kareem said. "Last week Frank Howell burned himself with fat from the deep fryer. Luckily, his burns were not bad."

Kareem constantly stresses safety with his staff. He knows that whenever you put hot cooking equipment and people in the same place, an accident may occur.

Phil Olsen, a new line cook, happened to be home when Kareem called looking for a replacement for Ellen. Phil agreed to come right in. Sometimes Kareem had to call three or four people before rounding up a substitute. Kareem isn't sure how well Phil has mastered their kitchen routine after just a short time on the job. He will be running the line, and Kareem may have to help out.

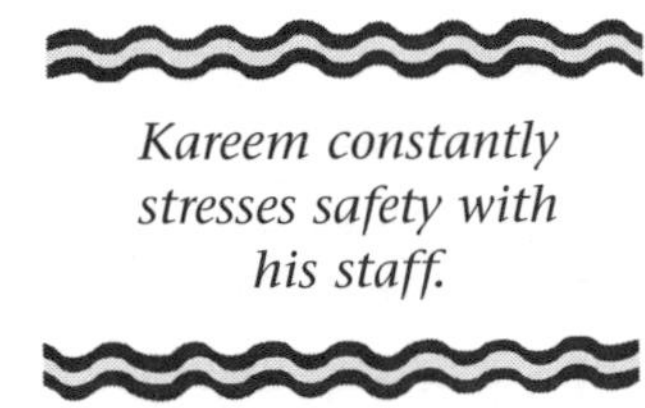

Kareem constantly stresses safety with his staff.

In the Kitchen

As Kareem walks through the kitchen, the pastry chef, Mario Petras, stops him.

"Just look at the fruit that Apex Produce sent over," Mario exclaimed. He's one of the best dessert and pastry chefs in town, so Kareem knows he must be upset for a reason. "These bananas are too soft for the flaming glazed bananas, so we'll have to drop that from the menu today. And these strawberries are better suited to jam than my fresh strawberry tart."

Kareem looks more closely at the bananas and agrees with Mario. Kareem makes a mental note to tell the servers about the menu change. Also, Kareem will tell the manager at some point because she likes to know what's going on, although she leaves most menu decisions to him. After all, Kareem is responsible for what comes out of the kitchen.

Then Kareem and Mario look at the strawberries and decide that Mario can make do. As Kareem walks away, he makes another mental note to call Apex Produce about the problem.

Finally, Kareem reaches Phil, who is checking a beef roast in the oven. "I'm doing okay, Kareem," he said, smiling. "I think the new Hungarian goulash is good. Do you want to taste it?"

"Excellent," Kareem said after picking up a spoon and sampling the food. "Increasing the grated lemon rind certainly adds to the flavor."

Cooking Up a Career

Kareem had been studying oceanography when he realized college wasn't for him. He dropped out and took the first job he could find–as a salad maker in a restaurant. He soon got tired of washing lettuce and chopping vegetables. But he was fascinated by the restaurant business and decided to get the training he'd need to run a kitchen.

Kareem was fascinated by the restaurant business and decided to get the training he'd need to run a kitchen.

He completed a two-year program in culinary arts, taking such courses as food chemistry, equipment technology, accounting, and management. Kareem then worked as an assistant chef in a hotel kitchen. After several years there, he accepted the job as chef at Peterson's Restaurant.

Even though Kareem pursued a formal education, he worked with many people who had high school diplomas. Most of them learned by working in restaurant kitchens and moving their way up through the various positions, starting as dishwasher or vegetable prep person.

In fact, he knew the owner of one of the most popular places in town was a self-taught chef who risked everything to open a restaurant of his own. Now that took confidence!

The Chef's Work Is Seldom Done

Kareem looks up at the clock and notices that it's time to fix lunch for the staff. Since Phil is new, Kareem decides to take care of that while Phil finishes his prep work. The staff normally takes their lunch break at 10:45 a.m. That's too early for some, but better than a chorus of growling stomachs that would have to otherwise wait until 3 p.m.

"The time always seems to fly by. Everyone is so busy there's hardly time to take a breath."

Kareem then checks to see if the pantry and dish stations are ready for service, makes sure the morning bread was delivered, and confirms that the dining room attendants have filled the coffee machine and put out the garnish trays.

By 11:45 a.m., the first food orders come in to the kitchen. As noon approaches, the restaurant becomes much busier, and the tempo of the work increases.

Kareem helps out wherever it's necessary. He garnishes the plates Phil puts up and gives occasional advice. The height of the lunch service passes quickly.

"The time always seems to fly by. Everyone is so busy there's hardly time to take a breath," Kareem said.

As the crowd in the dining room thins out, the pace of work in the kitchen slows. Kareem splits up the kitchen staff so that half can take a break while the others cover for them. When the first half comes back to their stations, the others can sit down and cool off for a few minutes. They will all start preparation for dinner in the time left before the night crew arrives.

A Break at Last

Kareem fixes a plate of food for himself and goes to a table in the back of the empty dining room to finish writing his comments on the food budget. "It certainly feels good to sit down," he said.

Soon Kareem is immersed in his estimate of food costs. He is startled to realize it's already 3:30 p.m. when Mario joins him at the table.

"About those bananas," Mario began. "I suppose I can use them for a Brazilian banana cake."

"Sounds like a good idea, Mario," Kareem said with a smile.

As the pastry chef walks away, Kareem remembered something. "One more thing to take care of," he said. He goes to his office, picks up the phone, and dials the Apex Produce Market.

"Hello, Mr. Yankelovich? This is Kareem Newsome at Peterson's Restaurant. Would you help me with a problem?"

PROFILE

Antonio Perez—Hairstylist

"There will always be work for hairstylists," Antonio Perez said. "Styles go in circles," he explained as he worked on a customer. "As long as people don't start wearing the same style, I'll be in demand.

Antonio enjoys customers' reactions when he creates a flattering look.

"Each person is unique and has his or her own look and style," Antonio said. "I always try to communicate with the client and exceed expectations."

Antonio has many clients who trust only him to cut their hair. When Antonio changed employers about two years ago, many clients followed him to his current workplace, a small but very busy salon.

Antonio offers a wide range of services, including shampooing, cutting, coloring, and styling hair. He advises clients on how to care for their hair.

"I always try to communicate with the client and exceed expectations."

"My salon also offers aromatherapy with essential oils and flowers," Antonio said. "Skin care is a big part of our business. For my continuing education, I learn about these personal services in small, hands-on workshops. That way I keep my license current.

"I worry about client allergies. If a chemical burns or skin gets itchy and blisters, I discontinue its use on that client. It's important to screen the client for all products."

Making the Cut

"I knew I was artistic, and I liked working with people," Antonio said. "So right after high school, I signed up with a well-respected academy. At the academy, I took numerous classes, saw many demonstrations, and worked on mannequins. When I completed half the required hours, I moved to the school's salon floor."

In the school's salon, Antonio put his training to work under the supervision of instructors. He practiced on customers who received haircuts and other services at reduced costs. He also cut hair for family and friends.

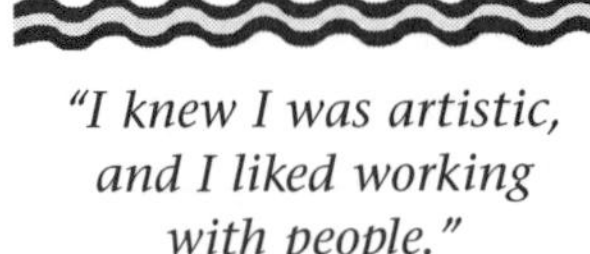

"I knew I was artistic, and I liked working with people."

After graduating from his training program, Antonio passed his state's licensing exam. He then went to work for a large chain of hair salons. "While it's possible to start by buying your own salon or establishing one in your home, it's better to work with other stylists. You learn from each other and from clients," said Antonio.

Growing into a Career

"When I first started, I would do whatever the client wanted, even if I thought it was not the most flattering look. Now I tactfully suggest that another style might be more suitable. It pays to be honest, because the clients I persuade are more likely to come back than the ones I merely please," Antonio stated.

"It takes years to build up your clientele," he said. "It's probably best to start at a franchise that pays you a salary while you get established. Otherwise you sit around waiting for clients. And it's nice to have other stylists to talk to, to learn from. We tend to be a talkative, friendly bunch.

"I tactfully suggest that another style might be more suitable."

"It's a tough job in the beginning. You don't earn much at first. If you start young and live at home, rent free, that helps a lot," Antonio said.

"The biggest temptation is to spend your tips right away. After all, it's cash and it's right there in your pocket. But you have to remember that tips are part of your income."

A Standing Schedule

"One occupational hazard is standing for an eight-hour stretch," Antonio said. "It strains the back, feet, and legs. Varicose veins plague hairstylists. At the end of a day of standing, my back and arms ache."

"Late or no-show customers are a problem also," Antonio said. "And I always work Saturdays. That's my biggest day."

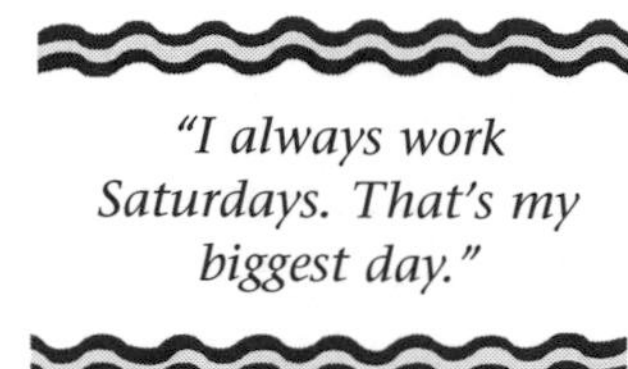
"I always work Saturdays. That's my biggest day."

"The rewards come when a difficult client likes what you've accomplished, and he or she comes back asking for you. That's a good feeling," Antonio said.

"Another good thing about being a hairstylist: You can move anywhere in this country and find work. The start-up costs aren't so high that the ordinary person can't work out of the home. But you do need to check on your state's requirements and local zoning ordinances, licenses, and so on. Different states do it differently.

"The ability to open a home salon is a dream come true for many parents. Being able to earn a decent living while keeping an ear open for the kids–it doesn't get much better than that."

Snippets for Success

Antonio has some advice about being a successful hairstylist. "Don't get too emotionally involved with your clients. This business operates on a very personal level. After all, I am touching strangers and running my fingers through their hair. When a client cries out his or her sorrows, I listen but move to a cooler emotional level.

"I don't talk too much. I can usually tell if people want to talk or not. Some just want you to take care of business and that's that."

What would Antonio do if he ever decided to stop working with clients? "Perhaps I could sell products to salons as a manufacturers' rep. And vocational schools *always* need teachers."

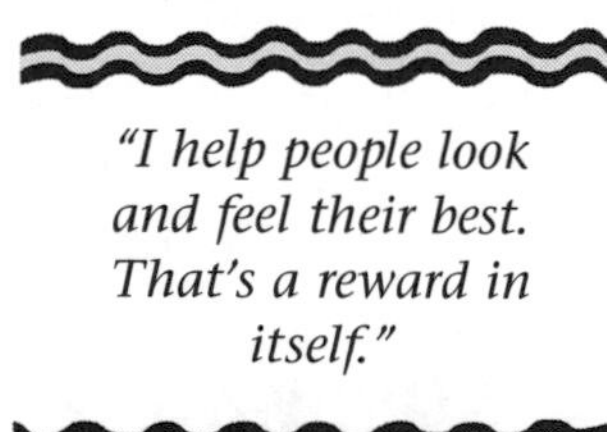
"I help people look and feel their best. That's a reward in itself."

For now, however, Antonio is content with his work. "I help people look and feel their best. That's a reward in itself."

PROFILE

Tim Penner—Janitor

Tim Penner, elementary school janitor, usually starts his work when many of the students are gone. He is responsible for cleaning and maintaining the school property.

Tim sets his own pace in cleaning the elementary school.

Tim carries much of his equipment with him. In one pants pocket he carries a Swiss army knife. In another he stores a screwdriver. Keys hang from his belt. He's stashed a flashlight in another pocket. Rags dangle from a rear pocket.

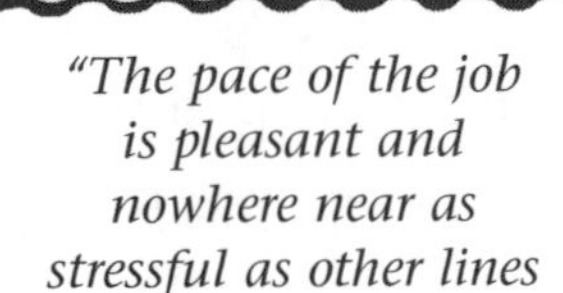

"The pace of the job is pleasant and nowhere near as stressful as other lines of work."

He carries a dry mop in one hand and hauls a pushcart with the other. On the cart, he stores a wet mop, a pail filled with soapy water, hand towels and toilet paper for the bathrooms, and assorted other items.

"One of the good things about this job is that I plan what to do and when. I take breaks when I want. In that sense, I'm my own boss. I could work until all the dirt is gone before I take a break. But if I do that I'll burn out," Tim said.

"So I take breaks when I need them and work hard the rest of the time, and everything gets done. The pace of the job is pleasant and nowhere near as stressful as other lines of work."

Knowing the Basics

"When I first started, I ate more dirt than I do these days. I'm more efficient now at not stirring the dust. I plow it out of the building like a snow plow. Each night I spray the mop I'll use tomorrow so the dust clings to it. These are things you learn on the job."

Tim points out that janitors should have some mechanical knowledge, such how to use tools and repair various machines. "Janitors should also know some chemistry and how to read directions. You'll need to mix cleaning supplies, which could be toxic if not used correctly," Tim said. "And you need good people skills to provide service to occupants of the building."

Janitors should have some mechanical knowledge, such how to use tools and repair various machines.

Tim learned most of this knowledge on the job. He started as a trainee, working with an experienced janitor. Later, he took on more responsibility and more difficult jobs.

Constantly on His Toes

Tim's job is hard work and much more. There are some potential dangers. Since he's always mopping and creating wet surfaces, he must take care not to slip and fall, especially when he's alone in the building.

Occasionally the heat goes out. The water in pipes could freeze and that presents a special danger–the boiler could explode.

"I constantly listen to the building," he said. "I never have the radio on. If it's too quiet, or there are unusual sounds, I take immediate steps to find out why."

"It's a very physical job, where I'm standing or walking for hours at a time. The work is repetitive, so if your back aches every time you bend over to mop, there's not much you can do but keep on mopping until the job is done.

"I constantly listen to the building. I never have the radio on."

"But injuries are rare. When you think about the lifting, bending, and such, and how we work with chemicals all the time, you would think more

accidents would happen. But that's part of what you learn at the very beginning, how to be careful, how to stay safe. And if you're smart, you'll do just that."

A Much-Needed Job Everywhere

"I like working in the school because I like kids, and they seem to like me. A lot of the little ones draw me pictures, which I tape to the door of my office.

"I enjoy the fact that everyone in the building needs me and depends on me."

"I also enjoy the fact that everyone in the building needs me and depends on me. When the principal lost her keys and I was able to find them, she said that the school couldn't manage without me. I don't think too many people hear that in their jobs.

"I especially like not having a boss watching me all the time. As long as the work gets done, no one tells me how to do it."

Every building in every town needs some kind of janitorial maintenance. The skills that Tim uses on a daily basis translate across the entire country. "If I moved to Alaska or Hawaii, I could do this job. I might have to learn a few things about the climate, but the rest is all right here," he said, pointing to his head.

"If you work for a large company, you may have the chance to be promoted within the janitorial department. Your chances are better if you have your high school diploma or GED.

"You could also work toward a supervisor's position," Tim explained, "but you need experience and additional ongoing training. If you ever want to be your own boss, you can always open your own janitorial business."

Ready for Anything

Overnight a foot of snow falls. In the dark, Tim drives to school with fifty pounds of cat litter in his trunk for added traction. The entrance to the school is drifted over with ten feet of snow. Although school has been canceled today, he has a job to do.

Tim puts gas in the snow blower and watches as the snow billows out and over, clearing the way for tomorrow, when the children will return to school.

Although school has been canceled today, Tim has a job to do.

There has been talk that a new school building may be built the following year. A modern heating plant would make Tim's job easier, but the need for cleaning will just be transferred to the new building.

"I'm ready for anything," Tim said, as he finishes clearing the school's entrance.

PROFILE

Cindy Arora—Waitress

Cindy enjoys interacting with customers. On return visits to the restaurant, some customers ask to be seated at her tables.

The theater crowd was in full swing. Guests were having dinner before heading off to the shows. Stilts Restaurant was alive with the delicious aromas of fresh-baked bread, sizzling salmon, and sauces. Cindy Arora moved between tables, her arms heavy with plates.

"Cindy, table 14 just arrived," said a waiter, Kevin, as he brushed past her.

"Thanks!" Cindy called as she put down the last of the plates. Then she saw the familiar faces at table 14–the couple known privately to the wait staff as The Crabcakes.

An Encounter with The Crabcakes

"Good evening, so nice to see you again. May I get you something from the bar?"

"We didn't get any of that garlic bread," the man grumbled.

"I'll get you some right away," Cindy smiled. "Your drink orders?"

Cindy memorized their choices. This was the custom at Stilts: no writing down orders. "I'll get those right away. First, let me review our specials tonight. We have a delicious fish dish . . ."

"Forget it! We already know what we want."

Cindy smiled even more widely. This was another custom at Stilts: the customer is always right. "Of course. I'll just get your drinks, and . . ."

"We have to order our food now," the man interrupted. "We're due at the theater at 8 p.m."

"I'll try to push your order through, sir," Cindy said, wondering if Tony, one of the cooks, was in the mood to do her a favor.

"I'll have the salmon, thoroughly grilled, with the vegetables on the side," said the man.

Kevin appeared with a basket of bread for the table and winked at Cindy. She smiled back her appreciation.

It was Mrs. Crabcake's turn to order. It seemed she wanted everything specially prepared. Cindy struggled to remember the details.

"Anything else?" Cindy asked.

Thankfully, there wasn't. She still had to take an order at table 13, clear table 15, and check up on tables 11 and 19.

Such is a demanding night for a four-star restaurant waitress. And no one can appreciate the demands of the job better than Cindy, a veteran of five restaurants.

"Restaurant work can be stressful, all right," Cindy admitted.

Cindy memorized the customers' food choices. This was the custom at the restaurant: no writing down orders.

Freedom and "Family"

For Cindy, it's also worth it. Her schedule of graduate school, art projects, and volunteer tutoring leaves her no time for a nine-to-five job. The service industry gives her a flexible work schedule, excellent take-home pay, and the ability to leave her job at the restaurant door. In addition, employees are welcome to free salads and breads and reduced prices on the main courses.

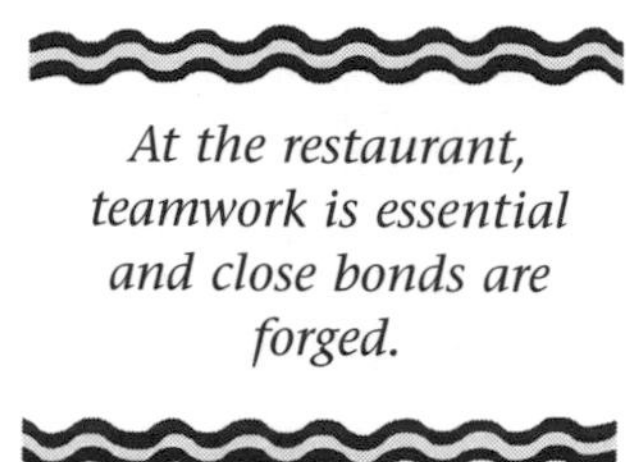

At the restaurant, teamwork is essential and close bonds are forged.

"I eat like royalty," laughed Cindy.

Cindy enjoys the support and attention of her "second family" at the restaurant, where teamwork is essential and close bonds are forged.

Cindy recalled one night, after closing, when the kitchen staff began banging on pots and singing. "Soon, *everybody* was playing some makeshift instrument or singing or dancing. It was a great way shake off stress."

Serving Up a Successful Day

Cindy arrives at work at 4 p.m., an hour early. Dressed in her uniform of perfectly pressed black trousers, a clean shirt, and flat black shoes, Cindy first orders her own dinner.

While she waits for her food, she checks in with the host or hostess to find out where her section will be. A section usually consists of five or six tables in a common area of the restaurant.

Cindy believes the best way to ensure a successful evening is to be prepared. "I check my tables before the customers start to arrive. I make sure they all have clean silverware, nicely folded napkins, and the correct number of chairs," said Cindy.

She greets a table of guests within five minutes of their seating. She then takes drink orders, describes the specials, and, finally, gets the drinks or greets another table. With five or six tables going at once, the process can be a tricky acrobatics act.

"You have one table ordering drinks, another ordering food, another with their meals ready at the line, another waiting for their check."

Waiting on five or six tables at once can be a tricky acrobatics act.

Stilts relies on a computer system for food and drink ordering and check printout, as do most upscale restaurants.

"You may need extensive training to master these complex ordering systems," Cindy said.

After guests are served and their table is cleared, Cindy must verify the entries on the bill and carefully handle all credit card and cash transactions. That's a lot to deal with, and sometimes mistakes are made. Of course, some patrons arrive in a bad mood.

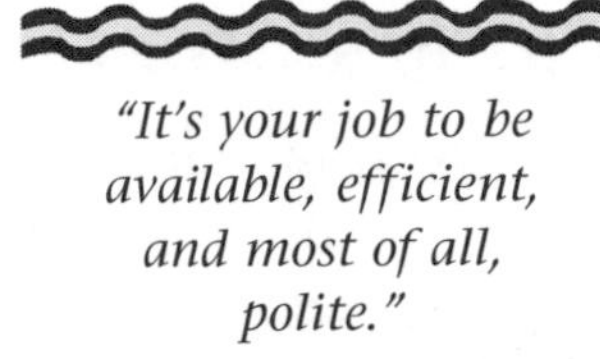

"It's your job to be available, efficient, and most of all, polite."

"An experienced server can recognize the difference between a valid complaint and a grumpy complainer and respond appropriately. In the first case, I smile and ask questions. If the guest is simply rude, I bring the problem to my manager.

"Whatever kind of day you are having or *they* are having, it's your job to be available, efficient, and most of all, polite."

The First Order of Business

According to Cindy, the best way to begin waiting tables is to apply at local diners or at restaurants that cater to lower or middle-level budgets. These restaurants usually use notepads for ordering and allow wait staff to carry food trays. They also offer on-the-job training.

"You may find you prefer the casual diner with a high-turnover crowd to the upscale restaurant, though you probably won't find the pay as inviting.

"After six months to one year of experience, you'll have the proper background to approach four-star establishments. But be prepared for tough interviewing. I went through three interviews with Stilts," Cindy said.

Those interested in waiting tables should have physical endurance. "You're on your feet and moving for five or six hours at a time," Cindy noted.

Personality is also important. "You have to be a team player, number one," she emphasized. "It can save you in this job."

Organization and good prioritizing are high on Cindy's list of necessary skills for a service position.

Cindy also suggested that a good memory is helpful. "Even if you are allowed to write orders down, you may forget which customer gets what appetizer, that sort of thing. Speaking of customers, it's also helpful if you can remember the names of your regulars."

Organization and good prioritizing are also high on Cindy's list of necessary skills for a service position. And last but not least is patience. "I quietly count to ten a lot," Cindy admitted.

Cindy's "Tips"

Patience may also be a helpful trait if you're interested in a long-term career in the service industry. Restaurants often promote from within. Experienced waiters and waitresses, as well as chefs, bartenders, and hostesses, can move up to assistant manager.

"Somehow, and I can't explain it, this job is satisfying," she said. "It's the little things. There are moments when I really feel good about the job I do.

"Once I discovered that a man had left his credit card at the table. I ran after him and caught up to him in the parking lot as he was about to drive off.

"That man and his family have since become regular customers. And when they come in," she said, "he always asks for me."

SKILL SAMPLER

Tamika Jones—Hotel Desk Clerk

Tamika Jones is a hotel desk clerk at the Sailor's Inn, a large resort hotel. She helps visitors get checked in and answers any questions they have. "Smiling customers are what really make my job rewarding."

For Tamika, the job's evening schedule allows her to attend college during the day. Tamika talked about some of the skills needed by a hotel desk clerk. She suggested the following tips to help you decide if this is a job you want to pursue.

Tamika has always enjoyed meeting and helping people.

Hotel desk clerks deal with the public all day.

- Do you like meeting people?
- Do you start conversations with people you don't know?
- When you see people having trouble carrying a package or finding their way, do you offer to help before they ask?

Hotel desk clerks must look nice and be pleasant while they are at work.

- Do you care about how you look?
- Do you like to wear clean, neat clothes to school?
- Are you polite and cheerful to others, even when you aren't feeling completely happy or well?

Hotel desk clerks must remain calm and helpful with angry guests.

- Can you let someone else have the last word in an argument?
- Have you ever excepted blame for something you didn't do?
- Do you follow your teachers' instructions when you complete school assignments, even if you think you know a better way?

Hotel desk clerks' activities change very little from hour to hour and day to day.

- Are you comfortable with routine activities?
- Do you have a daily schedule?
- Have you ever delivered newspapers, sold candy, collected money for a charity, or had another job that involved doing the same thing over and over?

Hotel desk clerks must be able to remember and give directions and other detailed information.

- If someone calls your home with a message for your parents, can you relay the message correctly?
- Do you remember the names of people and places?
- Would you be able to give someone clear directions for driving to a certain place?

Hotel desk clerks must keep track of many things at once. They must be able to work quickly without making mistakes.

- Do you have a system for keeping track of your homework assignments and computer files?
- Do you generally finish tests on time?
- Do you enjoy games that require a good memory?

Now learn about all major jobs in the Recreation, Travel, and Other Personal Services interest area→

Facts About All Major Jobs Related to

RECREATION, TRAVEL, AND OTHER PERSONAL SERVICES

In addition to the jobs covered in the profiles and skill sampler, other careers in the Recreation, Travel, and Other Personal Services interest area may appeal to you. This section describes and gives facts about all major jobs in the Recreation, Travel, and Other Personal Services interest area. For an explanation of the $, ★, and 🚹 symbols, see page 6.

MANAGERIAL WORK IN RECREATION, TRAVEL, AND OTHER PERSONAL SERVICES

These workers manage all or part of the activities in restaurants, hotels, resorts, and other places where people expect good personal service. Some of them manage services that keep a building clean. Within the guidelines of their organization, they set goals, monitor resources, and evaluate the work of others.

Aircraft Cargo Handling Supervisors. Direct ground crew in the loading, unloading, securing, and staging of aircraft cargo or baggage. Determine the quantity and orientation of cargo and compute aircraft center of gravity. May accompany aircraft as member of flight crew, monitor and handle cargo in flight, and assist and brief passengers on safety and emergency procedures. **Education and Training:** Work experience in a related occupation. **Skills:** Math—Medium. English—Medium. Science—Medium. **Yearly Earnings:** $$$ **Job Growth:** ★★★★ **Yearly Openings:** 🚹

First-Line Supervisors/Managers of Food Preparation and Serving Workers. Supervise workers engaged in preparing and serving food. **Education and Training:** Work experience in a related occupation. **Skills:** Math—Medium. English—Medium. Science—Medium. **Yearly Earnings:** $$ **Job Growth:** ★★★ **Yearly Openings:** 🚹🚹🚹🚹🚹

First-Line Supervisors/Managers of Housekeeping and Janitorial Workers. Supervise work activities of cleaning personnel in hotels, hospitals, offices, and other establishments. **Education and Training:** Work experience in a related occupation. **Skills:** Math—Medium. English—Medium. Science—Medium. **Yearly Earnings:** $$ **Job Growth:** ★★★ **Yearly Openings:** 🚹🚹🚹

First-Line Supervisors/Managers of Personal Service Workers. Supervise and coordinate activities of personal service workers, such as supervisors of flight attendants, hairdressers, or caddies. **Education and Training:** Work experience in a related occupation. **Skills:** Math—Medium. English—Medium. Science—Medium. **Yearly Earnings:** $$ **Job Growth:** ★★★ **Yearly Openings:** 🧍🧍

Food Service Managers. Plan, direct, or coordinate activities of an organization or department that serves food and beverages. **Education and Training:** Work experience in a related occupation. **Skills:** Math—Medium. English—Medium. Science—Medium. **Yearly Earnings:** $$$ **Job Growth:** ★★★ **Yearly Openings:** 🧍🧍🧍🧍

Gaming Managers. Plan, organize, direct, control, or coordinate gaming operations in a casino. Formulate gaming policies for their area of responsibility. **Education and Training:** College degree plus work experience. **Skills:** Math—Medium. English—Medium. Science—Medium. **Yearly Earnings:** $$$$$ **Job Growth:** ★★★★ **Yearly Openings:** 🧍

Gaming Supervisors. Supervise gaming operations and personnel in an assigned area. Circulate among tables and observe operations. Ensure that stations and games are covered for each shift. May explain and interpret operating rules of house to patrons. May plan and organize activities and create friendly atmosphere for guests in hotels/casinos. **Education and Training:** Postsecondary career and technical education. **Skills:** Math—Medium. English—Medium. Science—Medium. **Yearly Earnings:** $$$ **Job Growth:** ★★★ **Yearly Openings:** 🧍

Housekeeping Supervisors. Supervise work activities of cleaning personnel to ensure clean, orderly, and attractive rooms in hotels, hospitals, educational institutions, and similar establishments. Assign duties, inspect work, investigate complaints regarding housekeeping service and equipment, and take corrective action. May purchase housekeeping supplies and equipment, take periodic inventories, screen applicants, train new employees, and recommend dismissals. **Education and Training:** Work experience in a related occupation. **Skills:** Math—Medium. English—Medium. Science—Medium. **Yearly Earnings:** $$ **Job Growth:** ★★★ **Yearly Openings:** 🧍🧍🧍

Janitorial Supervisors. Supervise work activities of janitorial personnel in commercial and industrial establishments. Assign duties, inspect work, and investigate complaints regarding janitorial services and take corrective action. May purchase janitorial supplies and equipment, take inventories, screen applicants, train new employees, and recommend dismissals. **Education and Training:** Work experience in a related occupation. **Skills:** Math—Medium. English—Medium. Science—Medium. **Yearly Earnings:** $$ **Job Growth:** ★★★ **Yearly Openings:** 🧍🧍🧍

Lodging Managers. Plan, direct, or coordinate activities of an organization or department that provides lodging and other accommodations. **Education and Training:**

Work experience in a related occupation. **Skills:** Math—Medium. English—Medium. Science—Medium. **Yearly Earnings:** $$$ **Job Growth:** ★★ **Yearly Openings:** 👤👤

Meeting and Convention Planners. Coordinate activities of staff and convention personnel to make arrangements for group meetings and conventions. **Education and Training:** Bachelor's degree. **Skills:** Math—Medium. English—Medium. Science—Low. **Yearly Earnings:** $$$ **Job Growth:** ★★★★ **Yearly Openings:** 👤

RECREATIONAL SERVICES

These workers provide services to help people enjoy their leisure activities. They may lead people in recreational activities such as exercise, crafts, music, or camping. Or they may help people engaged in recreation by performing such services as dealing cards, guiding tourists, taking tickets, or operating thrill rides.

Amusement and Recreation Attendants. Perform variety of attending duties at amusement or recreation facility. May schedule use of recreation facilities, maintain and provide equipment to participants of sporting events or recreational pursuits, or operate amusement concessions and rides. **Education and Training:** Short-term on-the-job training. **Skills:** Math—Medium. English—Medium. Science—Low. **Yearly Earnings:** $ **Job Growth:** ★★★★ **Yearly Openings:** 👤👤👤👤

Gaming and Sports Book Writers and Runners. Assist in the operation of games such as keno and bingo. Scan winning tickets presented by patrons, calculate amount of winnings, and pay patrons. May operate keno and bingo equipment. May start gaming equipment that randomly selects numbers. May announce number selected until total numbers specified for each game are selected. May pick up tickets from players; collect bets; and receive, verify, and record patrons' cash wages. **Education and Training:** Postsecondary career and technical education. **Skills:** Math—Medium. English—Medium. Science—Low. **Yearly Earnings:** $ **Job Growth:** ★★★★ **Yearly Openings:** 👤

Gaming Dealers. Operate table games. Stand or sit behind table and operate games of chance by dispensing the appropriate number of cards or blocks to players or operating other gaming equipment. Compare the house's hand against players' hands and pay off or collect players' money or chips. **Education and Training:** Postsecondary career and technical education. **Skills:** Math—Medium. English—Medium. Science—Low. **Yearly Earnings:** $ **Job Growth:** ★★★★ **Yearly Openings:** 👤👤👤

Motion Picture Projectionists. Set up and operate motion picture projection and related sound reproduction equipment. **Education and Training:** Short-term on-the-job training. **Skills:** Math—Low. English—Low. Science—Low. **Yearly Earnings:** $ **Job Growth:** ★ **Yearly Openings:** 👤

Recreation Workers. Conduct recreation activities with groups in public, private, or volunteer agencies or recreation facilities. Organize and promote activities such as arts and crafts, sports, games, music, dramatics, social recreation, camping, and hobbies, taking into account the needs and interests of individual members. **Education and Training:** Bachelor's degree. **Skills:** Math—Low. English—Medium. Science—Medium. **Yearly Earnings:** $ **Job Growth:** ★★★ **Yearly Openings:** 🚶🚶🚶

Slot Key Persons. Coordinate/supervise functions of slot department workers to provide service to patrons. Handle and settle complaints of players. Verify and pay off jackpots. Reset slot machines after payoffs. Make minor repairs or adjustments to slot machines. Recommend removal of slot machines for repair. Report hazards and enforce safety rules. **Education and Training:** Short-term on-the-job training. **Skills:** Math—Medium. English—Medium. Science—Medium. **Yearly Earnings:** $$ **Job Growth:** ★★★★ **Yearly Openings:** 🚶

Tour Guides and Escorts. Escort individuals or groups on sightseeing tours or through places of interest, such as industrial establishments, public buildings, and art galleries. **Education and Training:** Short-term on-the-job training. **Skills:** Math—Medium. English—Medium. Science—Low. **Yearly Earnings:** $ **Job Growth:** ★★ **Yearly Openings:** 🚶🚶

Travel Guides. Plan, organize, and conduct long-distance cruises, tours, and expeditions for individuals and groups. **Education and Training:** Moderate-term on-the-job training. **Skills:** Math—Medium. English—Medium. Science—Medium. **Yearly Earnings:** $ **Job Growth:** ★★ **Yearly Openings:** 🚶🚶

Ushers, Lobby Attendants, and Ticket Takers. Assist patrons at entertainment events by performing duties such as collecting admission tickets and passes from patrons, assisting in finding seats, searching for lost articles, and locating such facilities as restrooms and telephones. **Education and Training:** Short-term on-the-job training. **Skills:** Math—Medium. English—Low. Science—Low. **Yearly Earnings:** $ **Job Growth:** ★★★ **Yearly Openings:** 🚶🚶🚶

TRANSPORTATION AND LODGING SERVICES

These workers help visitors, travelers, and customers get acquainted with and feel at ease in an unfamiliar setting. They are charged with the safety and comfort of people who are traveling or vacationing. They may register travelers at hotels, book trips for passengers, or carry travelers' luggage. These workers find employment with air, rail, and water transportation companies; hotels and restaurants; retirement homes; and related establishments.

Baggage Porters and Bellhops. Handle baggage for travelers at transportation terminals or for guests at hotels or similar establishments. **Education and Training:**

Short-term on-the-job training. **Skills:** Math—Medium. English—Medium. Science—Medium. **Yearly Earnings:** $ **Job Growth:** ★★★ **Yearly Openings:** 🧍🧍🧍

Concierges. Assist patrons at hotel, apartment, or office building with personal services. May take messages; arrange or give advice on transportation, business services, or entertainment; or monitor guest requests for housekeeping and maintenance. **Education and Training:** Short-term on-the-job training. **Skills:** Math—Medium. English—Medium. Science—Medium. **Yearly Earnings:** $$ **Job Growth:** ★★★ **Yearly Openings:** 🧍

Flight Attendants. Provide personal services to ensure the safety and comfort of airline passengers during flight. Greet passengers, verify tickets, explain use of safety equipment, and serve food or beverages. **Education and Training:** Long-term on-the-job training. **Skills:** Math—Medium. English—Medium. Science—Medium. **Yearly Earnings:** $$$ **Job Growth:** ★★★ **Yearly Openings:** 🧍🧍

Hotel, Motel, and Resort Desk Clerks. Accommodate hotel, motel, and resort patrons by registering and assigning rooms to guests, issuing room keys, transmitting and receiving messages, keeping records of occupied rooms and guests' accounts, making and confirming reservations, and presenting statements to and collecting payments from departing guests. **Education and Training:** Short-term on-the-job training. **Skills:** Math—Medium. English—Medium. Science—Medium. **Yearly Earnings:** $ **Job Growth:** ★★★★ **Yearly Openings:** 🧍🧍🧍🧍

Reservation and Transportation Ticket Agents. Make and confirm reservations for passengers and sell tickets for transportation agencies such as airlines, bus companies, railroads, and steamship lines. May check baggage and direct passengers to designated concourse, pier, or track. **Education and Training:** Short-term on-the-job training. **Skills:** Math—Medium. English—Medium. Science—Low. **Yearly Earnings:** $$ **Job Growth:** ★★★ **Yearly Openings:** 🧍🧍🧍

Reservation and Transportation Ticket Agents and Travel Clerks. Make and confirm reservations and sell tickets to passengers for large hotel or motel chains. May check baggage and direct passengers to designated concourse, pier, or track; make reservations; deliver tickets; arrange for visas; contact individuals and groups to inform them of package tours; or provide tourists with travel information, such as points of interest, restaurants, rates, and emergency service. **Education and Training:** Short-term on-the-job training. **Skills:** Math—Medium. English—Medium. Science—Medium. **Yearly Earnings:** $$ **Job Growth:** ★★★ **Yearly Openings:** 🧍🧍🧍

Transportation Attendants, Except Flight Attendants and Baggage Porters. Provide services to ensure the safety and comfort of passengers aboard ships, buses, or trains or within the station or terminal. Perform duties such as greeting passengers, explaining the use of safety equipment, serving meals or beverages, or answering questions related to travel. **Education and Training:** Short-term on-the-job training. **Skills:** Math—Medium. English—Medium. Science—Low. **Yearly Earnings:** $ **Job Growth:** ★★★ **Yearly Openings:** 🧍

BARBER AND BEAUTY SERVICES

These workers cut and style hair and provide a variety of other services to improve people's appearance or physical condition. They may specialize in one activity or perform many different duties.

Barbers. Provide barbering services, such as cutting, trimming, shampooing, and styling hair; trimming beards; or giving shaves. **Education and Training:** Postsecondary career and technical education. **Skills:** Math—Low. English—Low. Science—Low. **Yearly Earnings:** $ **Job Growth:** ★ **Yearly Openings:** 🚹

Hairdressers, Hairstylists, and Cosmetologists. Provide beauty services, such as shampooing; cutting, coloring, and styling hair; and massaging and treating scalp. May also apply makeup, dress wigs, perform hair removal, and provide nail and skin care services. **Education and Training:** Postsecondary career and technical education. **Skills:** Math—Medium. English—Medium. Science—Medium. **Yearly Earnings:** $ **Job Growth:** ★★★ **Yearly Openings:** 🚹🚹🚹🚹

Manicurists and Pedicurists. Clean and shape customers' fingernails and toenails. May polish or decorate nails. **Education and Training:** Postsecondary career and technical education. **Skills:** Math—Low. English—Low. Science—Medium. **Yearly Earnings:** $ **Job Growth:** ★★★★ **Yearly Openings:** 🚹

Shampooers. Shampoo and rinse customers' hair. **Education and Training:** Short-term on-the-job training. **Skills:** Math—Medium. English—Medium. Science—Medium. **Yearly Earnings:** $ **Job Growth:** ★★★ **Yearly Openings:** 🚹

Skin Care Specialists. Provide skin care treatments to face and body to enhance an individual's appearance. **Education and Training:** Short-term on-the-job training. **Skills:** Math—Medium. English—Medium. Science—Medium. **Yearly Earnings:** $$ **Job Growth:** ★★★ **Yearly Openings:** 🚹

FOOD AND BEVERAGE SERVICES

These workers prepare and serve food. Some of them cook or do other tasks to prepare food in kitchens of restaurants or institutional cafeterias. Others aid in the preparation process by cutting meat, baking bread and pastries, or decorating cakes. The various kinds of workers who serve food and drink may wait on tables, serve diners at a counter, bring meals outside at drive-ins, or tend bar. Other workers play a supporting role by greeting diners as they enter a restaurant, by washing dishes, or by keeping the dining room set up with clean linens and silverware.

Bakers. Mix and bake ingredients according to recipes to produce breads, rolls, cookies, cakes, pies, pastries, or other baked goods. **Education and Training:** Long-term on-the-job training. **Skills:** Math—Medium. English—Medium. Science—Medium. **Yearly Earnings:** $ **Job Growth:** ★★★ **Yearly Openings:** 🚹🚹🚹

Bakers, Bread and Pastry. Mix and bake ingredients according to recipes to produce small quantities of breads, pastries, and other baked goods for consumption on premises or for sale as specialty baked goods. **Education and Training:** Long-term on-the-job training. **Skills:** Math—Medium. English—Low. Science—Medium. **Yearly Earnings:** $ **Job Growth:** ★★★ **Yearly Openings:** 🧍🧍🧍

Bartenders. Mix and serve drinks to patrons directly or through waitstaff. **Education and Training:** Short-term on-the-job training. **Skills:** Math—Medium. English—Medium. Science—Low. **Yearly Earnings:** $ **Job Growth:** ★★★ **Yearly Openings:** 🧍🧍🧍🧍

Butchers and Meat Cutters. Cut, trim, or prepare consumer-sized portions of meat for use or sale in retail establishments. **Education and Training:** Long-term on-the-job training. **Skills:** Math—Medium. English—Medium. Science—Medium. **Yearly Earnings:** $$ **Job Growth:** ★ **Yearly Openings:** 🧍🧍🧍

Chefs and Head Cooks. Direct the preparation, seasoning, and cooking of salads, soups, fish, meats, vegetables, desserts, or other foods. May plan and price menu items, order supplies, and keep records and accounts. May participate in cooking. **Education and Training:** Postsecondary career and technical education. **Skills:** Math—Medium. English—Medium. Science—Medium. **Yearly Earnings:** $$ **Job Growth:** ★★ **Yearly Openings:** 🧍🧍🧍

Combined Food Preparation and Serving Workers, Including Fast Food. Perform duties which combine both food preparation and food service. **Education and Training:** Short-term on-the-job training. **Skills:** Math—Medium. English—Medium. Science—Low. **Yearly Earnings:** $ **Job Growth:** ★★★★ **Yearly Openings:** 🧍🧍🧍🧍🧍

Cooks, Fast Food. Prepare and cook food in a fast food restaurant with a limited menu. Duties of the cooks are limited to preparation of a few basic items and normally involve operating large-volume single-purpose cooking equipment. **Education and Training:** Short-term on-the-job training. **Skills:** Math—Medium. English—Low. Science—Medium. **Yearly Earnings:** $ **Job Growth:** ★ **Yearly Openings:** 🧍🧍🧍🧍🧍

Cooks, Institution and Cafeteria. Prepare and cook large quantities of food for institutions, such as schools, hospitals, or cafeterias. **Education and Training:** Short-term on-the-job training. **Skills:** Math—Medium. English—Medium. Science—Medium. **Yearly Earnings:** $ **Job Growth:** ★★ **Yearly Openings:** 🧍🧍🧍🧍🧍

Cooks, Restaurant. Prepare, season, and cook soups, meats, vegetables, desserts, or other foods in restaurants. May order supplies, keep records and accounts, price items on menu, or plan menu. **Education and Training:** Long-term on-the-job training. **Skills:** Math—Medium. English—Medium. Science—Medium. **Yearly Earnings:** $ **Job Growth:** ★★★★ **Yearly Openings:** 🧍🧍🧍🧍🧍

Cooks, Short Order. Prepare and cook to order a variety of foods that require only a short preparation time. May take orders from customers and serve patrons at counters or tables. **Education and Training:** Short-term on-the-job training. **Skills:** Math—Medium. English—Medium. Science—Medium. **Yearly Earnings:** $ **Job Growth:** ★★ **Yearly Openings:** 👤👤👤

Counter Attendants, Cafeteria, Food Concession, and Coffee Shop. Serve food to diners at counter or from a steam table. **Education and Training:** Short-term on-the-job training. **Skills:** Math—Medium. English—Medium. Science—Medium. **Yearly Earnings:** $ **Job Growth:** ★★★ **Yearly Openings:** 👤👤👤👤👤

Dining Room and Cafeteria Attendants and Bartender Helpers. Facilitate food service. Clean tables, carry dirty dishes, and replace soiled table linens; set tables; replenish supply of clean linens, silverware, glassware, and dishes; supply service bar with food; and serve water, butter, and coffee to patrons. **Education and Training:** Short-term on-the-job training. **Skills:** Math—Low. English—Low. Science—Medium. **Yearly Earnings:** $ **Job Growth:** ★ **Yearly Openings:** 👤👤👤👤👤

Dishwashers. Clean dishes, kitchen, food preparation equipment, or utensils. **Education and Training:** Short-term on-the-job training. **Skills:** Math—Low. English—Low. Science—Low. **Yearly Earnings:** $ **Job Growth:** ★ **Yearly Openings:** 👤👤👤👤👤

Food Preparation Workers. Perform a variety of food preparation duties other than cooking, such as preparing cold foods and shellfish, slicing meat, and brewing coffee or tea. **Education and Training:** Short-term on-the-job training. **Skills:** Math—Low. English—Medium. Science—Low. **Yearly Earnings:** $ **Job Growth:** ★★★ **Yearly Openings:** 👤👤👤👤👤

Food Servers, Nonrestaurant. Serve food to patrons outside of a restaurant environment, such as in hotels, hospital rooms, or cars. **Education and Training:** Short-term on-the-job training. **Skills:** Math—Medium. English—Medium. Science—Medium. **Yearly Earnings:** $ **Job Growth:** ★★★ **Yearly Openings:** 👤👤👤👤

Hosts and Hostesses, Restaurant, Lounge, and Coffee Shop. Welcome patrons, seat them at tables or in lounge, and help ensure quality of facilities and service. **Education and Training:** Short-term on-the-job training. **Skills:** Math—Medium. English—Medium. Science—Medium. **Yearly Earnings:** $ **Job Growth:** ★★★ **Yearly Openings:** 👤👤👤👤

Waiters and Waitresses. Take orders and serve food and beverages to patrons at tables in dining establishment. **Education and Training:** Short-term on-the-job training. **Skills:** Math—Medium. English—Medium. Science—Low. **Yearly Earnings:** $ **Job Growth:** ★★★ **Yearly Openings:** 👤👤👤👤👤

APPAREL, SHOES, LEATHER, AND FABRIC CARE

These workers clean, alter, restore, and repair clothing, shoes, or other items made from fabric or leather. Their jobs are found in clothing stores, manufacturing plants, and specialty cleaning, alteration, and repair shops.

Custom Tailors. Design/make tailored garments, applying knowledge of garment design, construction, styling, and fabrics. **Education and Training:** Work experience in a related occupation. **Skills:** Math—Medium. English—Low. Science—Medium. **Yearly Earnings:** $$ **Job Growth:** ★ **Yearly Openings:** 🚹🚹🚹

Fabric Menders, Except Garment. Repair tears, holes, and other defects in fabrics such as draperies, linens, parachutes, and tents. **Education and Training:** Short-term on-the-job training. **Skills:** Math—Medium. English—Low. Science—Medium. **Yearly Earnings:** $$ **Job Growth:** No data available. **Yearly Openings:** No data available.

Laundry and Dry-Cleaning Workers. Operate or tend washing or dry-cleaning machines to wash or dry-clean industrial or household articles, such as cloth garments, suede, leather, furs, blankets, draperies, fine linens, rugs, and carpets. **Education and Training:** Short-term on-the-job training. **Skills:** Math—Medium. English—Medium. Science—Medium. **Yearly Earnings:** $ **Job Growth:** ★★★ **Yearly Openings:** 🚹🚹🚹🚹

Laundry and Drycleaning Machine Operators and Tenders, Except Pressing. Operate or tend washing or dry-cleaning machines to wash or dry-clean commercial, industrial, or household articles, such as cloth garments, suede, leather, furs, blankets, draperies, fine linens, rugs, and carpets. **Education and Training:** Moderate-term on-the-job training. **Skills:** Math—Medium. English—Low. Science—Medium. **Yearly Earnings:** $ **Job Growth:** ★★★ **Yearly Openings:** 🚹🚹🚹🚹

Precision Dyers. Change or restore the color of articles, such as garments, drapes, and slipcovers, by means of dyes. Work requires knowledge of the composition of the textiles being dyed or restored, the chemical properties of bleaches and dyes, and the effects of the bleaches and dyes upon such textiles. **Education and Training:** Postsecondary career and technical education. **Skills:** Math—Medium. English—Low. Science—Medium. **Yearly Earnings:** $ **Job Growth:** ★★★ **Yearly Openings:** 🚹🚹🚹🚹

Pressers, Delicate Fabrics. Press dry-cleaned and wet-cleaned silk and synthetic fiber garments by hand or machine, applying knowledge of fabrics and heat to produce high-quality finish. Finish pleated or fancy garments, normally by hand. **Education and Training:** Moderate-term on-the-job training. **Skills:** Math—Low. English—Low. Science—Medium. **Yearly Earnings:** $ **Job Growth:** ★ **Yearly Openings:** 🚹🚹🚹

Pressers, Hand. Press articles to remove wrinkles, flatten seams, and give shape by using hand iron. Articles pressed include drapes, knit goods, parachutes, garments, slip covers, and textiles such as lace, rayon, and silk. May block (shape) knitted garments after cleaning. May press leather goods. **Education and Training:** Short-term on-the-job training. **Skills:** Math—Low. English—Low. Science—Low. **Yearly Earnings:** $ **Job Growth:** ★ **Yearly Openings:** 👤 👤 👤

Pressers, Textile, Garment, and Related Materials. Press or shape articles by hand or machine. **Education and Training:** Moderate-term on-the-job training. **Skills:** Math—Medium. English—Medium. Science—Medium. **Yearly Earnings:** $ **Job Growth:** ★ **Yearly Openings:** 👤 👤 👤

Shoe and Leather Workers and Repairers. Construct, decorate, or repair leather and leather-like products, such as luggage, shoes, and saddles. **Education and Training:** Long-term on-the-job training. **Skills:** Math—Medium. English—Medium. Science—Medium. **Yearly Earnings:** $ **Job Growth:** ★ **Yearly Openings:** 👤

Shop and Alteration Tailors. Make tailored garments from existing patterns. Alter, repair, or fit made-to-measure or ready-to-wear garments. **Education and Training:** Work experience in a related occupation. **Skills:** Math—Medium. English—Low. Science—Medium. **Yearly Earnings:** $$ **Job Growth:** ★ **Yearly Openings:** 👤 👤 👤

Spotters, Dry Cleaning. Identify stains in wool, synthetic, and silk garments and household fabrics and apply chemical solutions to remove stain. Determine spotting procedures on basis of type of fabric and nature of stain. **Education and Training:** Short-term on-the-job training. **Skills:** Math—Low. English—Low. Science—Medium. **Yearly Earnings:** $ **Job Growth:** ★★★ **Yearly Openings:** 👤 👤 👤 👤

Tailors, Dressmakers, and Custom Sewers. Design, make, alter, repair, or fit garments. **Education and Training:** Work experience in a related occupation. **Skills:** Math—Medium. English—Medium. Science—Medium. **Yearly Earnings:** $$ **Job Growth:** ★ **Yearly Openings:** 👤 👤 👤

Upholsterers. Make, repair, or replace upholstery for household furniture or transportation vehicles. **Education and Training:** Long-term on-the-job training. **Skills:** Math—Medium. English—Medium. Science—Medium. **Yearly Earnings:** $$ **Job Growth:** ★ **Yearly Openings:** 👤 👤

CLEANING AND BUILDING SERVICES

These workers maintain the cleanliness of houses, various kinds of buildings, vehicles, and large equipment. They use detergents and other cleaning agents, vacuum cleaners, brushes, and specialized equipment to remove dirt, spills, and trash so the living or working environment is healthy, safe, and pleasant to be in. Some cleaners also do minor repairs, such as fixing leaky faucets. In hospitals, they may disinfect equipment

and supplies. Some of these workers provide other services for the convenience of people working or seeking recreation in a building, such as retrieving people's personal items in a locker room.

Janitors and Cleaners, Except Maids and Housekeeping Cleaners. Keep buildings in clean and orderly condition. Perform heavy cleaning duties, such as cleaning floors, shampooing rugs, washing walls and glass, and removing rubbish. Duties may include tending furnace and boiler, performing routine maintenance activities, notifying management of need for repairs, and cleaning snow or debris from sidewalk. **Education and Training:** Short-term on-the-job training. **Skills:** Math—Low. English—Medium. Science—Medium. **Yearly Earnings:** $ **Job Growth:** ★★★ **Yearly Openings:** 👤👤👤👤👤

Locker Room, Coatroom, and Dressing Room Attendants. Provide personal items to patrons or customers in locker rooms, dressing rooms, or coatrooms. **Education and Training:** Short-term on-the-job training. **Skills:** Math—Medium. English—Medium. Science—Medium. **Yearly Earnings:** $ **Job Growth:** ★★★ **Yearly Openings:** 👤👤

Maids and Housekeeping Cleaners. Perform any combination of light cleaning duties to maintain private households or commercial establishments, such as hotels, restaurants, and hospitals, in a clean and orderly manner. Duties include making beds, replenishing linens, cleaning rooms and halls, and vacuuming. **Education and Training:** Short-term on-the-job training. **Skills:** Math—Low. English—Low. Science—Low. **Yearly Earnings:** $ **Job Growth:** ★★ **Yearly Openings:** 👤👤👤👤👤

OTHER PERSONAL SERVICES

These workers provide personal services to people who need a lot of attention: young children, people with chronic health problems, people in mourning, or very busy people. They provide such services as companionship, bathing and grooming, simple meal preparation, organizing the household, running errands, and basic emotional support.

Cleaners of Vehicles and Equipment. Wash or otherwise clean vehicles, machinery, and other equipment. Use such materials as water, cleaning agents, brushes, cloths, and hoses. **Education and Training:** Short-term on-the-job training. **Skills:** Math—Medium. English—Medium. Science—Medium. **Yearly Earnings:** $ **Job Growth:** ★★★ **Yearly Openings:** 👤👤👤👤

Cooks, Private Household. Prepare meals in private homes. **Education and Training:** Short-term on-the-job training. **Skills:** Math—Medium. English—Medium. Science—Medium. **Yearly Earnings:** No data available. **Job Growth:** ★ **Yearly Openings:** 👤

Embalmers. Prepare bodies for interment in conformity with legal requirements. **Education and Training:** Postsecondary career and technical education. **Skills:** Math—Low. English—Medium. Science—Medium. **Yearly Earnings:** $$$ **Job Growth:** ★ **Yearly Openings:** 🚹

Funeral Attendants. Perform variety of tasks during funeral, such as placing casket in parlor or chapel prior to service, arranging floral offerings or lights around casket, directing or escorting mourners, closing casket, and issuing and storing funeral equipment. **Education and Training:** Short-term on-the-job training. **Skills:** Math—Low. English—Medium. Science—Low. **Yearly Earnings:** $ **Job Growth:** ★★★ **Yearly Openings:** 🚹

Personal and Home Care Aides. Assist elderly or disabled adults with daily living activities at the person's home or in a daytime non-residential facility. Duties performed at a place of residence may include keeping house (making beds, doing laundry, washing dishes) and preparing meals. May provide meals and supervised activities at non-residential care facilities. May advise families, the elderly, and the disabled on such things as nutrition, cleanliness, and household utilities. **Education and Training:** Short-term on-the-job training. **Skills:** Math—Medium. English—Medium. Science—Medium. **Yearly Earnings:** $ **Job Growth:** ★★★★★ **Yearly Openings:** 🚹🚹🚹🚹

Exploring Careers:

Education and Social Service

Start Your Journey Through Careers Related to

EDUCATION AND SOCIAL SERVICE

Careers in this area suit people interested in teaching others or in improving their social, mental, emotional, or spiritual well-being.

EXPLORING CAREER CLUES

Your interests give important clues for exploring career options. Think about your interests to learn if jobs in the Education and Social Service interest area may be worth further exploration.

Do you like the school subjects related to the Education and Social Service interest area? Here are some examples of related subjects:

- English
- Composition and writing
- Speech
- Foreign language
- Math
- Science
- Biology
- History
- Social studies
- Sociology
- Psychology
- Philosophy
- Computers
- Family and consumer sciences
- Child development
- Health
- Religion

Do you like the free-time activities related to the Education and Social Service interest area? Here are some examples of related free-time activities:

- Helping friends and others with homework
- Reading
- Writing
- Baby-sitting or caring for children
- Teaching siblings and small children how to play games, read, and learn new things
- Teaching, tutoring, or coaching others
- Collecting clothes, food, and supplies for needy people

- Volunteering at church, at school, the library, a hospital, a nursing home, or a retirement home
- Helping sick friends and neighbors
- Listening to friends and helping them with their problems
- Helping to organize or run school or community events
- Planning parties and outings
- Collecting and organizing books, CDs, and DVDs
- Researching topics that interest you

EXPLORING JOB GROUPS

Jobs related to the Education and Social Service interest area fit into three groups. Read through the list to see which groups sound interesting to you.

- Managerial Work in Education and Social Service
- Social Services
- Educational Services

EXPLORING CAREER POSSIBILITIES

You can satisfy your interest in the Education and Social Service area through jobs that help people learn about the world and improve their lives. Here are a few examples of career possibilities:

You may wish to teach students who may be preschoolers, retirees, or any age in between.

If you are interested in helping people sort out their complicated lives or solve personal problems, you may find fulfillment as a counselor, social worker, or religious worker.

Working in a library or museum may give you an opportunity to expand people's understanding of the world.

Turn the page to meet people working in the Education and Social Service interest area→

PROFILE

Jillian Winitsky—Curator

Jillian turned the corner, the stones from the road flying as her car sped by. She was on her way to a country antique show and wanted to get there before dark.

Jillian Winitsky is the curator of engineering at the Wood Museum. "I consider myself lucky to be working at a large museum such as the Wood, where I can concentrate on engineering history, my area of expertise," Jillian said. Most curators at the Wood Museum specialize in subjects like agriculture; textiles; mining; atomic energy; or political, cultural, or military history.

Acquiring Pieces

Jillian didn't count on finding anything at the show. She had gone to a number of antique shows in the five years she had worked at the Wood Museum, but she rarely found anything worth acquiring. Generally the museum relies on gifts of historical objects and of the money to purchase them.

She moved through the exhibit area, carefully noting each object on display.

Jillian walked into the hall where the antiques were. She moved through the exhibit area, carefully noting each object on display. An old rotary printing press in the center of the room stopped her in her tracks. The black metal press was somewhat worn and had a few cracks. Otherwise, it was in fair condition.

The museum had several other presses in its collection, but Jillian was excited about this one. It was about seventy years old. Jillian quickly found the manager of the antique show.

"I'm Jillian Winitsky, curator of engineering at the Wood Museum," she said. "I'd like to acquire that old printing press for the museum. Can you put me in touch with the owner?"

"Mrs. Cortland owns the press," the man replied. "You could probably reach her tomorrow." He handed Jillian a business card.

Jillian called Mrs. Cortland the next morning. She explained her interest in the press and suggested that they get together to talk more. Mrs. Cortland reluctantly agreed. She made it clear that she wanted to sell the press.

They met for lunch the following day. Jillian gave Mrs. Cortland a tour of the engineering section and gave her a brief but lively history of the printing press. She explained the historical significance of the press. Mrs. Cortland's resistance began to fade. After several more conversations, she agreed to donate the press to the museum.

Now, every time Jillian walks through the exhibit on printing technology, she remembers the antique show and the conversations with Mrs. Cortland.

A History of Involvement

"I grew up in the oldest house in the county and have been interested in history since I was young," Jillian said. Genealogy in particular fascinated her. She spent hours poring over records of her family's history in the county courthouse.

Jillian grew up in the oldest house in her county and had been interested in history since she was young.

Jillian hadn't planned to become a museum curator. Her background suits her well for the job, though. She finished college with a double major in history and engineering. She also has a master's degree in history. Curator jobs are few and far between, Jillian knows. She feels lucky to have a job that she likes so much. She realizes, too, that she'd probably need a Ph.D. to be hired at the Wood Museum today.

The Daily Details of Research

Jillian spends much of her workday dealing with letters, e-mails, and phone calls. One recent letter began, "I am writing a book, and I need photographs of several kinds of tunnels. Can you supply them?" Jillian usually can help with this kind of request. She checks the museum's photograph file and selects photos to fit the author's needs.

Two days ago, she got a letter from the director of a historic preservation society. The society plans to restore an old grist mill and wanted advice from Jillian. "I particularly enjoy restoration work, and I've had experience with grist mills," Jillian said. "I'd like to do this project, but the mill is three hours away."

She checks the museum's photograph file and selects photos to fit the author's needs.

Jillian referred the society to some books on the subject. She also gave them the names of other authorities who might be willing to help.

Today's paperwork taken care of, Jillian turns to the exhibit on industry in nineteenth-century America. "I've been working on it for nearly a year," Jillian said. "The exhibit will open next summer. It will include early industrial machinery, hand tools, company records, and other items."

Putting together an exhibit is a big job that involves a lot of detail. Jillian has acquired items from hundreds of sources: other museums, historical societies, archives, private collectors, antique dealers, and manufacturing firms.

"Much of my time has gone toward searching for historically significant items and negotiating with the owners for their acquisition," Jillian explained. "Documenting every item has been tedious and time-consuming. Now I'm preparing a catalog to be published when the exhibit opens."

Putting together an exhibit is a big job that involves a lot of detail.

Educating the Public

As a curator, Jillian educates and informs the public. She contributes articles to *Wood Light,* a newsletter for members of the museum. From time to time, she conducts special tours for dignitaries, reporters, students, and other groups. Normally, museum tours are conducted by volunteer guides. Jillian and other curators help train the volunteers. Last week, Jillian gave a talk at the museum on the history of textile manufacturing in New England.

"Doing research and keeping up with developments in the profession are important parts of my job. Last year, I devoted a lot of my free time to research on textile mill restoration," Jillian said. She presented a paper on the subject at the annual meeting of state historians.

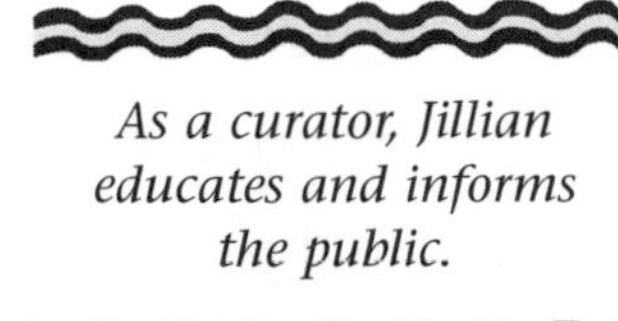

As a curator, Jillian educates and informs the public.

Jillian enjoys her work. She loves seeing people become totally absorbed in one of her exhibits. Jillian is proud, too, of being able to maintain and restore historic structures. Nevertheless, she feels pressure when she faces deadlines for opening an exhibit, completing a research report, or making a speech. The job has built-in frustrations, too. Recently, for example, she lost a chance to buy a very old drill press because the museum didn't have the funds.

"My job demands a commitment," she said. "I am expected to complete original research projects that require night and weekend work."

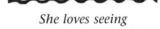

She loves seeing people become totally absorbed in one of her exhibits.

She must be "constructively aggressive" in looking for objects of historic value. She often attends auctions and flea markets in this never-ending search. Even while she's on vacation, Jillian investigates leads for new exhibit items. She knows that casual conversations can lead to major acquisitions.

"Because I find my job so interesting, I don't mind giving so much of my time to it. As a curator, I'm doing something that I want to do."

PROFILE

Judy Metzger—Librarian

"You may be surprised, but a librarian doesn't sit behind a desk all day speaking in hushed tones," Judy Metzger laughed.

Judy has been the head librarian at a public library for five years. "Some of us get out and do important things in the community–even around the world."

So Much for Stereotypes

Judy recently returned from a year in China teaching library techniques. She went at the invitation of a Chinese university, where they had learned of her ability to speak Chinese.

"I do a lot of public speaking," Judy said. "I talk about how to use the library, what new items we have, and what events we're planning.

"Many librarians write articles for local publications to promote their libraries. It informs the public of what goes on inside their library and helps raise funds.

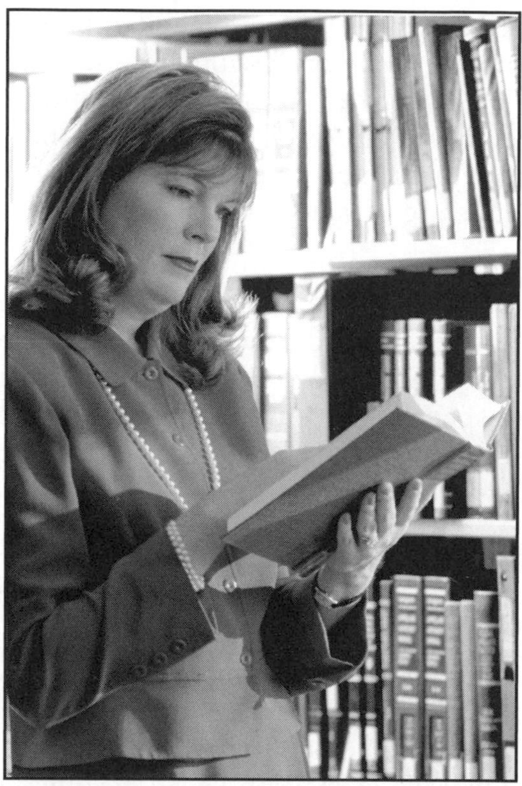

Judy has always loved books and reading.

"My day begins with management tasks and paperwork. Part of my day involves helping patrons with questions and checking out materials. In a large library, those tasks would be handled by a reference librarian and a circulation librarian.

"Most days, I work on preparing for the monthly board meeting, writing up a grant proposal, or preparing a presentation.

"I meet with my staff once a month to go over items brought up at the board meeting. These topics could be anything from changes in policy to budget issues."

How Do You Choose?

"It's important for me to have good communication with the patrons, too. Large libraries have librarians who do the book ordering. But here, I do it. I find out what patrons are reading and what they'd like to see at the library.

"When I order materials, I make an effort not to buy books just because they interest me. I consider bestseller lists, reviews, and patron comments.

"When I order materials, I make an effort not to buy books just because they interest me. I consider bestseller lists, reviews, and patron comments."

"I try to spread our limited funding into many areas–children's books, mysteries, nonfiction, reference materials, and so on. With magazines, it's the same story.

"We have to stay inside our budget. Some patrons believe we just don't *want* to carry a book or magazine they like. But it's usually because we have limited funds and space."

Hitting the Books

Judy earned her bachelor's degree and then obtained a master's degree in library science (MLS). She completed her graduate work in a one-year program. Some MLS programs, however, take two years.

"My bachelor's degree is in liberal arts, but there are many acceptable majors," said Judy. "Most good librarians I know have a broad range of interests."

Most librarians belong to the American Library Association (ALA) or a state association. The ALA hosts events such as conventions and workshops. The ALA offers seminars on cataloging, technology, personnel problems, and dealing with one's board of trustees or school board.

A Sticky Situation

"Occasionally, dealing with the public has taken creativity and a sense of humor," Judy related. "A few years ago, a retired professor made a large donation of books. We thanked him, of course.

"However, the books were outdated and in bad condition. With our limited space, we couldn't use them. So one morning I quietly tossed them out. Guess who walked in that afternoon, asking to see the display of his gift.

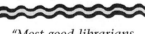

"Most good librarians have a broad range of interests."

"While one of my staff explained that his books hadn't been put out yet but were being kept in boxes, I ran out back and pawed through the big trash bin. I reboxed the books to show the gentleman. We kept them for a few years after that, but eventually those books paid another visit to the trash."

Libraries—They're Not Just for Books Any More

"Technology is changing the function and look of libraries," Judy said. "Microfilm and microfiche have been around for years. And most libraries, including ours, offer audiotapes, videotapes, and DVDs.

"Computers have had a huge impact. Books like encyclopedias are now available on CD. Most librarians must be able to use word-processing and database programs for research. Computers are also used for sharing information between libraries.

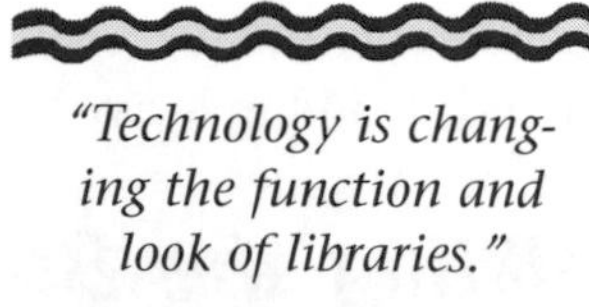
"Technology is changing the function and look of libraries."

"Home computer systems already are able, through the Internet, to gain access to information that previously was available only through books and library archives. Libraries are using computers in their operations, making them available on site for patrons. We also offer some books in electronic form—called *e-books.*

"Some people have never used computers or are anxious around them. Librarians help patrons learn to use computers.

"Still, several people have told me they hope we'll never get rid of the old, familiar card catalog system. Most libraries have done away with it in favor of the computerized version. I know that, eventually, we will too.

"Similarly, many people like having an actual text or magazine in their hands, rather than a CD or an e-book. For them, trying to read something on the computer monitor isn't the same. I understand their feelings.

"But there are important aspects of library science that most people don't think about. For example, paper doesn't last forever. We must preserve written treasures before they turn to dust. What good are books that can't be read?

"Electronic storage lets us preserve their content. What a tragedy it would be if the ideas, history, beauty, and wisdom from generations of authors should be lost."

Into the Future

Judy says that competition among librarians for jobs is tough. She points out that there are several options, however, for a librarian to pursue.

Besides university libraries and public libraries like hers, there are school libraries and corporate ones, such as those in law offices and hospitals.

"To someone considering the profession, I suggest earning a graduate degree. Keep up-to-date on the latest books, technology, and research materials.

"And practice your people skills. Learn how to work with all types of people. I like helping people. It's satisfying to know I've helped someone solve a problem, get a good grade, or find a new job."

"It's very satisfying to know I've helped someone solve a problem, get a good grade, or find a new job."

About the changes that technology is bringing, Judy is more excited than worried. "I think the new generation will be so comfortable with technology that they will push for more changes. After all, they're learning to use computers in grade school now.

"Complete home computer access to library holdings will probably occur at some point. But the function of the librarian will no doubt evolve along with these advances. I think it will be quite exciting."

PROFILE

Katie Hiebert—School Counselor

Students are waiting for Katie Hiebert when she arrives at her office at 7:30 every morning. "I have a full day scheduled even before it begins," laughed Katie. "But I wouldn't want to be doing anything else.

"I have to wear a lot of different hats in this job," Katie said. "I have to be parent, friend, advisor, all rolled into one, and still satisfy the standards set by my school district."

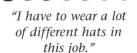

"I have to wear a lot of different hats in this job."

According to Katie, counselors are sometimes expected to fill in the gaps in a child's upbringing. It takes patience and a genuine affection for kids. They can spot a phony right away. In many ways, I treat kids like adults so I'm able to better earn their respect and trust.

"A major concern for me is that I'm required by law to report any signs of trouble, including depression or even a serious drop in grades. These can be indicators of problems, but it sometimes makes me feel like a cop. Kids often view this as breaking a confidence.

Katie enjoys listening to students and helping them solve their problems.

"What it also means, of course, is that counselors are on the leading edge, able to stop problems before they become too serious. This is important and works to the advantage of the kids. But you have to walk a fine line between doing a good job as defined by the teaching community and really being able to help the kids because you've earned their trust."

Becoming a Counselor

"I decided to be a high school counselor when I was a sophomore in high school. I was having problems with my grades and needed to talk with someone about improving them. I was assigned to a counselor whose interest in me was zero. I'd have had more response talking to the wall.

"I made up my mind right then to become a counselor," she said. "I had a real drive, so in college I took courses to get my degree in education and then went on to get my master's degree. Then I taught high school for a couple of years, which is an essential experience to being effective as a counselor."

The educational requirements for a counseling career vary by geographic area. For example, in many states a bachelor's degree in education is considered basic and a master's degree and state certification are essential.

"I taught high school for a couple of years, which is an essential experience to being effective as a counselor."

"A counselor who wants to pursue a different direction and is willing to take additional training can move into administrative positions with more responsibilities and perhaps better income. But it usually means longer hours, less time with your family, and being more distant from students. That personal contact is something I would miss very much."

Students researching the field should look up such job titles as educational, vocational, and school counselor; guidance counselor; educational adviser; and curriculum counselor.

Reality Check

"The paperwork for the job is overwhelming at times, and the deadlines can be stressful," Katie said. "This reduces the time we have for the kids. Things like scheduling, making out reports, reviewing courses, checking test results, correspondence with colleges and parents–it's important but takes you away from what you were trained to do. Still, it all has to be done.

"There are problem kids and sad cases," Katie said. "I do the best I can. And many of these kids have a hard time discussing their troubles.

"However, the toughest cases are also the rarest ones. Most of the time, I'm helping kids make little adjustments, like getting caught up on missing homework assignments or preparing the application for a scholarship.

"It's very satisfying for a counselor to help kids who want to succeed and work at it," Katie commented. "They provide us with about ninety-five percent of our bragging rights and only five percent of our counseling problems."

"It's very satisfying for a counselor to help kids who want to succeed and work at it."

A Counselor's Rewards

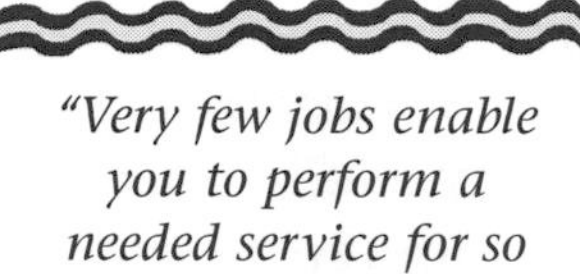

"Very few jobs enable you to perform a needed service for so many people."

Creative and communication skills are far more valuable to a counselor than mechanical skills. Some familiarity with a computer is required, but operations are usually limited to accessing records and schedules and knowing your way around word processing.

"Of course, there's room for improvement in high school counseling," she said. "But where else can I find a career that offers the opportunity to help young people?

"I have a stable vocation in an unstable society, no production pressures, and no day-to-day stresses that I can't handle. Very few jobs enable you to perform a needed service for so many people–a service that could change the rest of their lives."

PROFILE

Sidney Morrison—Special Education Teacher

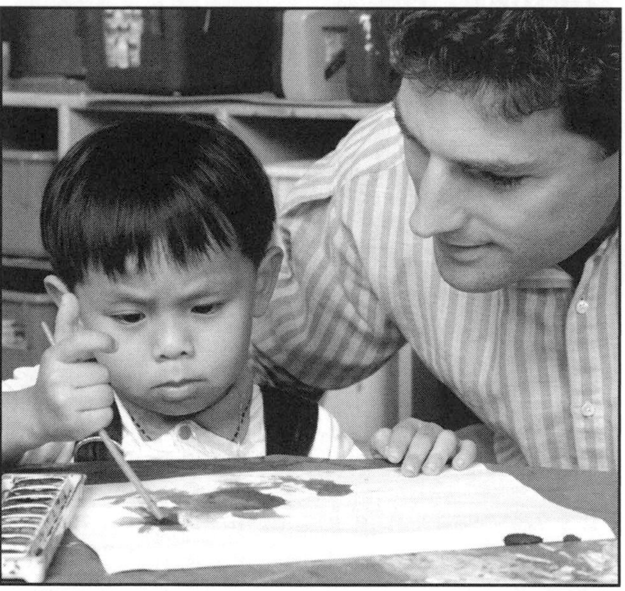

Sidney works one-on-one with his young students.

Sidney Morrison works one-on-one with students in his special education resource classroom. He has just finished helping a second-grade boy. "With these students, I determine their specific strengths. I identify their weaknesses and find ways to compensate for them."

"I have one child, Tony, who is overactive. He fidgets, bounces, taps, and roams constantly. Unless I sit beside him and give him individual

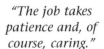

attention, his interest wanes. Tony's distractions don't materialize when he's with just one other person. They become more evident when he's in a group.

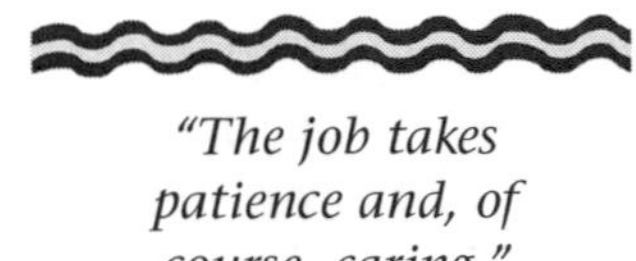

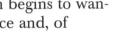

"The job takes patience and, of course, caring."

"I'm here to help kids overcome their problems or disabilities. We meet for a half hour one-on-one. I work these students hard. They don't have time to misbehave!

"While sitting next to Tony, I can sense when his attention begins to wander and I know I need to change direction. It takes patience and, of course, caring."

Getting Students on Track

Part of Sidney's job is to evaluate how the children are doing in both his special classroom and in the regular class. Sidney confers with the other teachers and writes evaluation reports.

"I believe we need to see more emphasis on human values in our schools. I try to teach respect for the person. If they learn anything, they learn that.

"We discuss feelings and manners. When they feel better about themselves, the rest often falls into place. All the book learning in the world can't replace heart. I show the kids I care. I'm interested and I believe in them.

"They are amazed at all the things they're able to do for themselves as I break down problems into small tasks and work on a step at a time. Goals are set so they can see them and almost touch them.

"In my evaluations, I may see that they've made enough improvement to no longer need the program," he said.

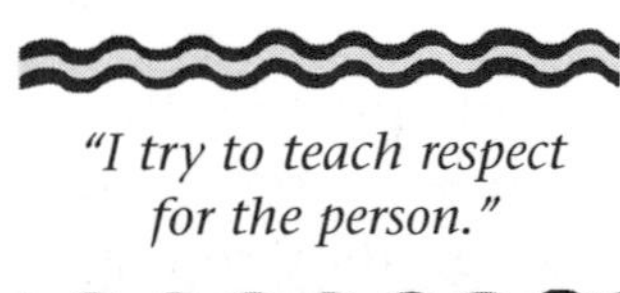

"I try to teach respect for the person."

More than Just Academics

Sidney continued, "A special education teacher is going to have to handle his or her share of tantrums. However, the temper tantrum doesn't work in my classroom. In some cases, I may be the first person the child has met who won't be budged by this tactic.

"As soon as they take that first deep breath, I tell them, 'That may work at home, but it won't work here with me. And we have a whole school year together.'

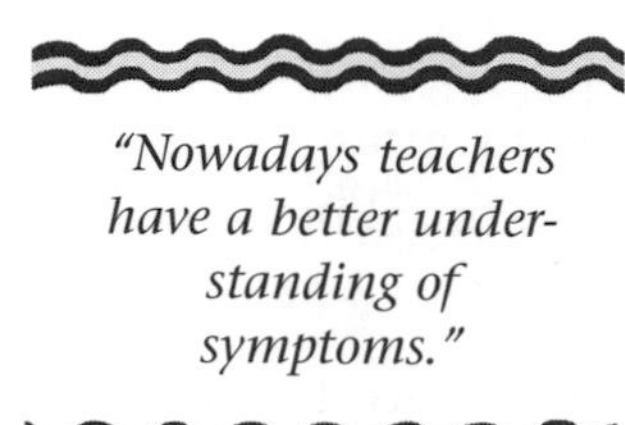
"Nowadays teachers have a better understanding of symptoms."

"Some tell me they don't like me. I hear them out, but I'm always in charge. They need to see an adult manage them without losing ground."

Working with Parents

Parent-teacher conferences are Sidney's show-and-tell time. Based on these oral report cards, he may decide to modify a child's educational program.

"Occasionally a parent realizes that he or she once had the same problem but it was never diagnosed as a learning disability. Some were told they were lazy or stupid.

"Nowadays teachers have a better understanding of the symptoms. It can lift a sense of failure off of the parents' backs. They can accept their child's condition, and progress can be made."

Understanding Individual Needs

If children can't read, Sidney tests them. "Test results can be misleading. Some children don't do well on tests but function well in class. Other children test well but don't finish assignments. These children often have a high IQ but perform below grade level," he said.

"Some people don't realize that children with learning disabilities have difficulty even though they're really trying."

"Some people don't realize or accept that children with learning disabilities have difficulty even though they're really trying."

Part of Sidney's job is to plan how to integrate a child into regular classes. Sidney tries to see that his students get a classroom teacher who understands their needs. He plans and conducts in-service training on how to help his students.

"Students can come to me individually and work on the areas that stump them. I can even enter their class and assist them while they work," Sidney said.

"Behavior disorders can overlap into learning disorders," continued Sidney. In the behavior disorders classroom, the children are rewarded with points for every fifteen minutes they are 'on task,' meaning sitting and working. Once they accumulate enough points, they get a treat like a pizza party.

"When they no longer need these periods of control, they're ready to go back into regular classes."

A Unique Field with Many Rewards

"Laws require schools to make special education available to meet not only the education needs but also the social, emotional, and vocational needs of kids with disabilities.

"The last government report I saw said that there is a shortage of teachers qualified in this specialized field. As long as that remains true, these kinds of jobs should be easier to find and keep."

Sidney went on to point out that the needs these kids have vary. "Every child is unique. They each have different learning styles, different personalities, different talents and abilities. Some have mental disabilities. Some have physical disabilities. Some have sensory problems, like hearing and vision. Some have health problems.

"You can see why a teacher has to have special training, a lot of patience, and a lot of heart to successfully develop each child's unique skills. We have to try to make these kids self-sufficient, contributing members of society. Sometimes we just can't. But often we do, and those successes are what make this profession so very worthwhile.

"Every child is unique. They each have different learning styles, different personalities, different talents and abilities."

"Even though I later specialized in learning disability teaching, I became a regular teacher first," Sidney said. "You need a bachelor's degree as well as a teaching license to teach, and some states require a master's degree. You do student teaching as part of your degree," Sidney said.

"There's nothing like the joy of recognizing when an awakening, a new thought, turns on in these kids' minds like a light. That's when learning disability teaching is so worthwhile."

SKILL SAMPLER

William Spencer—Clergy

In high school, William Spencer became interested in social issues. He turned his concern into social action and soon knew he had a calling. After college, he completed his seminary degree. He is now serving at St. Andrew's Catholic Church. "The ministry offers me a meaningful way to invest my life. I have an opportunity to reach many people."

Father Spencer talked about the skills that are important for clergy to have. He offers the following tips to guide you in considering whether you might want to enter the clergy.

Clergy must have a compelling sense that their life's work is to serve God and work for the betterment of humanity.

- Do you feel strongly about your faith and your religion?
- Are you active in your church?
- Are you interested in and concerned about problems in your community and in the world?
- Are you moved to action by problems such as poverty, hunger, poor housing, unemployment, injustice, and illiteracy in your own community?

Clergy must set an example of high moral and ethical conduct.

- Do questions and discussions about right and wrong interest you?
- Can you hold firmly to what you believe is right even when your friends don't agree?
- Do you treat others as you wish to be treated?
- Are you comfortable with the idea of people looking to you as an example?

- Would you mind having the public watching everything you do?
- Do you take your responsibilities seriously when you are elected to the student council, chosen to be yearbook or newspaper editor, or asked to chair a church or school club?

Clergy must be approachable and warm. Personal counseling is one of their prime responsibilities.

- Can you make a friend feel better about a problem such as failing a test or being turned down for a date?
- Do people come to you for advice?
- Are you able to keep a secret?
- Are your friends able to talk to you about whatever is on their minds?
- Are you able to put houseguests at ease?
- Are you able to talk to people you have just met?

Clergy must have the ability to inspire others.

- Have you ever changed a friend's viewpoint?
- Can you argue your point persuasively?
- Do your friends ask your opinion on things?
- Do you enjoy researching on the Internet or reading books about various theological and social issues?
- Are you able to get your way without seeming bossy?
- Do you sometimes praise a child when he or she behaves well, does a lesson correctly, or masters a skill?
- Are you comfortable praising adults sincerely?
- Can you help people help themselves?

Clergy must be able to command the attention of a group.

- Are you good at making class presentations?
- Is it easy for you to "get the floor" at club meetings or parties?
- Do your friends ever ask you to be the group spokesperson at going-away parties, victory celebrations, or birthday parties?

Clergy must be able to regulate their own reactions to the crises in people's lives.

- Can you remain calm when a friend or relative faces a serious problem?
- Can you remain calm when one of your parents is upset?
- Can you think and act quickly in a crisis situation?
- Does it upset you to visit people who are very sick?
- Can you comfort a friend or family member during a time of sorrow?
- Can you overcome your anger and keep from holding a grudge when someone hurts you?
- Can you maintain some sense of proportion about school rivalries?

Clergy must perform ceremonies and conform to traditional rituals.

- Do you enjoy initiation or recognition ceremonies?
- Do you think ceremonies such as confirmation, marriage, and graduation are important?

Clergy must be creative in communicating their ideas.

- Are you good at writing compositions or short stories?
- Can you write an interesting letter or e-mail to a friend?
- Do you like thinking of ways to interest children in their school work, in crafts or sports, or in Bible verses?

SKILL SAMPLER

Glenn Troutman—Farm Extension Agent

Glenn Troutman grew up on a dairy farm and was active in 4-H while he was in high school. He has a bachelor's degree in agriculture and five years of experience working for a farm supply company. He now works as a farm extension agent in the same area where he grew up. "I grew up on a farm, so it seemed natural to make agriculture my career."

Glenn described the skills farm extension agents need and offered the following tips to help you decide if this might be a good career for you.

Students interested in the field should research job titles such as agricultural extension agent and farm and home management advisor.

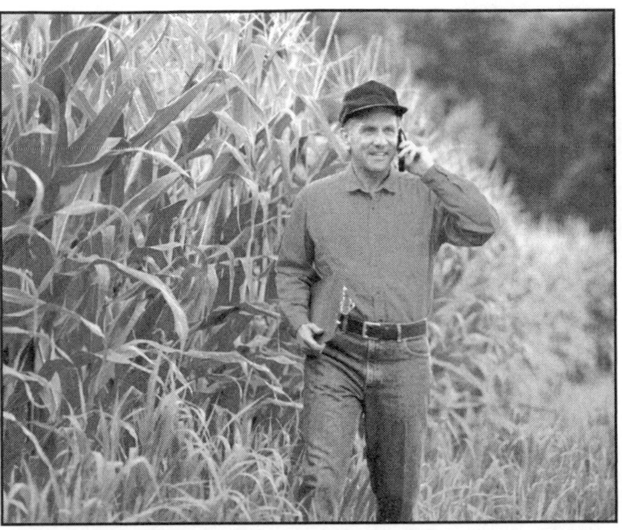

As a farm extension agent, Glenn helps farmers and keeps up with the industry.

Farm extension agents must be able to work with and gain the respect of other people.

- Do you listen to what your friends have to say?
- Do you enjoy participating in or leading group activities?
- Do you enjoy speaking in front of your class?
- Are you good at giving directions or organizing activities?
- Do people ever ask for your opinion?

Farm extension agents advise farmers on methods chosen from a wide variety of alternatives.

- Do you enjoy planning your time?
- When you have more than one option of what to do with your weekend, can you set priorities?
- Do you like considering social issues from various viewpoints?
- When buying clothes or other items, do you like to shop around for the best buy?

Farm extension agents must be able to express themselves well both orally and in writing.

- Do you keep a diary or journal?
- Do you write many letters or e-mails?
- Do you enjoy explaining things to people?
- Do you like writing themes in English class?

Farm extension agents must keep abreast of new developments in agricultural science and farming methods.

- Do you enjoy reading on your own?
- When you hear about something that interests you, do you enjoy learning more about the subject?
- Do you enjoy science classes?
- Have you ever done research on the Internet to find information about something that interests you?
- Are you interested in how things work?

Farm extension agents must provide help quickly and efficiently when farmers need it.

- Have you demonstrated to the people in your church, school, and clubs that they can depend on you?
- Do you get to class on time every day?
- Do you ever volunteer to help around the house?

SKILL SAMPLER

Mary Rodgers—Social Worker

Mary Rodgers is a social worker in one of the poorer sections of the city. She works in a senior center and finds places for elderly people to live when they have no home of their own. "I love spending my time talking to people, listening to their concerns, and helping them sort things out."

Mary shared several thoughts about what skills and knowledge a social worker needs. She gives the following tips for deciding if you should pursue a career in social work.

Mary helps senior citizens find housing and get government services.

Social workers must give people the confidence to deal with their problems. They must value the dignity and worth of the individual.

- Do you believe that you can learn something from everyone?
- Do you feel badly when a classmate is embarrassed?
- Do you think it's important that all people enjoy equal rights?
- Do you get personally involved in working against poverty, hunger, or hatred?
- Are you open-minded about other people's right to think, feel, and act in ways that may seem strange or wrong to you?
- Do you think people who are unhappy, mixed up, or in trouble can be helped?

Social workers must show their concern for people by being sympathetic yet objective.

- Are you able to see both sides of an argument?
- When something goes wrong, do you look for a solution instead of looking for someone to blame?

- Are you happy when good things happen to your friends?
- Are you concerned for the welfare of your friends and family?
- Do you like most people?
- Are you aware and considerate of the feelings of others?

Social workers must build a basis for trust.

- Are you able to maintain friendships over long periods of time?
- Do your friends confide in you and ask you for advice?
- Are you able to keep a secret?
- Do you make friends easily?
- When people visit you or your family, are you able to make them feel welcome?
- Are you able to put new students at ease?
- Can you work closely with others and be flexible enough to do things someone else's way?

Social workers must understand human behavior.

- Do you know your own strengths and weaknesses?
- Do you understand why you and your parents do the things you do?
- Do you know when to speak and when to listen?
- Are you able to feel what kind of mood a friend is in just by observing his or her facial and body expression or tone of voice?
- Do you judge people by their good points instead of by their faults?

Social workers must be able to speak the client's language. They must be good at communicating effectively in different situations.

- Can you talk to all kinds of people?
- Are you able to carry on a conversation with a child?
- Are you able to express your feelings to adults?
- Are you good at speaking in front of a group?
- Are you ever asked to be the spokesperson for a group?

Social workers must be able to express themselves clearly in the written record of their work.

- Are you good at organizing your thoughts for a school assignment or an essay question on an exam?
- Are you good at writing compositions, letters, or e-mails?

Social workers don't always see the results of their work immediately. Often they must remain supportive and helpful during times of slow progress.

- Do you appreciate small gains or progress?
- Do you have the patience to grow a garden?
- Do you have the patience to pursue projects such as learning a new computer software program?
- Are you able to stick with an exercise program?
- Can you be patient with people whose pace is slower than yours?
- Can you persist in the face of setbacks?
- Can you cope with failure?
- Are you realistic in your expectations even though you may be idealistic in your goals?

Now learn about all major jobs in the Education and Social Service interest area→

Facts About All Major Jobs Related to

EDUCATION AND SOCIAL SERVICE

In addition to the jobs covered in the profiles and skill samplers, other careers in the Education and Social Service interest area may appeal to you. This section describes and gives facts about all major jobs in the Education and Social Service interest area. For an explanation of the $, ★, and 🚹 symbols, see page 6.

MANAGERIAL WORK IN EDUCATION AND SOCIAL SERVICE

These workers are employed at colleges, school districts, corporations, parks, and social service agencies. They are responsible for planning, budgeting, evaluating results, and supervising workers. They need to balance their financial responsibilities against the educational and social service goals of their organizations and sometimes must make trade-offs. They enjoy helping people achieve their learning and social goals, but they are content to do so behind the scenes.

Education Administrators, Elementary and Secondary School. Plan, direct, or coordinate the academic, clerical, or auxiliary activities of public or private elementary or secondary level schools. **Education and Training:** College degree plus work experience. **Skills:** Math—Medium. English—High. Science—Medium. **Yearly Earnings:** $$$$$ **Job Growth:** ★★★ **Yearly Openings:** 🚹🚹🚹

Education Administrators, Postsecondary. Plan, direct, or coordinate research, instructional, student administration and services, and other educational activities at postsecondary institutions, including universities, colleges, and junior and community colleges. **Education and Training:** College degree plus work experience. **Skills:** Math—High. English—High. Science—Medium. **Yearly Earnings:** $$$$$ **Job Growth:** ★★★ **Yearly Openings:** 🚹🚹🚹

Education Administrators, Preschool and Child Care Center/Program. Plan, direct, or coordinate the academic and nonacademic activities of preschool and child care centers or programs. **Education and Training:** College degree plus work experience. **Skills:** Math—Medium. English—High. Science—Medium. **Yearly Earnings:** $$$$$ **Job Growth:** ★★★ **Yearly Openings:** 🚹🚹🚹

Instructional Coordinators. Develop instructional material, coordinate educational content, and incorporate current technology in specialized fields that provide guidelines to educators and instructors for developing curricula and conducting courses.

Education and Training: Master's degree. **Skills:** Math—Medium. English—High. Science—Medium. **Yearly Earnings:** $$$$ **Job Growth:** ★★★★ **Yearly Openings:** 🧍 🧍 🧍

Park Naturalists. Plan, develop, and conduct programs to inform public of historical, natural, and scientific features of national, state, or local park. **Education and Training:** Bachelor's degree. **Skills:** Math—Medium. English—Medium. Science—Medium. **Yearly Earnings:** $$$$ **Job Growth:** ★★ **Yearly Openings:** 🧍

Social and Community Service Managers. Plan, organize, or coordinate the activities of a social service program or community outreach organization. Oversee the program or organization's budget and policies regarding participant involvement, program requirements, and benefits. Work may involve directing social workers, counselors, or probation officers. **Education and Training:** Bachelor's degree. **Skills:** Math—Medium. English—Medium. Science—Medium. **Yearly Earnings:** $$$ **Job Growth:** ★★★★ **Yearly Openings:** 🧍 🧍 🧍

SOCIAL SERVICES

These workers help people deal with their problems and major life events. They may work on a person-to-person basis or with groups of people. Workers sometimes specialize in problems that are personal, social, vocational, physical, educational, or spiritual in nature. Schools, rehabilitation centers, mental health clinics, guidance centers, and religious institutions employ these workers. Jobs are also found in public and private welfare and employment services, juvenile courts, and vocational rehabilitation programs.

Child, Family, and School Social Workers. Provide social services and assistance to improve the social and psychological functioning of children and their families and to maximize the family well-being and the academic functioning of children. May assist single parents, arrange adoptions, and find foster homes for abandoned or abused children. In schools, they address such problems as teenage pregnancy, misbehavior, and truancy. May also advise teachers on how to deal with problem children. **Education and Training:** Bachelor's degree. **Skills:** Math—Medium. English—High. Science—Medium. **Yearly Earnings:** $$$ **Job Growth:** ★★★★ **Yearly Openings:** 🧍 🧍 🧍

Clergy. Conduct religious worship and perform other spiritual functions associated with beliefs and practices of religious faith or denomination. Provide spiritual and moral guidance and assistance to members. **Education and Training:** Professional degree. **Skills:** Math—Low. English—High. Science—Medium. **Yearly Earnings:** $$$ **Job Growth:** ★★★ **Yearly Openings:** 🧍 🧍 🧍

Clinical Psychologists. Diagnose or evaluate mental and emotional disorders of individuals through observation, interview, and psychological tests. Formulate and administer programs of treatment. **Education and Training:** Master's degree. **Skills:** Math—Medium. English—High. Science—Medium. **Yearly Earnings:** $$$$ **Job Growth:** ★★★ **Yearly Openings:** 🚹🚹🚹

Clinical, Counseling, and School Psychologists. Diagnose and treat mental disorders; learning disabilities; and cognitive, behavioral, and emotional problems using individual, child, family, and group therapies. May design and implement behavior modification programs. **Education and Training:** Master's degree. **Skills:** Math—Medium. English—Medium. Science—Medium. **Yearly Earnings:** $$$$ **Job Growth:** ★★★ **Yearly Openings:** 🚹🚹🚹

Counseling Psychologists. Assess and evaluate individuals' problems through the use of case history, interview, and observation and provide individual or group counseling services to assist individuals in achieving more effective personal, social, educational, and vocational development and adjustment. **Education and Training:** Master's degree. **Skills:** Math—Medium. English—High. Science—High. **Yearly Earnings:** $$$$ **Job Growth:** ★★★ **Yearly Openings:** 🚹🚹🚹

Directors, Religious Activities and Education. Direct and coordinate activities of a denominational group to meet religious needs of students. Plan, direct, or coordinate church school programs designed to promote religious education among church membership. May provide counseling and guidance relative to marital, health, financial, and religious problems. **Education and Training:** Bachelor's degree. **Skills:** Math—Medium. English—High. Science—Low. **Yearly Earnings:** $$ **Job Growth:** ★★★ **Yearly Openings:** 🚹🚹🚹

Marriage and Family Therapists. Diagnose and treat mental and emotional disorders, whether cognitive, affective, or behavioral, within the context of marriage and family systems. Apply psychotherapeutic and family systems theories and techniques in the delivery of professional services to individuals, couples, and families for the purpose of treating such diagnosed nervous and mental disorders. **Education and Training:** Master's degree. **Skills:** Math—Medium. English—Medium. Science—Medium. **Yearly Earnings:** $$$ **Job Growth:** ★★★★ **Yearly Openings:** 🚹

Medical and Public Health Social Workers. Provide persons, families, or vulnerable populations with the psychosocial support needed to cope with chronic, acute, or terminal illnesses, such as Alzheimer's, cancer, or AIDS. Services include advising family caregivers, providing patient education and counseling, and making necessary referrals for other social services. **Education and Training:** Bachelor's degree. **Skills:** Math—Medium. English—High. Science—Medium. **Yearly Earnings:** $$$ **Job Growth:** ★★★★ **Yearly Openings:** 🚹🚹🚹

Mental Health and Substance Abuse Social Workers. Assess and treat individuals with mental, emotional, or substance abuse problems, including abuse of alcohol, tobacco, and/or other drugs. Activities may include individual and group therapy, crisis intervention, case management, client advocacy, prevention, and education.

Education and Training: Master's degree. **Skills:** Math—Medium. English—High. Science—Medium. **Yearly Earnings:** $$$ **Job Growth:** ★★★★★ **Yearly Openings:** 👤👤

Mental Health Counselors. Counsel with emphasis on prevention. Work with individuals and groups to promote optimum mental health. May help individuals deal with addictions and substance abuse; family, parenting, and marital problems; suicide; stress management; problems with self-esteem; and issues associated with aging and mental and emotional health. **Education and Training:** Master's degree. **Skills:** Math—Medium. English—High. Science—Medium. **Yearly Earnings:** $$ **Job Growth:** ★★★★ **Yearly Openings:** 👤👤

Probation Officers and Correctional Treatment Specialists. Provide social services to assist in rehabilitation of law offenders in custody or on probation or parole. Make recommendations for actions involving formulation of rehabilitation plan and treatment of offender, including conditional release and education and employment stipulations. **Education and Training:** Bachelor's degree. **Skills:** Math—Medium. English—Medium. Science—Low. **Yearly Earnings:** $$$ **Job Growth:** ★★★★ **Yearly Openings:** 👤👤👤

Rehabilitation Counselors. Counsel individuals to maximize the independence and employability of persons coping with personal, social, and vocational difficulties that result from birth defects, illness, disease, accidents, or the stress of daily life. Coordinate activities for residents of care and treatment facilities. Assess client needs and design and implement rehabilitation programs that may include personal and vocational counseling, training, and job placement. **Education and Training:** Bachelor's degree. **Skills:** Math—Medium. English—Medium. Science—Medium. **Yearly Earnings:** $$ **Job Growth:** ★★★★ **Yearly Openings:** 👤👤👤

Residential Advisors. Coordinate activities for residents of boarding schools, college fraternities or sororities, college dormitories, or similar establishments. Order supplies and determine need for maintenance, repairs, and furnishings. May maintain household records and assign rooms. May refer residents to counseling resources if needed. **Education and Training:** Moderate-term on-the-job training. **Skills:** Math—Medium. English—Medium. Science—Low. **Yearly Earnings:** $$ **Job Growth:** ★★★★ **Yearly Openings:** 👤👤

Social and Human Service Assistants. Assist professionals from a wide variety of fields, such as psychology, rehabilitation, or social work, to provide client services as well as support for families. May assist clients in identifying available benefits and social and community services and help clients obtain them. May assist social workers with developing, organizing, and conducting programs to prevent and resolve problems relevant to substance abuse, human relationships, rehabilitation, or adult daycare. **Education and Training:** Moderate-term on-the-job training. **Skills:** Math—Medium. English—Medium. Science—Medium. **Yearly Earnings:** $$ **Job Growth:** ★★★★★ **Yearly Openings:** 👤👤👤

Substance Abuse and Behavioral Disorder Counselors. Counsel and advise individuals with alcohol, tobacco, drug, or other problems, such as gambling and eating disorders. May counsel individuals, families, or groups or engage in prevention programs. **Education and Training:** Master's degree. **Skills:** Math—Medium. English—High. Science—Medium. **Yearly Earnings:** $$ **Job Growth:** ★★★★ **Yearly Openings:** 🚶🚶

EDUCATIONAL SERVICES

These workers do general and specialized teaching, vocational training, and advising about education, career planning, or finances. Some provide library and museum services. Jobs are found in schools, colleges, libraries, and museums. ***Note:*** *The job growth for all jobs with "postsecondary" in their titles has been combined into one total. The yearly openings for all jobs with "postsecondary" in their titles have been combined into one total.*

Adult Literacy, Remedial Education, and GED Teachers and Instructors. Teach or instruct out-of-school youths and adults in remedial education classes, preparatory classes for the General Educational Development test, literacy, or English as a Second Language. Teaching may or may not take place in a traditional educational institution. **Education and Training:** Bachelor's degree. **Skills:** Math—Medium. English—High. Science—Medium. **Yearly Earnings:** $$$ **Job Growth:** ★★★ **Yearly Openings:** 🚶🚶🚶

Agricultural Sciences Teachers, Postsecondary. Teach courses in the agricultural sciences. Includes teachers of agronomy, dairy sciences, fisheries management, horticultural sciences, poultry sciences, range management, and agricultural soil conservation. **Education and Training:** Master's degree. **Skills:** Math—High. English—High. Science—High. **Yearly Earnings:** $$$$ **Job Growth:** ★★★★ **Yearly Openings:** 🚶🚶🚶🚶🚶

Anthropology and Archeology Teachers, Postsecondary. Teach courses in anthropology or archeology. **Education and Training:** Master's degree. **Skills:** Math—High. English—High. Science—High. **Yearly Earnings:** $$$$ **Job Growth:** ★★★★ **Yearly Openings:** 🚶🚶🚶🚶🚶

Architecture Teachers, Postsecondary. Teach courses in architecture and architectural design, such as architectural environmental design, interior architecture/design, and landscape architecture. **Education and Training:** Master's degree. **Skills:** Math—Medium. English—Medium. Science—Medium. **Yearly Earnings:** $$$$ **Job Growth:** ★★★★ **Yearly Openings:** 🚶🚶🚶🚶🚶

Archivists. Appraise, edit, and direct safekeeping of permanent records and historically valuable documents. Participate in research activities based on archival materials. **Education and Training:** Master's degree. **Skills:** Math—Medium. English—High. Science—Medium. **Yearly Earnings:** $$$ **Job Growth:** ★★★ **Yearly Openings:** 🚶

Area, Ethnic, and Cultural Studies Teachers, Postsecondary. Teach courses pertaining to the culture and development of an area (for example, Latin America), an ethnic group, or any other group (for example, women's studies, urban affairs). **Education and Training:** Master's degree. **Skills:** Math—High. English—High. Science—High. **Yearly Earnings:** $$$$ **Job Growth:** ★★★★ **Yearly Openings:** 🧍🧍🧍🧍🧍

Art, Drama, and Music Teachers, Postsecondary. Teach courses in drama, music, and the arts, including fine and applied art, such as painting and sculpture, or design and crafts. **Education and Training:** Master's degree. **Skills:** Math—Medium. English—High. Science—Medium. **Yearly Earnings:** $$$$ **Job Growth:** ★★★★ **Yearly Openings:** 🧍🧍🧍🧍🧍

Atmospheric, Earth, Marine, and Space Sciences Teachers, Postsecondary. Teach courses in the physical sciences, except chemistry and physics. **Education and Training:** Master's degree. **Skills:** Math—Medium. English—Medium. Science—Medium. **Yearly Earnings:** $$$$ **Job Growth:** ★★★★ **Yearly Openings:** 🧍🧍🧍🧍🧍

Audio-Visual Collections Specialists. Prepare, plan, and operate audio-visual teaching aids for use in education. May record, catalogue, and file audio-visual materials. **Education and Training:** Moderate-term on-the-job training. **Skills:** Math—Medium. English—High. Science—Medium. **Yearly Earnings:** $$$ **Job Growth:** ★★★ **Yearly Openings:** 🧍

Biological Science Teachers, Postsecondary. Teach courses in biological sciences. **Education and Training:** Master's degree. **Skills:** Math—High. English—High. Science—High. **Yearly Earnings:** $$$$ **Job Growth:** ★★★★ **Yearly Openings:** 🧍🧍🧍🧍🧍

Business Teachers, Postsecondary. Teach courses in business administration and management, such as accounting, finance, human resources, labor relations, marketing, and operations research. **Education and Training:** Master's degree. **Skills:** Math—Medium. English—Medium. Science—Medium. **Yearly Earnings:** $$$$ **Job Growth:** ★★★★ **Yearly Openings:** 🧍🧍🧍🧍🧍

Chemistry Teachers, Postsecondary. Teach courses pertaining to the chemical and physical properties and compositional changes of substances. Work may include instruction in the methods of qualitative and quantitative chemical analysis. Includes both teachers primarily engaged in teaching and those who do a combination of teaching and research. **Education and Training:** Master's degree. **Skills:** Math—High. English—High. Science—High. **Yearly Earnings:** $$$$ **Job Growth:** ★★★★ **Yearly Openings:** 🧍🧍🧍🧍🧍

Child Care Workers. Attend to children at schools, businesses, private households, and child care institutions. Perform a variety of tasks, such as dressing, feeding, bathing, and overseeing play. **Education and Training:** Short-term on-the-job training.

Skills: Math—Low. English—Medium. Science—Medium. **Yearly Earnings:** $ **Job Growth:** ★★★ **Yearly Openings:** 🧍🧍🧍🧍🧍

Communications Teachers, Postsecondary. Teach courses in communications, such as organizational communications, public relations, radio/television broadcasting, and journalism. **Education and Training:** Master's degree. **Skills:** Math—Medium. English—Medium. Science—Medium. **Yearly Earnings:** $$$$ **Job Growth:** ★★★★ **Yearly Openings:** 🧍🧍🧍🧍🧍

Computer Science Teachers, Postsecondary. Teach courses in computer science. May specialize in a field of computer science, such as the design and function of computers or operations and research analysis. **Education and Training:** Master's degree. **Skills:** Math—High. English—High. Science—High. **Yearly Earnings:** $$$$ **Job Growth:** ★★★★ **Yearly Openings:** 🧍🧍🧍🧍🧍

Criminal Justice and Law Enforcement Teachers, Postsecondary. Teach courses in criminal justice, corrections, and law enforcement administration. **Education and Training:** Master's degree. **Skills:** Math—Medium. English—Medium. Science—Medium. **Yearly Earnings:** $$$$ **Job Growth:** ★★★★ **Yearly Openings:** 🧍🧍🧍🧍🧍

Curators. Administer affairs of museum and conduct research programs. Direct instructional, research, and public service activities of institution. **Education and Training:** Master's degree. **Skills:** Math—Medium. English—High. Science—Medium. **Yearly Earnings:** $$$ **Job Growth:** ★★★ **Yearly Openings:** 🧍

Economics Teachers, Postsecondary. Teach courses in economics. **Education and Training:** Master's degree. **Skills:** Math—High. English—High. Science—High. **Yearly Earnings:** $$$$ **Job Growth:** ★★★★ **Yearly Openings:** 🧍🧍🧍🧍🧍

Education Teachers, Postsecondary. Teach courses pertaining to education, such as counseling, curriculum, guidance, instruction, teacher education, and teaching English as a second language. **Education and Training:** Master's degree. **Skills:** Math—Medium. English—Medium. Science—Medium. **Yearly Earnings:** $$$$ **Job Growth:** ★★★★ **Yearly Openings:** 🧍🧍🧍🧍🧍

Educational Psychologists. Investigate processes of learning and teaching and develop psychological principles and techniques applicable to educational problems. **Education and Training:** Master's degree. **Skills:** Math—High. English—High. Science—High. **Yearly Earnings:** $$$$ **Job Growth:** ★★★ **Yearly Openings:** 🧍🧍🧍

Educational, Vocational, and School Counselors. Counsel individuals and provide group educational and vocational guidance services. **Education and Training:** Master's degree. **Skills:** Math—Medium. English—High. Science—Medium. **Yearly Earnings:** $$$$ **Job Growth:** ★★★★ **Yearly Openings:** 🧍🧍🧍

Elementary School Teachers, Except Special Education. Teach pupils in public or private schools basic academic, social, and other formative skills at the elementary level. **Education and Training:** Bachelor's degree. **Skills:** Math—Medium. English—Medium. Science—Medium. **Yearly Earnings:** $$$ **Job Growth:** ★★★ **Yearly Openings:** 🚶🚶🚶🚶🚶

Engineering Teachers, Postsecondary. Teach courses pertaining to the application of physical laws and principles of engineering for the development of machines, materials, instruments, processes, and services. Includes teachers of subjects such as chemical, civil, electrical, industrial, mechanical, mineral, and petroleum engineering. Includes both teachers primarily engaged in teaching and those who do a combination of teaching and research. **Education and Training:** Master's degree. **Skills:** Math—High. English—High. Science—High. **Yearly Earnings:** $$$$ **Job Growth:** ★★★★ **Yearly Openings:** 🚶🚶🚶🚶🚶

English Language and Literature Teachers, Postsecondary. Teach courses in English language and literature, including linguistics and comparative literature. **Education and Training:** Master's degree. **Skills:** Math—Medium. English—High. Science—Medium. **Yearly Earnings:** $$$$ **Job Growth:** ★★★★ **Yearly Openings:** 🚶🚶🚶🚶🚶

Environmental Science Teachers, Postsecondary. Teach courses in environmental science. **Education and Training:** Master's degree. **Skills:** Math—Medium. English—Medium. Science—Medium. **Yearly Earnings:** $$$$ **Job Growth:** ★★★★ **Yearly Openings:** 🚶🚶🚶🚶🚶

Farm and Home Management Advisors. Advise, instruct, and assist individuals and families engaged in agriculture, agricultural-related processes, or home economics activities. Demonstrate procedures and apply research findings to solve problems. Instruct and train in product development, sales, and the utilization of machinery and equipment to promote general welfare. Includes county agricultural agents, feed and farm management advisers, home economists, and extension service advisors. **Education and Training:** Bachelor's degree. **Skills:** Math—Medium. English—High. Science—Medium. **Yearly Earnings:** $$$ **Job Growth:** ★★ **Yearly Openings:** 🚶

Foreign Language and Literature Teachers, Postsecondary. Teach courses in foreign (other than English) languages and literature. **Education and Training:** Master's degree. **Skills:** Math—Medium. English—High. Science—Medium. **Yearly Earnings:** $$$$ **Job Growth:** ★★★★ **Yearly Openings:** 🚶🚶🚶🚶🚶

Forestry and Conservation Science Teachers, Postsecondary. Teach courses in environmental and conservation science. **Education and Training:** Master's degree. **Skills:** Math—High. English—High. Science—High. **Yearly Earnings:** $$$$ **Job Growth:** ★★★★ **Yearly Openings:** 🚶🚶🚶🚶🚶

Geography Teachers, Postsecondary. Teach courses in geography. **Education and Training:** Master's degree. **Skills:** Math—Medium. English—Medium. Science—Medium. **Yearly Earnings:** $$$$ **Job Growth:** ★★★★ **Yearly Openings:** 🯅🯅🯅🯅🯅

Graduate Teaching Assistants. Assist department chairperson, faculty members, or other professional staff members in college or university by performing teaching or teaching-related duties, such as teaching lower-level courses, developing teaching materials, preparing and giving examinations, and grading examinations or papers. Graduate assistants must be enrolled in a graduate school program. Graduate assistants who primarily perform non-teaching duties, such as laboratory research, should be reported in the occupational category related to the work performed. **Education and Training:** Master's degree. **Skills:** Math—High. English—High. Science—High. **Yearly Earnings:** $$$$ **Job Growth:** ★★★★ **Yearly Openings:** 🯅🯅🯅🯅🯅

Health Specialties Teachers, Postsecondary. Teach courses in health specialties, such as veterinary medicine, dentistry, pharmacy, therapy, laboratory technology, and public health. **Education and Training:** Master's degree. **Skills:** Math—Medium. English—High. Science—High. **Yearly Earnings:** $$$$ **Job Growth:** ★★★★ **Yearly Openings:** 🯅🯅🯅🯅🯅

History Teachers, Postsecondary. Teach courses in human history and historiography. **Education and Training:** Master's degree. **Skills:** Math—High. English—High. Science—High. **Yearly Earnings:** $$$$ **Job Growth:** ★★★★ **Yearly Openings:** 🯅🯅🯅🯅🯅

Home Economics Teachers, Postsecondary. Teach courses in child care, family relations, finance, nutrition, and related subjects as pertaining to home management. **Education and Training:** Master's degree. **Skills:** Math—Medium. English—Medium. Science—Medium. **Yearly Earnings:** $$$$ **Job Growth:** ★★★★ **Yearly Openings:** 🯅🯅🯅🯅🯅

Kindergarten Teachers, Except Special Education. Teach elemental natural and social science, personal hygiene, music, art, and literature to children from four to six years old. Promote physical, mental, and social development. May be required to hold state certification. **Education and Training:** Bachelor's degree. **Skills:** Math—Low. English—Medium. Science—Medium. **Yearly Earnings:** $$$ **Job Growth:** ★★★ **Yearly Openings:** 🯅🯅🯅

Law Teachers, Postsecondary. Teach courses in law. **Education and Training:** Professional degree. **Skills:** Math—Medium. English—Medium. Science—Medium. **Yearly Earnings:** $$$$ **Job Growth:** ★★★★ **Yearly Openings:** 🯅🯅🯅🯅🯅

Librarians. Administer libraries and perform related library services. Work in a variety of settings, including public libraries, schools, colleges and universities, museums, corporations, government agencies, law firms, non-profit organizations, and health-care providers. Tasks may include selecting, acquiring, cataloguing, classifying, circulating,

and maintaining library materials and furnishing reference, bibliographical, and readers' advisory services. May perform in-depth strategic research and synthesize, analyze, edit, and filter information. May set up or work with databases and information systems to catalogue and access information. **Education and Training:** Master's degree. **Skills:** Math—Medium. English—High. Science—Medium. **Yearly Earnings:** $$$$ **Job Growth:** ★★ **Yearly Openings:** 🚶🚶

Library Assistants, Clerical. Compile records, sort and shelve books, and issue and receive library materials such as pictures, cards, slides and microfilm. Locate library materials for loan and replace material in shelving area, stacks, or files according to identification number and title. Register patrons to permit them to borrow books, periodicals, and other library materials. **Education and Training:** Short-term on-the-job training. **Skills:** Math—Medium. English—Medium. Science—Low. **Yearly Earnings:** $ **Job Growth:** ★★★ **Yearly Openings:** 🚶🚶🚶

Library Science Teachers, Postsecondary. Teach courses in library science. **Education and Training:** Master's degree. **Skills:** Math—Medium. English—Medium. Science—Medium. **Yearly Earnings:** $$$$ **Job Growth:** ★★★★ **Yearly Openings:** 🚶🚶🚶🚶🚶

Library Technicians. Assist librarians by helping readers in the use of library catalogs, databases, and indexes to locate books and other materials and by answering questions that require only brief consultation of standard reference. Compile records, sort and shelve books, remove or repair damaged books, register patrons, and check materials in and out of the circulation process. Replace materials in shelving area (stacks) or files. Includes bookmobile drivers who operate bookmobiles or light trucks that pull trailers to specific locations on a predetermined schedule and assist with providing services in mobile libraries. **Education and Training:** Short-term on-the-job training. **Skills:** Math—Medium. English—Medium. Science—Low. **Yearly Earnings:** $$ **Job Growth:** ★★★ **Yearly Openings:** 🚶🚶🚶

Mathematical Science Teachers, Postsecondary. Teach courses pertaining to mathematical concepts, statistics, and actuarial science and to the application of original and standardized mathematical techniques in solving specific problems and situations. **Education and Training:** Master's degree. **Skills:** Math—High. English—High. Science—High. **Yearly Earnings:** $$$$ **Job Growth:** ★★★★ **Yearly Openings:** 🚶🚶🚶🚶🚶

Middle School Teachers, Except Special and Vocational Education. Teach students in public or private schools in one or more subjects at the middle, intermediate, or junior high level, which falls between elementary and senior high school as defined by state laws and regulations. **Education and Training:** Bachelor's degree. **Skills:** Math—High. English—High. Science—Medium. **Yearly Earnings:** $$$ **Job Growth:** ★★ **Yearly Openings:** 🚶🚶🚶🚶

Museum Technicians and Conservators. Prepare specimens, such as fossils, skeletal parts, lace, and textiles, for museum collection and exhibits. May restore documents or install, arrange, and exhibit materials. **Education and Training:** Master's degree. **Skills:** Math—Medium. English—High. Science—Medium. **Yearly Earnings:** $$$ **Job Growth:** ★★★ **Yearly Openings:** 🚶

Nursing Instructors and Teachers, Postsecondary. Demonstrate and teach patient care in classroom and clinical units to nursing students. Includes both teachers primarily engaged in teaching and those who do a combination of both teaching and research. **Education and Training:** Master's degree. **Skills:** Math—Medium. English—High. Science—High. **Yearly Earnings:** $$$$ **Job Growth:** ★★★★ **Yearly Openings:** 🚶🚶🚶🚶🚶

Personal Financial Advisors. Advise clients on financial plans, using knowledge of tax and investment strategies, securities, insurance, pension plans, and real estate. Duties include assessing clients' assets, liabilities, cash flow, insurance coverage, tax status, and financial objectives to establish investment strategies. **Education and Training:** Bachelor's degree. **Skills:** Math—Medium. English—Medium. Science—Low. **Yearly Earnings:** $$$$$ **Job Growth:** ★★★★ **Yearly Openings:** 🚶🚶🚶

Philosophy and Religion Teachers, Postsecondary. Teach courses in philosophy, religion, and theology. **Education and Training:** Master's degree. **Skills:** Math—Medium. English—Medium. Science—Medium. **Yearly Earnings:** $$$$ **Job Growth:** ★★★★ **Yearly Openings:** 🚶🚶🚶🚶🚶

Physics Teachers, Postsecondary. Teach courses pertaining to the laws of matter and energy. Includes both teachers primarily engaged in teaching and those who do a combination of teaching and research. **Education and Training:** Master's degree. **Skills:** Math—High. English—High. Science—High. **Yearly Earnings:** $$$$ **Job Growth:** ★★★★ **Yearly Openings:** 🚶🚶🚶🚶🚶

Political Science Teachers, Postsecondary. Teach courses in political science, international affairs, and international relations. **Education and Training:** Master's degree. **Skills:** Math—High. English—High. Science—High. **Yearly Earnings:** $$$$ **Job Growth:** ★★★★ **Yearly Openings:** 🚶🚶🚶🚶🚶

Preschool Teachers, Except Special Education. Instruct children (normally up to five years of age) in activities designed to promote social, physical, and intellectual growth needed for primary school in preschool, day care center, or other child development facility. May be required to hold state certification. **Education and Training:** Bachelor's degree. **Skills:** Math—Low. English—Medium. Science—Medium. **Yearly Earnings:** $ **Job Growth:** ★★★ **Yearly Openings:** 🚶🚶🚶🚶

Psychology Teachers, Postsecondary. Teach courses in psychology, such as child, clinical, and developmental psychology, and psychological counseling. **Education and Training:** Master's degree. **Skills:** Math—High. English—High. Science—High. **Yearly Earnings:** $$$$ **Job Growth:** ★★★★ **Yearly Openings:** 🚶🚶🚶🚶🚶

Recreation and Fitness Studies Teachers, Postsecondary. Teach courses pertaining to recreation, leisure, and fitness studies, including exercise physiology and facilities management. **Education and Training:** Master's degree. **Skills:** Math—Medium. English—Medium. Science—Medium. **Yearly Earnings:** $$$$ **Job Growth:** ★★★★ **Yearly Openings:** 🚹🚹🚹🚹🚹

Secondary School Teachers, Except Special and Vocational Education. Instruct students in secondary public or private schools in one or more subjects at the secondary level, such as English, mathematics, or social studies. May be designated according to subject matter specialty, such as commercial teachers or English teachers. **Education and Training:** Bachelor's degree. **Skills:** Math—High. English—High. Science—Medium. **Yearly Earnings:** $$$$ **Job Growth:** ★★★ **Yearly Openings:** 🚹🚹🚹🚹

Self-Enrichment Education Teachers. Teach or instruct courses other than those that normally lead to an occupational objective or degree. Courses may include self-improvement, nonvocational, and nonacademic subjects. Teaching may or may not take place in a traditional educational institution. **Education and Training:** Work experience in a related occupation. **Skills:** Math—Medium. English—High. Science—Medium. **Yearly Earnings:** $$ **Job Growth:** ★★★ **Yearly Openings:** 🚹🚹🚹

Social Work Teachers, Postsecondary. Teach courses in social work. **Education and Training:** Master's degree. **Skills:** Math—Medium. English—Medium. Science—Medium. **Yearly Earnings:** $$$$ **Job Growth:** ★★★★ **Yearly Openings:** 🚹🚹🚹🚹🚹

Sociology Teachers, Postsecondary. Teach courses in sociology. **Education and Training:** Master's degree. **Skills:** Math—High. English—High. Science—High. **Yearly Earnings:** $$$$ **Job Growth:** ★★★★ **Yearly Openings:** 🚹🚹🚹🚹🚹

Special Education Teachers, Middle School. Teach middle school subjects to educationally and physically handicapped students. Includes teachers who specialize and work with audibly and visually handicapped students and those who teach basic academic and life processes skills to the mentally impaired. **Education and Training:** Bachelor's degree. **Skills:** Math—Medium. English—Medium. Science—Medium. **Yearly Earnings:** $$$ **Job Growth:** ★★★★ **Yearly Openings:** 🚹🚹

Special Education Teachers, Preschool, Kindergarten, and Elementary School. Teach elementary and preschool school subjects to educationally and physically handicapped students. Includes teachers who specialize and work with audibly and visually handicapped students and those who teach basic academic and life processes skills to the mentally impaired. **Education and Training:** Bachelor's degree. **Skills:** Math—Medium. English—Medium. Science—Medium. **Yearly Earnings:** $$$$ **Job Growth:** ★★★★★ **Yearly Openings:** 🚹🚹🚹

Special Education Teachers, Secondary School. Teach secondary school subjects to educationally and physically handicapped students. Includes teachers who specialize and work with audibly and visually handicapped students and those who teach basic academic and life processes skills to the mentally impaired. **Education and Training:** Bachelor's degree. **Skills:** Math—Medium. English—Medium. Science—Medium. **Yearly Earnings:** $$$$ **Job Growth:** ★★★★ **Yearly Openings:** 🚹🚹

Teacher Assistants. Perform duties that are instructional in nature or deliver direct services to students or parents. Serve in a position for which a teacher or another professional has ultimate responsibility for the design and implementation of educational programs and services. **Education and Training:** Short-term on-the-job training. **Skills:** Math—Medium. English—Medium. Science—Medium. **Yearly Earnings:** $ **Job Growth:** ★★★★ **Yearly Openings:** 🚹🚹🚹🚹🚹

Vocational Education Teachers, Middle School. Teach or instruct vocational or occupational subjects at the middle school level. **Education and Training:** Bachelor's degree. **Skills:** Math—High. English—High. Science—Medium. **Yearly Earnings:** $$$ **Job Growth:** ★★★ **Yearly Openings:** 🚹

Vocational Education Teachers, Postsecondary. Teach or instruct vocational or occupational subjects at the postsecondary level (but at less than the bachelor's level) to students who have graduated or left high school. Includes correspondence school instructors; industrial, commercial and government training instructors; and adult education teachers and instructors who prepare persons to operate industrial machinery and equipment and transportation and communications equipment. Teaching may take place in public or private schools whose primary business is education or in a school associated with an organization whose primary business is other than education. **Education and Training:** Work experience in a related occupation. **Skills:** Math—Medium. English—High. Science—Medium. **Yearly Earnings:** $$$$ **Job Growth:** ★★★★ **Yearly Openings:** 🚹🚹🚹🚹🚹

Vocational Education Teachers, Secondary School. Teach or instruct vocational or occupational subjects at the secondary school level. **Education and Training:** Bachelor's degree. **Skills:** Math—High. English—High. Science—Medium. **Yearly Earnings:** $$$$ **Job Growth:** ★★★ **Yearly Openings:** 🚹🚹

Exploring Careers: General Management and Support

Start Your Journey Through Careers Related to

GENERAL MANAGEMENT AND SUPPORT

Careers in this area suit people interested in making an organization run smoothly.

EXPLORING CAREER CLUES

Your interests give important clues for exploring career options. Think about your interests to learn if jobs in the General Management and Support interest area may be worth further exploration.

Do you like the school subjects related to the General Management and Support interest area? Here are some examples of related subjects:

- English
- Composition and writing
- Speech
- Foreign language
- Math
- Accounting
- Economics
- Business
- Marketing
- Computers
- Government
- Science
- Psychology
- Sociology

Do you like the free-time activities related to the General Management and Support interest area? Here are some examples of related free-time activities:

- Being on the debate team
- Serving as an officer of the student council, a club, or other organization
- Helping to organize and run school or community events
- Planning parties and outings
- Organizing your room, CDs, DVDs, tools, closets, books, desks, or other items and areas
- Budgeting your money
- Calculating sports statistics
- Helping friends and others with math
- Listening to friends and helping them with their problems

EXPLORING JOB GROUPS

Jobs related to the General Management and Support interest area fit into two groups. Read through the list to see which groups sound interesting to you.

- General Management Work and Management of Support Functions
- Management Support

EXPLORING CAREER POSSIBILITIES

You can satisfy your interest in the General Management and Support area by working in a position of leadership or by specializing in a function that contributes to an overall effort in a business, nonprofit organization, or government agency. Here are a few examples of career possibilities:

If you especially enjoy working with people, you may find fulfillment by working in human resources.

An interest in numbers may lead you to consider accounting, finance, budgeting, or purchasing.

Or perhaps you would do well as the manager of a business.

Turn the page to meet people working in the General Management and Support interest area→

PROFILE

Krista Mujawa—Accountant

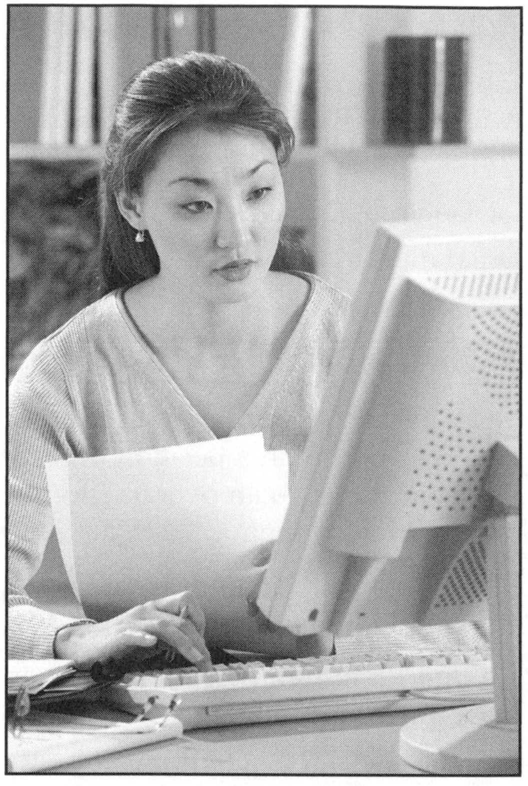

Krista never expected to become an accountant but loves the work.

"Believe it or not, I graduated from college with a degree in fine arts. I expected to work in advertising," said Krista Mujawa, a Certified Public Accountant and founding partner of a small accounting firm.

"No jobs were available. I took a job as a secretary for an accounting firm. When tax season hit, the firm asked me to try a few tax returns. I had never done my *own* return, much less somebody else's. But I was game.

"I enjoyed it! I loved the challenge and excitement of learning something new.

"Whenever I had any questions–and I had plenty–a kind partner sat me down in his office and explained words like 'capital gains,' 'depreciation,' and 'tax shelters.'

"By the end of the tax season, I had completed more than two hundred returns. I got a raise, and the firm asked me to do their payroll and books. As an accountant, I'd have a chance to learn the non-tax part of accounting.

"I barely knew the difference between a debit and a credit. I hadn't taken any business courses in college, but I am a walking, talking example of 'it's never too late to change.' After three years with the firm, I went for my CPA. That would give me a professional credential and more income."

"I loved the challenge and excitement of learning something new."

Earning Her Credentials

"Becoming a CPA involves meeting requirements in education, experience, and the passing of required exams. I had already exceeded the two-year work experience expected in my state.

"I went back to school part time. My accounting experience gave me an extremely helpful background from which to study for the exam. I passed on the first try. However, if I hadn't, I could have tried again.

"The final step in my exam was the ethics portion. This was a take-home open-book test. When I successfully completed that, I was licensed in my state as a CPA."

A Service Business

Now, some five years later, Krista works at an accounting firm as a full partner.

Returning from a meeting, Krista flips through her stack of messages. "An important part of my job is to return phone calls promptly. Accounting is a service business, and clients call for specific reasons and expect us to respond.

"They may have information we need to prepare their taxes, or they might need some advice on whether to purchase or lease a car. Once they have our answer, they can make their decisions. In the heart of the tax season, things get pretty hectic at any accounting firm," Krista said. "About sixty percent of our work is done in the first four months of the year. That's tax work for you.

"A public accounting firm like ours performs audits and prepares taxes and other financial reports for individuals and businesses. Accountants may also work for private firms, performing the bookkeeping, financial analysis, and other accounting functions. This is usually called private accounting."

A Variety of Jobs

"A person can pursue accounting at several levels," Krista explained. "The first level is bookkeeper, which requires a high school education. A bookkeeper maintains the books on a day-to-day basis.

"The position of accountant requires more education, usually a college degree, and would involve tax preparation and other accounting procedures under the supervision of a CPA.

"A CPA can act independently or practice in a firm."

"With the necessary credentials, a CPA can act independently or practice in a firm. You don't have to be a CPA to have a career in accounting. We have staff accountants who've been here for fourteen years and earn good salaries.

"Almost all accounting firms, from the small two-person firms to the huge international firms, need bookkeepers and staff accountants as well as higher-level CPAs.

"Accounting is a stable field," added Krista. "Even in tough times, accountants are needed. Taxes must be paid and financial statements prepared. An accountant is often consulted to help analyze a company's financial status, to suggest solutions to problems, or, if necessary, to help establish a value if the business needs to be sold.

"Sometimes accountants are called on to solve some pretty good mysteries," Krista said. "It often involves working as a team with other professionals such as attorneys, bankers, and insurance agents."

Skills Needed in Math and Logic

"A good accountant should have the ability to think logically and to be organized. We have to understand and show the technical and mathematical skills needed in working with the computer. We have to know bookkeeping and accounting concepts. We perform tax-related research and use forms.

"A good accountant should have the ability to think logically and to be organized."

"As my career progressed, I found my managerial skills took on more importance. I was in the role of analyzing the management of my clients' businesses, supervising the personnel reporting to me, and eventually managing my own business.

"Interpersonal skills are very important. That means getting along with people. A psychology course or two wouldn't hurt while taking the usual business and accounting courses," Krista said.

"Our business clients sometimes come in to bounce around ideas about expanding their businesses," Krista continued.

A Firm Approach

"All of our staff have an opportunity to work with clients. Our clients have a consistent contact person who knows the ongoing situation.

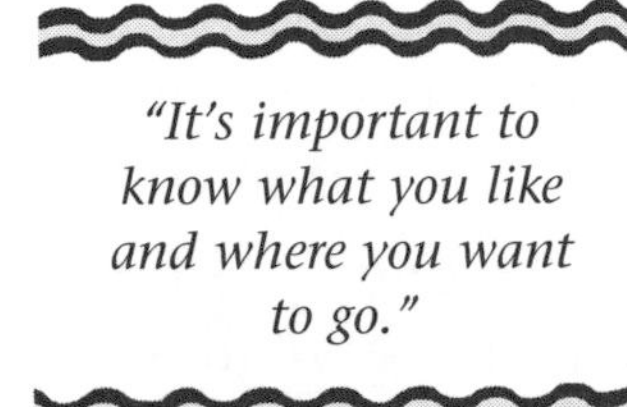
"It's important to know what you like and where you want to go."

"Not all firms work this way. With some of the large international firms, client contact might only come at the partner level. In a small firm, a staff member might be responsible for all the work for a particular client. In large firms with huge corporate clients, a staff member might be responsible for a small segment of the work.

"One of the biggest mistakes people make at the early stages is being improperly matched with the firm in which they work. It's important to know what you like and where you want to go.

"The factors vary depending on the management and philosophy of each firm. It's important to learn as much as possible about the firm's philosophy before signing on.

"Confidentiality is an important part of our professional ethics. Individuals' financial records are as confidential as their medical records. In the world of big business, the stakes are extremely high, and privacy can be vital to competitiveness and viability."

Adding Up the Future

"Anyone hoping to enter this field must be computer literate. We do research using books and, even better, we have references on CD-ROM. We rely more and more on computer technology to get our job done. We prepare tax returns on the computer and use word-processing software for correspondence.

"I feel rewarded by working with people of different ages and backgrounds, in being able to help them develop a business or provide for their family."

"Change is constant in this business, so we must keep up-to-date. A staff member reads professional literature and updates us at staff meetings.

"To maintain our certification each year, there are state continuing education requirements. Our professional organization–the American Institute of Certified Public Accountants (AICPA)–often offers continuing education. So do local state societies.

"Differences in requirements between states are not significant enough to prevent a person from being geographically flexible," Krista said.

"I've enjoyed prestige and respect being a CPA. And there's more flexibility than one might expect. I can work my schedule around my family's life. I know people who go full bore during tax season and work part time in the off-season so they can attend school. Some just work part time during tax season. Others have fully committed careers. As far as income is concerned, you can earn a comfortable living as a CPA.

"I feel rewarded by working with people of different ages and backgrounds, in being able to help them develop a business or provide for their family.

"As long as there are people, businesses, money, and taxes, there'll be a need for accountants."

PROFILE

Paul Romani—Funeral Director

"Romani Funeral Home? This is Good Shepherd Hospital. We had a death last night. The family asked that you handle the arrangements. They'll call you soon. When can you remove the remains?"

"We can have a vehicle there by 3 p.m. Whom should the driver contact when he arrives? Also, I'd like the family's name and phone number. I want to be sure of their plans," said Paul Romani.

Thus began Paul's day. He has been a funeral director for five years. In this instance, Paul knew the family of the deceased and knew that the grandmother had had emphysema.

"She was a frail lady," Paul said. "It's probably a blessing that she passed away in her sleep last night." The phone rang. "I'll bet that's her husband now," Paul said.

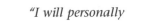

"I will personally handle the arrangements. It will be a beautiful service."

"Romani Funeral Home. Yes, Bill, I just heard the sad news from the hospital. I'm so sorry. I know how close you were. I will personally handle the arrangements. It will be a beautiful service just like Mary would have wanted.

"I need to meet with you soon, Bill, to discuss plans. When can you come to my office?" They set an appointment.

Many Aspects to the Job

Paul said, "A family needs to make many decisions, unless they've planned ahead. Will the person be cremated or buried? For a burial, what kind of casket do they want? Where is the cemetery? When is the funeral? Will there be flowers? Will there be a religious ceremony? Who will officiate?"

Paul said there is a lot of paperwork involved in the funeral home business. For example, the doctor must sign the death certificate and copies must be filed.

"I take extra care to be sure that communications happen," Paul said. "This is a stressful time for families. They're upset, and details of conversations or arrangements are easily confused, misunderstood, or forgotten.

"I take extra care to be sure that communications happen."

"I make it a point to remain cool and organized. I try to be the focal point of communications."

The Importance of Dignity and Respect

"In this business, reputation is everything. Those who take advantage of grieving people won't be around for long. If a funeral home is caught with its integrity down, people won't come there.

"From the moment a family approaches me about funeral arrangements, I consider my image. I must be sensitive to their needs and realize that anger, denial, and frustration over the death of a loved one may get taken out on me. Through it all, I stay cool and maintain my dignity.

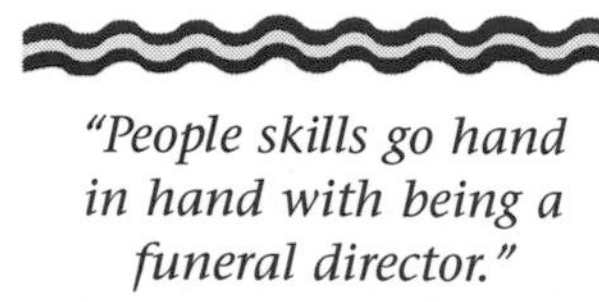

"People skills go hand in hand with being a funeral director."

"People skills go hand in hand with being a funeral director." Paul added. "In my funeral home, remains are always treated with dignity and respect."

It's Still a Business

Paul said that it's sometimes difficult to bring up the subject of costs with families at such an emotionally draining time. Their thoughts are occupied with their loss.

"To discuss money at such a time may seem crass and unfeeling, and funeral directors should remember that they're dealing with people at a low point in their lives.

"But at the same time, I have to remember that I am running a business. I must maintain a caring yet businesslike posture and not let people take advantage of me."

According to Paul, the average funeral home does about two hundred arrangements a year. Larger homes may do as many as five hundred.

"My income comes in clumps," Paul said. "Some days, we have nothing to do. But the other side of the coin is that I'm on call twenty-four hours a day, seven days a week. I live by my cell phone. Other days, we may have three arrangements.

"I have to remember that I am running a business."

"Anyone coming into this business needs to be able to budget their time and money. It takes business skills and people skills."

Religious Wishes Must Be Considered

Paul noted that it's very important for a funeral director to ask the family questions about their religious needs and wishes. "I am not personally involved in the religious aspects or service, but I need to know what arrangements I need to make. I also need to know about any special restrictions or requirements.

"Basically, I have to know what my position and involvement should be. I've handled the arrangements for all major religions and some I'd never heard of. Some funerals have no religious aspect at all.

"I have to know ahead of time, and that's why a personal meeting with the family is so important."

Education and Background

Paul has worked at his family's funeral home since he was a teenager sweeping floors and answering phones.

Paul said that in his state, an associate's degree in any subject is required in order to enter a mortuary science school. Some states require a bachelor's degree. There are about twenty such schools in the country. Some colleges and universities also offer courses of study.

Usually it's a two-year program, but some students can finish in one year if they really apply themselves. Grants and scholarships are available.

Courses in mortuary science usually include microbiology, chemistry, pathology, embalming, funeral directing, restorative art, anatomy, and physiology. Personal relations may also be offered. Paul advises that a course in general business management is a good idea as well.

"When I finished school, I had to take a state test. It was not easy. In most states if you fail, you can take it again, but if you still don't pass, you have to go back to school."

When you pass the state test, the state issues a license. Paul cautioned that some cities also have an exam and require a city license. "In my case, the city exam was tougher than the state," he said. "When you get your licenses, keeping them is usually just a matter of paying an annual fee."

Paul said there are continuing education programs. In his state, both funeral directors and embalmers are required to accumulate continuing education credits. Classes are often available through funeral directors' associations, and seminars are held throughout the country.

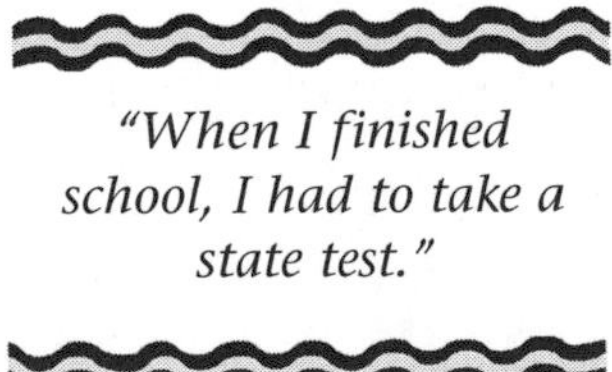
"When I finished school, I had to take a state test."

Getting Started in the Field

"This business isn't for everyone, and the time to learn if it's for you is early on."

Those interested in entering the mortuary sciences field should invest some time in being sure it's really what they want to do. Paul advised starting on the fringes–perhaps volunteer some time to answer phones or help out at wakes.

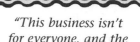

"This business isn't for everyone, and the time to learn if it's for you is early on. Find a good funeral home in your area to talk to. You have to work in the atmosphere of the business for a while before you know if you want to do it."

Paul said that in such jobs you will not make any actual arrangements, do any selling, or work with human remains in any way. "Only a licensed funeral director or embalmer can do that," he said.

The Process of Events

"There's great job satisfaction in comforting people and helping them through a difficult time."

Paul explained that embalming is a science that all funeral directors must be taught and licensed to perform. The embalming process takes about two hours, and when it's complete, the remains are dressed, made up, and placed in the casket, if the family has selected one.

This is followed by the visitation, the funeral service, and the burial or cremation. Cremation, of course, may have occurred before the service.

"If you're a fair and honest person with a real desire to be of service to people in the stressful time surrounding a death, this can be a great business. The majority of people won't have the opportunity or feel they couldn't do it," Paul said.

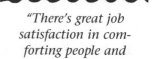

"There's great job satisfaction in comforting people and helping them through a difficult time. And that's what I do most of the time."

PROFILE

Diana Joplin—Human Resources Manager

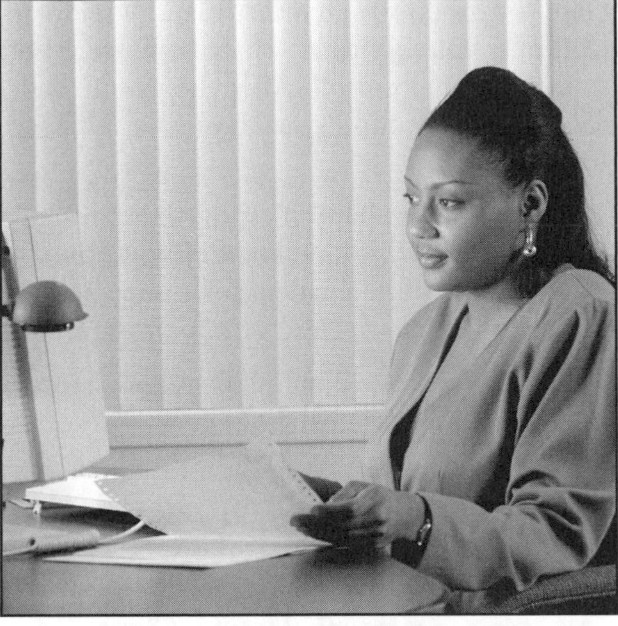

A human resources manager must be knowledgeable about company benefit plans.

Diana Joplin entered the human resources department offices thinking of a dozen activities that needed doing. As human resources manager, Diana had no doubt the day would bring her a dozen more. She greeted the receptionist in the sunny atrium.

"Good morning, Sheila. Are you going to the company picnic? By the way, did you know that Mike is in the hospital? Some of us are visiting him at lunch. Can you come?"

Sheila said, "That's a shame. I wish I could go, but I can't. Tell Mike I'm thinking about him. I'll try to see him soon. I'll be at the picnic, though."

Sheila introduced a new employee. "This is Tony Lansing, Diana. Do you remember each other from when he applied for the chemical engineer job? I told him you'd want him to fill out some forms this morning."

Tony shook Diana's hand. "Sure, you gave me the overview of the company's benefits."

"Oh, yes! Come into my office, Tony. We'll set up your W-2 forms."

She greeted everyone on the way to her office, as was her habit, and introduced Tony. After so many names, he looked confused. "Don't worry. You won't be tested on this until Monday!" Diana said.

They breezed into Diana's office. A secretary hovered near Diana's desk. The phone rang before Diana got her coat off. After the phone call, which concerned someone's vacation, she returned to Tony.

The phone rang before
Diana got her coat off.

She handed him pamphlets on the company's health and dental plan. "Read these and let me know if you have any questions. We offer personal life insurance and accident insurance equal to half the life insurance amount you select. Here's the pamphlet for that.

"After one year here or 1,000 hours of work, you're eligible for profit sharing. If you join, in profitable years we contribute to your account. It adds up."

After filing Tony's paperwork, Diana escorted him to the lab and introduced him to his new coworkers.

On the Job: A Busy Day

Nursing a cup of coffee, Diana headed into the plant. Vats of pesticides and bins of fertilizers lined up in rows. The pungent odors of chemicals clung to her clothing. Pallets groaned under the combined weight of many gallons of pesticides. Her company sold pesticides and fertilizer to commercial organizations.

Diana checked her appearance in the mirror. She had to give a speech to the plant's managers about discrimination. She looked over her notecards and the points she would have to cover. Speechmaking made her a little nervous.

She entered a conference room. The lecture was mostly a formality. Diana stood in front of the room.

As voices quieted, she began, "Management has asked me to make sure you understand that some behavior, if it exists here, has to stop. As you know, we can't discriminate according to sex, age, physical impairment, race, religion, or ethnic background.

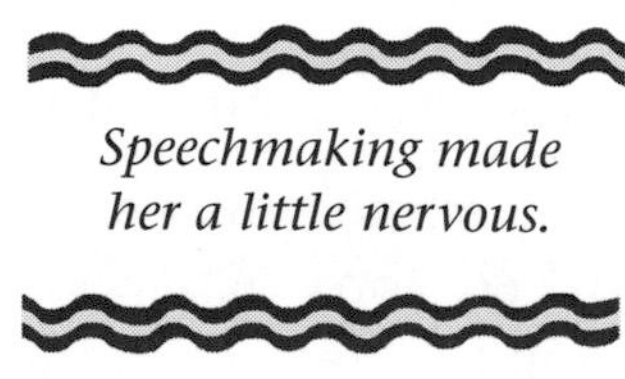
Speechmaking made
her a little nervous.

"Some of you may not be aware that ethnic jokes also come under that umbrella. I know you know some good jokes, but they can be very hurtful even if you don't mean them to be. So please keep them to yourselves.

Diana must be familiar with all the plans and be able to explain them in detailed but understandable terms.

"Management also wants to emphasize that it frowns upon sexual harassment, however mild. The offending party can be terminated."

Diana talked in broad terms. However, she knew that two people on the staff had lodged complaints against one of the managers in the room. "So consider yourselves warned, folks. Any questions?"

Many Administrative Responsibilities

What are the duties of a director of human resources? The list of responsibilities and the detailed knowledge required staggers the mind. Diana ticked off the list of benefits. They included health care, life insurance, profit sharing, and retirement plans, among others.

Diana must be familiar with all the plans and be able to explain them in detailed but understandable terms. She has to keep current on changes that occur, initiated either by her company or by changing regulations.

She continued, "Each plan has its own paperwork. Many have several options from which an employee can choose."

A human resources manager needs a good memory. Diana must be up-to-date on the laws. With the advice or aid of legal and tax specialists, she has to discuss their ramifications with employees as well as executives.

"There's a lot to remember and keep track of. As it concerns money for the company and the employee, it's crucial," Diana emphasized.

Helping Employees

Ben entered Diana's office, limping. He was the company's top-selling salesperson. He had option two of the long-term disability plan. Ben wanted to discuss his medical situation. He'd been in an automobile accident while selling pesticides and fertilizer.

Now every step hurt, but Ben was back for half days. He asked, "Can I change my option on the medical plan?" Diana knew the answer.

"You can increase your option by one level," she told him. "You're allowed to do this now because it's time for your annual change of coverage option."

After Ben left, a coworker stopped by who was moving closer to the plant and needed to change her tax forms and credit union. Diana gave her forms for that.

Career Path and Personality Traits

When she was just out of college, the company hired Diana to work in the billing department. In two years, she was promoted to billing supervisor. From there, she moved into the human resources department and was later promoted to manager.

When the company hires human resources staff, they often look for certification. From a two-year or four-year program, a person can earn accreditation with a personnel association.

"When I started, personal computers in business were new. I had to learn about them on the job. Over the years, I've taken personal computer courses through the local community college. First I learned a popular word-processing program. It helps me with my letters, memos, and reports. Then I mastered a spreadsheet program. Now I teach these to company employees whose jobs require them.

"Over the past few years, many changes–especially on-the-job attitudes–are not for the better," Diana said.

"The hardest part of my job comes when the company must downsize. Sometimes I have to lay off people I've known and worked with for a long time. That causes me real anguish.

"This job requires a lot of hard work, attention to detail, and a really good memory. But most important is a caring attitude, a genuine concern for the people you're working with and for. Liking people is important for being a good human resources manager.

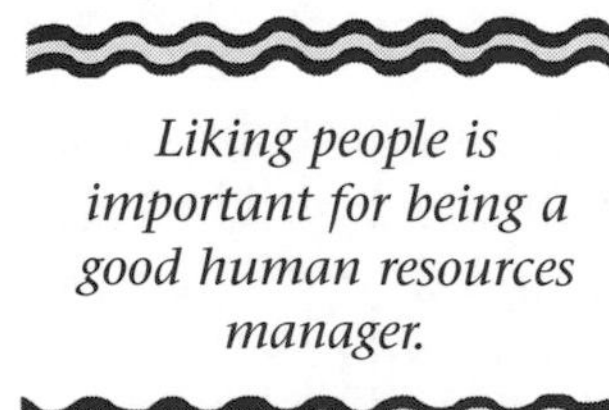
Liking people is important for being a good human resources manager.

"Without that, human resources work is probably not for you. But with it, you should find it interesting, enjoyable, and personally rewarding."

PROFILE

Tammy Carlisle—Property Manager

Tammy Carlisle hurried along the hall in the apartment building that she manages for Top Properties, a property management company.

At the top of the stairs, she saw a sack of garbage outside a door. "That looks awful!" she said. She scooped it up, making a mental note to phone the tenants.

"Normally, I don't pick up people's trash. If I do it for them, they assume it is a routine service we offer. I'm showing this apartment to prospective tenants this afternoon, and I want the place to look presentable."

A property manager shows apartments, collects rent, and handles tenant issues.

A Day on the Job

Tammy explained that Top Properties runs Fernwood Apartments, an apartment complex with six maintenance workers.

"It's a busy time right now. There is a lot of turnover in early summer when the students leave. This complex draws graduate students and their families because we're close to the university.

"Our maintenance people are busy painting and repairing units to get them ready for new tenants. I have three moveouts this week alone," Tammy said.

As Tammy continued through the complex, she explained that making rounds is an important part of the job. “I walk the grounds each day and look for any problems, like broken glass or excessive water runoff.”

Continuing through the building, she came to Apartment 10. There was a plaque on the door: Fernwood Apartments Manager. Opening the door, she said, “Welcome to the manager’s unit.”

“I like people–and what a great mix of them we have here.”

While coffee brewed, Tammy sat in her sunny kitchen and talked about her job. “I like people–and what a great mix of them we have here,” she began.

“Students, retired couples, lots of single mothers, and families from all over the world–we have a wonderful community. Fernwood Apartments is a great place to live.

“These buildings are only twelve years old, and we charge a fair rent.” Tammy explained. “We have a waiting list of people wanting to rent here. We only take people with good references and an excellent credit rating.

“Sometimes, though, even after all that checking, we have a hard time collecting the rent from tenants.

“My management company, Top Properties, is terrific,” she continued. “They help me work with tenants who lose a job or suddenly have huge medical bills. Not all management companies do that.

“Eviction is a last resort. I’ve never had to evict a tenant, but I’ve served three-day warning notices. They always manage to come up with the money at the last minute.”

Tammy keeps copies of three-day notices, warnings about lease violations, and complaints in case they are needed in court. Most of my tenants are responsible. The others–well, a verbal warning is generally sufficient. Nobody wants to get kicked out.

“The best part of being the manager is getting this apartment rent free.”

"The best part of being the manager is getting this apartment rent free," Tammy said as she rose to pour the coffee.

"As manager, I have to hold people to the rules. I can't be meek when I'm telling rowdy students to turn down the music."

Opening the Door

Getting started in the business is relatively easy, according to Tammy. Although some complexes want managers with college degrees, Tammy started out as an assistant manager at another complex run by the same company.

"Becoming a leasing agent with a property management company is another way to start. They find renters to fill vacancies. It's good experience, and they're often the first to find out when a resident manager position opens up.

"Liz, my supervisor, is wonderful," she said. "We've worked out a flexible schedule. I work a thirty-hour week plus emergency calls. This company has always treated me very fairly.

"Managers are only called during off hours if it is an emergency. Most emergencies happen at night when everyone is giving their plumbing a workout. The tenants page the maintenance person who is on call. Then maintenance decides if it's an emergency."

Students interested in the field should research such job titles as property, real estate, and community association managers; condominium association manager; and trailer park manager.

The Right Personality Is Needed

"I am, by nature, a rather reserved person," Tammy explained, "but I've developed a tougher side. As manager, I have to hold people to the rules. I can't be meek when I'm telling rowdy students to turn down the music."

The phone rang and Tammy answered it. After she hung up, she said, "That was Rob, our maintenance man. He'll be over this afternoon to inspect a vacant unit and see what repairs it needs.

"Come on, I'll show you my office," Tammy said. She entered a small room lined with file cabinets. The wooden desk was covered with a computer and a stack of files.

Collecting the Rent and Other Important Tasks

"I took a crash course in accounting from my supervisor. I keep ledgers on each tenant and each month's rental payments.

"The most important part of my job is collecting and depositing rent checks," said Tammy. "I'm busiest the first week of each month. I tally the checks, update ledgers, and get after people who are slow to pay.

"I also keep a complete record of the work done on every apartment," she added. Opening a folder, she pointed to a maintenance checklist.

"This office is also used to interview prospective renters or meet with tenants. I spend a lot of time making phone calls, talking to service people, or counseling tenants who are having disputes with their neighbors.

"If I didn't have good listening skills before, I do now!" said Tammy.

One drawback of being the manager, Tammy explained, is having to keep a professional distance from her neighbors. "It's important for me to be impartial. If I become too friendly with a tenant, it's hard to tell them to keep the TV down."

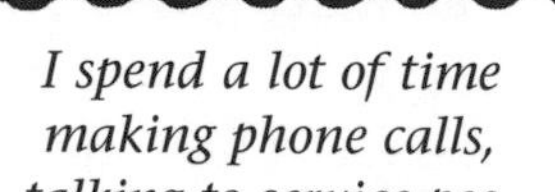

I spend a lot of time making phone calls, talking to service people, or counseling tenants who are having disputes with their neighbors.

Tammy unlocked a cabinet. Inside were rows of keys, each clearly labeled. "The keys I carry include a master key that lets me into every apartment, but the individual apartment keys are locked in this cabinet.

"The answering service has a list of numbers to call, including my supervisor, if they can't reach me. I carry a cell phone only when I'm on duty. Otherwise I'd never get any time to myself."

Building on Success

Tammy hopes to make a career of property management and is taking business courses at the nearby university. "I have only one more year to

go for a bachelor's degree," she said. "But you can usually qualify for the job without a degree. You need basic math skills, people skills, and common sense.

"I get so much satisfaction knowing I am part of a team that provides safe and well-maintained homes for our tenants."

"If you want to go into higher levels of management, it's a good idea to get a degree.

"Housing is a basic need for everyone. I get so much satisfaction knowing I am part of a team that provides safe and well-maintained homes for our tenants.

"I was lucky to hook up with a good management company," Tammy continued.

"After I get my degree, I'd like to stay on with apartment management as an administrator or manage a larger complex. "By that time I'll have the knowledge and experience to handle the additional responsibility.

"The job suits me. And you can't beat the commute!"

SKILL SAMPLER

Nina Lupovich—Bank Officer

Nina Lupovich is a bank officer in the consumer lending division of First National Bank. "Helping customers gives me more pleasure than any other aspect of my job."

Nina talked about the skills that are important for bank officers.

Bank officers must always show their best side to customers.

She lists the following tips that can help you decide if a career in banking interests you.

Students interested in the field should research such job titles as financial manager and bank director.

Bank officers must show their best side to customers.

- Do you like meeting and talking with people?
- Do you enjoy making new friends?
- Do you like to talk on the telephone?
- Can you remain friendly and courteous when other people are upset or when something is troubling you?

Bank officers must evaluate financial records, but they must also understand people.

- Are you a good judge of character?
- Can you tell when someone isn't telling the whole truth?
- Do you question things you read or hear that don't seem right?

Bank officers deal with large sums of money and with information about people's private lives. They must be honest and trustworthy.

- Are you careful with another person's belongings and valuables?
- Do you spend money wisely?
- Have you proven to your friends and family that they can trust you?
- Can you keep a secret?

Bank officers are part of a team. They must be able to get along with their coworkers.

- Do you enjoy working on group projects with other students?
- Do you like tennis, volleyball, and other team sports?
- Are you willing to follow another person's instructions?

Bank officers work with detailed financial statements. They must read and write carefully.

- Do you enjoy working with numbers?
- Do you read the instructions before taking a test?
- Do you check your homework before handing it in?
- Do you use spreadsheet software to keep track of your savings and to plan what you will use your money for?
- Do you have a system for organizing your activities and responsibilities?

Bank officers often have to refuse loans, even to customers they would like to help.

- Are you able and willing to turn down offers to be involved in activities you know are not right?
- When you are baby-sitting or working with a group of children, do you stand firm even if the children beg or cry?

Now learn about all major jobs in the General Management and Support interest area→

Facts About All Major Jobs Related to

GENERAL MANAGEMENT AND SUPPORT

In addition to the jobs covered in the profiles and skill sampler, other careers in the General Management and Support interest area may appeal to you. This section describes and gives facts about all major jobs in the General Management and Support interest area. For an explanation of the $, ★, and 🚹 symbols, see page 6.

GENERAL MANAGEMENT WORK AND MANAGEMENT OF SUPPORT FUNCTIONS

These workers are top-level and middle-level administrators who direct all or part of the activities in business establishments, government agencies, and labor unions. They set policies, make important decisions, and determine priorities. They use a variety of skills, including math, critical thinking, communications, insight into human nature, and computer applications. They have a good knowledge of how their industry operates and what laws and regulations they must follow.

Chief Executives. Determine and formulate policies and provide the overall direction of companies or private and public sector organizations within the guidelines set up by a board of directors or similar governing body. Plan, direct, or coordinate operational activities at the highest level of management with the help of subordinate executives and staff managers. **Education and Training:** College degree plus work experience. **Skills:** Math—Medium. English—Medium. Science—Medium. **Yearly Earnings:** $$$$$ **Job Growth:** ★★★ **Yearly Openings:** 🚹🚹🚹

Compensation and Benefits Managers. Plan, direct, or coordinate compensation and benefits activities and staff of an organization. **Education and Training:** College degree plus work experience. **Skills:** Math—Medium. English—Medium. Science—Medium. **Yearly Earnings:** $$$$ **Job Growth:** ★★★ **Yearly Openings:** 🚹🚹🚹

Farm, Ranch, and Other Agricultural Managers. On a paid basis, manage farms, ranches, aquacultural operations, greenhouses, nurseries, timber tracts, cotton gins, packing houses, or other agricultural establishments for employers. Carry out production, financial, and marketing decisions relating to the managed operations following guidelines from the owner. May contract tenant farmers or producers to carry out the day-to-day activities of the managed operation. May supervise planting, cultivating,

harvesting, and marketing activities. May prepare cost, production, and other records. May perform physical work and operate machinery. **Education and Training:** Work experience in a related occupation. **Skills:** Math—Medium. English—Medium. Science—Medium. **Yearly Earnings:** $$$ **Job Growth:** ★★ **Yearly Openings:** 🧍🧍🧍

Financial Managers. Plan, direct, and coordinate accounting, investing, banking, insurance, securities, and other financial activities of a branch, office, or department of an establishment. **Education and Training:** College degree plus work experience. **Skills:** Math—Medium. English—Medium. Science—Medium. **Yearly Earnings:** $$$$$ **Job Growth:** ★★★ **Yearly Openings:** 🧍🧍🧍🧍

Financial Managers, Branch or Department. Direct and coordinate financial activities of workers in a branch, office, or department of an establishment, such as branch bank, brokerage firm, risk and insurance department, or credit department. **Education and Training:** College degree plus work experience. **Skills:** Math—High. English—High. Science—Medium. **Yearly Earnings:** $$$$$ **Job Growth:** ★★★ **Yearly Openings:** 🧍🧍🧍🧍

Funeral Directors. Perform various tasks to arrange and direct funeral services, such as coordinating transportation of body to mortuary for embalming, interviewing family or other authorized person to arrange details, selecting pallbearers, procuring official for religious rites, and providing transportation for mourners. **Education and Training:** Associate's degree. **Skills:** Math—Medium. English—Medium. Science—Medium. **Yearly Earnings:** $$$$ **Job Growth:** ★★ **Yearly Openings:** 🧍

General and Operations Managers. Plan, direct, or coordinate the operations of companies or public and private sector organizations. Duties and responsibilities include formulating policies, managing daily operations, and planning the use of materials and human resources, but are too diverse and general in nature to be classified in any one functional area of management or administration, such as personnel, purchasing, or administrative services. Includes owners and managers who head small business establishments whose duties are primarily managerial. **Education and Training:** College degree plus work experience. **Skills:** Math—Medium. English—Medium. Science—Medium. **Yearly Earnings:** $$$$$ **Job Growth:** ★★★ **Yearly Openings:** 🧍🧍🧍🧍🧍

Government Service Executives. Determine and formulate policies and provide overall direction of federal, state, local, or international government activities. Plan, direct, and coordinate operational activities at the highest level of management with the help of subordinate managers. **Education and Training:** College degree plus work experience. **Skills:** Math—High. English—High. Science—Medium. **Yearly Earnings:** $$$$$ **Job Growth:** ★★★ **Yearly Openings:** 🧍🧍🧍

Human Resources Managers. Plan, direct, and coordinate human resource management activities of an organization to maximize the strategic use of human resources and maintain functions such as employee compensation, recruitment, personnel policies, and regulatory compliance. **Education and Training:** College degree plus work experience. **Skills:** Math—Medium. English—Medium. Science—Medium. **Yearly Earnings:** $$$$$ **Job Growth:** ★★★ **Yearly Openings:** 🯅🯅🯅

Legislators. Develop laws and statutes at the federal, state, or local level. **Education and Training:** Work experience in a related occupation. **Skills:** Math—Medium. English—Medium. Science—Medium. **Yearly Earnings:** $ **Job Growth:** ★★★ **Yearly Openings:** 🯅

Postmasters and Mail Superintendents. Direct and coordinate operational, administrative, management, and supportive services of a U.S. post office or coordinate activities of workers engaged in postal and related work in assigned post office. **Education and Training:** Work experience in a related occupation. **Skills:** Math—Medium. English—High. Science—Medium. **Yearly Earnings:** $$$$ **Job Growth:** ★ **Yearly Openings:** 🯅

Private Sector Executives. Determine and formulate policies and business strategies and provide overall direction of private sector organizations. Plan, direct, and coordinate operational activities at the highest level of management with the help of subordinate managers. **Education and Training:** College degree plus work experience. **Skills:** Math—Medium. English—High. Science—Medium. **Yearly Earnings:** $$$$$ **Job Growth:** ★★★ **Yearly Openings:** 🯅🯅🯅

Property, Real Estate, and Community Association Managers. Plan, direct, or coordinate selling, buying, leasing, or governance activities of commercial, industrial, or residential real estate properties. **Education and Training:** Bachelor's degree. **Skills:** Math—Medium. English—High. Science—Low. **Yearly Earnings:** $$$ **Job Growth:** ★★★★ **Yearly Openings:** 🯅🯅🯅

Public Relations Managers. Plan and direct public relations programs designed to create and maintain a favorable public image for employer or client or, if engaged in fundraising, plan and direct activities to solicit and maintain funds for special projects and nonprofit organizations. **Education and Training:** College degree plus work experience. **Skills:** Math—Medium. English—Medium. Science—Medium. **Yearly Earnings:** $$$$$ **Job Growth:** ★★★★★ **Yearly Openings:** 🯅🯅

Purchasing Managers. Plan, direct, or coordinate the activities of buyers, purchasing officers, and related workers involved in purchasing materials, products, and services. **Education and Training:** College degree plus work experience. **Skills:** Math—Medium. English—Medium. Science—Medium. **Yearly Earnings:** $$$$$ **Job Growth:** ★ **Yearly Openings:** 🯅🯅🯅

Storage and Distribution Managers. Plan, direct, and coordinate the storage and distribution operations within an organization or the activities of organizations that are engaged in storing and distributing materials and products. **Education and Training:**

Work experience in a related occupation. **Skills:** Math—Medium. English—Medium. Science—Medium. **Yearly Earnings:** $$$$$ **Job Growth:** ★★★ **Yearly Openings:** 👤👤👤

Training and Development Managers. Plan, direct, or coordinate the training and development activities and staff of an organization. **Education and Training:** College degree plus work experience. **Skills:** Math—Medium. English—Medium. Science—Medium. **Yearly Earnings:** $$$$ **Job Growth:** ★★★ **Yearly Openings:** 👤👤👤

Transportation, Storage, and Distribution Managers. Plan, direct, or coordinate transportation, storage, or distribution activities according to governmental policies and regulations. **Education and Training:** Work experience in a related occupation. **Skills:** Math—Medium. English—Medium. Science—Medium. **Yearly Earnings:** $$$$$ **Job Growth:** ★★★ **Yearly Openings:** 👤👤👤

Treasurers, Controllers, and Chief Financial Officers. Plan, direct, and coordinate the financial activities of an organization at the highest level of management. Includes financial reserve officers. **Education and Training:** College degree plus work experience. **Skills:** Math—High. English—High. Science—Low. **Yearly Earnings:** $$$$$ **Job Growth:** ★★★ **Yearly Openings:** 👤👤👤👤

MANAGEMENT SUPPORT

These workers plan, manage, analyze, evaluate, and make decisions about personnel, purchases, and financial transactions and records. They use mathematics, logic, psychology, computerized tools, and knowledge of industry practices and government regulations that apply to their specific fields. They provide information and recommendations that help higher management accomplish the goals of the organization. They supervise clerical and sometimes technical staff that support them.

Accountants. Analyze financial information and prepare financial reports to determine or maintain record of assets, liabilities, profit and loss, tax liability, or other financial activities within an organization. **Education and Training:** Bachelor's degree. **Skills:** Math—High. English—High. Science—Low. **Yearly Earnings:** $$$$ **Job Growth:** ★★★ **Yearly Openings:** 👤👤👤👤

Accountants and Auditors. Examine, analyze, and interpret accounting records for the purpose of giving advice or preparing statements. Install or advise on systems of recording costs or other financial and budgetary data. **Education and Training:** Bachelor's degree. **Skills:** Math—Medium. English—Medium. Science—Medium. **Yearly Earnings:** $$$$ **Job Growth:** ★★★ **Yearly Openings:** 👤👤👤👤

Appraisers and Assessors of Real Estate. Appraise real property to determine its fair value. May assess taxes in accordance with prescribed schedules. **Education and Training:** Postsecondary career and technical education. **Skills:** Math—Medium. English—Medium. Science—Medium. **Yearly Earnings:** $$$ **Job Growth:** ★★★ **Yearly Openings:** 👤👤

Appraisers, Real Estate. Appraise real property to determine its value for purchase, sales, investment, mortgage, or loan purposes. **Education and Training:** Postsecondary career and technical education. **Skills:** Math—Medium. English—Medium. Science—Medium. **Yearly Earnings:** $$$ **Job Growth:** ★★★ **Yearly Openings:** 🧍🧍

Assessors. Appraise real and personal property to determine its fair value. May assess taxes in accordance with prescribed schedules. **Education and Training:** Postsecondary career and technical education. **Skills:** Math—Medium. English—Medium. Science—Low. **Yearly Earnings:** $$$ **Job Growth:** ★★★ **Yearly Openings:** 🧍🧍

Auditors. Examine and analyze accounting records to determine financial status of establishment and prepare financial reports concerning operating procedures. **Education and Training:** Bachelor's degree. **Skills:** Math—High. English—High. Science—Medium. **Yearly Earnings:** $$$$ **Job Growth:** ★★★ **Yearly Openings:** 🧍🧍🧍🧍

Budget Analysts. Examine budget estimates for completeness, accuracy, and conformance with procedures and regulations. Analyze budgeting and accounting reports for the purpose of maintaining expenditure controls. **Education and Training:** Bachelor's degree. **Skills:** Math—High. English—High. Science—Medium. **Yearly Earnings:** $$$$ **Job Growth:** ★★★ **Yearly Openings:** 🧍🧍

Claims Adjusters, Examiners, and Investigators. Review settled claims to determine that payments and settlements have been made in accordance with company practices and procedures, ensuring that proper methods have been followed. Report overpayments, underpayments, and other irregularities. Confer with legal counsel on claims requiring litigation. **Education and Training:** Long-term on-the-job training. **Skills:** Math—Medium. English—Medium. Science—Medium. **Yearly Earnings:** $$$$ **Job Growth:** ★★★ **Yearly Openings:** 🧍🧍🧍

Claims Examiners, Property and Casualty Insurance. Review settled insurance claims to determine that payments and settlements have been made in accordance with company practices and procedures. Report overpayments, underpayments, and other irregularities. Confer with legal counsel on claims requiring litigation. **Education and Training:** Long-term on-the-job training. **Skills:** Math—High. English—Medium. Science—Medium. **Yearly Earnings:** $$$$ **Job Growth:** ★★★ **Yearly Openings:** 🧍🧍🧍

Compensation, Benefits, and Job Analysis Specialists. Conduct programs of compensation and benefits and job analysis for employer. May specialize in specific areas, such as position classification and pension programs. **Education and Training:** Bachelor's degree. **Skills:** Math—Medium. English—High. Science—Medium. **Yearly Earnings:** $$$$ **Job Growth:** ★★★ **Yearly Openings:** 🧍🧍

Cost Estimators. Prepare cost estimates for product manufacturing, construction projects, or services to aid management in bidding on or determining price of product or service. May specialize according to particular service performed or type of product manufactured. **Education and Training:** Bachelor's degree. **Skills:** Math—High. English—High. Science—Medium. **Yearly Earnings:** $$$$ **Job Growth:** ★★★ **Yearly Openings:** 👤 👤 👤

Credit Analysts. Analyze current credit data and financial statements of individuals or firms to determine the degree of risk involved in extending credit or lending money. Prepare reports with this credit information for use in decision-making. **Education and Training:** Bachelor's degree. **Skills:** Math—Medium. English—Medium. Science—Medium. **Yearly Earnings:** $$$$ **Job Growth:** ★★★ **Yearly Openings:** 👤 👤

Employment Interviewers, Private or Public Employment Service. Interview job applicants in employment office and refer them to prospective employers for consideration. Search application files, notify selected applicants of job openings, and refer qualified applicants to prospective employers. Contact employers to verify referral results. Record and evaluate various pertinent data. **Education and Training:** Bachelor's degree. **Skills:** Math—Medium. English—Medium. Science—Medium. **Yearly Earnings:** $$$ **Job Growth:** ★★★ **Yearly Openings:** 👤 👤 👤

Employment, Recruitment, and Placement Specialists. Recruit and place workers. **Education and Training:** Bachelor's degree. **Skills:** Math—Medium. English—Medium. Science—Medium. **Yearly Earnings:** $$$ **Job Growth:** ★★★ **Yearly Openings:** 👤 👤 👤

Financial Analysts. Conduct quantitative analyses of information affecting investment programs of public or private institutions. **Education and Training:** Bachelor's degree. **Skills:** Math—High. English—High. Science—Medium. **Yearly Earnings:** $$$$$ **Job Growth:** ★★★★ **Yearly Openings:** 👤 👤 👤

Insurance Adjusters, Examiners, and Investigators. Investigate, analyze, and determine the extent of insurance company's liability concerning personal, casualty, or property loss or damages and attempt to effect settlement with claimants. Correspond with or interview medical specialists, agents, witnesses, or claimants to compile information. Calculate benefit payments and approve payment of claims within a certain monetary limit. **Education and Training:** Long-term on-the-job training. **Skills:** Math—Medium. English—High. Science—Medium. **Yearly Earnings:** $$$$ **Job Growth:** ★★★ **Yearly Openings:** 👤 👤 👤

Insurance Appraisers, Auto Damage. Appraise automobile or other vehicle damage to determine cost of repair for insurance claim settlement and seek agreement with automotive repair shop on cost of repair. Prepare insurance forms to indicate repair cost or cost estimates and recommendations. **Education and Training:** Long-term on-the-job training. **Skills:** Math—Medium. English—Medium. Science—Medium. **Yearly Earnings:** $$$ **Job Growth:** ★★★ **Yearly Openings:** 👤

Insurance Underwriters. Review individual applications for insurance to evaluate degree of risk involved and determine acceptance of applications. **Education and Training:** Bachelor's degree. **Skills:** Math—High. English—Medium. Science—Medium. **Yearly Earnings:** $$$$ **Job Growth:** ★ **Yearly Openings:** 🚶🚶🚶

Loan Counselors. Provide guidance to prospective loan applicants who have problems qualifying for traditional loans. Guidance may include determining the best type of loan and explaining loan requirements or restrictions. **Education and Training:** Bachelor's degree. **Skills:** Math—Medium. English—Medium. Science—Medium. **Yearly Earnings:** $$$ **Job Growth:** ★★★ **Yearly Openings:** 🚶

Loan Officers. Evaluate, authorize, or recommend approval of commercial, real estate, or credit loans. Advise borrowers on financial status and methods of payments. Includes mortgage loan officers and agents, collection analysts, loan servicing officers, and loan underwriters. **Education and Training:** Bachelor's degree. **Skills:** Math—Medium. English—Medium. Science—Medium. **Yearly Earnings:** $$$$ **Job Growth:** ★★ **Yearly Openings:** 🚶🚶🚶

Logisticians. Analyze and coordinate the logistical functions of a firm or organization. Responsible for the entire life cycle of a product, including acquisition, distribution, internal allocation, delivery, and final disposal of resources. **Education and Training:** Bachelor's degree. **Skills:** Math—Medium. English—Medium. Science—Medium. **Yearly Earnings:** $$$$$ **Job Growth:** ★★★★ **Yearly Openings:** 🚶🚶🚶

Management Analysts. Conduct organizational studies and evaluations, design systems and procedures, conduct work simplifications and measurement studies, and prepare operations and procedures manuals to assist management in operating more efficiently and effectively. Includes program analysts and management consultants. **Education and Training:** College degree plus work experience. **Skills:** Math—Medium. English—High. Science—Medium. **Yearly Earnings:** $$$$$ **Job Growth:** ★★★★ **Yearly Openings:** 🚶🚶🚶

Market Research Analysts. Research market conditions in local, regional, or national areas to determine potential sales of a product or service. May gather information on competitors, prices, sales, and methods of marketing and distribution. May use survey results to create a marketing campaign based on regional preferences and buying habits. **Education and Training:** Bachelor's degree. **Skills:** Math—High. English—High. Science—Medium. **Yearly Earnings:** $$$$$ **Job Growth:** ★★★★ **Yearly Openings:** 🚶🚶🚶

Personnel Recruiters. Seek out, interview, and screen applicants to fill existing and future job openings and promote career opportunities within an organization. **Education and Training:** Bachelor's degree. **Skills:** Math—Medium. English—Medium. Science—Medium. **Yearly Earnings:** $$$ **Job Growth:** ★★★ **Yearly Openings:** 🚶🚶🚶

Purchasing Agents and Buyers, Farm Products. Purchase farm products for further processing or resale. **Education and Training:** Work experience in a related occupation. **Skills:** Math—Medium. English—Medium. Science—Medium. **Yearly Earnings:** $$$ **Job Growth:** ★★★ **Yearly Openings:** 🚹

Purchasing Agents, Except Wholesale, Retail, and Farm Products. Purchase machinery, equipment, tools, parts, supplies, or services necessary for the operation of an establishment. Purchase raw or semi-finished materials for manufacturing. **Education and Training:** Bachelor's degree. **Skills:** Math—High. English—High. Science—Medium. **Yearly Earnings:** $$$$ **Job Growth:** ★★★ **Yearly Openings:** 🚹🚹🚹

Tax Examiners, Collectors, and Revenue Agents. Determine tax liability or collect taxes from individuals or business firms according to prescribed laws and regulations. **Education and Training:** Bachelor's degree. **Skills:** Math—High. English—High. Science—Medium. **Yearly Earnings:** $$$$ **Job Growth:** ★★ **Yearly Openings:** 🚹🚹

Training and Development Specialists. Conduct training and development programs for employees. **Education and Training:** Bachelor's degree. **Skills:** Math—Medium. English—Medium. Science—Medium. **Yearly Earnings:** $$$$ **Job Growth:** ★★★ **Yearly Openings:** 🚹🚹🚹

Wholesale and Retail Buyers, Except Farm Products. Buy merchandise or commodities, other than farm products, for resale to consumers at the wholesale or retail level, including both durable and nondurable goods. Analyze past buying trends, sales records, price, and quality of merchandise to determine value and yield. Select, order, and authorize payment for merchandise according to contractual agreements. May conduct meetings with sales personnel and introduce new products. **Education and Training:** Bachelor's degree. **Skills:** Math—Medium. English—Medium. Science—Low. **Yearly Earnings:** $$$ **Job Growth:** ★ **Yearly Openings:** 🚹🚹🚹

Exploring Careers:

Medical and Health Services

Start Your Journey Through Careers Related to

MEDICAL AND HEALTH SERVICES

Careers in this area suit people interested in helping people be healthy.

EXPLORING CAREER CLUES

Your interests give important clues for exploring career options. Think about your interests to learn if jobs in the Medical and Health Services interest area may be worth further exploration.

Do you like the school subjects related to the Medical and Health Services interest area? Here are some examples of related subjects:

- Science
- Chemistry
- Biology
- Physics
- Psychology
- Sociology
- Math
- Computers
- Health
- Family and consumer sciences
- Child development
- English
- Physical education

Do you like the free-time activities related to the Medical and Health Services interest area? Here are some examples of related free-time activities:

- Raising, training, and caring for pets and other animals
- Baby-sitting or caring for children
- Serving as a volunteer in a hospital, nursing home, or retirement home
- Helping sick relatives, friends, and neighbors
- Learning first aid and CPR
- Listening to friends and helping them with their problems
- Participating in science fairs and doing experiments
- Staying fit, eating right, and taking care of your health
- Going to museum exhibits on science and technology

- Watching television shows about medicine, health, science, and technology
- Participating in sports and outdoor activities
- Reading about topics related to medicine, science, health, nutrition, and technology

EXPLORING JOB GROUPS

Jobs related to the Medical and Health Services interest area fit into eight groups. Read through the list to see which groups sound interesting to you.

- Managerial Work in Medical and Health Services
- Medicine and Surgery
- Dentistry
- Health Specialties
- Medical Technology
- Medical Therapy
- Patient Care and Assistance
- Health Protection and Promotion

EXPLORING CAREER POSSIBILITIES

You can satisfy your interest in the Medical and Health Services area by working in one of many careers that help people stay healthy, cope with illness and injury, or regain their health. Here are a few examples of career possibilities:

You can satisfy your interest in this field by working in a health-care team as a doctor, therapist, or nurse. You might specialize in one of the many different parts of the body or in one of the many different types of care. Or you may wish to be a generalist who deals with the whole patient.

If you like technology, you might find satisfaction working with X rays or new methods of diagnosis. You might work with healthy people, helping them stay in condition through exercise and eating right.

Turn the page to meet people working in the Medical and Health Services interest area→

PROFILE

Roberta Jo Weilhammer—Medical Lab Technologist

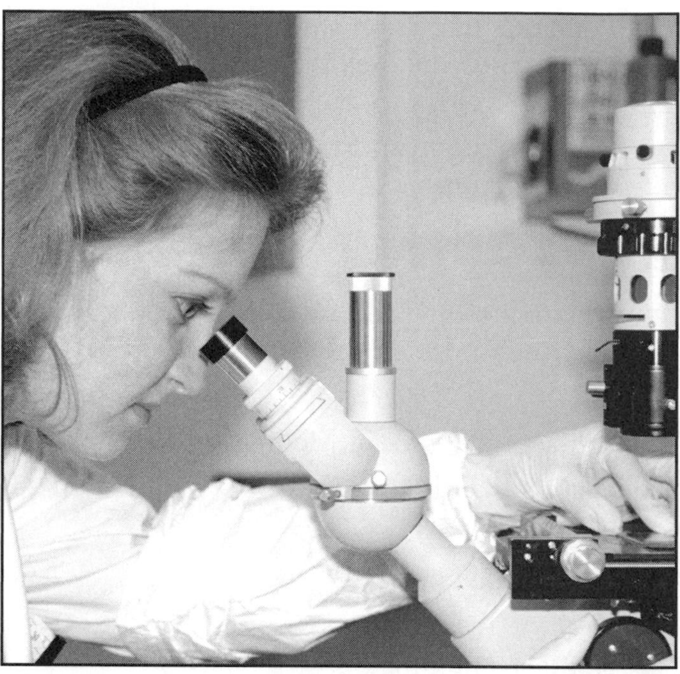

Roberta Jo must do accurate testing. "A patient's life could depend on it."

Roberta Jo Weilhammer is a medical lab technologist at St. John's Hospital. The medical laboratory where she works does tests to find out exactly what's wrong with people who are sick. Doctors need to know what the problem is to take care of it.

The medical laboratory is divided into four departments: clinical chemistry, bacteriology, hematology, and the blood bank. Roberta Jo has been in bacteriology since she started at St. John's, but her training covered all of the areas.

A Natural Chemistry

Roberta Jo became interested in chemistry during her freshman year in college. "I did so well in it that my professor encouraged me to consider a career in science. I visited a local laboratory and talked to some of the people there. I decided to become a medical lab technologist. I have a bachelor's degree in medical technology," Roberta Jo said.

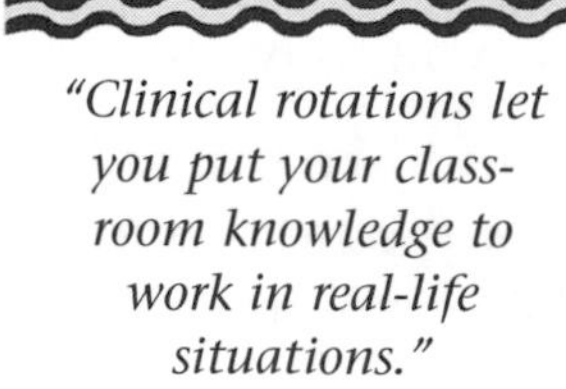

"Clinical rotations let you put your classroom knowledge to work in real-life situations."

"During my senior year in college, I worked at City Hospital. I rotated among the departments of

the medical laboratory. Clinical rotations let you put your classroom knowledge to work in real-life situations," Roberta Jo said. After she graduated, she took an exam to become registered as a medical technologist. Registration helps in getting a job and, sometimes, a higher salary.

Physicians have samples sent to bacteriology when they suspect an infection or a disease.

Students interested in the field should research such job titles as medical and clinical laboratory technologist and technician, blood bank technologist and technician, cytotechnician, immunohematologist, and serology technician.

A Day in the Lab

A pathologist is in charge of the medical laboratory. Pathologists are physicians who study the ways in which disease shows up in body tissues and fluids. About seventy people work in the medical laboratory at St. John's. In addition to medical lab technologists like Roberta Jo, there are technicians and assistants who take care of routine lab work. Most of them took one or two years of training.

Yesterday was a typical day in the bacteriology department. They had the usual sorts of things to test: samples of urine, spinal fluid, throat cultures, material from wounds, and blood. Physicians have samples sent to bacteriology when they suspect an infection or a disease.

This morning, a throat culture came in. The doctor wants to find out which antibiotic to prescribe for the patient's sore throat. An antibiotic destroys bacteria. There are many kinds of bacteria that make people sick and antibiotics to combat them. The first step is to find out exactly what they're dealing with. That's where the lab comes in.

The culture arrived on a swab in a sterile tube. Roberta Jo placed some of it in a dish with nutrients that make bacteria grow. She then put the dish in a warm incubator. Tomorrow morning she will try to identify the bacteria by using chemicals. She'll make slides and examine them under a microscope. Then she'll experiment to find out which antibiotic works against the strain of bacteria she has identified.

She'll make slides and examine them under a microscope.

When she finishes the tests the doctor has asked for, she'll record the results and notify the doctor. The results come up within forty-eight to seventy-two hours. When test results don't make sense to the patient's physician, they run tests on another specimen.

"You can't be too careful in a medical lab," Roberta Jo said. "But mistakes sometimes happen, and test results can be wrong. That's why the human factor–judgment–is so important."

Other Jobs in the Lab

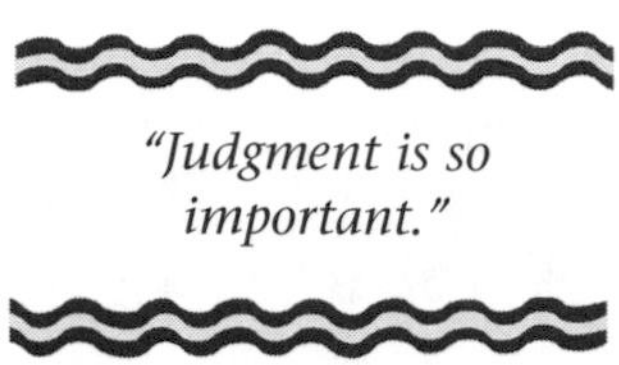
"Judgment is so important."

Jessica just started working in the lab last week. She's in the clinical chemistry department and operates machinery that tests blood for sugar, salt, fat, and protein content and for disease.

She's testing for sugar content right now. She begins by placing tubes of blood in a machine that spins so fast that the blood cells fall to the bottom of each tube. The material that remains on top is the serum. It looks like water and contains the sugar. Chemicals in the machine make the sugar turn blue. Knowing whether or not a patient's blood has the proper amount of sugar helps a doctor treat the patient.

Many of the machines Jessica works with are linked to a computer. It enables her to run thousands of different tests in a short period of time. Computers have made a big difference in medicine.

Fritz is in hematology, where they specialize in testing blood. Fritz does blood counts much of the time. He's concerned with the number of red cells and white cells in the blood. Red cells carry oxygen and white cells fight infection.

Fritz operates machinery that places drops of a blood sample on a slide, stains the sample with colored dyes to help identify the cells, and smears the blood across the slide. Then he sets the slide under a microscope and looks closely at the white blood cells. Red cells all look alike, but white cells don't.

Fritz can differentiate among white cells. His count of the various kinds of white cells in the patient's blood gives the physician an idea of whether or not something is wrong.

Wanda works in the blood bank. Wanda and the other technologists in the lab draw blood from blood donors–healthy people who donate blood to the blood bank. The blood is refrigerated in plastic bags and stays good for twenty-one days. The laboratory receives blood samples of patients who are scheduled to undergo surgery. Doctors need to have blood available for transfusions. Medical technologists in the blood bank find donors' blood that is compatible with patients' blood samples sent to the lab.

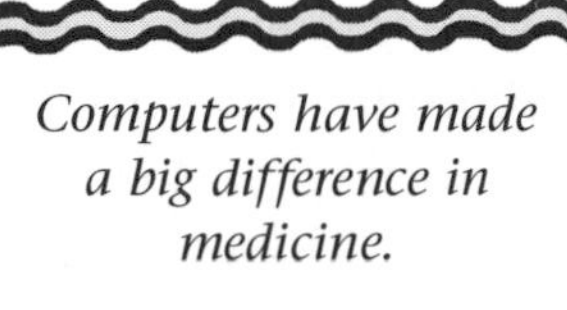

Computers have made a big difference in medicine.

Technologists determine the type and Rh factor of blood in the sample. They then find stored blood that matches the blood in the patient's sample. They retest it to be safe. To be usable, the stored blood must be exactly like the patient's blood. If no compatible blood is in storage, the technologists contact the Red Cross to get the type they need.

"Accuracy is essential in the blood bank."

Accuracy is essential in the blood bank, and workers are under pressure to avoid mistakes. "If the lab makes an error in testing and a patient receives the wrong blood during an operation, he or she could die. That's an awesome responsibility," said Roberta Jo.

Examining Her Future

Last fall, Roberta Jo supervised some medical technology students during their senior year clinical rotation in the biochemistry department here. "I was surprised to discover that I enjoy teaching," she said. "I'm thinking of going back to school for a master's or Ph.D. I eventually want to teach in a university program in medical technology."

Although her job can be routine at times, it doesn't intrude on her personal time. Also, Roberta Jo knows enough science to understand what the tests really mean. "Once I run some tests, I often have an idea of what's going on inside the body of a patient. That makes the work interesting," she said.

"I like being part of a team effort to help sick people."

Roberta Jo also likes the day-to-day contact with the hospital staff. "I like being part of a team effort to help sick people."

PROFILE

Jeannette Huck–Optometrist

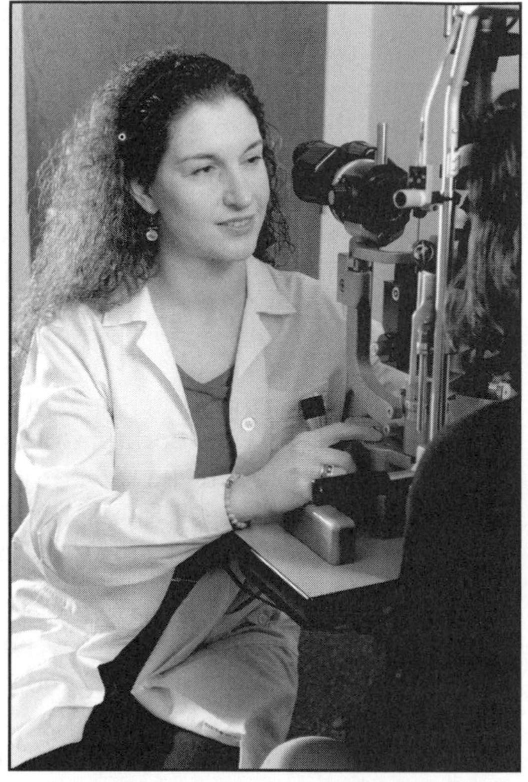

Dr. Huck works with patients until their prescriptions are perfect.

Jeannette Huck, doctor of optometry, has an office in a suburb of a midwestern city. Behind a counter at the end of the comfortable reception area sits Barry Jameson, her receptionist.

"Good morning!" Barry said to Ms. Fitzpatrick, who had just walked in. "Here to pick up your new glasses?"

Barry leads her to a well-lit, cheerful room, with racks of glasses lining the walls. After retrieving the new glasses from a drawer, he calls in Dr. Huck. With practiced eyes and hands, Dr. Huck quickly checks Ms. Fitzpatrick's glasses for fit and makes some minor adjustments to the earpieces.

Ms. Fitzpatrick is thrilled with her new look–and with what she can see now–and follows Barry back to the counter, where he calculates her bill on the computer.

More Than Meets the Eye

"Most people," Dr. Huck said, "think that this is all an optometrist does. Checks vision and fits glasses. Period. That's a big part of the job, but there's more to it than that.

"Optometrists can be the first line of detection for many medical problems. We aren't M.D.s and can't give medical advice beyond our area of practice. But we *can* catch problems early and refer our patients to medical doctors for further diagnosis.

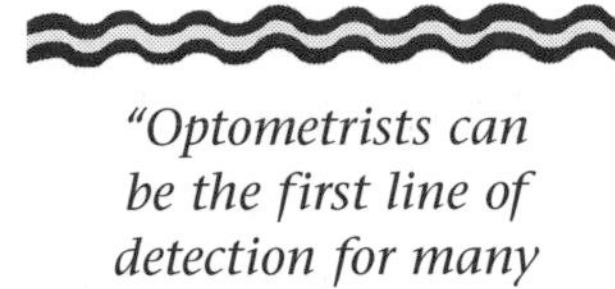

"Optometrists can be the first line of detection for many medical problems."

"Such things as high blood pressure, diabetes, and multiple sclerosis aren't so much *about* the eyes but can often be detected *through* examining the eyes. Spotting a serious problem in time to help somebody is very rewarding.

"And of course, there are many diseases and conditions of the eyes themselves that we detect, such as glaucoma, eye infections or injuries, and cataracts."

Dr. Huck said that the profession of optometry has undergone changes. For one thing, in the past, only an ophthalmologist, who is an M.D., could prescribe drugs. Now many states allow an optometrist to prescribe drugs to fight infection and inflammation and to relieve pain.

Ophthalmologists have more education in treating diseases of the eye, Dr. Huck pointed out, but optometrists have more training in testing vision and prescribing and fitting corrective lenses and contacts.

A continuing trend that Dr. Huck has observed is commercialization. Optometry groups have joined with large retail stores–with big advertising budgets and fast turnaround times on delivering lenses.

"I think it's beginning to change again," she reflected. "I've had many patients come back to me because they missed the personal service and the extra time I give them."

Being Your Own Boss

Optometrists have more training in testing vision and prescribing and fitting corrective lenses and contacts.

Dr. Huck walks to a long, narrow, somewhat darkened third room, with a chair at one end for the patient. At the other end is a small projection screen. An impressive array of instruments, one looking like goggles from outer space, stand ready to measure a patient's vision, test for glaucoma, and perform other routine procedures.

"Just look around at all this equipment. This costs a lot. I also have to pay for its maintenance, lease a good office space, pay my staff, and buy insurance.

An impressive array of instruments stand ready to measure a patient's vision, test for glaucoma, and perform other procedures.

"I also have to keep up the inventory. Everybody wants something that looks different or fashionable," Dr. Huck continued. "And now there are many merchandisers competing for business.

"In good economic times, my patient load can be almost more than I can keep up with. When money gets a little tight, however, they just won't come in unless they're in distress.

"Not having a steady paycheck and being responsible for so many business decisions can be drawbacks. The other side of that coin is that I have my independence. My decisions are mine and mine alone. For example, I can set up my practice anywhere I like–and not worry about being transferred."

Envisioning a Career

"My interest started when as a youngster I had my first eye exam and got my first pair of glasses. My parents were pushing for me to go to college, and I decided I wanted to be an optometrist. It's a decision I've never regretted."

Dr. Huck said that a person usually needs first to have a four-year bachelor of science degree in a subject such as biology, chemistry, or physics. Then, another four years of optometry school are necessary. Dr. Huck also believes that a college student should take business courses, whether required or not.

"I should also point out that some students who enjoy and excel at the technical, scientific aspects of this profession fall apart when they have their first hands-on experience with real people. You've got to really like working with and helping people to be a successful optometrist.

"My decisions are mine and mine alone."

"We've talked about aptitude for science and business. You've also got to have lots of mechanical skill," Dr. Huck said. "You need it to do the fitting and adjusting that lenses require–from handling contact lenses to those tiny little screws in glasses frames.

"You've got to really like working with and helping people to be a successful optometrist."

"Getting back to education, it's important to know that in optometry, as in most professions, the education process never stops," Dr. Huck continued. "To renew my license to practice, I'm required by the state to take twenty-four hours of study–and be tested on them!–every two years. Six of those hours must be from an accredited college of optometry.

"A good optometrist also reads about advances and attends seminars. They offer a good chance to learn new things as well as to meet some of your professional colleagues."

A Bright Outlook

"It's important to know that in optometry, as in most professions, the education process never stops."

"An optometrist just starting out might be well advised to go into a group practice," said Dr. Huck. It would cut the costs of inventory, rent, and utilities by sharing these costs. That also has the advantage of giving you someone to cover for you when you're sick or want to take a vacation.

"You're not limited to private clinical practice, either. For example, some optometrists take salaried jobs in hospitals, with HMOs, or in retail stores' optical shops. One of my former classmates works as a consultant in eye-safety programs at industrial plants. Or you might work somewhere that makes optometric products."

Dr. Huck feels that the future looks bright for optometry. "The older generation is swelling rapidly, and that means an increase in eye diseases and an optometrist's patients."

The Rewards Are Clear

"This profession also brings personal rewards you can't measure in dollars and cents, of course," Dr. Huck noted.

"Let me tell you about Tommy. He's a fourth-grader who never realized he couldn't see very well. He'd never known anything different all his life. But his teacher noticed it, and she referred him to me. I put him through an exam, and he sure needed glasses.

"I put his new glasses on the fourth-grader, and you should have seen his face light up."

Dr. Huck motioned to the window. "When they came in yesterday, Tommy and his mother sat in those chairs over there. I put his new glasses on him, and you should have seen his face light up.

"'Wow, Mom!' he said. 'I can see leaves on the trees.'

"Small moments like that are when I get a great deal of pleasure out of what I do for a living."

PROFILE

Nick Badua—Pharmacist

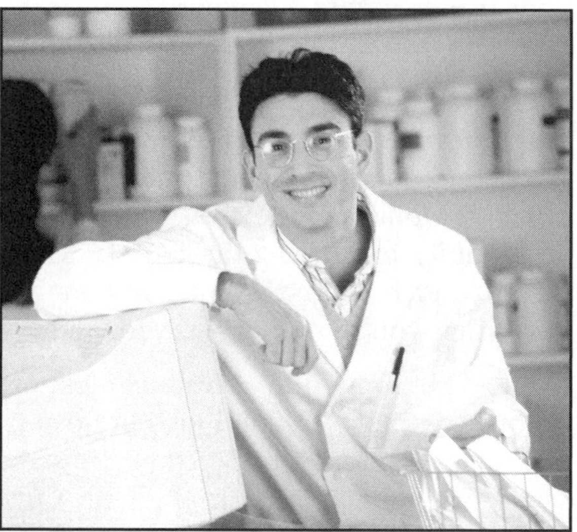

Nick fills prescriptions and advises people on the proper use of medications.

The phone was ringing as Nick Badua opened the pharmacy in the retail store. A dozen people sat in the waiting area.

He grabbed the phone. "Good morning. SmartMart Pharmacy, Nick Badua speaking."

"This is Mrs. Dickinson. I need a prescription filled for my son."

"Good morning, Mrs. Dickinson. Hold on a moment. I'll check to see if your doctor has phoned in the prescription."

Nick put the call on hold and almost immediately another line began to ring. The people in the waiting area were lining up at the counter. Most of

them were trying to get their prescriptions filled before they had to be at work.

Nick recognized the first patient in line at the window.

A Day at the Pharmacy

The phone was insistent. "Good morning. SmartMart Pharmacy, Nick Badua speaking."

"This is Dr. Wilmot's office. The doctor would like to talk to you about a prescription for Rasheed Kellogg." Nick briefly discussed the prescription with the doctor and then went back to Mrs. Dickinson, who had been on hold.

"Mrs. Dickinson? I have the prescription here. It should be ready for pick-up by 10:30."

Nick turned to the line at the counter. His assistant, Mindy, was just arriving. Mindy quickly started filling the waiting call-in prescriptions. She was a good assistant, able to fill prescriptions quickly and accurately. She was also good with the patients, which is important.

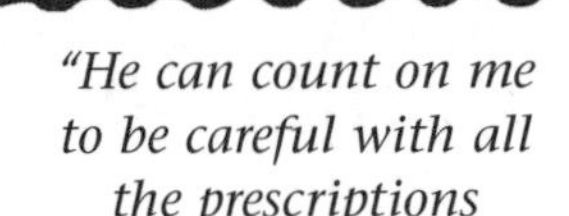
"He can count on me to be careful with all the prescriptions I fill."

Nick recognized the first patient in line at the window. He had been a good customer for years. "Good morning, Mr. Fremont. How can I help you?"

"My son is out in the car with a high fever. Here's a prescription the doctor gave me yesterday."

"We'll fill it as soon as we can. Please have a seat and we'll call you."

Nick handed the prescription slip to Mindy, who was on the phone. Nick handled each patient in turn. By 9:30 the waiting area was empty of all but one patient, who hobbled over on crutches to ask him a question.

"He trusts me," Nick said. "He can count on me to be careful with all the prescriptions I fill. He also knows that I check out side effects or reactions with any medications he's already taking. If I find any, I warn him about them or double-check with his doctor.

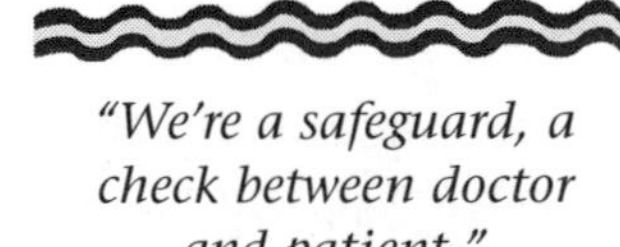
"We're a safeguard, a check between doctor and patient."

"I do this with all my patients. We enter patient records in the computer, which links with our entire chain. It can spot a drug allergy or some other problem instantly, some of which can be fatal. In that respect, it can save lives.

"I treat my patients as if they were my friends, as indeed many of them have become over the years.

"We're a safeguard, a check between doctor and patient. We check a prescription's directions, strength, conflicts with other drugs, and age appropriateness, for example. We're here to protect and serve the public, and I consider it a very important part of our profession," Nick said.

A Prescription for Success

Nick has a B.S. degree in pharmacy, which was a five-year curriculum. Pharmacy programs today, however, offer a Doctor of Pharmacy (Pharm.D.), which is a six- or seven-year curriculum. Some colleges require applicants to take the Pharmacy College Admissions Test.

Nick listed anatomy, pathology, and cellular biology as among the courses that students take. He also mentioned courses that teach how drugs break down in the body, how they interact with other drugs, and how they may affect different organs.

"You should expect to take some law courses, as there are a lot of regulations. Internships are helpful, too.

"After receiving your degree, you take a state board exam to receive your license. This is usually a written exam, and it lasts two days," he said. "Your license must be displayed publicly at the pharmacy where you work and must be renewed every two years."

Opportunities Abound

"There's always a window of opportunity to work in this field."

"Most pharmacists work in retail. By 'retail,' I mean dispensing drugs to fill prescriptions, usually as part of a big national chain.

"But there are other opportunities for pharmacists, too. Some work in hospitals and nursing homes.

Pharmacists do research work, represent drug manufacturing companies, sell to doctors and hospitals, and do respiratory and home IV work. There's always a window of opportunity to work in this field."

Record-keeping is important.

Nick said that anyone wanting to be a retail pharmacist should take a realistic view of the profession. What the customer sees at the counter is the tip of an iceberg.

"I rarely get to go on vacation, and I have to be prepared to work on holidays. This situation, plus having to deal with ill patients and insurance companies, can produce stress," Nick continued.

Pharmacists and the Law

Nick describes pharmacy as a "complicated profession." State and federal governments have strict mandates regulating the dispensing of drugs and how a pharmacist practices the profession.

Pharmacists have access to some very powerful and addictive drugs. As a result, record-keeping is important, Nick said. The government must be able to track quantities dispensed, how often and to whom.

"There is another point of law that would-be pharmacists should be aware of. If you make a mistake in dispensing, you can be held personally responsible. Similarly, warning labels on the pill bottles are fine, but I like to explain warnings personally."

Nick pointed out that security in the pharmacy business has to be extremely tight. "Nobody has a key to the pharmacy but me. Any time the door to the pharmacy is unlocked, a pharmacist must be there."

Prescription forgery happens surprisingly often. "Altering a prescription is a felony, and we have ways that we can spot one most of the time."

Career Thoughts

Nick recommends pharmacy as a career. "I'm comfortable with it. There usually isn't a problem finding a position. But the burnout rate is high.

"I know many pharmacists who like the satisfaction of advising people on the proper use of medications and the knowledge that they're really helping make sick people better.

"This is a profession that you should scrutinize closely. You may love it and do well. Just be sure you have real-world facts before you commit."

PROFILE

Julia Stovall—Physical Therapist

Two patients are in the waiting area when Julia Stovall arrives early in the morning in the physical therapy (PT) department of the hospital. An elderly man is sitting quietly in a wheelchair, and a young man is lying on a transport bed. Julia greets them and the receptionist and then proceeds to the treatment rooms. There, two other physical therapists are preparing for patients.

George Sopoci is working with a burn patient. Nicki Bathista, the other therapist, is setting up the parallel bars. Her first patient lost his leg in a construction accident. He has just been fitted with an artificial leg, and Nicki will help him learn to walk normally with it.

Julia is bound for room 514. "I hope the swelling in Mark's leg is down today," Julia thinks as she waits for the elevator. After a short ride, the elevator doors open onto the fifth floor and Julia heads down to 514.

"Good morning, Mark," she says brightly as she looks over his chart. "How is the leg?"

"It hurts a lot."

"Well, when the swelling goes down, that will improve," Julia explained. "The exercises we're doing this morning have been designed to reduce the swelling."

The patient's injuries are extensive, and Julia wants no chance for an error in his treatment.

The exercises Mark performs are prescribed by a physician. After the emergency surgery on Mark's injured leg, the surgeon wrote an "order," or prescription, for Mark to receive physical therapy.

Ordinarily, Julia would know exactly what to do after reading the order. But Mark's injuries are extensive, and Julia wants no chance for an error in his treatment. So, before she visited with Mark for the first time, she consulted with the physician and discussed her goals for Mark's treatment.

Important Work That Improves Lives

"Physical therapy is teaching patients how to help themselves," said Julia. "The best part of my job is enabling patients to make progress in their healing process."

Julia explains a recent case involving a five-year-old with cerebral palsy. Although no one ever expected her to be able to walk, Julia was able to teach her first to roll over, then sit up, and finally to walk. Julia and her patient's mother both burst into tears at the sight of the girl walking for the first time.

"The best part of my job is enabling patients to make progress in their healing process."

"Working in the health care system as a whole is rewarding, too," Julia said. "This is important work. When I confer with doctors and nurses about the correct treatment for someone who is relying on us to improve his or her life, I'm awestruck at the responsibility involved.

"And no matter how difficult a patient may be or how hopeless a case appears to be, I never feel like giving up. You never know if that the next session will be the breakthrough. And I'm certainly never bored."

A Hard Job Requiring Compassion

"It's hard work to keep an upbeat attitude when so many of the patients are sick and unhappy. Of course, I remind myself that they are in pain or scared that their condition will never improve. I try to put myself in their place."

"I try to put myself in the patient's place."

Julia said some therapists complain about the need to stand for so many hours. "There are days when I don't sit down for more than ten minutes," she said.

"Even though we schedule ourselves carefully, and we certainly don't have the demands that an emergency room worker does, there are still unplanned problems, like consults with doctors at the last minute. Standing so much can be hard on the back."

"I would advise students to study their high school science courses very carefully."

Starting Out As a Volunteer

"I started out doing volunteer work when I was in high school," Julia said. "I worked at a hospital near my home and was assigned to the physical therapy department. I liked the work so much that I majored in physical therapy when I went to college.

"College was a lot of science. I had courses in chemistry, biology, physics, neurology, physiology, biomechanics, neuroanatomy. Psychology was required too, and that proved to be very helpful. A course in the psychology of individuals with disabilities really opened my eyes to how many disabled people view the world. It helped me understand some of their hopes and fears."

Julia went on to explain the hands-on assignments she had during college. "That was valuable experience. The assignments gave me a taste of the day-to-day work in most of the specialty areas as well as the general practice."

Julia points out that accredited physical therapist programs are required to offer degrees at the master's level and above. Graduates must pass a license exam before they can practice. Julia must take continuing education courses as well to keep up with the latest treatment methods.

"I would advise students to study their high school science courses very carefully, because that will start them on the right road."

Qualities for Today and Tomorrow

"First and foremost, physical therapists must have patience. Many of the people you are trying to help will be resistant. It's up to you to persuade them that you're trying to help them help themselves.

"Along with that, you must be self-assured, resourceful, and able to work with many different kinds of people. You must be able to look at a patient with perfect confidence and say, 'We'll soon have you up and about.'

"Along with this is the ability to hear what people are saying and to make yourself heard when telling them something. How can you help someone if you're aren't listening to him or her describe their pain or stiffness or whatever? And if you can't get the patient to hear what you're saying, it will be hard for that person to follow through on the proper treatment course. They go hand in hand."

Physical therapists are here to stay, according to Julia. "More and more people need our services each year. As injuries like carpal tunnel syndrome occur, physical therapists will be instrumental in helping people to continue to function and work, even with such conditions."

SKILL SAMPLER

Catherine Rodriguez—Registered Nurse

Catherine Rodriguez responds calmly to the tense, highly charged atmosphere of the intensive care unit.

Catherine Rodriguez works as a registered nurse in a hospital intensive care unit. She takes care of patients who are in serious condition following surgery. "I observe every little thing about my patient's condition, and I have to understand what I see."

Catherine discussed the skills and knowledge needed by registered nurses. She offers several tips to help you decide if you are suited for a career in nursing.

Registered nurses must be concerned about good health.

- Do you eat a well-balanced diet?
- Do you get enough sleep?
- Do you see the dentist regularly?

- Do you pay attention to warnings about alcohol, drug, or tobacco use?
- When you ask someone how he or she is feeling, are you really concerned?

Registered nurses must have an interest in science.

- Do you like science?
- Do you enjoy doing projects for a science class or science fair?
- Do you read magazine or newspaper articles about science?
- Do you like to visit museum exhibits on science and technology?
- Do you enjoy watching medical programs on television?

Registered nurses must be able to tolerate unpleasant sights and sounds.

- Does the sight of blood upset you?
- Does it bother you to change a diaper?
- Would you feel comfortable going with an injured friend to the emergency room of a hospital?
- Do the signs and smells bother you when you visit people in a hospital or nursing home?
- Does the idea of dissecting a frog in a science class bother you?

Registered nurses must be very observant. They must recognize danger signals right away.

- Can you tell when your pet isn't feeling well?
- Can you tell when you have had too much sun?
- Do you notice when the ink in a computer printer cartridge starts to fade?
- Can you tell when a car needs a tune-up?
- Do you notice minor changes in television or radio reception?
- Can you tell when something is missing from your room?

Registered nurses must carry out instructions precisely. There's no room for error when they give measured doses of medicine to patients.

- Are you good at following written instructions for assembling things?
- Can you remember road directions when someone gives them to you over the phone?
- Do you remember jokes and funny stories?
- Can you memorize plays and coaches' instructions in football, basketball, and other sports?
- Can you remember a teacher's exact instructions for a homework assignment or test?

Registered nurses should care about people. They deal with patients who are at their worst due to an illness or accident.

- Do you mind hearing people complain?
- Do you visit relatives or neighbors when they are sick?
- Are you patient with your younger brothers or sisters when they are tired or irritable?

Registered nurses must stay calm during emergencies. They might have to set up an oxygen tent, administer artificial respiration, or treat a patient having a heart attack.

- Could you keep calm and get help right away if your kitchen caught fire?
- Would you know what to do if an infant got hurt or stopped breathing while you were baby-sitting?
- Would you act sensibly if a pet were injured?
- Would you know what to do if a friend injured himself or herself in the hall at school?

Registered nurses function as part of a health team. They must be good at giving and taking instructions. They also must understand the limits of their authority.

- Can you enforce your parents' rules when caring for your younger brothers and sisters?
- When you are in a place of leadership, are you good at getting people to do what you ask without getting angry?
- Do you respect the law, even when it is dealing with relatively minor offenses such as littering or jaywalking?
- Can you judge how far you can go when talking with a teacher about a grade you don't agree with?

Registered nurses must have stamina. They spend a lot of time on their feet.

- Do you like to be active most of the time?
- Do you enjoy activities such as sports, hiking, backpacking, dancing, or gardening?

Registered nurses must keep accurate records of patient information such as medication, blood pressure, and temperature.

- Do you use your computer to keep your schedule, money, and responsibilities organized?
- When you're an officer in a club, do you keep good records?
- Do people ask you to keep score in bowling and other activities?
- When you look back at notes you take in class, are they clear?

Registered nurses must have manual dexterity to handle patients and medical equipment.

- Do you like working with your hands?
- Are you accustomed to using tools for work around the house?
- Are you good at setting up displays for class projects or school exhibits?
- Do you enjoy playing a wind instrument or keyboarding?

Registered nurses cannot afford to become emotionally involved with their patients.

- Can you remain calm when a friend or relative tells you about a serious problem?
- Does it upset you to visit someone who is very sick?
- Can you comfort a friend or family member during a time of sorrow?
- Can you make your point calmly in a heated discussion?

Registered nurses keep their medical knowledge current by reading professional literature and attending lectures and conferences.

- Do you like to read, especially popular science magazines?
- Do you show initiative in doing research on subjects of personal interest?
- When you are curious about something, do you go to the library or search online to learn more about it?
- Do you use a dictionary to look up words you don't understand?
- Do you like to browse in the new-books section of your library?

Now learn about all major jobs in the Medical and Health Services interest area→

Facts About All Major Jobs Related to

MEDICAL AND HEALTH SERVICES

In addition to the jobs covered in the profiles and skill sampler, other careers in the Medical and Health Services interest area may appeal to you. This section describes and gives facts about all major jobs in the Medical and Health Services interest area. For an explanation of the $, ★, and 🯅 symbols, see page 6.

MANAGERIAL WORK IN MEDICAL AND HEALTH SERVICES

These workers manage medical activities. Some primarily supervise doctors, nurses, therapists, and other health care workers. Others provide leadership for all aspects of a hospital or nursing home, including finance and physical facilities. Some make decisions about how an autopsy is to be conducted. They do planning, budgeting, staffing, and evaluation of outcomes. They work for hospitals, health insurers, and government agencies.

Coroners. Direct activities such as autopsies, pathological and toxicological analyses, and inquests relating to the investigation of deaths occurring within a legal jurisdiction to determine cause of death or to fix responsibility for accidental, violent, or unexplained deaths. **Education and Training:** Work experience in a related occupation. **Skills:** Math—Medium. English—High. Science—High. **Yearly Earnings:** $$$$ **Job Growth:** ★★ **Yearly Openings:** 🯅🯅

Medical and Health Services Managers. Plan, direct, or coordinate medicine and health services in hospitals, clinics, managed care organizations, public health agencies, or similar organizations. **Education and Training:** College degree plus work experience. **Skills:** Math—Medium. English—High. Science—Medium. **Yearly Earnings:** $$$$$ **Job Growth:** ★★★★ **Yearly Openings:** 🯅🯅🯅

MEDICINE AND SURGERY

These workers diagnose and treat human diseases, disorders, and injuries. They work in such places as hospitals, clinics, health facilities, industrial plants, pharmacies, and government agencies. Some are professionals who make life-and-death decisions, perform invasive procedures, and prescribe drugs. They may specialize or work in

general practice. Many are self-employed and have their own offices. Other workers in this group provide care under the supervision of professionals.

Anesthesiologists. Administer anesthetics during surgery or other medical procedures. **Education and Training:** Professional degree. **Skills:** Math—Medium. English—High. Science—High. **Yearly Earnings:** $$$$$ **Job Growth:** ★★★ **Yearly Openings:** 🯅🯅🯅

Family and General Practitioners. Diagnose, treat, and help prevent diseases and injuries that commonly occur in the general population. **Education and Training:** Professional degree. **Skills:** Math—High. English—High. Science—High. **Yearly Earnings:** $$$$$ **Job Growth:** ★★★ **Yearly Openings:** 🯅🯅🯅

Internists, General. Diagnose and provide non-surgical treatment of diseases and injuries of internal organ systems. Provide care mainly for adults who have a wide range of problems associated with the internal organs. **Education and Training:** Professional degree. **Skills:** Math—High. English—High. Science—High. **Yearly Earnings:** $$$$$ **Job Growth:** ★★★ **Yearly Openings:** 🯅🯅🯅

Medical Assistants. Perform administrative and certain clinical duties under the direction of physician. Administrative duties may include scheduling appointments, maintaining medical records, billing, and coding for insurance purposes. Clinical duties may include taking and recording vital signs and medical histories, preparing patients for examination, drawing blood, and administering medications as directed by physician. **Education and Training:** Moderate-term on-the-job training. **Skills:** Math—Medium. English—Medium. Science—Medium. **Yearly Earnings:** $$ **Job Growth:** ★★★★★ **Yearly Openings:** 🯅🯅🯅

Obstetricians and Gynecologists. Diagnose, treat, and help prevent diseases of women, especially those affecting the reproductive system and the process of childbirth. **Education and Training:** Professional degree. **Skills:** Math—High. English—High. Science—High. **Yearly Earnings:** $$$$$ **Job Growth:** ★★★ **Yearly Openings:** 🯅🯅🯅

Pediatricians, General. Diagnose, treat, and help prevent children's diseases and injuries. **Education and Training:** Professional degree. **Skills:** Math—High. English—High. Science—High. **Yearly Earnings:** $$$$$ **Job Growth:** ★★★ **Yearly Openings:** 🯅🯅🯅

Pharmacists. Compound and dispense medications following prescriptions issued by physicians, dentists, or other authorized medical practitioners. **Education and Training:** Professional degree. **Skills:** Math—High. English—High. Science—High. **Yearly Earnings:** $$$$$ **Job Growth:** ★★★★ **Yearly Openings:** 🯅🯅🯅

Pharmacy Aides. Record drugs delivered to the pharmacy, store incoming merchandise, and inform the supervisor of stock needs. May operate cash register and accept prescriptions for filling. **Education and Training:** Moderate-term on-the-job training.

Skills: Math—Medium. English—Medium. Science—Medium. **Yearly Earnings:** $ **Job Growth:** ★★★ **Yearly Openings:** 🚹🚹

Pharmacy Technicians. Prepare medications under the direction of a pharmacist. May measure, mix, count out, label, and record amounts and dosages of medications. **Education and Training:** Moderate-term on-the-job training. **Skills:** Math—Medium. English—Medium. Science—Medium. **Yearly Earnings:** $$ **Job Growth:** ★★★★★ **Yearly Openings:** 🚹🚹🚹

Physician Assistants. Provide healthcare services typically performed by a physician, under the supervision of a physician. Conduct complete physicals, provide treatment, and counsel patients. May, in some cases, prescribe medication. **Education and Training:** Bachelor's degree. **Skills:** Math—Medium. English—High. Science—High. **Yearly Earnings:** $$$$$ **Job Growth:** ★★★★★ **Yearly Openings:** 🚹

Psychiatrists. Diagnose, treat, and help prevent disorders of the mind. **Education and Training:** Professional degree. **Skills:** Math—Medium. English—High. Science—High. **Yearly Earnings:** $$$$$ **Job Growth:** ★★★ **Yearly Openings:** 🚹🚹🚹

Registered Nurses. Assess patient health problems and needs, develop and implement nursing care plans, and maintain medical records. Administer nursing care to ill, injured, convalescent, or disabled patients. May advise patients on health maintenance and disease prevention or provide case management. Licensing or registration required. Includes advanced practice nurses such as nurse practitioners, clinical nurse specialists, certified nurse midwives, and certified registered nurse anesthetists. Advanced practice nursing is practiced by RNs who have specialized formal post-basic education and who function in highly specialized roles. **Education and Training:** Associate's degree. **Skills:** Math—Medium. English—High. Science—High. **Yearly Earnings:** $$$$ **Job Growth:** ★★★★ **Yearly Openings:** 🚹🚹🚹🚹🚹

Surgeons. Treat diseases, injuries, and deformities by invasive methods, such as manual manipulation or by using instruments and appliances. **Education and Training:** Professional degree. **Skills:** Math—Medium. English—High. Science—High. **Yearly Earnings:** $$$$$ **Job Growth:** ★★★ **Yearly Openings:** 🚹🚹🚹

Surgical Technologists. Assist in operations under the supervision of surgeons, registered nurses, or other surgical personnel. May help set up operating room, prepare and transport patients for surgery, adjust lights and equipment, pass instruments and other supplies to surgeons and surgeon's assistants, hold retractors, cut sutures, and help count sponges, needles, supplies, and instruments. **Education and Training:** Postsecondary career and technical education. **Skills:** Math—Medium. English—Medium. Science—Medium. **Yearly Earnings:** $$ **Job Growth:** ★★★★ **Yearly Openings:** 🚹🚹

DENTISTRY

These workers provide health care for patients' teeth and mouth tissues. Most dentists are general practitioners, performing a variety of oral-care tasks. Others specialize: Orthodontists straighten teeth; prosthodontists make artificial teeth and dentures; oral and maxillofacial surgeons operate on the mouth and jaws. Dental hygienists clean teeth and teach people how to take care of their teeth. Dental assistants provide chair-side help, get the patient and equipment ready, and keep records.

Dental Assistants. Assist dentist, set up patient and equipment, and keep records. **Education and Training:** Moderate-term on-the-job training. **Skills:** Math—Medium. English—Medium. Science—Medium. **Yearly Earnings:** $$ **Job Growth:** ★★★★★ **Yearly Openings:** 🧍🧍🧍

Dental Hygienists. Clean teeth and examine oral areas, head, and neck for signs of oral disease. May educate patients on oral hygiene, take and develop X rays, or apply fluoride or sealants. **Education and Training:** Associate's degree. **Skills:** Math—Medium. English—Medium. Science—High. **Yearly Earnings:** $$$$$ **Job Growth:** ★★★★★ **Yearly Openings:** 🧍

Dentists, General. Diagnose and treat diseases, injuries, and malformations of teeth and gums and related oral structures. May treat diseases of nerve, pulp, and other dental tissues affecting vitality of teeth. **Education and Training:** Professional degree. **Skills:** Math—Medium. English—High. Science—High. **Yearly Earnings:** $$$$$ **Job Growth:** ★★ **Yearly Openings:** 🧍

Oral and Maxillofacial Surgeons. Perform surgery on mouth, jaws, and related head and neck structure to execute difficult and multiple extractions of teeth, to remove tumors and other abnormal growths, to correct abnormal jaw relations by mandibular or maxillary revision, to prepare mouth for insertion of dental prosthesis, or to treat fractured jaws. **Education and Training:** Professional degree. **Skills:** Math—Medium. English—High. Science—High. **Yearly Earnings:** $$$$$ **Job Growth:** ★★ **Yearly Openings:** 🧍

Orthodontists. Examine, diagnose, and treat dental malocclusions and oral cavity anomalies. Design and fabricate appliances to realign teeth and jaws to produce and maintain normal function and to improve appearance. **Education and Training:** Professional degree. **Skills:** Math—Medium. English—High. Science—High. **Yearly Earnings:** $$$$$ **Job Growth:** ★★ **Yearly Openings:** 🧍

Prosthodontists. Construct oral prostheses to replace missing teeth and other oral structures to correct natural and acquired deformation of mouth and jaws, to restore and maintain oral function, such as chewing and speaking, and to improve appearance. **Education and Training:** Professional degree. **Skills:** Math—High. English—High. Science—High. **Yearly Earnings:** $$$$$ **Job Growth:** ★★ **Yearly Openings:** 🧍

HEALTH SPECIALTIES

These workers are health professionals and technicians who specialize in certain parts of the human body. They are employed in private practices, vision-care chains, hospitals, and long-term health care facilities. Optometrists diagnose various diseases, disorders, and injuries of the eye, but opticians specialize in using lenses to correct imperfections in how the eye focuses. Podiatrists maintain the health of the feet and lower extremities. Chiropractors adjust the spinal column and other joints to prevent disease and correct abnormalities of the human body believed to be caused by interference with the nervous system.

Chiropractors. Adjust spinal column and other articulations of the body to correct abnormalities of the human body believed to be caused by interference with the nervous system. Examine patient to determine nature and extent of disorder. Manipulate spine or other involved area. May utilize supplementary measures, such as exercise, rest, water, light, heat, and nutritional therapy. **Education and Training:** Professional degree. **Skills:** Math—Medium. English—High. Science—High. **Yearly Earnings:** $$$$$ **Job Growth:** ★★★★ **Yearly Openings:** 🚶

Opticians, Dispensing. Design, measure, fit, and adapt lenses and frames for client according to written optical prescription or specification. Assist client with selecting frames. Measure customer for size of eyeglasses and coordinate frames with facial and eye measurements and optical prescription. Prepare work order for optical laboratory containing instructions for grinding and mounting lenses in frames. Verify exactness of finished lens spectacles. Adjust frame and lens position to fit client. May shape or reshape frames. **Education and Training:** Long-term on-the-job training. **Skills:** Math—Medium. English—Medium. Science—Medium. **Yearly Earnings:** $$ **Job Growth:** ★★★ **Yearly Openings:** 🚶

Optometrists. Diagnose, manage, and treat conditions and diseases of the human eye and visual system. Examine eyes and visual system, diagnose problems or impairments, prescribe corrective lenses, and provide treatment. May prescribe therapeutic drugs to treat specific eye conditions. **Education and Training:** Professional degree. **Skills:** Math—High. English—High. Science—High. **Yearly Earnings:** $$$$$ **Job Growth:** ★★★ **Yearly Openings:** 🚶

Podiatrists. Diagnose and treat diseases and deformities of the human foot. **Education and Training:** Professional degree. **Skills:** Math—Medium. English—High. Science—High. **Yearly Earnings:** $$$$$ **Job Growth:** ★★★ **Yearly Openings:** 🚶

MEDICAL TECHNOLOGY

These workers use technology mostly to detect signs of disease. They are employed by hospitals, long-term health care facilities, HMOs, physicians' offices, and specialized diagnostic laboratories and practices. They perform tests requested by

physicians, and the findings they report help the physicians to diagnose disease and formulate a therapy.

Cardiovascular Technologists and Technicians. Conduct tests on pulmonary or cardiovascular systems of patients for diagnostic purposes. May conduct or assist in electrocardiograms, cardiac catheterizations, pulmonary-functions, lung capacity, and similar tests. **Education and Training:** Associate's degree. **Skills:** Math—Medium. English—Medium. Science—High. **Yearly Earnings:** $$$ **Job Growth:** ★★★★ **Yearly Openings:** 🚶

Diagnostic Medical Sonographers. Produce ultrasonic recordings of internal organs for use by physicians. **Education and Training:** Associate's degree. **Skills:** Math—Medium. English—Medium. Science—Medium. **Yearly Earnings:** $$$$ **Job Growth:** ★★★★ **Yearly Openings:** 🚶

Medical and Clinical Laboratory Technicians. Perform routine medical laboratory tests for the diagnosis, treatment, and prevention of disease. May work under the supervision of a medical technologist. **Education and Training:** Associate's degree. **Skills:** Math—Medium. English—Medium. Science—High. **Yearly Earnings:** $$ **Job Growth:** ★★★ **Yearly Openings:** 🚶🚶🚶

Medical and Clinical Laboratory Technologists. Perform complex medical laboratory tests for diagnosis, treatment, and prevention of disease. May train or supervise staff. **Education and Training:** Bachelor's degree. **Skills:** Math—Medium. English—High. Science—High. **Yearly Earnings:** $$$$ **Job Growth:** ★★★ **Yearly Openings:** 🚶🚶🚶

Medical Equipment Preparers. Prepare, sterilize, install, or clean laboratory or healthcare equipment. May perform routine laboratory tasks and operate or inspect equipment. **Education and Training:** Short-term on-the-job training. **Skills:** Math—Medium. English—Medium. Science—Medium. **Yearly Earnings:** $$ **Job Growth:** ★★★ **Yearly Openings:** 🚶

Nuclear Medicine Technologists. Prepare, administer, and measure radioactive isotopes in therapeutic, diagnostic, and tracer studies utilizing a variety of radioisotope equipment. Prepare stock solutions of radioactive materials and calculate doses to be administered by radiologists. Subject patients to radiation. Execute blood volume, red cell survival, and fat absorption studies following standard laboratory techniques. **Education and Training:** Associate's degree. **Skills:** Math—High. English—Medium. Science—High. **Yearly Earnings:** $$$$ **Job Growth:** ★★★★ **Yearly Openings:** 🚶

Orthotists and Prosthetists. Assist patients with disabling conditions of limbs and spine or with partial or total absence of limb by fitting and preparing orthopedic braces or prostheses. **Education and Training:** Bachelor's degree. **Skills:** Math—Medium. English—Medium. Science—Medium. **Yearly Earnings:** $$$$ **Job Growth:** ★★★ **Yearly Openings:** 🚶

Radiologic Technicians. Maintain and use equipment and supplies necessary to demonstrate portions of the human body on X-ray film or fluoroscopic screen for diagnostic purposes. **Education and Training:** Associate's degree. **Skills:** Math—Medium. English—Medium. Science—Medium. **Yearly Earnings:** $$$ **Job Growth:** ★★★★ **Yearly Openings:** 🚹🚹🚹

Radiologic Technologists. Take X rays and CAT scans or administer nonradioactive materials into patient's bloodstream for diagnostic purposes. Includes technologists who specialize in other modalities, such as computed tomography, ultrasound, and magnetic resonance. **Education and Training:** Associate's degree. **Skills:** Math—Medium. English—Medium. Science—Medium. **Yearly Earnings:** $$$ **Job Growth:** ★★★★ **Yearly Openings:** 🚹🚹🚹

Radiologic Technologists and Technicians. Take X rays and CAT scans or administer nonradioactive materials into patient's bloodstream for diagnostic purposes. Includes technologists who specialize in other modalities, such as computed tomography and magnetic resonance. Includes workers whose primary duties are to demonstrate portions of the human body on X-ray film or fluoroscopic screen. **Education and Training:** Associate's degree. **Skills:** Math—Medium. English—Medium. Science—Medium. **Yearly Earnings:** $$$ **Job Growth:** ★★★★ **Yearly Openings:** 🚹🚹🚹

MEDICAL THERAPY

These workers care for, treat, or train people to improve their physical and emotional well-being. Most persons in this group work with people who are sick, injured, or disabled. Hospitals, nursing homes, and rehabilitation centers hire workers in this group, as do schools, industrial plants, doctors' offices, and sports organizations.

Audiologists. Assess and treat persons with hearing and related disorders. May fit hearing aids and provide auditory training. May perform research related to hearing problems. **Education and Training:** Master's degree. **Skills:** Math—Medium. English—High. Science—High. **Yearly Earnings:** $$$$ **Job Growth:** ★★★★★ **Yearly Openings:** 🚹

Massage Therapists. Massage customers for hygienic or remedial purposes. **Education and Training:** Postsecondary career and technical education. **Skills:** Math—Medium. English—Medium. Science—Medium. **Yearly Earnings:** $$ **Job Growth:** ★★★★ **Yearly Openings:** 🚹🚹

Occupational Therapist Aides. Under close supervision of an occupational therapist or occupational therapy assistant, perform only delegated, selected, or routine tasks in specific situations. These duties include preparing patient and treatment room. **Education and Training:** Short-term on-the-job training. **Skills:** Math—Medium. English—Medium. Science—Medium. **Yearly Earnings:** $$ **Job Growth:** ★★★★★ **Yearly Openings:** 🚹

Occupational Therapist Assistants. Assist occupational therapists in providing occupational therapy treatments and procedures. May, in accordance with state laws, assist in development of treatment plans, carry out routine functions, direct activity programs, and document the progress of treatments. Generally requires formal training. **Education and Training:** Associate's degree. **Skills:** Math—Medium. English—Medium. Science—Medium. **Yearly Earnings:** $$$ **Job Growth:** ★★★★★ **Yearly Openings:** 👤

Occupational Therapists. Assess, plan, organize, and participate in rehabilitative programs that help restore vocational, homemaking, and daily living skills, as well as general independence, to disabled persons. **Education and Training:** Bachelor's degree. **Skills:** Math—Medium. English—Medium. Science—Medium. **Yearly Earnings:** $$$$ **Job Growth:** ★★★★ **Yearly Openings:** 👤

Physical Therapist Aides. Under close supervision of a physical therapist or physical therapy assistant, perform only delegated, selected, or routine tasks in specific situations. These duties include preparing the patient and the treatment area. **Education and Training:** Associate's degree. **Skills:** Math—Medium. English—Medium. Science—Medium. **Yearly Earnings:** $ **Job Growth:** ★★★★★ **Yearly Openings:** 👤👤

Physical Therapist Assistants. Assist physical therapists in providing physical therapy treatments and procedures. May, in accordance with state laws, assist in the development of treatment plans, carry out routine functions, document the progress of treatment, and modify specific treatments in accordance with patient status and within the scope of treatment plans established by a physical therapist. Generally requires formal training. **Education and Training:** Associate's degree. **Skills:** Math—Medium. English—Medium. Science—Medium. **Yearly Earnings:** $$$ **Job Growth:** ★★★★★ **Yearly Openings:** 👤👤

Physical Therapists. Assess, plan, organize, and participate in rehabilitative programs that improve mobility, relieve pain, increase strength, and decrease or prevent deformity of patients suffering from disease or injury. **Education and Training:** Master's degree. **Skills:** Math—Medium. English—High. Science—High. **Yearly Earnings:** $$$$$ **Job Growth:** ★★★★ **Yearly Openings:** 👤👤

Radiation Therapists. Provide radiation therapy to patients as prescribed by a radiologist according to established practices and standards. Duties may include reviewing prescription and diagnosis; acting as liaison with physician and supportive care personnel; preparing equipment, such as immobilization, treatment, and protection devices; and maintaining records, reports, and files. May assist in dosimetry procedures and tumor localization. **Education and Training:** Associate's degree. **Skills:** Math—Medium. English—Medium. Science—High. **Yearly Earnings:** $$$$ **Job Growth:** ★★★★ **Yearly Openings:** 👤

Recreational Therapists. Plan, direct, or coordinate medically-approved recreation programs for patients in hospitals, nursing homes, or other institutions. Activities include sports, trips, dramatics, social activities, and arts and crafts. May assess a patient's condition and recommend appropriate recreational activity. **Education and Training:** Bachelor's degree. **Skills:** Math—Low. English—Medium. Science—Medium. **Yearly Earnings:** $$ **Job Growth:** ★★ **Yearly Openings:** 🧍

Respiratory Therapists. Assess, treat, and care for patients with breathing disorders. Assume primary responsibility for all respiratory care modalities, including the supervision of respiratory therapy technicians. Initiate and conduct therapeutic procedures; maintain patient records; and select, assemble, check, and operate equipment. **Education and Training:** Associate's degree. **Skills:** Math—Medium. English—Medium. Science—High. **Yearly Earnings:** $$$ **Job Growth:** ★★★★ **Yearly Openings:** 🧍

Respiratory Therapy Technicians. Provide specific, well defined respiratory care procedures under the direction of respiratory therapists and physicians. **Education and Training:** Postsecondary career and technical education. **Skills:** Math—Medium. English—Medium. Science—Medium. **Yearly Earnings:** $$$ **Job Growth:** ★★★★ **Yearly Openings:** 🧍

Speech-Language Pathologists. Assess and treat persons with speech, language, voice, and fluency disorders. May select alternative communication systems and teach their use. May perform research related to speech and language problems. **Education and Training:** Master's degree. **Skills:** Math—Medium. English—High. Science—High. **Yearly Earnings:** $$$$ **Job Growth:** ★★★★★ **Yearly Openings:** 🧍

PATIENT CARE AND ASSISTANCE

These workers are concerned with the physical needs and welfare of others. They may assist professional workers. These workers care for people who are very old, are very young, or have handicaps, frequently helping people do the things they cannot do for themselves. Jobs are found in hospitals, clinics, daycare centers, nurseries, schools, private homes, and centers for disabled people.

Home Health Aides. Provide routine personal healthcare, such as bathing, dressing, or grooming, to elderly, convalescent, or disabled persons in the home of patients or in a residential care facility. **Education and Training:** Short-term on-the-job training. **Skills:** Math—Medium. English—Medium. Science—Medium. **Yearly Earnings:** $ **Job Growth:** ★★★★★ **Yearly Openings:** 🧍🧍🧍🧍🧍

Licensed Practical and Licensed Vocational Nurses. Care for ill, injured, convalescent, or disabled persons in hospitals, nursing homes, clinics, private homes, group homes, and similar institutions. May work under the supervision of a registered nurse. Licensing required. **Education and Training:** Postsecondary career and technical

education. **Skills:** Math—Medium. English—Medium. Science—Medium. **Yearly Earnings:** $$ **Job Growth:** ★★★ **Yearly Openings:** 🧍🧍🧍🧍

Nursing Aides, Orderlies, and Attendants. Provide basic patient care under direction of nursing staff. Perform duties such as feeding, bathing, dressing, grooming, or moving patients or changing linens. **Education and Training:** Short-term on-the-job training. **Skills:** Math—Medium. English—Medium. Science—Medium. **Yearly Earnings:** $ **Job Growth:** ★★★★ **Yearly Openings:** 🧍🧍🧍🧍🧍

Psychiatric Aides. Assist mentally impaired or emotionally disturbed patients, working under direction of nursing and medical staff. **Education and Training:** Short-term on-the-job training. **Skills:** Math—Medium. English—Medium. Science—Medium. **Yearly Earnings:** $$ **Job Growth:** ★★★ **Yearly Openings:** 🧍🧍🧍

Psychiatric Technicians. Care for mentally impaired or emotionally disturbed individuals, following physician instructions and hospital procedures. Monitor patients' physical and emotional well-being and report to medical staff. May participate in rehabilitation and treatment programs, help with personal hygiene, and administer oral medications and hypodermic injections. **Education and Training:** Postsecondary career and technical education. **Skills:** Math—Medium. English—Medium. Science—Medium. **Yearly Earnings:** $$ **Job Growth:** ★★ **Yearly Openings:** 🧍🧍

HEALTH PROTECTION AND PROMOTION

These workers help people maintain good health and fitness. They educate and advise people to help them live healthier lifestyles, eat well, and get into better physical condition.

Athletic Trainers. Evaluate, advise, and treat athletes to assist recovery from injury, avoid injury, or maintain peak physical fitness. **Education and Training:** Bachelor's degree. **Skills:** Math—Medium. English—Medium. Science—Medium. **Yearly Earnings:** $$$ **Job Growth:** ★★★ **Yearly Openings:** 🧍

Dietetic Technicians. Assist dietitians in the provision of food service and nutritional programs. Under the supervision of dietitians, may plan and produce meals based on established guidelines, teach principles of food and nutrition, or counsel individuals. **Education and Training:** Moderate-term on-the-job training. **Skills:** Math—Medium. English—High. Science—Medium. **Yearly Earnings:** $$ **Job Growth:** ★★★★ **Yearly Openings:** 🧍

Dietitians and Nutritionists. Plan and conduct food service or nutritional programs to assist in the promotion of health and control of disease. May supervise activities of a department providing quantity food services, counsel individuals, or conduct nutritional research. **Education and Training:** Bachelor's degree. **Skills:** Math—Medium. English—High. Science—High. **Yearly Earnings:** $$$ **Job Growth:** ★★★ **Yearly Openings:** 🚶

Health Educators. Promote, maintain, and improve individual and community health by assisting individuals and communities to adopt healthy behaviors. Collect and analyze data to identify community needs prior to planning, implementing, monitoring, and evaluating programs designed to encourage healthy lifestyles, policies, and environments. May also serve as a resource to assist individuals, other professionals, or the community, and may administer fiscal resources for health education programs. **Education and Training:** Master's degree. **Skills:** Math—Low. English—Medium. Science—Medium. **Yearly Earnings:** $$$ **Job Growth:** ★★★★ **Yearly Openings:** 🚶 🚶

Appendix A

Core Subjects and Your Career

Students often wonder why they must study subjects that seem unrelated to their career goals. Why does a future engineer need to take English classes? How does math help an air traffic controller direct planes? When do chefs or cooks use science and technology in the kitchen?

This appendix explains the importance of English, math, and science in your career preparation. For students with an interest or aptitude in a subject, the sections explain the link between that subject and a number of careers. Each section also describes how we use English, math, and science in everyday life and lists occupations requiring various levels of competence.

Of course, you should consult detailed references, such as this book or the *Occupational Outlook Handbook*, in making career decisions. But this appendix may serve as a reminder that a good foundation is essential for success.

ENGLISH AND YOUR CAREER

Reading and writing are basic skills we begin learning at a young age. So why do we need to continue studying them in high school and beyond? Taking English classes improves communication skills, which are essential to every job.

Communication is the ability to understand information other people give us and to have other people understand what we tell them. In addition to being fundamental for most jobs, the ability to communicate clearly and effectively can help us in every area of our lives. Every time we write a letter, make a phone call, or give someone instructions, we use communication skills. Studying English helps us develop our reading, writing, speaking, and listening skills, all of which play some part in our everyday lives.

Taking English in High School and College

In high school English classes, most students study basics such as vocabulary, spelling, composition, reading, and grammar. Learning how to construct sentences and paragraphs lays the groundwork for writing effective letters, essays, term papers, and reports. English classes also include exposure to literature, which teaches students to analyze other people's words and provokes thought by providing insight into the human condition.

College-level English courses are designed to refine the skills learned in high school. Subjects such as literature, writing, and grammar are taught as individual classes. These courses provide additional study and practice of communication.

How English Relates to Careers

You may think English classes only relate to a few occupations, such as writing or editing. But every job requires workers to understand instructions quickly and to explain problems to supervisors and other workers.

Good communication is essential for most occupations, even those that require little interaction with others. A problem cited by employers of engineers, for example, is that some technically competent workers are unable to explain what they are doing, to understand or explain what their part of a project is, or to relate their task to what others are doing.

Jobs Requiring Basic Communication Skills

Basic communication requires the ability to interact with others and to follow simple oral and written instructions; high school English classes are helpful but not essential in developing this level of skill.

The following jobs require basic communication skills:

Bank tellers

Bus drivers

Cashiers

Correctional officers

Counter and rental clerks

Court reporters, medical transcriptionists, and stenographers

Dispatchers

Flight attendants

Funeral directors

General office clerks

Homemaker—home health aides

Hotel and motel desk clerks

Interviewing and new accounts clerks

Loan clerks and credit authorizers, checkers, and clerks

Nursing aides and psychiatric aides

Occupational therapy assistants and aides

Physical and corrective therapy assistants and aides

Postal clerks and mail carriers

Prepress workers

Preschool teachers and child care workers

Proofreaders

Receptionists

Reservation and transportation ticket agents and travel clerks

Routing and receiving clerks

Service representatives

Taxi drivers and chauffeurs

Telephone operators

Title searchers

Typesetters

Typists, word processors, and data entry keyers

Visual artists

Many occupations require frequent communication. Sales workers must be able to speak effectively both on the telephone and in person to present their company's products well. Lawyers and managers need to express themselves clearly and analyze large amounts of information to be successful. Health care workers must be able to understand their patients' questions and concerns and help patients understand how to maintain their health. Psychologists and psychiatrists must be able to listen and communicate effectively.

Developing Communication Skills

The best way to begin developing communication skills is to take high school English classes. Reading outside of class is also a good way to develop those skills and build an effective vocabulary. In addition, getting involved in extracurricular activities improves communication because of the interaction required. Some activities target specific abilities: Joining the school newspaper or yearbook staff is a good way to work on writing skills; the debate team is ideal for developing speaking skills.

Jobs Requiring Intermediate Communication Skills

Intermediate communication requires the ability to accurately give and follow instructions, to persuade people to a particular point of view, and to write in an organized and grammatically correct manner; both high school and college English courses are helpful in developing these skills.

The following jobs require intermediate communication skills:

Adjusters, investigators, and collectors
Architects
Clerical supervisors and managers
Construction and building inspectors
Construction and building managers
Designers
Employment interviewers
Financial managers
Health information technicians
Health services managers
Hotel managers and assistants
Industrial production managers
Insurance agents and brokers
Library technicians
Licensed practical nurses
Paralegals
Pharmacists
Physical therapists
Police, detectives, and special agents
Private detectives and investigators
Property managers
Real estate agents, brokers, and appraisers
Receptionists

Recreation workers
Recreational therapists
Registered nurses
Respiratory therapists
Restaurant and food service managers
Retail sales worker supervisors and managers
Retail sales workers
Secretaries
Securities and financial services sales representatives
Service sales representatives
Social and human service assistants
Travel agents
Travel guides

Jobs Requiring Advanced Communication Skills

Advanced communication requires a strong ability to communicate both orally and in writing; college-level English courses are recommended.

The following jobs require advanced communication skills:

Actors, directors, and producers
Administrative services managers
Adult education teachers
Agricultural scientists
Biological and medical scientists
Chemists
Engineering, science, and computer systems managers
Foresters and conservation scientists
Geologists and geophysicists
Government chief executives and legislators
Lawyers and judges
Librarians
Management analysts and consultants
Manufacturers' and wholesale sales representatives
Marketing, advertising, and public relations managers
Meteorologists
Optometrists
Pharmacists
Physician assistants
Physicians
Physicists and astronomers
Podiatrists
Psychologists
Public relations specialists
Radio and television announcers and newscasters
Reporters and correspondents
School teachers, kindergarten, elementary, and secondary
Social scientists
Social workers
Special education teachers
Speech-language pathologists and audiologists
Urban and regional planners
Veterinarians
Writers and editors

The accompanying lists show occupations that require advanced, intermediate, or basic communication skills. Advanced communication requires a strong ability to communicate both orally and in writing; college-level English courses are recommended. Intermediate communication requires the ability to accurately give and follow instructions, to persuade people to a particular point of view, and to write in an organized and grammatically correct manner; both high school and college English courses are helpful in developing these skills. Basic communication requires the ability to interact with others and to follow simple oral and written instructions; high school English classes are helpful but not essential in developing this level of skill.

MATH AND YOUR CAREER

Math skills help us cope with today's complex world. We use math to carry out everyday tasks such as balancing a checkbook, shopping for groceries, cooking, and creating a personal budget. Other important skills we learn from studying math include problem solving, analysis, and estimating. And math knowledge is essential for earning a living in many occupations, including most higher-paying occupations.

About 15,500 mathematicians are employed in the United States, but millions of workers have jobs in which mathematics is a necessary part. In fact, almost all jobs require at least some understanding of basic mathematics. For example, carpenters must be able to measure lengths and angles when installing wood trim. Machinists need to understand and manipulate angles and dimensions. Loan officers must determine applicants' debt-equity ratios before approving mortgage applications. And math skills are required for any science, engineering, computer, and technical occupation.

Math is also an important part of a well-rounded education. Most high schools require students to take at least two years of math to graduate. And most colleges require some proficiency in math for all applicants, regardless of their intended majors.

Careers for People Interested in Math

Although most occupations require basic math skills, some jobs rely on math more heavily than others. If you have taken many math courses, have a high aptitude for math, or major in math in college, you might be interested in some of the following occupations.

Actuaries. Actuaries answer questions about future risk, formulate investment strategies, and make pricing decisions. They may design insurance, financial, and pension plans by calculating probabilities of events such as sickness, disability, or death based on known statistics.

A bachelor's degree in mathematics or statistics is required for an entry-level position in a life or casualty insurance company. Applicants must be proficient in several mathematics subjects, including calculus, probability, and statistics, and have passed the beginning actuarial exams.

Mathematicians. Mathematicians use their mathematical knowledge and computational tools to create mathematical theories and techniques. They use these theories and techniques to solve economic, scientific, engineering, and business problems. Mathematicians often work with computers to solve problems, develop models, analyze relationships between variables, and process large amounts of data.

Mathematicians need a minimum of a bachelor's degree. People with bachelor's degrees may assist senior mathematicians or work on less advanced problems. Most mathematicians in the private sector need a master's or doctoral degree.

Operations research analysts. Operations research analysts are problem solvers who usually work for large organizations or businesses. They help these organizations operate more efficiently by applying mathematics principles to organizational issues. They work on problems such as facilities layout, personnel schedules, forecasting, and distribution systems. They often use mathematical models to explain how things happen within an organization and to determine how to organize things more effectively.

Most employers prefer to hire analysts who have a master's degree in operations research, industrial engineering, or management science.

Statisticians. Statisticians collect, analyze, and present numerical data. They also design, carry out, and interpret the results of surveys and experiments. Statisticians use mathematics techniques to predict things such as economic conditions or population growth, to develop quality control tests for manufactured products, and to help business managers or government officials make decisions and evaluate the results of new programs.

For most beginning jobs in statistics, a bachelor's degree in mathematics or statistics is the minimum requirement. Many research positions require a master's or doctoral degree.

Jobs Requiring General Mathematics Skills

Occupations in the general math skills category require basic arithmetic such as addition, subtraction, multiplication, and division.

The following jobs require general mathematics skills:

- *Bank tellers*
- *Billing clerks and billing machine operators*
- *Bindery workers*
- *Bookkeeping, accounting, and auditing clerks*
- *Bricklayers and stonemasons*
- *Brokerage clerks and statement clerks*
- *Cashiers*
- *Counter and rental clerks*
- *Drywall workers and lathers*
- *Glaziers*
- *Interviewing and new accounts clerks*
- *Library assistants and bookmobile drivers*
- *Loan clerks and credit authorizers, checkers, and clerks*
- *Manufacturers' and wholesale sales representatives*
- *Medical assistants*
- *Metalworking and plastic-working machine operators*
- *Order clerks*
- *Payroll and timekeeping clerks*
- *Plasterers*
- *Postal clerks and mail carriers*
- *Precision assemblers*
- *Prepress workers*
- *Printing press operators*
- *Private detectives and investigators*
- *Reservation and transportation ticket agents and travel clerks*
- *Roofers*
- *Secretaries*
- *Stock clerks*
- *Structural and reinforcing ironworkers*
- *Taxi drivers and chauffeurs*
- *Teacher aides*
- *Tilesetters*
- *Traffic, shipping, and receiving clerks*

Careers Requiring Strong Math Skills

Some other jobs require a strong background in math. The following occupations are among those in which strong math skills are very important.

Physical and life scientists. Physical and life scientists, including biologists, physicists, chemists, and geologists, work to discover the basic principles of how the earth, universe, and living things operate. The ability to use mathematical relationships to understand and describe the workings of nature is vital.

Most scientists need a doctoral degree in their field, especially those who work in basic research, but some scientists in applied research may need only a bachelor's or master's degree.

Jobs Requiring Practical Application of Mathematics

Occupations in the practical math category may require algebra and geometry in addition to general math skills.

The following jobs require the practical application of mathematics skills:

Air traffic controllers
Aircraft mechanics, including engine specialists
Automobile mechanics
Automotive body repairers
Blue-collar worker supervisors
Boilermakers
Broadcast technicians
Carpenters
Concrete masons and terrazzo workers
Diesel mechanics
Dietitians and nutritionists
Electric power generating plant operators and power distributors and dispatchers
Electricians
Electronic equipment repairers
Elevator installers and repairers
Farm equipment mechanics
Funeral directors
General maintenance mechanics
Heating, air-conditioning, and refrigeration technicians
Industrial machinery repairers
Inspectors, testers, and graders
Jewelers
Landscape architects
Machinists and tool programmers
Millwrights
Mobile heavy equipment mechanics

(continues)

(continued)

Motorcycle, boat, and small-engine repairers
Ophthalmic laboratory technicians
Photographers and camera operators
Purchasers and buyers
Sheet metal workers
Stationary engineers
Tool-and-die makers
Water and wastewater treatment plant operators
Welders, cutters, and welding machine operators

Social scientists. Social scientists perform research that helps us understand how individuals and groups make decisions, exercise power, and respond to change. Many social scientists, especially economists, describe behavior with mathematical models. Also, much of social scientists' research depends on gathering and understanding statistics that describe human behavior.

As with physical and life scientists, many jobs involving research require a doctorate. However, many social science jobs involving applied research require only a bachelor's or master's degree.

Computer scientists and systems analysts. Workers in computer science occupations design computer systems and perform research to improve these systems. They may also program computers. Advanced mathematics skills might not be necessary for computer programming; however, training in mathematics helps develop an ability to think logically–a necessary qualification for working with computers.

Most of these workers have bachelor's degrees in computer science, information systems, or computer engineering. Some research positions require a master's or doctoral degree.

Engineers. Engineers use the theories and principles of mathematics to help solve technical problems. They also use mathematics to design machinery, products, or systems. Most entry-level engineering jobs require a bachelor's degree.

Science and engineering technicians. Science and engineering technicians use the principles and theories of science, engineering, and mathematics to solve technical problems in research and development, manufacturing, and other areas. Their jobs are more limited in scope and more practically oriented than those of scientists and engineers, but technicians rely heavily on mathematics techniques in their work.

There are many different ways of qualifying for a position as a science and engineering technician, but most jobs require at least some training beyond earning a high school diploma.

Jobs Requiring Applied Mathematics Skills

Occupations in the applied math skills category include those in which workers need to understand mathematical concepts and be able to apply them to their work; in these occupations, knowledge of statistics and trigonometry may also be needed.

The following jobs require applied mathematics skills:

Accountants and auditors
Administrative services managers
Aircraft pilots
Budget analysts
Chiropractors
College and university faculty (nonmathematics)
Computer programmers
Construction and building inspectors
Construction contractors and managers
Cost estimators
Dentists
Dispensing opticians
Drafters
Education administrators
Engineering technicians
Farmers and farm managers
Financial managers
General managers and top executives
Government chief executives and legislators
Industrial production managers
Insurance agents and brokers
Insurance underwriters
Loan officers and counselors
Management analysts and consultants
Optometrists
Pharmacists
Physician assistants
Physicians
Podiatrists
Psychologists
Real estate agents, brokers, and appraisers
Respiratory therapists

(continues)

(continued)

School teachers, kindergarten, elementary, and secondary
Science technicians
Securities and financial services sales representatives
Special education teachers
Surveyors and mapping scientists
Urban and regional planners
Veterinarians

Other Careers that Require Math Skills

Math skills are useful in a number of other occupations. For example, most jobs in the financial industry use math skills. Bank tellers must have strong math skills to be both accurate and efficient. Accountants need proficiency in math to calculate and analyze numbers. Air traffic controllers need to understand maps and geometry when directing planes. Managers of all kinds use math skills; for example, hotel managers and assistants must be able to estimate costs for items the hotel needs to order, such as food and drinks.

Preparing for Careers in Math

The accompanying lists show occupations that require different levels of math skills: advanced, applied, practical, or general. Occupations in the advanced or theoretical math skills category require an understanding of more complex math concepts such as calculus and linear algebra. Occupations in the applied math skills category include those in which workers need to understand mathematical concepts and be able to apply them to their work; in these occupations, knowledge of statistics and trigonometry may also be needed. Occupations in the practical math category may require algebra and geometry in addition to general math skills. Occupations in the general math skills category require basic arithmetic such as addition, subtraction, multiplication, and division.

Jobs Requiring Advanced or Theoretical Mathematics Skills

Occupations in the advanced or theoretical math skills category require an understanding of more complex math concepts such as calculus and linear algebra.

The following jobs require advanced or theoretical mathematics skills:

- *Actuaries*
- *Agricultural scientists*
- *Architects*
- *Biological and medical scientists*
- *Chemists*
- *Computer scientists, computer engineers, and systems analysts*
- *Economists and marketing research analysts*
- *Engineering, science, and data-processing managers*
- *Engineers*
- *Foresters and conservation scientists*
- *Geologists, geophysicists, and oceanographers*
- *Mathematicians*
- *Mathematics teachers (secondary school and college)*
- *Meteorologists*
- *Operations research analysts*
- *Physicists and astronomers*
- *Social scientists*
- *Statisticians*

SCIENCE AND YOUR CAREER

Studying science helps us understand the discoveries that affect our daily lives. Every time we use a telephone, television, or computer, we are using a product of science. We use our knowledge of science when making decisions about our health and diet. Even common hobbies, such as cooking, gardening, and photography, rely on scientific principles.

By studying science, we learn how the universe works; we learn to observe, classify, measure, predict, interpret, and communicate data; and we develop the ability to think logically and solve problems. The skills and knowledge that come from studying science are important in many occupations.

Almost 400,000 scientists are employed in the United States, but 21 million workers use science on the job. For example, mechanics use scientific procedures when repairing or testing equipment. Physical therapists use biology and physics to rehabilitate patients. Journalists use scientific knowledge when writing about technology, health, or the environment. And scientific problem-solving skills are necessary for most computer occupations.

Science courses are also important if you want an advanced education. College admissions officers often favor individuals who have taken science classes. Many colleges require at least two years of high school science courses, regardless of your intended major. If you want to be admitted into scientific and technical programs, you will probably need three or four years of high school science.

Careers for People Interested in Science

Although science skills are helpful in many occupations, some occupations rely heavily on science. If you have a strong interest in science, you might want to consider one of the following occupations.

Biologists. Biologists study living organisms and their relationship to each other and the environment. Most biologists specialize in one branch of biology–for example, microbiology, the study of microscopic organisms; zoology, the study of animals; or botany, the study of plants. These branches are then subdivided. For example, types of zoologists include mammalogists, who study mammals; ichthyologists, who study fish; ornithologists, who study birds; and herpetologists, who study reptiles and amphibians.

Jobs Requiring the Practical Application of Science Skills

Practical application occupations require familiarity with the basic principles of biology, chemistry, or physics; high school courses in these areas should be sufficient. The following jobs require the practical application of science skills:

Automotive body repairers
Automotive mechanics
Barbers and cosmetologists
Boilermakers
Chefs, cooks, and other kitchen workers
Dental assistants
Diesel mechanics
Electricians

- *Electronic equipment repairers*
- *Elevator installers and repairers*
- *Farm equipment mechanics*
- *Farmers and farm managers*
- *Firefighting occupations*
- *Fishers, hunters, and trappers*
- *Funeral directors*
- *General maintenance mechanics*
- *Heating, air-conditioning, and refrigeration technicians*
- *Home appliance and power tool repairers*
- *Industrial machinery repairers*
- *Jewelers*
- *Landscaping, groundskeeping, nursery, greenhouse, and lawn service occupations*
- *Machinists and tool programmers*
- *Medical assistants*
- *Millwrights*
- *Mobile heavy equipment mechanics*
- *Motorcycle, boat, and small-engine mechanics*
- *Nursing aides and psychiatric aides*
- *Ophthalmic laboratory technicians*
- *Pest controllers*
- *Pharmacy technicians*
- *Photographic process workers*
- *Physical and corrective therapy assistants*
- *Plumbers and pipefitters*
- *Prepress workers*
- *Printing press operators*
- *Stationary engineers*
- *Structural and reinforcing iron workers*
- *Tool-and-die makers*
- *Urban and regional planners*
- *Vending machine servicers and repairers*
- *Water and wastewater treatment plant operators*
- *Water transportation occupations*
- *Welders, cutters, and welding machine operators*

Chemists. Chemists search for new chemicals and find uses for existing ones. Their discoveries might be used to produce medicines or create stronger building materials. Some chemists specialize in one branch of chemistry. Biochemists, for example, study the chemical composition of living things. Physical chemists examine the physical characteristics of atoms, molecules, and chemical reactions.

Physicists. Physicists study the behavior of matter, the generation and transfer of energy, and the interaction of matter and energy. They study areas such as gravity, nuclear energy, electromagnetism, electricity, light, and heat. They might examine the structure of the atom or design research equipment such as lasers. Physicists might also work in inspection, testing, or other production-related jobs.

Agricultural scientists. Some types of scientists work to improve agriculture. Crop scientists study the genetic breeding and management of field crops. Soil scientists use soil physics, soil chemistry, and soil microbiology to enhance soil fertility and the growth of plants. Agronomists develop practical applications for discoveries in plant and soil science to produce high-quality food.

Other scientists. There are many other branches of science. Geologists study the history and composition of our planet, including volcanoes and earthquakes. Oceanographers study the oceans and their movements. Meteorologists study the atmosphere, and some make weather predictions. Astronomers study the universe, trying to gain knowledge about the stars, planets, and galaxies.

Jobs Requiring Applied Science Skills

Applied science occupations require workers to understand scientific principles and apply them to their work; some post-high school science training is needed.

The following jobs require applied science skills:

Aircraft mechanics, including engine specialists
Aircraft pilots
Broadcast technicians
Cardiovascular technologists and technicians
Clinical laboratory technologists and technicians
College and university faculty
Construction and building inspectors
Construction contractors and managers
Dental hygienists
Dental laboratory technicians
Dietitians and nutritionists
Dispensing opticians
Drafters
Electroneurodiagnostic technologists
Electronic semiconductor processors
Emergency medical technicians
Engineering technicians (all specialties)
Health information technicians
Health services managers
Licensed practical nurses
Nuclear medicine technologists
Occupational therapists

Occupational therapy assistants and aides
Photographers and camera operators
Physical therapists
Psychologists
Radiologic technologists
Recreational therapists
Registered nurses
Respiratory therapists
Science technicians
Speech-language pathologists and audiologists
Surgical technologists
Surveyors and mapping scientists

Although many scientists specialize, most need to have knowledge in more than one branch of science. Agronomists, for example, combine their knowledge of biology, geology, chemistry, and mathematics to find better ways to grow food and conserve soil. They may also work closely with other scientists, such as microbiologists, biochemists, meteorologists, and entomologists.

Engineers. Engineers use the principles and theories of chemistry, physics, and mathematics to solve practical problems. They develop new products and improve systems and processes. Engineers design computers, generators, helicopters, spacecraft, and other devices. Engineering has many specialties. The largest are mechanical engineering, electrical and electronics engineering, and civil engineering.

Mechanical engineers design and develop power-producing machines, such as internal combustion and rocket engines. Others design and develop power-using machines, such as refrigeration systems.

Electrical and electronics engineers design, develop, test, and supervise the production of electrical equipment. This includes computers, automobile ignition systems, and wiring and lighting in buildings. They also design communications, video, and radar equipment.

Civil engineers design and supervise the building of roads, bridges, tunnels, buildings, airports, harbors, and water supply, flood control, and sewage systems.

Jobs Requiring Advanced Science Skills

Advanced science occupations require a thorough knowledge of scientific principles; a bachelor's degree with a number of college science courses is usually the minimum requirement. But many of these positions require a master's or doctoral degree.

The following jobs require advanced science skills:

- *Agricultural scientists*
- *Architects*
- *Archivists and curators*
- *Biological and medical scientists*
- *Chemists*
- *Chiropractors*
- *Computer scientists, computer engineers, and systems analysts*
- *Dentists*
- *Engineering, science, and computer systems managers*
- *Engineers*
- *Forensic scientists*
- *Foresters and conservation scientists*
- *Geologists and geophysicists*
- *Landscape architects*
- *Meteorologists*
- *Optometrists*
- *Pharmacists*
- *Physical therapists*
- *Physician assistants*
- *Physicians*
- *Physicists and astronomers*
- *Podiatrists*
- *Respiratory therapists*
- *Teachers, secondary and college (sciences)*
- *Veterinarians*

Technicians and technologists. Science and engineering technicians carry out the plans of scientists and engineers–setting up experiments, recording results, or testing product quality. They may also design simple experiments. These workers use testing and measuring devices and have a solid understanding of laboratory techniques.

Other technician occupations include drafters, who prepare technical drawings of structures and products; broadcast technicians, who install, repair, and operate radio and television equipment; and air-conditioning, refrigeration, and heating technicians.

Other Careers that Use Science

Science skills are useful in many other occupations. For example, there are numerous occupations in health care, and all require knowledge of biology and other sciences. Physicians, nurses, dentists, veterinarians, and emergency medical technicians are just a few of the health occupations that require an understanding of science.

Many workers use chemistry and physics in their work. Chefs and cooks use chemistry when creating recipes and preparing food, because cooking ingredients are chemicals. Dietitians and nutritionists are also concerned with chemical content of foods. Farmers and horticulturists use fertilizers and pesticides, the products of chemistry. Electricians apply the principles of physics when wiring a building, and aircraft pilots use physics and meteorology to plot flight paths and fly planes.

Preparing for Careers in Science

Careers in science require orderly thinking, systematic work habits, and perseverance. If you are a student who is interested in scientific and technical careers, you should take as many science classes in high school as possible. Basic courses in earth science, biology, chemistry, and physics will form a solid foundation for further study. A strong background in mathematics is also important for those who want to pursue scientific, engineering, and technology-related careers.

The lists show occupations requiring different levels of scientific skill: advanced, applied, or practical application. Advanced science occupations require a thorough knowledge of scientific principles; a bachelor's degree with a number of college science courses is usually the minimum requirement. Many of these positions require a master's or doctoral degree.

Applied science occupations require workers to understand scientific principles and apply them to their work; some post-high school science training is needed. Practical application occupations require familiarity with the basic principles of biology, chemistry, or physics; high school courses in these areas should be sufficient.

From the *Occupational Outlook Quarterly* by the U.S. Department of Labor. Written by Nancy Saffer, an economist formerly with the Office of Employment Projections, BLS.

Appendix B

Career Tips for Students

Here are some important tips to keep in mind as you plan your education and training, your career, and your life.

Finish high school. *Nearly every job requires the basic communication and math skills you learn in high school.* Compared to workers at higher education levels, high school dropouts have more difficulty getting and keeping jobs. They also have lower earnings throughout their lives.

Consider continuing your education. *The more education you get, the higher your earnings are likely to be.* On average, high school graduates earn more than high school dropouts. Those who receive postsecondary training earn more than high school dropouts and graduates. And workers who have bachelor's or higher degrees usually earn more than those with less education.

Research career information. *A small investment of your time will help you make an informed career choice that could pay dividends throughout your life.* There are hundreds of occupations, so choosing and planning a career is a lot more complex than it may appear. The ideal career for you might be something you've never heard of or thought about. This book, the *Occupational Outlook Handbook,* and other career references are loaded with helpful information.

Plan your career. *Seek out information about occupations with favorable career prospects, high earnings, and other attributes that are important to you.* Having a solid career plan can affect your future prospects more than your level of education. True, college study increases opportunities for careers with above-average earnings–but not in all fields. Good opportunities await workers without college degrees who spend several years learning a sought-after skill or craft.

Develop basic computer skills. *Take advantage of every opportunity to acquire computer proficiency.* Regardless of whether you continue your education beyond high school, chances are that you will need at least minimal computer skills to do your job.

Value your personal interests and abilities. *You shouldn't shy away from a career that interests you just because it's competitive.* If your interests and abilities draw you to a field like acting, journalism, law, piloting, or another competitive occupation, go for it! Just be prepared for the challenges that may lie ahead.

Learn how to conduct a good job search and develop a resume. *No matter what you do after high school, you will have to market your skills as you search for a job.* Learning about resume preparation and job search techniques will help you get through the process more easily. Workers average more than eight different jobs by age thirty-two, so prepare to change jobs–even careers–until you find the one that's right for you.

Gain experience early. *Learning by doing is a great way to approach a prospective career.* Internships, part-time jobs, and volunteer work are some examples of ways to get hands-on experience while still in school. Not only do these opportunities help you make smarter career decisions, but they may also help you get hired after graduation; most employers value work-related experience.

Keep learning. *Take every opportunity to learn new skills.* The more you upgrade your skills to the constantly changing world of work, the more likely you–and your career–will adapt along with it.

From the *Occupational Outlook Quarterly* by the U.S. Department of Labor. Written by Jon Sargent, a supervisory economist in the Office of Employment Projections, BLS.

Appendix C

For More Information

Exploring Careers is a good source of career information. For more information on your career, education, and training options, other resources can be helpful as well. This appendix suggests several ways and places you can get good up-to-date career information.

BOOKS AND VIDEOS

Career-related books and videos can provide you with valuable information. Check with your school or public librarian for recommendations. In addition, here are descriptions of some helpful reference books. All are published by JIST Works.

- *Occupational Outlook Handbook.* This book by the U.S. Department of Labor is the most widely used source of job information. In addition to about 300 job descriptions, the *OOH* includes up-to-date details on pay, education, job growth, working conditions, and more. *America's Top 300 Jobs* contains the same information and may be easier to check out from the library. You can find the *OOH* job descriptions online at http://stats.bls.gov.
- *Guide for Occupational Exploration.* The *GOE* describes the 14 major career interest areas covered in *Exploring Careers* and gives more information on the jobs related to them.
- *Best Jobs for the 21st Century.* This book emphasizes jobs with fast growth, high pay, and many openings.

- *Career Guide to America's Top Industries.* This book reviews trends, jobs, and openings in major industries. It is helpful for career research if you are interested in working in certain industries.
- *America's Top Military Careers.* This book helps people who are considering military careers.
- *O*NET Dictionary of Occupational Titles.* This book provides in-depth descriptions of the more than 1,000 occupations included in *Exploring Careers.*

LIBRARIES

Most school and public libraries have some or all of the materials mentioned in this appendix. Your librarian will welcome the chance to help you. Ask about the best books and Web sites for career exploration and for your career interests. Talking to the librarian about career resources can save you a lot of time.

YOUR SCHOOL

Your teachers have a good understanding of who you are. They can suggest careers that might be of interest to you or how you can learn more about your future options.

Your guidance or career counselor can offer helpful career information, including suggestions for training, education, service learning, internships, job shadowing, part-time or summer jobs, and apprenticeships.

Don't be afraid to ask for help. Be willing to listen to what your teachers and counselors suggest. Think about the information they offer.

CAREER ASSESSMENTS

Career assessments can help you think more about your interests and skills and how they relate to careers. While no assessment can tell you what to do, assessments can help you think more clearly about a career

direction. Ask your counselor about career assessments. Two good assessments are *The World of Work and You* and *Career & Life Explorer.*

The World of Work and You, available from JIST Works, covers the same interest areas as *Exploring Careers* and leads you through possible career and learning options. *The World of Work and You* is a 48-page booklet packed with worksheets, checklists, and information on 250 jobs. You can work through this assessment on your own and keep it for future reference.

Career & Life Explorer, also from JIST Works, is a foldout assessment that helps you identify your key interests and abilities. You then use these "clues" to identify your top career interest groups and their related jobs. You summarize all information on a "My Ideal Job" poster that can be hung on a wall.

THE INTERNET

Most libraries provide free Internet access. Your school librarian or guidance counselor can suggest Web sites for career research. Or you can search the Internet using keywords such as *career* or *vocations.* You can also do a keyword search for specific careers.

For a list of recommended sites for career and education information, visit www.jist.com. Another great Internet resource is www.careeroink.com. This site provides descriptions of 14,000 jobs.

Finally, each job description in the *Occupational Outlook Handbook* has a section called "Sources of Additional Information." Use the table of contents to locate jobs that interest you. Read the descriptions of those jobs. Look for specific information about Web sites related to those jobs.

PROFESSIONAL ASSOCIATIONS

Professional associations exist for almost every career. The *Occupational Outlook Handbook* lists association contact information for most major jobs. Most of these associations provide free or inexpensive career material.

You will find additional help in books such as

- The Guide to American Directories
- The Directory of Directories
- The Encyclopedia of Associations

Check with professional and trade associations you are interested in. They can give you a list of schools that offer the preparation needed for jobs that interest you.

COLLEGES AND TRAINING PROGRAMS

Ask your counselor about your future education and training options. Contact colleges, schools, and training institutions directly or visit their Web sites. You will learn about admission requirements, courses offered, certificates or degrees awarded, cost, financial aid, and location and size of the school.

PEOPLE YOU KNOW

Think about your family and friends and other people you know. Remember that these people know a lot about you. They can be a big help in learning more about your career options.

The people you know may be able to answer your career-related questions directly. Or they may be able to put you in touch with someone else who can. Consider every suggestion you receive.

Also, locate and talk to people who have jobs that interest you. Ask them what they like and don't like about their work, how they got started, and the training and education they have.

Index of Job Titles

A

B

C

D

E

F

G

H

I

N

O

P

R

S

T

U

V

W

Z